Africa's
Urban Past

SCHOOL OF ORIENTAL AND AFRICAN STUDIES

University of London

ONE WEEK LOAN COPY

D1420323

Africa's Urban Past

EDITED BY
David M. Anderson
& Richard Rathbone

JAMES CURREY
OXFORD

HEINEMANN
PORTSMOUTH (N.H.)

First published in 2000 in the United Kingdom by

James Currey
73 Botley Road
Oxford
OX2 0BS

and in the United States and Canada by

Heinemann
A division of Reed Elsevier Inc
361 Hanover Street
Portsmouth, New Hampshire 03801–3912

1 2 3 4 5 04 03 02 01 00

British Library Cataloguing in Publication Data
Africa's urban past
  1. Urbanization – Africa – History 2. Cities and towns -
  Africa – History 3. Cities and towns – Africa – Growth
  I. Anderson, David, 1957-   II. Rathbone, R. J. A. R. (Richard
  John Alex Reuben), 1942-
307.7'6'096'09

ISBN 0-85255-760-4 (James Currey cloth)
       0-85255-761-2 (James Currey paper)

Library of Congress Cataloging-in-Publication Data available on file at the Library of Congress

ISBN 0-325-00221-5 (Heinemann cloth)
       0-325-00220-7 (Heinemann paper)

Typeset in 10/11 Bembo by Long House, Cumbria, UK
Printed in the United Kingdom by
Villiers Publications Ltd, London N3

Contents

List of Illustrations   viii
Preface & Acknowledgements   ix
List of Contributors   x

INTRODUCTION   1
Urban Africa: Histories in the Making
DAVID M. ANDERSON & RICHARD RATHBONE

PART ONE
Urban Archaeologies

1   19
Clustered Cities of the Middle Niger
Alternative Routes to Authority in Prehistory
RODERICK J. MCINTOSH

2   36
African City Walls
A Neglected Source?
GRAHAM CONNAH

3   52
Aksumite Urbanism
DAVID W. PHILLIPSON

PART TWO

Pre-colonial Towns in Transition

4   67
Mbanza Kongo/São Salvador
Kongo's Holy City
JOHN K. THORNTON

5   85
Ouidah: a Pre-colonial
Urban Centre in Coastal West Africa
1727–1892
ROBIN LAW

6   98
Merchants, Missions & the Remaking
of the Urban Environment in Buganda
c. 1840–90
RICHARD REID & HENRI MEDARD

PART THREE

Urban Economies

7   109
'*A Town of Strangers*'
or '*A Model Modern East African Town*'?
Arusha & the Arusha
THOMAS SPEAR

8   126
The Cost of Living in Lagos
1914–45
AYODEJI OLUKOJU

9   144
The City of Durban Towards a Structural Analysis
of the Economic Growth & Character
of a South African City
BILL FREUND

PART FOUR

Becoming Urban

Towns as Cultural Brokers

10

'But I know what I shall do'
Agency, Belief & the Social Imaginary
in Eighteenth-century Gold Coast Towns
RAY KEA

163

11

Gender in the City Women, Migration
& Contested Spaces in Tunis
c. 1830–81
JULIA CLANCY-SMITH

189

12

The Cultural Politics of Death & Burial
in Early Colonial Accra
JOHN PARKER

205

13

'Wo pe tam won pe ba' ('You like cloth but you
don't want children') Urbanization, Individualism
& Gender Relations in Colonial Ghana
c. 1900–39
EMMANUEL AKYEAMPONG

222

PART FIVE

The Politics of Urban Order

14

Land Alienation
& the Urban Growth of Bahir Dar
1935–74
SELTENE SEYOUM

235

15

Conservation & the Colonial Past
Urban Planning, Space & Power in Zanzibar
WILLIAM CUNNINGHAM BISSELL

246

16

The Urbanism of District Six,
Cape Town
RAFAEL MARKS & MARCO BEZZOLI

262

17

The Political Shaping of Sacred Locality in Brazzaville
1959–97
FLORENCE BERNAULT

283

Index

303

List of Illustrations

1.1	Location of sites and regions, Middle Niger	20
1.2	Components of the Jenne-jeno urban complex	24
1.3	Alternative routes to clustering at the Jenne-jeno complex:	30
	a. Single core (Jenne-jeno) priority	
	b. Multiple founding communities and daughter communities interact	
	c. Metallurgical antecedents	
2.1	African walled towns and cities	37
2.2	(a) Barth's plan of Kano, Nigeria; (b) Faras, Sudan	38
2.3	(a) Pate, Kenya; (b) Bigo, Uganda	41
2.4	(a) Hamdallahi, Mali; (b) Earthwork enclosures in Benin City	42
2.5	(a) Ife, Nigeria, with several phases of walling; (b) the fortified settlement of Mourgoula, Mali	44
2.6	Destruction of part of the innermost city wall at Benin City by removing earth for building purposes	46
2.7	Hypothetical section drawing, showing the archaeological potential of an earthwork consisting of a single ditch and bank	47
2.8	Excavated section through the innermost city wall at Reservation Road, Benin City, after completion in late May 1963	49
3.1	Inside the mausoleum: the central passage	54
3.2	Elite building at the 'Domestic Area', to the north of Aksum	56
3.3	Sixth-century non-elite buildings at the 'Domestic Area'	56
3.4	Aksumite walling in an area of non-elite occupation in Maleke Aksum	59
3.5	Cathedral Precinct, seen from the modern bell tower	59
3.6	Throne bases in the Cathedral Precinct	60
3.7	South wall of the podium on which the Old Cathedral stands	60
3.8	Aksum, showing principal sites and monuments	62
7.1	Arusha Town Plan (1930)	117
11.1	The Medina of Tunis, nineteenth century	193
15.1	Map of Zanzibar Town in the late colonial period	247
16.1	Map of the Cape metropolitan region showing District Six, 1997	263
16.2	The Bashew Brothers' shop in Aspeling Street, c. 1910	267
16.3	Map, District Six, 1940	269
16.4	Map, District Six, 1992	274
16.5	Aerial photograph of District Six after its destruction	276
17.1	Map showing Congo's political regions, 1992–5	284
17.2	Map showing Brazzaville's territories, 1992–5	286

Preface & Acknowledgements

The papers collected in this volume represent a selection of those first delivered at the conference on 'Africa's Urban Past', held at the School of Oriental and African Studies, University of London, in June 1996. That this meeting should have attracted more than 200 historians underlines the importance of urban history in current Africanist research. Participants in the conference discussed some 104 papers over four days, ranging across virtually every conceivable aspect of the social, cultural, economic, political, spatial and architectural history of African towns and cities. The 18 chapters assembled here offer a fair reflection of the rich variety of the conference, and they have been selected with an eye to those issues which seem to be of most immediate significance in current African historical research. This book reports the work of a conference, then, but more significantly we hope that it charts new directions in historical investigation.

We owe many debts of gratitude to those who have assisted in this project along the way. Of the many people who helped to organize the July 1996 meeting, Anna Debska deserves very special mention. As an administrator in the Centre of African Studies, under whose auspices the conference was organized, it fell upon Anna to deal with all bureaucratic matters, from booking flights, hotels, rooms and lecture halls, to coordinating caterers, cajoling advertisers and shepherding publishers. She also expertly edited the 124-page conference brochure that was distributed to each participant. As conference administrator she handled all these matters with consummate efficiency, and her seemingly endless store of good humour did much to smooth the ruffled feathers of those of us who admit to a less calm disposition. We owe her our deep and appreciative thanks.

Around Anna Debska were a team of helpers, all of whom were then graduate students in the History Department at SOAS. They have now gone on (or are going on) to greater things: we are grateful to Andrew Burton, Grace Carswell, Sandra Ferreira, Mike Jennings, Webby Kalikiti, Joyce Kannan, Arlette Leandro, Neil Overy and Richard Reid for having so willingly given up their time and for the many ways in which they each assisted in the running of the conference. In the History Department office, Carol Miles and Joy Hemmings-Lewis uncomplainingly fielded enquiries from our many visitors and were welcoming and hospitable to all.

A number of organizations provided funding to assist participants in attending the conference. We received grants from The British Academy, the Basler Afrika Bibliographien, the Institute of Archaeology of University College, London, the British Council, and the Anglo-American and De Beers Chairman's Fund. The SOAS Research Committee provided the seed monies which allowed us to get the whole idea up and running, and the SOAS History Department generously hosted a reception to welcome those attending the conference. The Calouste Gulbenkian Foundation must be singled out for special mention, as they most generously provided travel monies to enable several scholars from Angola and Portugal to attend the conference. The presence of so many historians of Lusophone Africa greatly enriched the proceedings, and we must thank Jill Dias especially for the commitment and energy she showed in helping to make this possible.

In bringing the book to publication Pedro Machado and James Whidden have assisted us with translations, Catherine Lawrence and Claire Iveson, resident cartographers in SOAS, have skilfully prepared several of the maps, and Mike Jennings has ably assisted in the final stage of preparing the manuscript for despatch to the publishers.

Lastly, we must thank the great majority of those who participated in the conference whose work is not represented directly here, but who may recognize in what follows some of the insights, ideas and excitements of the conference discussions in which they took part. We are grateful to them all for their contributions and their support.

David M. Anderson
St Albans, Hertfordshire

List of Contributors

Emmanuel Akyeampong is Associate Professor of African History, Harvard University

David M. Anderson is Senior Lecturer in History, SOAS, London

Marco Bezzoli teaches at the Cape Technikon, Cape Town

William Cunningham Bissell completed his doctorate at Chicago University in 1997

Florence Bernault is Associate Professor of African History, University of Wisconsin-Madison

Julia Clancy-Smith is Professor of History, University of Arizona, Tucson

Graham Connah is an Emeritus Research Fellow at the Australian National University, Canberra

Bill Freund is Professor of Economic History, University of Natal, Durban

Ray Kea is Professor of African History, University of California, Riverside

Robin Law is Professor of History, University of Stirling

Rafael Marks teaches at the Cape Technikon, Cape Town

Roderick J. McIntosh is Professor of Archaeology at Rice University, Houston

Henri Medard is a doctoral student at the University of Paris I

Ayodeji Olukoju is Senior Lecturer in History, Lagos University, Nigeria

John Parker is Lecturer in African History, SOAS, London

David W. Phillipson is Reader in African Archaeology, Cambridge University

Richard Rathbone is Professor of African History, SOAS, London

Richard Reid is Lecturer in History, University of Asmara, Eritrea

Seltene Seyoum is Lecturer in History, University of Addis Ababa, Ethiopia

Tom Spear is Professor of African History and Director of the Program of African Studies, University of Wisconsin-Madison

John K. Thornton is Professor of African History, Millersville University, Pennsylvania

INTRODUCTION

Urban Africa
Histories in the Making

DAVID M. ANDERSON & RICHARD RATHBONE

Rapid and dramatic urbanization has been the most significant and pervasive socio-economic trend across the African continent during the present century. By the year 2000, it is estimated that more of Africa's people will live in towns than live in the countryside; and, if present urban growth rates continue, by 2020 Africa's main conurbations will be amongst the world's largest cities.[1] Whilst urban development in other parts of the world is restrained increasingly by planning controls, in Africa the conurbations of Lagos, Nairobi, Johannesburg and many other larger cities continue to sprawl into their own hinterlands, their growth largely unregulated. It is in these cities that the changing face of modern Africa over the twentieth century is revealed most starkly: in 1900 much of the continent was characterized by an abundance of land, relatively thin population densities and hence a comparative lack of labour; now, as the millennium approaches, land scarcity is widespread and the pools of unemployed urban people grow ever larger.[2]

The fact that Africa's social and economic problems in the present era are increasingly identified as urban has given greater relevance and immediacy to research into the history of towns. Urban growth on such a scale is a profoundly modern phenomenon, but urbanization has been an important feature of Africa's history for over two thousand years. All African towns have their own distinctive histories; addressing their problems success-fully demands an understanding of these. In Africa's archaeological record, and in the descriptive documentary sources for pre-colonial history, towns and cities predominate as the arenas within and around which societies were organized – as centres of trade, economic activity and wealth accumulation; as the foci of political action and authority; as military garrisons and symbols of physical domination; as sites of ritual power and contact with the other-worldly, of ceremonial and display; and as places of refuge, shelter and collective security in troubled times. Africa's towns took many different spatial forms; some were highly visible with clearly demarcated boundaries, such as the walled cities of Sahelian West Africa or the stockaded villages found in parts of East Africa,[3] whilst others amounted to little more than 'a heap of huts' – clusters of scattered settlements interspersed with tracts of cultivation and pasture, seeming to lack order or formality to the visitor's unfamiliar eye.[4]

The vastness of Africa and its cultural pluralism defies a typology of urban settlements, and over so long a span of history as this volume covers it would be futile to attempt any classification. Africa has its trading towns and entrepots, its mining towns, its religious centres, its grand administrative capitals and its market towns, to be sure, but their histories are invariably complex, marked by the layerings of indigenous and external influences from ancient times to the present. For those who may think of Africa as a place of pre-dominantly rural cultures, the extent and depth of urbanization to be found in a survey of the history of the continent is remarkable.

In Egypt and in Nubia the Nile Valley kingdoms gave rise to monumental cities to rival any in antiquity. There is little evidence that the influence of Egyptian urbanism upon the rest of Africa was very great; but further up the Nile, beyond the Third Cataract, at Kerma and then at Meroe we find ancient cities whose connections to tropical Africa, in trade and in cultural and political influences, can be seen plainly in the archaeological record.[5] Along the coast of North Africa, the Phoenician city of Carthage was already trading to the south through Berber intermediaries before the Romans razed the city in 146 BC. Here, as in Egypt, Mediterranean culture appears not to have penetrated far to the south, but as commercial links across the desert expanded in the first milliennium AD it is clear that North Africa's towns absorbed more and more of the influences of Saharan and sub-Saharan Africa.[6] In the Horn of Africa, the ancient highland city of Aksum stood at the centre of yet another civilization built upon trade between tropical Africa and the wider world. From the first to the seventh centuries AD, Aksum's wealth was displayed in monumental stone temples, tombs and stelae. At its largest extent, the population of the city of Aksum may have numbered 10,000, and there were certainly many other contemporary Aksumite urban settlements whose archaeology remains to be investigated.[7] In tropical Africa fewer stone monuments survive, but numerous urban cultures have been identified none the less. On the middle Niger at Jenne-jeno[8] and Gao,[9] at Koumbi Saleh in ancient Ghana,[10] in the West African forest belt at Ife, Benin City and Old Oyo,[11] in the Great Lakes region at Bigo and Ntusi,[12] at Shanga, Gezira, Unguja Ukuu, Kilwa and Chibuene along the East African coast,[13] in the Zambezi valley and on the highland plateau of eastern Zimbabwe,[14] and in many other places besides, we can map complex urban settlements, many of which were contem-porary with Aksum and all of which were occupied before 1500.

For some of these towns the writings of Greek, Roman and especially Arabic-speaking travellers, such as Ptolemy, al-Bakri, al-Yakubi, al-Masudi and Ibn Battuta, give us early documentary evidence for Africa's urban heritage. Relating to the end of the tenth century, al-Bakri described the Maghrib region of Biskra, along the northern edge of the Sahara, as a district of many towns. These settlements grew up where there was water, and where that water could be used to irrigate the land. The capital of the region, Biskra itself, was a typical large oasis town, 'fortified with a wall and a ditch, and with three gates', the citizens drawing water from wells and from a nearby river.[15] In the suburbs, outside the walls among the palm groves, lived the bulk of the population. The people of Biskra were described as being 'of mixed race, half Latin and half Berber'. Patronage and clientage, mediated by powerful leading families of sedentarized Arabs, secured entry into the safety of the walled town and dictated its politics.[16] As in contemporary towns of the Maghrib up to the sixteenth century, such as Tripoli, Tunis, Tlemcen (Agadir), Marrakech and Fes, urban elites retained close contacts with the rural economy as well as participating in local commerce and longer-distant trade.[17] It was in the walled towns that Islam flourished. Tlemcen, in the south-western part of Oranie, was already 'an island of Muslim culture set in a predominantly Berber sea' in the tenth century, its well-cultivated fields feeding the population within its walls of mudbrick and lime, and its trade goods from the south moving through to the port of Oran.[18] Leo Africanus, who visited the city in the sixteenth century, found it then still to be a centre of Islamic scholarship and a place of considerable wealth, closely bound up with the trans-Saharan trade:

> [Tlemcen] is a great and royal city. During the reign of the Sultan Abou-Tesfin it contained some 16,000 households.... All the shopkeepers, merchants and industrial workers are concentrated in particular streets ... there are beautiful and well-built mosques. One also finds there five colleges, beautifully designed and decorated with mosaics.... There are a great number of caravanserais, including two which house merchants from Genoa and Venice. The city walls are high and strong with five well-built gateways, attached to which are quarters for officers and guards. Outside the city one sees fine farms and houses....[19]

At the other end of the trade routes that linked Tlemcen with Sudanic West Africa, the sources for the sixteenth century are similarly rich. There the largest towns of Gao, Timbuktu and Djenne had populations fluctuating between 15,000 and 80,000, depending upon the trading seasons. Katsina and Kano were also important trading towns at this time, and important centres of Islamic influence. In their principal functions and social composition, these Sahelian towns were little different from Tlemcen.[20]

On the east coast, Islamic traders from the Gulf also played a role in urbanization. When Ibn Battuta visited the town of Kilwa in 1331, for example, he described it as having a population of 10,000 to 20,000 people, a few of whom lived in stone houses while the greater majority occupied wood and thatch dwellings.[21] The wealth of Kilwa was based upon trade, the most important element of which was the gold brought from the plateau lands of central Africa. The earliest indications of a significant urban civilization in this region comes from the eleventh and twelfth centuries at Mapungubwe, on the Limpopo River. Many smaller urban settlements surrounded the main town on Mapungubwe Hill, indicating that the area was densely settled and intensively farmed. Gold was produced here, but it is unlikely that any great quantity was exported. Toutswe urban sites, further up the Limpopo into modern-day Botswana, were contemporary with Mapungubwe but the larger settlements here on the edge of the Kalahari appear to have been associated with wealth derived from cattle keeping.[22] Moving a little north, the stone enclosures of Great Zimbabwe mark the best-known urban centre of the region, inhabited from the eleventh to the sixteenth centuries, and thought to have had a population of 18,000 at its peak.[23] It was from this region that the bulk of Kilwa's gold came. Scattered around Great Zimbabwe, on the plateau between the Limpopo and Zambezi rivers, were more than 50 lesser settlements of similar design.[24] It seems likely that these walled enclosures held only an elite, whilst outside the stone walls were the wood and plaster houses of the ordinary population. The role of spiritual beliefs in the siting of Zimbabwe's stone enclosures seems to have been significant.[25] Many other densely settled sites are thought to be contemporary with Great Zimbabwe, but because these lack stone walls they have received less archaeological attention.[26]

From the fifteenth century, as the sailors of the Iberian peninsula began to take their ships around the coast of Africa, we begin to find an accumulation of written European sources on African towns. By the time the Portuguese reached the East African coast, in 1498, the old town of Kilwa had been abandoned, but other settlements had risen to take its place.[27] Like many other African towns, Kilwa has been made and remade. Before rounding the Cape, the Portuguese had encountered large, sophisticated and wealthy towns to rival Old Kilwa in West and West-Central Africa, particularly along what came to be called the Gold and Slave Coasts, and in the Kingdom of Kongo, close to the mouth of the great Zaire River. In these regions we find some of Africa's most deeply rooted and enduring urban cultures. In the Akan region, gold mining and trading laid the foundations for the growth of Begho and then Bono Mansa, both important towns by the fifteenth and sixteenth centuries.[28] Further to the west, the state of Benin then encompassed hundreds of towns, its capital a substantial walled city of some six kilometres across, within which there were dwellings, public buildings and large cultivation grounds.[29] A Dutch visitor to Benin City at the beginning of the seventeenth century was impressed by the 'very great' extent of the town, comparing its broad, straight thoroughfares to those of Amsterdam.[30] Ijebu Ode and Owo were other significant towns of this period, as was Oyo, the capital of the northern-most Yoruba state, lying within the savanna. These towns all offered richly varied social environments, their communities including agriculturalists, merchants and artisans who produced finely worked goods. Ife, for example, was a political capital and a religious centre, as well as home to a flourishing glass industry.[31]

Where the capitals of West African states tended to be fixed and permanent urban centres, the 'roving capitals' of sixteenth- and seventeenth-century highland Ethiopia held populations, perhaps larger than 20,000, gathered together in an 'amorphous mass of tents and grass huts sprawled over many miles'. The royal capital might encamp itself temporarily at any one of several sites, although the more important centres, such as Gondar, had permanent buildings and fortifications.[32] But in Ethiopia, as in much of Africa, urbanization took a number of forms. In contrast to the scale of the royal capitals, most of the rural population lived in small hamlets, consisting of households from the same landholding descent group. There were also permanent market centres. The most significant in northern Wallo from the seventeenth century was Saqota, a town with distinctive two-storey stone houses and walled streets, home to a small but industrious population of artisans and merchants who serviced the many trade routes that converged on the town. Other urban centres in this region combined commerce with a religious function, the most famous being Lalibala. The town contained ten individual churches and religious foundations and supported a large clerical community.[33]

Many African towns developed rapidly from the fifteenth century in response to the economic stimuli of overseas trade. At the vast, sprawling Kongo capital, Mbanza, slave plantations were established to feed the burgeoning population of the town, swelled by captives awaiting shipment to the Americas.[34] These difficulties in urban food supply led the Portuguese to introduce new, high-yielding American crops, such as maize, manioc and groundnuts, in the mid-sixteenth century.[35] When the first European factors and merchants began to settle along the coast, for the most part they joined African popula- tions who already had their own urban traditions. The 'trading towns' that evolved out of this relationship, at places such as St Louis, Cape Coast, Elmina, Ouidah, Bonny, Old Calabar, Loango, Malemba and Cabinda, may have become idiosyncratic and rather different from anything seen there before; but these places were not made initially in the image of contemporary European urbanization. The African inhabitants of these towns had their own ideas of urban aesthetics, their own cultural readings of landscape and understandings of space and place, and their own personal, socio-economic and political motivations for congregating in urban settlements. For these reasons purely functional interpretations of African urbanization will seldom suffice. As the impact of slave trading made itself felt in the inner basin of the Zaire River in the nineteenth century, for example, new forms of political authority came into being in the shape of African trading 'firms'. These groups gathered at strategic points on the river, forming towns. Urbanization, however, was by no means a novel social process even in this sparsely populated region; its roots can be traced back well before the sixteenth century in the capitals of the Kongo and Kuba states and at earlier river towns such as Basoko, where populations numbered above 10,000. But the river towns of the nineteenth century 'were remarkable for their size' and their number, many along the Zaire counting 'over 5,000 inhabitants and perhaps five surpassed the 10,000 mark'. In their structure, Jan Vansina describes these towns as 'villages writ large'. Undoubtedly their placement and extent were influenced by changing patterns of external trade – as at the large town of Bongo, described by one writer as 'the Venice of Africa', where the dwellings were built on artificial mounds to raise them above the water – but they were intrinsically African in their design, orientation and social and political organization.[36]

It may seem paradoxical that the ending of the disruptive and exploitative trade in slaves and the rise of 'legitimate' trade in the mid-nineteenth century should have brought with it greater European influence over urban forms along Africa's Atlantic coast; but it must be remembered that it also entailed massive commercial reorientation and this contributed to severe political disruption in many places. As former African state monopolies on exports proved impossible to sustain and European merchant houses took a firmer grip on the trade in vegetable oils and, later, cocoa along the West African coast, the cities of Dakar, Freetown, Accra, Lagos and Luanda became primary centres of commerce and grew dramatically at the expense of their smaller, less favoured neighbours. Some important towns from an earlier era, such as Ouidah and Old Calabar, managed to sustain their prosperity to the end of the century, but others, such as Badagry, declined.[37] Further inland, the towns and cities of Benin, Dahomey, Oyo and Asante were at the same time drawn more closely into the orbit of European commerce. By the nineteenth century some dozen towns in Yorubaland had populations above 20,000. At the largest, Ibadan, a city wall of 24 miles circumference contained at least 70,000 people. Further to the north, more than half the entire population of Hausaland was reckoned to be urbanized. The traveller Barth estimated the population of Kano at a regular 30,000, a figure which doubled at the height of the trading season.[38] Kumasi, the capital of the great Asante empire, was a town of 10,000 to 15,000 people in the early nineteenth century.[39] Kumasi was a complex and multi-functional town, the bureaucratic capital of a sophisticated polity, a spiritual and ritual centre, and an important commercial entrepot. It, too, had a greatly fluctuating population as regular festivals, state occasions and seasonal trades brought temporary visitors into the town. One such visitor, Bowdich, described the town as:

> an oblong of nearly four miles in circumference, not including the suburbs of Assafoo nor Bantama.... Four of the principal streets are half a mile long and from 50 to 100 yards wide. I observed them building one, and a line was stretched to make it regular. The streets are all named, and a superior captain in charge of each.... The palace was situated in a long and wide street running through the middle of the town from which it was shut out by a high wall.... The Ashantees persisted that the population of Commassie, when collected was upwards of 100,000 ... perhaps the average resident population of Commassie is not more than from 12 to 15,000.[40]

By the nineteenth century there were no indigenous urban civilizations in eastern or southern Africa to match the scale of those of North or West Africa, but there were many significant towns all the same. Urbanization had long been a prominent feature of the kingdoms of highland Ethiopia. Small towns were scattered throughout the Ethiopian highlands, most growing up around markets and along trade routes. The largest urban settlements remained the royal capitals, whose fortunes fluctuated with the shifting political economy. The early nineteenth-century Shawan royal capital of Ankober was a spectacular sight, 'perched at 2400 meters atop a volcanic cone above the steep escarpment of the eastern highlands'. It commanded a prosperous, cosmopolitan and culturally diverse polity. Founded as a frontier outpost in the late-eighteenth century, fifty years later Ankober stood amidst a rich agricultural area and controlled the Red Sea trade through regional markets such as Aliyu Amba. Visited by Muslim merchants and traders from the Mediterranean, and a busy ecclesiastical base of Orthodox theology, Ankober was a lively commercial and intellectual centre. In 1878 the town had a population of 6,000, but with the founding of Addis Ababa as a new, fixed royal capital in 1886 to take advantage of the new trade routes to the south, Ankober went into rapid decline and by 1894 it was already described as 'a dead town'.⁴¹ Ankober had been but one of several Shawan 'roving capitals' in the nineteenth century, the court moving seasonally between Ankober, Liche, Dabra Behran, and later Enewari.⁴² As a single and permanent capital, Addis Ababa grew more quickly in the twentieth century to a size far exceeding the towns of the nineteenth century.⁴³

Elsewhere in eastern Africa, the better-known towns of the nineteenth century existed, strung out from coastal entrepots along the main arteries of overland trade. Lamu, Mombasa, Bagamoyo, Zanzibar and Lindi were all centres of Indian Ocean commerce in the nineteenth century, whose communities included visiting Arab merchants and permanent immigrants from the Gulf. Along the trade routes the large stockaded villages found at Taveta, Baringo, Sonjo and elsewhere were impressive defensive structures, protecting populations of no more than 5,000 who cultivated the surrounding fields to supply passing caravans and neighbouring pastoralists with cereals and vegetables.⁴⁴ At the far end of the trade routes lay the towns of Ujiji and Kazembe. Situated on the shore of Lake Tanganyika, Ujiji had a population of probably no more than 5,000 in the mid-nineteenth century, and it was to grow only marginally by the end of the century. Kazembe, capital of the Lunda state further to the south-west, was a grander and more substantial town, described in 1832 as covering an area three kilometres across.⁴⁵ Other royal capitals nearer the coast, such as Vugha and Utengule Usafwa, did not match Kazembe's scale or importance.⁴⁶ None of these towns would outlive the colonial conquest, although the great capital of Buganda (the *Rubaga*), which had moved between several sites over the nineteenth century, would survive in easily recognizable form within the colonial conurbation of Kampala.⁴⁷

The colonial impact upon indigenous African towns was felt earlier to the south than in the east. From the early eighteenth century the Tswana areas were heavily urbanized, but here, as in Yorubaland, many townsfolk were also farmers. The Tswana capital of Latakoo was said to be as large as Cape Town by the early nineteenth century, 'its scattered huts housing 5,000 to 15,000 people'. At the same time Molokweni, the Kwena capital in Transvaal, was a large stone-walled town.⁴⁸ From the nineteenth century southern Africa's urbanization was very much a product of colonial intervention, although this, as at Mafeking, by no means excluded African influence upon the nature of that urbanism. Cape Town, founded in 1652, was the essence of a colonial town, yet by the nineteenth century its form had come to be shaped in larger part by its non-European inhabitants. In 1806 Cape Town's population was 16,000, made up of 7,000 free persons and 9,000 slaves. By 1875 the total figure had risen to 45,000, and by 1904 some 170,000 people lived within the town. Europeans dominated the government of the town, but this population was predominantly African, even if increasingly although not entirely segregated into the less desirable zones of the municipality.⁴⁹

Cape Town's *raison d'être* was that it was a port town. Durban, on the Indian Ocean coast, grew in the last quarter of the nineteenth century for similar reasons, supplying the great industrial cities of Kimberley and then Johannesburg on the Witwatersrand. Both these cities emerged as the direct consequence of the discovery of minerals, first diamonds at Kimberley and then gold on the Rand. These are rare examples of industrial cities in Africa, unique creations dramatically spawned in an unregulated and squalid clamour. Kimberley was famously ramshackle and rowdy, a frontier town where only the barest of essentials could be guaranteed.⁵⁰ Johannesburg's growth was latterly better controlled, but from the opening of the goldfields in 1886 it was estimated that more than 100,000 people had flooded into the fledgeling city by 1896. By the 1920s, with a population of more than 250,000, the sheer scale of Johannesburg made it quite unique within the continent.[51] Industry and its demands dominated the development of these towns, etching itself onto the lives of the Africans who gathered there. The roots of hard-edged segregation, of job reservation, the migrant labour system and the final elaborations of apartheid are to be found in the turbulent evolution of South Africa's industrial towns.[52]

It is all too easy to imagine that the segregation of African towns evident throughout much of the continent in the twentieth century was a consequence of colonialism, and particularly of its southern African brand. But many African towns, from antiquity to modern times, had been segregated between free and unfree, or between elites and commoners, or had set aside separate areas for merchant or immigrant communities of one kind or another. Urban spaces were often too important – too powerful, too filled with the symbolism of authority and wealth – to be freely opened to allcomers. African towns were always arenas in which identities were firmly maintained, as well as being newly made and remade. For example, around the heart of old Freetown, founded in 1794, there quickly grew up a series of settlements whose names betrayed the strong ethnic essentialisms of urban life: by 1880, the map of Freetown showed 'Kroo Town' in the western portion, with 'Congo Town' a little further out; 'Bambara Town', 'Foulah Town' and 'Kossoh Town' lay to the east, and 'Soldier Town' was, naturally enough, located in the shadow of the Tower Hill barracks.[53] In the capital cities of settler colonies, such as Salisbury (Harare) and Nairobi, this process was more obviously the deliberate product of colonial intervention. These towns, founded around the turn of the century, were regarded by their rulers as essentially European in form and function, set down to service a settler community. African and Asian residents were almost from the outset segregated and regulated, whether through the differential imposition of rating and renting regimes, or through sanitation controls, or through social segregation effected by zoning. From the perspective of those who governed, race was here the primary determinant of one's place within the social order of the colonial city, ethnicity only a secondary concern.[54]

By the early twentieth century the residence patterns and social map of cities such as Accra and Lagos were also being redrawn in the name of racial segregation and urban zoning. In making these attempts to redefine the urban order, European rulers were challenging the deep and long-standing historical, cultural and ethnic pluralism of African towns.[55] Only very rarely were African towns monolingual,[56] or inhabited solely by people linked by kinship. Towns grew and were constructed within multiple images of urbanism. In this respect, the historical towns of Africa, most especially those of the coasts, were very like other trading towns throughout the world. Like Amsterdam or Venice, London or Lisbon, trade and commercial expansion ensured that urban populations were drawn from many parts of the world as well as from other parts of Africa. For thousands of years trade *within* Africa was of far greater significance than trans-Saharan or maritime trade with the rest of the world. Merchants from the Sahel travelled to and lived in forest towns, just as traders from the forests were long used to residence in the towns of the southern fringes of the Sahara. This long history of temporary migrations would by the twentieth century include many other immigrants, forced migrants and economic refugees such as the Malays in Cape Town, Omanis and Hadramis in Zanzibar, Gujaratis in Nairobi, and Lebanese in Accra and Freetown. Each wave of immigrants brought their own cultural values and urban mores. All of these migrant communities were brought to Africa by imperialisms of a kind, but their absorption into the social and cultural fabric of African towns was very much part of an ancient, indigenous process.

Absorption and pluralism did not imply the abandonment of identity. Ethnicity, sometimes very recently constructed, was as much a factor in town as outside it. Modern African cities of the mid-twentieth century were not the cultural melting pots that some colonial officals feared: rather the opposite. Increasing competition – for jobs, for space and for power – hardened rivalries and in many places these struggles were configured in ethnic terms. A breakdown of Lagos's population in 1950 revealed that 73 per cent of those citizens questioned saw themselves as Yoruba, whilst 12 per cent were Ibo. No less than 37 per cent of the total urban population of 230,000 were estimated to have been born in the city, and a further 39 per cent had been born in the Western Region, more than half of these from the two neighbouring districts of Abeokuta and Ijebu. Only 11 per cent of Lagos's residents came from the Eastern Region, and only 8 per cent from the Northern Region. Lagos, like most larger African cities of this period, drew the bulk of it migrants from the immediate hinterland of the town.[57] In these circumstances, older, longer established residents and members of majority communities defended access to jobs and living space as 'theirs' against newcomers. Minorities banded closer together to garner what influence they could muster. Such divisions came to be significant aspects of the urban politics of the mid-twentieth century in Accra,[58] Brazzaville,[59] Freetown,[60] Kinshasa,[61] Douala and Libreville,[62] as well as in Lagos.

The growth of African cities has been spectacular throughout much of the continent since the 1940s. Lagos's population had stood at only 75,000 in 1939, but reached 230,000 by 1950, and 675,000 by 1962. Abidjan had a population of only 10,000 in 1931, but this had expanded to 180,000 by 1960. Accra grew between 1948 and 1960 from 135,000 to 325,000, and Dakar's population doubled to 400,000 over the same period. Bamako's population increased four-fold from 25,000 in 1945 to over 100,000 by 1970.[63] In eastern Africa, Nairobi's growth began during the Second World War; a town of 49,000 in 1936 reached 120,000 by 1948. By 1962 Nairobi's population was officially estimated at 267,000, although the real figure may have been considerably larger.[64] Alongside the huge expansion of the prime, capital cities, smaller market towns also grew in size and number. Africa was becoming an increasingly urban continent. By the mid-1960s 'Ethiopia sported some 200 towns of various sizes, which concentrated state power, held almost 10 per cent of the population' and were estimated to be growing at an annual rate of 7 per cent.[65] North Africa was by then the most urbanized region of Africa, perhaps one-third of the population living in towns.[66] In South Africa the most spectacular growth was in the 'squatter cities' that became home to Africans displaced from rural lands, Soweto being the largest and most infamous of many.[67] Everywhere the physical growth of African cities and towns in this period far outstripped the capacity of urban resources and services. Water supplies, sanitation, educational provision, health facilities, transport infrastructure and, most desperately of all, housing provision proved inadequate to support such dramatically burgeoning populations. From being places of accumulated wealth and prosperity, by the 1970s Africa's leading cities were increasingly coming to be seen as centres of poverty and social deprivation.

As some towns boomed, others slumped, even in this period of rapid urbanization over the continent. In West Africa, for example, the emergence of Accra as an adminis-trative capital marked the decline of Cape Coast, while the fortunes of the cocoa-boom town of Koforidua plummeted as the devastation of cocoa disease reduced its importance as a buying centre. In Equatorial Africa the growth of twentieth-century towns has generally been far less spectacular than elsewhere. Here towns hardly outstripped their pre-colonial dimensions. Abeche, in eastern Chad, had numbered 28,000 toward the end of the nineteenth century and was then the largest urban centre in the region. By 1939 Abeche had declined sharply, being replaced as the largest city of the region by Brazzaville with a population of only 45,000. Libreville, once a thriving French colonial trading port, could boast a population of only 11,000 in 1940. Against the trend elsewhere on the continent, Equatorial Africa was probably less urban in 1970 than it had been in 1870.[68]

In the late twentieth century, the larger African towns and cities may appear to have become more uniform than ever before. Colonial urban designs structured Africa's towns in new ways, regulating access, segregating space, and seeking to control and regiment in the name of 'order'. Such policies were seldom successful in all their grand ambitions, but they made their mark on the physical appearance of colonial towns.[69] In the post-colonial years, economic globalization has taken this a step further, most especially in the commercial sectors of the larger cities. There can be no city in Africa with streets without advertising hoardings for Coca Cola or Marlboro cigarettes and sound systems which pump out a familiar global melange of soul and rap.[70] But the surface 'sameness' towards which these influences appear to be pushing Africa's cities should not be allowed to mask the richly varied and diverse histories of urbanization. Even where colonial cities are explicitly modern creations, as are Nairobi and Lusaka, the peoples who have come to live in those places have brought their own cultural values and aspirations with them, fashioning distinctive forms of urbanism that remain to be explored adequately in their historical contexts.

Making Urban Histories

The 17 essays gathered together in this collection celebrate the variety of historical experience to be found in Africa's urban past, but they do not share a common methodology or theoretical approach. There is no one urban history of Africa, and no single paradigm that can be imposed to explain the growth, development or decline of African towns. In Africa, as elsewhere, the interpretation of pre-industrial urbanization necessarily differs sharply from that of the industrial city; and there are marked cultural influences evident in urbanism across the various regions of the African continent that cannot be ignored. That said, it seems to us appropriate and timely for historians now to look more closely at the character of urban history in Africa, and especially at the importance of urbanization as an historical force, and to move towards a greater awareness of those factors which may be unique to a particular urban experience, and those which may allow a more comparative approach to the history of Africa's towns.

To date, urban history as a recognizable sub-field has not made a significant impact upon African historiography, and the reasons for this need to be addressed.[71] In the first place there are familiar problems of definition. There are many historians of America, Europe and Asia, as well as Africa, who might share Eric Hobsbawm's worry that urban history can too easily degenerate into becoming 'a large container, with ill-defined, heterogenous and sometimes indiscriminate contents'.[72] Even when writing in praise of the pioneering work of the leading urban historian of Victorian England, H. J. Dyos, David Cannadine felt compelled to admit that 'It is, in practice, exceedingly difficult to see what *is* uniquely urban.'[73] Dyos himself recognized the difficulties that definition posed, but thought the answer lay in seeing the city itself as an organic field of study. 'The authentic measure of urban history', wrote Dyos,

> is the degree to which it is concerned directly and generically with cities themselves, and not with the historical events and tendencies that have been purely incidental to them; and that, whether concerned with cities as more or less isolated or systematic or universal phenomena, it is the study of the ... ways in which their components fitted together or impinged upon other things, that distinguishes urban historians from those who may be said to be passing through their territory.'[74]

But as the historical study of North American and European cities first came to prominence in the 1960s and early 1970s, there were relatively few scholars who wrote about urbanism and urbanization in the manner Dyos would have wished. Those 'passing through' the city, writing about events to which the urban environment was merely a backcloth, remained very much in the majority.

Historians of Africa were especially slow to pick up Dyos's challenge, and until the 1970s relatively few of them even bothered to 'pass through' the city. The evolution of urban research in Africa, as it emerged in the 1950s and gathered momentum in the 1960s, offers clues as to why this was so. Even though urban studies became a dominant feature of scholarship on Africa in these decades, towns and cities were then the pre-occupation not of the historian, but of geographers,[75] political scientists and urban sociologists.[76] Towns were perceived as the epitome of modernization. Urbanization was the shape of things to come, and, for better or for worse, 'traditional' Africa was being dis-assembled in the urban milieu of modern occupations, wage earning, transformed patterns of domesticity, class consciousness and education. Most significant of all the problems of urbanization, towns were perceived as the classic location in which 'detribalization' was occurring. The danger was seen to be one of order and control. Urban populations were growing dramatically in numbers, but were unstable. Many came to town only briefly, to earn money, before returning to the countryside. Circular migration and target working suggested that urban values and attitudes might be speedily and widely disseminated through the rural areas, undermining 'traditional' authority and heralding dramatic social change. Urban 'pull factors' vastly outweighed rural 'push factors' in most explanations of these migratory patterns.[77] In this interpretation – which it must be acknowledged was more evident in Anglophone literature on African urbanization than in its Francophone counterpart[78] – towns were essentially modern aberrations, characterized as representing a sharp break with the past. History had little place in towns, because towns had little history.

The great social surveys of the late colonial years reflected the functionalist emphasis of this urban research. Wilson's *Mombasa Social Survey*, Leslie's detailed study of Dar es Salaam's households, the Carpenter report on Nairobi, Ione Acquah's *Accra Survey*, and K. A. Busia's *Report on a Social Survey of Sekondi-Takoradi* were all imaginative works of sociological data collection, geared towards the better regulation and structure of the colonial and post-colonial town.[79] Troubled by the material evidence of the wretchedness of the lives of many urbanites, the authors of these studies tended to stress the importance of social welfare issues such as public health, housing and education.[80] Most especially in the work on East and Central Africa, 'detribalization' remained a key theme, as it was commonly argued that without 'traditional' supports African urban societies were less able to cater for their own needs and that government should therefore either provide enhanced urban welfare services or better-regulated access to the cities. The over-mighty influence of southern African anthropology also loomed large in all this, some of the most elaborate enquiries being prompted in the towns of the Copperbelt, as well as further south, under the auspices of the Rhodes Livingstone Institute.[81] The evolving discriminatory policy of the Bantustans, then emerging as the cornerstone of apartheid, gave these concerns an even greater sharpness in South Africa, where Meyer's *Townsmen or Tribesmen* ironically posed the seminal question confronting the Nationalist government as well as those who struggled against it.[82]

These trends are less obvious in the research generated in West Africa. Here there were social scientists who were less impressed by the impending tragedy of the city than by its exciting particularities.[83] Some scholars drew attention to the Eurocentric quality of supposing a stark opposition of town and country when periods in town employment appeared to be viewed by many rural Africans as part of the essential seasonality of rural production.[84] Others stressed that urbanism rather than 'detribalizing' seemed to thrive on the persistence of 'tribal' identities.[85] Above all, the city was seen as a key political arena in a period when rapid political change was in the process of transforming colonial West Africa into post-colonial West Africa.[86] J. D. Y. Peel, who more than any other social anthropologist has used history with remarkable success in his extensive work on the Yoruba,[87] has pointed out that the most illuminating social science of this period concerning West Africa was very much aware of the significance of history in its understanding of the present.[88]

Though exceptions can be found in works such as Peter Gutkind's splendid history of Buganda's *Rubaga*, or Christopher Fyfe's largely Freetown-focused *History of Sierra Leone*, before the 1970s very few historians, as opposed to social scientists, of Africa made the town the centre of their world. Those 'passing through' the town – writing about things that went on in the urban environment, but not being concerned with urbanism or urbanization – found plenty to interest them in the activities of an urban elite who were enmeshed in the struggles of political nationalism, but such studies in no way problema-tized towns historically.[89] For the vast majority of Africa's historians, it was the country-side that mattered: Africa's societies were consistedly presented as peasant societies first and foremost, and the impetus of historical research was channelled into agrarian studies.

Urban Africa was at last 'discovered' by historians in the later 1970s, partly as a consequence of the rise of the 'new' social history.[90] This did not emerge out of interest in urban issues *per se*, but out of the quest for a clearer understanding of African experiences of colonial domination and class oppression. Cooper's influential *Struggle for the City*, focusing upon modern urban social and labour history, set the tone, but the trailblazing study was unquestionably Charles van Onselen's majestic collection of essays on the social and economic history of the Witwatersrand in its formative years, between 1886 and 1914.[91] The many concerns of urban history 'from below' which had earlier been flagged by scholars such as George Rudé, Gareth Stedman Jones, David Levine and Herbert Guttman[92] – crime, policing, indigency, town-planning and public health to state only the most obvious topics – formed the core of van Onselen's analysis and set an example for others to follow. These themes quickly became central tenets in the elaboration of a new South African historiography in the 1980s, in which the social history of urbanization featured strongly.[93]

In the wave of writing on urban social history that has subsequently developed and spread over the African continent, two limiting tendencies have been apparent. First, Africa's historians have been too ready to accept the urban sociologist's presentation of the town as a colonial and relatively modern creation. This was particularly attractive to the social historian because it captured and bounded a segment of African humanity, who were at once more visible in the accessible historical record. In contrast to the burgeoning of modern urban histories in Africa, until very recently there has been little interest in pre-colonial urbanism other than through the work of archaeologists.[94] Second, the social histories of towns and cities have too often been viewed solely and narrowly from a regional (or even local) perspective. Linked into regional historiographies, and therefore reflecting the different emphases of research in different parts of the continent, opportunities for the comparative study of African towns have been hampered. And with the exception of South Africa, where some writers have preferred to peer into the North American mirror than look to other parts of Africa for a comparativist view, there has been relatively little awareness shown of the development of urban historiography in other parts of the world.

The studies collected in this volume suggest that the critical mass of urban historical research needed to make comparative studies meaningful within Africa has now been reached. To encourage such comparisons we have avoided either a regional or a strictly chronological format. The chapters which follow are linked by three broad themes, each of which spans the full historical range of the volume and each of which has relevance to current debates on African urbanization. Each theme raises substantive historical questions, which have been addressed by several contributors. The first is that of urban *transitions*: by what means were African towns transformed by external influences, such as new economic stimuli, conquest and warfare, or the demands of international capital; and what internal shifts have contributed to changes in the urban environment, such as the rise of new polities, changes in cultural, religious and social practice, and new desires and expectations on the part of urban populations? The second broad theme is *the making of urban cultures*: to what extent have African townspeople been distinct culturally from their rural kin? How has urban culture evolved, and by what markers has it been recognized? What are the particular characteristics of urban society, and how have these changed over time? *Regulating the city* forms our third theme: who has controlled the urban environment, and how has that control been regulated? How have people gained access to things that the city has to offer, and who has mediated that process? Who decides what happens in the city? These issues became particularly apparent under colonialism, but they were no less a feature of pre-colonial urban politics than the process of urban transition or the making of urban cultures.

The 17 chapters are organized into five parts. Part One offers three examples of the ways in which recent archaeological research has contributed to our understandings of urban forms in Africa; Rod McIntosh deals with the importance of cultural symbolism in interpreting the origins and placement of ancient urban settlements; Graham Connah provides a comparativist examination of the many different forms of city walls and argues for the urgent need to explore the archaeology of these structures more fully; and David Phillipson reports findings from the most recent excavations at the ancient city of Aksum.

The three chapters in Part Two monitor transitions in pre-colonial towns, beginning with John Thornton's survey of the political history of the great Kongo capital of Mbanza Kongo (latterly known as São Salvador). This chapter emphasizes the importance of ideas of spirituality, and of indigenous expressions of political and cultural symbolism in the longer history of urbanization. Robin Law next provides a survey of the economic and political transformations at Ouidah through its rise as a slaving entrepot to its role in 'legitimate' trade. Though Ouidah was a town made out of the engagement with Atlantic commerce, Law shows that it was never dominated by external influences. In the final chapter in this section, Richard Reid and Henri Medard give an account of the changing status of the royal capitals of Buganda in response to the evolution of the nineteenth-century political economy of the interlacustrine region. Here, it is argued that the Europeans who wished to dominate the city did so by adopting symbolic geography of the African urban landscape: Kampala would become the centre of a colonial administration, but it remained an African town.

Part Three focuses upon aspects of the commercial and economic histories of towns. Smaller towns have received less historical attention to date than have Africa's larger cities, but Tom Spear's study of the evolution of Arusha town, in northern Tanzania, examines the many ways in which a small market town and regional centre affects the cultural and economic lives of local communities. Here, the town itself has come to reflect contrasting cultural expressions of lifestyle among different groups of people. Ayodeji Olukoju's chapter on the cost of living in Lagos looks at some of the economic hardships of urban life, especially the high cost of urban foodstuffs, and at the problems of food supply. To close this section, Bill Freund provides an overview of the evolving political economy of Durban, exploring the many contradictions between social policies and economic aims to be found in South Africa under apartheid.

The four chapters comprising Part Four each examine the urban setting as an arena in which cultural forms and meanings have been remade. To emphasize that urban identities are not entirely modern constructs, Ray Kea draws upon the lives of Africans living in the urban settlements of the Gold Coast in the eighteenth century to suggest ways in which they made sense of their world. Dealing with that same social milieu, but two hundred years on, John Parker looks at the cultural politics of death and burial in the city of Accra. Julia Clancy-Smith's discussion of urban identities in nineteenth-century Tunis takes up the history of urban migration and the assimilation of migrants, looking especially at the significance of gender evident in these processes, both in materialist and in culturally, ethnically and racially symbolic terms. Gender, and the independence of urban women, is also the organizing theme of Emmanuel Akyeampong's study of urbanization in colonial Ghana which closes this section.

In Part Five, our four contributors each address questions of the politics of urban control and regulation. In his account of the urban growth of Bahir Dar, a town in highland Ethiopia that has undergone dramatic growth since the 1930s, Seltene Seyoum considers the way in which urbanization impacts upon traditional ideas of land tenure and property rights. Conservation and urban control are the linked themes explored in William Bissell's survey of the history of urban planning in Zanzibar Town. This chapter exposes the haplessness of colonial government in its attempt to make African urbanism conform to its vision of the 'regulated, orderly town'. The discussion of the recent past and possible future of Cape Town's District Six by Rafael Marks and Marco Bezzoli also reviews the history of urban planning. They make a strong plea that District Six's distinctive history should be drawn upon in devising the plans for its renewal and rebirth as a residential area. In the closing chapter, Florence Bernault shows how urban riots in Brazzaville have come to be an expression of the divisions and factionalism of the city itself, drawing upon a bewildering array of local, national and international symbols. Here the city no longer reflects older conflicts, but has reshaped them anew.

Some of these chapters are undoubtedly more self-conscious than others in their attempt to meet Dyos's demand that urban history 'should be concerned directly and generically with cities themselves', but all endeavour to place the city at the centre of the discussion. The themes they develop are often unexpected, particularly in the many ways in which African urbanism emerges as having been historically distinctive, and the sources they draw upon are surprisingly rich. Taken as a whole, the collection suggests that Africa's urban history offers very great potential for further research. In this important sense, this volume is intended not as a summation of what we know about African towns, but rather as a starting point for the writing of deeper and eventually more comparativist histories of Africa's urban past.

Notes

1 United Nations, *Global Report on Human Settlements* (Washington, 1996).
2 John Iliffe, *The African Poor: a History* (Cambridge, 1987), chapter 1, for a succinct statement of this.
3 Graham Connah, *African Civilisations. Precolonial Cities and State in Tropical Africa: an Archaeological Perspective* (Cambridge, 1987), remains by far the best synthesis of the subject. See also T. Shaw, P. Sinclair, B. Andah and A. Okpoko (eds), *The Archaeology of Africa: Food, Metals and Towns* (London, 1993).
4 The description is from Richard F. Burton, *The Lake Regions of Central Africa*, 2 vols (new edition, London, 1961), but we owe the citation to Justin Willis, '"A heap of huts"? Vugha and the nature of the Kilindi state', paper presented to the conference on 'Africa's Urban Past', SOAS, London, June 1996.
5 Derek A. Welsby, *The Kingdom of Kush: the Napatan and Meroitic Empires* (London, 1996), and David

N. Edwards, *The Archaeology of the Meroitic State* (Oxford, 1996), significantly update the earlier standard works by W. Y. Adams, *Nubia: Corridor to Africa* (London, 1977), and P. L. Shinnie, *Meroe* (London, 1967).

6 For an excellent illustration, see Richard I. Lawless and Gerard Blake, *Tlemcen: Continuity and Change in an Algerian Islamic Town* (London and New York, 1976).

7 Stuart Munro-Hay, *Aksum* (Edinburgh, 1991); Stuart Munro Hay (ed.), *Excavations at Aksum: An account of the research at the Ancient Ethiopian Capital, Directed in 1972–74 by the Late Neville Chittick* (London and Nairobi, 1989). For the most recent findings, David W. Phillipson and Andrew Reynolds, 'B.I.E.A. excavations at Aksum, Northern Ethiopia, 1995', *Azania*, 31 (1996), pp. 99–147, and chapter 3, below.

8 S. K. and R. J. McIntosh, *Prehistoric Investigations in the Region of Jenne, Mali*, 2 vols (Oxford, 1980), is the starting point, but see the more recent references cited below in Chapter 1.

9 Timothy Insoll, *Islam, Archaeology and History: Gao Region (Mali) ca. AD 900–1250* (Oxford, 1996).

10 John Iliffe, *Africans: The History of a Continent* (Cambridge, 1995), p. 51.

11 Graham Connah, *The Archaeology of Benin* (Oxford, 1975); Thurston Shaw, *Unearthing Igbo-Ukwu* (Ibadan, 1977).

12 J. E. G. Sutton, *A Thousand Years of East Africa* (Nairobi, 1990), pp. 6–16 for a fine survey. And for the results of the most recent excavations: Peter T. Robertshaw, 'Recent archaeological surveys in Western Uganda', *Nyame Akuma*, 36 (1991), pp. 40–6; Peter T. Robertshaw, 'Archaeological survey: ceramic analysis and state formation in Western Uganda', *African Archaeological Review*, 12 (1994), pp.105–31; D. A. M. Reid and J. E. K. Njau, 'Archaeological research in Karagwe district', *Nyame Akuma*, 41 (1994), pp. 68–73; and J. E. G. Sutton and Andrew Reid, *Ntusi* (forthcoming, 2000).

13 Mark Horton, *Shanga: The Archaeology of a Muslim Trading Community on the Coast of East Africa* (London and Nairobi, 1997) updates earlier works. But see also, Neville Chittick, *Kilwa: An Islamic Trading City on the East African Coast*, 2 vols (London and Nairobi, 1974); Neville Chittick, *Manda: Excavations at an Island Port on the Kenya Coast* (London and Nairobi, 1984); F. Chami, *The Tanzanian Coast in the First Millennium AD* (Uppsala, 1994); Paul Sinclair, 'Chibuene: an early trading site in southern Mozambique', *Paideuma*, 28 (1982), pp. 150–64.

14 Peter S. Garlake, *Great Zimbabwe* (London, 1973); Thomas N. Huffmann, *Snakes and Crocodiles: Power and Symbolism in Ancient Zimbabwe* (Johannesburg, 1996); Robert Soper, 'The Nyanga terrace complex of eastern Zimbabwe', *Azania*, 31 (1996), pp. 1–36.

15 Michael Brett, 'Ibn Khaldun and the dynastic approach to local history: the case of Biskra', *Al-Qantara: Revista de Estudios Arabes*, 12 (1991), p. 159.

16 Brett, 'Ibn Khaldun: Biskra', pp. 159–63, 176–7.

17 Michael Brett, 'The city-state in medieval Ifriqiya: the case of Tripoli', *Cahiers de Tunisie*, 34 (1986), pp. 69–94; Lawless and Blake, *Tlemcen*.

18 Lawless and Blake, *Tlemcen*, Chapter 1.

19 Quoted from Lawless and Blake, *Tlemcen*, p. 34.

20 A. G. Hopkins, *An Economic History of West Africa* (London, 1973), p. 19; John O. Hunwick, 'Songhay, Bornu and Hausaland in the sixteenth century', in J. F. A. Ajayi and M. Crowder (eds), *History of West Africa*, 2 vols (second edition, London, 1976), i, p. 265.

21 Iliffe, *The Africans*, p. 55; see also Chittick, *Kilwa*.

22 Martin Hall, *The Changing Past* (Cape Town, 1987), pp. 75–84; James R. Denbow, 'Cows and kings: a spatial and economic analysis of a hierarchical Early Iron Age settlement system in eastern Botswana', in M. Hall, G. Avery, D. M. Avery, M. L. Wilson, and A. J. B. Humphreys (eds), *Frontiers: Southern African Archaeology Today* (Oxford, 1984), pp. 24–39.

23 Iliffe, *The Africans*, p. 118.

24 Hall, *Farmers, Kings and Traders*, p. 91; Huffmann, *Snakes and Crocodiles*.

25 Huffmann, *Snakes and Crocodiles* offers the most cogent argument for this interpretation.

26 But see Paul Sinclair, 'Some aspects of the economic level of the Zimbabwe state', *Zimbabwea*, 1 (1984), pp. 48–55.

27 Iliffe, *The Africans*, p. 55; Chittick, *Kilwa*, for the archaeology, and G. S. P. Freeman Grenville, *The East African Coast: Select Documents* (Oxford, 1962) for documentary sources.

28 Iliffe, *The Africans*, p. 79.

29 Iliffe, *The Africans*, p. 85.

30 Hopkins, *Economic History*, p. 19.

31 Iliffe, *The Africans*, p. 78.

32 Ronald Horvath, 'The wandering capitals of Ethiopia', *Journal of African History*, 10 (1969), pp. 205–19.

33 James C. McCann, *From Poverty to Famine in Northeast Ethiopia* (Philadelphia, 1987), p. 24.

34 Jan Vansina, *Paths in the Rainforests: Towards a History of Political Tradition in Equatorial Africa* (London, 1990), pp. 211–12.

35 Vansina, *Paths in the Rainforests*, p. 211; Marvin P. Miracle, *Maize in Tropical Africa* (Madison, Milwaukee and London, 1966), pp. 87–95.

36 Vansina, *Paths in the Rainforests*, pp. 229, 118 and 106 for Bongo, citing G. Sautter, *De l'Atlantique au fleuve Congo: une geographie du sous-peuplement*, 2 vols (Paris, 1966), pp. 259–61.

37 Hopkins, *Economic History*, pp. 145 and 107–12 for a summary of the commercial histories of Whydah (Ouidah) and Old Calabar. For more on Ouidah, see Law, Chapter 6, below. See also, Robin Horton, 'From fishing village to city state: a social history of New Calabar', in Mary Douglas and Phyllis M. Kaberry (eds), *Man in Africa* (London, 1969), pp. 37–58.

38 Hopkins, *Economic History*, p. 19.

39 Iliffe, *The Africans*, p. 143.

40 T. E. Bowdich, *Mission From Cape Coast to Ashantee* (third edition, London, 1966), pp. 322–4.

41 James C. McCann, *People of the Plow: An Agricultural History of Ethiopia, 1800–1990* (Madison, 1995), pp. 109–15.

42 McCann, *People of the Plow*, pp. 200, 240: Horvath, 'Roving capitals'.

43 Peter P. Garretson, 'A history of Addis Ababa from its foundation in 1886 to 1910' (PhD thesis, University of London, 1974).

44 For contemporary accounts, see Thomas Wakefield, 'Routes of native caravans from the coast to the interior of East Africa', *Journal of the Royal Geographical Society*, 40 (1870); Joseph Thomson, *Through Masailand* (London, 1887), esp. p. 263 for Baringo; and L. von Hohnel, *Discovery of Lakes Rudolf and Stephanie*, 2 vols (London, 1894), for Baringo and Taveta.

45 A. C. P. Gamitto (trans. Ian Cunnison), *King Kazembe and the Marave, Chava, Bisu. Bemba, Lunda, and other peoples of Southern Africa* (Lisbon, 1960: originally published 1832), pp. 109–30.

46 John Iliffe, *A Modern History of Tanganyika* (Cambridge, 1979), p. 381.

47 P. W. Gutkind, *The Royal Capital of Buganda* (The Hague, 1963); and see Reid and Medard, Chapter 7, below.

48 Iliffe, *The Africans*, p. 118.

49 Vivian Bickford-Smith, *Ethnic Pride and Racial Prejudice in Victorian Cape Town: Group Identity and Social Practice, 1875–1902* (Cambridge, 1995), pp. 10–13.

50 Robert V. Turrell, *Capital and Labour on the Kimberley Diamond Fields, 1871–1890* (Cambridge, 1987), and William H. Worger, *South Africa's City of Diamonds: Mine Workers and Monopoly Capitalism in Kimberley, 1897–1895* (New Haven and London, 1987).

51 Charles van Onselen, *Studies in the Social and Economic History of Witwatersrand, 1886–1914* (Harlow, 1982), for a wonderfully vivid account of the early development of Johannesburg; Peter Kallaway and Patrick Pearson, *Johannesburg: Images and Continuities – a History of Working Class Life Through Pictures, 1885–1935* (Braamfontein, 1986); A. N. Porter (ed.), *Atlas of British Overseas Expansion* (London, 1991), p.225, for a map of the city *c.* 1897.

52 Iliffe, *African Poor*, pp. 260–8, for an excellent summary of the period 1948 to the early 1980s.

53 Porter (ed.), *Atlas of British Overseas Expansion* (London, 1991), p. 234.

54 Dane Kennedy, *Islands of White: Settler Society and Culture in Kenya and Southern Rhodesia, 1890–1939* (Durham NC, 1987), pp. 148–66; Anja Kervanto Nevanlinna, *Interpreting Nairobi: The Cultural Study of Built Forms* (Helsinki, 1997); Michael G. Redley, 'The Politics of a predicament: the white community in Kenya, 1918–32' (PhD thesis, University of Cambridge, 1976).

55 Kristin Mann, *Marrying Well: Status and Social Change among the Educated Elite in Colonial Lagos* (Cambridge, 1985); Sandra T. Barnes, *Patrons and Power: Creating a Political Community in Metropolitan Lagos* (Manchester, 1986); John Parker, 'Ga state and society in early colonial Accra, 1860s–1920s' (PhD thesis, University of London, 1995); and Parker, Chapter 13, below.

56 M. E. Kropp Dakubu, *Korle Meets the Sea: A Socio-linguistic History of Accra* (Oxford, 1997).

57 Peter C. Lloyd, *Africa in Social Change* (Harmondsworth, 1967), pp. 112–13.

58 Dennis Austin, *Politics in Ghana, 1946–60* (Oxford, 1964), and more generally Kropp Dakubu, *Korle Meets the Sea*.

59 Rene Gauze (trans. Virginia Thompson and Richard Adloff), *The Politics of Congo Brazzaville*

(Stanford, 1973), but for a more recent study of the social history of the city see Phyllis M. Martin, *Leisure and Society in Colonial Brazzaville* (Cambridge, 1995).

60 Joe A. D. Alie, *A New History of Sierra Leone* (Freetown, 1990); Akintola J. G. Wyse, *H. C. Bankole-Bright and Politics in Colonial Sierra Leone, 1919–1958* (Cambridge, 1990).

61 Crawford Young, *Politics in the Congo* (Princeton, 1965); Jean La Fontaine, *City Politics: A Study of Leopoldville, 1962–63* (Oxford, 1970).

62 Ralph A. Austen and Rita Headrick, 'Equatorial Africa under colonial rule', in David Birmingham and Phyllis M. Martin (eds), *History of Central Africa, Volume 2* (London and New York, 1983), p. 80.

63 Lloyd, *Africa in Social Change*, pp. 111–12.

64 Nevanlinna, *Interpreting Nairobi*, pp. 162, 188.

65 McCann, *People of the Plow*, p. 240.

66 Lawless and Blake, *Tlemcen*, p. 1.

67 Surplus People Project, *Forced Removals in South Africa, vols 1–5* (Cape Town, 1983); Gavin Maasdorp and A. S. B. Humphreys (eds), *From Shantytown to Township: An Economic Study of African Poverty and Rehousing in a South African City* (Cape Town, 1975); John Western, *Outcast Cape Town* (London, 1981).

68 Austen and Headrick, 'Equatorial Africa', p. 80.

69 Anthony D. King, *Colonial Urban Development: Culture, Social Power and Environment* (London, 1976); Philip Amis and Peter Lloyd (eds), *Housing Africa's Urban Poor* (Manchester, 1990), pp. 1–71; Nevanlinna, *Interpreting Nairobi*, pp. 157–203.

70 Anthony D. King, *Urbanism, Colonialism, and the World Economy: Cultural and Spatial Foundations of the World Urban System* (London, 1990); Anthony O'Connor, *The African City* (London, 1983).

71 But for a most useful survey, see Catherine Coquery-Vidrovitch, 'The process of urbanization in Africa, from the origins to the beginning of independence', *African Studies Review*, 34 (1991).

72 David Cannadine and David Reeder (eds), *Exploring the Urban Past: Essays in Urban History by H. J. Dyos* (Cambridge, 1982), p. 209, the quote being drawn from Cannadine's concluding essay.

73 Cannadine and Reeder, *Exploring the Urban Past*, p. 210.

74 The statement comes from Dyos's essay on 'Urbanity and suburbanity', Cannadine and Reeder, *Exploring the Urban Past*, p. 36.

75 A real pioneer in this field was the Nigerian geographer Akin Mobogunje, whose *Urbanization in Nigeria* (London, 1968) is unusual in having a great deal to say about pre-colonial urbanization as well as analyzing the nature of modern cities.

76 For example, Michael Banton, *West African City: A Study of Tribal Life in Freetown* (Oxford, 1957); Abner Cohen, *Custom and Politics in Urban Africa: A Study of Hausa Migrants in Yoruba Towns* (Berkeley, 1969); Kenneth Little, *West African Urbanization: A Study of Voluntary Associations in Social Change* (Cambridge, 1956); Peter Marris, *Family and Social Change in an African City* (London, 1962); and Leonard Plotnicov, *Strangers in the City: Urban Man in Jos, Nigeria* (Pittsburgh, 1967).

77 For example Lloyd, *Africa in Social Change*, Chapters 3, 4 and 8; and, for a more recent overview, Sharon Stichter, *Migrant Labourers* (Cambridge, 1985).

78 See Coquery-Vidrovitch, 'The process of urbanization'.

79 Gordon Wilson, *Mombasa Social Survey* (Nairobi, 1958); J. A. K. Leslie, *A Survey of Dar es Salaam* (London, 1963); *Report on the Committee on African Wages [Carpenter Report]* (Nairobi, 1954); Ione Acquah, *Accra Survey* (Accra, 1958); K. A. Busia, *Report on a Social Survey of Sekondi-Takoradi* (London, 1950).

80 John Iliffe is the only scholar who has yet begun to exploit the rich potential for comparative study presented by this near-contemporaneous collection of this data on African urban life. See his *African Poor*, Chapter 10.

81 Amongst the most influential of such works was J. Clyde Mitchell, *African Urbanization in Ndola and Luanshya* (Lusaka, 1954). See also A. L. Epstein, *Urbanization and Kinship: The Domestic Domain on the Copperbelt of Zambia, 1950–56* (London, 1981).

82 Philip Meyer, *Townsmen or Tribesmen: Conservatism and the Process of Urbanization in a South African City* (Second edition, Cape Town, 1971).

83 J. D. Y. Peel's review article, 'Urbanization and urban history in West Africa', *Journal of African History*, 21 (1980), pp. 269–77 remains an invaluable guide to the interface between social science and history.

84 Aronson's *The City is Our Farm* (London, 1978) draws on fine geographical data for an ethnographic account which has much to teach historians.

85 Banton, *West African City*.
86 See especially K. W. J. Post and G. D. Jenkins, *The Price of Liberty* (Cambridge, 1973); N. S. Hopkins, *Popular Government in an African Town: Kita, Mali* (Chicago, 1972); and J. Paden, *Religion and Political Culture in Kano* (Berkeley, 1973).
87 Such as his *Ijeshas and Nigerians* (Cambridge, 1983).
88 Peel, 'Urbanization and urban history', pp. 272–3.
89 Gutkind, *Royal Capital*; Christopher Fyfe, *A History of Sierra Leone* (London, 1962). For another important exception, see Post and Jenkins, *The Price of Liberty*.
90 Which included women's history, such as C. C. Robertson, *Sharing the Same Bowl: Women and Class in Accra* (Bloomington, 1984), and Luise White's *The Comfort of Home: Prostitution in Colonial Nairobi* (Chicago, 1990).
91 Frederick Cooper (ed.), *Struggle for the City: Migrant Labour, Capital and the State in Urban Africa* (Beverley Hills, 1983); van Onselen, *History of Witwatersrand*.
92 Herbert Guttman, *Work, Culture and Society in Industrializing America* (Oxford, 1977); David Levine, *Family Formation in an Age of Nascent Capitalism* (New York, 1977); Gareth Stedman Jones, *Outcast London: A Study in the Relationship between Classes in Victorian Society* (Oxford, 1971); George Rudé, *Paris and London in the Eighteenth Century: Studies in Popular Protest* (London, 1969).
93 For an overview, see William Beinart, *Twentieth Century South Africa* (London, 1995), and the special issue of the *Journal of Southern African Studies* (1996).
94 Conservation issues raise the most obvious exceptions. See Abdul Sheriff (ed.), *The History and Conservation of Zanzibar Stone Town* (London, 1995).

PART ONE

Urban Archaeologies

1

Clustered Cities of the Middle Niger
Alternative Routes to Authority in Prehistory

RODERICK J. MCINTOSH

An Archaeological Intangible: Authority

We are all familiar with the hoary, and terribly misleading, caricature of the Hairy-Chested versus the Hairy-Chinned archaeologist. The former, with Ramboesque pectorals and dull little eyes, lives to dig and dreads writing up; the latter sinks ever deeper over the years into his easy chair of abstract analysis. The 1996–7 season of excavations at Jenne-jeno (Mali) marked twenty years of investigations into urban prehistory in the Middle Niger.[1] This most recent season served, yet again, to show how far removed is the Hairy-Chested stereotype from the reality of the field situation. At every moment of excavation, empirical decisions and exigency hypotheses for testing bubble up from the research project's driving theory and from interpretative debates within the discipline. From the decision at the dawn of the excavation day to designate this ash lens a separate level or to pedestal that feature, to the obligatory whole-crew discussion after dinner each evening, the archaeologists investigating Middle Niger sites such as Jenne-jeno are continuously making empirical assessments against the evolving theoretical issues behind our current understanding of the emergence of urbanism.

Middle Niger urbanism does not conform comfortably with the expectations of urban archaeologists elsewhere around the globe. Archaeology here has the exciting potential to tweak the chin hairs of those speculating from their armchairs about preconditions of pre-industrial urbanism anywhere on the globe. Indeed, the African data have already encouraged researchers in northern China and in Mesopotamia to think in novel ways about their own discoveries. This chapter introduces to a general readership three intersecting planes of urban theory that drive our daily research decisions and empirical targets. All three planes intersect along an axis that archaeologists find chronically difficult to test: authority. Who made the decisions at these newly emergent towns, these historically experimental, heterogeneous social arenas? Authority may be a classic archaeological intangible, but after twenty years of work at Jenne-jeno and related sites, we can at least identify some of the pertinent theoretical issues. The three theoretical planes are definition, distinctiveness, and authority. Let us look at each in turn.

The first of our three intersecting planes concerns archaeologists' working definition

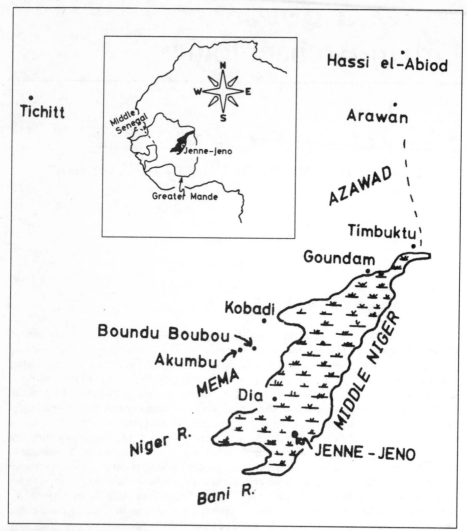

Figure 1.1 Location of sites and regions, Middle Niger

of an urban settlement. Can our experience gained uncovering the earliest cities along the Middle Niger help the larger search for an urban definition applicable not just to Africa? Can Africanists contribute to a definition of the city that is inclusive of the great variability of urban forms and historical particularities of long-term transformations out of rural landscapes that characterize the process of urbanism globally? Surveying the world literature, we have yet to find a better definition of a city than that proposed by a fellow Africanist, Bruce Trigger.[2] Towns are settlements with a diverse population engaged in providing specialized services and manufactures to a broader hinterland. This is a definition that does not specify a population threshold or minimum acceptable number of social or occupational strata (except relative to smaller-scale settlements in the hinterland). It is quite true that others still attempt to insert a power variable into a universal equation of urbanism. Take this 1997 example:

I consider an urban society as one with complex division of labor, that is, the existence of specialists in activities different from the production of subsistence goods; with specialists in decision-making that live in an urban center providing specific services to the surrounding region, such as the distribution of a large variety of goods.[3]

This may be quite adequate for the types of city, with unambiguous evidence of power elites, that archaeologists preferentially find in Mesopotamia, Central Mexico or the Andes: but where does that leave the large and heterogeneous settlements of the Middle Niger? These are sites as large as most in Mesopotamia, but they lack evidence of kings or other decision-making elites. In any definition, to specify the presence of those elites would be to eliminate by *fiat* a major component of urban diversity in Africa.

As we struggle with the issues of inclusiveness and variability in our definition, we find ourselves drawn along the intersection with our second theoretical plane: distinctiveness. What importance should we attach to the (distinctively) dispersed or clustered form of the earliest Middle Niger towns? What importance should we attach to the apparent lack of elites and of celebratory, monumental architecture at a clearly wealthy, densely populated site such as Jenne-jeno? The issue of distinctiveness is major contested ground in archaeology today. On one hand there are those who believe that the key prehistoric processes are already well and sufficiently known from the longer-researched Near East or Europe (or from ethnographic 'primitive' situations). Why investigate early urbanism in Africa, or South-East Asia or India, when developments in those places will be a pale reflection of the essential causes and circumstances known from the 'core civilizations'? Countering this privileging view is the argument that long-term transformations leading to food production, to settled life or to urbanism everywhere need not replicate the experience of Europe or Mesopotamia and that, as a general rule, world history and prehistory have taken much more diverse routes to the same destination than traditional models would allow.[4]

Proponents of the former, brilliant-core position tend to be strict functionalists. It is their view that narrow economic or demographic causation, once identified in Mesopotamia or Central Mexico, can be exported wholesale to the peripheral, less inventive parts of the globe. Others are more willing to look to extra, non-functional motivations for actions in the past. In the Middle Niger, urban clustering is both a functional response to a highly variable and unpredictable flood and climate regime and a distinctive distribution of urban space that grew out of a deep-time conception of authority (and which sustained a long history of resistance to centralization).[5] But what gave birth to authority at these cities – material and ecological constraints and poten-tialities, or the culture-specific world of beliefs and values? This is the third theoretical concern always in the mind of the urban archaeologist.

Clustering (non-aggregation) and lack, or underdevelopment, of social stratification are the Middle Niger developments that confront our most fundamental expectations about the nature of authority at the earliest moments of urbanism. When the archaeolo-gist thinks about what the distinctive form of Jenne-jeno might mean in terms of power and authority, of regulation of urban space, he or she must consider empirical tests of both functional and 'cognitive' motivations on the part of the prehistoric inhabitants. But, to speak of alternative routes to authority in pre-literate times necessarily takes us beyond the relatively straightforward problems of describing the Middle Niger clustered cities.

These descriptive problems are not to be dismissed. Enormous excavation resources have to be expended just to construct the basic chronology and culture history of these communities. Only after 20 years at Jenne-jeno have we begun to put a finger on the pulse of the place. Enormous efforts on survey (and complementary excavations of satellite sites) must still be committed to establish the contemporaneity of the many components of the integrated mass of settlement we now label the Jenne-jeno urban complex. To estimate population for different periods is to stick one's head (repeatedly) in the maw of speculation. And were our urban residents full-time specialists? What was their relation to the classically invisible communities of nomadic fisherfolk and trans-human pastoralists?

In considering alternative routes to authority in pre-literate times we must move beyond the purely functionalist analyses.[6] The Middle Niger's highly changeable climate and flood regime surely had enormous influence on the fortunes of these city dwellers.[7] Yet the art of reconstructing the so-called ecodynamics[8] of the human landscape (the reciprocal co-evolution of social and natural systems) is practised hesitantly even in those parts of the world where basic archaeology has a far longer history. The rules of inter-ethnic relations and persistent oral traditions of town and village dwellers pervasive in the Middle Niger today provide a working economic rationale that can be extrapolated back in time to the maturation and perhaps even to the growth of these clustered communities. Yet the ecological and functional explanations for clustering only hint at deeper, more complex 'cognitive' roots of authority. Clustered cities may well prove to be the supreme test of a thesis describing networks of horizontal, componential distribution of authority. These communities were the classic horizontal complex societies, long successful as the locus of resistance to the tendencies theorized by the social evolutionist:[9] centralization, social hierarchy and monopoly of decision-making.

Decision-making, authority, resistance to despotism – all these smack profoundly of dabblings in prehistoric motivations and intentionality. It would be foolish to deny the material motivations for control and regulation of urban space. The objectives of an archaeology of prehistoric intentionality need not be incommensurable with the more usual functionalist, economic, or ecological concerns of historians and archaeologists. Can we marry down-and-dirty excavation and survey, archaeomagnetism and palaeo-ethnobotany with research into ideology, symbols and social construction of reality – without (like the historian's nemesis of historicism) privileging the realm of ideology and 'inner rules' metaphysics? Can we speak of cumulative transformation of deep-time notions of authority (or sacrality) without succumbing to discredited habits of 'essentialism' and immanent change? These epistemological debates go to the very heart of our search for 2000-year authority at these cities.

In fact, archaeology now searches for a term – 'prehistory of mind', 'cognitive processualism', 'cognitive archaeology' – to describe the willingness in the 1990s to marry hard-data approaches to cross-cultural explanation in prehistory with a desire for testable research into past ways of thought as inferred from material things.[10] The search for alternative routes to authority at the earliest clustered cities of the Middle Niger (and at these cities' antecedent communities of the Late Stone Age) inserts us squarely into the debates about reconstructing deep-time (and pre-literate) intentionality. We begin with a review of evidence for urban clustering.

A Functional Diagnosis of Componential Cities

When first excavated in the 1970s and early 1980s, the Middle Niger cities of Jenne-jeno, Dia, and (near) Timbuktu were a puzzle. These communities were sophisticated in trade, had large specialist populations, and were at the high end of (peculiar) regional settlement hierarchies. All these are consonant with our classic definition of a pre-industrial town. According to conventional archaeological wisdom, these economic and demographic patterns should have grown in concert with demonstrable social ranking (including demonstrable measures of elite wealth and status monopolization) and of centralizing, if not coercive mechanisms of political integration.[11] To date, the elites remain stubbornly invisible. Perhaps the absence of the expected manifestations of political and social hierarchies allows us the freedom to experiment with the thesis that these cities were not a dense agglomeration of population focused on a single locale, but rather a network of specialized parts integrated by autonomous but linked spheres of authority.

In the functional thesis,[12] the clustered city was a stable solution (for more than 1,000 years) to the complementary ecological problems (physical and social) confronting Middle Niger communities, in the past as today: first, this is a superbly productive environment, but one marked by highly variable rain and flood regimes; and second, to combat climatic unpredictability, artisans and subsistence producers grow increasingly specialized, yet must be linked together into a generalized economy. The clustered city, then, becomes a segmented community of specialists who voluntarily come together to take advantage of the services of others and to exploit the larger market for their products, but who maintain physical separation in order to reinforce their separate identities.

In the apparent absence of elites and coercive control, who keeps the peace in such a congery of corporate groups, particularly when (by *c.* 800 AD) population at the Jenne-jeno urban complex may have exceeded 20,000? An exclusively functional approach to authority is inadequate to answer this critical question. This is why we cautiously enter into the domain of 'cognitive archaeology': This was a highly complex society organized horizontally, a heterarchy,[13] with multiple overlapping and competing agencies of resistance to centralization. The dispersed clustered city landscape was an instrument of that resistance. Such a view calls up profound Mande views of sacred power places distributed in a grid across the landscape, as will be argued below.

Before taking on these interpretative issues, however, we shall summarize the data to demonstrate the pervasiveness in time, and over space, of urban clustering as an organizing principle. Clustering evolves not as a dense agglomeration of population focused upon a single locale – as would be predicted by a long Western tradition of thinking about the origins of the pre-industrial city. Rather, these towns are networks of specialized parts. Urban complexes, the networks of physically distinct communities, can cover impressive areas – greater than fifty square kilometres in the case of the Jenne-jeno urban complex. Clustered cities can form a (peculiar) localized settlement hierarchy within a classic urban regional site hierarchy.[14] Who lived in these cities? We can detect corporate, ethnic and class differences amongst those who left behind evidence of varied subsistence tasks (net weights, cattle bones, sub-Saharan Africa's earliest *Oryza glabberima*, amongst other finds), of their artisan prowess (iron smelting furnaces, spindle whorls, fine-ware ceramics), and of differences of identity (burial customs, architectural styles, forms and themes of the sadly abused Middle Niger terracottas). But who made decisions in these populous, brazenly heterogeneous communities? Who regulated and controlled the urban space?

The anchoring sequence for understanding urban development in the Middle Niger comes from the Upper Delta (southern Middle Niger) site of Jenne-jeno. Results of the excavations at the principal site and at ten satellites in the urban complex, and of the survey in its hinterland, are available in several publications, so only the key elements will be highlighted here. Alone, the site of Jenne-jeno would have been sufficient testament to the indigenous development of urbanism in West Africa. As recently as the middle of the last millennium BC, this sector of the Middle Niger was uninhabited, or frequented only by nomadic pastoralists, hunters or fisherfolk. Ambiguous debris of their ephemeral presence is found encased within the upper alluvium beneath a very few sites. This and the independent geomorphological assessment of the region lead us to believe that the Jenne area was a paludial (more or less permanent swamp) if not long-seasonal lake

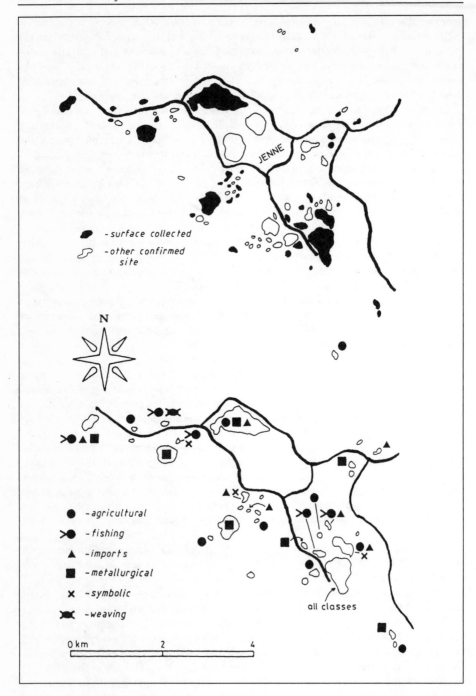

Figure 1.2 Components of the Jenne-jeno urban complex

environment until the great pan-tropical dry episode of *c.* 300 BC to AD 300.[15]

Permanent occupation begins shortly after the onset of that dry episode, when the swamps reduced in size and annual floods diminished. We know little of the first colonists, besides their physical kinship to groups occupying the Malian Sahara (Hassi el-Abiod) and Méma (Kobadi) and their ceramic affinities with the Tichitt lake-and-*falaise* dwellers of early in the last millennium BC.[16] In the first centuries of the settlement's existence, the community pioneered a mixed economy that remained remarkably stable during the 1,600-year sequence (rice, sorghum, millet and a high volume of wild grains; domesticated cattle and sheep/goats and a significant hunted component; and, of course, fish and aquatic reptiles and mammals). Trade in some volume tied earliest Jenne-jeno to communities in the Sahara (semi-precious stone for ornaments) and immediately adjacent to the Middle Niger alluvium (grindstones and iron ore).

The curious fact that, at 250 BC, the first colonists import iron ore (rather than a finished iron product or, at least, a bloom ready for final smithing) and conduct the smelt at the site itself begins a chain of speculation about the reasons this particular locale was selected and, perhaps, why it thrived. The Jenne vicinity is a wonder of highland and floodplain soils at the different elevations and bathymetric progressions necessary for high volume recessional (*décrue*) and paddy farming. The diversity of farmland provides a measure of security in this environment of high-interannual variation in rain (annual total, monthly distribution, date of onset) and flood (yearly height, onset, date and speed of evacuation, annual crop of rizophagenous fish). The Jenne vicinity is close to dune highlands necessary for keeping cattle in an active floodplain. And Jenne's merchants could exploit the maze of streams and major rivers (Niger and Bani) giving access to the towns and villages within the traditional hinterland as well as to distant commercial partners, such as Dia and Timbuktu. All the above were sufficient conditions but, of course, do not explain why Jenne-jeno was selected over many hundreds of other advantageous locales.

Perhaps Jenne-jeno was just one of hundreds founded virtually simultaneously by a wave of southern Saharan migrants. Dia, in a similar floodplain environment in the Macina, has extensive basal deposits of roughly the same date.[17] Oral traditions, however, suggest that founding communities saltated across the virgin floodplain to a few locales (Dia and Jenne most prominently mentioned), from which daughter communities spawned.[18] The satellite nearest Jenne-jeno, Hambarketolo, must have been founded within a few centuries of, if not virtually simultaneously with its parent city, whereas another satellite (Kaniana) has deposits only of the last phase of occupation (beginning *c.* AD 800). It would be difficult for any Mandeist to resist the temptation to see in these data older yet familiar notions of sacrality and of the attractions of locations steeped in occult power. Such a notion, if present, surely would have been at play in the decision to found a settlement at this particular place.

A blacksmith in the greater Mande lands is more than just a technician.[19] Blacksmiths manipulate and even create vast amounts of occult power, *nyama*, the life energy of the earth. The physical location of this act is highly important – both for the success of the smelt and for the attendant act of harvesting power from a network, or power grid that describes the Mande conception of occult geography. To smelt iron at Jenne-jeno at its foundation would be to make the extraordinary effort of shipping in ore from at least 75 kilometres, gathering wood and charcoal from some distance (trees being necessarily scarce in the middle of a floodplain), and putting up with the filth, noise (and potential polluting interference by the uninitiated) of the working furnace. A purely functional, rational-decision explanation seems highly unsatisfactory.

As Jenne-jeno grows from a minimum of 12 hectares at 250 BC, to at least 25 hectares three centuries later, to its final 33 hectares by *c.* AD 500, the locus of production for blacksmiths and perhaps for other specialists also shifts. Later in the first millennium, iron working takes place at several of the satellite mounds. The *tells* (deeply stratified mounds entirely of anthropogenic origin) that comprise the component sites of the Jenne-jeno urban complex are enormously expensive to excavate, and efforts have been concentrated on the principal Jenne-jeno site (the six units of the 1996–7 season bring the total to 17). Now, however, we have limited excavations at ten satellites,[20] auger coring at several others,[21] and four campaigns of recording surface ceramics, small finds and features at all satellites within a four-kilometre radius of Jenne. It is clear from this research that some degree of clustering was a feature of the very earliest urbanism here. Further, specialists occupied and conducted their business on many and perhaps most of the satellites. Until many more units are sunk into the lowest levels of a large sample of satellites, of course, it will be impossible to know if this occupational exclusivity characterized the first moments of clustering. But this seems entirely likely.

The process does evolve and accelerate with time. Smelting (but not smithing) moves off the largest site, Jenne-jeno, by the middle of the first millennium. By the end of the millennium, fully 69 satellites are in orbit about Jenne-jeno – and this number records only the *tells* (permanent settlements). Sadly, we too suffer from the classic Mesopotamian disease of seriously underrepresenting the affiliated, mobile segments of the community who seasonally set up temporary (and virtually invisible) camps in the vicinity. Under-counting the nomadic populations is just the beginning of our demographic difficulties.

Demographics are surely the bugbear of archaeologists.[22] There are numerous proxy measures of population: site size, numbers of houses, area enclosed within house walls, size of necropoli. None are entirely satisfactory. We have published population estimates for the late first millennium of between 7,000 and 13,000 persons for Jenne-jeno and between 15,000 and 27,000 persons for the principal site plus the 25 satellites within a one-kilometre radius.[23] It is highly probable (from the settlement distribution and oral tradition) that most if not all 69 *tells* of the Jenne-jeno urban complex were occupied simultaneously; the total occupied area in excess of 190 hectares gives a low-end population estimate of up to 42,000 persons. These gross estimates, of course, tell us nothing of the population parameter in which we are really interested: the nature of 'corporate' differences within this urban population.

The story becomes considerably more complicated with the results of the 1994 auger-coring project and excavations in 1996–7 at the previously lightly explored western precinct of Jenne-jeno. We had always favoured the local oral traditions that claimed a foundation and growth of modern Jenne town at the demise of Jenne-jeno (and its satellites) sometime after the twelfth or thirteenth centuries. We need to reconsider this history in the light of the ceramics from the 34 cores lifted from seven or more metres of anthropogenic deposits in Jenne town itself. There is no unambiguous evidence for occupation prior to Phase IV, so our preliminary conclusion is that Jenne was founded perhaps a millennium or more after the initial occupation of Jenne-jeno. It will require formal excavations at Jenne to know whether even this date is too conservative. Still, these results reveal several centuries of early second-millennium simultaneity of habitation at the 45-hectare Jenne, at a Jenne-jeno that admittedly was contracting slowly, and at a probable majority of satellites. An estimate of 50,000 persons seems a reasonable minimum estimate for the population here at the turn of the present millennium.

What of the early end of Jenne-jeno's history? The lengthy analysis of the 1996–7 results has only begun, but the earliest Upper Delta ceramics (Phase I, including fine ware) have been found in the lowest levels of units to the far west of the site. This may suggest that the settlement was one massive unity at or before the turn of the present epoch. Or, perhaps, that it began as two (or more) smaller hamlets that soon merged. Every season at the Jenne-jeno urban complex reminds us that we consistently tend to underestimate the size of the community.

Such a large population distributed in such a peculiar manner over the landscape might be explained away as an exception, were urban clustering not so widely distributed across Middle Niger's 170,000 square kilometres. Other instances are not as well documented as the Jenne-jeno urban complex, but we have only begun to inventory the clustered towns that functioned within an extensive, pre-trans-Saharan trade, commercial network of the first millennium AD. North-west from Jenne-jeno, across the Niger, is another town featured in the oral traditions of earliest colonization of the deep alluvium. If anything, Dia displays the urban clustering principle more vigorously than Jenne-jeno. Rather than the single site of Jenne-jeno, here two large sites have extensive basal deposits of the last centuries BC (three counting the unexcavated *tell* of modern Dia). These focus sites are orbited by over 100 satellites, distributed in long curvilinear bands along present or senescent distributaries. Could all these have been occupied at the same time? The sample surface recorded in 1986–7 appears to favour simultaneity, rather than sequentiality of occupation of this urban complex.

Similar conclusions are drawn from survey and surface recording along the Niger Bend, around Timbuktu and further downstream at Gourma Rharous.[24] This is a very different environment. In the constricted Niger floodplain to the south of Timbuktu, however, and along the (embayment) wadis coursing north from the river into the longitudinal dune field of the Azawad, there are a considerable number of clustered villages and (perhaps) towns. Particularly noteworthy is a cluster of nine satellites orbiting a 24-hectare focus site found thirteen kilometres up the wadi (El-Ahmar) linking Timbuktu to Arawan. Slightly upstream, in the Middle Niger Lakes Region around Goundam, informal survey also revealed a pronounced tendency to clustering of settlement and tumuli (funerary monuments).[25] Most of these sites were not fully urban, but at least one undated *tell* (Arham-jeno) is recorded at 100 hectares.

Further afield, the Malian archaeologist Téréba Togola has investigated urban clusters in the Middle Niger's 'dead delta'. The Méma is the now-senescent north-east alluvial basin that was possibly the first magnet to Saharan communities migrating out of their increasingly distressed homelands during the last two millennia BC.[26] Togola's urban complexes of Akumbu (eight *tells*) and Boundu Boubou (31 *tells*) are particularly important because of their supporting evidence of specialist occupation at some of the mounds. Togola's most recent work at the former shows that the Méma, and not the Jenne region, is the place to investigate the continuity of this settlement pattern between the Late Stone Age and the use of iron. Indeed, the 1989–90 Méma survey of Togola and Kevin and Rachel MacDonald carefully documented 28 second and first millennium (Late Stone Age) sites.[27] These show patterns in lithics and ceramics and in the remains of animals and fish that strongly suggest some degree of contemporaneous occupation of separate but adjacent sites by specialist hunters, fishers and pastoralists. All exchanged with one another. However articulated, these are still tiny communities without urban pretensions, although they do show the antecedent conditions of corporate 'distinctness, exchange and reciprocity'.[28]

Finally, a superficially similar pattern of clustering coexists along the first millennium AD Middle Senegal Valley.[29] For most of the occupation sequence, small villages chain the banks of the Senegal River, at regular intervals. During the latter half of the first millennium, however, we find at least one cluster of perhaps a dozen settlements. It is harder here to speak of true specialist exclusivity, although the evidence does not exclude this.

What is going on at these clustered towns? During twenty years of research in the Middle Niger we have tended to functional and ecological explanations. For the moment, this is our working definition of urban clustering: segmented communities of specialists or distinct corporate groups that voluntarily come together to take advantage of the services of others and a larger market for their products, but that make a demonstrable effort to preserve their separate identity by strategies of physical distinctiveness. The clustered city was a stable solution to the complementary ecological problems of the Middle Niger. The unavoidable reality was of life within a rich environment, but one marked by rain and flood regimes of high interannual variability. One solution to this problem would be for each community to remain perpetually generalized in subsistence regime, perpetually prepared to move on to more welcoming locales, perpetually the passive pawn moved about the ecologically checkered landscape by virtually chaotic outside forces. An alternative – and the one hit upon by the inhabitants of these clusters, we believe – was to combat unpredictability by many (and increasingly) specialized artisan and subsistence producers linked into a generalized economy.

If this thesis is correct, the clusters needed mechanisms of integration. To model this we have, in the past, relied frankly upon direct historical canons of cooperation and ethnic reciprocity among various Mande groups that maintain the modern ethnic mosaic of the Middle Niger. Extrapolated back into later prehistory, the occupation of separate mounds would be a strategy of physical segregation to complement foundation myths and ritual practices of integration.[30] These might include:

1 Privileges of 'first arrivals' – certain decisions vital to the subsistence or ritual life of one group can be made only by another, linking everyone in a network of reciprocity.
2 Bonds of fictive kinship – myths and legends of common origin and rules of obligatory common labour.
3 Undischargable debt – lore of extraordinary sacrifice by one group for others, under conditions of ecological stress – linking everyone in a fabric of expectations for future behaviour.

This functional-ecological explanation leads to a prediction of cultural innovations leading to true urban clustering: Late Stone Age communities will be encouraged to specialize (including those new practices that led to the domestication of African rice, sorghums, millets, and fonio, inter alia) if they have a season of joint occupancy of a shared locale with other (emerging) specialist groups.[31] If peaceful, predictable reciprocity succeeds among these groups, further specialization will be encouraged. So, too, will a progressive lengthening of the period of joint occupancy. In time, the seasonality of movement withers away. The security of the generalized economy encourages further in-migration. There will be normal population increases associated with sedentarism, if under salubrious conditions. Eventually the tiny, seasonal, componential hamlets of the second and first millennium BC in the Méma evolve into Akumbu and Boundou Boubou and, with further migrations of Mande-speakers into the live alluvial basins to the east, into Jenne-jeno and Dia of undisputed urban status.

The functional–ecological explanation of componential, specialist producers linked into a generalized economy has had some successes. It helped predict the Méma results for earlier periods. It allows us to compare similar urban clusters from distant parts of the globe. For example, compare the map of presumed specialist components at the Jenne-jeno urban complex with Chang's model of components at Shang capitals, such as An-yang[32] or Cheng-chou. At these northern Chinese sites, plenty of specialist producers are distributed in a 'non-agglomerated' way over an extensive landscape. But there are clear differences, too. These Middle Bronze Age state capitals have a walled royal precinct and many reminders – in the form of chariot burials, noble and elite hamlets, and so on – of coercive, centralized mechanisms dedicated to political control. These celebrations of despotic power and extreme social ranking throw their lack in the Middle Niger into greater relief. The comparison with Jenne-jeno becomes more pertinent, I believe, when we compare plans of Middle Niger settlement complexes with earlier, yet still large and complex Chinese 'neolithic' sites lacking enclosure walls and monumental 'structures, such as Erh-li-t'ou, Hsing-T'ai or Lo-yang.[33]

In Mesopotamia researchers have utilized interpretations of integrative mechanisms at the West African clustered cities in a reinterpretation of social and economic relations at a classic late Sumerian/early Babylonian city. Mashkan-Shapir, just north of Nippur, was a thriving entrepot, but lacks compelling evidence for vertical control structures.[34] The architectural features and tablets from this site suggest a horizontal social structure much more in keeping with the overlapping, competing, plural agencies of authority that we have posited for the Middle Niger urban complexes than with the rigid hierarchy and despotic control of the many by the few that is the more usual Mesopotamian urban thesis.

Despite these successes, the essential problem for archaeologists interested in the long-term transition to urbanism is that these explanations and models of componential networks of sub-communities are fundamentally synchronic. They describe an integrative state at discrete points in time. They do not provide a diachronic mechanism of change and evolution, with continuity, over the long periods of time.

It may be more helpful to move away from a representation of the dynamic urban clustering phenomenon as a static network diagram, as in the 'structural model' of Figure 1.2. Figure 1.3 presents an adaptation of cladistics (or results obtained by the statistical methods of the same name, the science of systematics). The sites in this figure are those from which we have the best data from surface features and small finds relating to occupational specialization. Cladistics – and, specifically, cladograms such as these that show ever-elaborating branching of related but differentiating organisms from common stems – are a tool to help us comprehend urban clusters as temporal sequences of branching relationships among component specialist communities. Cladistics are frequently used in ethnogenetic studies,[35] where language and cultural borrowings provide (often highly contested) windows on processes of historical contacts, borrowings and co-evolution.

On the positive side, cladograms do not presume a prestige or power ranking among the components. They allow us to depict stable heterarchy over the long term. Vertically oriented hierarchy diagrams will not do this.[36] In heterarchy, the relations between sub-groups are those not of coercion and control but of separate but linked, overlapping yet competing spheres of authority. It is a reasonable working hypothesis that these clustered Middle Niger cities are a physical expression of persistent, highly successful resistance to power and monopolized authority represented within a highly complex society. The branching diagrams of cladism may be the best way to represent the temporal elaboration of alternative routes to authority as these cities evolved.

But what was the core dynamic behind the systematics? Figure 1.3 illustrates three probable alternatives:

a Single core priority – a large and dominant central settlement (Jenne-jeno) spawns multiple daughter communities that subsequently specialize;
b Multiple founding communities – several early specialized communities (parts of an eponymous cluster) give birth to daughter communities as all interact liberally (rhizotic mode); and
c Metallurgical antecedents – the blacksmiths, with their industrial and occult powers drove the settlement pattern.

These are just three alternatives amongst the several imaginable. Little in the functionalist explanations offers us a means of evaluating one pathway over another. If we are willing

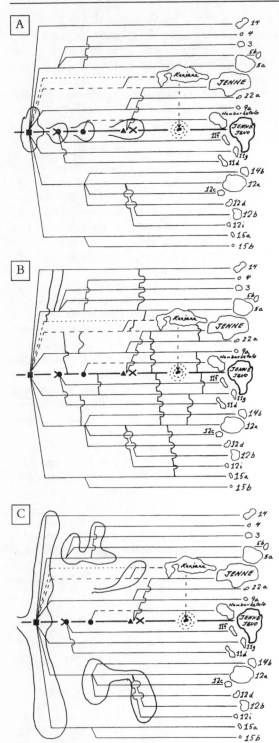

Figure 1.3 Alternate routes to clustering at the Jenne-jeno complex

A SINGLE CORE (JENNE-JENO) PRIORITY
B MULTIPLE FOUNDING COMMUNITIES
   AND DAUGHTER COMMUNITIES
   INTERACT
C METALLURGICAL ANTECEDENTS

to credit the idea of a perceived environment,[37] however, in which the group makes decisions about where to place their communities and how to use the land on the basis of values and symbolic abstractions, then there are several venerable Mande notions of the grid of occult power and authority laid over the landscape that can take excavation and survey into novel data fields. Here we tread upon the sacred landscape in deep time. We first have to confront the debates about an archaeology of mind.

Clustered Cities on the Mande Sacred Landscape

To understand the rise and interaction of the various corporate groups comprising the clustered city, one must appreciate an alternative route to authority amongst the Mande: how those groups harvest occult knowledge and, hence, power.[38] Authority is harvested by *nyamakalaw*, professional classes of artists and occupational specialists from a sacred landscape, a spatial blueprint of power in three dimensions. It is entirely reasonable that there is a very long pedigree to related notions of landscape, occult access to knowledge, and the translation of that knowledge into authority within the community. Possessing just settlements cast aside, and the garbage of the ages, how can the archaeologist test the impact of (antecedent) Mande beliefs and values upon behaviour at the founding of cities such as Jenne-jeno? Put a different way, the prehistorian's problem is to verify motivations and intentionality in the remote past. The test must be done *empirically*. In any hypothesis of deep-time intentionality, of persistent notions of authority or sacrality, we must, of course, guard against a reinvention of essentialism and the historicist's conceits; immanent change, privileging an 'inner rules' metaphysic, and history ruled by contingent forces.

All this suggests a future strategy for urban research, not just along the Middle Niger, but in Greater Mande generally, because of two fundamental inadequacies of the functional–ecological explanation. First, where are the elites, the chiefs, the kings, the early state bureaucracies? In other words, who keeps the peace? This is the first fundamental complaint raised by the distinctiveness of these towns with the traditional 'hierarchy as adaptive solution' approach to emerging complex society. To date, excavation at sites such as Jenne-jeno reveals no obvious signs of social stratification, as opposed to abundant evidence of (horizontal) social complexification. Where are the public buildings, the monuments, the shrines to state ideologies that classic preindustrial city theory tells us should be present?[39] One has the strong impression of a highly complex society, with multiple overlapping and competing agencies of authority and decision making, and of resistance to centralization. The city's lay-out – the dispersed cluster – was an instrument of that resistance.

This assertion that heterarchy, rather than hierarchy, is the better description of authority at these cities recalls persistent Mande notions of who has decision-making roles in society, notions very familiar to historians, social anthropologists and art historians. Authority is shared amongst many corporate groups rather than being the monopoly of a charismatic individual (in Weber's sense)[40] or of one bureaucratic lineage. Contrast the Middle Niger situation with Weber's interpretation of early Mesopotamian urbanism as conditional upon the prior monopolization of authority by the prince ('patrimonial kingship'), a social order within which no 'municipal associations' can develop.

This notion from the urban clusters of alternative, multiple paths to authority calls up the second fundamental complaint against functional or strictly ecological explanations. Such explanations ignore the persistent Mande view of sacred geography, power places in the landscape. This forces upon us a very different view of 'urban cladistics'. The long-term systematics of urban space are shaped by environmental concerns and by competition amongst sub-groups within the community for advantageous siting upon the power grid. In Mande thought, one can gain occult knowledge and harvest power either by taking a knowledge quest (*dalimasigi*) to visit distant masters or to power-invested points of the wilderness. Or, one can locate at and extract occult power (preeminently for smiths, by the act of the smelt) from locations loaded with occult power. In local tradition, the *marigots* (floodplain distributaries) encircling both Jenne and Dia are particularly noteworthy for their concentration of *faaro* (water spirits with whom Mande heroes entered into contracts).[41] In order to understand the rise and sustained interaction of the various corporate groups, one needs to appreciate how they differentially harvest occult power and, hence, authority from the power grid of the Mande landscape.

In ethnographic time, the ancient cities of Mande (including, amongst others, ancient Middle Niger cities such as modern Jenne or Dia) occupy a prominent position, in three dimensions, on the sacred landscape. That landscape may be thought of as a local power grid and a map for navigation in search for occult knowledge. Thus far, we are entirely in the realm of speculation when we extrapolate earlier versions of these notions back even to the time of the Mali empire. Nevertheless, there should be ways empirically to test the proposition that some recognizable (although greatly altered) conception of landscape as a spatial blueprint of power has a very long pedigree in the Middle Niger. If so, corporate groups, through their mythic founders and heroes, or through the agency of the knowledge-traveller well known amongst Mande smiths, sculptors, and bards,[42] conceivably would have been involved in the acquisition and maintenance of occult and political authority by harvesting it from that symbol-charged, dangerous landscape.

In Mande, authority derives not just from economic monopolies, but from multiple (and dangerous) sources differentially accessible to various groups. Weber's quasi-theocratic, charismatic prince would have a rough time of it. This is a road map to successful municipal associations – heterarchy as resistance to non-consultative power. This implies that we must open our minds to an archaeology of mind, a prehistory of deep-time intentionality that would throw light on the motivations for the foundation of urban clusters. This is certainly not an isolated call for an exercise in cognitive archaeology to supplement (never entirely to replace) functional, or economic, or ecological analyses. Chinese archaeologists, for example, are exploring the transformation by Middle Shang times of deep-time (late Neolithic) notions of shamanism. Shamans were repositories for local and lineage authority. Eventually such notions were transformed into the monopolized High Shamanism, with sumptuary ritual implements that were the signature of the king's ideological right to power.[43]

Of course, all of these explorations of deep-time transformations, and reinventions of ideologies and cross-cultural symbols, share the risk of falling into the same logical traps as have discreditied historicism.[44] Ultimately, if these traps are to be avoided we must find ways to test empirically the proposition that some, perhaps many, Middle Niger cities were founded and flourished because of the position they occupied on the perceived landscape of occult power, in the case of Jenne-jeno because smiths believed they could tap the potential of the high concentration in several nearby distributaries of *faaro* – those aquatic sprites whose images even today adorn the mud-flaps of Malian long-distance lorries. The task will not be easy, but indications elsewhere in the Mande region tend to reinforce the view that this may be a productive line of enquiry. Just to the west of the Méma is a palaeochannel, the Vallée du Serpent, long hypothesized as a natural route in about 300 BC, for distressed Saharan peoples to follow into the then recently habitable floodplain of the Middle Niger.[45]

A thorough survey of the Vallée du Serpent might have been expected to provide support for this, yet although it yielded abundant mid-Holocene remains, and many sites probably dating from the last century, nothing at all was found in between.[46] A purely functional-ecological explanation of this simply fails. Here archaeologists will have to test the negative proposition that prehistoric towns and villages would never have been found along the otherwise very attractive Vallée du Serpent because of the belief that the sacred snake, Bida of Wagadu, used this as an underground highway to travel from his lair, Mallaara, in Koumbi, to the Niger River.[47]

If we are to give any credence to the possibility of alternative routes to authority at the foundation of clustered cities we must be prepared to experiment, with all caution and scepticism, with research that might open a window upon ancient motivations. The earliest cities would appear to be amongst our best proxy evidence for those novel transformations of a landscape of power and authority.

Notes

1 The Middle Niger research is published in the following: S. K. McIntosh and R. J. McIntosh, *Prehistoric Investigations in the Region of Jenne, Mali*, Cambridge Monographs in African Archaeology, No. 2 (Oxford, 1980); S. K. McIntosh (ed.), *Excavations at Jenne-jeno, Hambarketolo and Kaniana: the 1981 Season,*. University of California Monographs in Anthropology, No. 20, (Berkeley, 1995); S. K. McIntosh and R. J. McIntosh, 'Archaeological reconnaissance in the region of Timbuktu, Mali', *National Geographic Research* 2, 3 (1986), pp. 302–19; H. Haskell, R. J. McIntosh and S. K. McIntosh, 'Archaeological Reconnaissance in the Region of Dia, Mali', final report to the National Geographic Society, 1987; T. Togola, 'Archaeological investigations of Iron Age sites in the Méma, Mali', (PhD dissertation, Rice University, 1993) and 'Iron age occupation in the Méma region, Mali', *The African Archaeological Review* 13, 2 (1996), pp. 91–110; S. K. McIntosh and R. J. McIntosh, 'Microstratigraphical Investigation at the Jenne-jeno Site Complex (Inland Niger Delta) and at Jenne Town, Mali', report to the National Geographic Society, 1994; R. J. McIntosh, P. Sinclair, T. Togola, Michael Petrèn and S. K. McIntosh, 'Exploratory archaeology at Jenne and Jenne-jeno, Mali', *SAHARA, 9* (1997), pp. 19–28 ; and R. J. McIntosh and B. Diaby, Djenne-djeno Archaeological Site, 1996–7 interim progress report to the Institut des Sciences Humaines and the World Heritage Monuments Fund (New York, 1997); and M. E. Clark, 'Site Structural Research at the Jenne-jeno Settlement Complex, Mali, West Africa', report to the Institut des Sciences Humaines and Mission Culturelle à Djenne, 1997.

2 B. Trigger, 'Determinants of growth in pre-industrial societies', in P. J. Ucko, R. Tringham, and D. E. Dimbleby (eds), *Man, Settlement, and Urbanism* (London, 1972), p. 577; S. K. McIntosh and R. J. McIntosh, *Prehistoric Investigations*, pp. 424–5; R. J. McIntosh and S. K. McIntosh, 'From *siècles obscurs* to revolutionary centuries on the Middle Niger', *World Archaeology*, 20, 1 (1988), pp. 149–50, S. K. McIntosh and R. J. McIntosh, 'Cities without citadels: understanding urban origin along the Middle Niger', in T. Shaw, P. Sinclair, B. Andah, and A. Okpoko (eds), *The Archaeology of Africa: Food, Metals and Towns* (London, 1993), pp. 625–7.

3 L. Manzanilla, 'Early urban societies. Challenges and perspectives', in L. Manzanilla (ed.), *Emergence and Change in Early Urban Societies* (New York, 1997), p. 5.

4 R. J. McIntosh, S. K. McIntosh and T. Togola, 'Archaeology of the people without history', *Archaeology* 42, 1 (1989) pp. 75–80, 107.

5 S. K. McIntosh (ed.), *Beyond Chiefdoms: Pathways to Complexity in Africa* (Cambridge, 1999).

6 Cf. B. Trigger, *A History of Archaeological Thought* (Cambridge, 1989), pp. 289–369.

7 R. J. McIntosh, 'Floodplain geomorphology and human occupation of the upper Inland Delta of the Niger', *Geographical Journal*, 149 (1983), pp. 149–201 and 'The Mande weather machine and its social memory engine', in R. J. McIntosh, J. Tainter, and S. K. McIntosh (eds), *The Way the Wind Blows: Climate, History and Human Action* (New York, forthcoming).

8 J. McGlade, 'Archaeology and the ecodynamics of human-modified landscapes', *Antiquity* 69 (1995), pp. 113–32; J. A. Tainter and B. B. Tainter (eds), *Evolving Complexity and Environmental Risk in the Prehistoric Southwest* (Santa Fe, 1996).

9 For example, A. W. Johnson and T. Earle, *The Evolution of Human Societies* (Palo Alto, 1987).

10 C. Renfrew and E. B. W. Zubrow, *The Ancient Mind. Elements of Cognitive Archaeology* (Cambridge, 1994); see the 'Viewpoints: What is Cognitive Archaeology' section of the *Cambridge Archaeological*

Journal 3, 2 (1993), pp. 247–70, particularly essays by C. Renfrew, pp. 248–50 and by K. Flannery and J. Marcus, pp. 260–7.

11 R. J. McIntosh, 'Early urban clusters in China and Africa: The arbitration of social ambiguity', *Journal of Field Archaeology*, 18 (1991), pp. 199–212; S. K. McIntosh and R. J. McIntosh, 'Cities without citadels', pp. 622–41.

12 Articulated most fully in R. J. McIntosh, 'The pulse model: genesis and accommodation of specialization in the Middle Niger', *Journal of African History*, 34 (1993), pp. 181–220; and R. J. McIntosh, *The Peoples of the Middle Niger* (Oxford, 1999).

13 Heterarchy is a concept of growing utility in the archaeology of emerging complex society as a contrast with hierarchy and centralization. Here the social or political elements of a community are unranked or are stratified horizontally, each maintaining a degree of autonomy in decision-making matters; see C. Crumley, 'Heterarchy and the analysis of complex society', in R. Ehrenreich, C. Crumley and J. Levy (eds), *Heterarchy and the Analysis of Complex Society* (Washington, DC, 1995), p. 3.

14 S. K. McIntosh, 'A tale of two floodplains: comparative perspectives on the emergence of complex societies and urbanism in the Middle Niger and Senegal Valleys', in P. Sinclair (ed.), *Urbanism in Africa from a Global Perspecive* (Uppsala, forthcoming).

15 R. J. McIntosh, 'Floodplain geomorphology' and P. Jacobberger, 'Geomorphology of the upper Inland Niger Delta', *Journal of Arid Environments* 13 (1987), pp. 95–112.

16 K. C. MacDonald, 'Tichitt-Walata and the Middle Niger: evidence for cultural contact in the second millennium BC', in R. Soper and G. Pwiti (eds), *Aspects of African Archaeology. Papers from the 10th Congress of the PanAfrican Association for Prehistory and Related Studies* (Harare, 1996), pp. 429–40.

17 H. Haskell, S. K. McIntosh and R. J. McIntosh, 'Archaeological reconnaissance in the region of Dia'.

18 S. K. McIntosh, 'A reconsideration of Wangara/Palolus, Island of Gold', *Journal of African History*, 22 (1981), pp. 145-58.

19 For example, P. R. McNaughton, *The Mande Blacksmith. Knowledge, Power and Art in West Africa* (Bloomington, 1988) and D. Conrad and B. Frank (eds), *Status and Identity in West Africa: Nyamakalaw of Mande* (Bloomington, 1995).

20 Tests at Hambarketolo and Kaniana are reported in S. K. McIntosh, *Excavations at Jenne-jeno*. The 1996–7 satellite excavations are reported preliminarily in M. E. Clark, 'Site Structural Research'.

21 R. J. McIntosh, *et al.*, 'Exploratory archaeology at Jenne'.

22 F. Hassan, *Demographic Archaeology* (New York, 1981); K. J. Schreiber and K.W. Kintigh, 'A test of the relationship between site size and population', *American Antiquity*, 61 (3) (1996), pp. 573–9.

23 S. K. and R. J. McIntosh, 'Cities without citadels', p. 633.

24 S. K. McIntosh and R. J. McIntosh, 'Archaeological reconnaissance in the region of Timbuktu'.

25 P. Schmit, *Les Sites de Buttes de la Région de Diré (Mali)* (Mémoire de DEA, Université de Paris I, 1986).

26 T. Togola, 'Archaeological investigation of Iron Age sites' and 'Iron age occupation'.

27 K. MacDonald, 'Socio-economic diversity and the origin of cultural complexity along the Middle Niger (2000 BC to AD 300)', (PhD dissertation, University of Cambridge, 1994).

28 I am gratified that this evidence appears within the time frame and geographic circumstances predicted in the 1993 article, 'The pulse model' (based upon functional-ecological analysis of clustering at the Jenne-jeno urban complex).

29 S. K. McIntosh, R. J. McIntosh and H. Bocoum, 'The Middle Senegal Valley Project: Preliminary results from the 1990–1991 field season', *Nyama Akuma*, 38 (1992), pp. 47–61.

30 R. J. McIntosh, 'The pulse model', pp. 206–12.

31 R. J. McIntosh, 'African agricultural beginnings', in J. O. Vogel (ed.), *The Archaeology of Sub-Saharan Africa: an Encyclopaedia* (New York, 1997), pp. 409–18.

32 K-C. Chang, *Shang Civilization* (New Haven, 1971), Figure 38, p. 130.

33 R. J. McIntosh, 'Clustered cities and alternative courses to authority in prehistory', in *Journal of East of East Asian Archaeology* (1999), pp. 1–24.

34 E. C. Stone and P. Zimansky, 'The tapestry of power in a Mesopotamian city', *Scientific American*, 272 (4)(1995), pp. 118–23.

35 J. H. Moore, 'Ethnogenetic theory', *National Geographic Research* 10, 1 (1994), pp. 10–23.

36 For a critical introduction, see K. W. Butzer, *Archaeology as Human Ecology: Method and Theory for a Contextual Approach* (Cambridge, 1982), 281–94, esp. Figure 15.3.

37 K. W. Butzer, *Archaeology as Human Ecology*, pp. 252–7. Of course, the overlay of the existential or symbolic landscape over the objective landscape has received a more respectful hearing in history recently (e.g., S. Schama, *Landscape and Memory*, New York, 1995) and human geography (e.g., D. Gregory, *Geographical Imaginations*, Oxford, 1994).

38 I begin to explore the archaeological applicability of these themes in *People of the Middle Niger, passim*.

39 S. K. McIntosh and R . J. McIntosh, 'The early city in West Africa: towards an understanding', *The African Archaeological Review*, 2 (1984), pp. 73–98; R. J. McIntosh, 'Early urban clusters in China and Africa: the arbitration of social ambiguity', *Journal of Field Archaeology*, 18 (1991), pp. 199–212; R. J. McIntosh, 'Western representations of urbanism and invisible African towns', in S. K. McIntosh (ed.), *Beyond Chiefdoms*, pp. 56–65.

40 M. Weber, *Economy and Society* (4th ed.) (New York, 1956), pp. 1244–5, 1282–90.

41 S. Haidera (Institut des Sciences Humaines, Bamako), personal communication, 1994; oral tradition collected in Jenne in 1977, 1981, 1994 by R. J. and S. K. McIntosh.

42 For example, P. R. McNaughton, 'Is there history in horizontal masks?' *African Arts*, 24 (1991), pp. 40–53, 88–90 and S. Brett-Smith, *The Making of Bamana Sculpture. Creativity and Gender* (Cambridge, 1994).

43 K-C. Chang, *The Archaeology of Ancient China*, (4th ed.) (New Haven, 1986), pp. 365–7 and *Art, Myth and Ritual. The Path to Political Authority in Ancient China* (Cambridge MA, 1983), pp. 44–8, 56–63, 114.

44 See S. K. Sanderson, *Social Evolutionism: A Critical History* (Oxford, 1992), especially Chapters 1 and 2.

45 R. J. McIntosh, 'The Pulse Model', p. 203; K. C. MacDonald, 'Tichitt-Walata and the Middle Niger', *passim*.

46 K. C. MacDonald and P. Allsworth-Jones, 'A reconsideration of the West African microlithic conundrum: new factory sites and associated settlement in the Vallée du Serpent', *The African Archaeological Review*, 12 (1994), pp. 73–104.

47 G. Dieterlen and D. Silla, *L'Empire du Ghana. Le Wagadou et les Traditions de Yéréré* (Paris, 1992), pp. 55–7.

2

African City Walls
A Neglected Source?

GRAHAM CONNAH

The purpose of this chapter is to suggest research that should be undertaken or, to be more accurate, undertaken on a far more substantial scale than seems yet to have been the case. The material reported here derives from an investigation of available published sources made by the writer in 1995, when invited to present a paper on African city walls at a conference at the University of Minnesota about city walls worldwide.[1] Because Africa was otherwise represented at that conference only by some limited consideration of its northern margins, an ambitious and perhaps outrageous attempt was made to review the evidence from the rest of the continent, although in the end attention was focused on tropical Africa in the strictest sense. It quickly became apparent that publications concerning specifically archaeological investigation of such structures, involving either excavation or survey, were less numerous than might have been expected and often limited in their scope. In particular, reliable maps of African city walls appeared to be the exception rather than the rule, a problem that Fletcher[2] has complained of with respect to African city and town plans generally. This situation seems especially regrettable for two reasons: first, because of the value of such structures as independent sources of information concerning the urban past in Africa; and, second, because as time goes on population increase and settlement growth, as well as natural erosion, will destroy the physical evidence at an ever-increasing rate.

African city walls, so-called, are part of a morphological continuum that extended from single households to large cities, and which varied in function from domestic protection to formal military defence, as well as serving a variety of other functions. Essentially they consisted of enclosures, sometimes single, sometimes multiple, that contained the community (or a large part of it) with which they were associated. Here we are interested only in those at the top end of the scale, those that surrounded settlements that in one sense or another might be called urban. Nevertheless, the character of these enclosing structures varied considerably: some consisted of stone or mud walls; others of earthen banks; still others of timber stockades, or merely grass fences; a ditch was often present as well. Clearly, the amount of evidence surviving for archaeological investigation in any particular case will depend on the materials used, although climate and the extent of subsequent human activity will also play a significant role. The writer's concern in this

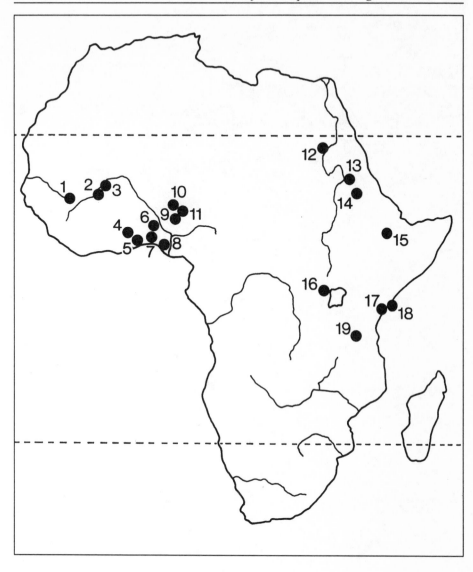

Figure 2.1 Walled towns and cities mentioned in the text.
Tropics of Cancer and Capricorn shown by broken lines.

1	MOURGOULA	8	BENIN CITY	15	HARAR
2	JENNE-JENO	9	ZARIA	16	BIGO
3	HAMDALLAHI	10	KATSINA	17	GEDI
4	KITARE	11	KANO	18	PATE
5	NOTSE	12	FARAS	19	KALENGA
6	OLD OYO	13	NAKHEILA		
7	IFE	14	KASSALA		

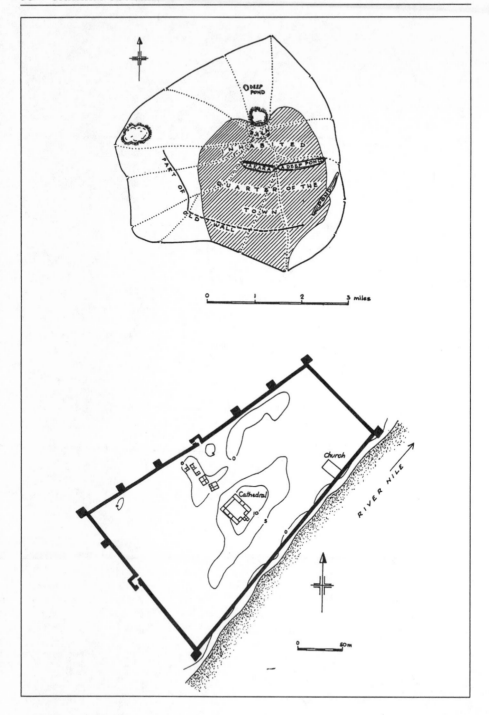

Figure 2.2 *Above:* Barth's 1851 plan of Kano, Nigeria (After Kirk-Greene 1962: Fig. 3).
Below: Faras, Sudan (After Karkowski 1986: Fig. 1).

paper is limited to structures of stone or mud or earth, often accompanied by a ditch, which might be expected to have left physical traces, other things being equal.

Despite such limitations, we are still left with a variety of structures, belonging to various dates within the last two millennia, and with a geographical distribution that includes both the savanna and forests of West Africa, the middle Nile region, part of the East African coast, and the interlacustrine area of East Central Africa (Figure 2.1).[3] With such a wide range through time and space, the potential of such structures as sources of information on Africa's urban past becomes immediately apparent. Although documentary and oral evidence will also be relevant to their investigation in many cases, it is the physical evidence of the structures themselves which is the focus here. The basic questions are: what sorts of things might such evidence tell us and what archaeological strategies should be adopted to extract the maximum information from such evidence?

Let us start with the first of these questions. African city walls were essentially containers and in many cases we would expect a container to tell us something about its contents. Thus the size and shape of the area enclosed should give some indication of the size and shape of the settlement around which the enclosure was constructed, even if no surface traces survive of that settlement. Admittedly the enclosed space may have included extensive open areas used for grazing or cultivation, such as Barth appears to have recorded at both Katsina and Kano (Figure 2.2), in Nigeria, in 1851,[4] but it is apparent that such areas must have been thought of as integral with the settlement in each case, otherwise why bother to enclose them within the wall? It follows that changes through time in the size and shape of the enclosed area may also reflect similar changes in the settlement, so that if we can reconstruct the history of a city's walls we may be able to understand something of the development of the city itself. A notable example of an attempt to do this, in a different geographical context, can be found in Biddle's work at Winchester in southern England.[5] African examples have been less successful, however, with the possible exceptions of Moody at Kano,[6] Ozanne at Ife,[7] Connah at Benin City,[8] Sutton at Zaria,[9] and Soper and Darling at Old Oyo,[10] all of these places being in Nigeria, as well as Quarcoopome at Notse, in Togo.[11]

Perhaps the most interesting example of these attempts is Moody's work at Kano. Even in Barth's map of 1851 it was apparent that the walled area had been smaller formerly than at that time, because of the survival of part of an old wall within the wall that Barth observed (Figure 2.2). By careful examination of the evidence on the ground as it was in the mid-1960s, and its assessment in the context of the oral and documentary record, Moody was able to identify three phases of growth in the Kano city walls. The first of these he dated to the eleventh–twelfth century AD, the second to the late fifteenth century, and the third to the seventeenth century.[12] This sequence of city wall phases documented the growing size and importance of the city as the present millennium progressed and did this within its environmental context. No excavations were carried out to test this chronological sequence and, so far as the writer is aware, there has been no attempt since Moody's work to reexamine his interpretation of the evidence, so that its accuracy is unknown. It remains, however, an important demonstration of the potential for African city walls to record urban transitions during the pre-colonial past. Such walls can constitute a physical record of change.

Similarly, the character of the enclosing structure can also give some indication of the character of the enclosed settlement. There is, for instance, a world of difference between the regular compact stone fortifications of Faras in the northern Sudan,[13] the irregular angularity of the stone city walls of Gedi[14] and Pate,[15] both in Kenya, and the extensive, meandering earthen banks and ditches of Bigo in Uganda.[16] In the same way the single enclosing mud wall of Hamdallahi, in Mali,[17] is very different from the nightmarish complexity of the multiple earthworks in the Benin City area of Nigeria.[18] The character of the enclosure or enclosures should, therefore, be able to tell us something of the socio-political organization of the enclosed settlement as well as its basic economy. Thus the formal defences of the small urban unit on the side of the Nile at Faras, with its central cathedral (Figure 2.2), suggests an administrative and religious centre, in a rather vulnerable location. In contrast, the somewhat chaotic informality of the wall at Pate (Figure 2.3) implies a rather loosely organized commercial centre unaware of any major threat, and the large multiple enclosures at Bigo (Figure 2.3) hint at an agrarian population as much concerned with cattle as with people. Also contrasting with one another are the large single enclosure of Hamdallahi, a short-lived specifically religious foundation centred on its mosque and palace (Figure 2.4), and the complicated aggregation of enclosures around Benin City (Figure 2.4), which are surely indicative of a longer-lasting, more dispersed urban development. These few examples suggest that African city walls also have the potential to inform us about the making of urban cultures, indicative as they are of urban distinctiveness, and to provide one of the markers by which urban culture might be recognized.

Furthermore, the very existence of such large and complex structures as city walls implies the presence of centralized direction or at least collective effort, as well as indicating labour availability and resource surplus even if only on a seasonal basis. Posnansky,[19] for example, estimated that the digging of the ditches at Bigo (Figure 2.3) would have required the removal of over 200,000 cubic metres of earth and rock; and Darling, not to be outdone, claimed that the vast network of banks and ditches in the Benin City area implied at least 150,000,000 person hours of work over a period of several centuries.[20] The innermost earthwork alone (Figure 2.4) could have required as many as 200 ten-hour days by 5,000 people to dig and construct it.[21] It is very likely that the number of workers was smaller than this, but in that case the time taken to complete the work would have been commensurately longer. Whatever the actual case, such an undertaking was obviously a major operation that would have required discipline and planning as well as the capacity to feed the labour force while the work was in progress. Thus the Benin City walls are eloquent of the power of the Oba of Benin, and of his chiefs and priests, as well as being indicative of a cohesive social organization within the Benin state and its principal city. The existence of such structures tells us something about the regulating of the city and about the character of its control. In addition, the fact that work could be undertaken on such a scale demonstrates the strength of the underpinning rain-forest economy of agriculture and trade that was able to support the massive communal labour that must have been involved. It should be added that African city walls served not only to keep people out but also to control those within and those who were allowed to enter. Thus in the middle of the nineteenth century Richard Burton noted that the gates at Harar, in Ethiopia, were locked at night so that nobody could leave the city till dawn,[22] and Paul Staudinger at Zaria, in Nigeria, in 1885 observed that every trader entering the city had to pay for permission to do business there.[23]

Nevertheless, one might wonder at the extraordinary degree of motivation that such large projects suggest, and consider the protective function of African city walls and their role also as status symbols and as territorial markers. Thus, for instance, they should be informative about the level of political stress and conflict, and about the existence or threat of warfare or the fear of warfare. Fear, after all, is a great incentive. It comes as no surprise, therefore, that two of the densest groupings of African walled cities occurred in Hausaland and Yorubaland, both of them Nigerian areas of high population where there was vigorous competition for resources and control of trade that periodically resulted in armed conflict. In 1904, for example, Frederick Lugard, who had recently taken control

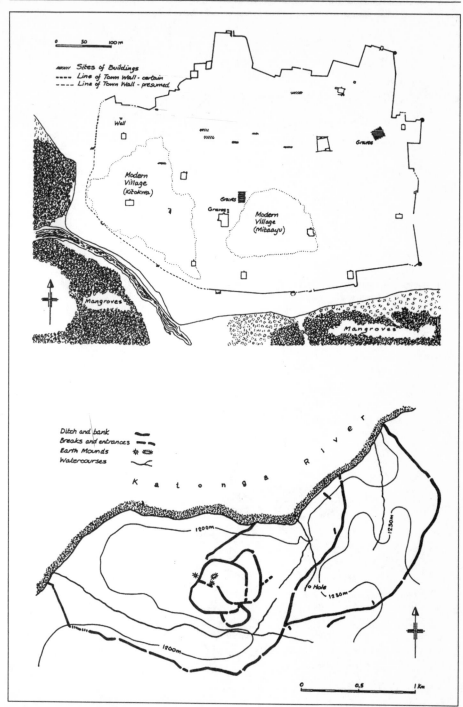

Figure 2.3 *Above:* Pate, Kenya (After Chittick 1967: Fig. 11).
Below: Bigo, Uganda (After Connah 1987: Fig. 9.6).

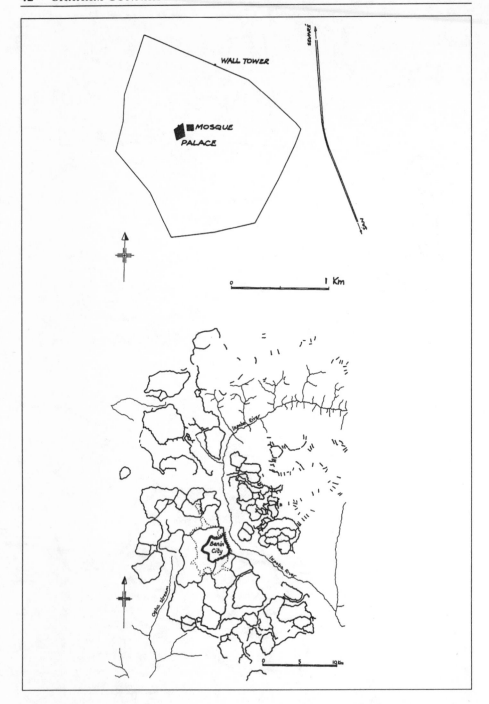

Figure 2.4 *Above:* Hamdallahi, Mali (After Galley *et al.* 1990: Fig. 4).
Below: Earthwork enclosures in the Benin City area, Nigeria, showing only the main part of the complex network, with the innermost city wall in thicker line (After Connah 1987: Fig. 6.6).

of the area on behalf of the British government, reported that there were 40 walled cities within 30 miles of Kano and 170 in the whole province.[24] Before his assault on Kano itself in 1902 he had indeed commented, of its towering city walls , that 'I have never seen, nor even imagined, anything like it in Africa'.[25] As often has been the case with defensive works in many other parts of the world, it seems that some African city walls were intended to impress and perhaps to intimidate the would-be attacker, who might then go away and seek an easier victim. In such a case, inevitably the status of both the citizens and their ruler must be enhanced by the very existence of the walls, without their needing to defend them – which given their frequently large extent would have been difficult to do. In addition to their defensive role, however, either real or psychological, African city walls also acted as territorial markers, and indeed in some instances this may have been their primary purpose. Much of the extraordinary network of interlocking earthworks in the Benin City area (Figure 2.4), for example, may have been concerned principally with the demarcation of sufficient land, around each enclosed settlement, to provide not only the farmland currently in production but also the considerable areas that had to lie fallow in a rotational cycle of some years' duration, as well as a share of 'wild forest' from which could be obtained a range of plant and animal resources.

In addition, the design and lay-out of such city walls surely should indicate something of the character of the warfare that was involved. The nine-metre-high mud walls of Kano recorded by Clapperton in the mid-1820s, for example, were presumably a response to the highly mobile cavalry forces of the West African savanna and the very real danger of siege by a substantial army.[26] Similarly, the multiple concentric walls of some Yoruba towns and cities, of which Old Oyo and Ife (Figure 2.5) are good examples, suggest that they were designed to provide defence in depth rather than a single strongly constructed barrier that might be held by the defenders against all odds. With such multiple walls, attackers on foot could be slowed down or even stopped temporarily, while the defenders retreated behind another defensive line, rallied their forces, and burst out in a counter-attack. In contrast, the walls of East African coastal towns and cities, such as Pate (Figure 2.3), have been described as generally 'more suitable for excluding dogs and wild pigs than any serious invaders',[27] suggesting that only small-scale and poorly organized attacks were thought to be likely. Furthermore, it might be argued that tropical African city walls in general suggest types of warfare involving only limited military technology, even as late as the nineteenth century. In particular, they appear not to have been designed to either withstand or deliver artillery gunfire, unlike some European military structures in Africa such as the late sixteenth-century Fort Jesus in Mombasa, Kenya.[28] Yet, surviving maps of the fortified town of Kalenga in Tanzania, captured by German forces in 1894,[29] or of the Mahdist *zariba* at Nakheila, scene of the British victory at the Battle of the Atbara in 1898,[30] provide examples which suggest that indigenous ideas of fortification adapted quickly in the face of colonial aggression.

African city walls should also be able to provide information on cultural identity and cultural relationships, specifically from similarities in design, materials and constructional methods. Thus a series of remarkable fortified settlements in western Mali and eastern Guinea, recorded by the French army in 1881,[31] had in common certain characteristics – such as mudbrick curtain walls with towers at intervals and often a central citadel – that reflected Islamic influences from North Africa and beyond. Mourgoula, in Mali (Figure 2.5), is a particularly remarkable example of this. In the same way, a plan dated 1860–4 of the walls of the fortified town of Kassala, in the Sudan, betrays the external influence of the 'Arab engineer' who designed them.[32] Nevertheless, most African city walls have clearly indigenous affiliations: the rambling earthworks of Uganda, the modest stone walls of Swahili cities and towns, the complex earthen networks of the Benin state, the neater

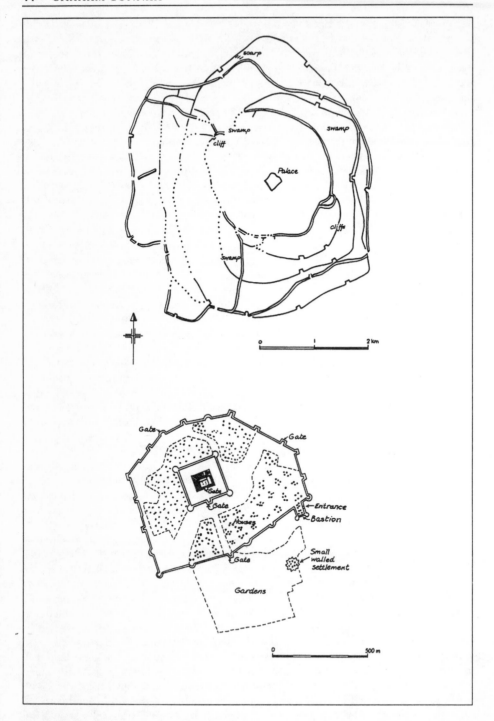

Figure 2.5 *Above:* Ife, Nigeria, with several phases of walling (After Connah 1987: Fig. 6.4).
Below: The fortified settlement of Mourgoula, Mali, in 1881 (After Meillassoux 1966: 33).

concentric enclosures of the Yoruba states, the high mud walls of Hausaland, such examples suggest themselves as distinctive cultural groups, although it has to be admitted that a great deal more field research and survey is needed before such generalizations can be accepted.

Other matters on which African city walls may throw light include past surveying skills, engineering expertise and building technology, sometimes resulting from external contact, as has been seen, but most commonly of indigenous origin. The very existence of these large and often complex structures, demonstrates specialized knowledge of these subjects. Finally, both the siting of African city walls and biological evidence encapsulated within their structures, have the capacity to inform us on environmental conditions and agricultural practices in the past and on changes in those conditions and practices through time.

The above has been a thumbnail sketch of the sorts of information that African city walls have the potential to provide, if subjected to appropriate archaeological investigation. Although an examination of the literature shows that there have been instances where this potential has been realized, at least in part, it would appear that the physical evidence in general has not been given the sort of scrutiny that it would merit. We have, then, a situation where an important source of information on Africa's urban past appears to have suffered from neglect. This brings us to our second question, the archaeological strategies that need to be adopted to extract the maximum information from this apparently neglected source. This question has to be addressed in terms of specifically archaeological field research methodology; it should be stressed that this methodology is far from novel in some parts of the world but nevertheless appears to have been applied insufficiently in the African situation.

The archaeological investigation of large-scale enclosing structures, such as city walls, requires a field research programme in which both extensive and intensive work are carefully integrated. The extensive work consists of survey and mapping, the intensive work comprises precisely targeted excavation. To do the former without the latter will commonly result in unresolved problems of chronology and structure; to do the latter without the former may provide detailed information on these and other matters but fail to relate it in any meaningful way to its context. The general research strategy that is appropriate was already clearly understood in European archaeology over half a century ago. It was frequently applied in the investigation of later prehistoric hill forts in Britain: for instance, a classic early example was Wheeler's work at Maiden Castle in Dorset.[33] The same approach was also used in the investigation of enclosed Roman and medieval towns and cities in Britain, a good example of the latter being the work of the Royal Commission on Historical Monuments on the defences of Wareham, also in Dorset.[34] The essential elements of this strategy consisted of accurate survey and careful mapping of the whole structure or set of structures, followed by the excavation of cross-sections of the bank, rampart or wall, and of any related ditch or ditches; these excavated sections were sited carefully both on representative parts of the structures and at points where features of apparently different date met or intersected. An additional part of the strategy, practicable only on deserted or near-deserted sites and involving heavy outlay of time and money, involved the selective stripping of extensive parts of the enclosed settlement, such as Alcock was able to undertake, at Cadbury in Somerset.[35] In general, however, the combination of mapping and sectioning was the basic recipe.

This recipe has been applied only rarely to African city walls. Such instances as Benin City, Ife, Old Oyo, Jenne-jeno and Bigo come to mind, but these examples are mostly from West Africa and even in some of these cases the work has been incomplete or inadequately published. In many other cases even survey and mapping *without* excavation either have not been attempted at all or have been done in such a manner as to produce something little better than a sketch map. For example, so far as this writer is aware, there

Figure 2.6 Destruction of part of the innermost wall at Benin City by removing earth for building purposes. This photograph was taken on 12 July 1962 at a time when the earthworks were already supposedly protected by legislation. Deliberate destruction of Africa's city walls as well as their general deterioration continues to be a problem, making their archaeological investigation an increasingly urgent matter.

is nowhere available a set of accurate archaeological maps of the important walled cities of Hausaland. Even for Kano there is only a rough map in publications difficult to find,[36] while a map of the Zaria city walls is in a publication so rare that recently a request to the author proved to be the only way of obtaining a copy.[37]

It may be objected that in some countries government survey maps adequately record the outline of city walls but these have been drawn, usually mechanically, from high-level aerial photography without consideration for archaeological criteria. The result is often less than satisfactory so far as detail is concerned and may be grossly incomplete, as was found to be the case with the Benin City 'walls' when their archaeological mapping was commenced in the early 1960s.[38] The problem is that conventional high-level aerial photography is often inadequate to the task, particularly in forested situations like that of the Benin City area. In addition, the cartographers who produce such maps are seldom concerned about archaeological matters. Nevertheless, much could be achieved in drier less vegetated areas of the continent if a systematic programme of low-level aerial photographic survey was conducted by archaeologists themselves. Unfortunately, however, this is often out of the question because of the sensitivity of many governments to security matters. Thus, for instance, a proposal in the early 1980s for the Cambridge aerial archaeologist, the late J. K. St Joseph, to conduct such a survey in Nigeria came to nothing. We may hope that this problem will begin to disappear in the near future, as it is realized that American satellites are watching all of us all of the time, anyway: indeed, some of their satellite imagery might well prove valuable in recording the plans of African city walls – in the unlikely event that researchers have lots of money!

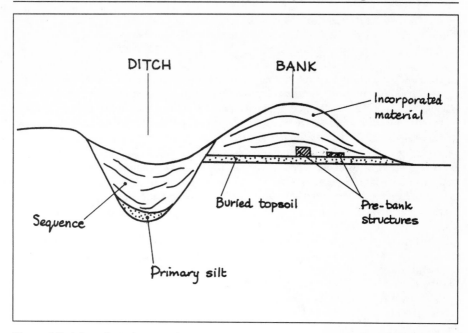

Figure 2.7 A hypothetical section drawing, showing the archaeological potential of an earthwork consisting of a single ditch and bank

Even so far as traditional archaeological ground survey is concerned, money is still a problem, which to some extent explains why we have so few decent archaeological maps of city walls. With such large-scale structures, it is not so much the cost of sophisticated surveying equipment that is the issue, for if necessary perfectly adequate survey can be conducted by means of a hand-held compass traverse, with a chain or steel band, a nylon tape for offsets, and a set of ranging rods.[39] Even with such simple equipment, however, the expense can be substantial, for working in such a slow manner requires a massive and costly input of time by archaeologists and their field assistants. Current trends in field research, moreover, are away from work that both archaeologists and their funding bodies tend to see (wrongly, in this writer's view) as recording exercises rather than explicative investigations. This is a serious situation because, as African cultural resource managers are all too aware, time is running out. Already a lot of the physical evidence has been lost and more will be lost every year (Figure 2.6). Systematic archaeological survey and mapping of African city walls, together with the publication of such work, requires more attention than it is getting and requires substantial funding. This matter is now urgent.

If the survey and archaeological mapping of African city walls have been neglected, their excavation has been virtually ignored. With some notable exceptions – Willett at Ife,[40] Posnansky at Bigo,[41] Mathewson at Kitare (Ghana),[42] Connah at Benin City,[43] and McIntosh and McIntosh at Jenne-jeno (Mali)[44] – such enclosing structures have not received much attention from excavators. Given some of the difficulties in finding substantial depths of undisturbed stratified deposits for the last two millennia in Africa, this is particularly unfortunate, the more so in that stratified evidence from city wall contexts could contribute importantly to our understanding of African urban history, as has been suggested above.

Ditches, where present, can be especially valuable in this regard (Figure 2.7). Almost irrespective of the geological material into which they have been cut, their primary silt would have accumulated quite rapidly, particularly in tropical rainfall conditions, and wood charcoal from this silt can provide radiocarbon dates that will give some indication of the date that a particular ditch was dug. Furthermore, soil chemistry, water content and oxygen level in such ditch-bottom deposits might on occasion be such that important datable environmental evidence could be preserved from that time, such as pollens, phytoliths, macroscopic plant remains, animal bones, beetle exoskeletons, mollusca, and so on. Indeed, ditch deposits of any substantial depth could present an entire stratified sequence of such evidence, from the time that the ditch was dug up to the recent past. In practice such excavation may need extraordinarily sensitive stratigraphic interpretation, in order to deal with the possibility that ditches have been recut or cleaned out in the past, or indeed intersected by other ditches. Ditch deposits can also be frustratingly sterile of cultural material, which it is obviously desirable to find in any datable stratigraphic sequence, but this probem can be minimized by locating excavated sections adjacent to parts of the enclosed settlement thought to have been occupied in the past, thus increasing the chance that garbage will have been thrown into the ditch. Overall, despite the problems attached to their excavation, ditch deposits are a most important source of archaeological evidence that we cannot afford to ignore.[45]

Walls, earthen banks, and ramparts surrounding cities can also provide valuable undisturbed stratified deposits (Figure 2.7). Both cultural and environmental material can become incorporated in the *pise* or mud bricks of which a wall is built, or even in the mud mortar of a stone wall or in its foundation trench, but it is the broader earthen bank or rampart that is more likely to contain such evidence.[46] The problem is that such materials are often sparse or even absent and can date from any time prior to the building of the structure, but the latest of them should give some indication of the earliest possible date that it was built. Much more important is the old ground surface that might have been sealed by the building of a bank or rampart (Figure 2.7); this can preserve a sample of the topsoil at the time of building, from which cultural and environmental evidence might again be recoverable, along with material for radiocarbon dating.[47] Thus, at the Reservation Road section of the innermost city wall at Benin City (Figure 2.8), the old topsoil buried beneath the six-metre-high earthen bank not only produced a date for the construction of the bank but also preserved the stumps of two mud walls of a building that had been overwhelmed by that construction.[48] Such buried surfaces and old topsoils obviously have the potential to preserve important selections of associated evidence from the past that can be directly related to the building of the enclosing structure and to the history of the settlement within. The excavator who undertakes to section city walls or earthen banks and ramparts must be prepared, however, to dig deep and to cut right across the structure, removing a considerable volume of frequently near-sterile deposits (Figure 2.8). Cultural resource managers may complain of damage to the archaeological resource, and funding bodies may complain of the lack of pretty artefacts to put in museum cases, but such an approach does have the capacity to throw light on urban history and that is what should be our principal concern in this case.

It has been argued that African city walls constitute a source of information concerning African urban history which has not been exploited sufficiently. Such information can only be extracted from the physical evidence adequately by the application of appropriate archaeological research strategies involving both field survey and carefully targeted excavation. Within the practical limits of reasonably available published material, it does not seem that such strategies have been attempted to the extent that the volume of evidence would seem to justify. It is unclear why this should be the case but the tendency

Figure 2.8 The excavated section through the innermost city wall at Reservation Road, Benin City, after completion in late May 1963. This photograph was taken from the outer lip of the ditch and gives some idea of the surrounding vegetation. The man crouching on part of the excavation timbering indicates the size of this earthwork.

among archaeologists working on Africa's recent millennia to focus on aspects of their data relevant to anthropological, sociological, ethnological, linguistic and symbolic matters, rather than addressing more straightforward and perhaps more answerable archaeological questions, may have something to do with it. In addition, the scale of survey, excavation and consequent funding necessary to tackle such large structures in the field may well have been a serious inhibiting factor. Whatever the actual reason, the apparent neglect of city walls as a source of information is unfortunate, particularly as much of the physical evidence is disappearing steadily because of both neglect and destruction. If we really do want to understand more about the past of Africa's cities, here is one way in which we could possibly do so.

Notes

1 Graham Connah, 'Contained communities in Tropical Africa', in J. Tracy (ed.), *City Walls* [provisional title] (New York, forthcoming).
2 R. Fletcher, 'Settlement area and communication in African towns and cities', in Thurstan Shaw, Paul Sinclair, B. Andah, and A. Okpoko (eds), *The Archaeology of Africa: Food, Metals and Towns* (London, 1993), p. 733.
3 Of the eight Figures that follow, Figures 2.2, 2.5 and 2.7 were redrawn from the sources given in their captions by Jack Simmons of Canterbury, in the United Kingdom, to whom my sincere thanks are due. Figures 2.1, 2.6 and 2.8 are by the author.
4 H. Barth, *Travels and Discoveries in North and Central Africa* (London, 1857–8). Not seen, cited from A. H. M. Kirk-Greene, *Barth's Travels in Nigeria: Extracts from the Journal of Heinrich Barth's Travels in Nigeria, 1850–1855* (London, 1962), Figures 2 and 3.
5 Martin Biddle, 'Excavations at Winchester, 1967: sixth interim report', *Antiquaries Journal*, 48, pp. 250–84, Figure 1.
6 H. L. B. Moody, 'Ganuwa – the walls of Kano City', *Nigeria Magazine*, 92 (1967), pp. 19–38; H. L. B. Moody, *The Walls and Gates of Kano City* (Department of Antiquities, Nigeria, n.d. [1970]).
7 P. Ozanne, 'A new archaeological survey of Ife', *Odu* (new series) 1 (1969), pp. 28–45.
8 Graham Connah, *The Archaeology of Benin: Excavations and other Researches in and Around Benin City, Nigeria* (Oxford, 1975).
9 John E. G. Sutton, 'The walls of Zaria and Kufena', *Zaria Archaeology Paper* 11 (1976), pp.1–18, plus two addenda.
10 Robert Soper and Patrick Darling, 'The walls of Oyo Ile', *West African Journal of Archaeology* 10 (1980), pp. 61–81.
11 N. O. Quarcoopome, 'Notse's ancient kingship: some archaeological and art–historical considerations', *African Archaeological Review*, 11 (1993), pp.114–16.
12 Moody, *Walls and Gates of Kano City*, pp. 39–41.
13 J. Karkowski, 'A few remarks on stone used in Christian constructions at Faras', in M. Krause (ed.), *Nubische Studien: Tagungsakten der 5 Internationalen Konferenz der International Society for Nubian Studies Heidelberg 22–25 September 1982* (Mainz am Rhein, 1986), pp. 311–19, Figure 1.
14 Graham Connah, *African Civilisations. Precolonial Cities and States in Tropical Africa: An Archaeological Perspective* (Cambridge, 1987), Figure 7.3.
15 Neville Chittick, 'Discoveries in the Lamu Archipelago', *Azania*, 2 (1967), pp. 37–67, Figure 11.
16 Merrick Posnansky, 'Bigo bya Mugenyi', *Uganda Journal*, 33 (2), 1969, pp. 125–50.
17 A. Gallay, et al, *Hamdallahi, Capitale de l'Empire Peul du Massina, Mali. Première Fouille Archéologique, Études Historiques et Ethnoarchéologiques* (Stuttgart, 1990).
18 P. J. Darling, *Archaeology and History in Southern Nigeria: The Ancient Linear Earthworks of Benin and Ishan* (Oxford, 1984), 2 vols.
19 Posnansky, 'Bigo bya Mugenyi', p. 144.
20 Darling, *Archaeology and History in Southern Nigeria*, Vol. 2, pp. 302–3.
21 Graham Connah, 'New light on the Benin City walls', *Journal of the Historical Society of Nigeria* 3 (4) (1967), p. 608.

22 Richard F. Burton, *First Footsteps in East Africa; or an Exploration of Harar* (London, 1856), p. 321.

23 P. Staudinger, *Im Herzen der Haussaländer* (Berlin, 1889). Translated by J. Moody as *In the Heart of the Hausa States*, 2 vols (Athens, Ohio, 1990), Vol. 1, p. 177.

24 Moody, *Walls and Gates of Kano City*, p. 18.

25 Frederick D. Lugard, *Northern Nigeria: Report for 1902*, Colonial Reports: Annual, No. 409 (London, 1903), p. 28.

26 D. Denham *et al.*, *Narrative of Travels and Discoveries in Northern and Central Africa, in the Years 1822, 1823, and 1824* (London, 1826), p. 50 (Clapperton's narrative).

27 James de Vere Allen, 'Settlement patterns on the East African coast, *c.* AD 800–1900, in R. E. Leakey and B. A. Ogot (eds), *Proceedings of the 8th PanAfrican Congress of Prehistory and Quatenary Studies, Nairobi, 5–10 September 1977* (Nairobi, 1980), p. 363.

28 James S. Kirkman, *Fort Jesus: A Portuguese Fortress on the East African Coast*, Memoir 4, British Institute in Eastern Africa (Oxford, 1974).

29 C. Gillman, 'An annotated list of ancient and modern indigenous stone structures in Eastern Africa', *Tanganyika Notes and Records*, 17 (1944), pp. 44–55, Plate 3.

30 H. Keown–Boyd, *A Good Dusting: a Centenary Review of the Sudan Campaigns 1883–1899* (London, 1986), p. 197.

31 Claude Meillassoux, 'Plans d'anciennes fortifications (*tata*) en pays Malinké', *Journal de la Société des Africanistes* 36, 1 (1966), pp. 29–43.

32 O. G. S. Crawford, *The Fung Kingdom of Sennar: With a Geographical Account of the Middle Nile Region* (Gloucester, 1951), p. 96.

33 R. E. M. Wheeler, *Maiden Castle, Dorset* (London, 1943).

34 Royal Commission on Historical Monuments (England), "Wareham West Walls', *Medieval Archaeology*, 3 (1959), pp. 120–38.

35 L. Alcock, *'By South Cadbury is that Camelot …': The Excavation of Cadbury Castle, 1966–70* (London, 1972).

36 Moody, *Walls and Gates of Kano City*.

37 Sutton, 'Zaria and Kufena', pp. 1–18, plus two addenda.

38 Connah, *Archaeology of Benin*.

39 See A. Ogundiran, 'Archaeological survey at Ipole–Ijesa, southwest Nigeria: a preliminary report', *Nyame Akuma*, 42 (1994), pp. 7–13, for a good example of such initiative.

40 Frank Willett, *Ife in the History of West African Sculpture* (London, 1967), but no details.

41 Posnansky, 'Bigo bya Mugenyi', pp. 125–50.

42 R. D. Mathewson, 'Kitare: an early trading centre in the Volta Basin', in H.J. Hugot (ed.), *Congrès Panafricain de Préhistoire, Dakar 1967, Actes de 6e Session* (Chambéry, 1972), pp. 182–5.

43 Connah, *Archaeology of Benin*.

44 S. K. McIntosh and R. J. McIntosh, 'Cities without citadels: understanding urban origins along the middle Niger', in T. Shaw, P. Sinclair, B. Andah, and A. Okpoko (eds), *Archaeology of Africa* (London, 1993), pp. 622–41.

45 See, for example, John G. Evans, *An Introduction to Environmental Archaeology* (London, 1978), pp. 114–16.

46 Evans, *Environmental Archaeology*, p. 117.

47 Evans, *Environmental Archaeology*, pp. 112–14.

48 Connah, *Archaeology of Benin*, p. 86.

3

Aksumite Urbanism

DAVID W. PHILLIPSON

Aksum lies in the highlands of Tigray in northern Ethiopia, at an altitude of 2,200 metres. Today, it is a town of some 40,000 inhabitants, a market and administrative centre, and a place of great importance to the Ethiopian Orthodox Church. During the early centuries AD, however, it was the capital of a major trading state which has been described as 'the last of the great civilisations of Antiquity to be revealed to modern knowledge'.[1] It has been designated a World Heritage Site by UNESCO.

In its heyday Aksum displayed great prosperity, organisational power, and technological sophistication. Wide-ranging trade contacts were maintained, through the Red Sea port at Adulis, with the Mediterranean lands and, in the opposite direction, at least as far as India.[2] On occasion its rule extended across the Red Sea to what is now Yemen.[3] Sections of its population were literate both in Ethiopic and in Greek.[4] From the third to the seventh century it issued a tri-metallic coinage without parallel in sub-Saharan Africa.[5] The kings of Aksum adopted Christianity during the second quarter of the fourth century, probably within a decade of the corresponding event in the Roman Empire.[6] Although Aksum had declined in prosperity and political importance by the seventh/eighth centuries, it has remained a major religious centre, dominated by the two Cathedrals of Saint Mary of Zion where, according to the traditions of the Ethiopian Orthodox Church, is kept the Ark of the Covenant brought to Ethiopia by Menelik, the son of Solomon and the Queen of Sheba.[7]

In 1993, the British Institute in Eastern Africa launched a five-year research programme designed to broaden understanding of Aksumite civilisation in its local as well as its international context.[8] This paper is based on some of the preliminary results obtained during the first four years of this project. It offers some tentative ideas about the nature of Aksumite urbanism and the socio-political and economic systems which supported it.

Aksum's antecedents remain poorly understood. Cultivation and herding are both of considerable antiquity in highland Ethiopia, where several indigenous crops were domesticated.[9] It was probably during the second quarter of the last millennium BC that there were established in the Tigray highlands of northern Ethiopia a number of settlements the material culture of which shows several features with affinities and antecedents in southern Arabia.[10] The best known of these settlements is at Yeha, some

50 km north-east of Aksum, where a remarkable building of superbly dressed masonry still stands to a height of 12 metres. Associated with this building are figurative sculptures and stone inscriptions, all of types not previously known in Ethiopia but with traceable antecedents in Arabia.[11] Such phenomena are known in several Tigray localities; but in each case their distribution is tightly circumscribed. One possible explanation is that they represent the settlements of immigrant groups who initially established discrete colonies in particularly fertile parts of the highlands, later becoming assimilated and dispersed.[12] Some of the earliest inscriptions, which are unvocalized, refer to a state or kingdom of D'MT (perhaps Daamat) which may have been centred at Yeha. These inscriptions, both in language and in script, belong to the South Semitic classification and are directly ancestral to the Amharic and Tigrinya speech and writing of today.[13]

Archaeologically, Aksum is best known both overseas and in Ethiopia itself for its series of monumental stelae. Over 140 are known in the central area, and there are hundreds more in the vicinity. Six of them are carved in representation of multi-storeyed buildings: they probably date from about the third or fourth centuries AD.[14]

Before 1993, such excavation as had been conducted at Aksum had largely concentrated on the city's monumental architecture and long-distance trade contacts.[15] The research currently being undertaken seeks to investigate Aksum as an urban centre, with emphasis on domestic buildings (which were effectively ignored by previous researchers) and on economic developments through time.

It is now appropriate briefly to describe some of the research results obtained since 1993. The Tomb of the Brick Arches is located close to the standing storeyed stela, but does not appear to have been directly associated with any particular stela now extant. It had been entered in 1974, when its general plan was recorded and the first of its four chambers largely excavated.[16] Its date was estimated then as falling in the late third or early fourth centuries AD.

The tomb is approached by means of an adit with 18 surviving stone steps. At the foot of these a horseshoe-shaped brick arch gives access to the tomb, which comprises four rock-cut chambers, their floor being almost ten metres below the modern ground surface. The complex was roughly carved out as a whole, then subdivided by the insertion of stone cross-walls incorporating brick arches built with lime mortar.

The tomb contained a mass of archaeological material, generally well preserved, despite having suffered some disturbance in ancient times. Large numbers of complete and broken pots were mixed with fragmented glass vessels, some of very fine quality which must have featured prominently among Aksum's luxury imports and which provide valuable dating evidence. Elaborate metalwork in bronze and iron was mostly of local manufacture, although one item (currently subject to specialist examination) may possibly be of Chinese origin.

Particular interest attaches to a substantial quantity of ivory, including two very large panels carved with elaborate representations of vines and animals. The two panels are virtual mirror images of each other; and the placement of the animals suggests that they were set with their points uppermost. This positioning, the holes for fixing, the carefully cut joints and associated ivory slats all suggest that these objects should be interpreted as having adorned the back of an elaborate chair or throne. We now have, for the first time, direct archaeological evidence for Aksumite involvement not only with trade in ivory (previously attested in written sources, notably the *Periplus of the Erythraean Sea*)[17] but also with the local working of that material at a very high artistic and technological level.[18]

The stelae themselves consist of single pieces of granite; and the largest, now fallen and broken, would have been 29.8 metres high and some 517 tonnes in weight.[19] It had been

Figure 3.1 Inside the mausoleum: the central passage

shown in 1974 that major tombs existed on either side of the stela.[20] That on the east side was investigated in 1993 and found to have a collapsed roof, so our work has been concentrated on the westerly tomb, which its discoverers had designated the 'Mausoleum'. This was entered through a monumental portal giving access to a passage 16.7 metres long and 1.9 metres wide, roofed with massive dressed granite slabs in which were cut three square apertures connected to stone-lined shafts that originally led to the ground surface. The passage has a height of 2.3 metres, and its stone-flagged floor is 5.9 metres below the modern surface (Figure 3.1). On each side of the Mausoleum's central passage were five side chambers, making ten in all, each 6.6 metres long by 1.7 metres wide. At the entrance to each of these had originally been a brick arch springing from dressed stone slabs: none remains intact although the slabs and substantial remains of the brickwork survive.[21]

Building on the results of previous work, it is now possible to offer a much amplified understanding of the central stelae area. During the first three centuries AD, it was gradually built up in a series of terraces and platforms, in and under which were subterranean tombs, many of them marked by stelae. The finely carved storeyed stelae were probably the last, dating to around the beginning of the fourth century AD. The largest of all was associated with tombs of great complexity and magnificence. There can be little doubt that these were the burial places of Aksum's elite – presumably royal. They symbolize not only the power, authority and technological expertise of the ancient kingdom, but also its capacity for the organization of manpower.

All the recent work described so far has focused on the funerary monuments of the Aksumite elite. As this phase of the research drew to its conclusion, efforts were concentrated in 1995 and 1996 on the archaeology of domestic occupation and on the lives and burials of lower-status individuals. Excavations were also conducted at the so-called Gudit Stelae Field, on the western edge of Aksum, apparently a burial ground for lower-status individuals. The site is demarcated by a terrace; and a trench excavated across this revealed a well preserved retaining wall with, behind it, a stone platform approached by a flight of steps. Several non-elite graves have been investigated, each comprising a simple pit containing only a few artefacts and marked by a small rough-hewn stela.[22]

Efforts to throw light on domestic living conditions and the subsistence economy have been concentrated in two areas. One (which we designated the 'Domestic Area') lies outside the modern town, near the track which leads northward to the Tombs of Kaleb and Gabra Masqal. The second area lies within the modern town, in the quarter known as Maleke Aksum.

At the first of these sites, a circumscribed settlement area has been defined.[23] Its earliest phases remain poorly known but, perhaps around the fifth century, an elite structure akin to that known at Dungur (on the western side of Aksum near the Gudit Stelae Field) was erected (Figure 3.2). This structure has not been investigated in detail, but appears to have been short-lived. After its abandonment, buildings were erected which clearly belonged to a lower order in the social hierarchy. Several successive phases have been recognized stratigraphically, but coin evidence suggests that most occurred during a period which did not greatly exceed the sixth century. The buildings, of rough-hewn stone laid in poorly defined courses, were subject to repeated modification (Figure 3.3). As a result, much of the associated archaeological material was not recovered from primary contexts. We can be reasonably certain, however, that food processing was carried out in the general vicinity through much, if not all, of the occupation. Sheila Boardman has recovered plant remains representing a wide range of cultivated plants, including barley, teff, finger millet, two varieties of wheat, lentils, flax, cotton, grape and

Figure 3.3 Sixth-century non-elite buildings at the 'Domestic Area'

Figure 3.2 Elite building at the 'Domestic Area' to the north of Aksum

the local oil-yielding plant known as noog.[24] Investigation of the 'Domestic Area' has provided our first view at Aksum itself of non-elite living conditions, material culture and domestic economy of the later Aksumite period. Broadly comparable settlements have been known for many years at Matara in Eritrea,[25] but have not been published in detail.[26]

Evidence from the 'Domestic Area' has been supplemented by small-scale investigations in Maleke Aksum, where rough stone buildings were preserved to a height of several metres (Figure 3.4). They also appear to date from about the sixth century. They were associated with debris from craft and industrial production: although analysis of the residues has not yet been completed it is possible that the activities practised in the vicinity may have included metalwork, glass-making and the lathe-turning of ivory.[27]

One aspect which has so far been mentioned only tangentially is the coming of Christianity which has played such a vital role in the history of Aksum since the fourth century. In 1994 permission was granted by the ecclesiastical authorities for a detailed survey of the cathedral precinct at Aksum (Figure 3.5).[28] Features of archaeological significance here include the throne-bases in the outer compound (Figure 3.6), and the great Aksumite podium (Figure 3.7) on which the present Old Cathedral was built in the seventeenth century but which is believed to date back at least to Aksum's first Christian church, the basilica erected by King Ezana in the fourth century.[29]

Such, in bare outline, are the primary results obtained so far from the current series of excavations. In conjunction with earlier discoveries and observations, what do they contribute to an understanding of Aksumite urbanism? Although much of the site is obscured by the modern town, it is possible to estimate the central area of ancient occupation as having been in the order of between 70 and 110 hectares – roughly the equivalent of a one- kilometre square, the equivalent of many Roman provincial cities of the same general period.[30] There is some evidence that this area was not all densely covered with buildings,[31] and that it included substantial areas devoted to elite burials and to religious purposes. Such buildings as have been investigated are almost all of an elite nature: detailed plans have been recorded in several instances and, although the proposed reconstructions may be a trifle fanciful, these were clearly very substantial buildings.[32] They are conventionally designated palaces, but we do not know their original function. Buildings of this type were present in outlying areas as well as in the centre.[33] So far, the main area of non-elite domestic occupation to have been investigated is in a peripheral location, although such occupation also took place more centrally and there were significant economic differences between the two zones.

Throughout its history, Aksum's domestic economy seems to have followed the general pattern which had been established in far earlier times, with the possible addition to the crop repertoire of grape and cotton, both now attested there in sixth-century contexts, with hints of the former some two centuries earlier.[34] Architecture, both monumental and domestic, followed traditions established long previously which were, in some cases, common to wide areas of north-eastern Africa.[35]

Much information about wider aspects of the Aksumite economy may be obtained through study of the coinage. Coins were struck in gold, silver and copper/bronze in the names of the kings of Aksum from, probably, the third quarter of the third century until the first quarter of the seventh.[36] These coins circulated far beyond the modern borders of Ethiopia and Eritrea; probably more Aksumite gold coins have been discovered in southern Arabia than on the African side of the Red Sea.[37] The first Aksumite coins bear the name of a King Endybis who is otherwise unknown. Both sides bear profile portraits, which presumably represent the king, framed (on the gold coins) between ears of corn. There has been controversy over the identity of the cereal represented which could be either barley or emmer wheat, both of which were grown in ancient Aksum; opinion now tends to favour the latter.[38] The inscriptions on all coins of this reign are in Greek. By about AD 300, Ge'ez began to be used, generally but not exclusively on the copper. Greek continued on the gold coins until the final issue in that metal, in the early seventh century. The general pattern of Aksumite coin types shows considerable stability. Weights, and the fineness of gold and silver, decrease fairly steadily although the copper coins were larger again from the end of the sixth century.[39]

It is noteworthy that the first Aksumite issues in gold followed the weight standard then prevailing in the Roman Empire; furthermore, they were inscribed in Greek. These points all suggest that the first Aksumite coins were intended primarily for circulation in the context of international trade. Subsequently, copper coins were issued in far greater numbers and were often, at least from the late fourth century, inscribed in Ge'ez. It is reasonable to conclude that the copper coins were intended for mainly local circulation, as is supported by the nature of the reverse inscriptions and by the frequent occurrence of these coins on domestic occupation sites at Aksum. Coinage, therefore, was originally issued at Aksum to support involvement in international trade; this remained the basic function of the gold, although use of copper denominations subsequently expanded locally, at least through the urbanized population. It seems likely that the end of the Aksumite coinage was shortly preceded by abandonment of the international gold currency and emphasis on domestic circulation.[40]

Let us now turn to less tangible matters. Religion in Aksum before the early fourth century seems, at least for the ruling elite, to have followed a pattern of South Arabian origin which probably had been established in Ethiopia for many centuries previously. In the second quarter of the fourth century, Christianity was adopted formally by Aksum's rulers. Whereas in the Roman Empire Christianity began as a popular religion and eventually was embraced by Constantine, in Ethiopia the opposite process is indicated: it was the king (Ezana) in the capital (Aksum) who first adopted the new religion and subsequently sought its expansion.[41] This process is demonstrated admirably in the coinage which, suddenly and emphatically half-way through Ezana's reign, replaced the crescent-and-disc symbol of the earlier religion with the Christian cross. On the copper issues which, it was argued above, were intended primarily for local circulation, but not on the internationally circulating gold, the cross became the major reverse type, often accompanied by inscriptions in Greek or, subsequently, Ge'ez, such as TOYTO APECH TH XWPA ('may this be pleasing in the countryside').

We know extremely little about the Aksumite political system. The hypotheses proposed by Yuri Kobishchanov,[42] almost entirely on the basis of written sources, are marred by the biases both of the sources and of the historian himself. A simple hierarchical model, with a monarch at the apex of authority, does not fit comfortably with the available data. The epistle of Constantius[43] and Ethiopian tradition both point to the possibility of a system of co-rulers, although this is not reflected in the coinage which is invariably – except for some anonymous issues – in the name of a single BACIΛEYC.[44] (It is just conceivable that those coins, mainly in gold, which bear a portrait on both obverse and reverse reflect such duality; but invariably only one king is named in the inscriptions.)

Let us now consider when, how and why Aksum came to be. Although earlier sites are known in the general vicinity, there is no archaeological evidence for settlement of Aksum itself until about the first century BC/AD. Around AD 40 or 50, the anonymous author of the *Periplus* records the existence of a 'metropolis of the people called Aksumites', ruled by one Zoscales.[45] The metropolis was located inland; its port, Adulis, was on the Red Sea coast a short distance south of the modern Massawa.[46] Although Zoscales is not mentioned in any known inscription or other source, archaeological

Figure 3.4 Aksumite walling in an area of non-elite occupation in Maleke Aksum

Figure 3.5 The Cathedral Precinct, seen from the modern bell tower. The Old Cathedral, standing on the Aksumite podium, is to the right of centre

Figure 3.6 Throne bases in the Cathedral Precinct

Figure 3.7 The south wall of the podium on which the Old Cathedral stands

deposits at Aksum itself contain artefacts of this period which are predominantly of local manufacture, but include imported materials analogous to those noted in the *Periplus*.

Despite the frequent application to Aksum of the term 'city', it seems preferable to retain the word 'metropolis' used in the *Periplus*. The place was of a size and importance to merit use of the term 'city'. However, there is no evidence that Aksum ever was a city in the sense that the term is sometimes understood. Its structures, as presently known, comprised large buildings of unknown purpose but clear elite associations, as well as funerary and other monuments, and religious buildings. On the few occasions when buildings or burial sites have been located which could have belonged to people from non-elite social strata, or been used in connection with the subsistence economy, they are usually in outlying positions apparently separated from the centre by open country. There is no evidence whatsoever that Aksum and its contemporary Ethiopian settlements were equipped with defensive walls or any similar physical demarcation from their hinterland. Use of the term 'city' in these circumstances could be misleading. The same point serves to distinguish Aksum from contemporary conurbations in the Mediterranean world, and to remind us of its specifically Ethiopian nature.

Aksum, then, was a place where elite and religious buildings, monuments and burials were grouped together (Figure 3.8). It had no defensive walls, but its limits to the east and north were marked, following the practice known also at Adulis, by bilingual inscriptions set up by the fourth-century King Ezana.[47] From the eastern entrance a line of monumental thrones led to the main religious and burial area in the northern part of Aksum. Elsewhere, particularly in the western half of the area, were large elite structures of unknown function: similar buildings also occurred in the immediate hinterland of Aksum. Likewise in the hinterland were agricultural centres, stone quarries and workshops where intensive processing of some material, perhaps ivory, was carried out. In short, Aksum seems to have been a political, religious and commercial centre.

It is noteworthy that such a centre may not have been unique within the Aksumite polity. It was, however, a phenomenon which was not continued into post-Aksumite Ethiopia, where the ruler's court was essentially peripatetic. If the 'metropolis of the people called Aksumites' was established in a country which lacked a prior tradition of permanent centralized settlement, it was not a mere implant, but at least in major part a development firmly based in local tradition. At the Aksumite site of Matara in southern Eritrea, imported amphorae were used as containers in which to bury babies,[48] in an interesting variation of a very widespread African practice.

Until the archaeology of the last three centuries BC in northern Ethiopia and Eritrea comes to be more clearly understood, we shall not fully understand the antecedents of Aksum.[49] There may have been an earlier capital, or earlier capitals. One candidate is Matara. Then why was it eventually moved to, or established at, Aksum? If the polity's prosperity was based·on international trade, why was the centre so far to the west, almost at the limit of the archaeologically attested distribution of Aksumite sites and so far from the main port at Adulis? One possible explanation is the source area of ivory, now seen as Aksum's principal export.[50]

With the decline in Aksum's prosperity, marked by the end of the coinage even for local circulation, early in the seventh century, we enter the period which Gibbon characterized as one of somnolence and amnesia.[51] From Gibbon's standpoint this may, in the eighteenth century, have been a justifiable diagnosis. As a summary of Ethiopian history it is grossly misleading. John Sutton has shown how these developments coincided with the rise of Arabian power and control of the Red Sea.[52] The achievements of post-Aksumite Ethiopia, important though they undoubtedly were, did not emphasize urbanism and are not relevant to the present paper.

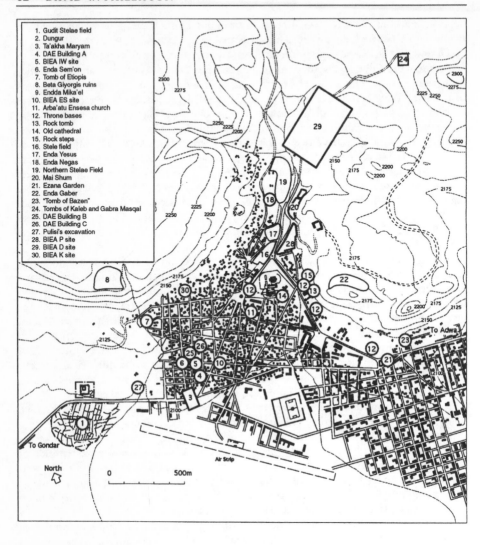

1. Gudit Stelae field
2. Dungur
3. Ta'akha Maryam
4. DAE Building A
5. BIEA IW site
6. Enda Sem'on
7. Tomb of Etiopis
8. Beta Giyorgis ruins
9. Endda Mika'el
10. BIEA ES site
11. Arba'atu Ensesa church
12. Throne bases
13. Rock tomb
14. Old cathedral
15. Rock steps
16. Stele field
17. Enda Yesus
18. Enda Negas
19. Northern Stelae Field
20. Mai Shum
21. Ezana Garden
22. Enda Gaber
23. "Tomb of Bazen"
24. Tombs of Kaleb and Gabra Masqal
25. DAE Building B
26. DAE Building C
27. Pulisi's excavation
28. BIEA P site
29. BIEA D site
30. BIEA K site

Figure 3.8 Map of Aksum, showing the principal sites and monuments considered in this chapter

Notes

1 The best overall account of Aksumite civilisation is S. Munro-Hay, *Aksum, an African Civilisation of Late Antiquity* (Edinburgh, 1991). See also D. W. Phillipson, *Ancient Ethiopia* (London, 1998).

2 S. Munro-Hay, 'The foreign trade of the Aksumite port of Adulis', *Azania,* 17 (1982), pp. 105–25.

3 Sergew Hable Selassie, *Ancient and Medieval Ethiopian History to 1270* (Addis Ababa, 1972).

4 A detailed compendium of inscriptions is by E. Bernand *et al. Receuil des Inscriptions de l'Ethiopie des périodes pré-Axoumite et Axoumite* (Paris, 1991).

5 S. Munro-Hay and B. Juel-Jensen, *Aksumite Coinage* (London, 1995).

6 Sergew, *Ethiopian History*; Phillipson, *Ancient Ethiopia*.

7 E. A. W. Budge, *The Queen of Sheba and her only son Menyelek being the Book of the Glory of Kings* (London, 1922); see also Phillipson, *Ancient Ethiopia*.

8 The Institute has received additional financial support from the Society of Antiquaries of London, the British Academy, the McDonald Institute for Archaeological Research in the University of Cambridge, the British Museum and, in 1995, the National Geographic Society. Preliminary reports have been published: D. W. Phillipson, 'The significance and symbolism of Aksumite Stelae', *Cambridge Archaeological Journal,* 4 (1994), pp. 189–210; D. W. Phillipson, 'Excavations at Aksum 1993–94', *Antiquaries Journal,* 75 (1995), pp. 1–41; D. W. Phillipson, A. Reynolds *et al.* 'B.I.E.A. excavations at Aksum, northern Ethiopia, 1995' *Azania,* 31 (1996), pp. 99–147; D. W. Phillipson and J. S. Phillips 'Excavations at Aksum, 1993-96: a preliminary report', *Journal of Ethiopian Studies,* 12 (1998), pp. 1–128. A detailed monograph on the results of the project will be co-published by the British Institute in Eastern Africa and the Society of Antiquaries of London.

9 D. W. Phillipson, 'The antiquity of cultivation and herding in Ethiopia' in T. Shaw *et al.* (eds), *The Archaeology of Africa: food, metals and towns* (London, 1993), pp. 344-57.

10 For an evaluation of affinities, see R. Fattovich, 'Remarks on the pre-Aksumite period in northern Ethiopia', *Journal of Ethiopian Studies,* 23 (1990), pp. 1–33.

11 The most comprehensive account of the Yeha temple remains that of the 1906 Deutsche Aksum-Expedition published by E. Littmann *et al., Deutsche Aksum-Expedition* (Berlin, 1913). For illustrations, including the sculpture, see Phillipson, *Ancient Ethiopia*.

12 Cf. S. Munro-Hay, 'State development and urbanism in northern Ethiopia', in Shaw *et al., Archaeology of Africa* (1993), pp. 609–21. Summaries of the known sites, with references, are provided by E. Godet, 'Répertoire des sites pré-Axoumites et Axoumites du Tigré,. Ethiopie'; *Abbay* 8 (1977), pp. 19–58 and *idem,* 'Répertoire de sites pré-Axoumites et Axoumites d'Ethiopie du Nord, IIè partie: Erythrée', *Abbay* 11(1982), pp. 73–113. See also Fattovich, 'Remarks on the pre-Aksumite period'.

13 Bernand *et al., Receuil.*

14 Again, the fullest account of the storeyed stelae is that of Littmann *et al., Deutsche Aksum-Expedition,* now translated, annotated and amplified in D. W. Phillipson, *The Monuments of Aksum* (Addis Ababa, 1997).

15 For a summary of earlier research, and a detailed account of that undertaken in 1972–74, see S. Munro-Hay, *Excavations at Aksum: an Account of Research at the Ancient Ethiopian capital Directed in 1972–74 by the late Dr Neville Chittick* (London, 1989).

16 Munro-Hay, *Excavations at Aksum.*

17 The best edition is that of L. Casson, *The Periplus Maris Erythaei* (Princeton, 1989).

18 Results of the excavations since 1993 are still being prepared for definitive publication. For preliminary accounts, see Phillipson, 'Excavations at Aksum 1993–94', Phillipson and Phillips, 'Excavations at Aksum 1993–96', and Phillipson, *Ancient Ethiopia*.

19 Phillipson, 'Significance and symbolism'.

20 Munro-Hay, *Excavations at Aksum.*

21 Again, results of the excavations since 1993 are still being prepared for definitive publication. For preliminary accounts, see Phillipson, 'Significance and symbolism', Phillipson, Reynolds *et al.,* 'B.I.E.A. excavations', Phillipson and Phillips, 'Excavations at Aksum 1993–96', and Phillipson, *Ancient Ethiopia*.

22 Excavations at the Gudit Stelae Field were supervised by Ato Ayele Tarekegn as part of a doctoral research project at the University of Cambridge. For a preliminary account see Ayele Tarekegn, 'Aksumite burial practices: the "Gudit Stelae Field", Aksum', in G. Pwiti and R. Soper (eds), *Aspects*

of African Archaeology (Harare: University of Zimbabwe Publications, 1996), pp. 611–19.

23 Phillipson, Reynolds *et al.*, 'B.I.E.A excavations'.

24 These identifications are provisional. See Phillipson, Reynolds *et al.*, 'B.I.E.A. excavations'; Phillipson and Phillips, 'Excavations at Aksum, 1993–96'. Boardman's research continues, partly supported by the Natural Environment Research Council.

25 F. Anfray, 'La première campagne de fouilles à Matara (Nov. 1959–Janv. 1960)', *Annales d'Ethiopie*, 5 (1963), pp. 87–166; *idem*, 'Matara', *Annales d'Ethiopie*, 7 (1967), pp. 33–88; *idem*, 'Deux villes axoumites: Adoulis et Matara', in *Atti IV Congresso Internationale di studi Etiopici* (Rome; Accademia Nazionale dei Lincei, 1974), pp. 745–65; F. Anfray and G. Annequin, 'Matara: deuxieme, troisieme et quatrieme campagnes de fouilles', *Annales d'Ethiopie*, 6 (1965), pp. 49–92.

26 Further relevant material is currently under investigation by Rodolfo Fattovich and Kathryn Bard at Beta Giyorgis, near Aksum. See Bard and Fattovich, 'The 1993 excavations at Ona Enda Aboi Zague (Aksum, Tigray)', *Nyame Akuma*, 40 (1993), pp. 14–17; *idem* 'The I.O.U./B.U. excavation at Bieta Giyorgis (Aksum): an interim report', *Nyame Akuma*, 45 (1995), pp. 25–7; Fattovich, 'Archaeological excavations at Bieta Giyorgis (Aksum, Tigray), 1994 field season: a preliminary report', *Nyame Akuma*, 43 (1995), pp. 34–7; Fattovich and Bard, 'Scavi archeologici nella zona di Aksum: C – Ona Enda Aboi Zague (Bieta Giyorgis)', *Rassegna di Studi Etiopici*, 35 (1993), pp. 41–71; *idem*, 'Scavi archeologici nella zona di Aksum: E – Ona Enda Aboi Zague e Ona Nagast (Bieta Giyorgis)', *Rassegna di Studi Etiopici*, 37 (1995), pp. 5–35.

27 Research on the residues is in progress.

28 Phillipson, 'Excavations at Aksum, 1993–94'. Additional research was undertaken by Michael Mallinson, who was able to make a detailed examination of the Old Cathedral and to offer advice on its maintenance and conservation.

29 For descriptions of these monuments, see Littmann *et al.*, *Deutsche Aksum-Expedition*; Phillipson, *Monuments of Aksum*.

30 For comparative African data, see R. Fletcher, 'Settlement area and communication in African towns and cities', in Shaw *et al.*, *Archaeology of Africa*, pp. 732–49. A wider perspective is provided by *idem*, 'Settlement archaeology: worldwide comparisons', *World Archaeology* 18 (1986), pp. 59–83.

31 This is indicated, for example, by test excavations undertaken in advance of proposed building work.

32 See Littmann *et al.*, *Deutsche Aksum-Expedition*; Phillipson, *Ancient Ethiopia*; Phillipson, *Monuments of Aksum*; D. R. Buxton and D. Matthews, 'The reconstruction of vanished Aksumite buildings', *Rassegna di Studi Etiopici*, 25 (1974), pp. 53–76; F. Anfray, *Les anciens Ethiopiens: siècles d'histoire* (Paris, 1990).

33 For example, Dungur and the elite building located at the 'Domestic Area', noted above.

34 Grape vines are, for example, depicted on ivory carvings from the Tomb of the Brick Arches, and on the base plate of the great standing stela (Stela 3). For further discussion, see Phillipson, *Ancient Ethiopia*.

35 This is particularly true of the stelae: R. Fattovich, 'Some remarks on the origins of the Aksumite stelae', *Annales d'Ethiopie*, 14 (1987), pp. 43–69.

36 For an up-to-date survey, see S. Munro-Hay and B. Juel-Jensen, *Aksumite Coinage* (London, 1995).

37 S. Munro-Hay, 'The al-Madhariba hoard of gold Aksumite and late Roman coins', *Numismatic Chronicle*, 149 (1989), pp. 83–100.

38 Phillipson, 'Antiquity of cultivation'.

39 Munro-Hay and Juel-Jensen, *Aksumite Coinage*.

40 For further discussion, see Phillipson, *Ancient Ethiopia*.

41 Sergew, *Ethiopian History*; Phillipson, *Ancient Ethiopia*.

42 Y. Kobishchanov, *Axum* (ed. J. Michels) (University Park, Pennsylvania, 1979).

43 J. M. Szymusiak, *Athanasius: Apologia ad Constantium Imperatorem (Sources Chrétiennes 56)* (Paris, 1958).

44 For a further discussion, including the identity of persons apparently named as co-rulers, see Phillipson, *Ancient Ethiopia*.

45 Casson, *Periplus*.

46 There is wide agreement on this location during the Aksumite period, although it has been suggested that the port may in earlier times have been located further to the north. See L. Casson, 'The location of Adulis', in L. Casson and M. Price (eds), *Coins, Culture and History in the Ancient World: Numismatic and other Studies in Honour of Bluma L. Trell* (Detroit, 1981), pp. 113–22.

47 One such inscription, beside the road into Aksum from the east (i.e. from Adwa) has been known

for many years. Significantly, it seems to have marked the beginning of the line of thrones leading to the central zone where the Cathedral and principal burial area were located. Another such inscription, virtually identical, was discovered in 1981 on the northern edge of Aksum: see E. Bernand, 'Nouvelles versions de la campagne du roi Ezana contre les Bedja', *Zeitschrift für Papyrologie und Epigraphik*, 45 (1982), pp. 105–14. Note also, in this connection, the 'Monumentum Adulitanum' described by Cosmas Indicopleustes at Adulis: W. Wolska-Conus (ed.), *Cosmas Indicopleustes: Topographie Chrétienne* (Sources Chrétiennes 241, 159 and 197) (Paris, 1968-73).

48 Anfray and Annequin, 'Matara'.
49 But see Fattovich, 'Remarks on the pre-Aksumite period'; and Munro-Hay, 'State development'.
50 See also D. W. Phillipson, 'Aksum in Africa', *Journal of Ethiopian Studies*, 23 (1990), pp. 55–65; L. Phillipson, 'A functional consideration of Gudit scrapers from Aksum, Ethiopia', paper presented at a conference on the Stone Age of north-eastern Africa, Poznan, Poland, August 1997.
51 E. Gibbon, *Decline and Fall of the Roman Empire*.
52 J. E. G. Sutton, 'Aksum, the Erythraean Sea, and the world of late antiquity: a foreword', pp. 1–6 in Munro-Hay, *Excavations at Aksum*.

PART TWO
Pre-colonial Towns in Transition

4

Mbanza Kongo/São Salvador
Kongo's Holy City

JOHN K. THORNTON

The city of Mbanza Kongo/São Salvadoré[1] sits on an impressive mountainous plateau some 600 metres above the sea in modern northern Angola. With the exception of a period of 30 years in the late seventeenth century when it was abandoned, it is the oldest continuously occupied town in West Central Africa, and one of the longest occupied in sub-Saharan Africa. In its heyday of the late sixteenth and early seventeenth centuries it was the largest city in West Central Africa and one of the largest in Africa. It was once close to the geographic centre of the old Kingdom of Kongo, and today remains the spiritual centre of the Kongolese people,[2] even those whose ancestors never recognized the king of Kongo as their ruler. Many Kongolese clans trace their ultimate origin to Mbanza Kongo, known in tradition as 'Kongo dia Ntotela' (Kongo of the Emperor) or 'Kongo dia Ngunga' (Kongo of the Bell) as well as its more prosaic Kikongo or Christian name.[3] Since the 1950s, a romantic strain in Kongolese nationalism has transported this point of origin to the 'other world' and away from the physical location in northern Angola.[4]

Mbanza Kongo's long history and prestigious position are a product of its status as a holy city – not just a political capital but a place of great religious significance – and the long period when it was a great centre of population. It was the religious element that made it a permanent place in a country where most of the population were shifting constantly in a slow-motion, rural restlessness increased since the mid-seventeenth century by civil discord.

The Kikongo word *mbanza*, town, forms a dichotomy with *vata*, or village, that reflects an ancient division between town and country in the language, and, since at least the seventeenth century, between crude and cultured, savage and civilized.[5] The origins of the dichotomy are ancient: recently archaeologist James Denbow unearthed evidence of a large settlement, perhaps an early *mbanza* surrounded by smaller ones (proto-*vatas*) at Kayes in Congo-Brazzaville that dates from the time of Christ.[6] On linguistic grounds we are led to believe that the *mbanza* got its distinctiveness from being a seat of government, a place of justice and a centre of wealth – and not just from its size.[7]

Mbanza Kongo, the capital of Kongo, was possibly founded in the late fourteenth century, at least if the evidence of seventeenth-century traditions about the founding of

Kongo is to be believed.[8] As Kongo grew into a major state, its capital grew too, soon surpassing other *mbanzas* in its orbit and becoming the largest settlement in West Central Africa. It was certainly such a place when the first Portuguese visitors described it in the late fifteenth century. An account of 1491, though brief, gives us some ideas about the significance of Mbanza Kongo, comparing it to the Portuguese city of Evora, and noting that its houses were 'better than found in all of Guinea'.[9] According to other accounts of 1491, the city was protected by a defensive palisade which King Afonso I made good use of 15 years later in a battle with his brother.[10] They also enclosed a great central plaza, the place where justice was carried out, visitors were received, coronations were proclaimed and carried out, and the royal palace, a complex of buildings within the walled area.[11] As a concentration of wealth and elite dwellings, it was a place where the earliest Portuguese visitors marvelled at the quality of construction of the houses, especially their cloth wall hangings.[12]

Economic and political significance was matched by centrality in a religious sense as well. Seventeenth-century traditions noted that even before the foundation of the kingdom, the site of Mbanza Kongo was the residence of a religious personage, known as the Mani-Cabunga, a sort of Summo Pontifice to whom people had recourse 'in their necessities, and water for their crops'.[13] In addition to this religous figure who clearly established his authority through the cult of territorial guardian spirits, Kongo was important in the cult of the ancestors. The immediate environs of the town contained the tombs of the early kings and their successors. Although Afonso I, in Christianizing the country, built the church of Our Lady of Victory on top of these remains soon after 1526,[14] he did not disturb them and the church retained the nickname *mbiro* – grave – for at least half a century later.[15]

Mbanza Kongo's impressive fifteenth-century architecture of the traditional style, largely of wood, woven and thatched grass, and bark textiles, was supplemented by stone soon after the Portuguese arrived. Portuguese masons assisted 'a thousand blacks' who carried the stone for the first church with voices raised in joyous song that could be heard 'two or three leagues away' in celebration of the baptism of King Nzinga Nkuwu, now João I, in May, 1491.[16] Afonso I, who succeeded his father in 1509, perhaps inspired by stories of the stone buildings of Europe, decided to make Mbanza Kongo into a stone city. Afonso constructed a great city wall, 15–20 feet high and between 2 feet 6 inches and three feet thick, around the royal quarter and a quarter assigned to the Portuguese. The work took a long time, for it was still progressing in 1529.[17] He also constructed new churches of stone, and a great stone palace for himself, work which took considerable time: commenced in 1509, it was still under construction in 1526.[18] In spite of his complaints and worries that the work would never be finished, Afonso not only completed the work of walling and church construction, but developed a cadre of local people who could construct and repair stone buildings. The Jesuits, who came to Kongo five years after Afonso's death, must have used such a team to erect three new stone churches in the city within a few months of their arrival.[19]

Although Afonso Christianized the town he was embellishing with stone buildings, he did not change its name; it remained the 'City of Congo' in the dateline of every letter that he and his successor Diogo I (1545–61) wrote.[20] In 1548 Jesuit priests erected a new church, dedicated to Jesus the Saviour,[21] and by the time of King Alvaro I (1568–87) rulers of Kongo sent their letters from 'Salvador' or 'São Salvador' after the name of this church.[22]

Afonso did not just anchor the city with stone construction and enhance its magnificence, but he and his successors also greatly enlarged its population. One mechanism for increasing the population size was bringing home slaves captured in the wars Afonso fought to expand the kingdom and punish rebels. As a result of such a war in about 1512, Afonso's agents exposed a substantial number of recently captured people for sale in the great public square, while other rebellious slaves wrought great destruction in the city.[23] These slaves and countless others were integrated into the town and its surrounding agricultural hinterland.

This population build-up did not mean that São Salvador was a highly nucleated city on the European model. Instead, it was more like a dense clump of population surrounding the palace, churches, the royal plaza and their enclosing walls. Dominican priests noted agricultural production even in the densely settled areas when they visited in 1610,[24] and the region of dense settlement extended for a considerable distance around the plateau and surrounding valleys for about 10 kilometres. Density within this area was at least 10 times greater than any other district of equivalent area in the kingdom.[25] The loose settlement pattern of the compounds ('palaces') of nobles scattered with the houses of commoners and fenced in animal shelters and even farmlands made it hard, as Duarte Lopes noted at the end of the sixteenth century, to see exactly what the extent of the city was, and one would be hard pressed to say exactly where it began and ended.[26] The settlement lacked clear demarcation, although undoubtedly some took the population within the city walls as representing the city, and others more generously counted the whole densely settled area. For this reason, population estimates fluctuate widely. Well-informed witnesses in 1595 gave its population at 10,000 households — perhaps 50,000 people — which probably included the whole settled area of the plateau,[27] while another equally knowledgeable witness in 1604 estimated just 2,000 households (approximately 10,000 people), probably only counting the people within the walls.[28]

The significance of the population build-up around Mbanza Kongo and São Salvador cannot be underestimated. The royal district around the city housed a significant professional army, and its size made control of the city all that was needed to remain King of Kongo. The magnificence of the city made the provincial nobles strive to live there, and most considered themselves ultimately citizens of the city, wherever they resided. Nobles tried to get appointments in the city which helped ensure royal power and the preservation of the centralization so noted by observers.[29]

The city reached its height under King Garcia II (1641–61), who restored many buildings and founded a major new complex for the Capuchin missionaries when they arrived in 1648.[30] Surrounded by stone walls, the city boasted a dozen churches and chapels including its cathedral (all with stone walls and thatched roofs). The cathedral dominated the main plaza, while the palace took one side and the smaller, walled Portuguese town the other. Elsewhere in the city was a Jesuit college which produced graduates — like the priest Manuel Robrerdo or Pedro de Sousa, Kongo's ambassador to the Low Countries — who were competent in Latin and religious law. The city was laid out along several streets, named perhaps for the churches along them; Dapper names one, Santiago Street that ran down to one spring that served the city. The streets were formed by the compound walls of the houses along them and both rich and poor surrounded their houses with some sort of fence that bordered those of their neighbours. This arrangement resulted in twisting lanes that snaked through the city rather than thoroughfares. As in earlier times, these compounds frequently enclosed gardens and even livestock. Houses were sometimes constructed of packed earth and whitewashed, others of wood and woven grass, while roofs were of thatch. Wealthy nobles who crowded the court had veritable complexes of houses for their servants, slaves and hangers-on, composed of patios, doorways and walls within their compounds, while those of common people were necessarily simpler.[31]

Kongolese clearly regarded this housing arrangement as more comfortable than making more substantial stone houses, perhaps because they could simply destroy or abandon them when they became old and vermin-infested. Even the king abandoned, for all its magnificence, the stone palace that Afonso had built; it lay in ruins while he resided in a walled compound with many dwellings within the precinct.[32] Thus only the walls and the churches, as ceremonial structures where no one lived, remained in stone and were maintained and repaired as required.

The only image of the city at its height, an engraving published by Olifert Dapper in 1668, is thus probably wrong in that it labels a large and prominent square building in the centre of the city as the 'king's palace' when it was ruined at the time. The engraving shows, however, a small round tower, labelled the 'citadel', which is not mentioned in any contemporary source. This tower was noted by nineteenth-century visitors as being located behind the cathedral on a stretch of the remaining town wall, suggesting that the engraving might have been based on a contemporary picture with some 'repairs' added.[33] António Agua Rosada, a royal official, told the German visitor Adolph Bastian in 1856 that the early kings proclaimed the law from the tower.[34] The religious elements and the stone buildings that kept São Salvador anchored contrasted sharply with the rest of the country where the population moved constantly from place to place. Kongolese residential construction, even in São Salvador, was light and easily destroyed and moved, but in the country the potential for mobility flourished as it could not in the great city. In writing about the strategy of house building in the 1660s, the Spanish Capuchin priest Antonio de Teruel noted how simple the construction of the average Kongolese house was, and remarked that this manner of building made it easy to move if danger threatened. Even elite buildings, though composed of a maze of walls, passageways and houses, were relatively easy to construct, and most nobles possessed enough slaves, subjects and retainers to build a residential complex adequate to house them all. Luxury tended to be represented in cloth wall hangings, arms and smaller material items rather than buildings.[35]

In addition to the potential mobility offered by construction techniques, the fact that Kongolese law did not recognize private property in land meant that the whole population, from the nobility to peasants, were not attached by property claims to particular pieces of land. In São Salvador, it was not rights in property, but the investment in stone and the sacredness of the place that kept the population from moving very far from the walls.

Although São Salvador reached its height as a capital and a settlement during the reign of Garcia II, it did not long outlast his reign. After Garcia's son António I was killed in the battle of Mbwila in 1665, a civil war broke out among his would-be successors. These successors were from two opposed branches of the royal family who gradually took over sections of the country. The Kimpanzu, supported by the Princes of Soyo, controlled areas in the west of the country; their rivals, the Kinlaza, had bases in the upper Mbidizi Valley in the Marquisate of Nkondo and south of the Zaire River in the district of Bula. Both groups sought to gain control of São Salvador and consequently their battles were often fought in or around the city. São Salvador was sacked as a result of these wars for the first time in 1668, and subsequently began shrinking rapidly in size. In a final great sack, by the forces of the Kinlaza pretender Pedro III in 1678, the city was abandoned altogether. Elephants, attracted by the untended fruit trees of the city's houses, moved in and slowly trampled much of the less substantial structures in the city down.[36]

The complete abandonment of the large, densely settled zone that made up São Salvador was occasioned by the insecurity of the spot, in spite of its ancient walls and the great ravines that surrounded the city on two sides. It was facilitated, however, by the fact that the Kongolese population was capable of considerable mobility without great loss. Security and military necessity outweighed the sacredness of the city and caused an exodus which, thanks to the prevailing patterns of residential architecture, even for the elite, was relatively easy. Some residents fled, doing as many of their rural counterparts had been doing for years, that is, simply moving their villages away from troubled or dangerous spots to safer ones. Others left at the orders of their political superiors, as kings deliberately abandoned or were driven from the city and took their followers – as many as they could persuade or compel – with them.

In the context of the civil war, the movement of people was facilitated by military law and changes in the way war was conducted. At the height of their power, Kongo's rulers could command every able-bodied person to serve in war, either as a combatant or as a part of the supply and support services,[37] and these rights were asserted by all the pretender kings during the civil wars. In actual fact, few mobilizations actually took everyone in spite of the somewhat grandiose language of one surviving mobilization order, that issued by António I in 1665, prior to the battle of Mbwila.[38] In the late seventeenth century, the actual fighting was usually done by relatively small numbers of professionals, although many civilians might be with the army to carry its baggage. Since baggage trains were not expected to fight, they included women and children, often the wives and families of the soldiers.[39]

Civil war conditions caused many more people to be mobilized than before the wars began, with several pretenders to the throne each trying to maximize the numbers of soldiers at his command. As the war developed, pretender kings of various lines established secure bases in mountainous areas in different parts of the country and built up regional states as they awaited the opportunity to reoccupy São Salvador and be crowned. The Kimpanzu took Mbamba Lovata in the south-west; in the east Kibangu became the centre of a new faction, the Agua Rosadas who were descended from both Kimpanzu and Kinlaza, while Kinlaza partisans occupied Nkondo in the south-east, and Lemba–Bula in the north. In establishing these strongholds, the pretender kings took their armies and the supply and support service with them, reconcentrating large sections of the population.[40] These people in turn simply established new villages, using their customary building techniques in these new locations.

This tendency to larger armies created by the conditions of civil war was augmented by military changes that also increased army sizes as the flintlock musket replaced the matchlock and imports of the new firearms increased. In Kongo, as elsewhere in Africa, the new weapons caused generals to mobilize larger armies equipped with the new weapons and changed tactics to reflect the larger number of combatants and the relatively lower levels of professional skill in hand-to-hand combat. Professional armies thus gave way to militias and as the military call-up became more important for armies, the tendency of the entire population to be involved in military operations increased.[41] These changes in turn made it more important for leaders to control large numbers of people.

If the leaders of the royal factions abandoned São Salvador out of military necessity and now lived among their militia armies in mountain fortresses, they could not abandon São Salvador as a political centre. Even as an abandoned site, its churches and city walls made it unique, while the cathedral and the tombs of the ancient kings made it a place of enduring religious significance. In the end, and in spite of the military problems involved, ideological reasons demanded that the city could not remain abandoned. No one could be king if they were not crowned in the capital, and the lure of the city was irresistible.

The mood was reflected in Girolamo Merolla's demand to the Kinlaza would-be king João II, based at Lemba in Bula just south of the Zaire River, that he reoccupy the city – in 1688, just ten years after his predecessor had abandoned it – before the Church would recognize him as king.[42] While not every pretender to the throne tried to be crowned in the capital – João did not risk it for years – increasingly towards the end of the seventeenth century, many did. The Kimpanzu leader Manuel I, with the support of the Princes of Soyo, was the first of the pretender kings to occupy the city and be crowned in 1690, but was soon forced to abandon it and retreat to a more secure position in the Mbidizi Valley.[43] In 1696, João II, goaded by his aunt Ana Afonso de Leao, the nominal head of the Kinlaza who sought to restore the country in his name, briefly occupied the capital, but quickly withdrew.[44] Similarly, later in the same year, Pedro IV Agua Rosada, João's principal rival ensconced in the mountain of Kibangu east of the city, also reoccupied the city. During his brief occupation Pedro's men cleared the undergrowth from the cathedral and the great central plaza in order to have a ceremony fitting a king. But a rumour that João's army was approaching caused Pedro to go scurrying back to his mountain.[45]

Forced to return to São Salvador by its religious and symbolic power, rulers therefore had to figure out how to manage the military problems of reoccupation. If any king wanted to reoccupy the capital permanently and win recognition from the Church and his peers, he would also have to repopulate it in order to have the means to defend it. Pedro IV decided that he would make his objective reoccupation and repopulation with loyal subjects and by extension with a significant military force that could protect the king. It was a daunting task; Pedro first announced his intention to reoccupy the city in this way at Saint James's Day celebrations in 1698, informing his subjects who lived along the Mufulege River in the northern part of his domains that they would move towards the city as a first step.[46] Pedro wished to proceed slowly, and over the following years he advanced more groups of colonists on the road to the city, where they paused along the way, for years at a time, building villages and planting and harvesting crops.[47] By 1703 the two principal columns at Manga and Mulumbi had been in place for several years, and expectation that the restoration would come and the wars be ended soon was very high.

Pedro's move set off an outpouring of emotional attachment to the city and hopes that its restoration would end the civil war among the common people of his colonizing columns. Thus Pedro's cautious, step-by-step approach to the reoccupation was upset by strong demands, even insistence from his people that he go faster. As evidence of the religious nature of this popular sentiment, a number of prophets appeared demanding restoration of the city, crowned by the appearance of D. Beatriz Kimpa Vita in August 1704, who made immediate reoccupation a cornerstone of her demands. Beatriz, who had been possessed by Saint Anthony, went to Pedro's court to tell the king that God would punish him if he did not go directly to São Salvador; rebuffed there, she sought support for this in João II's court at Bula. Failing there, Beatriz, who now had a large popular following, went to restore the city herself.[48]

In this way, the reoccupation of São Salvador in 1705 was led, not by a king, but by a prophet with a mass following. The lure of the city, its religious significance, and the yearning of the people for peace, had all contributed to this sentiment. It would explain why, from 1705 onwards, civil wars focused almost entirely on occupying the city and the regional headquarters were regarded simply as temporary bases for doing that. In the end, Beatriz's reoccupation precipitated its occupation by Pedro IV's armies, originally led by a traitorous general, Pedro Constantinho da Silva, who also managed partially to coopt the Antonian movement of Beatriz Kimpa Vita. It was not until 1709 that finally Pedro IV was able to defeat his former general and reoccupy the city fully.[49]

Following the reoccupation by Pedro IV, São Salvador would not be abandoned again, though vagaries of war gave it a fluctuating population. Reoccupation, however, would not mean restoration of the city in an architectural sense. In the early eighteenth century the churches of the city were in ruins,[50] and with the exception of the cathedral, which was occasionally reroofed, they were never rebuilt. But ruined or not, the old churches and tombs were noted and remembered, for it was they that gave the town its religious aura.

Although Pedro IV's restoration resulted in the permanent reoccupation of the city, it ended neither the factional struggles nor their use of regional bases to plot the overthrow of the king. Pedro IV's Agua Rosada family was well placed to make a compromise settlement, being descended from both Kimpanzu and Kinlaza, and he sought to reconcile the parties. He promised that a Kimpanzu would succeed him, so as to mollify the Kimpanzu who had supported Pedro Constantinho da Silva (and Beatriz) against him, and consolidated this promise with a dynastic marriage.[51] The focus on compromise rather than force meant that São Salvador was not the real military and political centre it had been under the kings of the early seventeenth century. Instead, the occupation and reoccupation of the city with loyal supporters drawn from secure areas of the countryside became critical.

The compromise worked at first; when Pedro IV died in 1718, the Kimpanzu leader Manuel Makasa, who had fought against Pedro in 1709, was crowned as King Manuel II in São Salvador. He moved to the city from his base at Mbamba Lovata on the south-west coast, probably bringing loyal supporters with him to ensure his security. When Manuel died in 1743, he was succeeded by Garcia IV, a Kinlaza from the northern branch.[52] Garcia had served as Marquis of Matari before becoming king and may have been drawn from a group of dissident regional nobles who supported Pedro IV in his rivalry with the Kinlaza king João II.[53] In any case, although Bula continued as a regional unit, its leaders abandoned their claims on the throne by the mid-eighteenth century, thus recognizing that São Salvador was the only capital of the country.[54]

Royal rivalry shifted in the last half of the eighteenth century to a contest between Kimpanzu leaders based in Mbamba Lovata and two Kinlaza factions, one from Garcia IV's northern section and the other from Nkondo in the Mbidizi Valley. In spite of their regional bases, their struggle was waged largely around the capital as each recognized unhesitatingly the critical role of possessing the city. In 1763 Pedro V, a Kimpanzu, took the throne but was quickly overthrown by Alvaro XI from the northern Kinlaza branch.[55] Although defeated, Pedro V maintained his claim; and even after his death a certain Alvaro was appointed regent to take up the throne in his turn.[56] This eventually led, after Alvaro XI's death about 1779, to a major showdown between the Nkondo Kinlaza under José I and the Mbamba Lovata faction, settled in favour of José at a major battle outside São Salvador in 1781, followed by a major movement of José's army, some 30,000 combatants strong, into the city.[57]

São Salvador in the 1780s was a sizable town and a real capital, even if its great stone buildings were mostly ruined and unoccupied. For all their disuse, Father Rafael Castello de Vide, resident from 1781 to 1788, was able to take a tour of the city during which he was shown the ruins of each church while receiving a brief lecture on its history. Like the medieval Romans, inhabitants of São Salvador lived amidst the ruins of a past splendour of whose history they were fully conscious. The Kinlaza victory was such that José's power was passed peacefully on to his brother Afonso V when José died in 1785. José and his pious brother effectively tore up Pedro IV's compromise, and by so doing sought to retain permanent control of São Salvador. But their ploy did not work for long. Already the northern Kinlaza were being treated as a separate faction by José I,[58] who would not enroll them in the Order of Christ, and by the time that Afonso V died – poisoned, it was rumoured, by his enemies – a complicated power struggle broke out.[59] Eventually this power struggle was settled by the intervention of the Agua Rosadas, who after Pedro IV's death had withdrawn to their mountain of Kibangu and left royal politics to the older factions. But the Agua Rosadas had married into the Nkondo Kinlaza as well as the Kimpanzu, and thus were positioned once again as mediators.[60] Prince Pedro Agua Rosada e Sardonia of Kibangu managed to establish a regency,[61] and, after some years, there emerged a complicated new arrangement under King Henrique I in the 1790s.

In this new arrangement, direct occupation of the city was modified by a symbolic occupation, while more powerful forces remained in regions closer to the city than the late seventeenth-century factional centres had been, but still far enough away to allow the compromise to work. Thus São Salvador became a symbolic centre with a token population while stronger forces hovered just beyond the valleys surrounding the town.

Henrique I, crowned in 1794, found most of his support and power outside the city – according to a later report, 'in a very large forest',[62] although we do not know where it was located or of what faction he was himself a member. His base was governed for him by a nephew while Henrique and a small number of soldiers and supporters occupied São Salvador.[63] His forces in the capital were small, but sufficient to force his choice on the electors and to maintain himself, presumably against hostile and potentially better equipped forces loyal to other factions, over which he had no power to either tax or command.[64] In addition, there was a special position of 'outside king' (rei de fora) chosen from one of the other factions with considerable powers in decision making and with whom the king must meet. This position was almost certainly held by Garcia Agua Rosada e Sardonia, based primarily in Kibangu and not always resident in São Salvador; perhaps it was now an institutionalized version of the regency of 1786. He held this position although he was quite hostile to Henrique, and clearly did not hold it at the king's will.[65] Equally important powers were wielded by the Mwene Vunda, who, according to da Dicomano, had to be elected from one of the major factions, perhaps the third of the three. Thus, although the king was honoured nominally, his power was hedged at every turn by restrictions on his activity and decision making.[66]

The factions with whom Henrique shared power were rooted in the struggles of the 1780s. The southern Kinlaza's seizure of power and their attempts to exclude all other factions, though it failed, probably reorganized the area under São Salvador's control. While virtually all the rulers of lands that had once been under the Kingdom of Kongo recognized themselves as subjects of the king, this submission was purely symbolic and nominal. Bit by bit, sections of the country ceased to play a role in the politics of the city and the kingdom; in turn, the kings exercised no real authority over them. The effect of the struggle had been to eliminate many players of the eighteenth century and to cause the game to be more and more focused on the areas immediately surrounding São Salvador itself. The three positions of king, outside king, and Mwene Vunda were held by three different factions, but they were probably not the factions of the 1770s; the Kimpanzu were not involved after their defeat by José I, for example. The Agua Rosadas had rejoined the battle, now as 'outside kings', and both northern and southern Kinlaza continued to be important.[67]

We know little about Henrique's reign after 1795, though it continued until 1802 or 1803. Apparently Henrique was not satisfied with the limited powers that the compromises of 1785–94 left him. He spent time trying to build a stronger personal base and exercise more exclusive authority. According to his successor and the author of our only account of these events, Garcia de Agua Rosada, Henrique was virtually apostate, constantly abusing and belittling the Christian faith, but his most important crime probably was plotting a more centralized government. Henrique alienated most of the other officials of the court and the surrounding lands held by their factions, and was driven from the court to his own lands. He raised one army and attacked the court unsuccessfully 'without killing anyone'; he returned later with 'another very large army' which was defeated with heavy losses; 'his brother, nephew, Master of Congo and many people were killed, outside of those who were seized and then killed, drawn and quartered and burned as God's punishment, for the war was unjust'.[68]

Garcia Agua Rosada succeeded as Garcia V and wrote to Angola to ask the governor to send a priest to crown him. Garcia was at pains to explain that the kingship in Kongo was elected, and that he was both properly descended from Afonso and duly elected to his office.[69] The old arrangements were dissolved; once again a single faction dominated the throne, and the size of the area controlled and able to contest the throne diminished.

São Salvador in the early nineteenth century, as the capital of the Agua Rosada kings, was a much smaller town that it had been in the eighteenth century. This was probably because the scale of its territory was smaller, and because of the custom of rival kings keeping their main forces just outside the city. As a regional capital that claimed the most nominal loyalty from the rest of the country, São Salvador was not the great city of the past, though it preserved its ruined buildings as a place of semi-religious awe.

When Cherubino da Savona visited São Salvador in the 1760s he thought it a well-populated place (though his own estimate of its size – 35,000 – need not be taken seriously), but when Pietro Paulo da Bene visited São Salvador in 1820 he saw the capital as a mere village of a few hundred inhabitants, mostly the king's own slaves. It remained a place of religious significance, nevertheless: the most permanent and committed population were the 'Hospice of Saint Anthony', slaves of the various religious organizations (including the Capuchins) whose settlement was on the south side of the city and included a well-made building housing images of the Saints, possibly those from the Capuchin hospice at Kibangu that came to the city with Pedro IV.[70]

When Garcia died in 1830 there was another struggle for the throne; Bernardo da Burgio, who came to São Salvador to bury him, was forced to leave before he could crown a new king. In the end, the winner of the struggle was D. André II, from a faction of the northern branch of the Kinlaza called the Kitumba Mvemba, according to a later tradition.[71] In 1842, however, he was overthrown by Henrique 'Fu kia Ngo' (Custom of the Leopard) Lunga, who was crowned as Henrique II. Henrique represented a new faction, the Kivuzi, formed from Agua Rosadas (since they bore the surname Agua Rosada) and the southern Kinlaza, and based in Madimba, their long-time core region.[72]

André survived the struggle and withdrew to the town of Mbanza a Mputo, some distance south-east of São Salvador, where his cause was taken up later by his relative Garcia Mbumba.[73]

The strength of each king still depended on his ability to raise large armies and to concentrate population. The process of gathering people and raising armies from them is well illustrated by the traditional account of Henrique II's rise to power, written down about 80 years afterwards. Expelled from his original home at Nsongela with only 30 soldiers after an accusation of witchcraft, Henrique began by founding villages, one at a time, from among a growing group of followers. After he had founded seven villages, variously governed by family members and allies, he approached the leaders of Nsongela with the proposal that he overthrow André. They gave their consent and the combined armies carried the day.[74]

Upon Henrique II's death in 1857 the Kivuzi fractured, and a civil war was carried on by a handful of small districts very close to the city. One fragment called the Kimpanzu'a Nkanga based in Nkunga, and led by Alvaro XIII Ndongo, temporarily came to power, only to be upset by the remaining Kivuzi leader, Pedro Lelo. Pedro visited the Portuguese post at Bembe to the south, arranged support from them and after some delay managed to storm the city and drive Alvaro out in 1860.[75] The fact that Pedro's partisans used Mbanza a Mputo as a base during this war suggests that he had made peace with Andre II's Kitumba Mvemba faction, albeit a fragile one, for in the 1880s Pedro and the Kitumba Mvemba leader Garcia Mbumba were said to hate each other.[76]

The factional battles of the nineteenth century were waged closer to the city and on a smaller scale than those of the eighteenth, but they reveal the continuing role of the spiritual elements of the capital in the fighting. Control of the Hospice of Saint Anthony remained important, giving slaves a crucial role in politics; a minor civil war broke out between the hospice slaves and those of one of Henrique II's supporters in 1841.[77] To the degree that they protected the sacred images, they were arbitrators of the city's consent to the king and an important force to win over. Later tradition attributed Pedro V's desire to unseat Alvaro XIII to the latter's desecration of Henrique II's grave, and, significantly, to his desire to remove the images of the saints from the Hospice of Saint Anthony to his own village[78] – no doubt to give him some of the sacred aura of the city while retaining the security of his territory and mass of followers.

Because of the reduced scale of royal authority and the tendency to keep the bulk of the loyal population outside the city itself, São Salvador did not grow to a very large size until a king was well consolidated. The mass of the population remained outside, although once a king had beaten or neutralized his rivals he might transfer fairly large numbers to the city. Thus while the estimate of 18,000 inhabitants in São Salvador in the best years of Henrique II's reign is probably exaggerated, it represents the continuation of the town as a population centre.[79] Even when a king won power other faction leaders, and deposed kings – such as André II, after his deposition by Henrique II, or Alvaro XIII, after his defeat by Pedro V – still retained military control of their bases, waiting for the opportunity to regain the throne for themselves or their faction. When Alvaro XIII established himself in Nkunga after his defeat by Pedro V, he issued orders to a large number of rulers in the Mbidizi Valley south and west of the city to refuse tribute and support to his rival.

During the mid-nineteenth century, however, this tendency towards concentrated population for military campaigns under faction leaders was intersected by another trend in population distribution which would create a new role for São Salvador. After 1839 the export of slaves, which had been an important part of the export economy of Central Africa, began to decline as a result of the steadily increasing British pressure south of the equator. A growing trade in new products took its place, especially in ivory but later also in wild rubber brought from the interior and carried to the coast. By the century's end, the Zombo highlanders alone were transporting some 200 tons of rubber to the coast, in loads of 40 kilograms each.[80] Unlike the slave trade which was managed through the state or large merchants and employed a relatively small number of military and semi-military guards, this trade was much less centralized and required a great deal of labour. People from villages all over Kongo began to travel eastward to participate in the trade. Successful traders founded new villages along the trade routes to store goods and to serve as stopping points, populating them with small numbers of clients, slaves and kin. When he travelled south of São Salvador in 1880, for example, Baptist missionary W. Holman Bentley found two villages that had been founded by traders from Zombo, one some time before as its leader was then an old man.[81] Others established quarters in existing villages along the trade routes, or developed reciprocal relations (sometimes through fictive kinship) with villages along these routes. These chains of villages tied by relations of kinship, slavery, and clientage formed *kandas* (clans)[82] of linked villages or sections of villages. Histories of these *kandas*, set out in writing in the early twentieth century, typically related the itinerary of a group of kinsmen, commencing at São Salvador or along the banks of the Zaire where the overseas commercial houses were located, and spreading through various villages in chains along the routes.[83] Territorial rulers with links to the older political system, like the rulers of the Marquisate of Nzolo in the Inkisi Valley, participated in the trade and founded trading villages and quarters of their own as a way of augmenting their strength beyond the traditional means.[84]

The tendency of the new trading economy, which involved more and more people as rubber boomed as an export from the late 1870s, increased demands for porters and led to increasing incentives to travel, trade and invest profits in slaves in order to found villages.[85] António Barroso, a Portuguese missionary who arrived in São Salvador in 1880, noted that the tendency of the trading economy was to decentralization as villages became smaller.[86] In fact, when the Swiss traveller Josef Chavannes crossed Kongo in 1884–5 he made a systematic survey of over 150 villages whose range was from about 50 to 75 inhabitants, while political capitals (with the name Mbanza) ran somewhat over 100 people.[87] But wealthy traders and contenders for power might still manage concentrations of people and resources, though with difficulty.

Makuta, lying on the trade route to the Pool north-east of São Salvador, was an important new commercial centre of the time, founded, according to its traditions set down in the early twentieth century, by a simple nobleman (*ngudi a nkama*) named Kuvo. By the 1870s, the district had grown to a powerful trading state when its ruler Garcia Bwaka Matu controlled one of the largest towns in Kongo – some 3,000 inhabitants – and was able to dominate trade and travel from São Salvador north and east. It is significant that Bwaka Matu is especially remembered in tradition for bringing peace to a disorderly market. But when Garcia died early in 1881, the state underwent strain.[88] A dispute between two of the subordinates in 1886 grew into a major stand-off in which Pedro V of Kongo sought to intervene.[89] By 1888 there were seven new villages that had been founded by people, 'running from their leaders [*sobas*]'.[90] Despite these troubles, Makuta was still a significant trading entity in 1896.[91]

Although the new commercial economy was a powerful decentralizing force, its ideological dimension continued to focus on São Salvador as the sacred city of origin. The trading *kandas* became so important that already by the 1850s they were seen as the ancient bedrock of the country, but they organized their histories placing São Salvador in the beginning. While earlier traditions of Kongo history focused on the foundation of the kingdom by invading kings and their history, Bastian recorded a tradition in 1856 that 12 clans elected the king when one died.[92] In 1910, Mpetelo Boka, a Kongolese author, wrote a tradition seeking to link all the *kandas* to a dispersal from São Salvador after receiving a commission from the king, a project which was taken up by other Kongolese historians as well as Belgian and Portuguese colonial administrators.[93]

Pedro V worked with all these factors as he re-established São Salvador as a major population centre as well as his capital. Because Alvaro XIII never gave up his opposition to the king, Pedro was reluctant to occupy the capital fully, even though a Portuguese fort and garrison helped maintain his security until it was withdrawn in 1866. At that point, Pedro kept most of his demographic strength in his core region of Madimba, ruled by a son,[94] and by 1868 the city was estimated to have no more than 300–400 people.[95] But Pedro hoped to resurrect the town using its time-honoured strengths. He invited priests and missionaries to come, first giving English Baptists a place in 1879, then allowing the Portuguese to restore their mission under António Barroso the next year.

When Barroso came in 1880 there were only 600 people in the city, but the king had been benefiting from making the town a centre of trade as well as religion, attracting traders from far afield in Africa and managing to get European companies to establish themselves in his capital.[96] 'Almost every day,' the English missionary Thomas Comber wrote of the city when he arrived in 1878, '"chimbukas" or caravans of 20–30 each pass from Ambriz and Ambrizette taking down groundnuts and perhaps ivory. These chimboukas come from Zombo, Banza, Umpuka and Makouta.'[97] By the mid-1880s it had grown to over 3,500 people, its growth based partially on an influx of slaves, and traders based there were employing up to 5,000 porters per year.[98]

Pedro's position was never secure, however, and he feared for his Kivuzi faction in the event of his death. Alvaro XIII's nephew Rafael, of the Kimpanzu a Nkanga, continued to press the claims of his faction from its base at Nkunga, even when the former king died in 1875.[99] André II's successor of the Kitumba Mvemba faction, Garcia Mbumba, also continued to press that lineage's claim from Mbanza a Mputo.[100] In this environment, by 1883 Pedro felt that a renewal of his alliance with Portugal was desirable.[101] This was met with Portuguese support, as they were now ready to resume their garrison in São Salvador to make good the 'effective occupation' demanded by the Congress of Berlin, and pressed on the Lower Zaire region by the Congo Free State.[102] To assure the Portuguese of his utility, and perhaps to enlist their support in the expansion of his powers, Pedro V annulled treaties made by rulers around Noki with the Congo Free State in 1884.[103] Then, in 1888, Pedro V accepted a renewal of his bond of vassalage, sworn in 1860 to gain Portuguese support in his war with Alvaro XIII, and once again welcomed Portuguese soldiers to his capital. But Pedro paid a heavy price for this support. He surrendered his rights to collect dues from merchants and rents from resident foreigners and missionaries in exchange for a salary of less value and less future potential,[104] though perhaps offset by a substantial bank account in his name in Luanda.[105]

When Pedro died in 1891 his calculation paid off. A Kivuzi successor, Alvaro XIV de Agua Rosada, followed him; Garcia Mbumba was disallowed from the kingship on the grounds of having become a Baptist convert, but was mollified with the title Noso Principe, a variant of the 'outside king' of the late eighteenth century.[106] Soon Alvaro was restless under Portuguese control, however, although rumours that he would attempt to massacre the garrison were unfounded.[107] With Portuguese soldiers on their side, the Kivuzi managed to retain the throne without effective challenge from other factions, but the city shrank: by 1896, its population was only 1,200.[108] Portugal, content that these arrangements had made Kongo a part of its colony of Angola, began in the early decades of the twentieth century to make its rule more effective, while Kivuzi kings cooperated. Portuguese administrators, accompanied by various Kivuzis, often holding commissions in the Portuguese army, fanned out into the country and effectively expanded the authority of the Kongo kings.[109] The Portuguese went beyond simply establishing royal authority, for they began collecting taxes directly from the population, and also forced the recruitment of carriers for Portuguese export houses that established branches in the newly founded posts,[110] something which the rulers of São Salvador had not been able to do outside their own territories since the seventeenth century. Moreover, in 1910 the administrator began forced recruitment of workers for the island of São Tomé.[111] This was done in the name of the king, then the Kivuzi Manuel III Kiditu, and through royal agents backed by Portuguese troops if necessary. In 1910 the tax burden had become so great that a league of local leaders formed in Madimba itself, seat of the Kivuzi, to refuse payment; they were soon joined by their counterparts in Zombo.[112] In this environment people bypassed the Portuguese areas in their trading, and population shifted further into hundreds of small, independent villages. By 1914 the population of São Salvador had shrunk to 700, as royal councillors withdrew and the king's status and income declined.[113]

In 1913 it led to a revolt, led by Alvaro Buta, and the virtual siege of the city by Buta's partisans over the next year. In the complex negotiations that followed, Portuguese troops intervened in strength and systematic campaigns finally reduced the country to obedience.[114] São Salvador was damaged in the attack, but quickly recovered, as it was still an administrative capital in the area and had not lost its commercial significance. It had ceased, however, to be a Kongolese capital and had become a Portuguese one in an increasingly authoritarian colonial state.

Notes

1 The city was known as Mbanza Kongo until around 1570, when its name was changed to São Salvador. It remained São Salvador until 1975 when the government of Angola changed the name back to Mbanza Kongo.

2 I use the term 'Kongolese' for convenience of non-Kikongo speakers. The inhabitants of the town and the former kingdom usually call themselves in Kikongo 'Esikongo' (singular 'Mwisikongo'), though since about 1910 it is not uncommon for the term 'Bakongo' (singular 'Mukongo') to be used, especially in areas north of the Zaire river, and by intellectuals and anthropologists adopting a standard nomenclature for Bantu-speaking peoples. I also pluralize all Kikongo words by adding 's' to the singular word, with its class marker, according to English rules. For the remaining orthography of Kikongo I follow the standards of Redemptorist mission orthography as used in their newspaper, *Kukiele* (Tumba-Matadi, since 1930) and found in such works as Jean Cuvelier (ed. and compiler) *Nkutama a mvila za makanda* (Tumba,1934 and fourth edition, Matadi, 1972) and Joseph de Munck, *Kinkulu kia nsi eto Kongo* (second edition, Matadi, 1971 [first edition,1956]).

3 For traditional histories of over 500 clans, primarily in the Zairean section of the old kingdom, see Cuvelier (ed. and compiler), *Nkutama a mvila za makanda* [Catalogue of Praise Names of Clans]. Not all trace their origin to Mbanza Kongo, but many who give an ultimate origin elsewhere have their ancestors pass through the ancient city.

4 Wyatt MacGaffey, *Custom and Government on the Lower Congo* (Berkeley and Los Angeles, 1970).

5 Older orthographies (and Angolan Portuguese) use *libata* for village, reflective of the coastal dialect in the sixteenth century, where the class 5 prefix was still used. For the linguistic dichotomy in seventeenth century sources, see John Thornton, *The Kingdom of Kongo: Civil War and Transition. 1641–1718* (Madison,1983), pp. 15–17.

6 James Denbow, 'Congo to Kalahari: data and hypotheses about the political economy of the Western Stream of the Early Iron Age', *African Archaeological Review*, 8 (1990), pp. 139–75. Denbow has clarified this more thoroughly, and proposed dating for the start at AD 100–350, in a personal communication, 9 January 1995.

7 See the attempt to fix its meaning, as 'place of authority' through historical linguistics in Jan Vansina, *Paths in the Rainforest: Toward a History of Political Tradition in Equatorial Africa* (Madison, 1990), pp. 271–2, cf. C. Grégorie, 'Le champ sémantique du thème bantou *-bánjá', *African Language*, 2 (1976), pp. 1–12.

8 For the argument about dating, based on traditions of 1624–7, see John Thornton, 'The Kingdom of Kongo,1390–1678: development of an African social formation', *Cahiers d'études africaines*, 23 (1981), pp. 332–4.

9 Letter of Milanese Ambassador in Lisbon, 6 November 1491, published in Adriano Capelli, 'A Proposito di Conquiste Africane', *Archivo Storico Lombardo* (1896), p. 461.

10 João de Barros, *Asia*, Dec. 1, Bk 3, Cap. 10, *MMA* 1, pp. 144–5. This account of the battle is probably based on one sent to Portugal by Afonso himself, *c.*1509.

11 Rui de Pina, Cronica Cap. 60, 61 *MMA* 1, pp. 113–14,130 (plaza and royal palace), Cap. 62, *MMA* 1, p. 122 (reception of the Portuguese in 1491), de Barros, *Asia*, Dec. 1, Bk 3, Cap. 10 *MMA* 1, p. 144 (coronation of Afonso I).

12 Rui de Pina, Cronica cap. 60, *MMA* l, p. 114.

13 [Mateus Cardoso], 'História do reino do Congo', (1624), Cap. 2, fol. 2v, in António Brósio (ed.), *História Ro Reino do Congo (MS 8080 da Biblioteca Nacional de Lisboa)* (Lisbon,1969). A French translation by François Bontinck establishes the author and marks the original pagination, *Histoire du royaume de Congo (1624)* (Brussels,1972).

14 Afonso to João III, 25 August 1526, *MMA* l, p. 476.

15 Christováo Ribeiro, 1 August 1548, *MMA* 15, p. 161.

16 de Pina, Cronica, Cap. 61 *MMA* 1, p. 130.

17 João III to Afonso (ca. end of 1529), *MMA* 1, p. 529, noting partial completion of the city walls. For the overall plan of the walls, see Lopes, writing 70 years later, Filippo Pigafetta, *Relatione del Regno di Congo e circonvince contrade* (Rome, 1591. Facsimile CA. Lisbon, 1949. Modern critical edn, Milan, 1978), p. 40; The dimensions of the wall were estimated from remains standing in the late nineteenth century by W. Holman Bentley, *Pioneering on the Congo* (London, 1914), p. 140.

18 Afonso to Manuel I, 5 October 1514, *MMA* 1, pp. 304–6 (work had been going on 5 years then); Afonso to Manuel I, 13 June 1517, *MMA* 1, p. 410 (Portuguese masons working too slowly); Afonso to João III, 25 August 1526, *MMA* 1, p. 476 (request for more workers to complete palace and start new churches).

19 Jacome Dias letter, 1 August 1548, *MMA* 15, p. 158.

20 See Diogo's letter of 28 January 1549, dated 'City of Congo' and the same formula is employed in the legal inquest of 1550, *MMA* 2, pp. 227 and 248. There are no later letters from Diogo or the kings who followed him to Alvaro I to allow us to say for sure when this formula was abandoned.

21 Jacome Dias letter, 1 August 1548, *MMA* 15, p. 154.

22 Alvaro to Garcia Simóes, 27 August 1575, *MMA* 3, p. 128.

23 Afonso to Manuel I, 5 October 1514, *MMA* 1, pp. 313–14.

24 Luis de Cáegas and Luis de Sousa, *Historia de S. Domingos* (Lisbon, 16), Pt 2, Bk 4, Cap. 12, in *MMA* 5, p. 610; similar implications occur in Duarte Lopes's description (city as observed in 1578–83), recorded and edited by Pigafetta, *Relatione,* p. 40 (pagination of original).

25 For a full discussion, including relevant population estimates, see John Thornton, 'Demography and history in the Kingdom of Kongo, 1550–1750', *Journal of African History,* 18 (1977).

26 Pigafetta, *Relatione,* p. 40.

27 'Interrogatoria de Statu Regni Congensis', 1595, *MMA* 3, p. 502 (testimony of Antonio Vieira, Kongolese ambassador, 10,000 households [focos]), p. 511 (testimony of Martinho de Ulhoa, bishop of São Tomé, 10,000 households).

28 Simon Rodrigues Rangel, 16 January 1604, *MMA* 5, p. 71.

29 Documented more fully in Thornton, *Kingdom of Kongo.*

30 Biblioteca Nacional de Madrid, MS 3533, fols 35, 49–50, António de Teruel, 'Descripcion Narrativa de la mission de los Padres Capuchinos ... en el reyno de Congo' (1664).

31 This description is complied from that of Dapper, *Naukerige Beschrijvinge van Africa gewesten* (Amsterdam, 1668, 2d ed. 1676), [German edn, pp. 545–46] based on observations of 1642, and Antonio de Teruel,1650–64, Biblioteca Nacional de Madrid, MS 3533, fols. 179–83.

32 Biblioteca Nacional de Madrid, MS 3533, fol. 182, de Teruel, 'Descripcion Narrativa'. On the rationale for making rather impermanent housing structures, see fol. 180.

33 Bentley, *Pioneering,* p. 141. One might make the same observations about the engraving of the city of Benin, which seems uncannily correct on the roof structures of the city (inadequately described in the sources), yet obviously in error concerning the walls, shown as fence-like structures rather than the moat and ditch system visible to archaeologists.

34 Adolph Bastian, *Ein Besuch in San Salvador der Hauptstadt der Königreichs Congo* (Bremen, 1859), p. 124.

35 Biblioteca Nacional de Madrid, MS 3533, de Teruel, 'Descripcion Narrativa', fols 179–80.

36 Thornton, *Kingdom of Kongo,* pp. 75–83.

37 John Thornton, 'The art of war in Angola, 1575–1680', *Comparative Studies in Society and History,* 30 (1988), pp. 362–3.

38 Manifesto de guerra de D. António, 13 July 1665, in Brásio, *MMA* 12, pp. 549–50. Original document published in Mercurio Portuguesa, 1666.

39 Thornton, 'Art of war', pp. 368–71.

40 Thornton, *Kingdom of Kongo,* pp. 98–103.

41 For eighteenth-century military affairs, see John Thornton, 'African soldiers in the Haitian Revolution', *Journal of Caribbean History,* 25 (1991), pp. 65–8; and for somewhat earlier periods, John Thornton, 'African Roots of the Stono Rebellion', *American Historical Review,* 96 (1991).

42 Girolamo Merolla da Sorrento, *Breve e succinta relatione del viaggio nel Congo* (Naples, 1692), pp. 200, 211, 216, 224.

43 Marcellino d'Atri, 'Giornate Apostoliche fatte da me Fra Marcellino d'Atri ... nelle messioni de Regni d'Angola e Congo ...', fol. 253, published with original foliation marked in Carlo Toso (ed.) *L'anarchia Congolese nel sec. XVII. La relazione inedita di Marcellino d'Atri* (Genoa,1984); Luca da Caltanisetta, 'Relatione della missione fatta nel Regno di Congo...', 13–14, published with original foliation marked in Romain Rainero, *Il Congo agli inizi del settecento nella relazione di P. Luca da Caltanisetta* (Florence, 1974). A French translation with the original foliation marked was published by François Bontinck as *Diaire congolaise, 1690–1701* (Louvain, 1970); Letter of Pedro Mendes,

1710, in Levy-Jordão, Vicecomte de Paiva Manso, *História de Congo* (Lisbon,1877), p. 352.
44 D'Atri, 'Gionate Apostoliche', fol. 127.
45 Da Caltanisetta, fol. 26v.
46 D'Atri, 'Giornate Apostoliche', fol. 369.
47 D'Atri, 'Giornate Apostoliche', fol. 371 (1698), pp. 510–11 (1701).
48 On Beatriz's early career and occupation of São Salvador, see Bernardo da Gallo, 'Relazione dell'ultime guerre civili ... 12 December 1712', fols 294, 298v, 299–99v published with original foliation in Teobaldo Filesi, 'Nazionalismo e religione nel Congo all'inizio del 1700', *Africa (Roma)*, 9 (1971), pp. 267–303, 463–508, 645–68; a French translation with original foliation appears in Louis Jadin, 'Le Congo et la secte des antoniens. Restauration du royaume sous Pedro IV et la "Saint Antoine" congolaise (1694–1718)', *Bulletin, Institut historique belge de Rome*, 33 (1961), pp. 411–615.
49 For a fuller history, see Thornton, *Kingdom of Kongo*, pp.107–13.
50 Lorenzo da Lucca, Lettera Annua, 1706, in Archivo Provinciale dei Cappuccini di Toscana, Florence; Filippo Bernardi da Firenze, 'Ragguaglio del Congo', pp. 296–8, French translation with original pagination by Jean Cuvelier, *Relations sur le Congo du P. Laurent de Lucques* (Brussels: Memoires de l'Institute royale coloniale belge, 32, 1954).
51 Cherubino da Savona, 'Breve Ragguaglio', fol. 41.
52 Instituto Histo'rico e Geogra'fico Presileiro (Rio de Janeiro). Late 6, parta 2, Catalogo dos Reis do Congo (1758), fol. 5. This source does not mention Garcia IV's factional membership, but it is established by the fact that his son Manuel, ruler of Enlele in 1760, was called 'di Quimulaza' in da Savona, 'Breve ragguaglio', fol. 45v.
53 Cuvelier (compiler and ed.), *Nkutama*, p. 72. This tradition was collected about 1928, probably from a local manuscript composed in Kikongo in the early twentieth century at Matadi, and is a brief account of the successive rulers who controlled Matadi. It relates that Garcia was 'a son of Nlaza' and gives his Kikongo name as Nkanga a Mvemba (according to the Cattalogo his name was Nkanga a Mbanda). He was thus a Kinlaza but not a direct descendant of João II.
54 Da Savona, 'Breve Ragguaglio', fol. 44v.
55 Da Savona, 'Breve Raguggalio', fol. 41; Alvaro's home was in Mpangu, then a part of a larger district called Manga, probably shaped from an alliance of northern Kinlaza who were independent of Bula and had perhaps shaped Garica IV's reign, see da Savona, 'Breve Ragguaglio', fols 41v, 42, 45v.
56 ACL MS Vermelho 296, de Castello de Vide, 'Viagem', pp. 80, 95.
57 *Ibid.*, pp.118–22.
58 *Ibid.*, p.142.
59 *Ibid.*, p. 260.
60 Da Savona, 'Breve Ragguaglio', fols 43, 45.
61 ACL MS Vermelho 296, de Castello de Vide, 'Viagem', p. 296. This new prince gave his name in a letter to de Castello de Vide in 1788, reproduced in *ibid*, p. 308.
62 Garcia V to Governor of Angola, 6 July 1803, pp. 56–7.
63 Raimondo da Dicomano, 'Informaçao do Reino do Congo', (1798), fol. 108. The foliation is to the Portuguese manuscript translation found in the Biblioteca Nacional de Lisboa, edited by António Brásio in 'Informaçao do Reino do Congo de Frei Raimondo de·Dicomano', *Studia*, 34 (1972), 19–42: French translation, Louis Jadin, 'Relation sur le Congo du P. Raimondo da Dicomano, missionaire de 1791 1795', *Bulletin de l'Académie Royale des Sciences Coloniales* N. S., 3 (1957), pp. 307–37: and Italian translation Carlo Toso, *Informazione*. Susan Broadhead discovered the original Italian version (which closely resembles Toso's modern Italian edition) in the Arquivo Histórico Ultramarino, Angola, maço 823.
64 Da Dicomano, 'Informaçao', fols 108, 109.
65 Almeida e Vasconcelos to Melo e Castro, 3 March 1794, in Toso, *Informazione*, p. 90.
66 Da Dicomano, 'Informaçao', fols 108v–110v.
67 ACL MS Vermelho 296, de Castello de Vide, 'Viagem', pp. 127,131, da Dicomano, 'Informaçao', fols 107v, 108v and 115, note 8; all these factions claimed descent from Afonso I though their names are not given in the sources. When Garcia Agua Rosada e Sardonia claimed powers as Garcia V in his letter to the governor of Angola in 1802, he anchored the claim on his descent from Afonso, Garcia V to Governor of Angola, 6 July 1803, p. 57.
68 Garcia V to Governor of Angola, 6 July 1803, pp. 56–7.

69 *Ibid.*

70 Henrique II to Governor of Angola, 30 August 1845, in António Brásio, *Angola: Spiritana Monumenta Historica* (Pittsburgh and Louvain,1966) vol. 1, p. 26 mentions the slaves of the hospice. For a fuller description of the hospice and its buildings in 1856, Alfredo de Sarmento, *Os sertões d'Africa (Apontamentos de Viagem)* (Lisbon,1880), pp. 56–7; and a short time later, Bastian, *Besuch,* p. 190.

71 De Munck, *Kinkulu,* p. 46. This section is probably based on traditions that de Munck collected, perhaps in manuscripts, in his trip to Angola in 1960, see de Munck, 'Notes sur un voyage au Kongo dia Ntotila', *Ngonge,* 3 (1960), No. 8. His northern antecedents come from the itinerary of the clan, originating in Sumpi and Manga and moving southward to found villages north of São Salvador.

72 On the origin and early history of the Kivuzi, see Cuvelier, *Nkutama,* p. 70; and another version probably from the same MS in French translation in 'Traditions Congolaises', *Congo,* Vol. 2, No. 2 (September 1931), pp. 205–6; see also, a similar version, but from a different MS or source, in de Munck, *Kinkulu,* pp. 46–7.

73 De Munck, *Kinkulu,* p. 46. On the later history of Garcia Mbumba, see Bentley, *Pioneering,* pp. 298, 304; Graham, *Under Seven Congo Kings* (London, 1931), pp. 41–2; Faria Leal, 'Memorias', pp. 319–20. Graham calls his faction Mbumbuzi; de Munck's informants gave its name as Kitumba Mvemba.

74 This Kikongo manuscript was published by Cuvelier in 'Mambu ma Kinzu Nkulu mu Nsi a Kongo', *Kukiele,* 5 (1931), p. 55. (A partial French translation in Cuvelier, 'Traditions', pp. 205–6). A shorter version, perhaps from a different source and of later date is found in de Munck, *Kinkulu,* p. 46.

75 The specifics of this conflict are worked out best in François Bontinck, 'Pedro V, roi de Kongo face au partage colonial', *Africa (Roma),* 37 (1982), pp. 6–17. His clan membership is given as Kimpanzu a Nimi in Cuvelier, *Nkutama,* p. 71 and 'Traditions congolaises' p. 206 (same original MS source) and Kimpanzu a Nkanga in de Munck, *Kinkulu,* p. 46 and Graham, *Under Seven Congo Kings,* Appendix II.

76 Bentley, *Pioneering,* p. 298.

77 Henrique II to Governor of Angola, 30 August 1845, in António Brásio, *Angola: Spiritana Monumenta Historica* (Pittsburgh and Louvain, 1966) Vol. 1, p. 26; Copia do oficio do capitão António Joaquim de Castro ao Governador Geral de Angola, 27 July 1845, in Mario António Fernandes de Oliveira and Eduardo dos Santos, *Angolana (Documentaao sobre Angola)* 3 vols (Lisbon, 1968–76), Vol. 3, pp. 469–70.

78 De Munck, *Kinkulu,* p. 46; see also Cuvelier, 'Mambu', p. 55.

79 A. J. Castro for 1845.

80 Faria Leal, 'Memorias', *Boletin da Sociedade de Geographia de Lisboa,* 15 (1915), p. 359.

81 Bentley, *Pioneering,* pp. 200–1.

82 Kikongo: *kanda,* plural *makanda,* a word with a broad semantic field. It is not strictly a family term, for it is used to express concepts such as ethnic group or race. It might also include non-kin who are connected to a leader, such as clients, allies and slaves.

83 Hundreds of these village *kanda* traditions were collected, both in oral form and from manuscript Kikongo documents, by Jean Cuvelier in 1927–8; they are printed, along with a variety of other traditions, in *Nkutama.* In editing these texts, Cuvelier usually eliminated the mythical and magical stories that illuminated and sometimes accounted for the migrations, though full versions of a few are found in MS and TS form in the Redemptorist archive in Leuven. One school of thought has projected these migrations back to ancient (fourteenth century and before) times and made the *kanda* the bedrock of society and government in Kongo at the height of the kingdom (for an early example, see Joseph van Wing, *Études Bakongo* [Brussels,1920] and a more recent one, João Castodio Gonsalves, *Lineages contre l'état* [Lisbon,1985]). This analysis sees the *kanda* traditions of modern times as fairly recent and linked to trading rather than as ancient and linked to folk movements.

84 Cuvelier, *Nkutama,* p. 70. Written at some time before 1928, a history, of the dynasty – probably founded in the early eighteenth century from older territorial rulers under the kings of Kongo – also includes a list of villages in a chain, as well as a list of all the villages in the district itself.

85 António Barroso, 'O Congo: Seu passado, presente e futuro' (1889) in António Brásio (ed.), *D. António Barroso. Missionário. cientista missiólogo* (Lisbon,1961), pp. 105–7.

86 Barroso, 'Congo', p. 107.

87 Josef Chavannes, *Reisen und Forschungen im alten und neuen Kongostaate* (Jena, 1887), pp. 506–7.

88 Tradition in Cuvelier, *Nkutama*, p. 67 (which gives Bwaku Matu's Christian name as 'Galasia'). On 'Bwaka-Matu' in the late 1870s, see Baptist Missionary Society Archives (Oxford), A/12 Comber papers, Comber to Barnes, 24 November 1878, Comber thought that Makuta had 2000 more people than São Salvador; Bentley, *Pioneering*, Vol. 1, pp. 81, 83, 213 (often quoting Comber).

89 António Barroso to Governor General of Angola, 20 October 1886, Arquivos de Angola ser. 2, 11 (1954), pp. 286–7.

90 Barroso, 'Congo', p. 107.

91 Bentley, *Pioneering*, Vol. 2, p. 370.

92 Bastian, *San Salvador*, p.124. Bastian uses the term 'nationen' which could be translated more easily as nations or even tribes in English. This interpretation relies on his being told they were *kandas*, which in Kikongo can mean a wide variety of things, including nations and tribes, as well as the specific type of social organization referred to here.

93 The master text of this interpretation is Archief der Redemptoren Vaters, Leuven, Mpetelo Boka, 'Nsosani a Kinguli. Luzailu lua Makanda Yezimvila Zazonsono' (15 September 1910) [Research into matrilinearity]. Information on all clans and praise names pp. 87–8, 93–4, partial French translation in Cuvelier, 'Traditions', pp. 480–4 and partial publication in Kikongo in *Nkutama*. (*passim* under the names of the clans mentioned in the master tradition). On the Kongolese and administrative search for a perfect genealogy which would unite all the clans to the original 12 that left São Salvador, see Wyatt MacGaffey, *Custom and Government on the Lower Congo*, pp. 17–35.

94 Chavanne, *Reisen*, p. 277.

95 Bontinck, 'Pedro V', p. 38, citing a report by Zacharias da Cruz of 1858; Report of Antonio Leite Mendes, 29 November 1868, in Brásio, *Angola*, pp. xviii–xix. In 1877, Boaventura dos Santos noted that the city's small population was due to the insecurity of the city and Alvaro XIII's withdrawal, Louis Jadin, 'Recherches dans les archives et bibliothques d'Italie et du Portugal sur l'Ancien Congo', *Bulletin des Séances. Academie royale de Sciences d'Outre Mer*, 2 (1956), p. 977.

96 Already notable in spite of the small size of the settlement in 1873 when William Grandy visited, 'Report of the ... Livingstone Congo Expedition', *Proceedings of the Royal Geographic Society*, 19 (1874–5), pp. 102–3.

97 Baptist Missionary Society Archives, A/12, Comber to Barnes, 17 August 1878.

98 Barroso, 'Congo', pp. 105–7. Joseph Chavanne, a Swiss visitor in 1885, actually counted houses in the city, coming up with 212, which he estimated held only 765 people, but his estimate was only for the core settlement, and he noted that many people were away at all times for commercial reasons, Chavanne, *Reisen*, pp. 276, 506.

99 Faria Leal, 'Memorias', pp. 305–6; Bontinck, 'Pedro V', pp. 16–17, reviewing various theories of the year of Alvaro's death and settling on this one based on Pedro V to Bishop of Luanda, 25 August 1875, in Brásio, *Angola*, Vol. 3, p. 588.

100 Bentley, *Pioneering*, pp. 298, 303; Graham, *Under Seven Kongo Kings*, pp. 41–2; Faria Leal, 'Memorias', p. 320, notes his death on 23 April 1911.

101 Pedro V to Governor General of Angola, 3 June 1883, *Arquivos de Angola* ser. 2, 11 (1954), pp. 211–12.

102 See Faria Leal, 'Memorias', pp. 299–303; 390–2.

103 Pedro V to Governor General of Angola, 6 June 1884, *Arquivos de Angola* ser. 2, 11 (1954): p. 239.

104 Oficio 411 of Governo General de Angola, 22 August 1887, *Arquivos de Angola* ser. 2,11 (1954), p. 293; José Heliodoro de Faria Leal, 'Memorias d'Africa', *Boletim da Sociedade de Geographia de Lisboa*. 32 (1914–15), p. 304.

105 Chavannes, *Reisen*, p. 276.

106 Graham, *Under Seven Congo Kings*, p. 45.

107 It seems to me that the idea of Alvaro as a nationalist, a backward-looking royalist, or an excessively cruel tyrant, found alternately in Rene Pelissier's account of his reign, are exaggerated, perhaps from Baptist sources that saw him as anti-Protestant, or from nervous Portuguese sources: *Les guerres grises. Résistance et révoltes in Angola, 1845-1941* (Orgeval, 1977), pp. 207–9.

108 Faria Leal, 'Memorias', p. 75.

109 Faria Leal, 'Memorias', pp. 384–96.

110 Faria Leal, 'Memorias', pp. 394–6. By 1910 they were collecting tax, but only from areas north of

São Salvador; the south was completely insubmissive, *ibid.*, p. 399.

111 Pelissier, *Guerres grises*, pp. 226–32.
112 Faria Leal, 'Memorias', pp. 406–7.
113 Faria Leal, 'Memorias', pp. 75–6.
114 Outlined in detail in Pelissier, *Guerres grises*, pp. 232–48, who sees too much pan-Kongo national-
    ism in it, I think, though there is no doubting that general grievances over the extension of Portu-
    guese power in northern Angola led to various uncoordinated revolts in many localities.

5

Ouidah A Pre-colonial Urban Centre in Coastal West Africa 1727–1892

ROBIN LAW

Ouidah (or, in the form of the name more familiar in English sources, Whydah) is a town situated in what is today the coastal area of the Republic of Benin (formerly Dahomey), on the section of the West African coast known to Europeans in pre-colonial times as the Slave Coast. Although nowadays economically marginalized, in earlier times it was the principal commercial centre in the region. In particular, it was a major centre for European trade, especially in slaves, from the late seventeenth to the mid-nineteenth centuries. Over this whole period perhaps as many as a million slaves were exported through Ouidah, making it the most important single embarkation point for the trans-Atlantic slave trade in West Africa.

Strictly, Ouidah is not an Atlantic port, although often described as such, being situated on the northern bank of the lagoon which runs parallel to the coast; slaves and other commodities had to be taken from the town across the lagoon to be embarked from the seashore. Indeed, its commercial importance was due as much to its lagoon-side situation as to its proximity to the coast, slaves being brought for shipment there by canoe from other lagoon ports to both east and west.[1]

'Ouidah', it should be noted, is not, strictly, the correct indigenous name for the town, but rather a name given by Europeans. The local name, used even nowadays when speaking in Fon rather than French, is Glehue. Ouidah (more correctly, Hueda) is more properly the name of the kingdom to which Glehue originally belonged, whose royal capital was at Savi, a few miles inland.[2] In 1727, however, the Hueda kingdom was conquered, and its capital Savi destroyed, by the hinterland power of Dahomey. Glehue itself was attacked and partially destroyed during this Dahomian conquest, but survived as a commercial centre. It remained subject to Dahomey, and served as its principal outlet for the Atlantic trade, until the French colonial occupation in 1892.

From the mid-nineteenth century, slaves were replaced by palm oil (and later also palm kernels) as the principal export from the region. This shift coincided with a decline in Ouidah's commercial importance, relative to Porto-Novo to the east, and the rise of the new port of Cotonou, which served as an alternative outlet for the trade of Dahomey itself as well as for Porto-Novo. Ouidah's decline was compounded by the fact that it was Porto-Novo which became the centre of French colonial power from the 1860s; and, even more critically, by the construction of deep-water port facilities at Cotonou from the 1890s.

Ouidah in the pre-colonial period was more than simply a centre for the European trade. Even in narrowly economic terms, it was also a centre for fishing and salt production (by evaporation from sea water), as well as for local trade (especially trade along the lagoons). It also served as a Dahomian provincial administrative centre and as a military garrison town. But its central function was in trade with Europeans: this is not merely a European perception, but evidently was shared by the Dahomians themselves, as is reflected in the fact that the title of the Dahomian administrator of the town, Yovogan, meant literally 'Chief of White Men'.

The writer is currently engaged in research on the history of Ouidah during the period of Dahomian rule, 1727–1892. Among other topics, the study will of necessity deal with the development and character of Ouidah as an urban community, including its demographic and spatial growth, its changing economic base, its local administration and its relationship to the wider Dahomian polity. This chapter is a preliminary attempt to indicate the ways in which the pre-colonial urban history of Ouidah can be approached, together with a provisional (and necessarily tentative) outline of some aspects of this history.

Sources

The source material available for the study of pre-colonial Ouidah is both substantial and varied in character. Because of its role, over a long period, as a centre of European commerce in the region, there is a mass of detailed information in contemporary European records. During the period of the slave trade, the British, French and Portuguese all maintained permanent fortified trading posts in the town, whose records (though incompletely preserved) provide massive documentation of their day-to-day activities and interactions with the rest of the community. Among the records of the French fort there is even a crude map of the town dated 1776.[3] With the legal abolition of the slave trade, these forts were all abandoned – the French fort in 1797, the English in 1812, the Portuguese apparently after the Anglo-Portuguese treaty banning Portuguese slave-trading north of the Equator in 1815; though the Portuguese fort was reoccupied in 1865 and remained a Portuguese possession until 1961, forming an anomalous foreign enclave within French Dahomey throughout the colonial period. During the nineteenth century, documentation of the town's affairs is provided by the records of the British and French governments (the former maintained a Vice-Consulate at Ouidah in 1849–52 and the latter from 1863) and by Christian missions which resided in the town, the British Methodists in 1855–67 and French Roman Catholics in 1861–71 and again from 1884.[4] There are also a number of detailed published accounts by European visitors to Ouidah, of which the most informative are perhaps those of the British naval officer Frederick Forbes in 1849–50 and the Consul (and pioneer anthropologist) Richard Burton in 1863–4.[5]

There is also a corpus of local source material, mainly in the form of oral traditions relating to the history of the town and (more substantially) of its component wards and families. A significant body of local traditions was collected and recorded by two French colonial officials in Ouidah, in surveys of 1913 and 1917;[6] this and other material was collated into a substantial published history of the town by a local writer, Casimir Agbo, published in 1959.[7] There are also three published histories of particular Ouidah families: the de Souzas, descended from the Brazilian slave-trader Francisco Felix de Souza, who settled in Ouidah in *c.*1818 (and died there in 1849); the Dagba family, descended from a man who served as Yovogan of Ouidah for an exceptionally long period during the nineteenth century (1823–*c.*1875); and the Quénums, who were the most prominent indigenous Dahomian merchants in Ouidah in the second half of the nineteenth century.[8] There are also some contemporary written sources of local provenance for the pre-colonial period, notably correspondence of another Brazilian slave trader settled in Ouidah, José Francisco dos Santos, relating to the 1840s and 1860s.[9]

A further important 'source' for the history of Ouidah is the town itself, as it survives to the present. One fortunate consequence of Ouidah's commercial marginalization in the twentieth century ('fortunate', that is, for the historian, if not for the community itself) is that it was not subject to radical redevelopment during the colonial or post-colonial periods. There were, of course, some important changes: notably, the elimination of the office of the Dahomian governor, the Yovogan, together with his official residence whose site was given for the construction of the Roman Catholic Cathedral in 1901; the demolition of the French fort (now a public square) in 1908; the covering of the principal market in 1896. But the basic lay-out of the town as it existed at the end of the nineteenth century was preserved; the major colonial developments were added on to the town, as an extension of it (to the north-west), rather than disturbing the character of its historical centre. A detailed survey of the architectural 'heritage' of Ouidah was recently undertaken by a joint project of the Benin government with the French Institute of Overseas Development.[10] Given this continuity of occupation, and the consequent ease of identification of historically significant sites within the town, archaeological evidence is also potentially a significant source of information on the history of the town – though hitherto excavation efforts have been concentrated on Savi, the capital of the pre-Dahomian kingdom of Hueda, rather than on Ouidah itself.[11]

The Development of the Town: Foundation of Quarters

The clearest insight into the development of Ouidah as an urban community is afforded by the history of the foundation of its component quarters. As it existed at the end of the nineteenth century, the town comprised twelve quarters, each with its own distinct identity and historical origins. It may be noted that no European observer in the pre-colonial period ever grasped the ward organization of Ouidah in its entirety, so that for this approach the historian is dependent primarily upon local oral traditions, though these can to some extent controlled and supplemented by the more fragmentary information in contemporary sources.

According to local tradition (which, although uncorroborated, seems in this respect entirely credible), Ouidah existed as a settlement before Europeans began to trade there in the seventeenth century. The original, pre-contact village is identified today with the Tovè quarter, in the east of the modern town. The shrine of the supposed founder of the town, Pase, is located in this area – though it should be noted that there is no record of the tradition of Pase, or of the existence of his shrine in Ouidah, in contemporary accounts before the 1840s. The tradition is supported by a contemporary account, of the 1720s, which indicates that the indigenous village was situated to the east of the French and English forts, which is at least approximately the location of modern Tovè.[12]

Subsequently Ouidah was extended geographically through the foundation of the three European fortified trading factories: from west to east (which is also the chrono-logical order of their establishment), the French (known as Fort Saint Louis de Glegoy [i.e. Glehue]), English (William's Fort, Whydah), and Portuguese (Fort São João Baptista de Ajuda [Ouidah]). Of these, the French factory was originally established in 1671; it was destroyed in a local war in 1692, but re-founded (and at the same time fortified) in 1704.[13] The English initially established their factory in the royal capital Savi, but moved it to Glehue probably c.1684; this factory was fortified from 1692 onwards. The Portuguese fort was constructed in 1721. Each of these forts became the centre of a quarter of the town, occupied by families in the service of or associated with the fort; the French quarter was called Ahouandjigo, the English Sogbadji, the Portuguese Docome, though these names are not attested in the contemporary record before the nineteenth century. Even after the abandonment of these forts in the late eighteenth/early nineteenth centuries, the quarters associated with them retained their distinctive identity, and continued to be dominated by families descended from those formerly associated with the forts: Sogbadji, for example, by the Lemon family, descended from a British soldier, identifiable with Raymond [= Lemon] Quillie, who came to Ouidah as a gunner in 1779 and was still there when the fort was abandoned in 1812; Ahouandjigo by the Bonnaud family, descended from Pierre Bonnaud, a freeman of Afro-European descent, left behind in titular charge of the French fort when it was abandoned in 1797.[14]

In the Dahomian wars of conquest in 1727–8, the town of Ouidah was partially destroyed. The three European forts, however, together with their associated quarters, although attacked by the Dahomians, survived. The records of the English fort note explicitly that in 1728 the Dahomians agreed to spare 'the people belonging to the crooms [i.e. villages] near the forts, as servants and cargadores to the whites'.[15] The three quarters of Ahouandjigo, Sogbadji and Docome thus survived to form the core of Dahomian Ouidah.

A second distinct section of the town comprised two quarters to the north of the European forts called Fonsarame and Caosarame, meaning the Fon (Dahomian) and Cao quarters. These represent the Dahomian administrative and military establishment in Ouidah. Fonsarame was the site of the residence of the Dahomian governor, or Yovogan, and also includes the shrine of Dangbe – the royal python and the national deity of the Hueda kingdom – formerly located in the capital, Savi, and re-established by the Dahomians in Ouidah after the conquest. The establishment of this quarter dates from 1733, when the first Dahomian Viceroy was appointed, as recorded in contemporary European accounts, 'to reside among the Forts' at Ouidah. The Cao was the commander-in-chief of the local Dahomian garrison, constituted as a separate office from that of Yovogan, to judge by the contemporary records, in 1747.[16] Although today absorbed within the town, the Cao's encampment is shown on the map of 1776 as a separate settlement outside it.

A third distinct section of Dahomian Ouidah was formed by Tovè, which as noted earlier was the indigenous pre-Dahomian settlement. According to tradition, this was destroyed in the Dahomian conquest of 1727, but subsequently resettled by elements of the indigenous population; a contemporary account corroborates this resettlement of some of the pre-Dahomian population, 'under the protection of the Portuguese fort', which corresponds with the location of Tovè, adjacent to the Portuguese quarter of Docome.[17] Although apparently this was destroyed again when the Dahomians attacked and destroyed the Portuguese fort in Ouidah in 1743, presumably it was resettled once more thereafter. There are, however, some grounds for believing that the Tovè quarter was of only limited importance within Ouidah before the nineteenth century, its rise to prominence being associated (as will be seen hereafter) with the establishment in it of the Adjovis, nowadays the leading family in the quarter, probably in the 1840s.

The other six quarters of Ouidah were founded by leading merchants or commercial officials of the town. The earliest of these was Ganvè, which was in origin a sub-section or extension of the French quarter, Ahouandjigo, which it adjoins immediately to the west. Joseph Ollivier de Montaguère, Director of the French fort in 1775–86, married an Afro-European woman, Sophie, by whom he had children, who remained in Ouidah when he returned to France, founding a family which still exists in Ouidah and bears the name of its French ancestor (though nowadays generally given the Portuguese form d'Oliveira). His eldest son, Nicolas Ollivier, set up as a trader in Ouidah, and is credited with the foundation of Ganvè quarter, named with his praise name ('importer of metal'). Local tradition recalls that he secured the concession to settle there from the Dahomian King Kpengla (r. 1774–89); at any rate, he was certainly established there by 1818, since he is recalled to have given lodging there to Francisco Felix de Souza when the latter settled in Ouidah.[18]

The principal extension of the town in the nineteenth century was associated with this same Francisco Felix de Souza.[19] Brazilian in origin, de Souza had been an official of the Portuguese fort at Ouidah, but following the Portuguese abolition of the slave trade in 1815 he had left to become a private merchant outside Ouidah, mainly at Anecho (Little Popo) to the west. After financing the *coup d'état* which overthrew King Adandozan of Dahomey in favour of his brother Gezo in 1818, he was appointed by Gezo as his agent at Ouidah, with the title Chacha. He at first lodged with Nicolas Ollivier in Ganvè quarter, but later established his own settlement, in what became known as the Brazil (Brésil) quarter, to the south-west of the existing town; apart from the de Souza family itself, the inhabitants of this quarter are descended from slaves and, to a lesser degree, Brazilian associates of the founder.

De Souza is also credited with the creation of two other quarters, to the west of Brazil, called Maro and Zomai. Of these, Maro was settled, according to local tradition, by freed slaves from Brazil, who were granted land to settle by the first de Souza. These were mainly of Hausa and Yoruba origin, and included many Muslims, so that this quarter was the original Muslim quarter of the town (and contains the oldest mosque). The name 'Maro' seems to reflect the Hausa/Muslim element in the quarter, being that given to Muslim quarters in towns in the interior of Benin, north of Dahomey. This Brazilian immigration seems to derive from the deportation of free Blacks from Bahia in Brazil, following the uprising of Muslim slaves there in 1835.[20] In contemporary sources, this Hausa/Yoruba Brazilian quarter was first noted in 1845 by the Scots explorer John Duncan, who reported that, in addition to the 'real Portuguese', there were 'numerous' ex-slaves from Brazil, who had been expelled from there 'on account of their being concerned in an attempted revolution amongst the slaves there'.[21]

Zomai, further west again, is said to have been built by the first de Souza as a country retreat; like Brazil quarter, it is occupied by families descended either from Brazilians or from slaves of de Souza. The name Zomai ('Fire prohibited') is said to allude to the fact that de Souza stored his gunpowder there. In contemporarary sources, the existence of 'some large stores' on the 'outskirts' of Ouidah belonging to de Souza (and also including his billiard room) was noted in 1847; and the actual name Zomai first recorded (as that of a 'street' of the town) in 1850.[22]

Two other quarters in the west of Ouidah also appear to date from this period, and to be associated in their origins with the career of de Souza. First, Boyasarame, or Boya quarter (situated between Brazil and Ahouandjigo). Boya was the title of a leading commercial official in Ouidah, responsible for handling the sale of slaves on the king's behalf. This title certainly existed from the mid-eighteenth century,[23] but it is doubtful whether the Boya quarter goes back so early. The most circumstantial version of local tradition attributes its foundation to a later holder of the office, Boya-Cisse, a resident in the Dahomian capital Abomey who was party to the alliance between King Gezo and de

Souza in 1818, in reward for which he was installed at Ouidah as an associate of the latter in the operation of the slave trade. He is said to have lived originally in Brazil quarter, but Gezo then granted him a new site, which became the present Boya quarter.[24] Second, the Quénum quarter, occupied by the family of that name, to the south of the Brazil quarter, out of which it appears to have been carved. The foundation of this quarter is credited to Azanmado Quénum, an indigenous Dahomian trader, who originally was associated with de Souza and settled in the Brazil quarter under his patronage; de Souza family tradition, indeed, maintains that Azanmado was originally a slave of de Souza, though the Quénums claim a free ancestry, members of the family having earlier served as officers in the Dahomian army (in this they are supported by contemporary evidence, which attests a member of the family as a Dahomian military officer in the 1780s). In the mid-1840s Azanmado Quénum broke with de Souza, however, and set up as an independent trader.[25]

A further and final quarter whose rise to prominence, if not its origins, seems to be linked to de Souza is Tovè, the indigenous Hueda quarter of the town, to the east. Although, as noted earlier, the resettlement of Tovè is said to date back to the early years of Dahomian rule, its rise to importance is linked with a merchant called Adjovi, who originally served de Souza as warden of his slaves, but moved from Brazil quarter to settle in Tovè; according to de Souza tradition, he made his fortune by stealing slaves belonging to de Souza destined for export, and employing them instead in agricultural production – the context being the development of exports of palm oil in the 1840s.[26] Although the Adjovis claim descent from the earlier heads of Tovè quarter, and ultimately from the pre-Dahomian kings of Savi (and owed their influence to their control of the shrine of the founder-ancestor Pase, as well as to their commercial wealth), this is disputed by the de Souzas and other local rivals, who often impute slave origin to the family. Forbes's allusion in 1850 to 'a new town lately built to the eastward' may refer to Tovè, lately expanded and risen to prominence under Adjovi.[27]

It may also be noted that contemporary sources of the nineteenth century attest to the existence of at least one further quarter of Ouidah, which evidently did not survive and whose existence is no longer recalled in local tradition, occupied by ex-slave repatriates from Freetown in Sierra Leone. The British missionary Freeman in 1843 alludes to the existence in Ouidah of a group of Christian emigrants from Sierra Leone, who had arrived there 'two or three years' earlier; Duncan in 1845 confirms the presence of a 'few families' from Sierra Leone, who had built 'a small town' on land donated by the King of Dahomey; and Forbes in 1850 likewise noted the existence of 'towns' of freed slaves from Sierra Leone, as well as from Brazil. By 1864, however, this community evidently no longer existed, Burton then noting that British subjects in Ouidah numbered only a dozen, mostly from Fante and Cape Coast.[28] Precisely what happened to this Sierra Leonean community in Ouidah is uncertain (though light may be thrown on this issue by research in the archives of the Methodist Mission); maybe they migrated to Lagos after the establishment of British influence there in 1852.

One thing which emerges clearly, even from the sketchy and preliminary account offered above, is the enormous heterogeneity of origins of the population of Ouidah, including indigenous and Dahomian, as well as Brazilian and other Afro-European elements. The heterogeneity was, indeed, even greater than might appear at first sight, since the 'indigenous' element was itself of disparate origins, including Hula (originating from Grand Popo to the west) as well as Hueda;[29] and the 'Dahomian' element was likewise heterogeneous in its remoter ancestries, including families which traced their origins from outside Dahomey or from originally distinct communities absorbed within it only by recent conquest – the Quénums, for example, claim descent from the kings of Weme, conquered by Dahomey in the early eighteenth century. The African slaves and free labourers employed in the European forts (descendants of some of whom remain *in situ* to the present) likewise included many brought from other (and sometimes distant) areas: the French quarter Ahouandjigo, for example, includes two families descended from former 'servants' of the French fort whose founders came from Bariba country, in northern Benin; and the English quarter Sogbadji has a family called Kocu (or Kweku, traceable in contemporary accounts of the eighteenth century), whose founder was a canoeman who came to Ouidah from the Gold Coast.

It also appears that Ouidah was, demographically, largely a community of slave origin. The African personnel of the European forts were mainly slaves (though some freemen were employed also); and the large households of local traders, whether Afro-European, Brazilian or African, likewise included many slaves. European observers in the nineteenth century generally gained the impression that the population of Ouidah consisted pre-dominantly of slaves, although their accounts sometimes suffer from conceptual imprecision, including pawns and perhaps even free clients within their definition of 'slave'. Forbes in 1850 thought that no more than 10 per cent (20,000 out of 200,000 according to his estimate) of the population of Dahomey were free, the remainder slaves; while the French merchant Béraud in 1866 stated that 'two-thirds of the population are slaves'.[30] Although presented as applying to Dahomey in general, it seems likely that these estimates were based on the specific case of Ouidah, with which Europeans were most familiar. The British explorer Skertchly in 1871 thought that no less than four-fifths (8,000 out of 10,000) of the population of Whydah were 'slaves, or [introducing the conceptual ambiguity] dependent upon the caboceers [officials] and merchants in the place'.[31]

The Growth of the Town: Quantitative Measures

Contemporary accounts also provide occasional evidence on the size and population of Ouidah, which can be compared with the picture suggested by the history of the founda-tion of its component quarters. Such quantitative estimates are, of course, subject to a number of problems of interpretation and evaluation, notably, conceptual uncertainty over how precisely the town was defined: for example, whether including or excluding physically separate but sociologically dependent farming hamlets in the surrounding countryside.

Estimates of the physical extent of the town are relatively few, but at least may be assumed to be relatively reliable (the conceptual issue just noted apart), to the extent that they were based on actual walking of the distances computed. Pre-Dahomian Ouidah, in the early eighteenth century, was said to have a circuit of three-quarters of a league, or just over two miles, while Dahomian Ouidah in the 1780s was given a slightly smaller circuit of 1.5 miles. By contrast, Burton in 1863/4 estimated the town to be two miles long (north-west to south-east) by half a mile in depth.[32] This is, at least, consistent with the extension of the town westwards in the first half of the nineteenth century, associated with Francisco Felix de Souza.

Population estimates are more frequent, but are also likely to be less reliable, since it is unclear on what, other than an impression of size (or at best, a count of buildings, multiplied by a hypothesized average number of residents), they could be based. The difficulties (and range of error) are illustrated by the fact that, of two members of a French mission to Dahomey in 1856, one estimated the population of Ouidah at between 20,000–25,000, but another thought that this should be reduced by a third.[33] There is the additional problem that the size of the population might be subject to significant short-term fluctuations: Burton, for example, noted that 'during war [the population] may be reduced to half', and Skertchly that it was reduced by 40 per cent (10,000 to 6,000) during the ceremony of the 'Annual Customs' at the capital, which many officials with their entourages were obliged to attend.[34] For what they are worth, the figures are given in Table 5.1.

Table 5.1 Estimated population of Ouidah, 1772–1913[35]

1772:	about 8,000
1776	under 2,000
1793:	6,000–7,000
1803:	about 20,000
1851:	25,000–30,000
1856:	20,000–25,000
	(or one third less: 13,300–16,700)
1862-3:	about 12,000
1863-4:	12,000
1866:	about 15,000
1871:	10,000
1913:	15,000

As regards the plausibility of these figures, it may be noted that the exceptionally low figure for 1776 is explained in the source as reflecting a drastic decline during the previous 7–8 years, the size of the Dahomian garrison in Ouidah alone during the same period allegedly falling from 8,000–10,000 (an improbably high figure) to only 300.[36] The high figure for 1803 has no obvious comparable explanation, and probably should be discounted. The fact that the figures for the 1850s–70s are generally higher than the earlier ones (apart from the aberrant figure for 1803) is, again, consistent with the documented westward expansion of the town associated with de Souza after 1818. It may also reflect the shift from slaves to palm produce in the town's export trade, since the latter demanded more labour for its transport. The apparent population decline between the 1850s and 1860s is also supported by the impressionistic evidence of the French missionaries resident in the town, reported by Burton in 1864, that 'the population diminishes',[37] and may reflect the beginnings of the town's commercial decline in that period.

Economic Tranformations

According to traditional etymology, the indigenous name of Ouidah, Glehue, alludes to its original status as a farm (gle). Contemporary European sources of the eighteenth century, however, do not suggest that Ouidah was, to any significant extent, an agricultural community; two pre-1727 accounts, for example, describe its inhabitants as 'fishers and porters', or 'fishers and canoemen'.[38] There was evidently some cultivation, but this was limited in extent: an account of 1776, for example, says that the land around Ouidah was planted with maize, but only for a distance of three-quarters of a league (just over two miles) around.[39] Another visitor to Dahomey, in 1803, observed that cultivation was done only 'generally in the immediate neighbourhood of their towns'; and, here again, it seems reasonable to suppose that this was based mainly, if not exclusively, on observation of the case of Ouidah.[40] Another account, in 1772, reported that the market at Ouidah was supplied with 'great quantities' of palm oil from Allada, in the interior; which implies (at a period when exports of palm oil were still minimal) that local production was insufficient to meet domestic demand.[41] It seems probable, indeed, as was certainly the case by the early colonial period, that Ouidah was dependent for its basic foodstuffs on importation from elsewhere, financed out of the profits of its trade (and also sales of fish and salt), rather than producing its needs locally.

In the nineteenth century, however, the economic basis of Ouidah was transformed, with the development of an extensive agricultural hinterland. Duncan in 1845 noted that the country around Ouidah was 'in many places well cultivated', to a distance of no less than 10–12 miles; much of this cultivation being undertaken by ex-slaves returned from Brazil. He also reports that the Dahomian authorities had recently issued orders that 'all the spare land in and round the town of Griwhee (Glehue) should be cultivated'. Duncan's own account suggests that the chief crops raised on these farms were maize and cassava, of which the latter at least was used mainly to provision slave ships.[42] The extension of cassava cultivation at this time was an aspect of Brazilian influence; local tradition, it may be noted, credits de Souza with having introduced into Dahomey the technique of processing cassava to make a palatable flour.[43] Beyond that, it may have been stimulated by the difficulties caused for the illegal slave-trade by Palmerston's Equipment Act of 1839, which authorized the British naval ships to intercept Portuguese ships equipped for slave trade, even if there were no slaves on board, which made it dangerous for slavers to take on foodstuffs prior to embarking their slaves.

Later in the 1840s, however, farms around Ouidah were devoted rather to the production of palm oil for export. Duncan, returning there as British Vice-Consul in 1849, found that 'the whole of the land in the immediate neighbourhood of the settlement, which three years ago was occupied solely for the production of farinha [i.e. cassava flour] for slave subsistence, is now occupied for other purposes'; and Forbes in 1850 refers to three palm oil plantations near the town, one owned by the Dahomian trader Adjovi, one by the Brazilian José Francisco dos Santos, and one by an unnamed liberated slave from Brazil.[44] These estates clearly employed slave labour on a large scale; already in 1844, it was reported that 'the inhabitants and black merchants' of Ouidah were using slaves to produce palm-oil, rather than exporting them; and in 1848 it was estimated that, in addition to slaves exported, around 1,000 a year were being imported from the interior for use in Ouidah and other coastal towns.[45] One implication of the shift from slaves to palm oil in Dahomey's export trade, which is clearly traceable in the contemporary record, therefore, was that the Ouidah merchants became large-scale slave owners. Forbes in 1850, for example, noted that the wealthiest indigenous merchants of the town, Adjovi, Gnahoui and Quenum, 'own thousands of slaves', Gnahoui alone owning 'upwards of a thousand slaves' – though not all of these slaves would have been in the Ouidah area, since Gnahoui also owned estates in the capital Abomey and other places in the interior.[46]

Administration and Identity: Ouidah and Dahomey

It is more difficult, on the basis of the available sources, to document and trace the development of Ouidah's self-image as a community. It is clear, however, that, although subject to Dahomey, Ouidah did not regard itself as fully part of that polity. Europeans in the nineteenth century noted that people going from Ouidah into the interior spoke of themselves as travelling 'to Dahomey'.[47] This was not, moreover, a merely geographical expression, since local Ouidah tradition presents an explicit portrayal of Dahomian administration as alien and exploitative, in effect as essentially colonial in character.[48] Ouidah seems, indeed, to have developed a sense of collective identity, despite the heterogeneity of origins of its population noted earlier, essentially in opposition to what was seen as the heavy hand of Dahomian rule.

The alien character of Dahomian rule was expressed, not only in its frequently arbitrary and oppressive behaviour, but also in the fact that normally the Yovogan and other senior offices were filled by appointments from the capital Abomey rather than by local men; they were also non-hereditary, so that normally they did not give rise to locally based office-holding families. This did change somewhat in the nineteenth century, partly because of the exceptionally long tenure of the office of Yovogan by Dagba (1823–c.1875), who in consequence did establish local roots, founding (as was noted earlier) a family which still resides in Ouidah to the present; but also (and more critically) because of the creation of new, essentially commercial offices which tended to rival and eclipse the power of the administrative hierarchy. The first of these was the office of Chacha, conferred on Francisco Felix de Souza in 1818; although in origin, of course, a foreigner, de Souza by his death had become effectively naturalized, marrying locally (polygamously) and founding an extensive Afro-Brazilian family, as well as acquiring an enormous retinue of household slaves. After the disgrace of the third Chacha (and the first de Souza's second son), Ignacio de Souza, in c. 1859, although the office of Chacha continued to exist, its power and prestige was much diminished. Power did not, however, pass back to the Yovogan, since around the same time King Glele of Dahomey raised Azanmado Quénum to the new title of 'chief of traders [ahisigan]' at Ouidah, in which office he was succeeded on his death in 1866 by his son Kpadonou Quénum.[49]

This localization of the political establishment, however, changed the form of the opposition between Ouidah and Dahomey, rather than mitigating it. Tensions between the Dahomian monarchy and the Ouidah merchant community were evident already in the eighteenth century, with recurrent executions and expropriations of wealthy merchants, and a major crisis provoked by the attempts of King Kpengla (1774–89) to establish a royal monopoly of the slave trade.[50] These tensions became much deeper in the second half of the nineteenth century, with the shift from slaves to palm oil in Dahomey's export trade. This had the effect, as noted earlier, that the Ouidah merchants began to produce oil for export locally, diminishing their dependence on the Dahomian monarchy for their commercial operations, and thereby heightening the contradiction of interest between them. At the same time, by undermining the revenues of the monarchy, the commercial transition also increased its propensity to arbitrary expropriatory attacks on the Ouidah merchant community. The second half of the nineteenth century was marked by the disgrace and execution and/or expropriation of several leading Ouidah merchants, beginning with the Chacha Ignacio de Souza, as noted earlier, in c. 1859 and including Kpadonou Quénum, who was detained in Abomey in 1877 and died still in prison there in 1887, his property in Ouidah being meanwhile confiscated. Although the politics of these events was complex, and in part reflected factional disputes within the Ouidah merchant community (and in particular the rivalry between the de Souzas and the Quénums), they also reflected the progressive alienation of the Ouidah merchants from the Dahomian monarchy.[51] In a context where Dahomey was increasingly under threat from European imperialism, while the Ouidah merchants of necessity were linked by interest to the European merchants, this was ultimately expressed in the politics of collaboration. When war broke out between Dahomey and France in 1890, Kpadonou Quénum's son Tovalou Quénum, then in exile at Porto-Novo, fought on the French side. Conversely, the Dahomian authorities, distrusting Ouidah's loyalty, took over 1,000 hostages from the community: carried off into the interior, many of them died in captivity, but the survivors were liberated by the French conquest of Dahomey two years later.

Epilogue

The expectations of the Ouidah merchant community that they stood to benefit from French colonial rule were disappointed, however, inasmuch as the town's commercial decline accelerated after the French occupation. Given the town's political and commercial marginalization from the 1890s, in favour of Porto-Novo and Cotonou, members of Ouidah families had to seek prosperity through migration elsewhere.[52] Only very recently, in the 1990s, has a serious attempt been made to construct an alternative role for the town, which would form the basis for its economic regeneration, in the development of 'heritage tourism', invoking its central role in the history of the Atlantic slave trade and thereby in the creation of the African diaspora.[53]

Notes

1 Cf. more generally, Robin Law, 'Between the sea and the lagoons: the interaction of maritime and inland navigation on the pre-colonial "Slave Coast"', *Cahiers d'Études Africaines*, 29 (1989), pp. 209–37.

2 For the history of the Hueda kingdom, see especially Robin Law, '"The common people were divided": monarchy, aristocracy and political factionalism in the kingdom of Whydah, 1671–1727', *International Journal of African Historical Studies*, 23 (1991), pp. 201–29.

3 In Archives Nationales, Paris: C6/27bis.

4 Published accounts of these missions are, however, not very informative for the social history of Ouidah. The only published study of the Wesleyan mission focuses on its relations with the Dahomian state: Rev. Paul Ellingworth, 'Christianity and politics in Dahomey, 1843–1867', *Journal of African History*, 5 (1964), pp. 209–20. The principal account of the French Catholic mission deals only briefly with the nineteenth century, and in any case is focused more on the missionaries than on the people they envangelized: Christiane Roussé-Grosseau, *Mission catholique et choc des modèles culturels en Afrique: L'exemple du Dahomey (1861–1928)* (Paris, 1992).

5 Frederick E. Forbes, *Dahomey and the Dahomans* (2 vols, London, 1851); Richard Burton, *A Mission to Gelele, King of Dahome* (2 vols, London, 1864).

6 Both published, as 'Note historique sur Ouidah par l'administrateur Gavoy (1913)', *Études Dahoméennes*, 13 (1955), pp. 45–70; 'Ouidah: organisation du commandement [by Reynier, 1917]', *Mémoire du Bénin*, 2 (1993), pp. 30–70.

7 Casimir Agbo, *Histoire de Ouidah du XVe au XXe siècle* (Avignon, 1959).

8 Simone de Souza, *La famille de Souza du Bénin-Togo* (Cotonou, 1992); Léon Pierre Ghézowounmè-Djomalia Dagba, *La collectivité familiale Yovogan Hounnon Dagba de ses origines à nos jours* (Ouidah, 1982); Maximilien Quénum, *Les ancêtres de la famille Quénum* (Langes, 1981).

9 Published in French translation in Pierre Verger, *Les afro-américains* (Dakar, 1952).

10 *Ouidah et son patrimoine* (ORSTOM/SERHAU, Paris/Cotonou, 1991); cf. also Alain Sinou, *Le comptoir de Ouidah: une ville africaine singulière* (Paris, 1995).

11 Ken Kelly, 'Transformation and continuity in Savi, a West African trade town: an archaeological investigation of culture change on the coast of Bénin during the 17th and 18th centuries' (PhD thesis, University of California, Los Angeles, 1995).

12 Jean-Baptiste Labat, *Voyage du Chevalier des Marchais en Guinée* (second edition, 4 vols, Amsterdam, 1731), Vol. 2, 34.

13 See Simone Berbain, *Le comptoir français de Juda (Ouidah) au XVIIIe siècle* (Dakar, 1942).

14 For Raymond Quillie, see personnel registers in Public Record Office, London: T70/1161-3; for Pierre Bonnaud, see Berbain, *Le comptoir français de Juda*, p. 54.

15 Robin Law (ed.), *Correspondence of the Royal African Company's Chief Merchants at Cabo Corso Castle with William's Fort, Whydah, and the Little Popo Factory, 1727–1728* (African Studies Program, University of Wisconsin-Madison, 1991), No. 22: Thomas Wilson, Whydah, 12 July 1728.

16 Robin Law, *The Slave Coast of West Africa 1550–1750* (Oxford, 1991), pp. 336, 338.

17 Robert Norris, *Memoirs of the Reign of Bossa Ahadee, King of Dahomy* (London, 1789), p. 29.

18 Reynier, 'Ouidah', pp. 58–9.

19 For whom, see esp. David Ross, 'The first Chacha of Whydah: Francisco Felix de Souza', *Odu*, new series, 2 (1969), pp. 19–28.

20 Cf. João José Reis, *Slave Rebellion in Brazil: the Muslim Uprising of 1835 in Bahia* (Baltimore, 1993), p. 220, recording 200 deported from Bahia to Ouidah in 1835.

21 John Duncan, *Travels in Western Africa* (2 vols, London,1847), Vol. 1, pp. 138, 185, 202.

22 Archibald Ridgway, 'A journey to Dahomey', *New Monthly Magazine*, 81 (1847), p. 196; Forbes, *Dahomey*, Vol. 1, p. 117.

23 Law, *Slave Coast*, p. 337.

24 Reynier, 'Ouidah', p. 58.

25 *Ibid.*, p. 63; Quénum, *Les ancêtres de la famille Quénum*, pp. 60-1. For the Quénum of the 1780s, cf. Archibald Dalzel, *The History of Dahomy* (London, 1793), p. 184; PRO, T70/1162, Day Book, William's Fort, Whydah, 5 December 1788.

26 De Souza, *La famille de Souza*, pp. 33–4.

27 Forbes, *Dahomey*, Vol. 1, p.105.

28 T. B. Freeman, *A Journal of Various Visits to the Kingdoms of Ashantee, Aku and Dahomi* (London, 1844), p. 242; Duncan, *Travels*, Vol. 1, p. 117; Forbes, *Dahomey*, Vol. 1, p. 105; Parliamentary Papers [hereafter PP], Slave Trade, 1864: Burton, 23 March 1864.

29 There are some grounds for believing that Ouidah was originally a Hula settlement, only later absorbed under the rule of the Hueda kings of Savi; this is suggested, among other things, by the acknowledged primacy of Hu (the Sea), the national deity of the Hula, among the divinities worshipped in Ouidah – ahead even of Dangbe, the national deity of the Hueda.

30 Forbes, *Dahomey*, Vol. 1, p. 14; Médard Béraud, 'Note sur le Dahomé', *Bulletin de la Société de la Géographie*, 12 (1866), p. 380.

31 J. A. Skertchly, *Dahomey As It Is* (London, 1874), p. 45.

32 'Relation du royaume de Judas en Guinée' (Archives d'Outre-Mer, Aix-en-Provence [hereafter AOM], Fortifications des Colonies, Côtes d'Afrique, 104), p. 2; Paul Erdman Isert, *Letters on West Africa and the Slave Trade* (ed. Selena Axelrod Winsnes, Oxford, 1992), p. 100; Burton, *Mission*, Vol. 1, p. 60.

33 F. Vallon, 'Le royaume de Dahomey', *Revue Maritime et Coloniale*, 1 (1860), pp. 333, 343; Dr Repin, 'Voyage au Dahomey', *Le Tour du Monde*, Vol. 1 (1863), p. 70.

34 Burton, *Mission*, Vol. 1, p. 61; Skertchly, *Dahomey*, p. 45.

35 Sources: Norris, *Memoirs*, p. 62; De Chenevert and Bullet, 'Reflexions sur Juda' (AOM, Fortifications des Colonies, Côtes d'Afrique, 111), p. 19; John Adams, *Remarks on the Country Extending from Cape Palmas to the River Congo* (London, 1823), p. 50; John Mc'Leod, *A Voyage to Africa* (London, 1820), p. 13; Auguste Bouet, 'Le royaume de Dahomey', *L'Illustration*, 20 (1852), p. 40; Vallon, 'Le royaume de Dahomey', pp. 333, 343; Repin, 'Voyage au Dahomey', p. 70; PP: Despatches from Commodore Wilmot, respecting his Visit to the King of Dahomey (1863), p. 13; Burton, *Mission*, Vol. 1, p. 61; Béraud, 'Note', p. 372; Skertchly, *Dahomey*, p. 45; Gavoy, 'Note historique', p. 63.

36 De Chenevert and Bullet, 'Refléxions', p. 4.

37 Burton, *Mission*, Vol. 1, p. 61.

38 'Relation du royaume de Judas', p. 2; Labat, *Voyage du Chevalier des Marchais*, Vol. 2, p. 33.

39 De Chenevert and Bullet, 'Refléxions', p. 19.

40 Mc'Leod, *Voyage*, p. 18.

41 Norris, *Memoirs*, p. 71.

42 Duncan, *Travels*, Vol. 1, p. 185, 192; Vol. 2, p. 268-9.

43 A. Le Herissé, *L'ancien royaume du Dahomey* (Paris, 1911), p. 327.

44 PP (Slave Trade 1849-50): Duncan, 17 August 1849; Forbes, *Dahomey*, Vol. 1, pp. 114–15, 123.

45 De Monleon, 'Le Cap de Palmes, le Dahomey et l'Île du Prince en 1844', *Revue Coloniale*, 6 (1845), p. 72; PP: Missions to the King of Ashantee and Dahomey (1849): Report of B. Cruickshank, 9 November 1848.

46 Forbes, *Dahomey*, Vol. 1, p. 113; Vol. 2, pp. 174-5.

47 Abbé Borghero, 30 September 1861, in 'Missions du Dahomey', *Annales de la Propagation de la Foi*, 25 (1862)
48 See esp. Agbo, *Histoire de Ouidah*, pp. 53–6.
49 Reynier, 'Ouidah', p. 63.
50 See further Robin Law, 'Royal monopoly and private enterprise in the Atlantic trade: the case of Dahomey', *Journal of African History*, 8 (1977), pp. 555–77.
51 See further Robin Law, 'The politics of commercial transition: factional conflict in Dahomey in the context of the ending of the Atlantic slave trade', *Journal of African History*, 38 (1997), pp. 213–34.
52 Bellarmin C. Codo and Sylvain C. Anignikin, 'Ouidah sous le régime colonial', in *Union Générale pour le Développement de Ouidah, Almanach de Ouidah: Les voies de la renaissance de Ouidah* (Caen, 1985), pp. 103–14.
53 Marked by the designation or creation of several monuments to the history of the Atlantic slave trade; and also by the organization of two major international conferences at Ouidah, on links between Africa and the Americas (1992) and on the slave trade (1994).

6

Merchants, Missions & the Remaking of the Urban Environment in Buganda c.1840–90

RICHARD REID & HENRI MEDARD

Religion, politics and trade are closely interwoven and dominating themes in the history of nineteenth-century Buganda. From the 1840s, when Islam was introduced by traders coming from the domain of the Sultanate of Zanzibar on East Africa's coast, Buganda's social and political order was ever more intensively shaped by interactions with external forces. Following the trade routes, European explorers arrived in 1862 in search of the source of the Nile. In their wake came the first Christian missionaries in the 1870s, French Catholics and then British Protestants, both keen to spread the gospel in the densely settled lands of Buganda. New religions speedily became enshrined in older politics. When the *Kabaka* of Buganda briefly adopted Islam, largely as a means of fostering commercial links with his new trading partners from the coast, religion became a matter of politics. Islam and Christianity both won converts among Ganda, and as the new ideas and technologies they helped to introduce became increasingly pervasive and thereby greatly more difficult for the *Kabaka* to effectively control, new conflicts emerged. By the 1880s, the political struggles within Buganda had taken shape as 'religious wars' in which political factions were identified by their affiliations to a creed. And out of this religious conflict was to come the colonial conquest of the 1890s.

All of these dramas were played out in the arena that was Buganda's capital and largest urban settlement, where the *Kabaka* held his court and where commercial and clerical emissaries came to pay him tribute and show their respect for his authority. Visiting merchants, missionaries and the Ganda elite were all congregated at the capital. The new configurations of religion, politics and trade that emerged in Buganda from the 1840s were therefore most visible, and had their greatest impact, within the confines of the capital. As interested parties competed for the control of commerce, and as political factions then formed around different religions, significant changes in the meaning of the urban settlements around the court of the *Kabaka* became evident. This was partly physical, but also symbolic, reflecting both the tangible control of resources and the imageries of power that could be invoked. By the mid-1890s, when British colonial power was firmly established over the capital, and by implication over the kingdom as a whole, the pre-colonial capital of Buganda had been replaced by something quite different and altogether more permanent.

The transformation of the pre-colonial urban environment occurred in two phases, the first driven predominantly by the lure of long-distance commerce, the second, beginning after the mid-1880s, influenced by the growing importance and authority of foreign religions. The effects of developments in commerce will be considered in the first part of this chapter. During the reigns of Suna (*c.* 1830–57) and Mutesa (1857–84), the Ganda capital became by far the most important urban centre in the entire interlacustrine region, largely as a result of its domination of long-distance trade by land and water. Up until the mid-nineteenth century, the Ganda capital had been peripatetic, the *Kabaka* and his court periodically relocating their business around the kingdom as sanitation and general health concerns, worries over military defence, or the need to assert royal authority might dictate.[1] From the 1850s, the need to monopolize and control external trade anchored the capital more firmly to the area around modern-day Kampala. Lake trading routes were especially important, and the Kampala area offered advantages for the control of the water-borne trade as well as a good political base, strategically placed at the heart of the kingdom. As long-distance traders visited Buganda more regularly, the commercial importance of the capital was enhanced. It also played an administrative and military role in Ganda life, giving a broad occupational base to the urban population that was remarkable by the standards of the East African interior. As settlement became more permanent, the physical area of the capital extended into suburban areas, and others were attracted into its growing commercial orbit. The high agricultural productivity of Buganda, coupled with a relatively densely settled rural population, enabled the capital to rely upon the countryside for its food supplies. Utilizing all of these factors, the capital site around Kampala quickly developed in terms of geographical size, population and political importance, and in the second half of the century there can be little doubt that it should be described as a 'town'.

Between the late 1870s and the 1890s, during the reign of *Kabaka* Mwanga (1857–88, 1889–97), religion had a profound influence upon the development of the capital, and this will be examined in the second part of this chapter. The European missionaries who came to settle at the capital had their own ideas about the definition of urban spaces, and in the religious wars that developed between their supporting factions a new symbolic geography of the capital was apparent: the battle for political and cultural authority was now increasingly expressed through the spatial organization of the town. Where previously the capital had been viewed as a manifestation of royal potency – the urban environment was indeed a creation of the royal presence – the new religions struggled to gain control of urban symbols and spaces and in so doing demonstrated that such things were no longer the monopoly of the *Kabaka*. As we shall see, especially in the case of the White Fathers, what successes the missionaries had in claiming symbolic authority in the capital largely depended upon their ability to harness and adapt already existing Ganda notions of power.

Trade and the Expansion of the Pre-colonial Capital

Reliable and detailed data on the pre-Suna (*c.* 1830) capitals of Buganda is difficult to come by; in a sense this makes constructive comparison between the nineteenth century and an earlier period somewhat problematic. There is, however, sufficient data relating to the 50 years or so prior to the establishment of colonial rule to identify certain key developments, enabling us to draw tentative conclusions about the changes wrought on the pre-colonial capital and to suggest ways in which these represented a marked break from what had gone before. The expansion in the scale of commercial activity during the nineteenth century seems to have had a corresponding effect on the pre-colonial urban environment. The increasing stability and enlargement of the capital may have been part of a process already in motion when the Ganda were first directly exposed to long-distance trade in the 1840s, but the forces of commercial change at the very least hastened this process.

Suna probably became *Kabaka* in around 1830 and built a new capital at Mulago, where he lived, according to Kagwa, 'for many years'.[2] By the time the first Arab traders arrived in Buganda in 1844, however, Suna's capital was at Nabulagala, near Kasubi in present-day Kampala.[3] Nabulagala was thus the site of the first direct contact with the long-distance commercial system of which Suna and his successor Mutesa would seek to be at the centre. Kagwa also tells us that, apparently in the mid-1840s, Suna 'extended his capital so largely that it reached as far as Namirembe hill'.[4] In 1862, Speke passed the site of Suna's *Kibuga* on his way to that of Mutesa, which came into view a day later.[5] In the vicinity of Suna's old enclosure was 'a large range of huts said to belong to [Mutesa's] uncle, the second of the late king Sunna's brothers, who was not burnt to death when he ascended the throne'.[6] This suggests that during the nineteenth century these old sites were not abandoned but represented rambling suburbs, forming part of what might be termed the 'greater *Kibuga*'.

Nabulagala was an immensely important capital. This is clear from the descriptions of the site given to Burton by coastal merchants:

> Kibuga, the settlment, is not less than a day's journey in length.... The sultan's palace is at least a mile long.... Bells at the several entrances announce the approach of strangers, and guards in hundreds attend there at all hours.... The harem contains about 3000 souls – concubines, slaves, and children. No male or adult animal may penetrate, under pain of death, beyond the Barzah, a large vestibule or hall of audience where the king dispenses justice and receives his customs....[7]

The dimensions given here were not mere hyperbole. As the area covered by the capital included the hills of Kasubi and Namirembe, it cannot have been much less than two miles in diameter, and was probably much more. The population of Nabulagala undoubtedly varied; throughout the nineteenth century there would have been a constant flow of people to and from the capital. But a royal entourage alone of around 3,000, in addition to the '2,000 guards' stationed outside the *Kabaka*'s enclosure,[8] points to a total of perhaps 10,000 in the early 1850s.[9]

It is likely that the capital had always attracted 'alien' groups: diplomatic missions from Busoga or Bunyoro, foreign traders and imported craftsmen in royal or chiefs' service were a common feature of the capital and its environs. Indeed, the Soga appear to have had a permanent embassy, surrounded by plantations, on the outskirts of the capital.[10] But the arrival of coastal merchants, not to mention European missionaries and travellers, lent a new cosmopolitan atmosphere to the urban environment, although it was probably only after *c.* 1860 that the Arabs had a permanent quarter in the capital. Yet the welcome received by the trader Snay bin Amir in 1852 suggested the manner in which the capital was to expand to accommodate these exciting new visitors. Burton wrote:

> When the report of arrival was forwarded by word of mouth to Suna, he issued orders for the erection of as many tents as might be necessary. The guest who was welcomed with joyful tumult by a crowd of gazers, was conducted to the newly-built quarters, where he received a present of bullocks and grain, plantains and sugar-cane....[11]

The symbolic, if not the geographical, centre of the capital was of course the *Kabaka*'s own enclosure, which probably dominated the fledgling town in much the same way as did the castles of medieval England. In normal circumstances, it was here that the *Kabaka* conducted political business, pronounced judgements on legal matters, and consulted with chiefs on military expeditions or tribute collection. It was also where the coastal merchants were received, and where such traders conducted commerce with the most powerful indigenous trader in the kingdom.

The evidence concerning Suna's strict enforcement of sanitary laws, and the suggestion that he expanded the capital to cover a large proportion of what is now Kampala, indicates that the 'modern' capital had its origins during his reign.[12] But the expansion of long-distance trade was critical in this regard. Nabulagala had become an important commercial centre, almost exactly contemporaneous with Tabora, and for some time it would remain the terminus of the winding trade highway which began on the coast opposite Zanzibar. Its value as a commercial entrepot lent the Ganda capital a new significance. Physical expansion would quickly follow, as would its growing importance as a meeting place for traders and emissaries from throughout the lacustrine region and beyond.

Importantly, too, the capital would never again be moved too far from the lake shore. This was no coincidence, for it was Suna who developed the Ganda navy and who perceived that control of the lake would be critical to the furtherance of Ganda commercial and military interests. From the 1840s onward the capital became inextricably linked to the lake. But we would be stretched to describe the capital itself as a port: even at the height of Buganda's naval power, it remained some twenty miles from the shore. Nonetheless, the capital's lacustrine connections can be discerned clearly during the second half of the nineteenth century. The growth of ports along the shore, most famously at Entebbe, was a reflection of the capital's own growth, both geographical and emblematic. Roads linked these ports to the capital: they were, perhaps, distant suburbs, the *Kibuga*'s furthest-flung gatehouses, waiting to welcome – and to control – the agents of the coast.

Shortly after Suna's death in 1856/7, Mutesa became *Kabaka*. Mutesa moved the site of his *Kibuga* several times during a long and eventful reign, but each site was close to the lake shore and most lay in close proximity to Nabulagala, which by the time of Mutesa's death in 1884 had been incorporated into a wider urban sprawl. By the time Speke arrived in 1862, Mutesa's *Kibuga* was at Banda, in the north-east of present-day Kampala and close to Nabulagala. Speke observed a 'whole hill ... covered with gigantic huts, such as I had never seen in Africa before'. His admiration swiftly dissipated when it was made clear that he could not go straight to the palace; rather, he 'was shown into a lot of dirty huts, which ... were built expressly for all the king's visitors. The Arabs, when they came on their visits, always put up here, and I must do the same'.[13] Indeed, this was by now a capital accustomed to the constant coming and going of strangers. It was a much more cosmopolitan environment than the capital first reached by Arab merchants in 1844. Speke was temporarily resident in the 'Arab quarter', an area of the capital reserved for the coastal merchants. There were several commercial expeditions during the 1840s and 1850s, but during this time traders appear not to have remained for any great length of time. They were refused entry during the interregnum following the death of Suna, but within a few years of Mutesa's accession, Arab traders seem to have been a permanent feature at the capital.[14] Despite his annoyance at having to stay in what he saw as a 'slum' area of the capital, however, Speke could not conceal his wonder at the lay-out of town. He described how he walked

> up the broad high road into a cleared square, which divides Mutesa's domain on the south from his Kamraviona's, or commander-in-chief, on the north, and then turned into the court. The palace or entrance quite surprised me by its extraordinary dimensions, and the neatness with which it was kept. The whole brow and sides of the hill on which we stood were covered with gigantic grass huts, thatched as neatly as so many heads dressed by a London barber, and fenced all round with the tall yellow reeds of the common Uganda tiger-grass; whilst within the

enclosure, the lines of huts were joined together, 'or partitioned off into courts, with walls of the same grass....[15]

The European had walked from an outlying area of the capital to the core of the *Kibuga*, a journey which reflected much of the stratification of Ganda society itself: from the Arabs' quarters past the huts of junior chiefs and of the *Kabaka*'s favoured wives, to the 'ante-reception court' where musicians played and sang for the pleasure of the *Kabaka*, should the latter choose to appear.[16] The coastal merchants were not always treated with the kind of respect they desired. They told Speke that 'from fear they had always complied with the manners of the court', while the European complained that 'my hut was a mile from the palace, in an unhealthy place, where he kept his Arab visitors'.[17] Speke eventually managed to bribe a leading chief to provide accommodation in a more suitable part of the capital, which he described, predictably, as the 'West End'.

By the end of the 1860s, Mutesa's *Kibuga* had returned to Nabulagala, but by the time the Egyptian envoy Chaille-Long arrived in 1874, the capital had spread south to include Rubaga hill, where the *Kabaka*'s enclosure was then located.[18] Again, it is unlikely that the old sites of royal enclosures were ever completely abandoned: they became, rather, part of the 'greater' *Kibuga*, which by the mid-1870s included much of present-day Kampala, such as the large hilly area between Nabulagala-Kasubi and Rubaga in the west, and Mulago, Banda and Nakawa in the north and east. Since the mid-1860s, the capital had become even more closely linked to the lake with the creation of a port and 'royal retreat' at Munyonyo.[19] Munyonyo quickly became one of the most important lake ports handling long-distance trade; it was also the site of a royal enclosure which Mutesa used to observe Ramadan or as a base to indulge in one of his favourite hobbies, the racing of canoes. The links between the lake shore and the urban hinterland were critical, both for the geographical growth of the capital and the increase in population. Both a cause and an effect of this expansion was the marked increase in cultivation in the environs of the capital. According to Roscoe, the land between the royal enclosure at Rubaga and the lake shore was given over to the royal women who cultivated plantains for the court's consumption. But the food produced for the court was also intended for wider consumption, as food distribution was one of the tenets of royal authority in the capital.[20]

The capital visited by Stanley in 1875 was a thriving regional centre: it attracted foreign diplomatic missions from as far away as Unyamwezi. Stanley observed, for example, 'the turbulent Mankorongo, king of Usui, and Mirambo, that terrible phantom who disturbs men's minds in Unyamwezi, through their embassies kneeling and tendering their tribute to [Mutesa]'.[21] The capital, moreover, was a place 'into which moneyed strangers and soldiers from Cairo and Zanzibar flocked for the sake of its supreme head'.[22] The attraction of the royal capital to foreign visitors itself led to further urbanisation. Traders, missionaries and travellers visiting Buganda rarely had sufficient land to grow enough crops to feed themselves or their large entourages of porters and guards. They relied in part on the exchange of gifts with the *Kabaka*, but increasingly they were able to buy food with the trade goods – for example, cowries and cloth – which they brought with them. The growing monetarization of commerce and the escalating demand for imported goods favoured the expansion of the capital as a market for local foodstuffs. Not surprisingly, therefore, missionary sources report that several markets opened in the capital during this period.[23]

The Church Missionary Society (CMS) missionaries claimed the credit for suggesting these measures to Mutesa. However debatable this point may be, there is little doubt that both the missionaries and the coastal traders had begun to influence the form of the capital. Permanent building materials were introduced; the form of the buildings themselves was altered, for example in the introduction of storeys; and the utilization of physical space within the capital was transformed with the development of larger markets. Yet such influence went beyond the merely physical. The growing importance of traders and, in particular, of European missionaries altered the ideology behind physicality; the location of missions in certain areas of the capital, especially in relation to the royal enclosure, challenged existing notions of urban hierarchy. This process had particular significance in the royal capital of Buganda where the organization of streets and residences was designed to reflect the political order of the kingdom at large. During the 1890s, therefore, the new religions influenced the symbolic structure of the town, and it is to this that we now turn our attention.

From the Kabaka's City to a Religious Capital

In 1890, Mwanga allowed his capital to become the major Christian centre of the region, but the royal exclusivity of the capital had been maintained prior to this date. It was the centre of the kingdom and the focal point of the royal cult, and as such was an expression of the *Kabaka's* power and glory: all roads in the kingdom pointed toward the capital, all avenues within the capital toward the palace. From the top of the hill, the royal enclosure or *lubiri* dominated the chiefs' enclosures; the *Kabaka's* buildings were larger, taller and more numerous. Indeed the only buildings which could compete with those of the *Kabaka* were the shrines of his ancestors. They were often located on the site of a former *Kibuga* which, as we have seen, increasingly after the 1840s formed the outlying suburbs of the expanding capital. The shrines of Mwanga's father and grandfather were at Kasubi and Wamala respectively, while none of the others were more than 15 miles to the west of Kampala. Many of the deceased *Kabaka's* wives or their heirs were settled at the tombs to serve their 'husband', and a number of faithful chiefs might eventually retire close to their late *Kabaka*. They all carried out ritual functions at the royal shrines. The size of the permanent populations at the shrines of Suna and Mutesa may have been quite extensive, and they added, by their vicinity to the *Kibuga*, to the urban character of the capital.

The religious shrines of minor divinities and the smaller shrines of major divinities were scattered throughout the kingdom, a pattern that was repeated in the capital. Namirembe, for example, where the Anglican mission was to be built, seems to have been the shrine of the spirit (*musambwa*) of a water well, located below the hill. But the major religious temples were invariably located away from the capital.[24] They were built along the seventeenth-century borders guarding the kingdom from foreign enemies. The majority of gods were based on the Sesse islands and watched over Lake Victoria. The temple of Kibuka, the chief god of war, protected the western border, and those of Kawumpuli and Nende watched over the northern and eastern frontiers respectively.[25] Ganda notions of their deities were replete with references to royal ideology. The most important temples were major constructions; the buildings and their settings were similar to those of the royal tombs, mostly in the form of enormous reed buildings located on hill-tops.[26]

Important gods were not, however, absent from the capital. The major deities had small shrines built opposite the main gate of the royal enclosure. They housed the head priests during their occasional visits to the capital.[27] These small, temporary structures were not meant for the general religious practices of the Ganda; rather, they were meant to serve and protect the *Kabaka*. The political and ideological hierarchy was clear. These religious buildings had nothing in common with royal architecture. The relationship between the *Kabaka* and the gods, however, was that of peers exchanging embassies.[28]

After around 1850, Muslim traders and Christian missionaries perpetuated this tradition through their ambiguous diplomatic status.

In the 1890s, *Kabaka* Mwanga's capital was to become the religious capital of the Christian ruling elite, who had gained power after defeating the Muslims during the religious wars of 1888–90. They restored Mwanga to the throne in 1890 but only as a figurehead. The Protestant and Catholic chiefs kept power firmly in their own hands.

The first weakening of the royal monopoly of the capital was initiated by Mutesa himself. He attempted to use Christianity and Islam to enhance his own religious authority and control. He tried during the 1870s to establish himself as the head of the new religious movements. He had mosques built at his enclosures, one of which, as we have noted, was at Munyonyo; in 1875 Mutesa had attempted to have one built with bricks. These buildings were used for the teaching of either Islam or Christianity, depending on which was in favour at any given time. They lost their importance once Mwanga realized that he could not control the new religions in the way that his father had hoped.[29] The missionary influence grew considerably after 1889. Ganda royal symbolism was used by the Christian churches: cathedrals were built on hill-tops which were formerly the exclusive territory of the *Kabakas*, living or dead, for example at Rubaga and Namirembe in 1891, and Nsambya in 1895.[30]

The religious domination was not only geographical, but also monumental. Between 1877 and 1888, the French and British missionaries had attempted with partial success to build their mission stations according to European standards. Mutesa and then Mwanga had maintained close control over these constructions, but after 1890 the missionaries were freed of all royal limitations. They endeavoured to erect great reed or brick cathedrals: never before in Buganda had such buildings been constructed, either in terms of size or labour.[31] St Mary of Rubaga is an enlightening example. The Roman Catholics settled deliberately on the site of one of Mutesa's most famous enclosures. Rubaga being a much higher hill, it dominates the nearby *lubiri* on Mengo. The cathedral was built where the main audience hall had once stood, in the former political heart of the kingdom. The missionaries were evidently aware of the political, as well as the religious, symbolism of their choice:

> Rubaga is far from being a peaceful desert. For the catechism classes altogether 3,000 people visit us on normal days, and 7 to 8,000 people on Sundays. Catechism is taught on the top of the plateau and our little hill looks over Mengo where the king is. Our poor king, who more than ever refuses to follow the movement, is terrorised when he hears or sees this crowd moving along. We are building a church with 420 columns on the plateau, exactly where the former great Baraza of Mutesa used to stand. We have established its columns. The Protestants, seeing us building there, also want to build their temple on a height with a view on Mengo. A third hill, Kampala, is occupied by the fort belonging to the English of the company. Our poor king, though surrounded on all sides, refuses to surrender.[32]

Because the royal cult was associated with pagan worship, the missionaries felt compelled to cleanse the hill with fire before using it.[33] But Ganda royal culture was extremely powerful. In August 1894, to enhance the prestige of the church, two drums of Kintu (traditionally the first *Kabaka* of Buganda and a major focus of the royal cult) were confiscated from his shrine at Magonga, west of Kampala.[34] They were kept as the cathedral's drums. Turning away from the supernatural aura of these drums, the Catholics used them as power symbols and as bells. These actions represented an attempt to place the church above the *Kabaka* and met with some success.

Prestige was placed ahead of comfort. The hill-top was not an obvious choice for the missionaries' houses: water had to be fetched from a distance half an hour away.

Travelling up and down the hill meant additional fatigue for the missionaries already severely tested by the climate.[35] But the symbolic meaning of the new construction was very well understood by the Ganda. Father Brard claimed that the Christian religious war erupted in 1892 because of the Cathedral: the Ganda believed that if the mission station was completed, the Catholics would have symbolically and practically taken over Buganda.[36] Ironically, the royal position of Rubaga was enhanced by the defeat of the Catholics in the 1892 war.

Following the British and Protestant victory, the capital was reorganized. Before 1892 the capital had represented the kingdom of Buganda in miniature. The town house of a chief was ascribed to him according to the conjunction of a number of politically symbolic factors. He should be settled on the road to his province, and his importance and role should be reflected by his proximity to the palace:

> The capital spreads over several hills, Mengo, Kampala, Namirembe and Rubaga being the main ones. The capital constitutes a separate unit of the kingdom under the king's close control. The capital does not belong to any province in particular, but it belongs to all of them collectively, because each provincial chief, compelled by his duties to spend every year most of his time close to the king, owns in the capital a large estate divided in as many plots as he has sub-chiefs. These concessions of land, a privilege of all the important people of the kingdom, are called in the local language bibanja. All the bibanja together form the capital of Uganda. Therefore the top of Mengo is occupied by the king: on the top of Kampala stands the Fort, residence of the representative of England, but on the sides of these two hills are built numerous huts each one surrounded by a small banana plantation. These are the bibanja of the Kyagwe chiefs [...] The summit of Rubaga is occupied by the White Fathers' mission, but both sides of the hill are covered by the bibanja of the chiefs of Buddu, Mawokota [Roman Catholic counties] and Singo. On the top of Namirembe rises the Protestant mission, but the sides of the mountain are reserved for the bibanja of the chiefs of Bulemezi, Kitunzi and Kyaddondo.[37]

The changes in the setting of the capital were much slower than the change in internal political power among the chiefs. The enclosure of the *Pokino*, the chief of Buddu county, was distant from the royal palace. This position corresponded to the geographical distance of Buddu from the capital.[38] But Buddu was also the wealthiest province of Buganda. The *Pokino* was the most powerful county chief. His province was the most recent addition to the kingdom, being conquered in the late eighteenth century. Being a 'latecomer', the *Pokino* was settled on the periphery of the capital. Despite his actual power, his enclosure was behind those of chiefs of older, but smaller, counties. The capital thus came to express the new balance of power, but with some features of the older system remaining in place.

The weakening grip of tradition in the 1890s enabled some corrections to be made in the urban expression of political authority. The 1892 war did not change the logic of the arrangement of the capital: it only introduced a new religious factor. Catholics, Muslims and Protestants were separated in distinct neighbourhoods.[39] The Catholics were grouped at the foot of the Rubaga's mission.[40] Captain Lugard of the Imperial British East Africa Company settled the Muslims around Natete and Kampala fort.[41] The Protestants generally remained in the traditional setting. The new political balance of Buganda could be seen by all. The Protestants dominated and controlled the immediate vicinity of the royal palace, while the Catholics and Muslims were tolerated close to their respective protectors, the French White Fathers and the British administration.

The new locations belonging to the Catholic chiefs, for example, represented a clear message to the Ganda. Irrespective of the former importance of their titles, the Catholics were second to the Protestants. Stanislas Mugwanya, the head of the Catholic party, remained the second-ranking chief in the kingdom after, as before, 1892.[42] But from one of the closest enclosures to the royal compound on Mengo hill, he was sent to the neighbouring hill of Rubaga.[43]

Conclusion

The nineteenth-century capital of Buganda was unique in the East African interior, given its size, population, and political and commercial significance. It is likely that it already covered a considerable extent, and was expanding, before the arrival of the first coastal merchants; Suna's capital was, after all, important enough to draw long-distance traders in the first place. But there is little doubt that its exposure to commercial and religious forces for change radically transformed the capital into a complex and cosmopolitan urban centre which was also, in the decades preceding the establishment of colonial rule, an arena of tension and conflict. Ultimately, the struggles between old and new which were played out at the capital, and which represented the battle for the economic and political soul of the country, were reflected in the kingdom at large; in the urban environment, however, the conflict was characterized by an intensity unparalleled elsewhere in Buganda or indeed, arguably, in the lacustrine region.

The intensity of the struggle and the pace of change stemmed from the very nature of Ganda political organization. The pre-colonial capital represented the delicate and highly-structured order of Ganda political society: the hierarchy of *Kabaka*, *bakungu* and *bakopi* was carefully reproduced in the highways and suburbs, in the approach to the royal palace and on the hills surrounding the *Kabaka*'s enclosure. Yet, like the political structure itself, it proved flexible and prone to often violent transformation. The importance, indeed sanctity, of the kingship itself meant that wherever the *Kabaka* was established would become the metaphysical heart of the kingdom. Given the military and economic authority welded by the Ganda during much of the nineteenth century, this in turn made the capital a 'supranational' centre which served as a beacon to the Zanzibari merchants penetrating ever further from the coast, and to the Christian missionaries keen to gain a foothold in the verdant lake region. Ganda rulers were not the passive recipients of this fascination, but actively encouraged it as a means to strenthening themselves and, consequently, the kingdom as a whole.

During the half century before colonial rule, however, the fragility of the kingship, as reflected in the carefully ordered urban environment, was exposed: the kingship which attracted its first truly international visitors in the 1840s could not survive the influences which the latter brought to bear without changing itself radically, or being changed by others. These visitors, their successors and their indigenous adherents fulfilled this role and, in so doing, wrested authority away from the *Kabaka* in the very heart of his realm. The story of urban transformation in this period reflects this clearly. The reconstruction of roads and sweeping highways; the reordering of architectural deference and hierarchy; the accommodation of strangers in burgeoning suburbs; and, perhaps most importantly of all, the battle for the urban symbols so essential to the maintenance of royal potency: all these tell the story of Ganda adaptation to rapid change. The urban history of Buganda, therefore, is to some degree a metaphor for the kingdom as a whole.

Notes

1 See also Kiwanuka's comments in Apolo Kagwa [trans. and ed. M. S. M. Kiwanuka], *The Kings of Buganda* (Nairobi, 1971), pp. 189–90.

2 *Ibid.*, p. 115.

3 *Ibid.*, pp. 119–20.

4 *Ibid.*, p. 120. Namirembe lies directly to the south of Kasubi.

5 J. H. Speke, *Journal of the Discovery of the Source of the Nile* (Edinburgh and London, 1863), p. 238. *Kibuga* is taken in this essay to refer to the royal enclosure, rather than the capital in its entirety, which seems prudent with regard to the pre-colonial urban environment. Yet Gutkind is surely right to suggest that 'there are many interpretations of this word which has undoubtedly meant different things to different categories of people at different times': P. C. W. Gutkind, *The Royal Capital of Buganda: a Study of Internal Conflict and External Ambiguity* (The Haugue; 1963), p. 9.

6 Speke, *Journal*, p. 281.

7 Richard F. Burton, *The Lake Regions of Central Africa* (London, 1860), ii, p. 188.

8 *Ibid.*, p. 194.

9 See also Gutkind, *Royal Capital of Buganda*, p. 15. Wrigley points out that the capital would have been the focus of a 'floating population of corvee labourers and of provincial chiefs': C. C. Wrigley, *Kingship and State: the Buganda Dynasty* (Cambridge, 1969), p. 59. These would have periodically swelled the overall population, while not residing permanently at the capital. Also J. Roscoe, *The Baganda: an Account of their Native Customs and Beliefs* (London, 1911), pp. 200–1.

10 J. Roscoe, *Twenty-five Years in East Africa* (London, 1921), p. 246.

11 Burton, *Lake Regions*, ii, pp. 193–4.

12 Kagwa, *Kings*, pp. 117–8.

13 Speke, *Journal*, pp. 283–4.

14 See J. H. Speke, *What Led to the Discovery of the Source of the Nile* (London, 1864), p. 259.

15 Speke, *Journal*, p. 287.

16 *Ibid.*, p. 288.

17 *Ibid.*, pp. 288, 303. The 'Arab quarter' later moved to Natete, to the west of present-day Kampala.

18 Kagwa, *Kings*, pp. 159, 164.

19 *Ibid.*, p. 158.

20 Roscoe, *Twenty-five Years*, p. 89.

21 Stanley, *Dark Continent*, Vol. 1, p. 193.

22 *Ibid.*, p. 194.

23 White Fathers: Rubaga Diary 2, 31 January 1882, 2 February 1882 and 26 February 1882; Church Missionary Society, G3 A6/0 1882/56, O'Flaherty to Wigram, 15 March 1882.

24 K. Moon, *St Paul's Cathedral, Namirembe: a History and Guide* (Richmond, 1994), p. 4.

25 Benjamin Ray, *Myth, Ritual and Kingship in Buganda* (New York, 1991), pp. 132, 152–3.

26 Roscoe, *The Baganda*, pp. 273, 276–7

27 Ray, *Myth, Ritual and Kingship*, p. 136.

28 Michael Kenny, 'Mutesa's crime: hubris and the control of African kings', *Comparative Studies in Society and History*, 30 (1988), pp. 604–5.

29 A. Oded, *Islam in Uganda* (New York, 1974), pp. 69–70.

30 Margery Perham (ed.), *The Diaries of Lord Lugard* (London, 1959) Vol. 2, pp. 27–8.

31 Moon, *St Paul's Cathedral*.

32 White Fathers: C13/495-525, Hirth to a colleague, 1 January 1892.

33 'Rubaga is a beautiful hill on which the capital of the whole of Uganda used to stand; fire overcame all the horrors this hill had witnessed for so many years. I hope the cult of Mary will soon replace Satan's': White Fathers: Casier 303, Hirth to his parents, 15 March 1891.

34 White Fathers: P199/2, Lefebvre, 'Kintu and Magonga', pp. 13, 48.

35 White Fathers: C12/533 Denoit to Livinhac, 5 December 1890.

36 'The station's transfer to the top of the hill of Rubaga meant to [the Ganda] the taking over of Buganda by Catholicism': White Fathers: C14/441 Brard to Hirth, 30 May 1892.

37 White Fathers: 84-3-b Streicher to Ledochowski, 10 October 1897. Also Roscoe, *Twenty-Five Years*, pp. 192–3.

38 Walker's map from 'Notes', *Church Missionary Society Intelligencer*, March 1893, p. 197.

39 White Fathers: 81120–81124, Hirth to Livinhac, 28 January 1894.

40 T. Ternan, *Some Experiences of an Old Bromsgrovian* (Birmingham; 1930), p. 160.

41 J.R. Macdonald, *Soldiering and Surveying in British East Africa* (London; 1897), p. 214; R. P. Ashe, *Chronicles of Uganda* (London, 1894), p. 327; White Fathers: 82–216, Guillermain to Livinhac, 9 July 1892.

42 Stanislas's title changed, but his rank did not. Formerly the *Kimbugwe*, the second most important title in the kingdom, a new function was created for him: that of Catholic *Katikiro*. In other words, the position of *Katikiro* was divided in two. Stanislas remained the second ranking chief.

43 Walker's map from 'Notes', *Church Missionary Society Intelligencer,* March 1893, 197. Compare this with map PT/86/U/IV/32/13 (Kibuga), 1908; map PT/86/U/IV/32/14 (Kibuga), 190?; and map PT/86/U/IV/42/1 (Kibuga) 1909.

PART THREE
Urban Economies

7
'A Town of Strangers' or 'A Model Modern East African Town'?
Arusha & the Arusha

THOMAS SPEAR

Initially established in the early nineteenth century by Arusha farmers as a market for trading agricultural produce with pastoral Maasai and, later, with trade caravans proceeding up the Pangani River to western Kenya and Tanzania, Arusha subsequently became the site of a German fort, the British administrative headquarters for northern Tanzania, a commercial centre for white farmers settled around Mount Meru, a tourist centre, and the administrative headquarters of the East African Community during the course of the twentieth. As the town changed, however, it became increasingly divorced from its local origins as the Arusha market and Arusha farmers who continued to cultivate within the town's borders were slowly driven out and few Arusha took advantage of expanding economic opportunities in the town's market, shops, industries or government service. Arusha became, instead, 'a town of strangers' – European colonial officers, shopkeepers, hoteliers and settlers; Asian merchants; and Chaga, Pare, Somali and Swahili traders and workers – alienated from its rural hinterland.[1]

While Arusha continued to live in Arusha town throughout much of the colonial period, then, they rarely became people of the town. They remained within the town's precincts as farmers who claimed prescriptive rights to their land and homesteads scattered through the upper portions of town, not as workers or traders living in the African quarter in the lower end of town, and bitterly contested the changes taking place.

This presents us with a paradox. Given Arusha's commercial origins and the increasing appeal of colonial towns elsewhere in East Africa, one might have expected Arusha to exploit the commercial opportunities that a growing town presented.[2] That they did not forces us to probe deeper into the social imagination to explore the different visions that Arusha and Europeans entertained about urban living, about land use, and about the structuring of social space.

Arusha saw the area of town as their patrimony, theirs by virtue of the labour they and their ancestors expended in clearing it, and their homesteads sprawled over its landscape. The Germans, by contrast, saw Arusha as a garrison town from which to dominate the surrounding countryside. Their primary contribution to its development was the *boma*, or fort, that dominated the emerging town physically and politically. The British then sought to develop Arusha as a centre for district and regional administration, a commercial centre for European settlers and 'a model modern East African town'.

Arusha became a classic colonial town, with the main street sloping symbolically downhill from the *boma*, past expansive European residences on one side and more crowded Asian shops on the other, and thence through an uninhabited green belt to the African 'bazaar' and industrial zone in its swampy lowlands. Just as the imposing German *boma* looming over the plains sought to impose German political and moral order over the 'disorderly' African landscape, so the British colonial town, with its hierarchically segregated residential, commercial, and African areas, was a manifestation of British attempts to dominate Africans politically, economically, and culturally.

European attempts to regulate land use and impose their own concepts of space, however, conflicted with Arusha attempts to preserve their own uses of land and space, and the two periodically engaged in protracted struggles over the land that each needed to realize its particular social and moral vision. The struggle over land, then, was a moral as well as a political and economic struggle over the kinds of social spaces in which people would live their lives.[3]

Colonial Visions

While the literature on African urbanization is extensive, it has focused almost exclusively on primate cities and urban social processes 'rather than on smaller towns or urban history.[4] Much of the literature on small towns concerns their putative role in economic development[5] or the politicization of ethnicity in towns.[6] Few deal specifically with urban-rural interaction,[7] the history of town development,[8] or the struggles to control and socialize the new spaces towns created.[9]

Most colonial towns in Africa generally, and in East Africa in particular, were sited with little regard for economic factors. They were not located at pre-existing political centres, at commercial centres or along established trade routes, or near exploitable natural resources. Rather, they were primarily political creations, established initially as military and administrative centres to maintain political dominance over the surrounding countryside. With a military garrison or district headquarters at their centre, and often a mission alongside, they resembled Sjoberg's model of pre-industrial cities organized around centres of political and ritual power; and like them, they were inherently 'crucibles of power' for projecting imperial dominance, social control and cultural hegemony over their colonized hinterlands.[10]

Colonial towns were also 'new towns', carefully planned in accord with prevailing colonial ideologies. The practice of residential segregation had long been established in India as a means of colonial social control in which urban topography, like that of pre-industrial cities, expressed imperial dominance. European headquarters usually overlooked and physically dominated 'native' settlements, while Europeans preferred to live in picturesque hillside locations with 'a breeze and a view' that dominated those below them, socially and culturally. The perceived need for such segregation flowed easily from racist assumptions concerning the importance of preserving racial purity, of affirming European cultural identity among the small displaced colonial population, and of protecting Europeans from the noise, clutter and pestilence of local settlements.[11]

Colonial town planning was further marked by European iconographies of status and modernist visions of the 'garden city'.[12] Government offices were located at the central and often highest point in town along broad, tree-lined streets and surrounded by exuberant tropical gardens. Nearby were the expansive European suburbs, modelled on those of the landed gentry at home, with individual plots carefully stratified by rank and social status in official Warrants of Precedence. At a safe distance was the medium-density commercial district consisting of combination shops and houses inhabited largely by Asians, Lebanese, or Greek traders, while below the broad green belt (often a park or golf course) protecting Europeans from disease, noise, and congestion lay the crowded 'native quarter', or 'medina'.[13]

European thinking about the design of colonial towns was encapsulated best, perhaps, in contemporary medical theories that explained tropical diseases in social and environ-, mental terms and seemed to provide a firm 'scientific' basis for social policy. Colonial doctors argued that tropical diseases brought on by foul air ('miasma'), by 'emanation' from the soil, or by the odour of decomposing vegetation were then transmitted from immune Africans to vulnerable Europeans by mosquitos and other vectors. They thus concluded that European and African housing should be separated physically from one another by a broad *cordon sanitaire* to inhibit the spread of diseases from Africans to Europeans. Similarly, European housing should be sited uphill and upwind of African housing to be well ventilated and dispel deadly contagion, and individual houses should be built off the ground to prevent 'emanation' of diseases from the soil. While such misguided attempts to control disease were supplanted by quinine, mosquito control and public sanitation by the early 1920s, the image of endemic African pestilence remained a powerful justification for continued residential segregation throughout the colonial period.[14]

The tripartite spatial hierarchy of colonial towns thus accurately mapped colonial social structure at the same time as it reflected colonial attempts to establish hegemony over colonized peoples through physical and symbolic control over the design and use of urban social space. But such attempts to redefine space were sharply contested by Africans who had long occupied the spaces Europeans sought to colonize and who had their own ideas about how space should be organized. Asserting prescriptive claims to prior settlement, many Africans continued to farm, herd cattle and live within urban boundaries in defiance of European social distinctions or rules of hygiene. At the same time, however, other Africans crowded into the new towns and asserted their own claims to the new spaces they provided.

Africans' concepts of space fundamentally challenged those of Europeans and undermined colonial attempts to impose order on 'unruly' African social and physical landscapes. Free-flowing African homesteads sprawled over the landscape, anchored by ancestral ritual sites, periodic markets, or the homes of powerful patrons, while individual Africans organized their residential spaces around family compounds surrounded by fields, cattle, work places and the compounds of close kin. Within each compound, space was segregated by gender, age and function into separate quarters and work places for men, women and children. African socio-spatial organization thus contrasted dramatically with the meticulously squared forms of colonial streets and architecture, the functional division of the colonial town between work and residence, and the allocation of residential space by race and class.[15]

Thus, if we wish to understand the development of colonial towns, we must first explore the different, and often diametrically opposed, ways in which Europeans and Africans sought to socialize the physical landscape. Social and cultural differences between them were manifested in the different built environments that they sought to impose on the landscape to give meaning and order to their lives. The following is thus not a history of the town, *per se*,[16] but an attempt to understand the ceaseless struggle over land that characterized its development, constrained its growth, and influenced the forms that urban society would take as different peoples sought to implant their own particular social visions on the lower slopes of Mount Meru.

Homesteads and Markets: Arusha in the Nineteenth Century

The present site of Arusha town was first settled in the 1830s by Arusha Maasai from Arusha Chini (Lower Arusha) south of Mount Kilimanjaro. Arusha Chini was one of a number of small agro-pastoral communities, such as Taveta, Kahe, Nguruman and Chamus, established on the edges of the plains by people displaced during the pastoral wars of the early nineteenth century. Such oasis communities played a vital mediating role in the region, providing agricultural foodstuffs, ironwork, honey and refuge to pastoralists in times of drought, famine or loss of cattle.[17]

During the 1830s some Arusha left Arusha Chini to establish a new settlement at Arusha Juu (Upper Arusha) at the base of Mount Meru.[18] Some Arusha say they were recruited by Supeet, the Maasai loibon settled nearby at Ngosua, to provide foodstuffs and labour for pastoral Kisongo Maasai, but the new location also provided an abundance of fertile well-watered land on the adjacent slopes of the mountain. Settling initially at Olasiti on the Burka River west of the modern town centre, Arusha also established a market at Sanguwezi on the Engare Narok River to the west, where they traded grains, honey, beer and tobacco with Kisongo in exchangè for livestock, milk, meat and skins. Arusha capitalized on their position astride the gradient linking pastoralism on the plains with productive mountain agriculture, and they continued to maintain interdependent social and economic relations with pastoral Kisongo through joint trade, intermarriage, age-sets and raids.[19]

New customers for Arusha foodstuffs began to arrive in the 1860s with the extension of the Pangani Valley trade route to Old Moshi, Arusha Juu and thence to western Kenya. Located near the edge of the Rift Valley, Arusha Juu was the last place caravans heading west could obtain supplies for the two to four week trek across the arid Maasai Steppe, and Arusha quickly became known for being able to provision caravans of up to 2,000 people for the long journey. The ability to supply such large quantities of food dependably gives some indication of the productivity of Arusha agriculture. Arusha raised bananas, maize, beans, sorghum, cassava, sugar cane, sweet potatoes, yams, tobacco, cattle and small stock on the fertile, well-watered and irrigable fields and pastures surrounding their homesteads on the edge of the plains.[20]

Arusha prospered and their settlements soon covered Burka, the site of the future town, and the surrounding areas. Each homestead, or engisaka, was ordered in Maasai fashion, with individual beehive-shaped houses arrayed around a central cattle kraal, the eldest male at the head and his wives and their children residing in alternating order along the sides. Each engisaka thus embraced the people living within it in flowing forms that knitted them into a social and economic unit.

Surrounding each homestead were permanent groves of bananas, annual fields of maize, beans and other crops, and pastures for cattle. Each wife was given her own fields so that, as a man and his sons married, their fields expanded outwards until they reached those of their neighbours, at which point younger sons left to clear and settle their own homesteads further up the mountain. Control over land was vested in the men who cleared and settled it, allocated its use to their wives, and ultimately passed control of it to their descendants, while the availability of land further up the mountain meant that all were guaranteed sufficient land to establish their own homesteads. Those who cleared the land had an inalienable right to its use, while everyone had a moral right to sufficient land to establish his own engisaka. Rights to engisaka thus lay at the very centre of Arusha economic, social, and moral well-being.[21]

New land was usually cleared and settled by age-mates after they retired from being warriors, married, and settled down to farm. Neighbourhoods were thus composed of close friends and allies, men who had forged strong bonds with one another during their initiation and service, and local leaders were drawn from the ranks of the leading age-set spokesmen (*laigwenak*).

While the expanding Arusha population thus became dispersed over the slopes of the mountain, people maintained close links with neighbours, age-mates, and kin. The original settlement at Burka remained densely populated; Olasiti became an important ritual centre where uninitiated youth from throughout Arusha gathered during their initiation; and the market at Sanguwezi remained an important regional market where Arusha, pastoral Maasai and passing caravans met to trade.[22] Arusha Juu was not yet a town, but it was an important regional centre; it already bore a number of urban features, features that would be profoundly altered following the German conquest in 1896–97.

Garrison Town: 1900–20

Arusha were conquered by the Germans after they killed the first two missionaries to attempt to settle on Mount Meru in 1896, and succeeding German punitive expeditions swiftly destroyed their crops, burned their food stores and confiscated their livestock.[23] A permanent German presence was not established in Arusha until 1900, however, when the Germans forced Arusha to build a fortified *boma* in the middle of densely populated Burka and garrisoned troops there.

The *boma* was a solid statement, meant to impress German political and moral order on the surrounding countryside. Set on a rise overlooking the plains, the fortress-like building dominated the surrounding landscape. One approached along 'a fine wide road … carefully marked off in kilometres', John Boyes noted on a visit in 1903:

> The road led to a place called Arusha, and as we approached it we came to our astonishment in sight of a truly marvellous building, erected in European style and surrounded by a moat…. The *boma* was a one-storey building of stone and mortar, with a huge tower in the centre, and the whole glistened bright in the sunlight, like an Aladdin's Palace transported from some fairy-land and dropped down in the heart of the tropics. Emblazoned on the front of the tower were the Royal Arms of Germany, which could be seen nearly a mile off…. The station was walled off and, being furnished with a Maxim and a machine gun, made a formidable stronghold.[24]

One entered the *boma* through a portal flanked by stone buildings on either side, emerging into a large walled courtyard, at the rear of which lay the Swahili-style houses of the African troops. Inside the main structure, Boyes continued:

> Water from neighbouring gullies was laid on throughout the building, and a plentiful supply was available for all purposes…. The inside of the station was paved with stone; the living rooms were fitted with electric bells; and Herr Küster said he hoped to install electric light at an early date…. Attached to the fort was a splendid kitchen garden in which grew almost every kind of European vegetable, and next to that a coffee plantation.[25]

Some thirty Indian, Greek, Arab and Swahili shops were arrayed either side of a wide path leading down from the fort. They sold cloth, trinkets, soap, enamelled plates and bowls, beads and copper wire; and one even had a sewing machine on its porch to produce jackets and trousers for the German soldiers and more progressive natives.[26] Boyes enthused that he had discovered 'a real oasis in the wilderness':

> Everything about Arusha was equally surprising, the streets being well laid out with fine side-walks, separated from the road by a stream of clear water flowing down a cemented gully-way…. The township was spotlessly clean and we saw Natives with small baskets picking up any

litter lying about, as though the place were the Tiergarten of Berlin and not the wild interior of the Dark Continent.[27]

While Boyes was deeply impressed with the Germans' ability to impose discipline on the 'wild interior of the Dark Continent', Arusha gained different impressions. The *boma* was set in the midst of the 'lush plantations of the Waarusha', many of whom had been forcibly displaced from ancestral *engisaka* and forced to dig lime or carry stones for its construction. Arusha referred to the German officer as Bwana Fisi, Mr Hyena; later, they would recall the senseless and amoral cruelty of the Germans in taking their land for Afrikaner and German settlers, chaining people together and whipping them like slaves, and forcing people to climb trees that the Germans then ordered cut down, killing the people in them.[28]

Thus alienated from the Germans, Arusha maintained their farms interspersed through the German settlement, while other people – coastal Swahili, Somali, and other Muslims – entered the emerging town to trade and work. As the town increasingly became a 'place of strangers', Arusha continued to farm in its midst, trade with Maasai on the plains, and supply foodstuffs to the new settler farms springing up around the base of the mountain.[29] Arusha thus remained predominantly rural, participating little in urban life, as the Germans appointed local 'chiefs' to collect taxes and recruit labour, and Lutheran missions and schools were established on the mountain itself, some distance from the town.[30]

Administrators and Settlers: 1920–60

The British capture of Arusha from the Germans in 1916 was followed by a temporary lapse in colonial control as German officials fled, the British deported German missionaries and settlers, and local government came under a skeletal military administration. Slowly through the 1920s, however, the British began to reassert control. Civilian administration was implemented; American missionaries replaced the Germans; British and Greek settlers occupied the ex-German farms; and the town began to expand.

The town still consisted of little more than the *boma* in 1921, when a settler reported: 'It is a funny little place consisting of a fortified *Boma*, a good store run by Hubble Thompson and a few Bungalows'.[31] It began to grow, however, after the British shifted the regional headquarters from Moshi to Arusha to take advantage of Arusha's altitude, cool climate and desirable location, as Clement Gillman noted in 1924:

> Arusha, at an altitude of 1400 m, has the advantage over New Moshi that it is situated high up on the lower slopes of the mountain, right in the cultivated zone, just as Old Moshi was formerly placed on Kilimanjaro.... The little garden town is really wonderfully situated. Its founders have had the good taste not to make the outlay interfere with existing configuration of the ground, nor with vegetation, and the result is that European and native quarters alike lie as in a large natural park.[32]

Gillman's preference for natural vegetation and mixed settlement was hardly shared by his colleagues, however, who quickly developed a carefully ordered town plan, but the placement of the town in the midst of Arusha farms would continue to cause them endless problems in the future.

The expansion of the administration was followed by that of commercial interests linked to the district's settler community, and later, to the development of tourism and the East African Common Services Organization. The extension of the railroad from Moshi in 1928–9 precipitated a flurry of commercial activity. Sixteen European residential, twelve commercial, 114 bazaar, and 140 'native' plots were let in 1927 in anticipation of its completion, while two banks, a first-class hotel, several garages, new government offices, an airport, and a golf course all opened in 1928–9. The depression quickly intervened, however, precipitating numerous defaults on land rents and mortgages, causing a number of businesses to close, and leaving many buildings half-completed. The overall population was still less than 2,000 in 1940, and there were only three small flour mills, two banks, two hotels and some small shops in the European commercial district.[33]

Table 7.1 Population of Arusha Town[34]

	1938	1948	1957
European	180	435	878
Asian	500	1,8816	4,096
African	1,000	2,946	5,161
Arusha (%)	7%	6%	
Total	1,680	5,262	10,135

Urban growth resumed during the war, and a new flour mill, two cinemas, a power station, three hotels, a large meat packing plant, ten office blocks, 43 new European houses, some 60 shops, and two new clubs were built during the course of the 1940s. Available town plots were rapidly exhausted, and the overall population grew to over 5,000. Ten years later, on the eve of independence, population surged past 10,000 on the heels of the expanding tourist trade and the growth of the East African Community headquartered in Arusha.[35]

'A Model Modern East African Town'

The expansion of the town put increasing pressure on the small amount of land available as well as on British relations with Arusha. Every attempt to develop the town became a bitter struggle, as British and Arusha each sought to define social space and land use in their own terms.

The British laid out a new town plan in 1927 that capitalized on the town's rolling topography to superimpose colonial hierarchies and values on the African landscape. Rivers flowing off the mountain either side of the *boma* sharply divided the town into three sections. The upper section between the rivers was set aside for administrative offices flanking the *boma*, with a hospital sited to the west and the European residential district located across the Temi River to the east. The commercial district, reserved largely for Asian traders, flanked the main road below the *boma*, and it continued across the Nauururu River into the African market and housing area below. The King's African Rifles (KAR) lines, later redeveloped as the industrial area, lay far to the south.[36]

The European residential district east of the *boma* was carefully separated from the rest of town by the Temi floodplain. It was marked out into large acre plots arrayed along broad tree-lined streets interspersed with churches and sports clubs for the European population. Land rent averaged Shs240/- annually in 1927, twice that of other towns, and building regulations mandated that residents had to erect substantial single family houses worth at least Shs20,000/-, in order to retain their rights of occupancy, thus effectively restricting the area to members of the administration and wealthier Europeans.[37]

The commercial district, by contrast, was more closely laid out in the area between the rivers below the *boma*, and called for mixed shops and housing. Its upper reaches around the clock tower were easily accessible to the administrative offices and European residential area and were set aside for European shopkeepers, banks, and hoteliers, while its lower reaches extending across the Naururu River and into the African market were intended for Asian traders. In spite of smaller plot sizes, rentals averaged Shs740/-, but the requirements for building were much less onerous than in the European residential area.[38]

The African 'bazaar' was safely isolated from the other areas by being placed across the steep gorge of the Naururu River. It was laid out in small housing plots surrounding the market renting for Shs180/- and covered with densely packed rooming houses for single male workers designed to maximize the income from each plot.

The town plan thus carefully reflected colonial thinking in segregating European, Asian and African areas from each other and mandating different residential patterns and forms of development for each. The higher elevation and windward location of the European residential area was meant to protect Europeans from the spread of malaria and other diseases as well as to shield them from the noise and disorder of the bazaar. Colonial dominance, racial difference and social status were also manifested physically in the design of the different districts in order to assert Europeans' dominance over others while carefully preserving their own social identity and status.

The Politics of Space and Land Use

British planning rapidly collided with African realities, however, as Arusha living within the town's boundaries refused to conform to the new forms. The Germans had placed the *boma* in the midst of Arusha farms. And while they had legally proclaimed that the town's boundaries extended a mile and a half from the *boma*, encompassing some 4,520 acres, the town actually consisted of only 1,100 acres, at least three-quarters of which were effectively occupied by Arusha.[39] Thus the British found in 1930 that the north-east and south-east quadrants adjacent to the European residential area (Areas A and C) were both 'fully occupied by natives', as were substantial parts of the north-west quadrant (Area F) containing the African bazaar and housing. Only the immediate administrative and European housing areas, the commercial zone, and the African bazaar itself were free of Arusha farms.[40]

Thus little development was possible without displacing Arusha long settled within the town's precincts. The Germans had forcibly dispossessed resident Arusha whenever they needed to acquire land, paying only minimal compensation for buildings and crops, and the British pursued similar policies through the 1920s. A number of Arusha were evicted from the bazaar area in 1924–5 without compensation; the new town plan caused the administration to dispossess Arusha farming in the intended European residential and commercial areas in 1927; the 1928–9 railroad boom brought further evictions; and 331 acres were seized from Arusha in 1931 alone.[41]

Arusha opposition mounted as the dispossessions grew. Some Europeans applied for an unoccupied piece of land outside of town for a cricket ground in 1928, but no sooner had they started to clear it than an Arusha chief sent people to clear and build on the site, thus effectively laying claim to it. The Provincial Commissioner, G. F. Webster, fumed that the chief's action was 'unreasonable', but indicated 'how very suspicious and jealous the Waarusha are of their tribal lands'. Two years later a number of Arusha complained

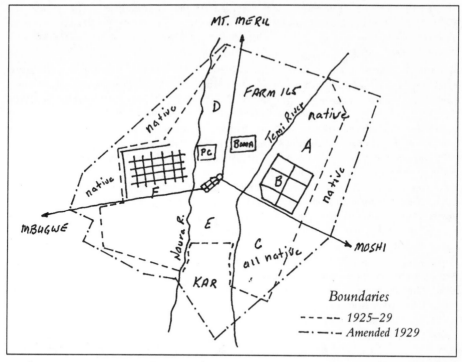

Figure 7.1 Arusha Town Plan (1930)

that they had not been compensated for land seized earlier by the Germans and, lacking German records to the contrary, the Administration was forced to pay.[42]

Arusha argued that they had prescriptive rights to land that their ancestors had cleared and settled long before the town was established. Moreover, land belonged to individual families by virtue of the labour they had invested in clearing it and planting permanent groves of bananas. Land was not simply an economic commodity that could be bought and sold, they asserted; it was *engisaka*, the focus of Arusha social and economic life. Arusha thus refused to consider moving unless they were offered full compensation for the land, their crops and buildings, and land of comparable quality was provided elsewhere.[43]

Since the Germans and British had already alienated most of the available land surrounding the mountain to settlers, little land of equal quality was available. The British were thus faced with a problem, a problem that became an intractable dilemma in 1930 when they formally recognized Arusha prescriptive claims and refused to permit future expropriations unless comparable land was made available elsewhere.[44] Their dilemma was then compounded when they also acknowledged that Arusha held individual tenure to land, thereby foreclosing the possibility of negotiating communal transfers with the chiefs and forcing the administration to negotiate individually with each family involved. Since few families were willing to move on British terms, future development of the town was effectively stymied.[45] The administration could only solve its dilemma by seeking to evict Arusha on other grounds, foremost among which was health and sanitation. Noting that Arusha continued to 'live in tribal style', Webster argued that their homes posed a threat to public health:

They plant a grove of bananas, and in the centre of this they build beehive shape huts of banana leaves. The huts are the home of the owner of the bananas and of his family. The same huts shelter the family cattle. Sanitation is unknown and at the present season of year conditions about the huts are filthy.[46]

Since bananas were also thought to harbour mosquitos carrying malaria, the township mandated that all standing crops within 440 yards of any residence had to be uprooted, effectively rendering Arusha farming within the town illegal, but it was unable to enforce the rules against prescriptive Arusha rights.[47]

Webster also argued strenuously against recognizing Arusha land rights. Arusha claims to freehold tenure were 'ridiculous' on the face of it, he asserted; by freely exchanging land with one another without payment, Arusha acknowledged that they held land in communal tenure. And if land was held communally, then Arusha had no grounds for objecting to exchanging it for comparable land elsewhere. Further, by refusing to recognize the town authority, the *Liwali*, Arusha forfeited any claim to urban land rights. Finally, Arusha voided their claims to land as necessary for their livelihood by loaning it to Somalis and other 'alien natives'. Arusha claims should only be recognized, he concluded, if 'the land is beneficially occupied by the claimant or his family or *essential for their livelihood*'. The Chief Secretary denied Webster's claims, however, and reaffirmed Arusha rights to individual tenure, emphasizing that land could only be expropriated legally through formal zoning controls over land use, payment of full compensation and provision of comparable land elsewhere.[48]

In seeking to dismiss urban land rights for Arusha, Webster also asserted the primacy of orderly administration. In the tortured logic of Indirect Rule, rural 'tribesmen' (or 'indigenous natives') came under the authority of chiefs and 'customary law' that mandated communal tenure, while urban 'townsmen' ('alien' or 'foreign natives') fell under the authority of the *Liwali* and township regulations that mandated individual tenure. Arusha living in town 'in tribal style' transgressed these categories and thus were in danger of being neither 'tribesmen' nor 'townsmen', potentially risking corruption by 'detribalized' 'foreign natives', threatening 'tribal discipline', and undermining chiefly authority.[49]

Failing in all these arguments, however, administrators were forced to search for comparable land to offer dispossessed Arusha.[50] Finding none, they fell back on simple coercion to evict Arusha from town and gain additional land outside the town's boundaries for expansion. After Arusha chiefs rejected a government offer in 1930 to exchange distant grazing land for agricultural land bordering the town, the District Officer cynically suggested that the government wait until impending drought and rinderpest forced Arusha to change their minds. Alternatively, he suggested exploiting Arusha class differences by urging wealthy Arusha cattle owners to buy land near the township, thereby dispossessing poorer farmers, and then exchanging it with the government for more expansive grazing land elsewhere.[51]

When the administration forcibly evicted 136 Arusha to acquire 331 acres the following year, it offered less than Shs120/- an acre in compensation, one twentieth the amount it had offered unsuccessfully to a neighbouring Greek farmer.[52] And when the government agreed to sell Arusha five farms on the plains in 1934 to relieve congestion on the mountain, it insisted that they relinquish a fifty-yard strip along the eastern border of the town in return. Individual Arusha evicted received less than Shs200/- each for their land, houses, and crops.[53]

The administration finally decided in 1934 to resolve the problem once and for all by expropriating all remaining Arusha, then occupying 436 acres. It first proposed excising land in the predominantly Arusha south-eastern and southern areas from the town and then expropriating the 142 families remaining at a total cost of over £2,046. Failing to gain Arusha acceptance, however, the administration then set about 'cleaning up the town': evicting 'alien natives' from Arusha land, clearly demarcating town boundaries to prevent further Arusha encroachments, and moving the Arusha livestock market south of town. [54]

The administration tried again in 1941 to evict Arusha from town, but found that the compensation required outstripped likely returns and that there was no land available to give in return.[55] Then, in 1944–5, it once more proposed to settle the problem for good. Again claiming that farming and keeping cattle in town were a danger to health and that the continued presence of 'tribal natives' in town was prejudicial to 'tribal discipline', the administration sought to acquire four small European farms on which to resettle them. When the settlers demanded prices the administration considered extortionate, however, it shifted to offering to pay Arusha much higher compensation (£12,000) in lieu of providing alternative land elsewhere. While the administration finally succeeded in pressuring Arusha to accept its terms, it was not without bitter protests accompanied by Arusha attacks on European farms outside the town.[56]

The difficult task of clearing the last Arusha farmers from town was no sooner completed, however, when township authorities petitioned to double the overall size of the town by acquiring an additional 1,100 acres from Arusha surrounding the town.[57] Some in the administration found the proposals 'embarrassing', given the bitter legacy of the recent evictions and the mounting political problems of land all across the mountain, but they considered it necessary none the less.[58]

The debate over expansion dragged on without resolution until 1949, when the administration suddenly seized 1,800 acres and 120 homes from 500 rural Arusha living north of town to build a new road from Moshi through Arusha to Namanga. The same year, it also expropriated 120 acres for a meat packing plant east of town. Arusha vehemently protested the evictions, sabotaged survey work, and refused to accept compensation, causing the District Commissioner to fear that the Kilimanjaro Union or immigrant Kikuyu might fan 'subversive interests' in the Arusha community and put the expansion plans on hold.[59]

A visit by the Governor in 1950 soon revived the issue, however. In a major address, he expressed his disappointment that the struggling dusty town was unworthy of its beautiful setting and called for a 20–30 year plan to bring it up to the standards of 'a model modern East African town'.[60] But while members of the administration were quick to seize on the Governor's initiative and to enumerate long lists of desired improvements, they remained unable to resolve the thorny political issue of finding sufficient land to resettle Arusha from around the town's boundaries.[61] A suggestion to expropriate local settler farms was deemed 'not practical politics at this juncture' and an attempt to develop a resettlement area in Nduruma Chini was less than successful.[62]

The temporary solution was to develop the existing town more densely by rationalizing land use, reducing lot sizes, and mandating two-storey buildings in the commercial area while secretly developing plans to more than double the size of the town at Arusha expense. A number of officials dissented from the expansion plans, including the Government Anthropologist, Henry Fosbrooke, who questioned the justification 'for expropriating a self supporting peasantry to make room for a rapidly expanding non-productive urban population'.[63]

And Arusha protests poured in despite the attempts at secrecy. Arusha refused to participate in government surveys on the grounds that the land was theirs by right of settlement: it was their home; no other land was available; those forced to move earlier had still not found land; money was no substitute for land; and the people would not benefit from expansion of the township.[64]

Forced to drop its plans for expansion once more, the administration again resorted to redeveloping government land and increasing densities in the township instead. The administration's problems were only resolved finally in 1957, when it was able to purchase two nearby settler estates totalling 7,134 acres. Future expansion of the township was ensured, and the remaining 149 Arusha in town willingly accepted resettlement on the estates after being compensated with three acres for each acre lost together with £16,000 in cash. The town authorities and Arusha seemed to find common ground at last, though dramatic growth following independence reopened old wounds and Arusha continued to resist further expansion of the town.[65]

Visions of Town

The ongoing struggle to clear Arusha from town, combined with the ceaseless struggles over land elsewhere on the mountain throughout the colonial period, carried a high political price for the British, but to what end? Most of the evictions were from areas of town surrounding the European residential area, and the land obtained was used largely to provide green spaces, in the form of golf courses, parks, and sports facilities, to separate Europeans from Africans, rather than for commercial development. The fifty-yard strip acquired in 1934 served solely as a *cordon sanitaire,* while the hard-fought expropriations in 1945 were used to develop a golf course, playing fields, and a park along the eastern boundaries of town separating Europeans from Arusha living outside the town limits.[66] Land was also acquired for additional European residences and social facilities, such as schools, sports clubs and a vacation lodge for the Governor. Hence, most of the land acquired was employed to enhance racial segregation, with such European social amenities as parks, sports facilities and golf courses justified on medical grounds.

In resolutely seeking to develop their 'model modern East African town', however, the British administration found itself in perpetual conflict with Arusha who had long farmed within its borders, especially when Arusha saw the fruits of their labour being turned into golf courses and playing fields. Arusha farm land was increasingly in short supply throughout the twentieth century, but rather than abandoning the land for a life as townspeople, Arusha tenaciously defended their rights to land and to their way of life. For, as Arusha argued endlessly, land belonged to those who worked it, one's homestead was a prerequisite of one's social life and cultural identity, and everyone had a right to sufficient land to build his own homestead. In the words of an Arusha today, Arusha were 'a people of plenty' who had no desire to join 'a town of strangers':

> People who have plenty do not want to work as servants.... If they had worked in town, they would have had to buy cattle. But they already had cattle and could use them to buy what they needed.... Arusha were not born to be sweepers! They could not take such jobs in town. People in town are pushed and ordered around. Arusha will not tolerate that. Had Arusha taken those jobs, they would have lost their identity.[67]

Arusha economic livelihood, social relations, and cultural values were encapsulated by *engisaka,* its free-flowing form encompassing their wealth in bananas, cattle and people. European concepts of social space, by contrast, were manifested by the German *boma* built in 1900 and by the British town plan drafted in 1927. Both sought to discipline the rank physical landscape by sculpting it into orderly lines and square corners, just as they sought to tame the 'unruly' social landscape along lines neatly ordered by race and class.

The two conceptions of social space were fundamentally at odds. Thus the cattle, bananas and sprawling family homesteads that were the quintessential symbols of Arusha prosperity were also the essential European symbols of filth, disease and the disorder of the wild. Thus every attempt by Europeans to bring order to their environs was seen simultaneously by Arusha as an assault on their moral values, economic well-being and social prosperity, while every attempt by Arusha to defend their homesteads was viewed by Europeans as offensive to civilized life and modern economic development.

While the British ultimately did determine the shape the town took, Arusha never accepted the European conceptions of social space manifested by the town, but chose instead to defend their own social visions, retreating into the rural hinterland when forced. The people who did become townsmen were not Arusha but immigrant Swahili, Chaga, Pare and others attracted to the economic opportunities and social spaces it provided.[68] Arusha town remained an urban anomaly, a colonial town alienated from its own hinterland, and as such it differed markedly from other East African towns, such as Moshi or Nyeri, whose urban populations came largely from their own rural hinterlands and actively developed social and economic linkages between their rural homesteads and town.[69] But the modernist colonial vision had little appeal for Arusha, who continued to prefer their own visions of the good life.

Notes

1 I owe much to Mesiaki Kilevo, who first initiated me into the town and its environs; to Richard Waller, who has, as always, been a perceptive and sympathetic critic; to Jan Vansina, who helped me understand the complexities of colonial towns; to Abdul Sheriff, N. N. Luanda, Wolfgang Alpelt, UTAFITI, and the National Archives of Tanzania for facilitating my research in Tanzania; and to the National Endowment for the Humanities and Williams College for funding.

2 Carl Dutto, *Nyeri Townsmen* (Nairobi, 1975); Allen Green, 'A Political Economy of Moshi Town, 1920–1960' (PhD thesis, UCLA, 1986); but cf. Joan Vincent, *African Elite* (New York, 1971).

3 For recent analyses of the moral significance of land, see Parker Shipton and Mitzi Goheen, 'Understanding African land-holding: power, wealth and meaning', *Africa*, 62 (1992), pp. 307–25; Thomas J. Bassett, 'The land question and agricultural transformation in Africa' in T. J. Bassett and D. E. Crummey (eds), *Land in African Agrarian Systems* (Madison, 1993), pp. 3–31; and Parker Shipton, 'Land and culture in tropical Africa: soils, symbols, and the metaphysics of the mundane', *Annual Review of Anthropology*, 23 (1994), pp. 347–77. On the broader struggle for land in Arusha, see Thomas Spear, 'Struggles for the land: the political and moral economies of land on Mount Meru' in G. Maddox, J. L. Giblin, and I. N. Kimambo (eds), *Custodians of the Land* (London, 1996), pp. 213–40; Spear, *Mountain Farmers* (London and Berkeley, 1977), Chs 9–11.

4 J.D.Y. Peel, 'Urbanization and urban history in West Africa', *Journal of African History*, 21 (1980), pp. 269–78. See also, Catherine Coquery-Vidrovitch, 'The process of urbanization in Africa (from the origins to the beginnings of independence)', *African Studies Review*, 34 (1991), pp. 1–98.

5 See, e.g., E. J. Soja, *The Geography of Modernization in Kenya* (Syracuse, 1968); Aidan Southall (ed.), *Small Urban Centers in Rural Development in Africa* (Madison, 1979); Aidan Southall (ed.), 'Small Towns in Africa Revisited', special issue of *African Studies Review*, 31 (1988), pp. 1–113; Jonathon Barker (ed.) *Small Town Africa* (Uppsala, 1990); J. Barker and P. Petersen (eds), *The Rural-Urban Interface in Africa* (Uppsala, 1992).

6 See, e.g., Vincent, *African Elite*; Nicholas Hopkins, *Popular Government in an African Town* (Chicago, 1972); Enid Schildkrout, *People of the Zongo* (Cambridge, 1978).

7 But see David Parkin (ed.), *Town and Country in Central and Eastern Africa* (London, 1975); Jane Guyer (ed.), *Feeding African Cities* (Bloomington, 1987). Both deal largely with cities rather than towns, however.

8 But see Akin Mabogunje, *Urbanization in Nigeria* (London, 1968); Dutto, *Nyeri Townsmen*; Green, 'Political economy of Moshi'; R. Launay, *Beyond the Stream* (California, 1992); Phyllis Martin, *Leisure and Society in Colonial Brazzaville* (Cambridge, 1995).

9 But see Frederick Cooper (ed.), *Struggle for the City* (Beverly Hills, 1983).

10 G. Sjoberg, *The Pre-Industrial City* (New York, 1960); T. C. McGee, *The Urbanization Process in the Third World* (London, 1971), pp. 50–55; Anthony King, *Colonial Urban Development* (London, 1976), pp. 14, 40–56; J. R. Rayfield, 'Theories of urbanization and the colonial city in West Africa', *Africa*, 44 (1974), p. 179; Joan Vincent, 'The changing role of small towns in the agrarian structure of East Africa', *Journal of Commonwealth and Comparative Politics*, 12 (1974), pp. 261–4; Bruce Fetter, *Colonial Rule and Regional Imbalance in Central Africa* (Boulder, 1983), pp. 27–9; Frederick Cooper, 'Introduction', *Struggle for the City*, pp. 17–18; Coquery-Vidrovitch, 'Process of urbanization', pp. 17–18, 33–5.

11 King, *Colonial Urban Development*; John Cell, 'Anglo-Indian medical theory and the origins of segregation in West Africa', *American Historical Review*, 91 (1986), pp. 307–35. Cf. Bill Freund, this volume.

12 Catherine Coquery-Vidrovitch, 'Reality and myth of the garden–city in colonial Africa', and Odile Goerg, 'From Hill Station (Freetown) to Downtown Conakry (1st Ward): comparing French and British approaches to segregation in colonial cities' (both papers presented to the conference on 'Africa's Urban Past', SOAS, London, June 1996).

13 King, *Colonial Urban Development*, pp. 123–53, 163–75, 223–6, 235–48; Philip Curtin, 'Medical knowledge and urban planning in tropical Africa', *American Historical Review*, 90 (1985), pp. 594–6; Cell, 'Anglo-Indian medical theory', pp. 307–12; Gwendolyn Wright, 'Tradition in the service of modernity: architecture and urbanism in French colonial policy, 1900–1930', *Journal of Modern History*, 59 (1987), pp. 291–316.

14 Raymond Betts, 'The establishment of the Medina in Dakar, Senegal, 1914', *Africa*, 41 (1971), pp. 143–52; King, *Colonial Urban Development*, pp. 103–20; Maynard Swanson, 'The sanitation syndrome: bubonic plague and urban native policy in the Cape Colony, 1900–1909', *Journal of African History*, 18 (1977), pp. 387–410; Curtin, 'Medical knowledge and urban planning', 594–613; Cell, 'Anglo-Indian medical theory'.

15 Dutto, *Nyeri Townsmen*, pp. 167–75; Betts, 'Establishment of the Medina'; King, *Colonial Urban Development*, pp. 44–56; Susan Denyer, *African Traditional Architecture* (London, 1978). Cf. Seltene Seyoum, this volume, and Allen Howard, 'Contesting urban spaces: Freetown and the surrounding centers' (paper presented at the conference on 'Africa's Urban Past', SOAS, London, June 1996).

16 A study currently being undertaken by Rona Peligal. See her 'Conflicting constituencies in the creation of Arusha Town, 1920–1945', African Studies Association, Orlando, 1995.

17 Arusha Historical Traditions (AHT); Thomas Spear, 'Being "Maasai", but not "People of Cattle": Arusha agricultural Maasai in the nineteenth century', in T. Spear and R. Waller (eds), *Being Maasai* (London, 1993), pp. 120–36; Spear, *Mountain Farmers*, Ch. 2.

18 While Meru farmers had long been settled on adjacent slopes of the mountain to the east, there is little indication that they were also involved in trade or that they subsequently partook in the development of the trading centre and town: Spear, *Mountain Farmers*, Ch. 1. I will thus focus here on Arusha.

19 Philip Gulliver, *Social Control in an African Society* (London, 1963), pp. 10–12; AHT; Richard Waller, 'The lords of East Africa: the Maasai in the mid-nineteenth century' (PhD thesis, Cambridge, 1979), pp. 43, 92–3, 285–6, 314–5; John Berntsen, 'Pastoralism, raiding, and prophets: Maasailand in the 19th century' (PhD, Wisconsin, 1979), pp. 161–71; Berntsen, 'Economic variations among Maa-speaking peoples' in B. A. Ogot (ed.), *Ecology and History in East Africa (Hadith 7)* (Nairobi, 1979), pp. 120–1; Spear, 'Being "Maasai"'; Spear, *Mountain Farmers*, Ch. 2. Such settlement patterns had long been characteristic of the area: Peter Robertshaw, *Early Pastoralists of South-Western Kenya* (Nairobi, 1990).

20 Thomas Wakefield, 'Routes of native caravans from the coast to the interior of East Africa', *Journal of the Royal Geographical Society*, 40 (1870), p. 305; J. F. Farler, 'The Usambara country in East Africa', *Proceedings of the Royal Geographical Society*, 1 (1897), p. 96; Farler, 'Native routes in East Africa from Pangani to the Masai country and Victoria Nyanza', *Proceedings of the Royal Geographical Society*, 4 (1882), pp. 731–4; G. A. Fischer, *Das Masailand* (Hamburg, 1885), p. 100; Ludwig von Höhnel, *Discovery of Lakes Rudolf and Stefanie* (London, 1894), pp. 165–6.

21 P.H. Gulliver, 'Structural dichotomy and jural processes among the Arusha of Northern Tanganyika', *Africa*, 31 (1961), pp. 19–35; Gulliver, *Social Control*, pp. 71–5; Spear, *Mountain Farmers*, Chapter 2.

22 Other early settlements at Elerai and Eor e Ngapio also became important ritual centres.

23 Max Schoeller, *Mitteilungen über meine Reise nach Äquatorial-Ost Afrika und Uganda, 1896–97* (Berlin, 1901), Vol. 1, pp. 154–7. Anton Lukas Kaaya [Meru Historical Tradition (MHT) 1]; Kirilo Japhet Ayo (MHT 2); Yohanes ole Kauwenara (AHT 2); Lodenaga Lotisia (AHT 3). John Iliffe, *A Modern History of Tanganyika* (Cambridge, 1979), p. 102; Berntsen, 'Pastoralism, raiding , and prophets', pp. 305–6; N. N. Luanda, 'European commercial farming and its impact on the Meru and Arusha peoples of Tanzania, 1920–1955' (PhD thesis, Cambridge, 1986), p. 39; Thomas Spear, 'Blood on our land: stories of conquest' in R. Harms, *et. al.* (eds), *Paths Toward the Past* (Atlanta, 1994), pp. 113–22; Spear, *Mountain Farmers*, Ch. 4.

24 John Boyes, *The Company of Adventurers* (London, 1928), pp. 169–71.

25 Boyes, *Company*, pp. 170–1. See also Krause in *Evangelisch-Lutherisches Missionsblatt*, [ELMB] 57 (1902), p. 279.

26 Fokken, *ELMB*, 60 (1905), p. 392.

27 Boyes, *Company*, p. 170.

28 Krause, *ELMB*, 57 (1902), p. 279; Müller, *ELMB*, 57 (1902), p. 458; AHT.

29 Colonial authorities generally acknowledged that Arusha refrained from participating in urban activities, and the first authoritative censuses conducted in 1948 and 1957 placed Arusha at only 6-7 per cent of the urban African population, the smallest percentage of local people anywhere in Tanzania. Descriptions of Arusha continuing to farm in town are found in: Krause, *ELMB*, 57 (1902), p. 279; Müller, *ELMB*, 57 (1902), p. 458; Boyes, *Company of Adventurers*, pp. 169–72; Fokken, *ELMB*, 60 (1905), p. 392; Clement Gillman, *Tanganyika Diaries*, VIII/65/ 16 November 1924 [Rhodes House (RH): MSS.Afr.s.1175]; Dep. Provincial Commissioner [DPC]/Northern Province [NP] to Provincial Commissioner [PC]/NP, 9 May 1930, Tanzania National Archives [TNA]: 26147]; NP, Annual Report, 1931 (TNA: 11681); Donald C. Flatt, *Man and Deity in an African Society* (Dubuque, 1980), pp. 328–9; Jonathan Kidale (AHT 7).

30 Müller, *ELMB*, 57 (1902), p. 458; Fokken, *ELMB*, 68 (1913), 162; Spear, *Mountain Farmers*, Chs 4–5.

31 L.B. Boyd-Moss, *Diaries,* Tanganyika, 18 August 1921 (RH: MSS.Afr.r.37).

32 Gillman, *Diaries,* VIII/65, 16 November 1924, p. 124.

33 NP, Annual Report, 1927–9 (TNA: 11681). PC/NP to Arusha Coffee Planters Assoc. (ACPA), 2 May 1927 (TNA 10068). Land Officer (LO) to Chief Secretary (CS), 8 September 1927; PC/NP to LO, 28 March 1930 (TNA: 10068).

34 Sources: Municipal Secretary to CS/DSM, 13 April 1938 (TNA: 18989); East African Statistical Department, *African Population of Tanganyika Territory: Geographic and Tribal Studies* (Nairobi, 1950); East African High Commission, *Tanganyika African Population Census, 1957* (Nairobi, 1958), p. 131; East African Statistical Department, *Tanganyika African Population Census, 1957: Analysis* (Nairobi, 1958).

35 Executive Officer (EO)/Arusha Township Authority (ATA) to CS, 25 June 1951 (TNA: 472). Meeting of District Representatives, 1949 (TNA: 9/8/1). Minutes, District Commissioners' (DC) Conference, NP, 28 June 1956 (TNA: 472).

36 Map D523, 6 May 1930 (TNA: 12516/II). DPC/NP to PC/NP, 9 May 1930 (TNA: 26147).

37 PC/NP to ACPA, 2 May 1927; ACPA to PC/NP, 25 May 1927; PC/NP to LO, 7 June 1927 (TNA: 10068).

38 NP, Annual Report, 1927 (TNA: 11681).

39 I estimate that Arusha effectively occupied at least 800 acres in 1920, based on unspecified expropriations in 1924–25, 1927, and 1928–29, 331 acres taken in 1931, and 436 acres in 1945-46, as detailed below.

40 Map D523, 6 May 1930 (TNA: 12516/II). Dep. PC/NP to PC/NP, 9 May 1930 (TNA: 26147). PC/NP to CS, 13 May 1930 (TNA: 12516).

41 NP, Annual Reports, 1927-31 (TNA: 11681). DPC/NP to PC/NP, 9 May 1930 (TNA: 26147). District Officer (DO)/Arusha District (AD) to PC/NP, 27 January 1931; PC/NP to CS, 22 May 1931 (TNA: 12516).

42 PC/NP to CS, 18 October 1928 (TNA: 10058/I). DPC/NP to PC/NP, 9 May 1930 (TNA: 26417). DO/AD to LO, 31 July 1930 (TNA: 10068). LO to DO/AD, 10 August1930 (TNA: 69/AR/II). DO/AD to LO, 24 September 1930 (TNA: 10068 & 69/AR/II). NP, Annual Report, 1931 (TNA: 11681)

43 See, for example, footnote 63 below.

44 PC/NP to CS, 13 May 1930 (TNA: 12516). CS to PC/NP, 20 April 1934 (TNA: 12516). DO/AD to PC/NP, 17 August 1934; PC/NP to CS, 2 October 1934 (TNA: 12516/II). CS to PC/NP, 10 April 1942 and reply 28 April 1942 (TNA: 12516/III).

45 DPC/NP to PC/NP, 9 May 1930 (TNA: 26147). PC/NP to CS, 12 June 1930 (TNA: 10068). DO/AD to PC/NP, 26 Aug 1931 & PC/NP to DO/AD, 2 Sept 1931 (TNA: 69/45/4). CS to PC/NP, 20 Oct 1934, correcting PC/NP to CS, 8 June 1934 (TNA: 12516).

46 PC/NP to CS, 13 May 1930 (TNA: 12516).

47 NP, Annual Report, 1933 (TNA: 11681).

48 PC/NP to CS, 8 June 1934 and reply 20 October 1934 (TNA: 12516). Emphasis in original. See also PC/NP to CS, 12 June 1930 & minute by A.E. Kitching, 10 Oct 1930 (TNA: 10068).

49 PC/NP to CS, 8 June 1934 (TNA: 12516). See also, DO/AD to PC/NP, 10 December 1943; PC/NP to CS, 8 May 1944 and 19 July 1944 (TNA: 12516/III). See also footnote 55 below.

50 The administration sought to acquire ex-German farms adjacent to the township, but held back because the owners were asking too much and it was not politically expedient to dispossess Europeans. PC/NP to CS, 12 May 1930 and 2 July 1930 (TNA: 26417). It also sought to obtain 300 acres of forest reserve for resettlement, but the Conservator of Forests (CF) rejected its request. CS to CF, 24 September 1934, and reply, 27 September 1934 (TNA: 12516).

51 DO/AD to PC/NP, 26 August 1931 (TNA: 69/45/4). The PC subsequently refused to either sell or finance the required grazing land, however. PC/NP to DO/AD, 2 September 1931 (TNA: 69/45/4).‹

52 DO/AD to PC/NP, 27 January 1931, and PC/NP to CS, 22 May 1931 (TNA: 12516).

53 DO/AD to PC/NP, 26 August 1921 and reply, 2 September 1931 (TNA; 69/45/4). Agreement between H.R. Gilbert, DO/AD, and Arusha Elders, 5 January 1934 (TNA: 69/602).

54 DO/AD to PC/NP, 17 August 1934; PC/NP to CS, 2 October 1934 (TNA: 12516/II). NP, Annual Report, 1934 (TNA: 11681).

55 DC/AD to PC/NP, 17 December 1941; PC/NP to CS, 24 January 1942; CS to PC/NP, 10 April 1942; PC/NP to CS, 28 April 1942; DC/AD to PC/NP, 21 August 1942 (TNA: 12516/III).

56 DO/AD to PC/NP, 10 December 1943; PC/NP to CS, 8 May 1944 (TNA: 12516/III). CS to PC/NP, 27 June 1944; PC/NP to CS, 19 July 1944 (TNA: 25369). DC/AD to PC/NP, 13 Dec 1944, PC/NP to CS, 25 January 1945; CS to PC/NP, 19 February 1945; PC/NP to CS, 14 April 1945; CS to PC/NP, 3 May 1945; PC/NP to CS, 19 May 1945; Memo for Standing Finance Committee, 22 May 1945; CS to PC/NP, 8 June 1945; Minutes of Standing Finance Comm., 6 July 1945; Certified Agreements, 4 July 1945–1 Feb 1946; PC/NP to CS, 15 April 1947 (TNA: 12516). NP, Annual Report, 1945 (TNA: 19415). Elders of Two Native Courts of Burka and Ilboro to His Excellency, the Governor, 7 January 1946; DC/AD to PC/NP, 15 January 1946 (TNA: 69/602).

57 EO/ATA to PC/NP, 22 March 1946; PC/NP to CS, 26 March 1946 (TNA: 12516).

58 For land problems elsewhere on Mount Meru, see Spear, 'Struggles for the Land'; Spear, *Mountain Farmers*, ChS 9–11.

59 Minutes, Meetings of District Representatives, 6 January 1949–8 Dec 1949 (TNA: 9/8/1). DC/AD to PC/NP, 6 July 1950 (TNA: 472/-). NP, Annual Report, 1950 (TNA: 19415). AD, Annual Report, 1952 (TNA: 472/-).

60 Note by His Excellency, the Governor, on his visit to Arusha, 12–18 January 1950 (TNA: 472/-).

61 A new town plan drafted in 1948 called for additional administrative facilities (new Provincial, District, and Municipal headquarters, a police station, fire station, post office, and tsetse fly control unit) and industrial sites; more housing, a nursery school and social facilities (a club, British Legion and sports club) for Europeans; housing, a mosque and four schools for Asians; and a hospital and health centre, sports ground, stadium, car park, bus station and two schools for Africans. Interestingly, the plan included no provision for additional African housing on the grounds that Africans could settle outside the town, thus confounding the separation of 'foreign' from 'indigenous natives' that the administration had long sought to achieve by evicting Arusha from town and putting additional pressure on Arusha land. Chief Town Planning Officer (CTPO) to Member for Local Government (MLG), 22 February 1950 (TNA: 472/-).

62 Minutes, Meetings of District Representatives, 29 April 1950 (TNA: 9/ADM/11 & 9/8/1). CTPO to EO/ATA, 22 June 1950; Memo. on Expansion, DC/AD to PC/NP, 6 July 1950 (TNA: 472/-).

63 Henry Fosbrooke to DC/AD, 14 December 1950 (TNA: 472/NA/48). Memo on Expansion of

Arusha Township Boundaries, President, ATA to Governor, 25 October 1951; PC/NP to MLG, 16 November 1951; Supplementary Memo on the Expansion of Arusha Township Boundaries, nd; DC/AD to PC/NP, 2 July 1952; PC/NP to DC/AD, 12 July 1952; (TNA: 472/-).

64 O. Simeon Laiser to His Excellency, the Governor, 14 September 1951; Ol-Karsis Simeon Laiser to PC/NP, 28 November 1951; Note on Survey of Area for Proposed Expansion of Township to the West and South, DC/AD to PC/NP, 7 November 1952 (TNA: 472/-).

65 CTPO to MLG, 4 March 1952; Memo. of Discussion, 20 March 1952; Governor to CS, 27 March 1952 (TNA: 18989). NP, Annual Reports, 1957–9 (TNA: 471/R.3/2). Land Ranger to DC/AD, 9 January 1958 (TNA: 472/ANR/1/57).

66 DO/AD to PC/NP, 5 January 1934 (TNA: 69/602). DO/AD to PC/NP, 10 December 1943 (TNA: 12516/II). PC/NP to CS, 12 May 1930 and 2 July 1930 (TNA: 26147). See also footnote 60 for a detailed list of proposed developments in 1948.

67 Jonathan Kidale (AHT 7).

68 Such townsmen struggled to control their own social spaces in town, of course, but they are not the subject of this paper.

69 Dutto, *Nyeri Townsmen*; Green, 'Political economy of Moshi'.

8
The Cost of Living in Lagos 1914–45

AYODEJI OLUKOJU

The port-city of Lagos, declared a British colony in 1861, had become pre-eminent along the West African coast by the third quarter of the nineteenth century.[1] Its population rose steadily as migrants moved into the city in response to the growth of maritime trade and to other factors in the hinterland.[2] The steady increase in the population of Lagos was matched by the rising cost of urban living. This neglected theme in the literature on Lagos up to the Second World War,[3] will be examined here principally through the views expressed in the Lagos press on the local and external factors that affected the cost of living in the city, and the ways in which urban residents coped with the expenses of urban life. Prices of local and imported foodstuffs form the main element of the study, but rents and wage levels will also be considered. A chronological approach has been adopted to permit an appreciation of the undercurrents of colonial history, and the broader fluctuation in the colonial political economy. The opening section will consider the effects of the First World War upon the Lagos economy, and the second part will focus on the inter-war years, concentrating upon the economic fluctuations between 1918 and 1922 and the effects of the 1930s depression. The last section will examine the experience of Lagosians during the 1939–45 war. The central argument of the study is to emphasize the vulnerability of Lagos to a combination of the vagaries in local supply of foodstuffs, and the fluctuations in the international economy affecting the value of commodities exported through the port and the costs of imports, including foodstuffs.

Developments up to 1918

That Lagos was an 'expensive' city was common knowledge by the turn of the century.[4] Wage levels were generally low, in part the result of colonial policy, and food prices high. Urban wages ranged between nine pence and one shilling per day. Acting-Governor Boyle had noted in 1910 that: 'The town of Lagos has rightly earned the reputation of the 'Liverpool' of British West Africa.... Perhaps the principal drawback to a most satisfactory condition is the increasing cost of living which is a natural sequel to increasing population and prosperity.'[5] Population and prosperity were indeed key elements but other factors played a part. As Hopkins has shown, the period 1906–14 was one of commercial prosperity in contrast with the era of trade fluctuations between 1893 and 1905. Over these years produce prices rose with demand from the external markets of Lagos and inflationary trends dominated both the internal retail business and external trade till the outbreak of the First World War.[6] As the city grew in scale, the problems of meeting the food requirements of its population became more acute. The sandy and swampy terrain of Lagos was not conducive to the cultivation of foodstuffs, and the port city was almost entirely dependent on its hinterland. Towards the end of the nineteenth century Lagos had already come to rely heavily on supplies from Abeokuta, via the Ogun River waterway. 'By the 1880s', Hopkins notes, 'commercial specialisation, combined with the growth of population, meant that Lagos had become almost completely dependent on outside sources of food supply.'[7] The implication was vulnerability to crises in the foodcrop economy and politics of the interior. In any year of bad weather or poor harvests, Lagosians were compelled to pay more for diminished supplies. Not even the existence of farms in the immediate hinterland, in the Agege-Ota region, could stem the tide of scarcity, high prices and attendant hardships.

In considering the rise in the cost of living in Lagos, a distinction has to be made between local foodstuffs and imported ones, the former being the staple of the majority of the city's population. Although a number of imported items such as sugar, bread and biscuits had assumed great importance in the diet by the end of the nineteenth century, *gari* or *farina* (cassava flour) remained the chief staple of Lagosians, and its price was the most reliable index of the cost of living in the city. Price fluctuations of *gari* resulted largely from problems of production and distribution.

These difficulties were especially apparent during 1910. A newspaper report of March 1910 claimed that the prices of foodstuffs in the city had 'gone up to something fabulous', naming *gari* among the listed items.[8] It was said that *gari* which previously had sold at five shillings per bag now sold for nine. Foodstuff prices continued to be 'high' throughout the month, with vegetables being especially scarce owing to low rainfall.[9] As the drought persisted over several further months, Lagos's food supplies became ever more precarious. By April the price of *gari* had shot up to thirteen shillings per bag, and the *Lagos Weekly Record* warned that 'the wolf is at the door for the great bulk of the people'.[10] According to the newspaper, poor rainfall was not the only cause of scarcity and high prices: traders were reported to be profiteering from the scarcity. 'Spasmodic fluctuations' in prices were attributed to 'cunning moves' on the part of market women, who were allegedly themselves holding up supply to keep prices artificially inflated. By May this seemed to be a popular explanation for the rise in the price of a bag of *gari* to fifteen shillings and that of pepper from six pence a measure to 'the fabulous sum' of ten shillings! 'Such a thing', the newspaper bemoaned, 'is unprecedented in the history of Lagos.... [The] public have become the victims of an unscrupulous set of sharpers and require to be protected'.[11]

In the pre-war years it is apparent that the cost of living in Lagos fluctuated appreciably, largely in response to periodic scarcity of foodstuffs such as occurred during 1910. It is difficult, therefore, to agree completely with Hopkins that food prices remained stable during this period, though one cannot dispute his claim that prices for the period 1905–1910 were lower than between 1880 and 1885. He concedes, however, that house rents were increasing in the opening decade of the century as farm incomes rose.[12] The outbreak of the First World War complicated the picture considerably. Soon after the commencement of hostilities, in August 1914, scarcity and high prices of staple foodstuffs were evident in Lagos. Imports were, not surprisingly, most affected. Rice and sugar were reported to be 'particularly scarce' and the 'dependency of Lagos on the outside world for food' was widely lamented. 'Surrounded by good and fertile soil, [and] blessed with population', the *Nigerian Pioneer* concluded, 'it is bordering on madness that such a state of things can be possible'.[13] So worried was the colonial government, that a Committee of Control was appointed to monitor the supply and sale of foodstuffs. Government also organized the baking of bread for sale at Broad Street to make the most of a limited supply of flour.[14] At its peak, the bakery was producing 600 loaves a day. The supply of a local staple, *ogi* (corn flour), was also eased by the cereal mill installed at Abeokuta, which milled maize for government and supplied Lagos with tons of corn flour.[15] At the same time government issued laws to prevent the export of *gari* from the Lagos region, to ensure that all available supplies were consumed within the city.[16] The situation in Lagos stood in stark contrast with that in Abeokuta, where foodstuffs were said to be so 'very plentiful' that enterprising traders there contemplated exporting *gari* to the Cameroons.[17] When controls on food supplies were removed by government in November 1914, prices immediately rocketed, imported foodstuffs rising by as much as 20 to 50 per cent. The *Pioneer* denounced the sharp rise in prices and demanded the resumption of price regulation.[18] The Comptroller of Customs, T. F. Burrowes, who had also been chairman of the Committee of Control, declared the newspaper to be 'misinformed', claiming that the report had exaggerated the increases and that prices of certain items had actually fallen.[19] Despite the conflicting claims, there is no doubt that prices of most foodstuffs remained high.

The fragility of foodstuff pricing in the city was exposed regularly by disruption to the agricultural economy.[20] In January 1917, for example, it was again noted that prices had 'gone up very considerably of late and the cost of living becoming increasingly dearer':[21] the price of three tubers of yam had risen from one shilling to 1s 3d and a cigarette tin of *gari* from seven pence to 1s 6d. The 'dry weather', the greater export of foodstuff, and farmers' increasing preference for cocoa at the expense of foodcrops were all cited as contributory factors. The *Pioneer* lamented that a country that could and did grow sufficient rice should be 'dependent on places abroad for that commodity', and demanded that the indigenous rulers be organized and exhorted 'to see to the growing of foodstuff on a large scale' and that '[a]ll loafing in Nigeria must cease'.[22] In an editorial of May 1917, captioned 'Is the Supply of our Foodstuffs Adequate?', the *Pioneer* expressed apprehension that the preoccupation with cash cropping was creating food scarcity. Producers were moving into cash crops such as coffee and cocoa at the expense of staple food crops: 'Whole districts formerly supplying yams and corn are now abandoned to the cultivation of cocoa,' the newspaper claimed.[23]

Price increases during the war years were all the more significant as workers' wages were still at pre-war levels. A contemporary account stated that 'the working classes are suffering terribly [as] their pay has not gone up by a farthing, whereas the prices of necessities of life have gone up enormously'.[24] By 1918 concern over low urban wages was widespread, and government and private employers were being urged to alleviate the hardship faced by the wage-earners and the lower classes. The *Pioneer* pleaded for 'a living wage' for workers, reporting that recently some merchant houses had raised the pay of labourers from one shilling to 1s 6d per day in view of the 'high rise in the price of food'. The 50 per cent pay rise was considered a 'generous windfall' to a class of worker, the majority of whom 'scarcely know what meat or fish is, and have to go content on 'Gari' soaked in water': 'Imagine living on tapioca soaked in water', the newspaper lamented. Another commentator, who deplored the 'undesirable high prices' of foodstuffs, urged government to control the prices of local foodstuffs as it did those of imports which only the Europeans and affluent Africans consumed. It was the poor who were most vulnerable to fluctuations in the prices – of basic foodstuffs.[25]

As the war drew to a close, the limited price control measures imposed by government did not appear to have solved the problem, and Lagosians devised their own means of cutting costs. Convinced that profiteering contributed to the high prices of foodstuffs, the *Pioneer* counselled its readers to take the suburban train to the outlying agricultural settlements of Agege, Alagbado and their environs 'to avoid our petty profiteers': a bag of *gari* that cost between 10s 6d and 11s 9d in Lagos could be had for 7s 6d at the most in these places. Other foodstuffs could also be obtained for 'about two-thirds the price' obtaining in Lagos. After fares and other incidental expenses had been deducted, the adventurous Lagosian would have been 'richer by several shillings'.[26]

Table 8.1 Pre-War and Wartime Prices of Local Foodstuffs and Firewood in Lagos[27]

	Pre-war	Sept 1918		Pre-war	Sept 1918
Three Yams	1s	2s 6d	Palm oil (bottle)	2d	3d
Cowsfoot	1.5d	9d	Native Rice (pan)	1s	3s 6d
Corn (pan)	5d	1s 6d	*Eyo* (spinach) (bundle)	1d	3d
Native pepper (pan)	6d	2s	Shrimp (dried) (pan)	2s	8s
Beef (lb)	9d	2s	*Gari* (pan)	2d	6d
Elubo (yam flour) (pan)	6d	2s	Firewood (5 bundles)	3d	6d
Ordinary size fish	1s	2s 6d			

A comparison of pre-war prices with those prevailing in the closing months of the war shows an increase of up to 400 per cent in some cases (see Table 8.1). Although prices had also risen in Abeokuta and other markets outside Lagos over the same period, the difference was more pronounced in the city. For example, a measure of *gari*, which went for four pence at Abeokuta before the war cost nine pence by September 1918, an increase of only 125 per cent compared with the 200 per cent increase reported for Lagos; and the price of *elubo* (yam flour) rose 100 per cent from six pence to one shilling at Abeokuta, compared with a 300 per cent increase in Lagos. Similarly, a measure of maize at Lagos was dearer by a margin of almost 300 per cent compared with less than 100 per cent (7.5d to 1s 1d) at Abeokuta.[28]

The Inter-War Years

Hopes that the conclusion of the war would bring an easing of the cost of urban foodstuffs were dashed by the artificial prosperity and inflation of the opening phase of the inter-war years. But the brief boom of 1918–20 was quickly followed by the slump of 1920–2, and Nigeria's economy entered a period of instability and fluctuation that would culminate in the Great Depression of the early 1930s.[29]

The boom of 1918–20 was characterized by unprecedented increases in produce prices in Lagos. By June 1919, foodstuff prices in Lagos had advanced on the already high wartime levels: 'no sooner were the restrictions [price controls] withdrawn than prices went up by leaps and bounds'.[30] Increasing prices of imports from Britain were attributed to high labour costs in the metropole, and it was alleged that local traders followed the

European merchants in squeezing prices upwards. For example, a barrel of flour landed in Lagos at £5, went for £8 in the local market. Local African traders justified such a move because the prices of imported merchandise, such as building materials, cooking utensils and clothing, had climbed by about 300 per cent.[31]

Once again the local press was prompted to accuse traders and merchants of profiteering, but on this occasion it was the European merchant houses who came in for the sharpest criticism. Viewed from Lagos, the editor of the *Lagos Weekly Record* thought the strains of the imperial economy a poor excuse for the failure of government to restrain local inflation. Post-war demobilization of servicemen in Britain should have eased labour supply problems, and shipping lines had reduced ocean freights which, with more regular sailings than during the war, had cut transport costs. Moreover, prices in Britain had fallen. Given these circumstances, it was argued that European importers had no justification for charging high prices in Lagos. At the same time, the *Record* also castigated African traders for profiteering.[32] But African traders and their sympathizers sought to justify the high prices on the grounds that rail transport was still difficult and that some foodstuffs were diverted to other parts of Nigeria and to neighbouring colonies, notably Dahomey and the Gold Coast.

The debate which ensued in the Lagos press around this issue was varied and lively. One writer lamented the increased cost of production in the fishing industry, caused by the development of the harbour.[33] Another blamed the high cost of beef upon the monopoly of the cattle trade by the Levantine merchant, Michael Elias, and the insufficiency of railway wagons required to convey cattle from Northern Nigeria. Yet another contributor criticized the colonial government for chasing shadows by sending policemen to the market to enforce price control. This was like 'looking to the leaves [while]...the roots are left unnoticed'.[34] This same writer highlighted several connected causes for the rise in prices: first, the phenomenal rise in the price of cassava, from five shillings to £2 per bundle of 200 sticks, was bound to affect the price of *gari*. Second, poor rainfall in the preceding year had affected harvests: many crops dried up in the parched soil and those that survived gave poor yields. Third, the cost of agricultural labour had risen remarkably: labourers who used to earn five shillings a month were no longer available for four times the price, and big farmers had been compelled to reduce the size of their labour force by as much as eighty per cent in some cases, while small farmers could no longer afford to employ labour at all. Fourth, a scarcity of silver coins meant that one paid £1 in currency notes for what should have cost half that sum in silver coins. The foodstuff retailer, who had to discount his currency notes to purchase his merchandise, had to include the ten-shilling discount on every pound, his transport fare and a margin of profit in the retail price demanded for the commodity. Finally, delays in the rail transport of foodstuffs made consignments arrive months behind schedule, by which time prices might have fallen or the goods spoilt. As either of these might ruin the foodstuff trader, he was obliged to create a safe margin for himself.[35]

Others saw a cause in the preoccupation with cash cropping. The development of the cocoa industry in Yorubaland was widely blamed for the predicament in which Lagos found itself. *The Nigerian Pioneer* again deplored 'the craze for cocoa [which] has caused farmers to neglect the growing of foodstuffs, coupled with the dearth of hands'.[36] The lack of farm labour at this time was linked to the popularity of porterage work within the city. A contemporary observer claimed that 'lands within easy reach of Lagos and other large and populous centres on which food was previously grown ... is now under cocoa'.[37] Lagos was thus confronted by the paradox that while cocoa exports enriched the economy of the city, the cultivation of the crop threatened the very supply of foodstuffs upon which the city depended.

Lagos's post-war food supply crisis undoubtedly arose from an unusual combination of factors. The result was a very steep inflationary spiral in retail prices. Compared with the September 1918 prices (indicated in Table 8.1), those prevailing by August 1919 were higher in some cases by 300 per cent. The price of a pan (measure) of *gari* had risen from 6*d* to 9*d*, that of palm oil from 3*d* to 10*d*, and a bundle of firewood was now 6*d* compared with the same price for five bundles in 1918.[38] The *Record* opined that the prices suggested that 'the greater part of the people are being underfed', asking the government to again control the prices of at least the most important food items. The clamour for government intervention intensified in the first half of 1920. The *Pioneer* cited the precedent of Lord Allenby's order under the Martial Law administration in Egypt that cultivators who rooted up cereals for cotton should pay a fine of £100 per acre. While acknowledging that such heavy-handed intervention was likely to cause deep resentment on the part of the producers, the newspaper contended that the Lagos situation was critical enough to be 'handled in a similar manner'.[39] The *Record*, which pictured the 'poor consumer' sandwiched between the devil of the local foodstuff producer and the deep blue sea of the European merchant, argued that the 'merry game' had gone on long enough and it was time for the government to step in and protect the hapless consumer: 'If the Government would only control the prices of imported goods, such as food and clothing,' it stressed, 'the prices of local necessities will fall automatically'. In regard to this point, much was made in the Lagos press of the speech by the King to the British Parliament on 23 December 1919, in which the monarch had acknowledged that the 'continued high cost of living with all its evil consequences [had] … caused distress throughout the world'. While admitting that the cost of living rates were 'lower in the British Isles than elsewhere', the King referred to measures taken particularly 'to prevent the charging of unreasonable prices for necessary articles'. The *Record* wondered when the Attorney-General would 'overhaul the invoices and daily sales books of the European firms in Lagos, and so prevent in Nigeria, the charging of unreasonable prices for necessary articles….'[40]

Some two months later, the newspaper declared that the situation had become 'very critical, and living … more than a problem'. The price of *gari*, 'the people's chief food', had, in a matter of a few weeks, gone up from one shilling to 2s 6*d* a measure – a quantity just enough to make about three meals for 'a healthy man with a normal appetite'. The cost of palm oil, an indispensable food ingredient, had risen from four pence to one shilling per bottle (of about one pint). Beef now cost about a shilling per six ounces while the price of fish ranged from two shillings upwards. The prices of imported articles such as croydon, baft, candles, tobacco, soap and kerosene were reported all to have gone up over 300 per cent above pre-war levels. Prices were said to be rising every day, 'two different prices being asked for the same article within the space of a few hours'. Things had reached the point where the people were 'beginning to talk strongly about it'. Reacting to a Reuters report that a committee of the British cabinet which was considering the question of rising prices was about to recommend food control, the *Record* again took its lead from developments in London to urge that government act in the interest of consumers.[41]

The Lagos strike of January 1920 brought matters to a head for at least some of the low-paid urban workforce, resulting in a sharp rise in the wages of porters (*alaaru*), agricultural labourers and railway workers.[42] But the improvement in wages had no effect in bringing down food costs, and if anything may have added another inflationary element to the urban economy. In the face of the apparent inability of government to influence the situation, in July 1920 a call was made for the consumer boycott of expensive items to force down prices in Lagos, as had been done in Britain.[43] Charges of official complicity in the alleged profiteering were made at this time and cannot be ruled out, even though the available evidence cannot sustain the accusation.[44] That said, two extenuating circumstances must be admitted which serve to explain the government's predicament: the fall in the purchasing power of the currency in the aftermath of the war; and the universality of the high post-war cost of living. Regarding the depreciation of the currency, it was claimed that sterling was worth only about a third of its pre-war value.[45] Hence, the rise in prices might be explained away as a normal feature of inflation which was compounded by the currency crisis of this period. In any case, Lagos was not alone in this predicament. Contemporary reports indicate that prices were similarly high in the towns of Ibadan and Kano. It was said of Kano in January 1920 that:

> Foodstuffs, poultry, firewood and other necessaries are now very dear and which the want of silver currency has helped to make dearer. Chickens three years ago cost 4d to 6d, today they could not be got under 1/6 to 2s. Indeed the rise in prices is mostly due to the stupid and selfish competition carried on by those who export foodstuffs from Kano to Lagos specially.[46]

In the case of Ibadan, some 100 miles up the railway line, it was stated in April 1920 that there was 'very little difference in the prices (of foodstuffs) between here and Lagos'.[47] It might be argued that such slight differences were crucial in the context of the times, as was suggested by the efforts of people who still went into the hinterland to procure food for the Lagos market at a reasonable profit. The behaviour of a few local traders in supplying the Lagos market with cheaper produce underlined the point. Lagos Stores Limited, for example, brought five tons of yams to Lagos for sale in February 1920, setting charges of only 16s per hundredweight and 2d per lb. which other Lagos traders claimed to be unremunerative.[48]

The situation began to change from the middle of 1920. By this time the slump that would run through to 1922 had set in, and by July 1920 there were reports of a 'slight fall' in the prices of foodstuffs and 'fairly good supplies' of corn and vegetables reaching the markets. The depression also eased shortage of farm labour, as urban workers returned to rural employment. Those who had worked as port labourers could no longer earn the daily wage of 10s–15s that had been possible during the boom of 1918–20 (compared with the pre-war wage of 8d–10d). While farm produce prices slipped back, the price of fish – another important element in the local diet – remained high at 2s to 2s 6d per pound. Since there had been 'abundant catch of late', and the fishermen 'were never at any time hard bargainers' (as they were eager to dispose of their catch whilst it was still fresh), the *Record* again saw the familiar hand of the profiteering villain behind this – the 'shrewd avaricious middlewoman' was accused of keeping the price so high.[49]

As the slump in the produce export market affected the local economy, the *Pioneer* expressed the forlorn hope that, with the 'timely rains', farmers 'will put down plenty of foodstuffs and let Cocoa have just a bit of rest'.[50] The recovery of export commodity prices soon laid any such move to rest, but there was no recurrence of the war-time and immediate post-war urban foodstuff crises over the rest of the 1920s. Failed harvests could still play a part in disrupting urban supplies, however, and periodic reports of shortages – such as the ban on the export of *gari* outside Ijebu-Igbo, a major centre of production in the adjoining Ijebu Province, owing to its 'great scarcity' there in 1926 – indicates that the food economy of the city remained vulnerable.[51]

When the Great Depression descended at the end of the decade, Lagos's foodstuff prices did not fall immediately. In September 1929, the price of *gari* stood at 9d per measure, three small tubers of yam cost sixpence and a measure of corn fetched five pence.[52] But by May 1930 the price of *gari* had risen by 50 per cent, a trend exacerbated by locust infestation in the regions around Lagos.[53] By June of the following year, *gari* was down to 7*d* per measure.[54] As Table 8.2 indicates, 1930 prices were generally lower than those reported from 1923. As the importation of foodstuffs from outside the colony became more difficult, the city's dependence on food from the hinterland became more complete. Once again, scarcity was apparent in Lagos.

Table 8.2 Comparison of Retail Market Prices in Lagos in 1923 and 1930[55]

Article	1923 Prices		1930 Prices	
Fowls (each)	2s 6d–5s		2s–3s 6d	
Eggs	3d–5d	(3–5)	1s–1s 6d	(dozen)
Yams	2s–3s 6d	(3 tubers)	1s	(10–16 lbs)
Beef (per lb)	1s 6d		1s	
Fish (fresh)	3s 6d–4s	(family ration per day)	1s–1s 6d	(per lb)
Fish (dried)	5s	(family ration per day)	4s 6d–9s	(dozen)
Rice	3s	(3 lb measure)	1s 9d–2s 3d	(9.5 inch bowl)
Gari	9d	(2.5 lb measure)	5d–7d	(9.5 inch bowl)
Pepper	3s 6d		1s 9d–2s 3d	
Locust seeds	2s 6d–3s		1s 9d–2s 6d	
Groundnut oil	1s 3d	(quart)	1s 3d–1s 6d	(gin bottle)
Palm oil	4d	(quart)	5d–6d	(gin bottle)
Cassava	1s 6d	(measure)	9d–1s 2d	(flour)
Vegetables	3d–6d	(measure)	3d–6d	(measure)
Plantains	3d	(four)	3d	(ripe)
Oranges	1d	(two)	1d	(three)

Recession brought in its train a slow but steady fall in urban wages, from one shilling to between eight and ten pence per day.[56] With housing rents remaining at previous levels, many bachelor labourers resorted to sharing accommodation at a cost of between 2s 6d and 4s each per month.[57] Married labourers commonly lived in single rooms, let out at 10s per month. The minimum cost of feeding a couple with two children for a month was estimated at £1. The diet of such low-income earners consisted essentially of *gari*. Artisans and skilled men who might earn 3s to 4s per day had a higher standard of living, and moving up the economic scale clerks, who earned between £36 and £400 per annum, occupied the better accommodation – three- or four-bedroomed houses for those who were married – paying rents ranging between £25 and £30 per annum. Available figures suggest that during the 1930s rents absorbed up to a third of the incomes of many Lagosians. Although rents were gradually squeezed down as economic conditions deteriorated, they remained relatively high as a proportion of the household budget. Moreover, urban rents tended to move with local commercial trends, especially in areas where there was a scarcity of accommodation, and even in the 1930s increases were reported in certain districts of the city for the years in which trade improved. Overall, the average cost of living in the city in 1932 was calculated at 1s 6d per day for a single person and 3s for the family man.[58]

In the face of economic depression, Lagosians generally adopted 'a simpler mode of living'. Cheaper, locally produced goods were substituted for the imported products that consumers may have desired, and people 'made do'. Products of the local weaving industry were patronized to an unprecedented level as 'the virtues of native woven cloth' were rediscovered in the depths of recession. At the Victoria Street market in Lagos, 'native woven cloth of excellent design' were observed to be 'ousting that of foreign manufacture' as it had become 'fashionable for a woman to be seen wearing them'.[59] Ancillary industries, such as capmaking, also experienced a resurgence. As the consumption of imported liquor declined, palm wine again enjoyed greater patronage; 'illicit' liquor was also smuggled into Lagos from Izon (Ijo) territory, via the creeks.[60] Belt tightening was evident as the consumption of meat and the sale of fineries diminished, and school attendances dropped as parents found it harder to raise the fees. As purchasing power fell, there was greater demand in the city for low-denomination coins (especially the tenth-penny coin) which were required for the purchase of smaller quantities of foodstuffs and condiments. Sellers correspondingly reduced their measures for the sale of items such as dye, while the smaller tomato purée tin replaced the cigarette tin as the lowest retail measure for salt and rice. In districts bordering Lagos, people intensified the cultivation of foodstuffs over the 1930s, contributing to a falling trend in urban prices of these crops over the period.[61] Consumers' preferences remained strong, however, as is indicated by the rapid upsurge in the purchase of imported goods and produce as soon as economic conditions showed improvement in 1936.[62]

There is some evidence to suggest that the effects of the Great Depression may have been more sharply felt in Lagos than in other parts of the colony. The experience of Lagos can be contrasted with Abeokuta, for example, where, by 1931, food was reported to be 'plentiful and cheap', meat was 'very good' and available at a 'reasonable price', while palm oil was 'to be had plentifully'. The price of gari at two pence a pan in Abeokuta was half that in Lagos.[63] These happier conditions at Abeokuta persisted into 1932, even as the depression deepened, and were attributed to the food-planting campaign championed in the previous year by the Alake (paramount ruler) of Abeokuta. Until then, there had been cases of serious shortages bordering on starvation. The shift to food cultivation in consequence of lowered export produce prices was a feature of these years that has also been noted for Northern Nigeria.[64]

The Second World War

The immediate consequence of the outbreak of war in September 1939 was reflected once again in a significant rise in the prices of Lagos imports, most markedly essential raw materials and manufactures. The price of a bag of cement increased from £2 11s to £9 6s in the second week of September; the prices of bicycles, sewing machines and bedsteads advanced by £1 on existing levels. The cost of 26-gauge corrugated iron sheets moved from £2:11:2 to £4 2s, and that of the less robust 35-gauge sheets went from £1 15s to £2 10s.[65] Colonial officials were quick to appreciate the destabilizing potential of these sharp increases, but opinion was divided over the most appropriate steps to take to regulate the urban economy. Not all officials considered price control a workable solution, especially as the Lagos Chamber of Commerce, representing the mercantile community, seemed strongly opposed to any such interference. While the Comptroller of Customs seemed confident that the merchants would be 'reasonable' enough not to exceed acceptable limits, the Administrator of Lagos Colony strongly advocated price controls. As early as October 1939 he declared his opinion that the European firms were 'utterly unscrupulous' and were 'already indulging in profiteering'.[66]

Perhaps learning from past experience in the city, the colonial government eventually decided in favour of controlling the prices of imported merchandise. The import price control scheme, instituted under the Emergency Powers (Defence) Act, 1939, took effect from 19 January 1940, when the colonial governor signed it into law. The criteria adopted in calculating prices under this scheme (the Duty Paid Landed Cost [DPLC]) were necessarily complex and detailed, having to include the primary cost of the article in the country of origin, the costs of freight and insurance, as well as all other costs entailed in the contract, right through to the advertising and marketing of the product. Central and local (Lagos) price regulation advisory committees, composed of representatives of mercantile, official and African interests, were constituted to monitor the operation of the scheme so as to ensure that retailers honoured the prices set.

The price control scheme did not function as well as had been envisaged, evidently because its success was bound to hurt certain business interests. The wide base of charges upon which the DPLC was calculated gave the merchant houses plenty of scope to cover their costs and maintain their profit margins. The Association of West African Merchants (AWAM), for example, insisted that a minimum of 19 per cent on the DPLC be allowed on all import costs to cover their overheads. The figure was allowed, even though the government not surprisingly considered it unduly high. A Colonial Office assessment of the claims of the AWAM later came to the conclusion that 13 per cent would have been a sufficient figure. There was, in truth, no easy solution to the problem of wartime price control in colonial cities such as Lagos, since the shortage of supplies in the presence of enhanced purchasing power had created a classic pattern of inflation.[67] An official of the Board of Trade admitted the utter hopelessness of the situation when he declared that even 'the most effective price control in the Colonies is not going to solve the problem completely'.[68]

Price controls were strengthened subsequently by the introduction of rationing of key articles and the classification of all imported articles into four groups, all of which were regulated in different ways. Prices were fixed for commodities including certain drugs and patent medicines, cement, bicycles, cigarettes, sewing machines, bicycle spares and accessories, flashlight batteries and photographic materials. The prices of articles in the second group were controlled on the basis of percentage profit: for example, corrugated iron sheets, tyres and tubes. In the third category were the bulk of imported foodstuffs (except the more important ones that attracted fixed prices), upon which 20 per cent wholesale and 30 per cent retail profit margins were set. The final group consisted of articles controlled under freezing orders: petrol and petroleum products, baft and shirtings. These elaborate arrangements regulated supply but did not lower prices, and the Lagos public suspected collusion between the government and the AWAM. The high visibility of the AWAM in the organization and running of the supply boards did not help matters, one official even remarking that the scheme 'does tend to be rather too much of a personal matter between the Supply Branch and AWAM'.[69]

But neither government nor the firms could be blamed for the acute scarcity of key items such as petrol, salt, sugar and milk, and all had to be rationed. To conserve petrol, efforts were made to divert traffic to the railways and the number of lorries and taxis permitted to operate in Lagos was restricted. New vehicles could only be registered for use if they directly replaced older vehicles being withdrawn from service.[70] Petrol was rationed to eliminate inessential traffic, in the hope that passenger traffic would fall by 75 per cent. Officials, merchants and private individuals were enjoined to share car rides, or take the railway. Even *Oba* Falolu, like other Lagosians, had a fixed allocation of petrol. When he complained that his ration was insufficient, it was increased from eight to twelve gallons per month; but it was made clear that this was the 'maximum ration' he could expect.[71] Salt, sugar and milk were likewise in very short supply from 1942 onwards. The salt ration for Lagos, a pound of salt for 60 persons, was based upon, but slightly higher than, the approved ration for prisoners, one pound for 80 persons per day.

With an estimated population of 170,000, the city's daily and weekly requirements were put at 2,833 lbs and 19,831 lbs (221 ninety-pound bags) respectively. Lagos fared better than other places in the allocation of salt, but there was still great scarcity in mid-1942. One police report from this period suggested that retailers were 'profiteering' in salt as a means of paying their old debts! Another police report commented upon a woman seen begging for salt from house to house along Bucknor Street after she had failed to get any from the market.[72] Over 40 years later the journalist Tai Solarin recalled that he had to do without salt altogether, such was the gravity of the situation.[73]

Meanwhile, the scarcity and high prices of imports had their complement in the local foodstuff market, and both escalated the cost of living in wartime Lagos. There were several aspects to this. The tendency on the part of farmers to be preoccupied with export crop production at the expense of foodstuffs was implicitly encouraged by the government's wartime production drive. The loss of actual and potential agricultural labour to the mines and the military affected foodstuff prices in many localities. The presence of troops in the city also contributed to inflation; it was reported that the soldiers, unfamiliar with local market prices, 'usually paid too much at a time, three or four times the correct prices'. It was more generally observed that the 'very control' of imported food stuff prices 'had the effect of forcing up the prices of local foodstuffs'.[74] Changes in the price index of the major foodstuffs for the period 1939–43 (as calculated by the office of the Commissioner of Labour) represented in Table 8.3, illustrates the dramatic extent of these price rises.

Table 8.3 Changes in the Price Index of Major Foodstuffs in Lagos, 1939–43[75]

Article	September 1939	April 1942	October 1942	April 1943
Fish	100	163	161	202
Yams	100	150	184	184
Shrimps	100	133	133	93
Bread	100	100	100	150
Ogi	100	100	100	200
Agidi	100	100	100	100

In an attempt to gain greater control over the situation, and to restrict the opportunities for profiteering in foodstuffs, in 1941 the government instituted the Pullen Scheme of food price control in Lagos.[76] Public Notice 15 of 1941 fixed maximum selling prices (as indicated in Table 8.4) for all staple foods and established special markets for the sale of these foodstuffs. Prices were calculated by obtaining the price of an article at the point of production, to which were added all charges up to the railway terminus at Iddo Station. The wholesale price was then determined by adding 10 per cent to the landed cost at Iddo, while the retail price was obtained by adding a margin of 20 per cent to the landed cost. The profit margin for perishable items like vegetables was fixed at 25 per cent, to cover losses.

Gari was the staple of the overwhelming majority of Lagosians, and its scarcity presented the most severe problem in the city. To prevent shortfalls in urban supply, the government intervened directly at the point of production in Ijebuland. As price controls were introduced in Lagos, producers in Ijebuland diverted supplies to the Northern Nigerian market, which was not subject to restrictions. To prevent this, and as a mechanism to 'steer' produce toward Lagos, government prohibited the export of gari outside the

Province except under permit.[77] Prices of *gari* were fixed for the Ijebu-Ode and Shagamu markets at 3.5 pence per *olodo* pan and 6s 6d per bag. Ijebu producers reacted by hoarding and smuggling their *gari* in order to secure prices higher than those fixed by the government. This action compelled government to placate the farmers with higher prices and an increase in the number of permits issued to cover exports to places other than Lagos. A statutory fine of £10 or two months' imprisonment with hard labour was duly prescribed for convicted smugglers. Despite all efforts, the Ijebu traders still managed to smuggle *gari* into the city for retail on the black market at prices determined by themselves.

Table 8.4 Maximum Prices Fixed for Local Foodstuffs in Lagos, 1941[78]

Commodity	Wholesale (prices per hundredweight, unless specified)	Retail	Per *Oloruka*
Peppers	£2 6s 8d	£2 13s 4d	1s 3d
Coarse-grade *gari*	3s 4.5d	3s 8.5d	2.5d
Fine-grade *gari*	3s 10d	4s 4d	4d
White beans (N. Nig)	8s 9d	10s	7d
Local beans	7s 6d	8s 6d	6d
Shelled melon	16s	£1	
Local rice (per lb)		2d	
Beef (lb.)		6d	
Mutton (backlegs)		9d	
Mutton (other parts)		7d	
Pork (backlegs)		10d	
Pork (other parts)		8d	

Gari supplies to the city fell short of requirements throughout the duration of the war, and from time to time the situation threatened to become critical. On the last day of 1943, for example, the Director of Supplies was in desperate need of 50 tons of the commodity within a week to avert disaster in Lagos. To achieve this, he sought supplies from the Ondo and Warri Provinces so as to undermine the *gari* hold-up of the Ijebu traders who were determined to destroy the government marketing scheme.[79] But Ondo Province had no surpluses over local requirements and Warri Province could not afford risking the possible diversion of labour from its economic mainstay, the oil palm industry.[80] The *gari* scarcity in Lagos therefore reached a critical point in 1944 and the Director of Supplies stated that the colonial governor

> was determined to break the Black Market in Lagos at all costs, and to do so we must have supplies. If there is any hold-up in Ijebu-Ode we shall have to go elsewhere ... even if it does have an adverse effect on production of oil and kernels ... [F]ood supplies to Lagos market must in present circumstances take priority over everything.[81]

The acute scarcity did not begin to abate until the last quarter of 1944, in fact, and then it was only achieved through a rich harvest of yams and increased supplies of rice which combined to relieve the pressure of demand for *gari*.[82] This provided the opportunity for the government to build up *gari* stocks to obviate further serious shortages for the remainder of the war. But this proved difficult to manage effectively.

Owing to the perishability of the foodstuff and the abundance of supplies, stocks had to be disposed of in October 1944, and 500 tons of *gari* were railed to Northern Nigeria while prices fell in Lagos from 9s in October to 7s 6d and then to 6s in November. When government reduced the controlled price to 5s 6d per bag from 24 November, there was again a resurgence of black market activities.

By the end of the year, therefore, Lagos was pitched back into *gari* scarcity once more. Captain A. P. Pullen, the Food Controller, was by then 'utterly exhausted' by the pressure of the *gari* crisis and what he saw as a lack of cooperation by the Resident of the Ijebu-Ode Province,[83] whose staff had been overstretched severely by the task of mobilizing the production of the commodity and policing its legal marketing and movement. In 1945, government resorted to outright coercion, imposing quotas on communities and threatening local chiefs with prosecution should their district fail to meet the set quota. But neither this nor the offer of higher prices at Ijebu-Ode (7s 6d per bag of 186 lbs.) and Lagos (11s) in February 1945 succeeded in drawing the necessary quantities into the government stores. Instead, the black market continued to boom at £1 per bag, double the official price.[84]

In desperation, the government looked further afield – to Northern Nigeria, the Gold Coast, Gambia, Portuguese Guinea and Angola – for additional supplies. But apart from a quantity of grain from Northern Nigeria, and 68 tons of *gari* from the Gold Coast, help was not forthcoming. Further coercive measures also failed to extract more *gari* from the Ijebu Province, and a senior official was forced to admit that:

> every possible effort has been made to obtain maximum production by compulsion. It is now, however, clear that the present system has not only failed to obtain the best results, but that it has created a political situation of some gravity, which will probably react adversely on production in the future.[85]

In July 1945, the Governor frankly acknowledged the seriousness of the situation:

> owing to high produce prices and serious shortage of consumer goods, [the] public is spending more on foodstuffs than ever before. Food consumption has therefore increased and this coupled with failure of early maize and yam crops has created food shortage especially in Lagos and larger centres ... No immediate question of starvation but further adverse factors would result in [the] situation becoming out of hand with serious results on internal economy and exports of oilseeds.[86]

It was not until the conclusion of the war, in August 1945, that the futility of price controls was finally admitted. As soon as price controls and restraints on the movement of *gari* outside Ijebuland (except the traffic to the North) were abolished, food was reported to be 'abundant and cheap' in Lagos, while *gari* could be 'bought in every part of the town'.[87]

The abolition of controls made foodstuffs more easily available in the open market, but it did not halt the upward trend in prices. A major reason for this was the increased demand generated by the rapidly rising population of Lagos. By 1944, it was estimated that the urban population had risen by a third over the pre-war level.[88] This had generated increases in house rents. By 1941, the presence of military contingents and a decline in the rate of real estate development had already caused a rise of between 33 and 50 per cent in Lagos rents, compounded by the 200 per cent increase in the prices of building materials since the outbreak of war. This prompted the *Daily Service* to demand government intervention 'with a view of destroying the hydra-headed monster of profiteering which seems to be rearing its rent-head'.[89] It was supported by the *Daily Times*, which argued that 'tenants ... should not be left entirely at the mercy of the unscrupulous landlord who, unfortunately, is of a type largely predominating in this community'.[90]

As in their efforts to control food supplies and imported merchandise, government intervened in 1942 by establishing the Rent Assessment Board. The Board was expected to tackle the matter of high rents, but, as the *West African Pilot* reported, the general impression of Lagosians was that the Board was merely a tool of the landlords. In a series of no fewer than five editorials on the subject, the newspaper asked the government to act on behalf of the 'poor tenants': only legislation could solve the problem, as landlords and their agents were already demanding as much as £1 5s per month for accommodation which had been let out for only 5s before the war. The *Pilot* suggested a flat rate of 12s 6d for a room having a dimension of ten by twelve feet and fitted with electricity in houses built before January 1940); houses constructed after that date should attract monthly rents of 17s 6d per room where electricity was installed, and 15s 6d where it was not.[91] Despite the Pilot's vigorous campaign, it was not until 1944 that the government instituted a Committee to consider comprehensive measures for controlling rents in Lagos. A member of that Committee, who was also Deputy Commissioner of Labour, forecast the difficulties they would face:

> If exhorbitant rents are being charged in the Township, as I am convinced they are, the problem of control will be a very big one … [For,] the vast majority of landlords are restrained by no sense of decency or scruple and demand just as much as they think they can get. I fear, therefore, that unless we are careful we are likely to arouse a ho[rn]met's [sic] nest…. [L]et us either adopt a scheme which will give the people a chance to help themselves or leave things as they are, without introducing timorous compromises which can only affect the fringes of the subject.[92]

The accuracy of these prophetic words was soon apparent, as the committee quickly came to the realization that it would be extremely difficult to impose a flat rate for single room accommodation all over the metropolitian area.[93] Instead, a control scheme was proposed allowing for geographical location, type of structure, and dimensions of room. On the first criterion, Lagos was divided into three zones, the first being Lagos Island, the second comprising the Yaba Estate, and Ebute Metta East and West; and the third covering the rest of the township. The structures were classified into four types, and a rent set per ten square feet of living space. Table 8.5 sets out the renting system proposed under this scheme.

Table 8.5 Rents Proposed by Government Committee in 1944[94]

	Lagos Island	Yaba, Ebute Metta East and West	Rest of the township
(a) Rooms of brick (cement rendered) or cement	1s 3d	1s	9d
(b) Rooms of brick (unrendered) or mud (cement rendered)	1s	10d	7.5d
(c) Rooms of mud (unrendered)	9d	7.5d	6d
(d) Rooms of bamboo, galvanised iron or mat walls	6d	6d	5d

Note: Values per 10 square feet of living space

Even with such measures in place, there was little that the government could effectively do to impose the rent limits or to check profiteering by landlords. Indeed, rather than co-operate in the imposition of new regulations, landlords claimed that they were 'suffering to a greater extent than the tenants' by the operation of rent control measures.[95] A deputation of the landlords, which included L. B. Agusto, the first Muslim lawyer in Lagos, complained about tenants' violations of agreements and suggested that the government should instead fix a maximum rental based on 10 per cent of the capital value of the property. This proposal was, of course, impracticable as the government would have had to undertake the onerous task of evaluating every house in Lagos.

Lagosians were to some extent successful in winning concessions from government to ameliorate the effects of the rising cost of living experienced in the city during the war years. Most notably, organized labour, spearheaded by the Railway Union under the leadership of Michael Imoudu, agitated for a Cost of Living Allowance (COLA) for city-based workers. This was won in 1941, with government awarding an increase 'to meet the need for immediate financial relief to workmen in the lower paid categories' – those whose annual wages did not exceed £36 being granted a flat rate cost of living bonus of three pence per day from 1 October 1941.[96] This victory marked the beginning, rather than the end of workers' struggle in the city during wartime. A further development took place in 1942, when the allowance was paid to three categories of wage earners: daily paid labour, those whose daily pay was collected at the end of the month, and workers whose income was based on a monthly or annual rate paid monthly. While the lowest paid workers (on daily pay) earned a COLA of one shilling per day, a salary earner whose annual income exceeded £220 but was less than £226 got COLA at a rate which would take his total annual income to £226. The COLA awards were made retrospective to 1 October 1941 and all workers received ten months' arrears.[97]

These increases failed to keep pace with the rising cost of living, and protests over pay and benefits continued over a wide range of industries, culminating in the General Strike of 1945 over workers' wages.[98] The General Strike led directly to the setting up of the Tudor Davies Commission, to enquire into the cost of living in the Colony and Protectorate of Nigeria. The Report, submitted in 1946, recommended a 50 per cent increase in the COLA as it stood at July 1945, implemented with effect from 1 August 1945.[99] The speedy concession of so large an increase served to emphasize the consider-able hardships that Lagosians had endured as a consequence of wartime inflation, but as one labour historian has commented, 'the much expected "paradise" did not follow the strike' and the COLA award of the Tudor Davies Commission.[100] Lagos remained a city whose food supply was vulnerable to the vagaries of disrupted supply, and whose limited resources would continue to be stretched by a burgeoning population into the remaining decade of colonial rule and beyond.

Notes

1 This essay is dedicated to my wife, Omowumi, and to generations of long-suffering homemakers in the expensive city of Lagos. I thank the Central Research Committee of the University of Lagos and CODESRIA, Dakar, for funding the primary research leading to this publication.

2 Population growth in Lagos has been analysed by P. O. Sada, 'Differential population distribution and growth in metropolitan Lagos', *Journal of Business and Social Studies (JBSS)*, I, 2 (1969), pp. 117–32; and Ayodeji Olukoju, 'Population pressure, housing and sanitation in West Africa's premier port-city: Lagos, 1900–1939', *The Great Circle: Journal of the Australian Association for Maritime History*, 15, 2 (1993), pp. 91–106.

3 The following, however, treat aspects of this subject for parts of this period: A. G. Hopkins, 'The Lagos strike of 1897; an exploration in Nigerian labour history', *Past and Present*, 35 (1966), pp. 133–55; Wale Oyemakinde, 'The impact of the Great Depression on the Nigerian railway and its workers', *Journal of the Historical Society of Nigeria (JHSN)*, 8, 4 (1977), pp. 143–60; Ayedele (correctly, Ayodeji) Olukoju, 'Maritime trade in Lagos in the aftermath of the First World War',

African Economic History, 20 (1992), pp. 119–35; *idem,* 'Population pressure'; and *idem,* 'The travails of migrant and wage labour in the Lagos metropolitan area in the inter-war years', *Labour History Review,* 61, 1(1996), pp. 49–70.

4 It was also an expensive port: Ayodeji Olukoju, 'The making of an 'expensive port': shipping lines, government and port tariffs in Lagos, 1917–1949', *International Journal of Maritime History,* 6, 1 (1994), pp. 141–59.

5 National Archives of Nigeria, Ibadan(NAI) CSO 1/19/45 18 of 10 January 1912, Boyle to Harcourt, encl. Financial Report for the year 1910.

6 A. G. Hopkins, 'An economic history of Lagos, 1880–1914' (PhD thesis, University of London, 1964), Chs. 4 and 6 for the respective periods.

7 *Ibid.,* 79.

8 *Lagos Weekly Record (LWR),* 12 March 1910.

9 *LWR,* 26 March 1910.

10 *LWR,* 9 April 1910.

11 *LWR,* 14 May 1910.

12 Hopkins, 'Lagos Strike', pp. 148–9.

13 *Nigerian Pioneer (NP),* 7 August 1914.

14 *NP,* 21 and 28 August 1914, Rambling Notes and News (RNN).

15 *NP,* 4 September 1914, Abeokuta Notes and News (ANN).

16 *NP,* 20 October 1914.

17 *NP,* 16 October 1914, (ANN).

18 *NP,* 13 November 1914.

19 *NP,* 1 December 1914, Burrowes to Editor.

20 For example, *NP,* 30 July 1915.

21 *NP,* 19 January 1917, RNN.

22 *NP,* 9 February 1917.

23 *NP,* 18 May 1917.

24 *NP,* 5 April 1918.

25 *NP,* 24 May 1918; *LWR,* 13–20 July 1918, Mary Bull to Editor.

26 *NP,* 23 August 1918.

27 *NP,* 13 September 1918.

28 *NP,* 8 November 1918.

29 Olukoju, 'Aftermath'; Kehinde Faluyi, 'The impact of the Great Depression of 1929–33 on the Nigerian economy', *JBSS,* IV, 2 (1981), pp. 31–44.

30 *LWR,* 24 June 1919.

31 *LWR,* 27 Dec. 1919, Adelayo to Editor.

32 *LWR,* 7 June 1919.

33 Ayodeji Olukoju, 'The development of the Port of Lagos, c.1892–1946', *The Journal of Transport History,* third series, 13, 1 (1992), pp.59–78.

34 *LWR,* 1 November 1919, 'K-Nut' to Editor, and 17 April 1920, 'Publicus' to Editor.

35 For the currency crisis, see Ayodeji Olukoju, 'Nigeria's colonial government, commercial banks, and the currency crisis of 1916–20', *International Journal of African Historical Studies,* 30, 2 (1997).

36 *NP,* 16 January 1920.

37 *NP,* 21 May 1920.

38 *LWR,* 9 August 1919.

39 *NP,* 30 April 1920 and 28 May 1920.

40 *LWR,* 24 and 31 January 1920.

41 *LWR,* 6 March 1920.

42 Details in Olukoju, 'Aftermath'; and *idem,* 'Travails'.

43 *LWR,* 31 July 1920.

44 Ayodeji Olukoju, 'Anatomy of business-government relations: fiscal policy and mercantile pressure group activity in Nigeria, 1916–33', *African Studies Review,* 38, 1(1995), pp. 23–50, for the dynamics of this relationship.

45 NA CSO 1/34/12, Confidential, 21 January 1919, Boyle to Milner.

46 *LWR,* 10 January 1920.

47 *LWR,* 3 April 1920.

48 *LWR*, 21 February 1920.
49 *LWR*, 24 July 1920.
50 *NP*, 9 July 1920.
51 *NP*, 26 May 1926: Ijebu-Ode Notes and News.
52 *NP*, 6 September 1929.
53 *Lagos Daily News (LDN)*, 23 May 1930.
54 *LDN*, 6 June 1930.
55 NAI COMCOL 1 698, 'Prices of Foodstuffs Obtaining in Markets', encl. in Administrator of the Colony to Revd J. P. Shrimpton, 2 May 1930.
56 *Colonial Reports – Annual, No. 1625 of 1933, Annual Report on the Social and Economic Progress of Nigeria 1932*, p. 50.
57 *Colonial Reports, No. 1569 of 1932, Annual Report for 1931*, p. 39.
58 *Colonial Reports, No. 1842 of 1938, Annual Report for 1936*, p. 31; *No. 1904 of 1939, Annual Report for 1938*, p. 30; *Report for 1932*, pp. 30, 51.
59 *Annual Report on the Colony, 1933*, paragraphs 25–6.
60 *Ibid.*, paragraphs 23 and 25.
61 NAI CSO 26/4 09512, Vol. X, report for 1934, paragraph 18, and report for 1933, paragraph 27.
62 NAI CSO 26/4 0512, Vol X, 'Annual Report on the Colony, 1933-35', Report for 1933, paragraph 25; Vol. IX, 'Annual Report on the Colony, 1932' paragraph 81; and Vol. XI 'Annual Report on the Colony, 1936' paragraph 19.
63 *NP*, 14 August 1931.
64 *NP*, 6 May 1932 and 15 December 1933.
65 NAI DCI 1/1 4031 Vol. I 'Control of Merchandise Prices', Minute to PAS, 11 September 1939.
66 NAI DCI 1/1 4031, Vol I, Acting Commissioner of the Colony (Comcol) to Chief Secretary to Government (CSG), 9 October 1939.
67 NAI DCI 1/1 4031, Vol. III, Creasy to Lockhart, 10 December 1941.
68 *Ibid.*, Willis to Creasy, 14 November 1942.
69 *Ibid.*, Mallinson to Director of Supplies, 30 August 1944.
70 NAI COMCOL 1 2275/S.l., Vol. III, 'Oil and Transport Control Correspondence', Williams to Petrol Controller, 17 April 1940; Acting Comcol to CSG, 18 May 1940.
71 NAI COMCOL 1 2275/S.l, Vol. IV, Comcol to Assistant Oil Control Officer, 31 May 1941.
72 NAI COMCOL 1 2283/S.10, Vol. II, 'Salt Rationing', Senior. Assistant Superintendent of Police, CID, to Comcol, 31 July 1942.
73 *Sunday Tribune*, 24 September 1989.
74 NAI DCI 1/1 4043/5.4, Vol. II, 'Price Fixing: Local Foodstuffs', Association of European Civil Servants to CSG, 2 December 1941; and Commissioner of Labour to Price Controller, 20 May 1941.
75 NAI DCI 1/1 4043/5.4, Vol. II, 'Price Fixing: Local Foodstuffs', Commissioner of Labour to Price Controller, 20 May 1941.
76 Wale Oyemakinde, 'The Pullen marketing scheme: a trial in food price control in Nigeria, 1941–1947', *JHSN*, 4, 4 (1973), pp. 413–23; and Olumuyiwa Ukweinde, 'Managing urban food crisis: The Lagos foodstuff marketing scheme, 1943–1946', in Kunle Lawal (ed.), *Urban Transition in Africa: Aspects of Urbanization and Change in Lagos* (Lagos, 1994), pp. 65–78.
77 Okuseinde, 'Food crisis'.
78 Public Notice No.15 of 1941 in Official Gazette No. 11, of 20 February 1941, adapted from Oyemakinde, 'The Pullen marketing scheme', p. 417.
79 NAI DCI 1/1 4041/5.35/C.2 vol. I 'Gari Supplies, Lagos Markets', Director of Supplies to Resident, Ijebu-Ode, 31 December 1943, and Supply Board to Resident, Ijebu-Ode, telegram, 10 January 1944.
80 *Ibid.*, Residents to Supply Board, 15 and 17 January 1944.
81 *Ibid.*, Colby to Secretary Western Provinces, 19 January 1944.
82 *Ibid.*, Minute to Director of Supplies, 7 September 1944.
83 *Ibid.*, Pullen to Director of Supplies, 28 December 1944.
84 NAI DCI 1/1 4041/5.35/C.2, Vol. II, Pullen to Director of Supplies, 3 May 1945.
85 NAI IBMINAGRIC S.2/AC 'Gari Control', Acting Secretary Western Provinces to CSG, 10 August 1945.

86 NAI DCI 1/1 4037/S.58, 'Food Supplies, Lagos', OAG Nigeria to Secretary of State, telegram No. 624, 2 July 1945.

87 NAI DCI 1/1 4037/5.58/C.3, 'Food Situation, Lagos Markets', Pullen to Director of Supplies, 25 October 1945.

88 NAI IBMINAGRIC S.2/AC, Minutes of Meeting between Pullen and officials of the Western Province, Ibadan, 5 February 1944.

89 *Daily Service*, 19 December 1941.

90 *Nigerian Daily Times*, 13 May 1942, editorial, 'The rent problem'.

91 *West African Pilot,* 26 May 1943, editorial, 'Rents in Lagos'; 7 July 1943, editorial, 'The rent problem'.

92 NAI COMCOL 1 2438, Vol. I, 'Rent and Premises Control', Holley to Commissioner of Labour, 16 February 1944.

93 *Ibid.*

94 *Ibid.*

95 *Ibid.*, Allen to Commissioner of Labour, 18 November 1944.

96 NAI COMCOL 1 2534/S.1, Vol. I, 'C.O.L.A. for Government Labour in Lagos and Colony', Acting Financial Secretary to COMCOL, 8 December 1941.

97 *Ibid.*, Acting Financial Secretary to Comcol., 27 July 1942.

98 Wale Oyemakinde, 'Michael Imoudu and the emergence of militant trade unionism in Nigeria, 1940–42', *JHSN*, VII, 3 (1974), pp. 541–61; *idem*, 'The Nigerian General Strike of 1945', *JHSN*, 7, 4 (1975), pp. 693–710; and Robin Cohen, *Labour and Politics in Nigeria* (London, 1974).

99 NAI CE/T9 W. Tudor Davies, *Enquiry into the Cost of Living and the Control of the Cost of Living in the Colony and Protectorate of Nigeria* (London, 1946), 17, para. 63 (a); *Ibid.*, Appendix: Despatch, Secretary of State to Governor of Nigeria, 9 July 1946.

100 Oyemakinde, 'General Strike', p. 710.

9

The City of Durban Towards a Structural Analysis of the Economic Growth & Character of a South African City

BILL FREUND

This chapter tries to do two things. For the most part, it is concerned to characterize the economic development (underpinning the spatial and social development) of the South African city of Durban. It is also, however, a prologomena to a wider research project which it means to introduce; the project will concern the post-1970 evolution of Durban economy and society. It proceeds through a general consideration of urban economic issues to work through a phased if sketchy history of relevant themes in Durban. It concludes with some paragraphs on more recent developments. I have been influenced by a host of theoretical considerations on the city, many of them picked up or clarified in a recent sabbatical in France. In time, a more refined analysis, informed by parts of the research, should emerge.[1]

Society and Economy in a City

Before considering the evolution of Durban, it may be useful briefly to address the economics of cities. The city as an environment for human activity is at once straight-forward and ambiguous when it is made into a subject of enquiry. On one hand, it is clear enough to us pragmatically what we mean by a city. On the other, as we aim for a definition, the city becomes surprisingly elusive. In fact definitions of the city vary and they vary in our perception as the nature of the city changes itself. Pre-industrial definitions of cities are not the same as our own; they privilege non-economic, political and even sacral factors. This is not only a question of the theatre-states of early South-East Asia or the world of the Mayas; in Europe too, cities were defined in terms of adminis-tration, of being the 'seat' of church structures rather than in terms of demography. A town that had fallen into ruin was still a town of significance on the mental map of Europeans conceptualizing geography. As an eminent French geographer has said of even eighteenth-century (Enlightenment and proto-modern) perspectives, 'the city is a machine of which the optimal usage, ordained by the government of men and things, assures at once the production of the necessary, the useful and the agreeable'.[2] A frequently used, defining modern book on cities, Lewis Mumford's *The City in History*, is held in sway by an idealized and somewhat scholastic picture of the classic *polis* of antiquity, the seat of learning and rich human intercourse, fount of creativity as well as a political model.[3]

With the industrial revolution, the city became more usually the object of economic enquiry and the question of the relationship between urbanization, urban structure and economic growth approached centre stage. On one hand, cities (especially old ones that are declining or deserve to do so) began to be seen as parasitical, at war with the productive forces of the countryside and to some extent the source of noxious ideas polluting a pure community. On the other (and here the advancing industrial centre was the new model), they were liberating and energizing, the wellspring of new productive processes that are transforming the world. In the colonial world and notably Africa, these ambiguities are especially striking. Towns conceptually were critical in the whole colonial venture for reasons of enforcing economic controls and establishing strategic hegemony over newly conquered territory.[4] At the same time many observers, given the ambiguous and often deeply conservative nature of colonial rule, saw them as a source for the unbinding of wholesome older ties that weld together real communities.[5] It was not difficult to perceive the colonial town as inherently extractive, cruel and corrupting. As Cooper and Coquery-Vidrovitch have pointed out, much Africanist scholarship has taken the town as also being somewhat extraneous to the 'real' Africa which is rural and communitarian.[6]

I would agree with Catherine Coquery-Vidrovitch that this anti-urban strand is especially strong in Anglophone scholarship in Africa, although more recently the city as a backdrop for social change, foregrounding for example the 'real economy' in which women participate so vivaciously, has become more significant.[7] To some extent this has been less true of South African scholarship. The contrast is notable with Francophone literature, however, which not only tends to maintain a much more cheerful view of cities, with the city as the source of diffusion of civilization and civilized values, but has included for some time the impressive work of social scientists, notably geographers, trying to encompass the city in all its variety and with every effort at reaching out to theory and to structure in order to explain urban activity.[8]

The reality is that Africa, albeit considerably behind the pace of Latin America or much of Asia, is beginning to urbanize quite rapidly and urban social and economic forms are becoming constantly more significant if one seeks to grasp the current dynamics of change in the continent; in answer a literature is beginning to emerge in English in tandem with that in French. One approach, perhaps an obvious one, is to stress the dysfunctionality of the new cities and even megalopolises such as Lagos and Kinshasa. Paul Bairoch's stunning world overview of urban history, which certainly pays its dues to the key role of cities in historic economic development, is pessimistic about contemporary 'Third World' cities: their growth seems to have leapt far ahead of any constructive economic role; they are not the seat of productive activity of a kind that builds up economies; their advance does not correlate with the increasing productivity of agriculture; and their economic growth seems unable, at first sight, to keep pace with the squalid and miserable conditions under which the accumulating population increasingly live beyond the structures initiated by colonial and post-colonial planners.[9] 'Thus not only has urbanisation in the Third World lost the essence of the positive components that it brings to economic development, but hyper-urbanisation also adds numerous and important obstacles to development to those already in existence.'[10] It is growth stimulated by negative changes on the land, extruding men and women from existing agrarian economic and social structures rather than positive change engendered by activities in the urban sphere as happened during the industrial revolution.

To some extent, this is a just picture and one would be foolish to underestimate the immense problems, both to the state and to the people affected, that prevail in the new megalopolises of which Africa is developing her share. It is possible to ask, however, whether the non-productive picture that this creates does not hark back unduly (moralistically, perhaps, rather than critically) to an earlier vision of the parasitic city. Even if we wish to decry contemporary urban growth, it seems essential to tie our understanding of it to a broader vision of changes in capitalism to which I shall refer below through the rubric of 'post-Fordism'. Contemporary scholarship on cities in Europe and America is in fact reflecting major structural changes that tie into these shifts and show real parallels, albeit at a higher level of material affluence, to the changes afflicting 'Third World' cities in crisis. The conditions of the nineteenth and even Eric Hobsbawm's 'short twentieth century' may be drawing to a close in important ways as technology and class relationships alter globally. The industrial city, even a city that has become as industrial as Durban has, is an increasingly flawed model for understanding what is going on. But perhaps the city can move on as an effective site of economic activity, even if classic industrial forms become less and less typical. Not all writers, however, see contemporary cities as unable to continue generating creative growth, even in apparently harsh circumstances in Africa. Parnell is correct in pointing out that there is 'a growing literature which stresses that cities are the vanguard of economic growth'.[11]

If one is trying to make sense at once of African and global discussions of the city, South African research can be extremely illuminating.[12] If there are symptomatic problems of Third World cities today, South Africa has them in abundance. At the level of social relationships, the literature on Africa remains very suggestive and valuable to the South African specialist. The South African economy, however, is not in severe crisis; it remains mercurial and capable of initiatives of considerable sophistication. Structural concerns about the reregulation of world centres[13] and technopoles planned effectively by modern states[14] are not irrelevant to conceptualizing change in the contemporary South African city.

This, however, brings us to a question which is surprisingly elusive for social scientists: exactly how to comprehend the economic significance of cities. Unlike more restricted economic phenomena, cities are unwieldy and vague economic units. In practice, planners work out boundaries for them, such as the currently operative Durban Functional Regional Boundary, but their efficacy is inevitably variable and inexact. Dreams of creating input–output function models for modern cities are belied by the limited quality of existing statistics. Indeed, experts more or less reluctantly acknowledge that post-Fordist cities, even in the West, are less and less able – by definition – to create reliable statistics of the sort needed. 'Urban economics' has developed along the lines of certain areas of interest such as the study of changing land values and the opportunity cost of transport systems.[15] It has long been acknowledged, however, that the real importance of cities economically belongs in the realm of the twilight zone, for economists, of 'externalities'.[16] Some writers are stressing that the key issue with regard to cities, in fact, has not been the raising of a measurable economic product but rather the intensification and interchange of knowledge, the importance of innovation and all that comes out of dense human interaction. The growing importance of the issue of knowledge acquisition and diffusion in economic theory highlights this trend.[17] I would add to this the observation that cities, even when dysfunctional in critical ways, may be precisely the source of *crisis* that is *surmountable*, and that through the exploration of solutions to urban problems, technical and social, in class as well as in economic terms, qualitative change may occur. In a sense this is why the question of parasitism in cities, even Third World cities, is often raised in ways that are insufficiently posed. Urban crisis could be a stimulus to development.

Perhaps a literature that tries to generalise easily about Third World, colonial or post-colonial urbanization is too much with us. Although themes recur in the history of such cities, and some writers are comfortable talking about 'colonial cities', the individuality of each city, or at least the establishment of a typology of different types of colonial cities and post-colonial trajectories, is important. This is the only way, certainly, that South Africans can contextualize their urban problems successfully and situate their cities in a global literature.

Durban is hardly an under-studied city. On the contrary, it has been an important site for the development of South African studies. A new book on its history, edited by Paul Maylam and Iain Edwards, *The People's City* (Pietermaritzburg, London & Portsmouth, 1996), demonstrates themes in its social history, especially that of the African population. The new project which I am inaugurating, however, may still hope to ask some new questions about the second most important demographic and economic agglomeration in South Africa. The literature on Durban that is available to me is rich in studies of 'racial' administration and social historical perspectives focused very largely on the African population.[8] This literature, rather necessarily, is mostly situated (critically) around the apartheid paradigm and the ravages of racism: the city as a site for control and repression, but also for resistance and organization. It needs, in my view, to be amplified and reconsidered now in the light of developmental and economic trajectories, as well as to be historicized in the sense of periodization. At the same time, however, a technical and positivist literature needs to be enriched by serious examinations of conflict, power and class. The discussion that is followed introduces the main elements of an economic history of Durban, looking both at structural and social features. It tries to establish a typology and develop descriptively a sense of a 'growth path'. The final section is intended to introduce questions to be pursued in understanding how the city is currently developing. What seems to be a master theme constructing the racialized, industrial and modern city that grew so fast in the 1960s is now a part of history. Therefore this section is infused with suggestions and questions that will be the subject of research.

Durban, the Trading Entrepot

It is impossible to see Durban as having developed from imperatives deriving purely from the social formations that emerged over the centuries on the south-eastern African seaboard. The original site, on low-lying and easily flooded ground between two shallow *vleis*, only made sense in terms of a new kind of commercial impetus. Its very existence has been bound up with the relationship between the broader region and the wider world opened up through ocean commerce. The first stage of this evolved very slowly from perhaps the sixteenth and certainly the seventeenth century. As with Cape Town, but at a later and slower pace over time, Durban began as a place where irregular ocean traffic arrived to pick up local cargo; ivory seems to have been the principal commodity beyond provisioning which could be desirable to such traffic. That traffic became more intense in the early nineteenth century. Actual settlement began in 1824. For eleven years, until 1835 when it was named for a British governor of the Cape, it was a free-standing frontier community which had at first to accept the suzerainty of the new Zulu state. This suzerainty calls to mind the kind of relationship which early forts and settlements in and beside the African coast had with rulers and polities in many parts of the continent in the pre-colonial period.

With the establishment of British control (following a short Boer interlude), much more directly for strategic than economic reasons, we can observe very clearly the role of a growing town as part of the physical dominance of a conquered terrain – the urban frontier.[19] The small settler population became active in an increasingly differentiated set of activities that were self-supporting as much as exploitative of the countryside, and derived ultimately from the new imperative of colonial control. The town was always of importance in Natal; at a time when scattered farmers struggled to find a dependent labour force, when transport was inadequate and expensive, and when experiments to find a valuable cash crop for the new colony remained fairly inconclusive, a high proportion of the white population was urban and able to sustain itself through commerce.[20] A remarkable feature of Natal was the failure in general to find a lucrative colonial commodity that would form the basis of wider imperial commercial linkages. This failure, indeed, was never remedied.

Assessing the production of goods for use outside the urban boundaries is critical for assessing how a city operates economically. For Durban, the key factor lay not in intensified integration in the world economy so much as in the formation of a national and regional economy. Natal's economy would finally 'take off' on the basis of the role it could play in the South African economy as a producer of sugar, that key ingredient in industrial food outlay, and of coal to fuel the railways. Even wattle was initially developed to provide timber for the mines. And Durban's growth was in some respects almost independent from that of the province as a whole from the time of the mineral revolution onwards.[21] It would come to dwarf any other urban settlements in Natal in the twentieth century and in fact until very recently Natal only sustained one other, fairly small city – Pietermaritzburg. The explanation, however, lay not so much in Durban's triumph in scooping up provincial wealth as in the reality that the rhythm of its growth was determined by the Witwatersrand and the national economy, while the regional economy only generated a limited need for urban development.

The social and cultural construction of the settlement saw it juxtaposed as the salient of a new force in the world vis à vis the indigenous population. Yet it held a substantial attraction for growing numbers of Africans who sought to make use of the access to foreign currency and who found in the ambiguous power relations between the Zulu polity and the new settlement a useful gap for their own purposes. In turn, their availability as workers had its uses for the settlers who nonetheless declined to lay out a town that would provide for such an outlandish population, an ambiguity which would remain until the conclusion of white rule in 1994. The dominant ruling class discourse equally felt that the Africans were more African and more wholesome on the land; the town only led to their corruption and degradation, a view held by many Africans themselves, the more so given the harsh conditions engendered by the lack of amenities and services.[22]

Durban: A Commercial Colonial Town Becomes a City

Discussion of Durban's earlier history is indebted to the work of the American historian, Maynard Swanson, who captured many of the key issues in his Harvard PhD of 1964, and the geographer R. J. Davies whose most pregnant work on the subject is an article written almost at the same time.[23] While Swanson's work points to a mid-century phase of development in which the still small and undifferentiated settlement began to acquire a sense of structure and internal political power (reflecting a more definite class composition), with municipal government being granted in 1854 (following the creation in the 1850s of a Chamber of Commerce, the first newspaper, the first bank, the Mechanics Institute),[24] Davies considers the pre-1860 period as 'formative'.[25] He indicates

1860 as the starting point of a long period of development stretching to approximately the creation of the Union of South Africa in 1910, distinct from the previous phase of settlement.[26] During this period, the population increased from approximately 8,000 to 115,000, counting the settled area around the city.

In urban economic and social history, the significance of accretion is always great. On one hand, the same physical site may be used for remarkably different purposes by an historically changing cast of characters. On the other, there are continuities not only in the *dramatis personae* but also in structure and purpose. Yet it seems crucial to stress that the constitution of Durban as a merchant-dominated colonial Victorian city, while the frontier closed by stages, represented a qualitatively new era. A key feature of the period was physical reconstruction of the site of Durban in important ways. Gradually, the collection of nightsoil (1860s) was systematized, water, sewage (the 1890s), gas and then electricity were laid on, and roads surveyed and eventually paved.The site was made substantially healthier. Residential neighbourhoods, notably rising on the Berea ridge parallel to the bay and thus taking advantage of the sea breeze, were constructed. This kind of spatial configuration is a classic feature in colonial town planning; it represented a reaction to the uncertain and potentially menacing natural and human environment around the colonial community. Low-lying regions were drained and isolated from the sea. Transport was improved, notably the Berea Road which led directly over the top of the ridge on into the interior and the colonial capital, Pietermaritzburg.[27] At the end of the century, a tram system was introduced.[28] The Congella-Point rail line was the first in sub-Saharan Africa when laid out in 1860.[29] From the 1870s, even more critical was the reconfiguration of the road system required by the construction of the railway which would make the link to the interior the lifeline of the economy.[30]

Until the railway reached Pietermaritzburg, that town was larger and more suitable for cornering the commerce of the interior of South Africa. It had cheap pasturage for oxen and was a logical terminus for the overland trade of the Boer republics and Lesotho. When the railway link was perfected, the commercial advantages of Pietermaritzburg largely vanished and Durban overtook it. Between 1879 and 1887, ox wagons largely disappeared from the roads leading to town.[31] The importance of the mining industry from 1885 was cardinal in intensifying this commercial linkage and turning Durban into a city. Finally, the problem of turning the Bay into a safe deep water port was solved following the Anglo-Boer War in 1904.[32]

Pietermaritzburg, however, remained the capital of Natal. An important part of Durban's character was that it lost early any administrative or military role of significance. This was a commercial town, exemplified by its lay-out, by the emphasis on commercial infrastructure and on the civic dominance of prosperous merchants who were characteristically the pool from which were selected councillors and mayors.[33] Manu-facturing began to develop from the middle of the nineteenth century but it was largely an extension of the commercial impulse; goods were manufactured when merchants found this convenient and profitable compared with a dependence on imported goods. There was no consistent physical focus for industry; it occurred on a small scale throughout the settled part of the town. A crucial aspect of Durban came from its physiognomy: the prevalence of streams and often steep hillsides gave a developmental importance to flat land which, once drained, was at a premium, especially behind the core town centre and along the inland side of the Bay and then to the south of it.

The social complexity of Durban was considerable but far from unusual amongst colonial cities. As is generally the case in South Africa, the questions of colonial adminis-trative power and of concentrated utilization of a native labour force (if not actual proletarianization) need to be supplemented, perhaps usurped, by those posed through the social imperatives and cultural imaginations of a white population, within which working-class and lower middle-class elements played a crucial role.[34] This population, if notorious for its loyalty to the Mother Country, was quick to reconceptualize itself in a new physical context. While riven by class conflict and considerable differences of wealth and status, it was quick to unite against the threat of 'outsiders' (although Durban perspectives on those closest to the whites, those of mixed race, including the descendants of the early founders of the city, were more ambiguous and tolerant). A remarkable feature of Durban was the heavy but transient presence of Africans. By contrast with other South African towns, 'reserves' intended for the African population could be found in walking distance of the commercial centre of Durban, both to the north-west and south-west.[35] Africans found cash and other resources in Durban to attract them, however, from much greater distances. Atkins, in her recent study of Pietermaritzburg suggests that Africans in a sense colonized nineteenth century towns for their own target purposes that continued to operate with a considerable integrity, but perhaps limited their claims on any stake as townsmen (or women).[36] Certainly as labourers – and this was codified into the *togt* system – thousands of workers passed through, 'eating' or farming the city, in order to get needed wages and perhaps experiencing new worlds of interest. The city fathers of Durban systematized the residence of thousands of Africans – working on the docks and railways, as domestics and in heavy unskilled chores in industry – through the institution of barracks for single men, but they did not try to establish even minimal possibilities for family housing or allow Africans civic rights. Women formed a very small part of this African presence in town;[37] men even predominated heavily amongst the domestic workers. While the exclusion of Africans from the civic culture that was propagated caused poverty and squalor, their continued tie to a rural culture with deep historical roots was to some extent a source of strength and a bargaining chip for them in social contestation.

The sugar interest was the key factor in the introduction to Natal of indentured labour from India under conditions where the indentured, after five years, had the right to remain in the colony as free individuals. Although the large majority of the indentured were male, there was a legal obligation to admit a minority of women. Indians in this situation experienced injustice and hardships in the sugar plantations but generally they were eager to remain in South Africa where they began to reconstruct family and community institutions, partially on a new basis.[38] A growing number found their way to the outskirts of Durban. Whereas a commercial Indian community agglomerated on the inland side of the centre of the city, predominantly Muslim and densely populated, the ex-indentured workers adapted to the kind of economic activities that contemporary Africanists like to call 'straddling', activities beyond and outside the discipline of the wage labour force and sometimes the law. Members of joint families involved themselves in market gardening (often on municipal land), fishing, petty commerce and other activities while living in shacks they constructed themselves and gradually extended.

An extraordinary feature of early Durban was that the borders laid out in 1860 for seventy years remained steady. Within the Borough, the municipal authorities had as much control as could be hoped for in a South African city. It was for long reluctant to sell off land, however, and a system of land lease beyond its borders became typical. A growing population, disproportionately Indian and African, grew alongside Durban either in weaker neighbouring muncipalities or outside municipal jurisdiction entirely. As early as 1863, African squatters on the banks of the Umgeni had come together and were being ejected as unwanted.[39] Yet this kind of sweep was never effective for long, despite the enactment of vagrancy legislation before 1870. For the authorities, this was a zone fraught with crime and illegality – interracial commerce engaged in transactions over liquor was the commonest image. An alternative way to understand outer Durban, that messy sea of shacks and wood-and-iron cottages that lay beyond the mayor's purview, was as a model developing urban centre where the costs of living were cheap; where water, fish, fruit and condiments were available virtually free; and where the built environment emerged in a random way that allowed for petty accumulation and enterprises free of control and regulation.[40] But there was a certain freedom, too, in the spaces that lay on the fringe of the white business core from which unwanted Indian rivals had been shamelessly eliminated late in the nineteenth century, notoriously through the application of licensing legislation and local ordinances. Here a kind of common Durban culture was diffused, that filtered through the discourse of men of all races, easily traceable in slang, in common amusements, in sport, in horse-racing.[41] Ethnic and racial clustering and defensive institutions were at the same time becoming stronger, although less starkly than they would after the Act of Union. The tripartite structure of the population – white, Indian, African – in roughly equal numbers was becoming marked by the time of Union.

Industrial Durban: the Racial Fordism Model

Davies views Durban after 1910 – up to 1970, I will suggest here – as a distinct second phase that he calls one of diversification.[42] Demographically, in this 60-year period, Durban grew from a small city to a large and necessarily complex one. By 1960, there were some 650,000 people living around Durban.[43] In 1970 Young estimated the population of greater Durban (within 30 miles of the centre) as 1.3 million people.[44] In this period the related themes of industrialization and modernization need stressing. First, Durban became an industrial centre. Not coincidentally, the era dawns with the formation of the Natal Manufacturing Association in 1905.[45] Thereafter industrial promotion became increasingly important to the strategies of municipal authorities.[46] Ever since, Durban's industrial vocation has been a key characterisic. Compared with Cape Town or Johannesburg, let alone the administrative cities of Pretoria or Pietermaritzburg, the weight of industry – of a proletarian culture as opposed to a bourgeois culture marked by the predilections of a commercial/professional stratum – has been very marked. The improvement of the transport infrastructure, integrating road and rail networks, and the quality and cost of water provision were important factors.[47] Gradually after 1910, favoured level ground concentrated industrial activities, first the Maydon Wharf area behind the harbour, then Mobeni and later Jacobs further south, then Pinetown and Clairwood.[48] The role of the city in providing inexpensive land earmarked for this purpose as well as other projects, such as the draining of the Umbilo and Umhlatuzana catchments to canalize the small rivers flowing into the Bay, was critical in creating and extending these concentrations.[49] The lay of the land required that Durban violate the positivist geographers' norms for how urban development expands and intensifies; only on flat land, which was so limited in the vicinity, could industry grow properly. Not only did industry in Durban concentrate physically, but it also became more capital-intensive and more concentrated in a financial sense. In some respects, it fitted into a planning model which was structured through the relationship between capital and the municipality. Davies referred to a system of 'planned layouts' in this regard.[50]

The most important published analysis of Durban industry, May Katzen's 1961 study, foreshadows current fashionable economic debates in trying to conceptualize Durban as an *industrial district* in the manner mapped out by Alfred Marshall. Undoubtedly, as Katzen found, industries of varying shape and size displayed some interconnections and some benefits of aggregation. Nonetheless, not only was the diffuseness and diversity of industry in Durban striking, but this became truer over time. In the inter-war years, Durban industry was dominated by consumer goods, usually at the modest end of the consumer spectrum, which relied on the transport advantages of the city to produce for a national market once the confines of local consumption were exceeded. In the 1930s, it was the production of cheap clothing, notably men's clothing, which grew most rapidly in this context. Yet the locational advantages were limited. In the 1920s and 1930s, the gap in size between the Reef and Durban as industrial centres increased markedly. A major reason for this was the drawing up of rail rates that blocked any advantage accruing to the coastal centres from their location until 1954.[51] At the same time, a second category of industries arose which benefited directly from the lower cost of imported material to Durban factories. The chemical industry and, at the end of this period, the automobile industry are key examples. After the Second World War, the chemical industry became more and more crucial to industrial growth in Durban. The key industries in Durban, however – Toyota, Frame (textiles), the big clothing and metal factories, Bakers (biscuits), Dunlop, the oil refineries, the paint factories, Unilever, Saiccor – are to this day diverse. They cannot really be said to rest on a virtuous circle of mutual attraction or on a competitive pool of particularly skilled labour.

The key to industrial success in Durban, which reached an unprecedented level in the 1960s when growth far surpassed the national average, lay in its access to both the national market (with the relative closeness of the Rand) and to ocean traffic. 'It is in the most favourable position of any of the coastal manufacturing centres to produce for a Union-wide market.'[52] Of almost equal importance was the presence of an inexpensive but free labour force, 'abundant and cheap' according to Katzen who was writing on the eve of the fastest historical growth rates attained, notably amongst the Indian population. The white working class, smaller than in Cape Town or Johannesburg, also waged fierce struggles in its structurally weak position between coloured competition and an energetic business class. With its hold on the craft unions and its influence on the state, however, it was able to secure a stabler place at the top of the labour market during the inter-war years. The Indian working class in Durban, meanwhile, found space working for the municipality and, in growing numbers, in consumer industries where the pay packet represented a major share of employer costs, particularly in competition with the Witwatersrand. Nonetheless I have argued elsewhere that white Durban manufacturers, who dreamt of excluding and expelling Indians, especially when Indians engaged in radical contestations with them, failed to take full advantage of their availability as workers, and that the dynamism of the industrial economy suffered as a result.

The second theme of the era can be summed up as modernization.[53] It is useful to consider the extent to which Durban entered into what, following Lipietz, we can call a Fordist era. If modernization can be taken as an ideologically driven set of ideas about economic and social values, Fordism is a way of discussing how the state and industry regulated the basic issues involving the production and reproduction of the key classes in an industrial society. This meant an intensification of service production based on the assumption of a large industrious male population, requiring the basic means of economic and social reproduction and able to buttress economic circulation through the capacity to consume mass-produced products. For such a working class, the provision of public transport, health, schooling and housing provision was often more practical and reliable than reliance on private enterprise. The state, and notably the local state, intervened in the sphere of reproduction that assured production. For Durban, given the dominance of secondary industry, this paradigm promises to be particularly useful.

The intensity of racial competition, however, and the definition of the state administering a 'plural society' comprised of races who needed to be kept apart, gave Fordism in

South Africa and in Durban a particular character. Steven Gelb, who first interested South African scholars and commentators in the concept, has written of 'racial Fordism' in South African social and economic regulation.[54] The model works particularly well in application to urban and consumption-related issues, though it is less useful in capturing the entire national picture, where the export of primary commodities remained fundamental (Fordism is hard to apply to the mining and agricultural sectors). Whites did not benefit from a European-style welfare state, which was hardly necessary given the racial constitution of the labour market. Nor were they sufficiently characteristic production line workers to justify Henry Ford and the Detroit automobile workers as models. What emerged, however, was a society where much of the city was set aside for whites, allowing for detached home ownership on a basis available to a large percentage. Inexpensive health care and schooling of reasonable quality, the possibility of very substantial consumer expenditure and virtually no fear of unemployment except in the worst years of the Depression became basic features. Extensive and racially exclusive suburbs extended on inland ridges and suburban lines of rail to cater to their needs. The Fordist order benefited a white population who were largely lower middle class or skilled workers. By contrast, people of colour, who actually formed the mainstay of the industrial order, were citizens in the Fordist order on sufferance.

Nonetheless, in the later phases of the industrializing period some of these conditions became available to the huge Indian working class, which far outnumbered its white counterparts. Indian workers were to a much greater extent domiciled in council houses placed in racially defined townships structured on class lines. Africans, who were for long outside the licit bounds of Fordism, were nonetheless assumed by the 1950s to be employed, resident in male-dominated households and in need of mass subsidized housing. Of course, this was not the case in reality, but it was a model which dominated the massive removals and creation of new townships that was to follow.[55] Even in early times the 'Durban system' whereby the revenues from municipal beerhalls were used as a way of paying for some elements of African welfare – and, more crucially, surveillance – represented a crude form of regulation of a working class that was at best half-wanted.[56]

It is crucial to recognize that Fordism in Durban rested only to a limited extent on the solid base of a consumer society, a mass market which could generalize and drive forward competition in a wide range of applied industries. This kind of consumer society made and continues to make capitalism so distinctive and intensely hegemonic in the land of Henry Ford. But important elements of it were present in South Africa. Moreover, it appeared to work. Despite the poor export capacity of South African – and Durban – industry, general conditions of economic and industrial growth were good through most of the 40 years of growth after 1933. It was an industry that responded to the needs of a national economy that flourished, apart from the inter-war depression troughs. In its heyday, during the 1960s, economic growth in Durban surpassed national averages and Durban drew level as an industrial employer with Cape Town. In one area, moreover, Durban benefited especially from this kind of social structure; with the development of mass leisure possibilities for whites, Durban as the seaside rail terminus became the principal holiday destination of white South Africa, particularly for the whites of the Witwatersrand. The 'Golden Mile' became the focus of a distinctive and important element in the city's economy.[57]

The establishment of effective controls over this mixed population was closely linked to an ideology that was concerned to keep the 'races' apart for their own good, although above all for the good of the whites, and to the notion of a 'modern' city, hygienic and planned.[58] Such a city needed to be designed on the latest models as a Garden City that would appeal to the white middle class with high levels of maintenance in low-density white suburbia and carefully zoned industry and commerce.[59] At the same time, it must be regulated to keep each 'race' in its place.

Through the eras of segregation and then apartheid, the search continued for controls appropriate to the regulation of an increasingly large and wealthy metropolitan area. The lands outside the Borough were an early target. In 1930 a Boundaries Commission made a crucial intervention that led to the extension of the city limits, permitting the whole range of apparently uncontrolled and illicit activity to come under the jurisdiction of the municipality of Durban, and considerably increasing the African and notably the Indian population as a result.[60] During the 1930s, however, beyond sporadic if intense waves of slum clearance, relatively little was done to enforce a new system or to plan a new way of life for Indians and Africans in Durban. After the Second World War, and stimulated by a hysteria during the war concerning the 'penetration' of white Durban by the Indian middle class, a much more massive restructuring was set into motion. The city was a prime mover in this combination of slum clearance and racial engineering and, more than in other South African municipalities, the role of the city, as opposed to an overlay of 'apartheid' from the central state, was clearly fundamental in this process.[61] McCarthy demonstrates that the local state also did its best to ensure that segregation would work for, rather than against, the interests of the local economy in its spatial planning.[62] Yet, as Maylam particularly has shown, conflicts rarely ceased between central state, local state and capital over how this control was to be implemented.[63] The terms of regulation were never out of dispute for long. Nor was it clear that this system of racial regulation actually paid; the best years of growth in Durban may have depended on the presence of substantial cheap labour which in large part lay outside the Fordist system.

The years from 1935 to 1960 were punctuated by intense strikes, largely by Indian workers in the first 15 years and then increasingly by African workers, although white labour was also restive, especially during the Second World War. These racial divisions, so crucial in structuring, defining, dividing and disciplining the working class of the city, were in fact often the cause, proximate or deeper, of the strikes as workers fought to prevent being undercut while committed activists aspired, in the end usually vainly, to find unity around disparate material interests.[64] In the context of the mid-1940s, while white workers were becoming less crucial to the equation as the economy expanded, Indian workers faced dismissals and replacement by apparently more docile migrant Africans, heightening tension between the two groups. From the transformation of Dunlop after 1942, through the struggles at Frame and in sugar milling in the mid-1950s, to the creation of Toyota in 1971, many firms deliberately sought to exclude troublesome Indian labour.[65]

The 'race riots' in 1949, which were at their worst in Cato Manor – immediately to the west of the city and in walking distance from the centre – and which seemed to suggest that the vibrant and racially mixed marginal communities that throbbed on the fringe of the city were sources of violence and disorder that needed to be broken up for good, were a powerful incentive to employers bent on tighter control. Cato Manor was the very centre of a new African urban life in Durban which, for the first time, included large numbers of women and youths, much political agitation and ferment on the part of small-scale accumulators, Indian and African, and was terrifyingly resistant to control from the state; it had expanded dramatically during the years of the Second World War and after.[66] It took the central state, however, partly concerned for reasons of security, to set up the funding base which would lead to the massive extension of Group Areas, especially after 1960, and result in the physical removal of several hundred thousand Indians and Africans. Huge new estates were created in Kwa Mashu and then Umlazi for Africans, in Chatsworth and then Phoenix for Indians. A recent University of Natal thesis itemizes very clearly for Phoenix the mixture of racism and modernism and (almost) late-model planning of this working class 'community'. The banner of the English New Towns flew over this massive housing scheme.[67] The transport model increasingly dominant was the costly, private, South African-built automobile, supplemented with private and public buses and trains servicing the big townships. Not only did this dismantle and disorganize opposition; it created the possibility – far more, admittedly, for coloureds and Indians than for Africans – for social promotion and reidentification of a type that is characteristic of housing transformations elsewhere.[68] Of course, in the intense if sporadic anti-apartheid struggles of the 1980s, townships could also foster a new form of solidarity. There proved, however, to be a big difference between Indian and coloured township resistance, which on the whole remained tied to specific struggles against City Hall, and African resistance which tied in to both work-place resistance (Durban became a major stronghold of FOSATU and then COSATU) and a national programme of insurrection.

Some of the removals affected areas of flat ground wanted for industrial development. This was already part of the logic of the expansion of the Borough in 1932.[69] Everywhere, however, the relatively spontaneous character of urban development that flourished in poorer and less controlled areas was under attack; the City Beautiful was to be a city without an informal sector, without markets, without unsightliness or shacks. The model imposed assumed that Durban could plan on a basis not unlike Amsterdam or Manchester; those features that could not be fitted into that model had to be swept aside, ruthlessly if need be. An expanding economy, however, made it possible for growing numbers to be fitted into the City Beautiful, even if not necessarily as first-class citizens. Indian unemployment, conventionally considered as a major social problem through the 1930s and 1940s, was 'solved' in the boom years with the entry of an increasingly literate Indian population into skilled posts vacated by whites. In the 1960s, the African population was largely employed, if very poor, and clearly an increasingly key element in the labour force of the city.

The Fordist Model Unravels; Towards a 'Post-Modern' City

Since 1970, perhaps since the important strike wave of 1973,[70] this modern Durban, the racial Fordist model typical of South Africa but distinctively Durban, has begun to unravel. It is much more difficult to generalize about what kind of city Durban has become or is becoming. This is, in fact, the burden of the research project in which I am beginning to engage and at this stage I consider my findings to be tentative indeed. A few key introductory points, though, may be put forward for consideration. First, as Morris and Hindson have insisted, the process of class compression in which colour was taken to be a useful token for position in the labour force and the social order, has been succeeded by a growing decompression. Indian workers, managers and capitalists have been able to encroach on previously white pastures. The Africans have become gradually more and more differentiated. The purely racial character of neighbourhoods, schools and other amenities has given way at least to a greater ambiguity.[71]

The bigger and more generalized issue, has been the evisceration of Fordism as a model for relating production to reproduction. Uneven growth in the 1970s has given way to slower growth if not outright stagnation, only apparently with better performances in the post-1994 context. Since the 1973 strike wave, but especially in the course of the early 1980s, a large proportion of African industrial workers have joined unions with a militant ethos, deeply hostile to their bosses. This has created a different form of cohesion and consciousness in the work place and has improved the situation of many workers; it is less easy to itemize the wider implications of unionization. There has been a shift in industrial composition whereby automobiles and chemicals, particularly tied in to the national market and import-dependent whilst using relatively small numbers of well-paid workers, have become more dominant. At the same time, the more localized and labour-intensive industries have experienced relative decline,[72] suggesting a corresponding decline in the industrial cohesiveness seen by Katzen and, to a lesser extent, Young, at the close of the Fordist era.[73]

The port has containerized. Although in periods of expansion it continues to make use of low-skilled migrants, its core workforce has substantially diminished. Even where factories expand, they do not take on equivalent numbers of new workers. As the size of the industrial workforce stagnates, workers are further threatened, despite recent growth, with the increasing possibility of seeing their handiwork swamped by cheaper and better-produced foreign imports. The ANC state is reluctant to retain tariff barriers to protect local industry and may well threaten the future of key elements in the industrial configuration that has been at the heart of the Durban economy from the point of view of employment. Even where laws remain in force, the actual capacity to police customs and regulate imports appears to have declined drastically in the last two years.

Yet the city continues to extend in physical size while the population increases. A recent estimate for the Durban Functional Region, which stretches to include Mpumalanga, Tongaat and Amanzimtoti, is 2.3 million, or approximately double the total 25 years earlier.[74] Durban is in the category of those cities where there is, as the capitalist sees it, a surplus population. Thus there is a declining economic logic to Fordist regulation and an increasing imperative for planning to be replaced by a more enterprising collection of individuals, on their own in terms of creating jobs – the so-called informal sector. Public facilities are increasingly unable to handle the demands made on them; the capacity and the will to make the affluent into 'cash cows' for the poor through taxes and rates is diminishing. The African population, previously physically penned in by the limitations of the space/transport system, are now mobile through the agency of a taxi industry that defies regulation. Above all, new so-called informal housing, spearheaded by land invasions, has sprung up on a scale far beyond that of the 1940s.[75] Apartheid was remarkably successful, as with the colonels in Greece, as with Mussolini in Italy, in blocking accumulation from below in the name of order. With the twilight of the apartheid order, the potential for new accumulators, Africans very much included, to emerge on the basis of providing poor people with transport, basic foodstuffs, building materials and other services has increased. Some of this has engendered violence as accumulators seeking exclusive control of some sort of turf or market niche (tied in to the availability of drugs and weaponry) square off. This feeds into the continued no-holds-barred rivalry between the Inkatha Freedom Party (IFP), itself already a patronage party created by the Bantustan policy which impacted on almost all the African residential areas around Durban from the 1970s, and the ANC, which is far from immune to such contagions of territory, influence and clientage.

It would be an error, however, to see post-Fordist urban growth as in any sense exclusively South African. It is not only here that a major shift is occurring in the order of cities, in the changing spatial dynamism of new economic activities that seem to be affecting country after country. There seems to be a widespread view that coherent urban planning of the old type, based on a definable city centre and allowing for an integrated urban structure to be organized from on top, is increasingly problematic. It may be argued that capital itself is only prepared to tolerate an overly powerful ringkeeper, excluding the sphere of profits from such a key area as the extension of the built environment, under special historical circumstances which are ceasing to prevail.[76] The quality of statistics may be declining, industry is decentring and many older industries are of dwindling importance; the stimulating dimensions of late twentieth-century capitalism may well be less and less amenable to inclusive, overall urban integration, social or spatial.[77] The nuclear family, much as it may be regretted, is of declining importance (like the extended African family and joint Indian family before it) as a basis for social construction while the autonomously defined work (and felt needs) of women are of growing importance as determinants in a 'regendered' urban space.[78] The modern city adapted for apartheid, which assumed the nuclear household model, increasingly seems dysfunctional to a late twentieth-century city.

The possibilities of accumulation in new ways are interesting and perhaps too easily dismissed as the evil work of 'shacklords' and warlords. A look at the construction of cities such as Istanbul or even Rome – and, one suspects in an earlier period Liverpool or Chicago – would also show the dynamic of accumulation working against the carefully laid plans of the state and out of harmony with the Fordist regulation that clearly represents a later phase of development. Otherwise, typically the expansion of the city has worked in tandem with the emergence of entrepreneurs, on a small scale to start with and dependent on patronage.[79] The continued dominance of a small range of big firms in the provision of food, clothing and shelter is an unusual feature of the South African growth path which may or may not endure.

It might be more useful to juxtapose this kind of accumulation with a new look at the view from the top. If we started with the picture of a growing nineteenth-century town comfortably dominated by a small interlocking stratum of enterprising merchant manufacturers, today there remains the world of big business, banks and City Hall, as well as the possessors of large tracts of land for urban use, whose history is somewhat shadowy. Contemporary planning is often based on the assumption that 'stakeholders' to take a treasured word from South African political vocabulary, or a 'growth coalition', which in South African language usually involves organized labour, can and will be the power brokers in growth and development. In fact, what is essential is to problematize the growth coalition and to try to understand how, notably since 1970 and the end of apartheid construction, it has functioned (or not, as the case may be). What are the key growth organizations and are they effective? How meaningful is it to talk about local capital and does it have a clear project of its own? It needs at least to be put forward as an idea that capital in Durban has become increasingly branch-plant in character and less rooted in the city, especially since the 1970s. What leads to successful projects such as the Convention Centre? What is at stake in problem areas such as the replanning of Cato Manor? What will the role be of the central state which continues to think in terms of regional planning (imitating in time the currently projected Maputo corridor for the Pietermaritzburg–Durban route)?[80] Can Durban look east towards the world of maritime Asia, the most dynamic in our contemporary economic world?

Or will the different regions and conurbations increasingly go their own way as the urbanist literature internationally is suggesting?[81] There is a growing interest in South Africa in the idea that cities and regions may be on their own, that the central government is limited in its capacity to generate growth and even more so in shaping the form it might take. At minimum, one may see cities competing (as with Cape Town and the Olympics) for advantage with the given and mobile forces of corporate capital, often in ways that, socially or financially, may disempower more than they empower. Alternatively, competitive advantage may be constructed through skills and infrastructure, human and physical, that have a sounder basis for generalized growth.[82] This has already been sketched out in a critique of constricted and business-led planning initiatives for Durban that marked the phase of political transition and negotiation.[83] That suggests that understanding Durban, not merely in terms of race but in terms of accumulation and of power juxtapositions, is what is needed to convey where the city is heading. It is increasingly obvious that modernist planning assumptions are not only undemocratic but also irrelevant to some aspects of current economic dynamism, and can lead to ludicrous misallocations of resources and energy.[84] From a completely different perspective, and thinking about the current fate of many African cities, may not initiatives from below subvert and transform the urban order, perhaps to the horror of the previously dominant classes? Contemporary critical literature on the city is indecisive and somewhat contradictory, if fascinating. It can be interpreted as suggesting that: (1) change is somewhat deceptive and national growth patterns are reasserting themselves; (2) the growth model for the future is regional or local and decentred; or (3) even urban growth is now disconnected, with connections between sectors in different cities becoming more important than connections within cities. These, for now, are hypotheses.

Notes

1 The 'City of Durban' project is intended to have a somewhat open-ended character. I am proposing to provide an overall theoretical framework and an historical thrust, while also researching the question of growth coalitions – the framing of actual political and economic power in the city. A range of other researchers will be considering topics on the changes in capital and the accumulation process on the one hand, and the emergence and development of new forms of accumulation – the second or 'real' economy – on the other. The goal is to strengthen our sense of what a post-apartheid city and an urban economy might mean in the South African context and to base our understanding of Durban in terms of meaningful temporal divisions that explain the rhythms through which economic development and social change have been punctuated. This chapter is a first effort at synthesizing some of the relevant ideas that will go into the project.

2 Own translation. Bernard Lepetit, *Les villes dans la France moderne 1740–1840*, (Paris, 1988), p. 74.

3 Lewis Mumford, *The City in History* (Harmondsworth, 1966). Another recent assessment on similar if apparently more radical lines is Murray Bookchin, *From Urbanization to Cities: Towards a New Politics of Citizenship* (London: 1995).

4 For a model of colonial urbanization in very general terms see Anthony King, *Urbanism, Colonialism and the World-Economy: Cultural and Spatial Foundations of the World Urban System* (London: 1990). Also Frederick Cooper's influential collection, *Struggle for the City* (Beverly Hills: 1983).

5 For a graphic lament that foreshadows the coming literature on 'urban bias', see Josef Gugler and Richard Flanagan, 'On the political economy of urbanisation in the Third World: the case of West Africa', *International Journal of Urban and Regional Research*, 1 (1977).

6 Catherine Coquery-Vidrovitch, 'The process of urbanization in Africa (from the origins to the beginning of independence)', *African Studies Review*, 34 (1991), pp. 8–9.

7 *Ibid.*, p. 18.

8 Philippe Gervais-Lambony, *De Lomé à Harare* (Paris, 1994); Guy Maïnet, *Douala: croissances et servitudes* (Paris, 1985); Marc Pain, *La ville et le cité* (Paris, 1984).

9 Bairoch specifically sees this phenomenon as in some way a return to manifestations found in cities before the industrial revolution in the Mediterranean world and elsewhere. Paul Bairoch, *De Jericho à Mexico; villes et economie dans l'histoire* (Paris, 1985).

10 *Ibid.*, p. 622. Own translation.

11 She refers to Durkheim's view of the 'city as the site of specialist production', Susan Parnell, 'South African cities; perspectives from the ivory tower of urban studies', *Institute of Advanced Social Research Seminar Papers*, 7 (University of the Witwatersrand), 1995. But of course Adam Smith, Weber and Marx were also very interested in the economic dynamism of urban economic activity. Braudel, commenting on European cities of the early modern period, envisioned them not as parasitic but as economic multiplier effect creators following Keynes: Lepetit, *Les villes dans la France moderne 1740–1840* (Paris, 1988), p. 85.

12 Parnell, 'South African cities'.

13 Susan Fainstein (ed.), *Divided Cities: New York and London in the Contemporary World* (Oxford, 1992).

14 Manuel Castells and Peter Hall, *Technopoles of the World: the Making of Twentieth Century Industrial Complexes* (London, 1994).

15 Alan Evans, *Urban Economics: an Introduction* (Oxford, 1985).

16 Rémy Prud'homme, 'Les comptes economiques des villes', *Revue economique*, 1972. See also the discussion in Laurent Davezies in *La Courrieur du CNRS*, 81, special issue on 'la ville'.

17 S. E. van der Leeuw and J. McGlade, 'Information, cohérence et dynamique urbaine', in Bernard Lepetit and Denise Pumain, *Temporalités urbaines* (Paris, 1993); Oliver Williamson, *Markets and Hierarchies: Analysis and Antitrust Implications* (New York, 1975).

18 For instance, Iain Edwards, 'Mkhumbane; Our Home' (PhD thesis, University of Natal, Durban, 1989); Joseph Kelly, 'Durban's Industrialisation and the Life and Labour of Black Workers 1920–50' (MA dissertation, University of Natal, Durban, 1989); Paul la Hausse, 'The Struggle for the City; Alcohol, the *Ematsheni* and Popular Culture in Durban 1902–36' (MA dissertation, University of Cape Town, 1985); Paul Maylam, 'The 'Black Belt', African Squatters 1935–50', *Canadian Journal of African Studies*, 17 (1983); Paul Maylam, 'Surplus people in a South African city: the contradictions of African urbanization 1920–50' (unpublished paper, Canadian African Studies Assocation, 1982); Tim Nuttall, 'Class, race and nation; African politics in Durban 1929–49' (D Phil thesis, Oxford University, 1991); Louise Torr, 'The social history of an urban African community; Lamont *c.*1930–60' (MA dissertation, University of Natal, Durban, 1985), but see also Leo Kuper *et al.*, *Durban; Study in Racial Ecology* (London, 1958); Bill Freund, *Insiders and Outsiders; The Indian Working Class of Durban 1910–90*, (Pietermaritzburg, London & Portsmouth, NH, 1995); Brij Maharaj, 'The spatial impress of the central and local states: the Group Areas Act in Durban', in David Smith (ed.), *The Apartheid City and Beyond*, (London, 1995); and Dianne Scott, 'Communal space construction: the rise and fall of Clairwood and district' (PhD thesis, University of Natal, Durban, 1994).

19 For parallels see the detailed study of Senegalese colonial towns in Alain Sinou, *Comptoirs et villes coloniales du Sénégal: Saint-Louis, Gorée, Dakar* (Paris, 1993).

20 Bill Guest and John Sellers (eds), *Enterprise and Exploitation in a Victorian Colony: Aspects of the Economy and Society of Natal* (Pietermaritzburg, 1985).

21 Maynard W. Swanson, 'The rise of multi-racial Durban: history and race policy 1830–1930' (PhD thesis, Harvard University, 1964), p. 271.

22 *Ibid.*, p. 403.

23 R. J. Davies, 'The growth of the Durban metropolitan area', *South African Geographical Journal*, 44 (1965), pp. 15–42.

24 Swanson, 'Rise of multi-racial Durban', pp. 126ff.

25 Davies, 'Growth of Durban', p. 17.

26 For the portrait of a similar economic structure manifested in the urban environment of a metropolitan city, see Roland Caty et Eliane Richard, 'Un négociant dans la ville; activités, fortune pouvoirs; Victor Régis à Marseille', in Michèle Collin (ed.), *Ville et port XVIIIe-XXe siècles* (Paris, 1994).

27 Swanson, 'Rise of multi-racial Durban', p. 168.

28 Bruce Young, 'The industrial geography of the Durban region' (PhD thesis, University of Natal, Durban, 1972), p. 61.

29 *Ibid.*

30 Davies, 'Growth of Durban', p. 31.

31 *Ibid.*, p. 33.

32 L. Heydenreych, 'Port Natal Harbour, *c.* 1850–97', in Guest and Sellars, *Enterprise and Exploitation*, pp. 17–43.

33 Swanson, 'Rise of multi-racial Durban', p. 144.

34 Gary Minkley, 'Border Dialogues: Race, Class and Space in the Industrialisation of East London *c.*1902–63' (PhD thesis, University of Cape Town, 1994).

35 Davies, 'Growth of Durban', p. 11.

36 Keletso Atkins, *The Moon is Dead! Give Us Our Money* (London and Portsmouth, 1993).

37 Under 10 per cent in 1911, Davies, 'Growth of Durban', p. 27.

38 Freund, *Insiders and Outsiders*.

39 Swanson, 'Rise of multi-racial Durban', p. 287.

40 Scott, 'Communal space'.

41 Freund, *Insiders and Outsiders*.
42 Davies, 'Growth of Durban', p. 17.
43 Swanson, 'Rise of multi-racial Durban', p. 2.
44 Young, 'Industrial geography', p. 24.
45 Scott, 'Communal space', p. 239.
46 Jeff McCarthy, 'Changing the definition of Natal's metropolitan areas: the case of Durban 1930–87' (unpublished paper, Workshop on Regionalism and Restructuring in Natal, Durban 1988).
47 Young, 'Industrial geography', p. 29.
48 May Katzen, *Industry in Greater Durban: Its Growth and Structure* (Pietermaritzburg, 1961), pp. 1 ff.
49 Scott, 'Communal space', pp. 260–1.
50 Davies, 'Growth of Durban', p. 24.
51 Katzen, *Industry in Greater Durban*, p. 7.
52 *Ibid.*, p. 8.
53 Parnell, 'South African cities'.
54 Steven Gelb (ed.), *South Africa's Economic Crisis* (Cape Town, 1991), Introduction, pp.13 ff.
55 G. G. Maasdorp and N. Pillay, *Urban Relocation and Racial Segregation: The Case of Indian South Africans* (Department of Economics, University of Natal, 1977); Edwards, 'Mkhumbane'.
56 Maynard W. Swanson, 'The Durban system; roots of urban apartheid in Natal', *African Studies*, 25 (1976), pp. 159–76.
57 Katzen, *Industry in Greater Durban*, p. 8.
58 Kuper et al., *Durban*.
59 Catherine Coquery-Vidrovitch, 'A propos de la cité-jardin dans les colonies', to be published in a forthcoming collection edited by Coquery-Vidrovitch and Odile Goerg.
60 McCarthy, 'Changing the definition'.
61 'Of all the major cities in the Union, Durban, through its City Council, has shown the greatest enthusiasm for compulsory segregation', Kuper et al., *Durban*, p. 34.
62 McCarthy, 'Changing the definition'.
63 Maylam, 'Surplus people'.
64 Freund, *Insiders and Outsiders*.
65 Vishnu Padayachee, Shahid Vawda and Paul Tichman, *Indian Workers and Trade Unions in Durban 1930–50* (University of Durban-Westville, Institute for Social and Economic Research, Report 20, 1985).
66 By 1951, almost a third of the African population registered in the city were women. Davies, 'Growth of Durban', p. 27. See also Edwards, 'Mkhumbane'.
67 David Bailey, 'The Origins of Phoenix, 1957–76: the Durban City Council and the Indian housing question' (MA dissertation, University of Natal, 1987).
68 Gérard Althabe et al., *Urbanisme et réhabilitation symbolique: Ivry, Bologne, Amiens* (Paris, 1984).
69 McCarthy, 'Changing the definition'.
70 Steve Friedman, *Building Tomorrow Today* (Johannesburg, 1987), pp. 37–68.
71 Mike Morris and Doug Hindson, 'The social structure and dynamics of metropolitan Durban' (Centre of Social and Development Studies Working Papers 13, University of Natal, Durban, 1995).
72 Consultative Business Movement Planning Forum, 'Report on the Durban functional region' (unpublished, Durban, c.1992).
73 It may be, however, that service production tied in to the big factories, such as auto parts makers, have become correspondingly more important.
74 Much higher estimates have been made. For example, the Urban Foundation some ten years ago went as high as 3.8 million but lately these figures have been discredited. See Consultative Business Forum, 'Report on the Durban Functional Region'. This estimate suggests that the growth of the city population is less out of line with economic growth than has been imagined. Durban Corporate Services, Urban Strategy Project, 'Population and housing in the Durban metropolitan area, 1995'.
75 Doug Hindson and Jeff McCarthy (eds), *Here to Stay; Informal Settlements in Kwa Zulu-Natal* (Durban, 1995).
76 Christian Topalov, *Capital et proprieté foncière: introduction à l'etude des politiques foncières* (Paris, 1973).
77 Amongst others, Cynthia Ghorra-Gobbin (ed.), *Penser la ville de demain: qu'est-ce que institue la ville?* (Paris, 1994).

78 Damaris Rose and Pierre Villeneuve, 'Work, labor markets and households in transition', in L. Bourne and D. Ley (eds), *The Changing Social Geography of Canadian Cities* (Montreal, 1989).

79 R. C. Fried, *Planning the Eternal City* (New Haven, 1973), on Rome; Kemal Karpat, *The Gecekondu: Rural Migration and Urbanisation* (Cambridge, 1976); Lila Leontidou, *The Mediterranean City in Transition; Social Change and Urban Development* (Cambridge, 1990), especially on Athens; and on nineteenth-century industrial cities, Ira Katznelson, *Marxism and the City* (Oxford, 1993).

80 Discussion, Ministry of Trade and Industry, May 1996.

81 Georges Benko et Alain Lipietz (eds), *Les régions qui gagnent; districts et reseaux: les nouveau paradigmes de la géographie economique* (Paris, 1992); Doreen Massey, *Spatial Divisions of Labour* (second edition, Basingstoke, 1995).

82 R. C. Hill, 'Economic crisis and political response in the motor city', in L. Sawers and W. K. Tabb (eds), *Sunbelt/Snowbelt*, (New York, 1984); Harvey Molotch, 'The city as a growth machine', *American Journal of Sociology*, 77 (1976); J. C. Perrin, 'Un bilan théorique et methodologique', in J. Federwisch et J. Zoller (eds), *Technologie nouvelle et ruptures régionales* (Paris, 1986).

83 Jennifer Robinson and Carlos Boldogh, 'Operation jump start: an urban growth initiative in the Durban functional region', in Richard Tomlinson (ed.), *Urban Development Planning* (Johannesburg, 1994), pp. 191–214.

84 G. Massiah et J. F. Tribillion, 'Les differents visages de la planification urbaine', *Politique africaine*, 27 (1985).

PART FOUR

Becoming Urban
Towns as Cultural Brokers

10

'But I know what I shall do'
Agency, Belief & the Social Imaginary
in Eighteenth-Century Gold Coast Towns

RAY KEA

What can be said about the values, thoughts, attitudes, and beliefs of social agents – individuals and groups – in eighteenth-century Gold Coast sea towns at the height of the trans-Atlantic slave trade, with its violence, displacements, compulsions and debasements? In what ways were expectations, grief, success, death, revenge, disasters and moments of achievement expressed in a mercantile world of international markets and the exploitation of materials and labour on an ever-expanding scale? Indeed, can anything at all be said about these matters? The major coastal towns, the locations of European castles, forts and factories, were commercially linked to the entrepots of western Europe and the plantations of the Americas. They were prosperous trading centres with warehouses, markets, commodities, currency reserves, credit facilities and intense commercial operations. The typical member of their dominant classes was a merchant broker.[1]

What did the processes of urbanization and state building on the Gold Coast and in its hinterland, and the sustained commercial interaction with the larger Atlantic world, signify in discursive, ideational and cognitive terms? What were social agents' imaginative perceptions of their societies and their 'everyday', and what discourses and narratives did they produce to express these perceptions? What intellectual and ideological profiles, if any, can be constructed on the basis of dominant and subordinate discursive formations? What was the language of honour, responsibility, respect, peace, good judgement, justice, security, companionship and belief? What were the controlling metaphors, categories, notions and norms that shaped the predominant conceptions of status, truth, morality and community? This study presents some broad reflections on these questions without proposing definitive resolutions or final conclusions. It is, above all, a preliminary investigation which attempts three things: to identify the Accra order's social imaginary and fields of intention – that is, the order's historical phenomenology and *mentalité* with references to historical *a prioris* and archives (in the Foucaultian sense); to understand how that order made sense of its own activities and experiences over time; and to conceptually frame the intersection and articulation of human agency and its larger historical circumstances. The guiding theoretical orientation is provided by Gramsci: 'The starting point of critical elaboration is the consciousness of what one really is, and is 'knowing thyself' as a product of the historical process to date which has deposited in you

163

an infinity of traces without leaving an inventory.' Four problems of a historiographical and theoretical nature are designated and these are pertinent to the matters under discussion in this study: (1) the problem of identity or the subject; (2) the problem of history; (3) the problem of ideology or culture; (4) the problem of knowledge or interpretation.[2]

The essay offers a particular kind of reading of the contemporary documentary sources in order to evoke the coastal entrepots' varied forms – of subjectivity/identity and thought/belief, of agency/capacity and practice/social action – in the broadest sense, the towns' cultural and ideological experiences. In particular, it looks at the utterances (énoncés) – the things-said – of certain persons, all men, as it turns out, resident in three Accra sea-towns (Gã: nshonamandshi; s. nshonoman). These persons include Hans Lykke (or Notei Doku), Kwaku, Asã (or Notei Sã), Noete Adowi and Christian Jacob Protten, all of Osu; Wetshe Odoi Kpoti of Labade (La); and Ni (or Note) Tshie of Teshi; Philip Quaque of Cape Coast and Johannes Eliza Capitein of Elmina. I present their practices and utterances – their specific ways of rationalizing the world and real life – in order to illustrate historically constituted forms of subjectivity (subject positionings) – self-activity and agency or their negation and denial – and the 'ordinary' ideological and cognitive experiences of persons in their class-being, their material and cultural locations, and in their orders of politicality.[3]

I have tried to read and constitute them in their internal heterogeneity, although the sources re-present them as unified intentionalities, in their politics of location, and their temporality of struggle. The utterances were among the texts of urban social life. If such texts are part of social being, and we can assume that this was the case, then they must be viewed, 'like other parts of social being, as multi-layered, complex, fractured, composed of incoherence, and silences, as well as the smooth flow of would-be authoritative discourses'.[4] The point is to ascertain the 'historical dimension of the culturally divided self struggling to create a livable life in the midst of contingencies'.[5]

'Over time the Aquamboes became worse and more harsh towards the Accras and others subject to them'

The Lutheran priest Johannes Rask, who resided at Christiansborg Castle, Osu, in the service of the Danish West Indies and Guinea Company from 1709 until 1713, writes:

> Many have told me about a black from Orsu, the town that lies under Christiansborg: he is called Hans Lykke after a colonel who formerly lived at Christiansborg. This black often wished that he were dead, so that he could meet the devil, for the devil, he said, makes or keeps one merry every day with spirits, palm wine, and other good drink; he has many women; he owns large cannon and much gunpowder with which one can amuse one's self, and he [Lykke] would gladly be in such company. He says he is perfectly suitable to play the part of a devil's imp. The Aqvambus decapitated him during their campaign in 1709, a little before my arrival.[6]

Lykke's death occurred in February 1709 and according to a contemporary Danish account he was shot while engaged in a war against the Akwamu regime.[7] He imagined good fortune, honour, and material possessions for himself in the world of the 'ancestral shades' sasa (in Rask), or, perhaps, more correctly, sisaman, 'town of departed spirits'.[8] If a discursive formation is a process by which a conceptual field is constructed and a domain of language use structured as a unity by common assumptions, what discursive formation engendered the world of sisa?[9]

But, first of all, who was Hans Lykke? There seems little doubt that he is to be identified with the Noete Doku of the nineteenth-century historian C. C. Reindorf and the Note Doku of the anthropologist M. J. Field. Using data collected in the 1930s, Field writes that the Osu people migrated from Osudoku:

> Odai Koto [of Nungwa] gave them a site to the north of the present Osu. They were skilful potters and traded their pots to the Accra people who were still on Okakwei Hill, and they had a famous pot-market in Osu. They arrived at Osu under the leadership of Note Doku, the *wulomo* of their god *Nadu*.[10]

In his capacity as the *Nadu wulomo*, (*wulomo* carries the meaning 'guardian' and 'representative'), Doku introduced *Me* worship, originally based in Osudoku-Shai, to the Osu community.[11] He was, in effect, the chief administrator of the ceremonies pertaining to the worship of *Nadu*.

Reverend Carl Christian Reindorf, in an earlier and longer version of the history of Osu, relates that a woman named Namole and her brother Noete Doku, a chief in Osudoku, travelled with their people from Osudoku-Shai to Osuko in order to see Okai Koi, the ruler of the Great Accra kingdom. They believed royal adjudication would settle the bitter quarrel that had forced them to leave Osudoku. Through the intervention of Noete Shai, an interpreter for Danish factors at Christiansborg Castle, Namole and Doku were brought before the governor, 'Erik Oehlsen' (d. 1698) in Christiansborg in Osu.[12] (This is Eric Olsen Lygaard, who served as governor at Christiansborg on two separate occasions: in 1698 and from 1705 to 1711.)[13] My interpretation is that Doku became the *lumo* ('ruler', 'king') of Osu in 1698; he did not arrive in Osu at that time. Danish Company records imply that he was the ruler of Osu in 1700. According to Reindorf, 'Noete [Doku] founded the seven huts known as Buiateng in [Osu]'.[14] The 'butuiateng' (from *bu aten*, 'to judge, to decide, pass sentence'?) was apparently a public place of adjudication where cases (palavers) were judged and settled. It was presumably set up as a new judicial institution by Doku after he became *lumo*.[15]

That Doku physically migrated from Osudoku-Shai (the La polity?) is doubtful. His connection to Osudoku-Shai may be attributed to the fact that he introduced *Me* worship to Osu, probably in the 1670s before the Accra polity was conquered by Akwamu.[16] He was probably initiated into and trained as a ritual specialist in *Me* worship in Osudoku-Shai itself. He had another explicit connection: the traditions link him to Osudoku-Shai pottery production and the selling of pottery in Accra towns.

Danish accounts first refer to Lykke/Doku in the 1680s. They do not associate him in any way with Osudoku-Shai. It seems he was a protégé of the Danish factor and governor Hans Lykke who served on the coast, first at Fort Frederiksborg in the coastal town of Amanfro in the Afutu polity and later at Christiansborg Castle, between 1681 and 1687, the year of his death. In a *Daghregister* of 1688–89 he was acknowledged as one of the leading political figures (*cabuseer*) in the town: he was a *numo* ('elder').[17] Osu was a community in which merchant capital was dominant and the political economy of credit and debt was integral to its social relations.[18] It was a community that had developed systems of measure and monetary (cowrie-gold) valuation and calculation, essential for the economic management of the entrepot. On one side, there were 'timeless' ideologies and, on the other, the circulation of currencies, an exchange economy, the exploitation of servile labour, monetary accounting and the like.[19]

What sites did Lykke/Doku occupy which made it possible for him to make statements about an afterlife of pleasure? In his various practices as a public figure, between 1687 and 1709, as an elder (*numo*), a captain and caboceer (*lumo*), a broker (*massever* or *makelaer*), a religious specialist (*wulomo*), Lykke enjoyed privileged access to the structured plenitude of Osu. They were social-ideological practices in Osu civic space, which defined specific discourses, strategies, and relations that allowed him to speak with authority and with legitimacy.[20] His sensibilities and cultural orientation were embedded in certain metaphysical regimes of truth: the Me and Kpele cults with their intellectual and religious traditions and practices.

Lykke/Doku seems to have come to prominence as a public figure in Osu in the years following the Akwamu defeat of the army of Okai Koi and the conquest of the Great Accra state between 1677 and 1681. In the ensuing decades Akwamu's musket-bearing armies embarked on regular campaigns to the east, north, and towards the coast. One contemporary factor wrote of these conquests that the akwamuhene Ansa Sasraku (d. 1689) 'extends his power over the Blacks along the sea for above twenty leagues, notwithstanding that these have kings of their own; and therefore are adjoined to this country of Akwamu'.[21] The forcible establishment of the Nyanaoase regime over culturally knowing and aware populations raises the question of the regime's acceptance and intelligibility among them.

The Akwamu heartland itself was a site where history was performed – politics, warfare, commerce and state-building – and where intensive and extensive forms of power were exercised, discourses were enabled and social-cultural practices were situated. It functioned as a social structure and as a cultural pattern of constraint on social and political practices among the conquered.[22] Akwamu governmentality marked out its subject population in specific disciplinary ways; it appropriated and directed its socialities and various spheres of activity within the technical capabilities of its mechanisms of domination.[23] During the reign of Sasraku's successor, Basua (1689–99), the mode of governance and tribute collecting defined the predatory nature of the Akwamu political order:

> The People who live under their rule are miserably tormented by them, being daily robbed by the Akwamu soldiers, against whom they dare not undertake anything with violence, out of fear of the Akwamu king who would not hesitate to punish heavily those who were to mistreat his soldiers, as they are all … his relatives or slaves.[24]

Akwamu political practice represented an ongoing efort to impose order and jurisdictional claims on conquered populations.[25] In 1709 the Akwamu military commander, Amputi Brafo, a hero (owurafram: 'one who knows how to use a musket') of Akwamu's earlier conquests, defined the political limits of tribute paying nkoa and rationalized the social hierarchies produced by the conquests in a terse statement to the Danish factors at Christiansborg Castle. He expressed the way in which notions of military agency placed themselves in the construction of a dominant political order.[26] He gave 'voice' to Akwamu symbolic power, that is, 'the power to constitute the given by stating it'.[27]

The social and political construction of Akwamu domination in the 1680s and 1690s represented a structural shift from the territorialism of the monarchic Great Accra kingdom to a civic (municipal) social-political order of semi-autonomous entrepots.[28]

> The first Aquambo kings' government was especially mild towards the Accras, and all of the other conquered; the Accras could not settle in their land again more than one and a half [Danish] miles from the sea, but should live under the European forts. The Accras became brokers for the trade which the Akwamus brought to the Europeans....[29]

How did Lykke live this experience of dominium and appropriation as an Akwamu akoa ('subject') when some of the Osu elite regarded the members of the ruling Akwamu military-political class as nothing more then 'coarse peasants' who knew 'nothing' except how to wage war? We may suggest that he lived it through two religious organizations. In addition to his position as wulomo of the Me deity Nadu, he was also a devotee of the Kpele dzemawon (oracle-deity) La Kpa of Labade.[30] The Me and Kpele cults were areas of relection and orientation in the Accra towns, where gbatsin ('god's houses') and aklabatsha ('a grove or tree temple') of La Kpa were the central locus of worship for all. The two cults were cultural apparatuses and interpellating devices which enabled subjectivities to invigilate events, relationships, practices, and the like. On the one hand, they were self-identified entities and systems of signification and categories of knowlege; on the other, they were constituted in practice and through events.

How did *Me* and *Kpele* work as cultural practices and cultural and symbolic capital? Perhaps we can attribute their importance, especially that of *Kpele La Kpa*, in this period to the reform project of constituting a post-Okai Koi societal order. Their representational economies, which produced the network of meanings attached to crossroads, bodies of water, rocks, termite mounds and trees, were grounded in the existing political, material, and hierarchical practices, social conflicts and tensions.[31] *Me* and *Kpele* located geographical space in a cultural and symbolic realm where significations spoke truths, mediated the excesses of unknowability and contingency, and countered 'natural' instabilities. The Akwamu military defeat of Great Accra existed not just in dispersed, individual memories, but in its multiple effects. For Lykke and his contemporaries the consequences of this defeat were impossible to erase. The singularity of defeat, subjugation, depopulation, enslavement, and widespread ravages was incontestable. Through *Me* and *Kpele* this past was engaged and the Akwamu-dominated social world, with its structured relations of inequality, interrogated. As cultural formations, they constituted subject positions within symbolic and discursive fields: they validated personal individuation.

Did Lykke slide into self deception with his fantasies regarding an afterlife in *sisaman*? The development of *Me* and *Kpele* as historically specific (urban-based?) forms of worship and spiritual organization occurred as individuals and groups in the Akwamu-dominated Accra towns internalized sometimes ineffable cultural ingredients and social relations and were alienated by the demands of their collective conditions of life. In his aesthetic of despair Lykke sought to transcend these conditions by imagining a continuous ritual (?) celebration which honored *sisa*, his departed and illustrious ancestors. Was this his *homowo*-festival, 'the outcrying or mocking of hunger', a political imaginary of revolt against Akwamu rule?[32] As a broker and merchant, he was located in the profitable commercial sector of the Akwamu political economy, although, like other *nkoa*, he faced regular exactions and appropriations. At another level this aesthetic was (unconsciously?) connected to the monarchical past of Great Accra. The experience of Akwamu dominance entered the Accra cultural and symbolic order by pointing to another, absent, historical moment, the conquest of Great Accra itself. That moment, encapsulated in military and political organizations and commercial strategies, brought into being and enabled overt acts of tribute collection and wealth accumulation, and these were recreated and played out in texts of fantasy and ritual(ized) actions, violence and destruction, dispossession and displacement.

In August 1708, at the annual eight-day New Year's (*Homowo*) celebration in the town of Labade, the *La Kpa* oracle proclaimed before the celebrants, who came from the various Accra towns, that now they were oppressed by Akwamu but in time they would become a powerful people and would have their own king again as in the past. The implication was that Akwamu's days of supremacy were numbered. This confident and uncompromising assertion – implicating an alternative Accra royalism – was tantamount to a delaration of war aginst Akwamu suzerainty. In 1708 an Akwamu army destroyed the *La Kpa* shrine and grove.[33] But this happened after the Accra towns – Osu, Labade, Teshi, Nungwa, and others – openly rebelled against the *akwamuhene* Akonno (1702–25). Who within the Akwamu polity could legitimately produce the authoritative speech acts which would represent institutional statements? The priesthood of the *La Kpa* oracle-*dzemawon* was not allowed to make public utterances that contested the ruling authority of the *akwamuhene*, his court, and grandees. If *dzemawon* worship was a form of cultural re-production, it was also an area of struggle, a form of political resistance, a source of knowledge, and a site for the achievement of security.

In 1705 and 1706 an Akwamu military force was campaigning in an Adangme district near the Volta River, evidently to quell a rebellion. In October 1706, having restored his authority, the *akwamuhene* Akonno decided to march his army through Osu on his way back to his capital. The Accras, according to a Danish report of January 1707, bought up muskets and other goods, alarmed that an Akwamu army was about to attack and destroy their towns. The feared attack did not take place. Instead, in February 1707 Akonno directed his military once again towards Adangme and from there inland against Kwahu and Krepi. He was still on campaign in July the following year.[34]

Lykke/Doku was one of the principal leaders in the 1708–9 uprising against Akwamu rule. He placed himself in committed and active political opposition to the policies and rule of the Akwamu elite. Through the oracular foretelling of *La Kpa* (and its priesthood) he identified the rebirth of the Great Accra monarchy as a unified trajectory and a master sign. Perhaps even before the rebellion he had already begun to meditate on death. He rejected the *akoa* position imposed by the sovereign authority of the Akwamu *oman* (polity). In this formulation he was not an *akoa* subject to the legal authority and coercive apparatus of the *akwamuhene*. The inauthentic character of *akoa*-ship produced discontent, bitterness, anger, hopes of revenge and an implacable oppositional stance; in other words it called, on the part of the Accra *nkoa*, for a new moral economy in an imagined community. The rebellion was a movement of political restoration, as articulated by the *La Kpa* oracular complex – itself a system of collective subjectification. It sought to enact an alternative political text while the Akwamu army was engaged in heavy fighting in the interior.

While travelling from the coast to the Akwamu capital, Nyanaoase, in September, 1708, the *akwamuhene*'s wives, children, servants and retainers were attacked by armed Accras. Many were murdered; the remainder were taken captive and sold at the different trading stations on the coast. Not long after this event, Lykke/Doku and the Osu *numo* Yeboah brought ten Akwamu prisoners into Christiansborg, some of whom were immediately sold to slavers. Lykke/Doku apparently sold other prisoners to the Danes and also to the Dutch, possibly as many as thirty. All of the prisoners were sold under the cover of darkness.[35]

Akonno's response was swift. In October he pledged to destroy the Accra towns. On 28 November his army arrived to put down the uprising and remained on the coast until April 1709, having plundered and burned down Osu, Labade, Teshi and Nungwa, and killed or captured many of the rebellion's leaders and their supporters. All of the rebel towns were heavily fined.[36] Those Akwamu prisoners still remaining in Christiansborg – who seem to have been court retainers or servants – were ransomed from the Danes. Lykke/Doku was dead and the uprising was broken.

Who was Hans Lykke/Noete Doku? His identity was a complex field of belief, politics, warfare, music, food, dance, trade, oracles, relations of subordination and domination, palavers, patronage and clientage, customs, adjudication, speech and so on.[37] Death and a life of pleasure in the *sisaman* pervaded Lykke/Doku's thoughts in the final years of his life. Were these, in the final analysis, metaphors for other classifications, social divisions and hierarchies? Could he only act by putting his activity under the dominion of 'alien' things – death and *sisa*? Was his social *imaginaire* an effect of alienation and the dominant mode of symbolizing, in the way described by Jean-Joseph Goux?

> [Marx] approaches the imaginary alienation as an effect of the mode of symbolizing. For the human subject is dispossessed of himself not openly through his submission to the gods but, first and above all, through his reified relation to the state, to property, to commodities.[38]

'But I know what I shall do'

A 'history from below' perspective is often difficult to achieve, since the available sources provide few direct and detailed references to subaltern groups and their 'hidden transcript'.[39] Fortunately, records of the Danish West Indies and Guinea Company from the 1740s and the account of the Gold Coast by the Danish factor L. F. Rømer published in 1760 provide useful information relevant to the construction and re-presentation of such a perspective. These sources refer to the protests and thoughts of three artisans employed at Christiansborg Castle as 'Inventory' or 'Company's slaves' (Gã: *nyondshi*; s. *nyon*). They provide evidence of the social world and symbolic universe of the mason Kwaku and the split lives of two blacksmiths, Kofi and his son Kwasi. For different reasons and in different ways, they rejected the Company's disciplinary practices, code of values and authoritarianism. What were the 'real problems' these individual producers were able to articulate concerning their life-existence, their lifeworld? What were their lived and ideological relations to their world of commercial centres and royal courts, of kin-ordered and slave-owning relations? For the bonded artisans one form of social necessity existed in direct, personal domination, the threat of force and of social or ideological sanctions. Kofi took his own life (1749); Kwasi was sold into Atlantic slavery (1750). Kwaku, on the other hand, contested the moral economy and the disciplinary regime of the work place without suffering dire punishment. In these lives one discerns historically specific forms of personal consciousness and social confrontation.

In the 1730s and 1740s the Danish chartered company employed at its different trading stations between 100 and 200 men, women and children. They formed the Company's unfree labour force – boatmen, blacksmiths, carpenters, coopers, masons, labourers, stone-blowers, gardeners, servants, and so on.[40] What was their lived relation to their work and to the mechanisms that made them dependent and unfree? Through what kind of cultural and discursive processes were they constituted as subjects? Their labour underlay the mercantile relations which bought and then transported 'chained slaves' to the American plantations. It was organized for the Company's business and profit. In this sense they were part of the Atlantic world's working class.[41] The social, cultural and ideological spaces within which they lived and interacted, the terrain of their everyday lives, was an effect of the Company's apparatus of power and institutional practices of subordination.

In his rather detailed account of belief and ritual in the Accra towns, the Danish factor L. F. Rømer records a conversation between the mason Kwaku and a Danish factor in 1739 (or possibly a little earlier). By recounting Kwaku's speech, Rømer attempted to illustrate the diversity of religious belief and practice in Osu and other Accra towns. What he manages to achieve is to specify the individuation of the Accra towns' repertoire of belief and thought.[42] Yet, it must be remembered that Kwaku's voice is heard in a narrative text he did not produce:[43]

> One of our black masons, a Company-slave [named] Qvacu, was still at work at 12 o'clock noon, while normally they are free from 11 [a.m.] until 2 [p.m.]. A European who was walking by asked him: Qvacu, why are you working? Isn't it noon?
>
> Response (with annoyance): 'Our master [the governor of the Danish trading stations] is acting very badly towards me today. He said I had not worked enough, and so, before I can stop, I must finish this job. But I know what I shall do.
>
> Question: 'What will you do?'
>
> Response: 'When I die, I will pray to God that he not send me into the world to work as a slave for whites and if my prayer is not answered I shall beat God.'

Question: 'What, then, will you be when you come into the world again?'

Response: 'Frempung's slave.' (Frempung was a great Akim king.)

Question: 'Why don't you pray to become Frempung himself?'

Response: 'No, that is not possible; for I know that as often as I have been in the world I have been a slave; and as often as I shall come I must be a slave.'

Kwaku's work as a mason – the space of his emplacement – was a central field of activity, emotion, and thought. His employment as an artisan and his status as a property of the Danish Company has to be seen in relation to the process of capital accumulation in Denmark. His mental universe, however, was dependent upon forces of culture and history that are not reducible to the social relations of mercantilist exchange. The spontaneous consent that he gives to the hegemony of slave-owning, his belief in a supreme being and in reincarnation, his longing for a situation as a page (Akan: *okra*) at the court of the Akyem ruler of Osu and Christiansborg, delineate Kwaku's interior life'(mentality), his consciousness as an artisan class-subject, his social construction of reality. These draw on local knowledges, belief systems and values, and the intellectual traditions of Osu and other Accra towns.

Unlike many of the Company's slaves, Kwaku had not been purchased by the Company's factors, but had been born a company *nyon*. Presumably, his parents, too, had worked for the Company as enslaved labour. At the time of his conversation with the Danish factor he was 33 or 34 years of age. He was very likely born between 1703 and 1706, when Hans Lykke/Noete Doku was *lumo* of Osu. He probably died in the late 1750s or the early 1760s. While he is listed among the slave labour force in 1755, he is not mentioned in the 1766 or later listings. He remained in servitude to the Company his entire life.[44]

Kwaku's world view incorporated a vision which was grounded in the material requirements of life and necessary services. Was he giving voice to an anonymous mode of thought, perhaps to be identified with various subaltern groups in the coastal entrepots? He occupied a determinate place in Osu's social space – as a slave, a space of personal dependence, and as an artisan a space of specialization and technical competence. The trans-Atlantic trade was not referred to in the conversation. Under the circumstances it must be regarded as a structuring absence.

Work and belief were central to Kwaku's self-identity as an unfree social subject. The articulation between work, his attitudes about work, and his belief in *Nyonmo* ('the supreme being'; the 'creator') and (*g*)*blanro* (the recurring cycle of death and re-birth: reincarnation), on one hand, and on the other his dream of life at the royal court of the powerful and wealthy Akyem ruler, Frimpong Manso (d. 1741) – who had been the political overlord of Osu from 1730 until 1732 and, until his death, one of Christiansborg's most important and valued merchants were frames of reference that defined his self awareness.[45] He defined himself in terms of the hegemonic slave-holding ideological order, but he renders his social subjectivity as a Company's slave more complex by rejecting his conditions of work, by challenging *Nyonmo*, and by constructing an imaginary life for himself as a court servant, or *okra*. This imaginary was both a refusal of the real and a higher level of immediacy.

Kwaku was situated in a chain of interpellations – God, prayer, death, re-birth, whites, work, Frimpong, and slave status – which gave him an 'identity and a functional role. It would seem, however, that *Nyonmo* provided the ultimate intelligibility of the world in which he lived. *Nyonmo* existed as the basic prerequisite for consciousness, as that intelligibility that enabled self-awareness, thus he prayed to *Nyoramo* about his wishes, he imagined *Nyonmo* if those wishes went unfulfilled: 'I shall beat God.' Kwaku placed himself as the final authority on his experiences of work, although he recognized that his social status was beyond his means to change.

At the level of the Atlantic world working-class, Kwaku's complaints about his hours and conditions of work belong to the career of absolute surplus value; they also belong to the history of concrete labour. He and the other Company slaves were subsumed under a transnational merchant capital. They did not exercise self-determination in their conditions of work. The routine of work was a permanent, relentless feature of daily life – a veritable force of history, of his personal existence that was external to him. But the routine was sublimated and transcended in thought and belief, in an alternative non-hegemonic point of view. Kwaku was able to transfigure this world of work into something it was not – he appropriated the values, symbols and beliefs of the Osu discursive, moral and cultural order – but without changing or removing the institutions and practices of enslavement and slavery. Kwaku did not attribute the difficulty of his assigned work to the Company's trade in 'chained slaves', but to the whites' harsh modes of time-work management. This trade in chattels was not the focus of his grievance, though it was the focus of the Company's operations on the Gold and Slave Coasts.[46]

Kwaku as a mason and Company slave was a site of work and trading capital; as a man with a world-view he was the site of the symbolic, discursive and ideological. These sites were historically and socially mediated, deriving from the urban division of labour. The world-view site developed and fulfilled itself through the work relationship and the lived experiences of the subject Kwaku. The world-view was part of Osu's structures of cognition. Its categories and ideas were manifest in different ways and combinations and configurations. It was a fundament of his social existence, which was grounded in an artisanate and Company slave cultural formation. It was, also, to borrow a phrase from Lukacs, 'a higher form of immediacy', which 'transcended' the social circumstances of the site of work and trading capital.[47]

In contrast with Kwaku's recriminations, Kwasi's opposition to the Danish Company was decidedly mutinous. The Company's disciplinary strategies, and relations of domination became a locus of social struggle and personal anxiety. Kwasi was implicated in a planned rebellion against the Danes in Christiansborg castle. In July 1749 his father, Kofi Kuma, a blacksmith and boatmaster, hanged himself to avoid being punished by the Danish governor.[48] While serving as a navigator and boatmaster, Kofi had sailed Christiansborg's 'last and best boat' onto the beach near the town of Ada and completely wrecked it. The cargo was either badly damaged or lost. The governor and other factors accused Kofi and the boat's crew of being constantly drunk while sailing along the coast. Kofi, in particular, was charged with being solely responsible for the accident and the drunken state of the crew. To avoid the shame and humiliation of public punishment Kofi took his own life by hanging himself. At the time, he was 45 or 46 years old. His son Kwasi was 25 or 26. Like the mason Kwaku, both men were born into Company servitude; both were property of the Company. Whether they shared Kwaku's world-view is not made clear in the documents. In contrast to Kwaku, there is reason to believe that until the misfortunes and tragedies of 1749 and 1750 the two men conformed to the disciplinary code of the Company: they were obedient, loyal, hard-working, compliant and dutiful.

Immediately after the boat accident, Kofi, accompanied by two crew members, made his way back to Osu. He went to the house of 'Soya', Sodsha Duomoro (died *c.* 1775), the chief *bofo* ('messenger') and assistant broker/linguist at Christiansborg and a socially prominent and wealthy *numo* who was the head of one of Osu's largest and most prosperous *akutshei* ('quarters'), Aneho. The conversation between the two men is recorded in a Company document:[49]

Soya told Cophi that he certainly knew under what conditions the fort's authorities had entrusted the boat to him: if anything were to happen to the boat he would be hanged. Cophi said he was aware of this and that he would save the authorities the trouble by hanging himself. He had one request to ask Soya: that he, Soya, would swear to take [and keep] all the goods that were in the sacks that Cophi and his accomplices [brought from the boat]. Soya asked if he had any other request. Cophi replied that [he] should take care of [his] children as if they were your own and if any were to get into trouble he would look after them the same way he would look after his own children. Soya swore to do this and Cophi went to his own house and hanged himself.

After the fateful shipwreck, Kofi could imagine unhesitatingly his own death at the hands of the Company's disciplinary regime. His act of desperation may be seen as an ideology effect of his subject position in the Company's code of values and disciplinary norms. But there was another side. He had also internalized the moral economy of Osu, with its relations of reciprocity, obligations and mutuality. Kofi's decision was to settle his family affairs by imposing a binding obligation on a social superior. He asked Sodsha to swear two oaths. What was an oath (Gã: *kita*)? As a social practice, it organized and coordinated people's actual activities; as an effect of a complex of social relations, it defined and organized in and across actual local sites of people's lives. Kofi was to die. What would happen to his children? His act of self-destruction would necessarily compel his children to change their domestic relationships completely; that is, Sodsha was to 'adopt' them as members of his *weku* ('house-group'). To the children, the oath had several implications: it meant new social and ideological relations, new cultural and social identities, and different practices, as they were to join the household of an eminent and influential *numo*.

One month after his father's death Kwasi, together with Anege and two other accomplices, broke into the Christiansborg warehouse and stole tobacco, musket balls, and flintstones. Within a relatively short time all of them were apprehended. They were interrogated while undergoing the bastinado; they were then placed in irons and put in the fort's dungeons. The council of factors decided not to hang them – they were esteemed good workers – but to send them to the West Indies instead. Kwasi's intention was to avenge his father by assaulting and killing one or more of the Danish factors; it is open to question, however, whether he intended to provoke a general uprising of the Christiansborg slaves with this act. This point is not made explicit in the interrogation, although there is the implication that the factors thought this was the plan.

Duomoro, together with some of the principal families of Osu and a number of the Company's slaves, asked for the prisoners' release. This was refused, whereupon Duomoro and the others swore an oath that they would compel the Danes to release Kwasi, Duomoro's 'son', and his fellow conspirators. Led by Duomoro, a few of the leading townspeople and the Company's slaves (among whom was probably Kwaku the mason) were to enter the fort at night and free Kwasi and the three other prisoners. Should they encounter any opposition from the sentry they would not hesitate to use force. Before they could act, however, one of the company's slaves revealed the plan to the Danish factors. Their first act was to execute the company slave 'Hotiafue' by firing squad, on the grounds that he, alone among Duomoro's protesters, had actually pledged to murder the fort's guards and all of the whites, single-handedly. No punishments were meted out to the other slaves who took part; Sodsha was relieved of his post as messenger and broker. Kwasi and his fellow accomplices were placed aboard the first Danish ship bound for the Danish Caribbean.[50]

The impropriety of the speech of the *nyon* subaltern revealed a social consciousness, a hidden transcript formed, in part, outside of the mercantile social relations that prevailed in Christiansborg. It cannot be separated from the cultural and social history of the Accra towns. The *nyondshi* were not the passive products of labour discipline and socialization.

They were in socially distinct ways active agents, but under conditions not of their own choosing.

'It is you, you whites, who have brought all wickedness among us'

The historical narratives of certain Accra notables (s. *nuntsho*: 'lord', 'master'), contemporaries of the *nyondshi* Kofi, Kwasi and Kwaku, incorporated a social imaginary which expressed a reflexive yet ambivalent attitude towards the Atlantic slave and commodity trade. The notables disavowed the political and military successes of dominant Others by disinvesting the social-political field of conquering military elites, like those of Akwamu and Akyem: the narratives delegitimized their political will, institutions and culture. The narratives offered an imaginary resolution of real conflicts in the political, social and material domains of Accra and, more broadly, Gold Coast life. This imaginary represented a Golden Age, a time of innocence, within the Accra elite's symbolic order and imagination.

The Danish factor Rømer provides details about the narratives in his book on the Gold Coast. He gained his information from four individuals, organic intellectuals, of influence and high status: *wulomo* Ni (Note) Tshie, the *lumo* of Teshi (died *c.*1751), Asã (Notei Sã), the *lumo* of Osu (d. 1769), *numo* Noete Adowi, the *mankralo* of Osu (d. 1767) and *wulomu* Wetshe Odoi Kpoti, the *lumo* of Labade (d. 1757). They were figures who commanded obedience and deference in the Accra public realm. They expressed a collective memory of political experiences, historical strategies and social struggles. As knowing and acting subjects with a strong historical sense, they were their own interpreters.

Ni Tshie and Wetshe Kpoti were younger contemporaries of Noete Doku/Hans Lykke, and both had been active and leading participants in the 1708–9 rebellion against Akwamu.[51] Kpoti was the chief priest of the *La Kpa* oracle and enjoyed the reputation of being the greatest priest on the entire Gold Coast. The prominence of Kpoti and the La Kpa oracle in the production and circulation of values, ideas, symbols and norms can be attributed, in large part, to their constitutive roles in the Accra and Gold Coast moral economies. Ni Tshie was the senior *wulomo* of *Ayiki*, one of the deities of the *Me* cult, and enjoyed a particularly high religious status among the Accras. Adowi was a man of considerable prestige in Osu, in part because he was the chief broker at Christiansborg Castle and in part because he was the *wulomo* of a powerful deity not identified in the Danish records. Possibly it was *Kumi*, a war god of the *Me* cult, or a war god of either the Fante-based *Otu* or the Akuapem-based *Akon* cults.[52]

The houses of these men formed a network of elite household administrations that encompassed the Accra district, as well as districts and polities beyond it. The bundles of rights and privileges they enjoyed over a range of resources – productive, commercial, cultural, human – were gained through a long-term process of patrimonial inheritance and prebendal grants.[53] The *nuntshei* were engaged in significant trade with the European mercantile organizations and all of them had heavy debts with the European companies.[54]

The Golden Age narrative – a cultural construct and the product of an intellectual praxis – represents their reflections on the conditions, past and present, of their land. I would suggest that these reflections were informed by the ideal interests that were held in eighteenth-century Accra towns: how to live the good and just life; how to acquire the power of command.[55] The lives of these men were shaped by historical contingencies. The intellectual grounds for their tempered opposition to the Atlantic trade rested on the historical and empirical perception that, for a 200-year period, the European trade had profoundly and negatively shaped the moral economy and political culture of society.

The narrative privileges the trade as a site of disruption but, paradoxically, it was also a site of acquisition, supplying merchandise that enhanced the material and social conditions of life. The utopian statements were not an iteration of simple nostalgia for an idyllic and distant past, but a mode of witnessing the possibilities and problems of common and shared experiences of violence, calamity and displacement. They represented both a critique of their status quo and a vision of an alternative and (presumed) superior way of life. The Accra *onukpai* ('grandees') created a cultural-political text that was always the imaginary unity of the present.

What were the intellectual and representational practices that enabled these men to conceptualize across time and space in their critical meditations (Rømer: *philosophere*: 'philosophizing') on the condition of their society? The Golden Age narrative, with its implied critique of its own political present, was an effect of many tendencies in Accra thought. The notables' re-presentation of history would seem to have drawn on an Accra historical archive. It postulated a cultural-political horizon opposed to the dominant political cultures with their strategies of military and territorial expansion and tribute collection. Kwaku, the *nyon* in life-long service to the Danish company, sought solace in the wealthy court of the rich and powerful Frimpong Manso, who had over 3,000 *akra* (Akan: 'pages') in attendance at his court, an imagined solace but a place he preferred to his Christiansborg work place.[56] In the ruminations of the Accra *onukpai*, royal courts, like Frimpong's, were responsible for the ruination that had plagued the country for more than a century. To the narrators of the Golden Age, historical disasters and catastrophes were not pre-eminently assessed at the level of military events, but rather in the logic of social action – commercial and military praxis over time – and the histories of political power, which produced their own subjective and political dispositions and forms of organization. Counterposed to this destructive development was the organic *weku* ('house-group'; 'family'; 'household') formation under the patriarchal authority of its housefather (Gã: *wetshe*) and the political authority of benevolent, just and honourable rulers. It opposed the violent and menacing effects of merchant capital. Trade established a new and contentious relationship between ruler and subject and between the *weku* and the market. In the history related by the *onukpai* the idealized *weku* is given its own cultural and social space and its own oppositional archive.

We might suppose that the history Rømer recorded was developed at the sites of the *we*, or house, and the *akrabatsha* ('sacred groves') of the principal *dzemawodshi* ('deities'). We might further suppose that they were dialogic spaces, locations of reciprocity and commonality constantly interacting with and interrogating the politically dominant.[57] The history signalled a story of economic decline, ecological destruction, massive depopulation, indebtedness, conquests and estrangement, both social and personal. Its inscribed values of honour, loyalty, service and respect, on one side, and self-contained, kin-ordered community headed by a *paterfamilias* lacking both gold and profit-making practices, on the other, were grounded in materialism and in the conflicts that history generated. Was it an expression of *wulomo* culture? More precisely, was the social imaginary of the 'Golden Age' narrative a component of eighteenth-century *Kpele* and *Me* thought?

In extended conversations with Accra *lumei* and *wulomei* over a number of years, Rømer learned that they had a shared perspective on the past and present condition of the Gold Coast lands:

> It is you, you Whites, who have brought all wickedness among us. Would we have sold each other had you not come among us? The greed we have for your enchanting merchandise and spirits has made it so that one brother does not trust another nor one friend another, indeed, even a father his son. From our forefathers, we know that only the malefactor who has committed murder twice would be stoned or drowned; otherwise, the usual punishment for

one who has committed a wrong had to carry a large log to the victim and go before his house for three successive days and beg for pardon on his bended knee. In our youth we have known many thousands of families here and there along the coast, and now one can only count a few hundred people. And what is worse is that you have become a necessary evil [*malum necessarium*] among us, for if you leave, then the inland Blacks would not allow us to live a half year, but would come and kill us together with our wives and children, and this hate they hold against us is your fault.[58]

All of this appears to be a denunciation of the *onukpai*'s own times, or status quo. On one hand, the social, political and domestic spheres of urban life were increasingly mediated by commodity relations. This was perceived as a fundamentally alienating relationship. On the other hand, inland ruling regimes were incorporated into the expanding frontier of commodified exchange and the establishment and re-production of this commercial connection involved an inescapable act of violence in the form of new kinds of warfare and military strategies.

Rømer continues: 'Because of the European presence, the Blacks, according to their own statements, have lost much of their former honesty, and have achieved nothing by helping the Dutch to drive away the Portuguese.'[59] Was this 'loss' one of the ways in which mercantile accumulation was internalized? There is the implication that the realm of social relations productive of a moral economy and symbolic order constitutive of 'honesty' in the acquisition of commodities and products was displaced by social relations which generated a moral economy and symbolic order constitutive of concerted struggles over the control and accumulation of commodities and products. Former times were decidedly better and more just:

[I] begin with the Blacks' golden age which was under the Benin government, before any Europeans had come here. One knows that before the Portuguese or other Europeans came to the coast, the king in Rio Benin was emperor over the entire Guinea Coast, up to Rio Gambia, and some say that his authority stretched just as far to the south of Rio Benin.... It is strange that in that time when the land had a thousand times more people than now there was no property with respect to farms and land, but, like now, [people] planted and sowed wherever they wished.

A Black had only his children and slaves, which comprised his wealth. His houses, if none of his ancestors were buried in them, he would sell for a few *rixdalers*, and with the help of one or more build himself another in another spot. Some muskets and cartridge boxes, a few boxes, some drinking vessels, calabashes, some pottery, a mirror are his entire household furnishings and furniture; besides, perhaps, a cat or a dog; anything else is unnecessary. His children and slaves were really his wealth, power, and protection; indeed, the more he had, the more he was esteemed in their *senatu gentium*, for in a land where *jus manus* is fully operational might must be repelled by might, or as they say one knife must stay another in its sheath. If there are fishers among his slaves or children, then everything they catch is his; at particular times some go and plant *millie* (Turkish corn), potatoes, beans, and more, others he employs in trading; he employs all of them in war....

About the Benin period one cannot write very much, as the Blacks at that time had no wars. [Today] they remember some of the laws of that time, which consisted of six articles, wherein they distinguished between a wife of free descent or of a slave family. In the first case the transgressor must for three mornings in a row bring to the victim a large log on his head and place it before the door, and on his knees beg for forgiveness. If the wife was a slave, once was enough. For unmarried persons there was no punishment in such circumstances. There was no law against theft, for it never happened, and there was no need for anyone to steal food, since the poor could ask for as much as they wanted.... They had no jewels and [other] valuables, except for aggrey beads and *contreterees*, which none dared to wear, unless they were granted the privilege by the [Benin] emperor. They had no need for clothes; they went completely naked, and wore only a loincloth around the waist. For them iron was rarer than gold, and when they couldn't get iron, they had to smelt gold in order to make axes and cutlasses with which to cut down the bush and clear the soil for seeding so they could plant.

The old Blacks talk about the millions of people who lived along the Accra coast for a distance of four [Danish] miles. And when one questions this and asks where did their food come from, they respond that both the sea and the land were more blessed than they are now. Noyte, the cabuseer of [Teshi] (who claims to have known the Portuguese at Accra...) declared that in former times the Accra coast had been full of coconut and palm trees and that he had seen whole forests in his youth.... It was not only the coast which was so populous, but one and a half [Danish] miles inland was Accra, where the king or the vice-kings had their residences. Two [Danish] miles beyond, where the [Akuapem] mountains begin, was full of towns and people.

The red *contreterre*, which some Blacks wear, were an imperial badge of honour; the old-fashion swords, which the Blacks deem a great privilege for their families to have, is proof that they descend from an imperial general or captain.... [O]n the Gold Coast are some families who can actually trace their descent from these great Benin generals, or viceroys, and they show as a great distinction, their horse tails, which have been and still are a great honour.

The old Accra king died: before his death, however, the Portuguese arrived on the coast and brought the Blacks spirits, swords and also gunpowder and muskets. Benin dominion declined, and the vice-kings, who before inherited their positions, except that the successor had to be confirmed from Benin, were the sovereign kings. The old Accra king's successor did not follow his predecessor's example, but made himself hated in his nation because of the evil deeds he committed while he was drunk.[60]

A consequence of the degradation of political culture and the moral corruption of the rulers was the spread and increasing brutality of warfare:

The Blacks contend that these bad customs [relating to war] have not been among them more than 100 years, and that the Aqvamboes [Akwamu) and their neighbours first started them. One knows that the Aqvambues did not take the head of the Accra king 150 years ago, and one knows that about 130 years ago the Assiantes [Asante] had war with the Akenists [Akyem]; but from that period the Assiantes have no heads of the Akim [Akyem] kings and great men, who were killed, to exhibit, but in the last two [wars] they had more than 4,000 Akim heads, which would be displayed. As might have been expected the Aqvamboes practised this custom and other nations developed a taste for treating their enemies in the same manner, so that they could make themselves more fearful and their enemies more contemptible, ignominious and disgraceful.[61]

Decapitation of the enemy was a hegemonic strategy whose desired and cumulative effect was to create among the conquered inferior and unequal social subjects.

The counter-text of the Accra *nuntshei* represents an intertwined history of culture and class, of the mercantile and the political, of frightening violence and dispossession. It challenged the dominant texts of the conquerors – Akwamu, Akyem, Fante, Asante – whose armies had, at different times, traversed and pillaged Accra lands. Yet the counter-text embodied paradoxes:

When our Accras talk about this time [of Akwamu domination], they are completely caught up with delight and desire as they imagine living once again in such a glorious time. We earned (they say) more in one day then than we earn now in a whole year. We could become as rich as we wanted, and had no need to work or worry ourselves about anything; our whites made so much profit that they could give without being asked an entire anchor of spirits, but now we must beg for a full glass and sometimes they simply show us the door.[62]

In the Akwamu historical conjuncture there was a discrepancy between the demands and desires of what was experienced – becoming rich through trade – and the internalized moral economy that rested on the integrity of a non-accumulating, wealth-denying *weku*.

We can propose several possible interpretations and readings of the historical narrative of Ni Tshie, Asa, Noete Adowi and Wetshe Odoi Kpoti. The four men elucidate a moral economy of the *weku*, that household group of slaves and children (*webii*) in service to a housefather, under the morally responsible rule of a distant but powerful monarch. It reinvented the *weku* where nothing necessary was lacking and nothing unnecessary was desired. Under the patriarchal guidance and authority of the housefather, the household group achieved self-sufficiency and internal discipline. Work, prosperity, loyalty, duty, respect, honour, honesty, integrity and security defined the *weku*'s moral economy. The *weku* constituted a 'social autarchy', endowed with its own economy, morality, language and time, articulated into labours, laws and charity towards the needy. This was the foundation of the political community. Affairs of government were in the hands of honourable, morally accountable and responsible generals and viceroys, who, in turn, were representatives of the 'great emperor'. There were no wars.

The Golden Age narrative foregrounded social practices and relations which encouraged a minimum exchange of goods and an absence of property in land and material riches: gold was used to make instruments of production (farming tools); it was not a medium of exchange. Accumulation of material riches was not a principle of *weku* social life. The European trade profoundly transformed all of this. Benin rule declined; its political representatives in Accra became tyrannical, corrupt and violent. Warfare plagued the land. The selling of enslaved persons for forced transportation to the Americas became the order of the day. The circuit of transnational and local trading capital produced a socio-cultural world of objects and subjects – that is, an alienating system independent of *wekumei* – and a system of general objective dependence, a 'necessary evil'. Certain goods had become essential and the integrity of the *weku* was compromised and subverted. Greed for trade goods undermined personal relationships and social solidarities. At the same time, the trade was a source of great wealth. The circuit of trading capital was independent of brokers, merchants, housefathers, rulers, slaves, children and so on; but, progressively, they were dependent on the movement of capital in varying degrees. Cultural order, at a certain level, became cultural pathology.

To understand the narrative and to appreciate its heteroglossic location in Accra civic space it is best to consider it not as a garbled and fanciful invention of the past but as a reflective critique of the present, not unified and coherently given, but ambiguous and historically and socially constituted. Can we read in it an opposition to the determinations of merchant capital? Did the narrative seek to control the real, to reduce reality to the knowable, which amounted to a censuring of the present? It is, perhaps, not unrealistic to see this *grand récit* as the expression of a utopian imagination, the group fantasy of certain Accra *lumei*, *wulomei* and *numei* who saw themselves as moral and political subjects. Their narrative can be said to relate the class-specific and historically submerged acts of primary wealth accumulation, recreated and played out in events of warfare, decapitation, greed, hate, drunkenness, anger, envy, dishonour and betrayal, and whose inherent dystopic and pathogenic qualities threatened and occasionally achieved social disharmony, political discord and worse. The *nuntshei* envisioned a self-sustaining, just society of collective well-being, without internal stresses and conflicts. The *weku* was valorized, the subject of the narrative. It represented the liberated, social subject – liberated from social and domestic strife, political oppression, injustice and brutalizing warfare. This utopian vision represented an imaginative alternative to the present world of warfare and slaving. It did not take the everyday for granted.

If the *nuntshei* told Rømer how this utopian order was to be realized, he failed to record it. My assumption is that they had no notion of an emancipatory force. The narrative's sub-text seems to be that the wise and just ruler (a metaphor?) is the only guarantor of justice, social cohesion and security. This, it would appear, was the dominant ideology behind the narrative.

'One can say in general that [Fante] is richer and more powerful than any other nation on the coast'

The period from the sixteenth to the eighteenth century was 'the political golden age of the great Akan kingdoms'.[63] This description seems apt for the mid-eighteenth century *mfantseman*, a dominant and prosperous polity comprising the Borbor and Ekumfi Fante. A federation of semi-autonomous principalities, Fanteland was the dominant political and military formation on the entire Gold Coast, a zone where trade constituted the principal form of capital accumulation. In the 1740s–50s the Fante narrative of origin configured the past and the logic and momentum of the society in terms of military and commercial successes. It was a vivid inscription of a complex historical experience of conquest, state building, and close ties to the mercantile operations of English trading agents, the Royal African Company:

> We the Braffoes and Curranteers, the Priests & Peoples of Fantee do declare that our Fathers under the Conduct of their Braffoe Imorah were brought by the English from the Country now Arcania and by them furnished with arms, ammunition, & money not only to take possession of the Lands now inhabited by us, but likewise to conquer all those little states around us at present subject to our Dominion.[64]

This statement represents the meta-narrative of a heroic military-merchant culture, an idea of a past, and a hegemonic view of a particular history. Rømer describes the perceptible material achievements of this history: 'Fante is especially populous; they trade, fish, and farm, and one can in general say that they are wealthier and more powerful than any other nation on the coast'.[65] This was Fanteland in the mid-eighteenth century.

The political head of the state was the *brafo*: he was a 'general' who 'commanded the highest authority in the entire nation'.[66] The emergence of a *brafo*-centered governance system is spelled out by A. A. Boahen:

> The system of government became truly federal and theocratic after the first phase of expansion.... The head of the federation was known as the *Braffo* who was elected from among the component states; a federal assembly consisting of representatives from the component states known as curranteers.... Over and above was the *Braffo* and the Assembly was the Fante national God – *Bura Bura Weigya* or *Nananom Mpow*; its decisions and pronouncements were binding on all Fante....[67]

Boahen places the emergence of this governmental form in the late seventeenth century. In the historical context of the eighteenth century, what was the basis of ethical and moral action in Fante society, and who or what defined its ethics and morality? Fante *abrafo*, *curranteers* ('delegates', 'political representatives'), *asofo* ('priests'), and *kwa-asafo* ('peoples'; 'commoners') celebrated the material and political benefits of trade for the *mfantseman* as a whole. Trade and alliances with the English enabled expansion and the transformation of Fante into the strongest of the coastal states. Trade was deemed a social and common 'good' and necessity,[68] but this trade meant the selling of war prisoners, the displaced and the dispossessed to English factors.[69] The common good exacted a terrible cost from these victims. Enslavement and the selling of the enslaved were themselves manifestations of historical processes, institutions and struggles. The titled and privileged classes of Fanteland could only express themselves as history by suppressing the histories of other kinds of social and explanatory strategies.

Territorial expansion and the presence of armed retainers and mercenaries defined Fante politics and the 'heroic' culture before the 1750s.' Fante mercenaries participated in the 1730 Akyem-Accra war against Akwamu, and again in 1741–2 in the Benda war in which Asante and Akyem fought.[70] In the middle decades of the eighteenth century this military aspect of Fante public life declined relative to the religious and commercial as organizers of the lifeworld. The institution of Nananom Mpow – the supreme shrine-oracle of Mankessim, the Fante capital – was decisive in this development.[71] A tradition recorded by E. J. P. Brown is instructive:

> Previous to the Asiantifu hiring Borbor Mfantsi, the latter had been approached by the Akyimfu and given their treasures and other belongings for safe custody, so that in case they suffered a defeat, their belongings could be received back intact. When the Asiantifu hired Borbor Mfantsi, the latter asked what would be their reward, but the former told them they could keep all the spoils they could get. Borbor Mfansti then said to themselves, 'We have already in our possession the treasures of the Akyimfu, and could keep them now as spoils.' The oracle of Nanam' remonstrated with them, and pointed out that their act was ungallant; but they adhered to their determination, and assisted the Asiantifu.[72]

This war marks perhaps the beginning of the end of Fante mercenary activity, at least on any significant scale. Over the next two or three decades there appears to have been a relative decline in the number of armed retainers, particularly among merchants. It seems that they were incorporated into urban militia units, whose numbers were greater towards the end of the century than in the 1710s or 1720s. During the same period the role of the *brafo* as an officiating priest (*osofo*) of Nananom Mpow (or Bura Bura Wigan) gained ascendancy over his role as supreme military commander.[73]

The contemporary counter-discourse of the Nananom Mpow hierocrats of Mankessim seems to have called for a reform of this political-military organization. Through the Nananom Mpow shrine-oracle the priests appear to have advocated a redefinition of the terms in which citizens and subjects interacted at a time when conquests were no longer the order of the day. In the priests' social imaginary a coherent civic life and public realm demanded a new moral and symbolic economy. What regimes of signification enabled the priests and other Fante notables to frame their world in two such distinct languages? Do we have a history of internal cultural capital accumulation by a priestly estate which called for a new kind of public civility and mannerliness in Fante society? The cultural and institutional consolidation of the *mfantseman* entailed the centring of dominant institutions, such as the *brafo*-ship, and this was part and parcel of a process of political centralization and the accumulation of property. The process was underpinned by the norms, rules and ratio advocated by the priesthood of Nananom Mpow.

Rømer's description of the *obosom* of Nananom Mpow indicates its symbolic and organizing significance:

> The Fante *Fetis* is ... the strongest [on the Gold Coast]. Two [Danish] miles from the sea, above Annamaboe, are several mountains of average height, convered with thick undergrowth and tall trees.... The mountains are regarded as so sacred that only on occasion some of the priests dare approach them, but then only to a certain distance. This *Fetis* comes three times a year, and if in the meantime anyone wishes to speak to it about anything, he replies through one of his priests or priestesses.... Offerings to the *Fetis* – people or livestock – are brought forward by fifty priests and priestesses, who sing.... The Blacks ... sit ten and sometimes twenty deep.... The Fante *Fetis* said: if you do not love what is good and do it, and do not hate what is bad and leave it, then I myself shall stand by your enemies so that they will murder you, like all the families living around you; it is only because of your pious forefathers' sake that you have been spared up till now.[74]

The dense growth of trees and bush, the location of this powerful *obosom* was, as McCaskie has noted, 'conceptualized as being part of that liminal zone or fringe area (*kurotia*) that separated the human society of the village (culture) from the unknown, anarchic and dangerous realm of the forest (nature)'.[75] The grove or thicket of trees and undergrowth 'embodied and expressed major categories of supernatural authority', and Nananom Mpow itself signified 'grove of the ancestors or forefathers. The purpose of this ancestor cult was to watch over the interests of the community, and it also served as a ubiquitous mnemonic of Borbor Fante historical identity.'[76] It was hegemonic in the realm of belief, morality and social life: 'It represented order in its command of communal and individual allegiances, and it encapsulated continuity in its determination of collective identity.'[77]

At the ceremony recorded by Rømer, the priest enjoined the worshippers to do good and eschew evil: by following this injunction they would escape misfortune and harm, ensuring the social harmony of society. Who were the enemies? They were most likely the conquered of the 'little states' who were now living under the dominion of the *abrafo* and *curranteers*. We might postulate that the Mankessim priestly estate, or a segment of it, sought to expand the role of the shrine-oracle in the moral and cultural life of society by promoting a vision of societal good based on the moral lives of the Fante citizenry. This was a movement against the commercial-martial ethos of the ruling, stool-holding Houses whose political head, the *brafo*, carried a military title. Thus Rømer, referring to political conditions in Fanteland around 1745, wrote that 'Fante is a republic, where every free Black is an absolute monarch; they have no leader. If they have an able general, then they kill him on the orders of the *Fetiss*. The Fantes have mutual hatred for each other and wish each others' ruin.'[78] No doubt, there is an element of exaggeration in the Danish factor's account of elite political behaviour. Nevertheless, he draws attention to certain subjective and structural features of the Fante political formation, particularly with reference to the powerful position of Nananom Mpow (Rømer's *Fetiss*), already well established in the 1740s.

Was the priesthood of the Mankessim shrine-oracle attempting to bring about the internal pacification of Fante society by having elite factional struggles for power rationally ordered through Nananom Mpow? Successful military leaders were rewarded with settlements, land, slaves, gold and prebends. Litigation and angry rivalries over land boundaries, claims to rights and privileges, and the like were sometimes violently settled. How to reduce and eliminate armed clashes among 'lords of the land', when there was a need to consolidate *brafo* and *curranteer* rule in the conquered territories, was the political question of the moment. The priesthood of the Mankessim *obosom* saw the need to pacify the land. The severe problems of the political order were not to be resolved by force of arms but by appeals to the judgements and exhortations of the Mankessim shrine-oracle. To mitigate internal crises brought on by intense political struggles over, for example, adjustments in the way status and wealth were distributed, the Nananom Mpow authority structure was the mediating means. The pacification process meant that the social disciplinary conventions and codes promulgated by the Nananom Mpow priest-hood had been internalized by the body politic. The priesthood's vision, one might suppose, was that social dialogue not hasty emotion engendered societal harmony.[79]

Were accumulating merchant families/households and their dependents the social basis of this development? Such families would appear to have formed a strong though differentiated constituency in the first half of the century. About 1745 Rømer reported that hundreds of Fante traders travelled to Akwamu for the purpose of buying slaves and ivory, which they would convey to Anomabo.[80] A Danish report of May 1753 relates that 'the Fantees, sometimes numbering in the hundreds, pass by on their way to Aquambue in order to buy up all of the slaves they can get, and we ourselves have reckoned that in the month of January there were more than 300 Fantees in Aquambue buying slaves'.[81] And in 1755 the English governor at Cape Coast Castle refers to a new group of active Fante merchants: 'The constant vent for slaves at our forts has raised a new set of traders who go to market every week and bring their slaves either to the fort or to the ship's boats in the road.'[82] Fante merchants resident in Cape Coast, Moure, Anomabo, Egya, Kormantse and other coastal and inland towns had the institutional and instrumental means to acquire slaves, ivory and gold from supplier markets like Akwamu and Asante. They had access to the credit facilities of the chartered trading companies and they had the ability to finance commercial business from Krepi to Cape Lahu on the Ivory Coast.[83]

What were the cultural archives and symbolic field of property-accumulating, ambition-focused traders and their families? What were their ideological practices? In the course of the first half of the eighteenth century merchants' households came to depend not on the authority of the *brafo* as a successful general but on the rules, pronouncements and revelations of the Nananom Mpow shrine-oracle. These were accepted as legitimate and adherence to them would lead to the good life. The moral exhortations, or sermons of the Mankessim *asofo* disseminated values, obligations and other forms of cultural capital, which established a standard for public decorum and speech, personal morality and self control. Thus, in 1751, it was reported that 'the priests of Bura Burum Weiga, who is the god of [Fante] country, utters oracles and governs that ... people with a more than despotic sway'.[84] Two years later one account comments that the Fante 'federal union' was 'founded on manners, customs, and religion, for they are all under the same subjection to the Father (or God) of Fantee'.[85] The rise of the Mankessim shrine-oracle to political prominence can be dated, perhaps, to the 1730s; by the 1740s it had a formidable reputation – this was its symbolic capital – throughout the Gold Coast and in the early 1750s was one of the principal institutions of governance in the *mfantseman*. Apropos the ascendant status of the shrine-oracle and its priesthood, Fynn writes:

> [I]t was during the second half of the eighteenth century that the Borbor Fante deliberately made Nananom Mpow the abode of gods.... From that time onwards Nananom Mpow was not only the ancestral shrine of the Borbor Fante but also the seat of an oracle to which men [and women] turned in their uncertainty about the future. Here, the priests and their abrafo healed the sick, practiced magic, and maintained an intelligence network that enabled them to obtain information on the private lives of their clients which is then given out as if it were a result of divination or revelation.[86]

Under this new ideological dispensation, the *brafo*-ship became an office serving the Nananom Mpow and representing its authority.[87] What was the context for the emergence of this symbolic field? Given the scale of and social weight of Fante merchant activity and its trading capital, one can postulate that Fante mercantilism represented itself in this historical alternative to militarism. In 1752, one letter reports, 'the Fantees declare ... that the more Europeans they have to trade with the better for their country'.[88] The rationalizing of the symbolic order was inextricably connected to commercial practices.

We can propose that the hegemonic Nananom Mpow *obosom* expressed and reflected the imagination and the social consciousness of the slave-trading merchant families, great and small, of Fanteland in the second half of the eighteenth century. The traders named in the trade book of Tantumkweri fort for the years 1776–8 assuredly had a sense of themselves, and the ideological and cultural means to handle their everyday experiences as traders and citizens.[89] They were an essential constituency for the Mankessim *obosom*. We cannot yet know what images such traders had of themselves or how they represented themselves in the public realm, but for the merchant families of the coastal entrepots the Mankessim *obosom*, pursuing a political-cultural strategy of demilitarizing the Fante public realm, embodied and articulated the imaginary and symbolic order of the society.

'[T]he (Gold Coast) mulattos and blacks who have been in Europe or were christened there'

Commenting on the role of European priests on the Gold Coast in the early nineteenth century, the Danish priest, H. C. Monrad wrote that 'it is incorrect to see the priest in Guinea as a missionary, as he is only a priest for the Europeans there, [and] for the mulattos and the Blacks *who have been in Europe or America and were christened there* [my emphasis]'.[90] In another place, he refers to merchants residing in Gold Coast towns: 'In many places in the towns are not only European traders, but also Mulattos and Blacks, especially those who have been in Europe and have received some kind of education [there]. They commonly have their factors at other towns, in the interior, but never too far inland.'[91] Throughout the eighteenth century 'Gold Coasters' had studied in Europe, but these Christian students have not yet become subjects in the historical investigation of modernity.[92] Thus, Paul Gilroy writes:

> The history of the black Atlantic ... continually criss-crossed by the movements of black people – not only as commodities but engaged in various struggles towards emancipation, autonomy, and citizenship – provides a means to reexamine problems of nationality, location, identity, and historical memory.... The intellectual and cultural achievements of the black Atlantic populations exist partly inside and not always against the grand narrative of Enlightenment and its operational principles.[93]

These considerations do not 'resuscitate' the voices of eighteenth-century West Africans educated in Europe and America.

Employed by Dutch, Danish and British transnational trading capital as chaplains (*asofo*) and/or schoolmasters, these men were committed Christians. Theirs was a shared religious faith with a lexicon which did not organize the dominant discourses and normative institutions in Fanteland and Accraland, but which were congruent with the transnational circuits of merchant capital. While they shared a general intellectual antagonism to *abosomsem* as an alternative cognitive possibility, they held differing views on the morality of the Atlantic slave trade. Was the language of this Christian 'pastorate' a cognitive mapping of commercial capital's commodity chains? What was their vision of life and how did they think their conditions of life?

The eighteenth-century writings of several Gold Coast Christians have survived. Some of these writings – in English, Danish, Dutch, Latin, Fante, and Gã – are useful in constructing a Christian religious imagination. The writers included Reverend Jacobus Eliza Johannes Capitein of Elmina (1717–47), Christian Jacob Protten of Osu (1715–69), Frederik Pedersen Svane of La and Osu (1710 or 1711–90), and Reverend Philip Quaque of Cape Coast (c. 1741–1816).[94] All of these men shared a strong belief in Christian evangelism. Svane and Protten, for example, were already committed pietists while they were still students at the University of Copenhagen. Neither completed his studies. Svane is said to have rebelled against the 'empty rationalism' of the Faculty of Divinity, refused to sit for his final exams and was expelled; Protten appears to have been part of this dispute and was also expelled.[95]

Capitein was born on the 22 June 1717, 'somewhere in Fantiland'. In 1726 he was taken to the Netherlands where he studied theology at the University of Leiden; he returned to the Gold Coast in 1742 and worked as a schoolmaster and chaplain in the service of the Dutch West Indies Company. His writings include sermons, published in Leiden in 1742 and in Amsterdam in 1744, letters, poetry, a public lecture, 'The Calling of the Gentiles' (1737) and a doctoral thesis, 'Dissertation on Political Theology in Which It Is Asked if Christianity Contradicts Evangelical Freedom,' (1742).[96] In his 1742 Leiden University dissertation, the clergyman Capitein argued that the institution of chattel slavery was not at variance with the principles of Christianity. He drew a distinction between 'spiritual' and 'bodily' (physical) freedom: 'So we distinguish between slavery of conscience and sin, from civil slavery; the law of heaven and that of the earthly court of law; and finally a spiritual freedom from bodily freedom: So that Christ speaks of heavenly law and spiritual slavery of conscience from which we are redeemed under the New Testament.' He continues that 'it is very certain that with the abolition of the institution of slavery, countless inconveniences would be created'.[97]

Capitein denied any juridical connection between Reformed Christianity and civic freedom on the grounds that Christian evangelical activity had primacy over the civic implications of Christian universalism. His imaginative vision was the 'spiritual conversion of all bondspeople in Christendom'.[98] Was Capitein's disquisition, in effect, a narrative of mercantile capital?

Svane and his friend Protten were both born in Osu (of Accra-Danish parentage) and grew up as *nkoa* ('subjects') of the ruler of the Akwamu kingdom; their Accra relations enjoyed high status as *nuntshei*. They received their early education at the Castle school at Christiansborg and in 1727 they traveled to Copenhagen to continue their studies. They entered the university in 1732 and joined the Faculty of Divinity where they studied theology.[99] In 1735, Protten joined the pietist religious community of the *Unitas Fratrum*, or Moravian Brethren, in Herrnhut, Silesia. He returned to the Gold Coast as a Moravian missionary in 1736, serving as the Guinea Coast missionary of the Evangelical Moravian Brotherhood – 'Herrnhuters'. Between 1740 and 1764 he lived in the Danish Caribbean for two years, and travelled frequently to Denmark and Germany from the Gold Coast, where he was employed as a schoolmaster in the Castle school at Christiansborg.[100] Protten kept a diary, or journal, during the early years of his travels; the Moravian missionary Oldendorp used it as a source in his 'ethnographical' study of the unfree population in the Danish West Indies.[101] He translated a short catechism in Fante and Gã together with a grammar of the two languages, published in Copenhagen in 1764.[102] According to Debrunner, Protten called himself 'a poor heart, as God himself knows' and the missionary-schoolmaster wrote: 'I know that I am not the man through whom the good Lord can achieve anything, yet I cling to our magnet (Christ) and cannot live without him.'[103]

Svane returned to the Gold Coast in 1735 as a 'free missionary'. He had no success as an evangelist, however, but was employed as schoolmaster at the Castle school and as 'Clerk of the Parish'. He also held the positions of deacon (Danish: *degi*) and catechist (Danish: *kateket*) at Christiansborg. He was closely associated with the house of Wetshe Odoi Kpoti. His brother, a constable at the Danish fort Fredensborg, was married to one of Kpoti's nieces. Because of the implacable hostility of some Christiansborg factors, Svane experienced considerable hardship, which included imprisonment in the castle's dungeons. In 1746, he returned to Denmark and lived there for the remainder of his life. In a formal complaint about his ill treatment at the hands of the Christiansborg authorities, he addressed a lengthy memorandum, or declaration, to the chairman of the West Indies and Guinea Company. This was in 1748. The declaration was 'partly autobiographical, and partly an account of events in Guinea from 1736 to 1746'.[104]

Quaque was born in Cape Coast in 1741 and was educated in London at the cost of the Society for the Propagation of the Gospel in Foreign Parts (1754–65). He was ordained an Anglican priest before returning to the Gold Coast in early 1766. He served as chaplain at Cape Coast Castle and served as schoolmaster at the Castle school.[105]

Unlike Capitein, Protten and Svane, Quaque was openly opposed to the Atlantic slave trade. In response to a letter from Reverend E. Bass of Massachusetts he wrote in July 1775:

In your Epistle You seem to lament bitterly of your Mother Country for Universal Liberty. You upon whom the light of the Gospel flourishes and abound, and if I may be allowed the Expression, as it were advancing daily towards the seat of Bliss, find the Hardships of Bondage and Oppression! Good God can this be possible when I behold with Sorrowful sighing, my poor abject Countrymen over whom You without the Bowels of Christian Love and Pity, hold in Cruel Bondage. This Iniquitous Practice methinks seems to set Religion aside and only making Room for the height of Ambition and Grandeur, the pride of Monarchs &c. to enter.[106]

Did Quaque's Christianity reveal the incommensurate aspects of mercantilist relations? In his 1748 declaration Svane expressed no misgivings about enslavement, slavery or the Atlantic slave trade. During his stay in Osu and Labade Svane owned a few slaves and engaged in the trade himself. Until Protten's numerous letters to the *Unitas Fratrum* of Herrnhut are examined nothing definitive can be said about his views on the matter. Unlike the others he was acquainted personally with life on a slave plantation, having spent an extended period of time on the Danish Caribbean island of St Thomas.

How are these persons, with their Christianity and European education, to be placed in the lifeworld of the Gold Coast entrepots? At another level, what is their historical position in the communities of discourse in the Atlantic world? Where do their ideas and publications fit in with respect to the existing social imaginaries and heteroglossia, which can be said to have emerged out of a merciless history?[107] And what historical possibilities do they represent in the early modern world of the trans-Atlantic slave trade?

Notes

Abbreviations
ADM   Admiralty Records
ARA   Algemeen Rijksarchief (General State Archives), The Hague
ANBKG Archief van de Nederlandsch Bezittingen ter Kuste van Guinea
       (Archives of the Dutch Settlements on Guinea Coast)
BM   Basel Mission Archives, Basel, Switzerland
CO   Colonial Office
FC   Furley Collection, Balme Library, University of Ghana
GK   Guinea Company 1765–1777
PRO   Public Records Office, London, England
RA   Rigsarkivet (National Archives), Copenhagen, Denmark
T   Treasury Records (at the PRO)
VgK   West-Indisk og Guineiske Kompagni 1674–1754 (The West Indies and Guinea Company)

1 For the European trading establishments on the Gold Coast see Albert van Dantzig, *Forts and Castles of Ghana* (Accra, 1980). For the Gold Coast ports see P. E. H. Hair, Adam Jones, and Robin Law (eds), *Barbot on Guinea, The Writings of Jean Barbot on West Africa 1678–1712* (London, 1992), Vol. 2, part two; Erick Tilleman (trans. and ed. Selena Axelrod Winsnes), *A Short and Simple Account of the Country of Guinea and its Nature* (Madison, 1994), Chapters 5 and 6, originally published as *En Kort og Enfoldig Beretning om det Landskab Guinea og dets Beskaffenhed* (Copenhagen, 1697); John Atkins, *A Voyage to Guinea Brasil and the West-Indies* (London, 1970: first edition 1735), see his section on the Gold Coast. Also Ludwig Rømer, *Die Handlumg Verschiedener Völker auf der Küste von Guinea und in Westindien* (Kopenhagen, 1758), Chapters 1–4.
2 Colin Mercer, 'Gramsci and Grammar', in Jeremy Hawthorne (ed.), *Criticism and Critical Theory* (London, 1984), pp. 78–9.
3 For the expression 'orders of politicality' and a discussion of its meanings see Cedric Robinson, *The Terms of Order* (Albany, 1980), Chapter 1.
4 Robert Gray, 'The deconstructing of the English working class', *Social History,* 11, 3 (1986), p. 367. Also Mercer, 'Gramsci and Grammar', p. 79.
5 Hermann Rebel, 'Cultural hegemony and class experience: a critical reading of recent ethnological-

historical approaches (Part One)', *American Ethnologist* 16, 1 (1989), p. 126.

6 Johannes Rask, *Ferd til og fra Guinea 1708–1713* (Oslo, 1969). Originally published in Danish in 1754, *En Kort og Sandferdig Reise-Beskiivelse til og fra Guinea*), p. 124.

7 RA. VgK. Negotie-Journaler fra Guinea 1698–1721, 1723–1754. Entry dated 30 April 1709. The presumption is that Lykke was shot and then beheaded. He may have been born in the 1660s or early 1670s.

8 *Sisa* (originally Akan) in the Gã language means 'ghost', 'spirit of departed men'. See Zimmermann, J., *A Grammatical Sketch of the Akra or Gã Language* (Stuttgart, 1858), p. 263. Also Protten, *Introduction* (Copenhagen, 1764), p. 57.

9 Duncum, 'Approaches to cultural analysis,' p. 11. See Foucault, *The Archaeology of Knowledge*, Part I, for a discussion of discursive formations.

10 M. J. Field, *Social Organization of the Gã People* (London, 1940), pp. 196–7.

11 Idem, *Religion and Medicine of the Gã People* (New York, 1979, first published in 1937), pp. 5–6, 64.

12 Rev. Carl Christian Reindorf, *History of the Gold Coast and Asante* (Basel, 1895), pp. 30–1.

13 J. Reindorf (ed. J. Simensen), *Scandinavians in Africa. Guide to Materials Relating to Ghana in the Danish National Archives* (Oslo, 1980), p. 135.

14 Reindorf, *History*, p. 30.

15 For *bu aten* see Zimmermann, *A Grammatical Sketch*, pp. 22, 36.

16 Field, *Social Oranization*, p. 197.

17 RA. VgK. Breve og Dokumenter fra Guinea 1683, 1648, 1689, 1689–1754. 'Vervolgh van het Daghs Register [1688–89].

18 See, for example, RA. VgK. Dokumenter vedk. diverse Københavnske Retsager II 1720–1728. F. Boye et al., Christiansborg, 9 October 1711, pp. 22, 47, 35–6, 48, 69, 71–2, 82, 85 [hereafter Boye]. (The document lacks pagination, which I have added.)

19 See RA. VgK. Breve og Dokumenter fra Guinea 1883, 1684, 1689, 1698–1754. 'Optegnelsis paa eendeel af Hedningenis Overtroe og Ugudelighed', 15 March 1724; Tilleman, *A Short and Simple Account*, pp. 112–13, 119–36, and Rask, *Ferd til og fra Guinea*, 57, 58–60, 115. Also Boye, [p. 22].

20 See Boye, *passim*, for various references to Lykke.

21 John Barbot, *A Description of the Coasts of North and South Guinea* in Churchill, *A Collection of Voyages and Travels,* 6 vols (London, 1732), Vol. 5, p. 181.

22 See Rask, *Ferd til og fra Guinea, passim*; Rømer, *Tilforladelig Efterretning,* pp. 118-43 *passim*; Reindorf *History*, pp. 58–60, 63–4, 70–1.

23 For example, Tilleman, *A Short and Simple Account*, pp. 28–30.

24 William Bosman, *A New and Accurate Description of the Coast of Guinea* (London, 1705), p. 70.

25 Cf RA. VgK. Breve og Dokumenter fra Guinea 1683, 1684, 1689, 1698-1754. 'Vervolgh van het Daghs Register [1688–9], *passim*; Tilleman, *A Short and Simple Account*, pp. 86–7, 102–10, 113–15.

26 Boye [p. 48; also p.57]. For *owurafram* see Rask, *Ferd til og fra Guinea*, p. 61 ('aurangfrang').

27 Pierre Bourdieu, 'Symbolic Power', *Critique of Anthropology,* Vol. 13/14 (1979), p. 82.

28 Rask, *Ferd til og fra Guinea*, p. 82.

29 Rømer, *Tilforladelig Efterretning*, pp. 122–3.

30 For twentieth-century accounts of *Me, Kpele*, and *La Kpa* see Field, *Religion, passim*; Kilson, *Kpele Lala, Gã Religious Songs and Symbols* (Cambridge, Mass., 1971).

31 For example, Tilleman, *A Short and Simple Account*, pp. 36–7.

32 For *homowo* see Rask, *Ferd til og fra Guinea*, pp. 51–2, and Zimmermann, *A Grammatical Sketch*, pp. 133, 134.

33 Sk, *Ferd til og fra Guinea*, pp.127–8, 131.

34 RA. VgK. Breve og Dokumenter fra Guinea 1683, 1684, 1689, 1698-1754. To the Directors from E. Lygaard, Christiansborg, 4 August 1705, 23 October 1706, 7 January, 18 May and 18 September 1707, and 23 February and 14 July 1708.

35 Boye [pp. 5,16–17, 22, 23, 29, 38, 51, 73, 75, 82–3]. It should be noted that the leaders of the rebellion pledged to live and die together in their struggle against the Akwamu regime. *Ibid.*, [p. 73].

36 RA. VgK. Breve og Dokumenter fra Guinea 1683, 1684, 1689, 1698-1754. To the Directors from E. Ligaard, Christiansborg, 3 and 11 May 1709 and 2 August 1710; Dokumenter vedk. Skibsekspeditioner til Vest-Indien og Guinea V 1706–1710 (1714, 1728). To Captain Hans Maas from E. Lygaard, Christiansborg, 25 March 1709 and To the Directors from Hans Maas, Christiansborg, 3 May 1709; Boye [pp. 29, 83]; Rømer, *Tilforladelig Efterretning* pp. 139, 140; Reindorf, *History*, pp. 70–1.

37 Boye, [pp. 3, 4, 11, 17, 22, 35–6, 47, 69, 71–2, 82, 85]; Rask, Ferd til og fra Guinea, *passim*.

38 Jean-Joseph Goux (trans. Jennifer Curtiss Gage), *Symbolic Economies. After Marx and Freud* (Ithaca, 1990), p. 153.

39 For a discussion of 'hidden' and 'public' transcripts, see James C. Scott, *Domination and the Arts of Resistance* (New Haven & London, 1990), Chapters 1–3.

40 For details about the Company's slaves and their wages and work see RA. VgK. Mandtal-og Gagebøger fra Guinea 1703–1705, 1727–1754.

41 For a discussion of this class see Peter Linebaugh and Marcus Rediker, 'The many-headed hydra: sailors, slaves, and the Atlantic working class in the eighteenth century,' *Journal of Historical Sociology*, 3, 3 (1990), pp. 225–52. In studies of the Atlantic working class, slaves employed in the West African forts and factories of the European chartered companies are never mentioned, let alone discussed. See Michael Twaddle (ed.), *The Wages of Slavery. From Chattel Slavery to Wage Slavery in Africa, the Caribbean and England* (London, 1993) and Paul E. Lovejoy and Nicholas Rogers (eds), *Unfree Labour in the Development of the Atlantic World* (London, 1994).

42 L. F. Rømer (trans. Mette Dige-Hess), *Le Golfe de Guinee 1700–1750* (Paris, 1989), pp. 56, 65–7, 69–71, 76–9, 83–6.

43 *Idem, Tilforladelig Efterretning*, pp. 104–5.

44 See RA. VgK. Breve og Dokumenter fra Guinea 1683, 1684, 1689, 1698–1754. 'Specification paa Compls. Slaver og Remidorer med deres Alder eftter Jugement samt hvad de nu kand Være af Værdie', E. N. Boris, Christiansborg, 14 November 1739; GK. Inventarium Overleverings Forretning, Mandtals-og Gageruller m. m. fra Guinea 1767, 1769–70, 1777–8.

45 RA. VgK. Breve og Dokumenter fra Guinea 1683, 1684, 1689, 1698–1754. To the Directors from A. Wærøe, Christiansborg, 24 December 1730; Negotie-Journaler fra Guinea 1698–1721, 1723–1754. Entry dd. 12 November 1732; Omkostningsbøger 1698–1721, 1723–1754. Entries for the 1730s; Rømer, Tilforladelig Efterretning, pp. 158–9,180, 244–5. For Frimpon's death see RA. VgK. Breve og Dokumenter fra Guinea 1883, 1684, 1689, 1698–1754. To the Directors from J. Jorgensen, Christiansborg, 2 April 1742.

46 See RA. VgK. Negotie-Hoveboger fra Guinea 1698–1754; Negotie-Journaler fra Guinea 1698–1721,1723–1754.

47 See Georg Lukacs, *History and Class Consciousness. Studies in Marxist Dialectics* (London, 1971), pp. 153–58; Frederic Jameson, *Marxism and Form* (Princeton, 1971), Chapter 3.

48 My account draws upon RA. VgK. Sekretprotokoller fort paa Christiansborg i Guinea 1723-1754. L.F. Rømer and C. Engman, Christiansborg, 3 July 1749 and J. Platfues et al,Christiansborg, 25 September 1749. For the ages of Kofi and Kwasi see RA. VgK. Breve og Dokumenter fra Guinea 1683, 1684, 1689, 1698-1754. ['List of Company's slaves'] Peter Salilgaard, Christiansborg, 3 May 1738.

49 For Duomoro see Reindorf, *History*, pp. 38–9, 98.

50 They were put aboard the *Crown Prince's Desire*, which arrived in the Danish West Indies in February 1750. For the ship see Waldemar Westergaard, *The Danish West Indies under Company Rule (1671–1754)* (New York, 1917), p. 324.

51 Reindorf, *History*, pp. 70–1; Rømer, *Tilforladelig Efterretning*, pp.139, 140.

52 For these men see Rømer, *Tilforladelig Efterretning*, pp. 9, 205, 300; idem, *Le Golfe de Guinee*, pp. 55, 69–71, 77–9; RA. VgK. 'En kort sandfærdig klar og tydelig omstændelig General Declaration og Underækning om ti Aars Begivenheder paa Fortet Christiansborg i Acra paa Custen af Guinea i Africa,' Friderich P. Svane, Kiobenhavn,1 June 1748, pp. 84–5; H. Bohner, 'La Lomo, der Fetisch-Prophet [Part Two]', *Evangelische Missions-Magazin 30ster Jahrgang* (1886), p. 202 and notes I and 2; Reindorf, *History*, p. 37. For the 'cults' in the twentieth century see Field, *Religion*, pp. 5–6, 39–40, 64–5, 73–5.

53 For example, Rømer, *Tilforladelig Efterretning*, pp. 16, 17, 102; Reindorf, *History*, pp. 96–8, 103–11.

54 See, for example, RA. VgK. Gældbøger 1723–1733, 1735–1754; FC. The Gold Coast 1731–1739. Extracts from the journals, correspondence with the out-forts, despatches, etc. of the Directors-General of the Netherlands West India Company, entry for 15 September 1733. Minutes of Council: 'List of outstanding debts at Accra due to the late upper factor Jacob de la Planque, this ulto. April 1731.

55 Cf. Rømer, *Tilforladelig Efterretning*, pp. 59–60, 205, 271.

56 For an account of Frimpong's court and gold mines see *ibid.* pp. 178, 180, 244–5.

57 Cf. *idem, Le Golfe de Guinea*, pp. 55–71, 76–9, 82–5, 86.

58 *Idem, Tilforladelig Efterretning*, p. 26. Cf. Habermas on the 'colonization' of the lifeworld by economic and political demands. Steven Seidman (ed.), *Jürgen Habermas on Society and Politics. A*

Reader (Boston, 1989), Chapters 8 and 9; Brand, *The Force of Reason*, Chapters 5 and 11.

59 Rømer, *Tilforladelig Efterretning*, p. 27.

60 *Ibid.*, pp. 16, 112–14, 115–16, 117.

61 *Ibid.*, pp. 132–3. Cf. *ibid.* p. 137.

62 *Ibid.*, pp. 126–7.

63 Bernard de Grunne, *Ancient Treasures in Terra Cotta of Mali and Ghana* (New York, 1981), p. 58. See also James R. Sanders, 'The political development of the Fante in the eighteenth and nineteenth centuries: a study of a West African merchant society' (PhD thesis, Northwestern University, 1980).

64 PRO CO 388/45. 'Fante treaty for excluding the French from making any settlement in the Fantee territory', Cape Coast Castle, 6 February 1753.

65 Rømer, *Tilforladelig Efterretning*, pp. 46, 217.

66 *Ibid.*, p. 84. For the different meanings of the term *brafo* see T. C. McCaskie, 'Nananom Mpow of Mankessim: an essay in Fante history', in David Henige and T. C. McCaskie (eds), *West African Economic and Social History. Studies in Memory of Marion Johnson* (Madison, 1990), pp.135–8.

67 A. Adu Boahen, 'Fante diplomacy in the eighteenth century', in R. Ingham (ed.), *Foreign Relations of African States* (London, 1974), pp. 27–8.

68 Cf PRO. ADM 1/1485. Captains' Letters 1751–1754. Letter from Matthew Buckle, *Assistance,* in Annamboa Road, 19 February 1752, pp. 4–5,10–11; CO 388/45. To the Earl of Halifax from Wm. Ansa Sessaracoa, son of John Currantee, Anomabo, 20 February 1752.

69 See, for example, Rømer, *Tilforladelig Efterretning*, pp. 110–11.

70 For these wars see ARA. ANBKG 97. Letter from D. Guichent, Bercoe, 5 March 1730; E. J. P. Brown, *Gold Coast and Asiante Reader*, 2 vols (London, 1929), Vol. 1, pp. 67–8. For Fante expansion before 1750 see Boahen, 'Fante Diplomacy,' pp. 27–39.

71 For a recent study of this institution see McCaskie, 'Nananom Mpow,' *passim*. Also J. K. Fynn, 'The Nananom Mpow of the Fante: myth and reality,' *Sankofa,* Vol. 2 (1976).

72 Brown, E. J. P., *Gold Coast and Asianti Redder* (London, 1929), Vol. 1, pp. 67–8.

73 For these and other 'roles' of the *brafo* see McCaskie, 'Nananom Mpow,' pp. 135–6, 137–8.

74 Rømer, *Tilforladelig Efterretning*, pp. 78–9, 80, 83. For a late eighteenth-century description of the shrine-oracle see J. A. de Maree, *Reizen op en Beschrijving van de Goudkust van Guinea*, 2 vols (The Hague and Amsterdam, 1817–18), Vol. 2, pp. 82–4.

75 McCaskie, 'Nananom Mpow', p. 135.

76 *Ibid.*

77 *Ibid.*, p. 142.

78 Rømer, *Tilforladelig Efterretning*, p. 272.

79 See McCaskie, 'Nananom Mpow,' p. 140; Fynn, 'The Nananom Mpow', p. 56.

80 RA. VgK. Relationer om Forholdene i Guinea 1733–1748. [L.F. Rømer,] 'En liden description af Rio Volta [ca. 1745].'

81 RA. Vgk. Breve og Dokumenter fra Guinea 1683, 1684, 1689, 1698–1705. To the Directors from C. Engman *et al.*, Christiansborg, 3 May 1753. See also *ibid.*, To the Directors from C. Engman, Christiansborg, 30 July 1753.

82 PRO T70/1523, To the Committee from Thomas Melvil, Cape Coast Castle, 17 March 1755.

83 John Hippisley, *Essays* (London, 1764), pp. 11–12 note 3; Ruth A. Fisher (ed.), *Extracts from the Records of the African Companies* (Washington DC, [1930?]), p. 58: 'The Council's answer to the return of the Lords of Trade [1749?].'

84 PRO T70/29, To the Committee from Thomas Melvil, Cape Coast Castle, 23 July 1751; also T70/30. To the Committee from Thomas Melvil, Cape Coast Castle, 14 March 1753.

85 PRO T70/30, To the Committee from Thomas Melvil, Cape Coast Castle, 14 March 1753.

86 Fynn, 'The Nananom Mpow,' p. 57. See also, McCaskie, 'Nananom Mpow,' pp. 138–9.

87 McCaskie, 'Nananom Mpow,' p. 138.

88 PRO T70/1518, To the Committee from .Thomas Melvil, Cape Coast Castle,14 March 1752; Sanders, 'The political development', pp. 312–17.

89 For these traders see PRO T70/1264, 'Slave barters 1772-76, Tantumquerry Fort', Richards Miles; T70/1265. 'Slave barters at Annamaboe Fort,1776-78', Richard Miles; T70/1266. '[Accounts] Tantumquerry Fort 1776–79'. Also George Metcalf, 'Gold, assortments and the trade ounce: Fante merchants and the problem of supply and demand in the 1770s', *Journal of African History*, 28 (1987) and *idem*, 'A microcosm of why Africans sold slaves: Akan consumption patterns in the 1770s', *Journal of African History*, 28 (1987).

90 H. C. Monrad, *Bidrag til en Skildring af Guinea-Kysten og dens Indbyggere, og til en Beskrivelse over de*

Danske Colonier paa denne Kyst (Kiabenhavn), p. 376.

91 *Ibid.*, p. 299 note.
92 Paul Gilroy, *The Black Atlantic. Modernity and Double Consciousness* (Cambridge MA, 1993); Robert Wuthnow, *Communities of Discourse. Ideology and Social Structure in the Reformation the Enlightenment and European Socialism* (Cambridge MA, 1989). Cf. Ntongela Masilela, 'The "Black Atlantic" and African modernity in South Africa', *Research in African Literatures* 27, 4 (1996), pp. 88–90.
93 Gilroy, *The Black Atlantic*, pp. 16, 48.
94 For biographical accounts of these men see H. W. Debrunner, *Presence and Prestige: Africans in Europe. A History of Africans in Europe before 1918* (Basel, 1979), pp. 81–5, 108–9.
95 See Debrunner, *Presence and Prestige*, p. 84; Poul Erik Olsen, '"Disse vilde Karle". Negre i Danmark indtil 1848' in Bent Blüdnikow (ed.), *Fremmede i Danmark* (Odense, 1987), p. 112.
96 See Kwesi Kwaa Prah, *Jacobus Eliza Johannes Capitein. A Critical Study of an Eighteenth Century African* (Braamfontein, 1989); Henri Gregoire, *On the Cultural Achievements of Negroes* (Amherst, 1996. originally published 1808), pp. 94–7; Allison Blakely, *Blacks in the Dutch Wolrd. The Evolution of Racial Imagery in a Modern Society* (Bloomington & Indianapolis, 1993), pp. 207–8, 218–19, 252–3; F. L. Bartels, 'Jacobus Eliza Johannes Capitein,1717–47', *Transactions of the Historical Society of Ghana*, Vol. 4 (1959). For his writings see Robert C. H. Shell (trans & ed.), *The Agony of Asar. Jacobus Eliza Johannes Capitein, 1717 to 1747. A Doctoral Thesis of an African Slave in the Twilight of Holland's Golden Age* (Princeton, 1997); 'J. E. J. Capitein's 1744 Fante catechism' in Protten, *Introduction*, pp. 59-66; Dr. A Eekhof, 'De Negerpredicant Jacobus Elisa Joannes Capitein,' *Nederlandsch Archief voor Kerkgeschiedenis* n.s. Vol.13 (1917), pp. 138–74, 209–76.
97 Prah, *Jacobus Eliza Johannes Capitein*, pp. 59–60. Also *The Agony of Asar*, passim.
98 'Editor's introduction' in *The Agony of Asar*, p. iii.
99 For a 1724 report of the Castle school, which had twenty pupils (twelve boys and eight girls), see the anonymous document which begins 'Melaterne...' and is dated 15 March 1724 in RA. VgK. Breve og Dokumenter fra Guinea 1683, 1684, 1689, 1698–1754. Protten's birthday is given as 1 September 1715 (he is called 'Uldrich Protten' in the report). Svane was said to be thirteen at the time, so was born in 1711 (or 1710). He is the 'Peder Pederson' mentioned in the report.
100 Debrunner, *Presence and Prestige*, p. 83; Olsen, '"Disse Vilde Karle"', p. 112; David Crantz, *Alte und Neue Brüder-Historie oder Kurzefasste Geschichte der Evangelische Brüder-Unität in den Ältern Zeiten und insonderheit in dem Gegenwärtigen Jahrhundert* (Hildescheim and New York, 1973, originally published 1772), pp. 293–4.
101 See C. G. A. Oldendorp, *History of the Mission of the Evangelical Brethren on the Caribbean Islands of St. Thomas, St. Croix, and St. John* (Ann Arbor, 1987, originally published in German, 2 vols, 1777), pp. 188–91. Protten's diary has never been published and is presently in the archives of the Moravian Brethren, Herrnhut, Germany – personal communication, Adam Jones, University of Leipzig.
102 The Danish title of his language study is: *En nyttig Grammaticalsk Indledelse til Tvende hidindtil gandske ubekiendte Sprog, Fanteisk og Acraisk (paa Guld-Küste udi Guinea) efter den Danske Pronunciation og Udtale*. For the English translation see note 16 above.
103 Debrunner, *Presence and Prestige*, p. 83.
104 *Ibid.*, p. 84; Reindorf, *Scandinavians*, p. 37. For the archival reference to Svane's manuscript, see note 87 above.
105 Debrunner, *Presence and Prestige*, pp. 81–2; Margaret Priestley, 'Philip Quaque of Cape Coast' in Phillip D. Curtin (ed.), *Africa Remembered. Narratives of West Africans from the Era of the Slave Trade* (Madison and London, 1968), pp. 99–112; Brown, *Gold Coast*, Vol. 2, pp. 126–32, 134–6.
106 Paul Edwards and David Dabydeen (eds), *Black Writers in Britain 1760–1890* (Edinburgh, 1991), p. 110. In a letter written in 1786 Quaque describes a slave revolt on board a ship in the Moure road. See also Priestley, 'Philip Quaque,' pp. 133–4.
107 See Aijaz Ahmad, *In Theory. Classes, Nations, Literatures* (London and New York, 1992), pp. 227–8.

11

Gender in the City Women, Migration & Contested Spaces in Tunis *c.*1830–81

JULIA CLANCY-SMITH

Offering one of the best natural harbours in the central Mediterranean, the Tunis region has for millennia welcomed peoples and products from all over the Middle Sea. In the early part of the nineteenth century, however, the vast majority of the city's population was Arabic-speaking and Sunni Muslim, although Tunis also had an important Jewish community.[1] The other identifiable micro-community were the Andalusians, Spanish Muslims and Jews who had come as refugees during the centuries-long *Reconquista* and retained a memory of Iberian origins.[2] The port city also enjoyed long-standing ties with the Ottoman Empire and eastern Mediterranean as well as with sub-Saharan Africa. Finally, there existed a small, resident Western European presence which by 1830 numbered no more than 30 families. They formed a closed, upper-crust mercantile class, however, kept distinct by endogamy over generations. Sexual politics and religious affiliation bounded this group, there being no indigenous Christian community in the Maghrib – in contrast to the situation in the Arab East.

After roughly mid-century, Tunis became the Ellis Island of the central Mediterranean as subsistence migrants from the impoverished edges of Southern Europe and its islands, particularly Malta, Sicily and Sardinia, poured into the city. They came in response to a number of complex push–pull and systemic forces operating around the Basin, particularly the ecological degradation of the Mediterranean mountain economy.[3] The single greatest political vector for subsistence migration to this part of the Maghrib, however, was the French conquest of neighbouring Algeria. By the 1860s, the percentage of European expatriates, male and female, permanently settled in Tunisia's capital region had increased enormously until they represented nearly 10 per cent of the population out of a total of some 100,000 people.[4] These new residents were, for the most part, of quite modest social means. As their numbers swelled, the Europeans spilled out of their older *funduq* (Christian residential quarter) in the medina to occupy the Bab al-Bahr neighbourhood near the old city's 'sea gate'; they also came to dominate whole sections of the port (Halq al-Wadi or La Goulette), referred to even today as 'the Sicilian quarter'.

Not only was the urban morphology of the capital transformed under the weight of the rapidly expanding immigrant presence but also older Islamic norms and institutions for managing socio-cultural and legal relations were eroded long before the 1881 imposition of the French Protectorate. Many of the newly arrived city residents were diplomatic protégés of various European powers vying for influence in the country – Italy, France and Great Britain. The Maltese, for example, were officially British protégés since the island had passed into British hands in 1801. Thus, in contrast with neighbouring Algeria, where military conquest had preceded European settler implantation, Tunis had a burgeoning population of unruly expatriate 'Europeans', espousing different cultural norms and enjoying dissimilar political privileges, decades prior to the arrival of the French army.

Tunis offers a particularly strategic site for investigating the multiple transformations occurring in a pre-colonial Mediterranean African port city due to the combined forces of European imperialism, world market integration and global population displacements. Yet, paradoxically, the social history of Tunis in the nineteenth century remains to be written. While there are numerous monographs devoted to the city – Lézine's *Deux Villes d'Ifriqiya* and Zbiss's *La Médina de Tunis* are examples – these tend to be of Islamic monuments and architecture.[5] In such studies, city dwellers are largely absent and, therefore, the changing uses and definitions of urban spaces and social environments are left unexplored. Abdelkafi's *La Médina de Tunis* does 'people' the medina but we hear little of the human flotsam and jetsam from across the sea – Maltese peasants without land, draft dodgers and bandits from Sicily, or prostitutes and smugglers – who settled in the capital or in other coastal cities and towns.[6]

Migration from southern Europe and the Mediterranean islands between 1850 and 1881 constituted a key transformative process in modern Tunisian history, particularly for Tunis. Indeed, from 1830, when France stumbled into Algeria, until the Great War, the North African littoral progressively became a frontier for southern European settlement.[7] Yet this particular migratory pulse has been neglected in world history largely because, in statistics-driven studies of nineteenth-century global movements, North Africa appears to be an outlying zone of interaction.[8] Thus, the progressive implantation of Europeans in the capital has not been the object of recent study.[9] In addition, the story of Mediterranean immigration to Tunisia is the history that no one wants. Tunisian scholars have ignored it. Post-1962 French scholarship has relegated it to historical forgetfulness – like the memory of Vichy France or of North African Muslims who served under the French flag.[10] In short, there is no historical study of Tunis comparable to Prochaska's *Colonialism in Bône, 1870–1920*, although his work is flawed by the fact that issues of women and gender are completely ignored.[11]

Colonial studies of Mediterranean migration to Tunisia undertaken at the end of the past century focused principally upon the problem of assimilating non-French Europeans to France and less upon the impact this settlement had upon the capital and its indigenous inhabitants. Finally, women, whether European or indigenous Tunisian, are absent from historical narratives of the nineteenth century – despite the fact that French diplomats fretted openly about the arrival of Maltese and Sicilian families in the *beylik*. Above all, it was the astonishing fertility of the Maltese women residing in Tunis that alarmed French imperialists.[12] For similar reasons, the city's Muslim notables, the *baldi* class ('urban bourgeoisie'), were also distressed by progressive Christian European immigration, above all by the presence of women of ordinary rank in the urban core.

In short, there exists a major contradiction in the literature on nineteenth-century pre-colonial and colonial North Africa. Settler colonialism is employed as the major explanatory device for all transformations, large and small, occurring in the Maghrib. Yet we know virtually nothing of how relations between North Africans and transplanted Europeans worked on the ground, in day-to-day encounters, exchanges and contestations. This is particularly true of ordinary folk and of those social elements straddling the fluid boundaries between the law-abiding and criminal. When it comes to women and gender in the colonial setting, our knowledge is even sparser – despite the fact that all the communities calling Tunisia home in the second half of the nineteenth century measured, evaluated and either approved of or condemned their urban neighbours by virtue of female public behaviour.

This chapter posits that the presence of Mediterranean folk, particularly women, in the medina – the locus of urbanity and *'umran* (civilization) for Tunisia and Tunisians – unleashed a process whereby the city's streets and public places increasingly became contested gender spaces. In response Tunisian notables formulated novel methods of city planning and urban micro-management; some measures were successful, others less so. Nevertheless, suggesting that indigenous authorities expanded their powers in the decades prior to 1881 is to argue against all the current literature. Scholarship on the Tunisian state in the period from Ahmad Bey (i.e., 1837–1855) onwards might be characterized as in the genre of 'oppression studies', a concept from women's history as practised over a decade ago. According to this model, ruling elites in Tunis heroically attempted to modernize the country but were thwarted in everything they sought to accomplish, forfeiting political, fiscal and legal ground to European powers and their diplomatic representatives in the capital. Thus, the 'Europeans' oppressed indigenous state actors, who in turn oppressed their own subjects – a view which deprives Tunisians and ordinary people of whatever background of agency.[13]

What has not been noticed by historians is that native urban elites began to assume novel institutional functions in the capital precisely because of European subsistence immigration.[14] Therefore, the Tunisian state invested – or attempted to – more and more social and economic spaces – and relationships which, in the older order of things, had been deemed 'private', non-state, or at least negotiable. In short, transnational and trans-Mediterranean forces had rendered definitions of the individual's and community's proper place in the capital city increasingly problematic; this was especially true for women.

In tracing the Mediterranean peopling of Tunis, it is necessary to follow three strands of analysis: the impact of subsistence migration upon residential and employment patterns; how the settlement of women of modest means provoked contestations over public spaces; and how the confluence of these forces for change resulted in the elaboration of new forms of urban social control which principally affected Tunisian Muslim women. Two suppositions underlie this study. First it could be argued that the colonial city was more or less in place prior to 1881; the imposition of the French Protectorate merely confirmed processes in motion since about 1850. It would be wrong, however, to characterize all the recent immigrants as colonial agents – indeed some groups, particularly the Sicilians, actually impeded France's imperial designs upon Tunisia because of the peculiar status enjoyed by Italians in the country. Second, conceptualizations of the modern 'colonial city' – located outside of the walls of the medina – as being utterly distinct from the 'traditional city' are misleading.[15] If we look not at where upper-class Europeans resided in the Tunis region (and their numbers were relatively small) but rather at the residential patterns of subaltern groups, we see that by 1900 a large proportion of the medina's population was of humble Mediterranean origins. When France set up her bureaucratic apparatus for governing the country after 1881, significantly and symbolically, that apparatus was not situated in *la nouvelle ville*, or the modern city stretching from the edges of the medina toward the port and sea. Rather the machinery of the Protectorate was placed in the heart of the medina, in the Qasbah, which had served as the political core of city and kingdom for centuries.

To calibrate the transformations unleashed by migration, we first must consider what Tunis represented in the collective cultural consciousness of its inhabitants as well as the configuration of the European minority in the period before human traffic from the central Mediterranean made the city into a mini Ellis Island. Compared with other Maghribi capitals, Tunis is somewhat unique. First, it has long been both the political and economic capital of Ifriqiya or Tunisia as well as the major intellectual-religious urban centre. Moreover, from the eighteenth century on, unlike Algiers, Tunis became associated with a single ruling dynasty, the Husaynids. Through intermarriage, the Turco-Ottoman commanders and indigenous Arab elites from the capital were intermingled; by the nineteenth century Husaynid rulers and institutions enjoyed virtually unquestioned legitimacy. Tunisia had 'Tunisified' its Ottoman conquerors; the regime drew much of its support from the *baldi* class who provided cadres and government officials. City inhabitants looked with disdain upon other Tunisian cities and especially upon the countryside. The two dichotomous terms, *baraniyya* ('foreigner' – those from other parts of Tunisia or from other regions in the Maghrib) and *baldi* capture the collective self-view of the population. The sobriquets of Tunis – *al-Hadira* or 'the capital' and *al-Khadra'* or 'the verdant' – suggest a conflation between the type of civilization only found in particular types of Islamic cities and the notion of 'garden' or 'paradise' with its subtle connotation of salvation. More explicit was the representation of Tunis as the North African or Ifriqiyan prototype of *al-Madina*, the city of the Prophet Muhammad and of Islam, the exemplary centre.[16]

The *axis mundi* of Tunis was, of course, the medina which boasted the Zitonna mosque-university, hundreds of guilds or artisan corporations producing luxury goods, palaces housing wealthy merchants and *ulama* families, and numerous religious edifices or shrines as well as rich libraries. While the medina was also home to ordinary people, the two adjacent *ribats* or suburbs, Bab al-Soniqa and Bab al-Jazira, were more popular in social composition, and tended to be associated with recent rural immigrants to the city as well as disorderly or even illicit activities. Public moderation, tranquillity, and circumspection were the behavioural attributes prized by the medina's largely, but not exclusively, Arab Muslim residents. Until the middle of the nineteenth century and the mass arrival of the Mediterranean Christians, the medina was a bustling commercial and religious centre by day. By night it was a relatively quiet area whose shops closed at sunset and whose inhabitants rarely ventured out of their homes after the deylical police force, responsible for keeping order in markets and streets during daylight hours, sounded the retreat at sundown. European travellers often noted with surprise that beggars were few on the streets, in contrast with capitals like London or Paris, and that the medina was a relatively quiet place after business hours when the gates of the city were closed.[17] As the Englishman, Godfrey Feise, observed during his years in service to the British consulate in Tunis: 'riots and cabals, so frequent in European cities, are here very uncommon; this may be attributed to the prohibition of wine and other strong liquors and although the Turks are in general very fond of the former (i.e., wine) in private, they seldom commit an excess'.[18] Finally, there were no theatres or permanent places of public amusement; street entertainment was confined to periodic religious or annual popular festivals that the Tunisian state increasingly suppressed or circumscribed as the century wore on.[19]

The original European community, as opposed to the newcomers, in Tunis went back at least as far as the twelfth century when Venetian/Italian merchants set up shop there; they were joined in later centuries by Jews from Livorno, and a small mercantile oligarchy from Marseilles. The Europeans were housed in their own *funduq* in the medina in what came to be known as the quarter of the 'Francs'.[20] Yet until the late eighteenth century, this was a very special kind of community composed exclusively of

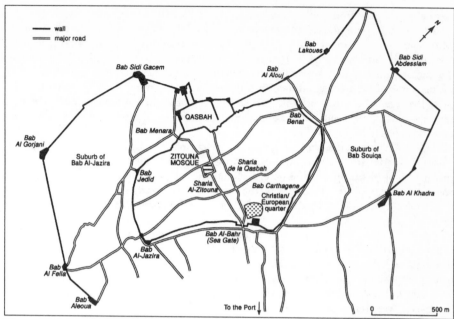

Figure 11.1 The Medina of Tunis, nineteenth century

males, mainly bachelors. According to treaty, resident European/Christian merchants were not allowed to bring families – no women, no children. This small European outpost was socially and sexually segregated from Arab-Muslim or Jewish city inhabitants since intermarriage between Christians, Jews and Muslims was forbidden by law. (During the heyday of Mediterranean corsair activity in the seventeenth and eighteenth centuries, 'European' Christian males settled in Tunis and other Ottoman port-cities but these renegades converted to Islam and intermarried with local families.)[20]

At some time late in the eighteenth century, the ban on bringing female spouses into the *beylik* was lifted – but only for specific social ranks of European merchants-cum-diplomatic representatives. The Tunisian state closely surveyed the arrival of Western European women into the realm by sea. Until 1837, Christian women could not disembark in the country without an appointed husband or male guardian. Even with a male protector of high rank and proven virtue, a woman had to obtain special written permission (*aman*) from the ruler to settle in the country. Authorization, even when requested by a friendly European power, was often refused by the beys.[21]

These regulations may appear to be an attempt by a Muslim state to guard the moral-sexual integrity of its populace; and indeed this was part of it. However, scrutinizing the various treaties subsumed under the rubric of Capitulations – an unlikely place at first glance to look for documentation on gender – reveals that prohibitions against women from European nations settling in Ottoman lands were in effect around the Mediterranean Basin. Moreover, it was not only Muslim authorities who desired this but also the 'Chambre de Commerce de Marseille', which had its own set of regulations regarding French women in Ottoman port cities. For example, in 1658 the heads of the French 'nation' in Smyrna complained to the Chamber in Marseilles about the presence of females and children among the merchant community there. An interdict was issued forbidding women from embarking to the Levant, particularly females from the artisan classes. Obviously the interdictions were not obeyed since they were repeatedly issued.[22] Moreover, the Chamber characterized women of humble station as 'vagabonds', 'disreputable', and 'undesirable' residents in France's overseas mercantile establishments. The debate in Marseilles over whether women should be allowed to travel to, or reside in, the Ottoman empire continued into the eighteenth century. It was argued that the presence of females would provoke 'disorder' and worse still – should a child be born in the Levant or Barbary, how could one give them to 'wet-nurse with [indigenous] nurses of Turkish or Jewish blood'?[23]

These Mediterranean-wide regulations governing the displacements of women, particularly from the common classes, have never been studied.[24] What they suggest is that the pivot of European commercial/diplomatic relations with the Ottoman Empire was the *droit de résidence*, guaranteed by the Capitulations, and that a critical element of the right of residence in Islamic realms revolved around the control of females. Also at stake implicitly was female sexuality and women's access to public spaces in societies where religious affiliation governed the individual's place in the socio-legal order as well as sexual or marriage partners. Finally, this brief foray into the 'pre-history' of gender relations in hybrid port cities underscores the immense change that the arrival of boatloads of Mediterranean women from the lowest orders of society meant not only for Tunisians but also for the European mercantile oligarchy. Negative attitudes towards lower-class Mediterranean women persisted well into the nineteenth century and shaped responses by the city's Arab-Muslim notables – as well as by European consular representatives – toward the social dangers posed by 'wanton' foreign females.

Port cities have long been regarded by government and religious authorities as well as by their prim hinterlands as particularly turbulent places whose ethnically heterogeneous populations are prone to sexual licence and deviant behaviour.[25] Moreover, such behaviour is frequently associated with newcomers. Tunis was no exception to this. In following patterns of Mediterranean settlement, it is necessary to consider not only how immigration transformed the physical morphology of Tunis but also how it insinuated itself into the cultural-symbolic or ideological spaces of urban life; in all these areas, gender loomed large. Moreover, using gender as a lens to evaluate how the immigrants were viewed by city inhabitants belies Woodford's assertion that the Maltese and Sicilian newcomers 'accepted the beldi system, taking their place in it, or on its fringes as best they could'.[26] In fact, these marginal folk were regarded as more than just a nuisance for they threatened the ideal of urbanity itself.

Until about 1850 residential patterns for the medina's civilian populace followed Islamic norms; urban space and identities, where one lived and worked, were largely a function of which religious community – or, in some cases, ethnic group – one belonged to. For example, the Jewish quarter was located in the medina's northern reaches near the shrine of Sidi Mahrez; Berber Algerians, who served in special military units, resided in their own separate neighbourhood.[27] Religious affiliation or ethnic identity in turn determined such critical matters as legal jurisdiction, civil status and employment possibilities. Fundamental to patterns of urban residence were issues of women, gender and collective honour – *'irdh*. The reputation of the patriarchal lineage was guaranteed by the strict sexual segregation of male/female spaces which were infused by religious norms, values and customary law. Thus, religious affiliation and socio-sexual boundaries were mutually reenforcing and regarded as the most significant relationship undergirding moral order in the city.[28]

Unlike the situation in the Arab East, for example in Cairo, Tunisian Muslim women did not normally appear in the public Friday communal prayer service, there being no *maqsura* in the Maliki mosques of the city.[29] While historians invariably mention the enclosed, inward-looking structure of the family compound in the Islamic city, other features of domestic architecture betray the concern with sexual spatial segregation. Many of the homes in the medina were equipped with several door knockers (*halqas*) of heavy iron rings; men exclusively used the knocker placed on the right; the one on the left was reserved for women. Visitors could be readily identified before the door was opened from the sound of the *halqa*. *Baldi* women rarely left their houses after the onset of puberty, with the exception of calling upon relatives or going to family graves or to the public baths.[30]

Nesbitt, however, writing in the early twentieth century, observed that upper-class women in the medina 'are never allowed to walk, do not seem, as in Algiers, to picnic in the cemeteries and seldom' are driven about the streets even in tightly closed carriages.[31] While little is known of individual acts of female rebellion among the urban bourgeoisie, it seems that recalcitrant women of the notable classes were quietly sent to houses of female obedience, *dar juwad*, located in hidden corners of the medina, until they acceded to their clans' wishes. As for Muslim and Jewish women of the popular classes, poverty meant that they were at more liberty to move around the city, although always veiled. Those women who had fallen into prostitution tended to be found in the Bab al-Jazira suburb; not surprisingly, they were mainly drawn from rural groups just arrived from the countryside or from the urban disinherited.[32] All European visitors to Tunis were amazed by the absence of indigenous women in the streets; as Feise once again observed: 'Few Moorish women are seen in the streets except such as abandon themselves indiscriminately to the Mahomedans but the Jewish women on the contrary are not so much confined to their homes.'[33] And the Englishwoman Nesbitt wrote that: 'Poor women are little seen in the streets, and those of their rich sisters who have no pretensions to rank are only permitted to walk about occasionally and then do so under the surveillance of servants and with such heavy silks [veils] that they must be almost smothered.'[34]

Evidence of the concern of city notables to maintain strict segregation not only between Muslim males and females in certain urban spaces but also to guard against cross-religious sexual contact is provided by a local Tunisian law in place until 1856. Until that year, when the law was repealed owing to European consular pressure, any sexual contact between a Christian or Jewish male and a Tunisian Muslim female was punished by death. Even urban prostitution and the common prostitute were supposed to observe moral-sexual boundaries constructed by religious confessionalism. The Jewish prostitute was only to have relations with fellow Jews; the Muslim prostitute was solely the domain of the Muslims, at least theoretically.[35]

Until 1837, resident Europeans, mainly merchants or consular representatives (or, frequently, both), were largely confined to the area around their *funduq* in the medina or had villas in the seaside suburb of La Marsa, far from the capital.[36] Then the modernization programme initiated by Ahmed Bey began to attract experts and advisers from Western Europe, which brought substantial if incremental changes to the city.[37] Christian edifices multiplied; the Church of the Holy Cross, previously located on Rue de la Qasbah, was moved to more spacious accommodation in the old hospital of the Trinitarians on Rue de l'Eglise. In 1831, an Italian school opened its doors and, in 1840, a Jewish school was founded; the Bourgade College was established in 1841. The whole quarter of the Place de la Bourse increasingly became European space. Outside the city's walls, the modern town started to creep eastwards towards the lake. The French consulate was moved in 1861 outside of the medina to the site where it stands today. Other consulates, however, – those of Great Britain, Italy and Spain – remained inside. From mid-century on, middle-class houses in the Christian quarter began to display architectural features and styles imported from Genoa and Florence.[38] Nevertheless, the European community in Tunis was highly stratified; indeed what constituted a 'European' in this period was less than certain since both the Maltese and Sicilians had long been viewed as belonging to 'the African race' and thus, at best, as only marginally from Europe.[39]

After mid-century, the ranks of the 'not-quite-Europeans' expanded precipitately and a new community, increasingly defined by social class and by the behaviour of its women, emerged in the medina. These people differed markedly from bourgeois Italian Jews, long-time residents who were financially independent and evinced a spirit of communal solidarity, or from the small but dominant Genoa-Marseilles trading oligarchy. 'Sicilians and Maltese had no financial resources and little of the same [communal] spirit. They came because life in their own countries had become too hard, or because they needed to escape the law, their despotic rulers or their equally despotic families.'[40] Of rural origins but largely unable to acquire land in Tunisia until the eve of the Protectorate, Maltese and Sicilian immigrants took up whatever occupations they could find as coachmen, messengers, builders and tavern owners, or in illegal trades like smuggling.[41]

Moreover, the migratory impulse to this part of North Africa may have been shaped in part by gender considerations.[42] As employment opportunities for lower-class females opened up in Tunis by mid-century, single women from Tuscany arrived alone, looking for work as nursemaids; married Sicilian females came with their menfolk, set up households, and looked for work. They laboured as domestic servants or laundresses for upper-class Europeans and in Tunisian notable households; some women kept shops, others begged on street corners.[43] Others found 'honest' work in the burgeoning flesh trade whose *liaisons dangereuses* the Tunisian state attempted to circumscribe.[44] In searching for implicit links between cultural-symbolic representations, lived environmeñts, and gender it is necessary to situate spatially the newly arrived village proletariat.

Until the post-colonial era, street names in this part of the old city bore witness to progressive Mediterranean settlement: 'Nahej Malta Sghira' ('Street of Little Malta') or 'Rue des Maltais' (Street of the Maltese) identified the north-eastern corner of the medina with newcomers from the island. The English consul observed in 1856: 'They [the Maltese] build for themselves hovels on the very brink of the city's common sewers where the noxious atmosphere causes frightful diseases and great mortality.'[45] The Maltese tended to inhabit the lower end of the medina at the very bottom of the gently rising city slope whose highest areas were dominated by the Qasbah and the instruments of rule – military garrisons and the Dar el-Bey or seat of the beylical government. Until about a decade before the Protectorate, city sanitation consisted of an open sewer system whose drainage gutters were located in the middle of the streets. Due to topography, the collection drains ran down in an easterly direction, spewing forth into a sewage canal built just outside the city walls and emptying eventually into the *buhaira* or Lac de Tunis. It was in that end of the medina – where sewage of all manner collected – that most of the destitute Mediterranean population lived.[46] Thus the topographical gradient of Tunis and the social 'gradient' of its inhabitants' residential space were nearly identical.

In addition, the vast majority of the newcomers were from villages. In consequence, their manner of life occasioned a 'ruralization' of certain quarters of the medina.[47] The villagers brought with them pigs which were allowed to roam around the Christian quarter, adding to the dirt and stench and, more importantly, bringing a sense of moral-spatial transgression to the city's Muslim and Jewish inhabitants alike. Other sorts of transgressions accompanied the Mediterraneans. In effect, the culture of public drinking was introduced progressively into the medina, its suburbs and the port; this represented not only an enormous change but also a major moral affront to urban Islamic sensibilities. Modest wine shops were opened by Sicilians and Maltese, despite the fact that alcohol is theoretically forbidden by Islam, although some Muslims elites consumed the proscribed beverage in private. After mid-century, the number of taverns in Tunis increased so that contemporary observers noted – perhaps with exaggeration – that the number of wine shops was greater per resident than in France.[48]

Another related source of anxiety for city fathers was the fact that crime increased dramatically in Tunis after mid-century. – or, at least, reports of crime multiplied. In part this precipitous jump can be attributed to the fact that some forms of behaviour were now branded as criminal.[49] It does appear, however, that immigration was directly responsible for an increase in crimes against persons and property, in turn related to the greater availability of firearms and gunpowder due to the contraband arms trade. The vast majority of criminal acts were committed by (or at least attributed to) the Mediterranean Christians. The link between urban insecurity, criminal behaviour and migration was made clear by the British consul who in 1861 blamed it on the Sicilian population pouring into the city.[50] European representatives recommended to city authorities that taverns, cafés and wine shops be closed at sunset, although enforcement of this was difficult for the Tunisians because of the immense problems posed by conflicting consular jurisdictions.[51]

Street violence, riots and nocturnal noise increased as the century wore on and as more impoverished Mediterranean folk crowded into the medina. In 1870, after a deranged Tunisian Muslim engaged in a series of random stabbings in the Christian quarter, Italian youths 'threatened to burn down the consulates if the consuls did not arrange for the Muslim stabber to be hanged on the gate of the Christian quarter'.[52] To combat crime and urban violence, the city council (to be discussed below) passed a number of ordinances from the late 1850s on. These regulations do not appear to have influenced the crime rate, though in the absence of any study whatsoever of crime, criminals and criminality in Tunisia during the past century, it is difficult to generalize.

Even when crimes were not committed, public tranquillity in the medina was increasingly compromised. Until the massive arrival of Mediterranean peoples, there was little night-time activity in the medina or its suburbs; patrols, composed of the residents from specific city quarters (*hawmat*) kept the peace.[53] L. Carl Brown has painted a portrait of the Tunis *baldi* class and of the virtues that were prized by the urban bourgeoisie: 'A baldi did not sing, eat, or in any other way call attention to himself while walking through the streets of Tunis. The sure mark of a hayseed was a man who conversed in a loud voice which could be overhead by passers-by. Among the leading notables it was even considered improper to be seen in public cafes.'[54] By the 1860s, this had all changed in some neighbourhoods; indigenous city inhabitants had to contend with unusual forms of night-time deportment – 'drunken brawling, random gunshots, and loud singing'.[55] Indeed, a city ordinance was passed prohibiting the playing of music after 10 p.m. This was directly tied to an incident during Christmas of 1860 when the Catholic Sardinians in the medina engaged in a riotous and noisy celebration of the new year.[56] Thus the Mediterranean migrants had invaded all manner of urban spaces – not only physical, residential space but also social places, the space of sound – which previously had been tranquil and inviolable, at least in the ideal order of things. The urban evolution of Tunis, therefore, did not follow a simple process whereby the 'city of vice' or the colonial city grew up alongside the 'city of virtue', the Muslim city as idealized by elite nineteenth-century writers. Within the medina itself, the Christian-Mediterranean quarter came to be associated in the collective consciousness of its native inhabitants with moral transgressions: prostitution, city sewage and disease, illicit economic behaviour, taverns and pigs.

Finally, disputes over love, honour, and dishonour invaded the streets of Tunis. To provide but one example: in 1877, Salvatore La Flora, a Sicilian of Palermo who resided in Tunis, fell in love with Francesca, the daughter of a Maltese tavern owner who operated a small wine shop in the medina. Marriage between a Sicilian man and Maltese girl was viewed by the Maltese community as *mésalliance* that threatened the integrity of the clan – in almost the same way that marriage between a Muslim and Christian did. There was but one solution for the star-crossed couple. Salvatore tried to elope with his beloved, only to be pursued through the medina by the girl's male relatives. A long and bloody street vendetta resulted from the foiled elopement.[57]

This seemingly innocuous incident offers insights into what may have been the most profound transformation effected by immigration into the capital – the presence of women in the streets, contests over females played out in public places, and female participation in street justice.[58] In any urban environment, 'street making' constitutes a cultural discourse on public (and by implication private) spaces which plots out a society's critical markers and boundaries, modified by social praxis and conflict. 'The street is not only the basic structuring device of the city's form but also the locus of its civilization.' Street discourse includes ritual, negotiation, and ideology.[59] The ideology of street use in nineteenth-century Islamic Tunis was heavily infused by gender proscriptions – indeed, the use and meaning of streets and other public domains was structured by gender first and foremost, more so than race, class or ethnicity. This fact has been largely ignored by scholars, or at best footnoted as evidence of Islam's concern with female chastity, and the deeper cultural significance of women in the streets, even foreign immigrants, has remained entirely unexplored.

'None but the most abandoned prostitutes can venture to be seen in the streets, and even then it would be a crime to walk publicly with the face uncovered,' wrote Feise in 1812.[60] Nearly a century later, Frances Nesbitt described the Tunisian women's market (*suq al-nisa'*) in the medina, near the old slave market: 'The souk ... like many others is a white tunnel lined with shops. It is very crowded in the early morning, and is almost the only place where many women are seen together. Some sit on the ground and sell their handiwork, others are busy bargaining for veils and embroideries. All are of the poorer classes and are heavily veiled.'[61] In effect, Tunis was a city constructed of walls within walls; the exterior monumental ramparts encircling the medina were fortified by interior cultural enclosures mapping out gendered places. The Tunisian women's market visited by Nesbitt was circumscribed – indeed immured ideologically – by social rank, sex and clothing. It was thus rendered a private public domain by those elements: access was restricted to veiled females only; involvement in its business transactions was the domain of the poor and humble. The same was not true of Maltese and Sicilian women's participation in the spaces of the local economy – whether in petty trade or in the public consumption of spirits – which threatened to breach the walls of the moral order.

Impecunious Mediterranean women frequently either worked in drinking establishments, serving alcohol to customers, or even operated and ran their own wine shops, selling spirits to both Christians and Muslims of the lower ranks of society. For example, an impoverished Maltese widow and her daughter Hanna earned their keep by selling wine out of a humble shop in the capital's market district, often after normal business hours in the evenings. Responding to a complaint in 1875 from the Tunisian authorities, the British consul reported: 'And being without the protection of any man, [the two Maltese women] are exposed to be insulted by the common people who frequent their shop; and in reply I beg to state that I have directed the woman Hanna to shut up her wine shop at the time the souk is shut up so as to prevent the common people from frequenting the shop at undue hours.'[62] Three years later, a local Muslim official complained to the English consul about a 'Christian' woman serving alcohol in a Maltese-owned tavern; because of the woman's presence in the tavern, 'the persons who frequent it at night quarrel and fight among themselves, thereby creating great disorders and disturbing the public peace'.[63] Finally, these establishments often offered more than just alcohol – gambling, prostitution and contraband were combined with tavern keeping.[64]

Evidence that this was not only deeply offensive to the refined urban sensibilities of the Tunis *baldi* class but also regarded as an assault upon the traditional ideology of street cartography is provided by the special interest accorded to such Mediterranean women in Tunisian government correspondence and even in didactic literature. In 1856 Ahmad Ibn Abi al-Dhiyaf, a high-ranking member of the bey's court, composed a 'treatise on woman', a highly unusual tract. Comparing women in Islamic law with European women, Ben Dhiyaf grapples with the concepts of *sitr* (to veil, hide, or shield from) and *tajahur* (to declare publicly, to bring to light).[65] This treatise might be seen as a riposte to Mediterranean settlement in the medina, the moral as well as political core not only of Tunis but also of the entire realm. What immigrants had done was to expose to view what previously had been concealed, thus giving public scandal. The appearance of women, even Christian women protected by foreign consuls, in taverns and streets, and the resulting disorder associated with their untoward behaviour, was the source of repeated protests by Muslim officials occupying the highest posts in the land until the eve of the Protectorate.[66]

As noxious as these transformations were, they offered opportunities for the capital's ruling elite to create new mechanisms for social control and municipal reorganization, often at the insistence of European consuls. In the older order of things, before 1837, the dey (or *dawlatli*) and his force of 100 agents had the responsibility for security in the capital during daylight hours. At night, however, the deylical security force was replaced by a local official, the *shaykh al-madina*, who was aided in maintaining nocturnal serenity by a *shaykh* from each of the two suburbs.[67] To restructure traditional urban society in the throes of a profound crisis, the city fathers created a municipal council, the *majlis*, in 1852, an entirely novel institution that betrayed the emergence of new concepts of urban space and collective identities. In 1858, the *shurta* or urban police was organized and patterned upon the Paris police. It was deployed in both the medina and suburbs; its agents were often recruited from the very social class that the authorities sought to better survey.[68] Agents could intervene in conflicts or crimes involving Europeans and Tunisians, men and women; they could not, however, issue arrests for Europeans.[69] It is indicative of the increased use and sale of alcohol in the medina that the operating budget of the *majlis* was partially financed by a tax on wine and spirits levied on Europeans residing in the medina.[70]

Many of the municipal council's ordinances were aimed at enhancing security for Tunisians and European alike, which also meant expanding state powers. One decree required all those circulating in the medina's streets after dark to carry a lantern. Class more than religious or ethnic difference was at work here since, as Cleveland has shown, the penalty for circulating the streets after sundown without a lantern was 'a night's detention unless he [the offender] be a respectable person and known to the police'.[71] Those of high social rank were not detained but merely escorted home by the police. Although not specifically mentioned in this ordinance, prostitution may have also been at play here because illicit sexual encounters were associated in the collective mind with dark city streets. In effect, daytime and night-time surveillance was enhanced and the movements of women, both Muslim Tunisian and Mediterranean, could be better controlled by the municipal council and police.

From the 1850s on, public works projects – for examples, improving sanitation, the water supply and street traffic – were launched, which also reconfigured the old city and its relationship to the surrounding environment.[72] Urban renewal projects always carry the notion, implicit or explicit, of a diseased body in need of medical intervention. This profound reconceptualization of core urban space and habitat has not yet been studied from the point of view of gender and social control. Nevertheless, there are suggestions that the Tunisian state evinced a new attitude *vis à vis* Muslim women and sought to intervene in new arenas of social control, most obviously in matters of female criminality and delinquence. The 1861 law and 1862 edict created special segregated prisons exclusively for women convicted of criminal acts. Arrested by the urban police, the nature of these women's crimes, or accusations of such, betray some of the changes in the city: for example, Fatima bint Muhammad Gharbi was condemned to four days in prison for going about in public at night in a state of drunkenness and without her veil.[73] As for rebellious women, they continued to be sent to the more informal houses of female obedience, *dar juwad*, hidden in corners of the medina or its suburbs; indeed, these houses appear to have multiplied in number during the past century, in rhythm with accelerating urban crises, and remained in existence until the eve of the Second World War. As significantly, it seems that the new municipal institutions created after 1852 were increasingly implicated in the maintenance of this much older method of dealing with recalcitrant Muslim females.[74]

Thus by the eve of France's invasion of Tunisia, two contradictory processes can be detected in the city of Tunis: on one hand, the penetration of urban spaces, places and moral cul-de-sacs by Mediterranean folk as well as by modern European technology, which opened up street making to negotiations and contestations; on the other, a modest expansion in Tunisian state and municipal powers which vigorously policed the medina, banned ancient public celebrations and popular street festivals for indigenous city inhabitants, and surveyed Muslim women more closely. Paradoxically, by the turn of the century 'the Tunisian woman' emerged as an ideological construct; this was new, for she did not exist in the middle of that century. The Tunisian woman became a site for contesting cultural authenticity – in the same way that the 'traditional' city, the medina, also became a signifier of Tunisian, Islamo-Arab historical authenticity in this period – despite, or because of, the fact that by 1900 many of the medina's residents were Mediterraneans of lower rank. In her work on early modern France, Sarah Hanley contended that the implicit 'state-family compact' meant that the state intervened in private family domains when it came to marriage alliances and particularly to female misconduct.[75] This was true in Tunisia in the nineteenth century; indeed, the state made the biggest inroads into areas concerning the control of Muslim women. But what about foreign women, the vast majority of whom were Mediterranean, mainly Catholic, and protected by European nations? Here I argue for a confluence of interests between European representatives and Tunisian notables – a sort of complicity of class which transcended the boundaries of religious affiliation. As southern Europe's 'ne'er-do-wells' poured into the country, modesty and the public comportment of certain women became matters of state and international diplomacy – for both Tunisian elites and high-ranking European diplomats. Not infrequently, diplomats cooperated with the indigenous ruling class even at the expense of their own protégés' interests; this was particularly true of the subsistence immigrants, and above all, of women from the 'not-quite-European' shores of the Mediterranean.

Notes

1 This chapter is part of a larger continuing study devoted to women, migration and contested identities in nineteenth-century Mediterranean North Africa; the author wishes to thank the following institutions for research support: The Virginia Foundation for the Humanities; The University of Arizona; the American Institute of Maghrebi Studies; and the Council for American Overseas Research Centers.

   On the Tunisian Jews, see Abdelhamid Largueche, 'Pauvres, marginaux et minoritaires à Tunis aux XVIIIè XIXè siècles', 2 vols (Thèse de Doctorat d'Etat en Histoire, Université de Tunis, 1996), 500–79; and Paul Sebag, *Histoire des juifs de Tunisie des origines à nos jours* (Paris, 1991).

2 Miguel de Epalza and Ramón Petit (eds), *Recueil d'Etudes sur les Moriscos Andalous en Tunisie* (Madrid, 1973).

3 John R. McNeill, *Mountains of the Mediterranean World: An Environmental History* (Cambridge, 1992).

4 Jean Ganiage, *La Population Européenne de Tunis au milieu du XXe siècle* (Presses Universitaire de France, 1960) provides some estimates of total population; however, Alexandre Lézine, *Deux Villes d'Ifriqiya: études d'archéologie d'urbanisme de démographie, Sousse, Tunis* (Paris, 1971), pp. 153–4, discusses the problem of accurate statistics for the city in the nineteenth and early twentieth centuries.

5 Lézine, *Deux Villes*; Slimane Mostafa Zbiss, *La Médina de Tunis* (Tunis, 1981); and Besim Selim Hakim, *Arabic-Islamic Cities: Building and Planning Principles* (London: KPI, 1986), among numerous other works.

6 Jellal Abdelkafi, *La Médina de Tunis: espace historique* (Tunis, 1989).

7 There are only two studies of Maltese migration – Marc Donato, *L'Emigration des Maltais en Algérie au XIXè siècle* (Montpellier, 1985); and Charles A. Price, *Malta and the Maltese: A Study in Nineteenth Century Migration* (Melbourne, 1954).

8 Taking the Mediterranean Basin as a unit of analysis in the *longue durée*, we see that population transfers from the European edges of the Sea, or its islands, to northern Africa between 1830 and 1900 represented the single largest movement of peoples since the expulsions occasioned by the Spanish *reconquista* centuries earlier.

9 Jean Ganiage's *La Population Européenne* is virtually the only study of the Mediterranean folk who settled in Tunis; Ganiage is less concerned with migration and settlement patterns, however, and more with demographic issues. European migration to other northern African or Levantine port cities during the past century has attracted surprisingly little scholarly attention; Leila Fawaz' *Merchants and Migrants in Nineteenth-Century Beirut* (Cambridge, MA, 1983) is an excellent study, mainly of internal migration from the Lebanese hinterland.

10 South to north migration in the present century – from the Maghrib to Europe – is extensively studied: Russell King, 'Migration and development in the Mediterranean Basin', *Geography* 81, 1 (January 1996), pp. 3–14; and Benjamin Stora, 'Locate, isolate, place under surveillance: Algerian migration to France in the 1930s', in L. Carl Brown and Matthew Gordon (eds), *Franco-Arab Encounters* (Beirut, 1996), pp. 373–91.

11 David Prochaska, *Making Algeria French: Colonialism in Bône, 1870–1920* (Cambridge, 1990); and also his 'History as literature, literature as history: Cagayous of Algiers', in *American Historical Review* 101, 3 (June 1996), pp. 670–708.

12 Studies of Mediterranean migration to Algeria and Tunisia were carried out as France became alarmed by the large numbers of Maltese and Sicilians residing permanently in the Maghrib; some examples are: Gaston Loth, *Le Peuplement Italien en Tunisie et en Algérie* (Paris, 1905); Jules Saurin, *Le Peuplement Français en Tunisie* (Paris, 1910); and Ernest Fallot's, 'Malte et ses rapports économiques avec la Tunisie', *Revue Tunisienne*, 3 (1896), pp. 17–38.

13 L. Carl Brown, *The Tunisia of Ahmad Bey, 1837–1855* (Princeton, 1974); and J . S. Woodford, *The City of Tunis: Evolution of an Urban System* (Cambridgeshire, 1990). While Brown's *Ahmad Bey* remains unsurpassed as a study of the political culture of the Tunisian ruling class in the middle of the past century, there is a tendency to underestimate the ability of that ruling class to fend off or manipulate to their own advantage foreign interference in the country's domestic affairs.

14 Michael J. Reimer, 'Ottoman-Arab seaports in the nineteenth century: social change in Alexandria, Beirut, and Tunis', in Resat Kasaba (ed.), *Cities in the World-System* (New York, 1991), p. 144, attributes too much power to local European consular representatives.

15 This conceptualization is found in Kenneth Brown, Michèle Jolé, Peter Sluglett, and Sami Zubaida (eds), *Middle Eastern Cities in Comparative Perspective* (London, 1986).

16 Jamila Binous, Fatma Ben Bechr and Jellal Abdelkafi, *Tunis* (Tunis, 1985); and Paul Lowy, 'Evolution des grandes Médinas tunisiennes', in *Présent et Avenir des Médinas (de Marrakech à Alep)* (Tours, 1982), pp. 103–20.

17 Godfrey Feise, 'Observations on the Regency of Tunis, 1812, 1813', unpublished mss, no. 15, 417, The British Library, 8–9, 16.

18 *Ibid.*, 11.

19 Mohamed El Aziz ben Achour, 'Islam et controle social à Tunis aux XVIIIe et XIXe siècles', in Abdelwahab Bouhdiba and Dominique Chevallier (eds), *La Ville Arabe dans L'Islam* (Tunis, 1982), pp. 137–47; and Dalenda Largueche, 'Loisirs et mutations socio-culturelles en Tunisie à l'époque ottomane', unpublished ms.

20 Zbiss, *La Médina*, p. 14.

21 Ganiage, *La Population*, p. 49.

22 Yves Debbasch, *La Nation Française en Tunisie* (1577–1835) (Paris, 1957), pp. 62–3.

23 *Ibid.*

24 The articles devoted to 'Port-Cities of the Eastern Mediterranean, 1800–1914', in *Review* 15, 4 (Fall 1993) make no mention of these regulations.

25 Indeed, the notion of the civilizing mission, wrongly associated with modern French colonialism in places like Africa, began in the sixteenth century with Jesuit missionary activity to port cities like Naples. Jennifer D. Selwyn, '"Procur[ing]" in the common people these better behaviors": the Jesuits' civilizing mission in early modern Naples, 1550–1620', *Radical History Review*, 67 (Winter 1997): pp. 4–34.

26 Woodford, *Tunis*, p. 130. By 'beldi' system, Woodford refers to the socio-behavioral and cultural norms adhered to by the Arabo-Muslim urban bourgeoisie of Tunis.

27 Lézine, *Deux Villes*, pp. 150–1.

28 *Ibid.*, p. 131.

29 *Ibid.*, p. 21. The *maqsura* was the upstairs gallery or balcony, where women could be isolated from the male worshippers below yet still be part of the service.

30 A portrait of how the women of the beys' harems lived in the nineteenth century is found in Julia Clancy-Smith and Cynthia Metcalf, 'A visit to a Tunisian harem', *Journal of Maghrebi Studies* 1, 1 (1993): pp. 43–9.

31 Frances E. Nesbitt, *Algeria and Tunisia Painted and Described* (London, 1906), p. 159.

32 Dalenda and Abdelhamid Largueche, *Marginales en terre d'Islam* (Tunis, 1992).

33 Feise, 'Observations', pp. 10–11.

34 Nesbitt, *Algeria and Tunisia*, p. 159.

35 In *Marginales*, 24, the authors also note that in 1744 anti-Christian riots broke out in the popular quarters of the medina after young, unmarried Frenchmen of the trading community brought Muslim prostitutes into their *funduq*. In 1852, however, Judah ben Levy, a Jewish English protégé, reported to the English consul in Tunis that a Jewish woman was receiving night-time visits from a Muslim male while her husband was absent from the house. PRO/FO Tunisia, 335/101/16, ben Levy to Baynes, 8 August 1852.

36 From the 1840s on, European consular representatives complained to the bey about the over crowded conditions of the Christian *funduq* and repeatedly requested more space in the medina for their protégés; for example, PRO/FO Tunisia, 335/95/7, Palmerston to Reade, 7 October 1848.

37 Some of the main political events in the history of nineteenth-century Tunisia need mention. First was the modernization programme of Ahmad Bey, partially patterned on the Ottoman Tanzimat, but which also included the abolition of slavery and the slave trade, and the manumission effected between 1840 and 1846. Next came the 'Fundamental Pact' of 1857, promulgated by Muhammad Bey (1855–1859) which sought to reorder relations between the bey and his subjects as well as between Tunisians and Europeans. This beylical decree freed Tunisian Jews from older restrictions based on religion. In 1861, the first constitution in the Islamic world was proclaimed in Tunisia, though many of its provisions were stillborn. Three years later, the largest revolt in modern Tunisian history broke out in 1864, followed by a series of financial, economic and other sorts of crises. These woes, followed by the bankruptcy of the Tunisian state in 1878, eased the way for the French take-over in 1881.

38 Robert Brunschvig, 'Tunis', *Encyclopedia of Islam* 1st edition (Leiden, 1913–1936) Vol. 8, p. 843;

Zbiss, *Médina*, pp. 14–15; and Abdelkafi, *Médina*, pp. 55–7.

39 Donato, *L'émigration*, p. 66.

40 Woodford, *Tunis*, p. 127.

41 On trans-Mediterranean contraband and smuggling in the nineteenth century, see Julia Clancy-Smith, 'Migration, markets, and contraband in Mediterranean Tunisia: the view from below, 1850–1900', in Dirk Vandewalle (ed.), *The State and Informal Economies in North Africa* (forthcoming). Arthur Marsden in *British Diplomacy in Tunis, 1875–1902* (New York, 1971), pp. 29–30, mentions that in 1863 the British consul, Richard Wood, had secured the right to own real property for his mainly Maltese protégés from the Tunisian government; yet land ownership did not substantially increase until later.

42 By 1850, the trans-Mediterranean 'labour transhumance' of 1830 to 1850 turned into permanent residence in Tunisia and Algeria. Until about 1850 male villagers from islands like Sardinia worked in various menial jobs along the North African coast, when labour demand in the villages back on the islands was low; their families, however, stayed behind and they returned to the islands when the harvest called. Also, Mediterranean peoples heading for French Algeria would often do so via Tunisia, at times remaining there. Others might proceed to Algiers, but then return to Tunisia. There is a constant *va et vient* between Mediterranean sending points and these two North African countries – a triangular trade in people.

43 Loth, *Le peuplement*, pp. 145–57.

44 Prostitution is rarely discussed in urban studies of North Africa cities; Lowy, 'Evolution', p. 117, mentions the *quartier réservé* in passing, but only with reference to Muslim prostitutes.

45 Public Record Office, FO/Tunisia, 102/50, Richard Wood, September 1856.

46 William L. Cleveland, 'The Municipal Council of Tunis, 1858–1870: a study in urban institutional change', *International Journal of Middle East Studies*, 9 (1978), pp. 22–61.

47 The ruralization of the medina's European sector during the pre-colonial period has never been studied, mainly since the economic forces 'pushing' rural island folk to Tunisia – environmental degradation, overpopulation and scarcity of land – have scarcely been considered.

48 Numerous British consular documents from nineteenth-century Tunisia attest to this; for example, Sir Thomas Reade's 1846 letter to London detailing the disorders in a tavern owned by a Maltese in Sousse; PRO, FO Tunisia, 335/92/5; Feise, 'Observations', p. 11, has information on the private consumption of spirits among Tunisian Muslim males.

49 Crime and the process of criminalization has never been studied for Tunis in the nineteenth century. Brown, *Ahmad Bey*, pp. 194–5, maintains that crimes of violence or theft were relatively rare in the medina proper in the early part of the nineteenth century before the arrival of Mediterranean immigrants; numerous European travellers note this as well, among them Feise in 'Observations'.

50 Cleveland, 'The Municipal Council', pp. 46–53; blaming Sicilians for crime and violence may have been an expression of prejudice on the English consul's part; nevertheless, many of the Sicilians emigrating to Tunisia in this period were draft dodgers or criminals fleeing the Italian police.

51 By this period, there were 14 different consulates in Tunis, each with wide powers *vis à vis* their nationals and protégés; they could administer justice and issue expulsion orders, particularly for unruly women.

52 Cleveland, 'The Municipal Council', p. 50.

53 *Ibid.*, pp. 35–7; and Brown, *Ahmad Bey*, pp. 194–5.

54 Brown, *Ahmad Bey*, p. 194; see also Ahmed Abdesselem, 'La sémantique sociale de la ville d'après les auteurs tunisiens des XVIIIe et XIXe siècles', in Bouhdiba and Chevallier (eds), *La ville arabe*, pp. 45–65.

55 Cleveland, 'The Municipal Council', p. 49.

56 *Ibid.*

57 Jean Ganiage, 'Les Européens en Tunisie au milieu du XIXe siècle', *Cahiers de Tunisie* 3, 9 (1955), pp. 389–421; for this incident, p. 397.

58 Samuel K. Cohn, Jr., 'Women in the streets, women in the courts, in early Renaissance Florence', in *Women in the Streets: Essays on Sex and Power in Renaissance Italy* (Baltimore, 1996), pp. 16–38, argues that even lower-class women lost access to Florentine streets in the fifteenth century, participating less in public festivals and street justice, due in part to the consolidation of the Renaissance state.

59 This section is inspired by the fine work of Zeyneb Celik, Diane Favro, and Richard Ingersoll (eds), *Streets: Critical Perspectives on Public Space* (Berkeley, 1994); the quotes are from the Foreword, pp.

204 • JULIA CLANCY-SMITH

1–7. The gendering of city spaces historically needs to be compared across cultures; for example, Elizabeth Wilson, *The Sphinx in the City* (London, 1991), p. 16, notes that in nineteenth-century Korean cities men were prohibited from roaming the streets after dark, with the exception of officials and blind men; women, on the other hand, were given access to the streets after city gates closed. Thanks to Gail Bernstein for this reference.

60 Feise, 'Observations', pp. 37–8, explained female seclusion which in Islam was common to all social ranks and carried to the utmost extent as the product of male jealousy.

61 Nesbitt, *Algeria and Tunisia*, p. 150.

62 Dar el-Bey, Tunis, correspondence between Great Britain and the beylical government, Richard Wood to the Tunisian Prime Minister, carton 228, dossier 413, 30 August 1875.

63 Dar el-Bey, Tunis, correspondence between Great Britain and the beylical government, Richard Wood to the Tunisian Prime Minister, carton 228, dossier 414, 20 July 1878.

64 The beylical government complained repeatedly to the consuls regarding public gambling by their protégés; see Richard Wood's letter to Mustafa Khaznadar about 'the assembling of individuals in the corners of [the medina's] streets for the purpose of gambling', Dar el-Bey, dossier 635, carton 58, 17 January 1863.

65 Ahmad Ibn Abi al-Dhiyaf, *Risala fil mara'a* (Tunis, 1968), which has not received the scholarly attention it merits. The one study of the 'treatise on woman' suggests that the impetus for its composition was Ibn Dhiyaf's state visit to France in 1846. Béchir Tlili, *Etudes d'Histoire Sociale Tunisienne du XIXe Siècle* (Tunis, 1974), pp. 93–160. He did not have to journey as far as Paris, however, to be confronted with the issue of women, gender and the street morality. All the Tunisian chronicler had to do was walk around the medina.

66 Dar el-Bey, Tunis, correspondence between Great Britain and the beylical government, cartons 227 and 228; for example, Richard Wood to the Tunisian Prime Minister, carton 228, dossier 414, 29 March 1878, regarding a Maltese woman, Consolata Scinga, accused of 'keeping a disorderly house'.

67 Brown, *Ahmad Bey*, pp. 123–4.

68 Both the municipal council and the police force were new to Tunisia. In typical fashion, the city fathers did not dismantle the older Islamic offices, but superimposed the police and council upon the *shaykh al-madina* structure.

69 The only study of the police force is Rida ben Rajab's, 'Al-Shurta wa Aman al-Hadira, 1861–1864' (Thèse du Doctorat, 3ème cycle, Université de Tunis, 1992).

70 Brunschvig, 'Tunis', p. 844.

71 Cleveland, 'The Municipal Council', p. 49.

72 *Ibid.*, pp. 53–8.

73 Largueche, *Marginales*, pp. 142–6.

74 *Ibid.*, pp. 99–108.

75 Sarah Hanley, 'Engendering the state: family formation and state building in early modern France', *French Historical Studies*, 16 (Spring 1989), pp. 4–27.

12

The Cultural Politics of Death & Burial in Early Colonial Accra

JOHN PARKER

Weku fe akotsa ni ame keba ju ohe ne, no hewo le keji ote le koni oya bo amanie.

This is the sponge of all your relatives which they brought to wash you, so that when you have gone you will be able to tell their story.[1]

In 1911, Yeboa Kwamli began to make preparations for his impending death. Although we do not know the year of his birth, Yeboa was widely regarded as the oldest and wisest man in Osu, one of the three original towns of Accra. Active in the politics of Accra's indigenous Gã community from the 1850s, he had been 'enstooled' in 1880 as Osu *mankralo*, the leading public office of the Asante Blohum quarter and second only to that of *mantse* in the chiefly hierarchy of Osu. As his long and distinguished career drew to a close, the old chief expressed a wish to be interred in a royal mausoleum in the countryside on the outskirts of the colonial capital. Applying to the British authorities for permission to begin the construction of the tomb, he reminded the Secretary for Native Affairs that other prominent office holders – including Gã *mantse* Taki Tawia, the late paramount chief of the entire Gã polity – had recently been accorded such a privilege.[2]

Yeboa Kwamli's funeral plans caused considerable consternation in the other three quarters of Osu. The burial of notables in mausoleums was a recent innovation in Gã mortuary practice, Yeboa's political opponents fearing that his tomb would become a symbol of the disputed authority of the *mankralo* stool. A series of heated public meetings failed to resolve the issue, Osu *mantse* Noi Ababio of the rival Kinkawe quarter leading the calls that the *mankralo* be interred not in his own mausoleum but in the municipal burial ground. In the face of mounting tension, the colonial government refused to sanction its construction. Following Yeboa's death on 27 July 1912, however, it was discovered that his Asante Blohum kin had surreptitiously dug a grave in the countryside outside the town boundaries. Curtailing the intricate funerary rites normally accorded a venerable chief, they succeeded in burying the *mankralo*'s remains according to his wishes. Caught unawares, Noi Ababio hurriedly mobilized his supporters in a vain effort to prevent the burial, requesting that a detachment of colonial police block the cortège. A new form of social action – 'mausoleum politics' – had begun to emerge in early colonial Accra.

This chapter explores the politics and dramaturgy of Gã mortuary practice and ritual festival from the 1880s to the 1920s. The setting is the city of Accra, the epicentre of the Gã polity and from 1877 the headquarters of the British colony of the Gold Coast (Ghana). It argues that death, burial and public ritual – major concerns of African anthropological literature – need to be appropriated from the ethnographic present and relocated within a context of historical change. Mortuary practice had long been central to the definition of the cosmological and social orders in Gã thought, a tradition of intramural sepulture shaping the ritual topography of urban Accra. Far from being timeless constructions, however, these ideas about the Gã world were characterized by reformulation, negotiation and innovation. By the late nineteenth century, much of this innovation arose in response to the encroachment of the expanding colonial state into ritual affairs in Accra. As the burial of Yeboa Kwamli in 1912 indicates, death and burial became highly politicized in the vigorously contested cultural space of the colonial city.

'Twixt Land and Sea: Gã Cosmology and Ritual Topography

Cosmology, as Wyatt MacGaffey notes in his study of the BaKongo of lower Zaire, has come and gone in African studies since the publication in 1954 of Daryll Forde's pioneering collection, *African Worlds*.[3] The location of African social action within a set of assumptions concerning the nature of the world and the place of men and women in it, however, has largely remained rooted in the ethnographic present. This is particularly evident with regard to issues of death, burial and funerary ritual; in other words, social action concerning the negotiation of the boundary between the world of the living and the world of the dead.[4] Whereas the various meanings of death and mortality have long featured in the anthropological literature on the peoples of southern Ghana, it is only recently that historians have begun to add a temporal dimension to these most funda-mental of human concerns.[5] Intimately linked to ideas about death and mortality are the great public festivals which in southern Ghana served as ritual affirmations of both the cosmological and social order. As is evident from recent contributions to an emerging literature, the historical reconstruction of public ritual provides a fruitful entry into the field of African thought and consciousness.[6] Struggles over mortuary ritual and festival, as McCaskie shows for pre-colonial Asante and Glassman for the nineteenth-century Swahili coast, represented major arenas for the contestation of political power.

How did the Gã peoples of Accra conceptualize the world and their place in it? The Gã identified a supreme being, Nyonmo, who occupied a distant, inaccessible world and was closely associated with the physical phenomenon of rain. Nyonmo was credited with creating the world, *jen*, divided into the realm of the living (*huluman*, lit. 'the sun's town') and the realm of the dead (*gbohiiajen*).[7] As in many African societies, everyday worship was directed towards more accessible 'gods of the world' (*jemawojii*; sing. *jemawon*), the most powerful of an extensive array of supernatural forces (*wojii*, sing. *won*) jostling for space throughout both realms of the world with mankind's living, dead and unborn. Although all three spheres of *huluman*, the skies, the earth and the sea, were crowded with *wojii*, it is significant that Accra's three principal tutelary deities were – like *Nyonmo* – all associated with water: Nai, the god of the sea, Sakumo, the war god identified with coastal lagoons, and Kole, a lagoon goddess recognised as the guardian of the Gã lands.

Gã cosmological categories reappear in the geographical and social ordering of the world of the living. The original locus of Gã settlement and state formation was not the coast but the hills which rise sporadically from the better-watered and more fertile northern fringe of the dry Accra plains. Following the destruction by Akwamu of the powerful centralized kingdom at Ayawaso hill in 1677, the focus of the Gã social formation shifted to a series of towns dotted along a twenty-mile stretch of the eastern Gold Coast. It is possible only to speculate on the extent to which this violent political rupture reshaped Gã epistemology, but all subsequent sources point to the sea (*nshon*) as the most salient parametric feature of the physical world. Whereas the south in Gã thought connotes the sea, the great god Nai, civilization and urban culture, the north represents land, lesser deities and rustic culture located in an essentially untamed and hazardous 'nature'.[8] These lateral associations conveyed by the north–south divide intersected with the east–west axis, the east being associated with the superior south and the west with the inferior north. The extent of Gã (and related Dangme) settlement was also defined by water: to the west the sacred Sakumofio lagoon, and to the east the great River Volta. *Gbohiiajen*, the world of the dead, Zimmermann's informants in the 1850s supposed, lay 'on the islands of and beyond the river Volta'- at the very margins of the known world.[9]

These ideas reflected the historical realities of life on the Accra plains. Gã cosmology was clearly shaped – and reshaped – by a narrow, precarious cultural niche between land and sea.[10] The lagoons which punctuate the open surf beaches of the eastern Gold Coast were not only physical manifestations of powerful deities but valuable economic resources, their rich harvests of salt and fish compensating for the limited agricultural capacity of the dry coastal plain. Indeed, the Gã historian and Basel Mission pastor Carl Reindorf noted that the Gã attributed their conquest by the Akwamu to Portuguese traders having converted one of Accra's sacred lagoons into a salt pit, 'a profanation which, they said, provoked the vengeance of the fetishes [i.e. *jemawojii*] upon them'.[11] Abandoned by their tutelary gods at a moment of national crisis, the Gã were forced to endure the successive overrule of the Akan kingdoms of Akwamu, Akyem Abuakwa and Asante for some 150 years. The final lifting of the 'Asante yoke' at the battle of Katamanso in 1826, Reindorf observes, was also popularly explained by the intervention of watery supernatural allies:

> It was God in heaven who mercifully defended our country. But our deluded people attributed the victory not only to their fetishes, but also to every cartilaginous, spinous, and testaceous creature in the sea, which they consider, to the present day, as warriors of their fetish Nai (the sea) and suppose to have taken part in the engagement and even, in some instances, to have got wounded....[12]

The superior culture of the Gã south – backed by the ritual power of the sea itself – had finally triumphed over that of the rustic, terrestrial, Akan north.

If cosmology gave shape to a perceived cleavage between the Gã world and that of their neighbours in the Akan forest zone to the north, then it also reinforced a fundamental divide within Gã society, that between town and country. The distinction between the civilized order of the town (*man*; pl. *majii*) and the untamed, potentially dangerous nature of the bush (*kose*) was conveyed by a variety of linguistic and cultural signifiers. The term *manbii* (lit. 'children of the town'), with its connotations of full citizenship, is typically used as 'townspeople' in contrast to *kosebii*, 'country people' or – perhaps better – 'bush people'. *Kosenyo*, bushman or farmer, is also rendered by Zimmermann as 'rough person', 'boor' or 'clown'.[13] As in Akan forest settlements, the boundary between town and country was an ambiguous and spiritually hazardous liminal zone, called in Gã *husu* or *husunaa*. The northern boundary of the two contiguous Accra *majii* of Kinka and Nleshi until the urban expansion of the late nineteenth century was a cactus-covered ridge which in the early colonial period became a major residential thoroughfare, Horse Road. Together with the Kole lagoon to the immediate west of Nleshi, the boundary was seen as the exit point for the souls of the dead from the town and the world of the living.[14]

Gã space was further defined by an intricate and shifting ritual topography which overlay this established moral geography. Whereas both town and country were crowded with diverse spiritual forces, urban space was characterized by the higher degree of control exercised over these forces by a built ritual infrastructure and by a hierarchy of religious specialists. This control was visibly apparent in the shrines (gbatsui; sing. gbatsu) which dotted the town quarters of pre-colonial Accra, conical-roofed structures dedicated to particular jemawojii and presided over by hereditary priests (wulomei, sing. wulomo). 'Religion' in Accra, organized into four main cults, was characterized above all by an uninhibited eclecticism. Three of the cults are non-Gã in origin: me is a Dangme and otu and akon are Akan cults, while the fourth, kple or kpele, is recognized as the original Gã belief system. The established pantheon of tutelary jemawojii coexisted with a multiplicity of localized deities worshipped in a more intimate manner by particular families, lineages or town quarters.[15]

Located on the interface between interior and maritime trades and closely associated with the three European forts around which they grew, the three nshonamajii, 'seaside towns', of Nleshi, Kinka and Osu[16] emerged in the eighteenth century as centres of Gã political power and mercantile wealth. Although both kinship and political institutions straddled the rural–urban boundary, linking farming communities to these cosmopolitan urban centres on the coast, socio-economic differentiation engendered by expanding trade deepened the divide between town and country in Gã thought. The perceived superiority of urban culture on the part of townspeople was heightened by the growing numbers of slaves and other dependants settled by their masters on the Accra plains following the collapse of the Atlantic slave trade in the early nineteenth century. It is important to emphasize, however, that the hegemony of Accra's urban elites did not go unchallenged. In a revealing exchange during a conflict in the coastal town of La in 1872, for example, the received association of the 'bush' with slavery was neatly turned on its head. 'We are farmers,' sneered a group of La kosebii at some of Osu's literate, Christian elite. 'When we take a single grass from the ground under that grass is five cowries. You don't like to cultivate therefore you have made yourself slaves to Europeans.'[17]

The most dramatic bridging of the divide between man and kose was – and is – Homowo, the great annual festival of the Gã ritual calender. A sequence of solemn civic and family-based rites framed by outbursts of riotous popular revelry, the climactic central week of the festival opened with the ceremonious entry of the rural population into the town. Meaning literally 'hooting at (ridiculing) hunger', Homowo was both a celebration of the ability of the Gã to prosper in their precariously constructed niche between land and sea and a reaffirmation of the social contracts seen to underlie that prosperity. At the heart of the festival lay the reassertion of the contract between the living and the dead, staged by each Gã lineage at its adeboo shia, 'ancestral house'. Interred under the floor of the adeboo shia were the corporeal remains of the ancestors, heightening its role as the most potent mnemonic for the origin of collective identities and the social order. If Homowo was a reaffirmation of the cultural unity seen to underlie the divisions in Gã society, however, it also served as an arena for both factional struggles and popular discontent with the established hierarchy. The Gã town may have been the realm of 'cultural order', yet it was also that of political power, and power meant not only hierarchy and order but also conflict and disorder.

Death and Burial in Gã History

In common with all human societies, Gã conceptions of the world and their place in it were informed by the certainty of mortality and physical death. The continuing influence of the dead over the affairs of the living meant that for the Gã the funeral was the most important of all *rites des passages*. Death and burial accordingly defined the ritual topography of the known world, forming an explicit link between landscape and memory, past and present.

At the very centre of this complex of ideas lay the custom of intramural sepulture. It is unclear exactly when the burial of the dead within the *adeboo shia*, the ancestral house, became established in Accra. Barbot makes no mention of it in his brief treatment of Gã funeral rites, and his description – based on information supplied in 1679 by the Danish commander at Osu and 'two black headmen' – implies that burials may have taken place outside.[18] A century later, however, Isert reports from Accra that 'every single Black is buried in the room in the house where he died'.[19] This observation is confirmed by mid-nineteenth century sources, with an important qualification: the bodies of slaves – probably a growing proportion of the population following the ending of the Atlantic slave trade – tended to be cast into the bush on the *husunaa*, the town boundary.[20] Pawns and heavily indebted members of the community were also often denied full burial rights, Daniell noting that unless some arrangement had been made with the creditor their bodies were exposed on elevated platforms on the edge of town, 'since the interment of the corpse would render his family liable for the payment [of the debt]'.[21] The impact of credit, debt and dependency on access to burial rights in Accra provides a striking illustration of social differentiation generated by the highly commercialized urban economy. The result was that growing inequality in the realm of the living was replicated in the realm of the dead.

Intramural sepulture underpinned the role of the *adeboo shia* as 'embodying' – literally – the historical identity of each Gã lineage, an identity firmly rooted in the cultural order of urban space. Owing in part to the multiple spiritual entities comprising a human being, the ultimate destination of the dead in Gã thought was somewhat ambiguous.[22] After a liminal period of about forty days during which the dead are in limbo between their biological existence and the afterlife, their spirits were understood to pass 'across the water' to *gbohiiajen*. That realm, however, intersected with the known world, departed spirits returning to their own houses – the location of their corporeal remains – to 'live' amongst their earth-bound families. The principal object of the complex succession of funerary rituals was to sever the ties between the living and the dead to ensure that this ongoing relationship would be trouble-free. The recently deceased were angry and easily offended, willing and able to harass the living if their departure was improperly managed.[23]

In contrast to the ritually managed urban space, the enclosing town boundary was understood to be frequented by the restless, vengeful spirits of those whose corpses were deposited there. Aside from serving as the graveyard of slaves and marginalized members of the community, it was also where the corpses of those deemed to have transgressed laws regulating the division between life and death were traditionally expelled from the culture of the town. Three categories of offenders stand out here: those accused of posthumous witchcraft, women who died in childbirth, and those who died during the *Homowo* season. The demise of two or three members of a family in quick succession, Daniell reported, was often blamed on the posthumous maleficence of the first to die. The corpse of the guilty party was summarily exhumed from its 'hallowed repository' and burned, the ashes scattered on the *husunaa* 'amid the mingled groans and execrations of the populace'.[24] The corpses of women who died in childbirth were also cast unburied into the bush, their property confiscated by the *wulomo* of Naa Dede Oyeadu, the goddess of birth and death.[25] Such a death occasioned a general trauma throughout Accra, representing a horrific confusion of the two carefully mediated passages between biological and other-worldly existence. Death during *Homowo* was also seen to sow grave confusion at a time when normal communication between the living and the dead was suspended and the powerful *jemawojii* were 'in the town'. It was referred to as *owu kase*, the 'accursed' or 'blasphemous' death.[26] It is important to stress, however, that far from being simply an evil place, the *husunaa* was a highly ambiguous liminal zone. Its charged supernatural environment was certainly hazardous, yet could also be carefully manipulated by ritual specialists to the benefit of the living.[27]

The salience of funerary practice in shaping mythic space ensured that the cultural politics of death and burial in Accra was historically contested. This is suggested by two oral traditions recorded by Reindorf in the late nineteenth century. The first tells of the regicide of Dode Akabi, a cruel and tyrannical regent who ruled over the Gã at Ayawaso before the succession of her son Okai Koi (d. 1677).[28] Ordering her subjects to dig a deep well (again, the salience of water can be noted), Dode Akabi was lured into the incomplete shaft, where the exploited Gã proceeded to bury her alive. The mode employed to kill Dode, Reindorf explains, was preserved in the ritual burial of animals or powerful medicines 'whenever an epidemic, war, death or any other misfortune is impending'.[29] Called *otutui* (sing. *otutu*), these sacred spots marked by conical mounds still dot the old quarters of Accra. Although Reindorf avoids the subject, Field's informants in the 1930s insisted that a human rather than an animal sacrifice was traditionally used in establishing the potent war *otutui* which served as foci for the intensive ritual preparation proceeding any military venture.[30]

The second tradition involves the burial of Okaija, the founder of the Gbese *akutso* (quarter) in Kinka and a dominant figure in mid-eighteenth-century Gã politics. Okaija's success in consolidating power following a series of conflicts within Accra in the late 1730s is reflected in the concentration of ritual authority in his new *akutso*, tradition holding that it was during this period that the shrines of Nai, Sakumo and Kole were all removed from the Asere *akutso* to neighbouring Gbese.[31] On the death of Okaija a serious dispute arose over the mode of his burial.[32] The Gã, it was held, had traditionally buried their dead wrapped in a woven mat, although following the advent of Europeans on the coast the use of wooden coffins became increasingly common. Despite this innovation, *mantsemei* ('chiefs') and *wulomei* ('priests') continued to be buried in mats. Some of Okaija's sons, however, had been educated by the Dutch and – perhaps influenced by Christian instruction – insisted that their father be interred in a coffin. Traditionalists within the family were outraged, and a violent struggle for the possession of the body ensued between a 'mat party' and a 'coffin party', the latter supported by the soldiers of Kinka's Dutch garrison. A number of protagonists were killed before the coffin party succeeded in interring the remains within the Dutch fort. Memory of the incident is enshrined in Gbese's official oath, uttered to enforce judicial obedience by evoking the spectre of the loss of life in past military conflict: '*Okaija adeka*'- 'Okaija's coffin'.[33]

These two traditions raise important issues regarding death and burial in pre-colonial Accra. The first involves the custom of human sacrifice. An established practice amongst the neighbouring Akan kingdoms and those of the Slave Coast to the east, the immolation of slaves and wives at the funerals of chiefs and other 'big men' was clearly a feature of Gã mortuary ritual.[34] In common with the Akan, the Gã regarded the social order of *gbohiiajen*, the realm of the dead, as approximating that of the known world, the spirits of powerful men requiring the continuing services of a retinue of dependants. The extent and magnitude of human sacrifice, however, remains unclear, as does the willingness and ability of the English, Dutch and Danish forts to intervene to prevent mortuary slayings in their respective spheres of influence in Accra. It is likely that the European forts, especially the more assertive British presence at James Town, had some impact on the practice of human sacrifice even before the Bond of 1844 clarified the legal jurisdiction of the British Crown on the Gold Coast. The Bond, by which the chiefs of the British enclaves consented to the trial of criminal cases by the Queen's judicial officers, signalled the growing determination of the British to stamp out customs considered 'morally repugnant' and incompatible with English law.[35]

By the 1850s human sacrifice in British Accra – which now included the old Danish headquarters of Osu – and in the Dutch enclave of Kinka appears to have been in decline, although sources agree that the immolation of slaves continued to be practised in secret.[36] Daniell, whose ethnographic material was compiled in about 1850, writes that the 'sacred obligation' of human sacrifice at funerals had until recently been 'fully authorised', citing the immolation of two young slaves – one male and the other female – on the death of a powerful chief of Kinka.[37] The two victims, he records, were killed on the edge of the grave, the corpse of the male being placed below and that of the female above the remains of their master. Gã funerary ritual observed by Field in the coastal town of Nungwa in the 1930s retained a striking residue of this pattern. Prominent in the funeral procession of the town's *mantse* were a boy and girl, 'shorn of their hair and finger-nails, whitened with clay, and richly dressed'.[38] The pair, Field was informed, represented those who in earlier days would have been buried with the *mantse*. In an elaboration of the older custom they endured only a mock execution, their hair and finger-nails being interred in the grave.

This leads on to a second and more general point arising from Reindorf's two oral traditions: death and burial in Accra, like religion and belief generally, had long been characterized by contest and innovation. By the final quarter of the nineteenth century the context for this change was the expansion of British colonial power, as the long era of informal, mercantile colonialism on the Gold Coast gave way to a new imperial age. The departure of the Danes in 1850 followed by the Dutch in 1868 signalled the gradual consolidation of British authority in Accra, a process which accelerated in 1874 with the formal creation of a Crown Colony and the abolition of slavery. In 1877 Accra succeeded Cape Coast as the headquarters of the British colonial administration. Herein lay a tension that would shape Gã ritual action throughout the colonial period and beyond: Accra was both the colonial capital and a long-established African urban centre. The reformulation of cultural space was contested by a multiplicity of interest groups – Gã townsmen and women, newly arrived migrants, Christian converts, Muslim traders, colonial rulers – all of whom possessed contrasting visions of the colonial city.

Two conflicting visions of Accra most concern us here. On one hand there is that defined by the cosmology and ritual topography of the Gã world, and on the other hand there is that of colonialism's 'official mind'. Neither of these visions were monolithic, nor were they immune from change. Their fundamental antagonism, however, can be expressed quite simply: whereas Accra represented the political, cultural and sacral epicentre of the Gã world, British officials viewed the colonial capital as an essentially European domain, unfit for a 'proper' African state. African affairs, officials repeatedly opined, were best conducted in the bush, not in the urban showcase of expatriate enterprise and ordered modernity. Many regarded Gã political institutions as either borrowed piecemeal from the Akan kingdoms or irreparably damaged by long exposure to outside influences, a sentiment forcefully expressed by Margaret Field in the 1930s.

The structuration of town and country in the official mind closely informed the emerging ideology of indirect rule, a policy which never fully came to terms with the existence of an African polity in the heart of the colonial capital.

Much of the effort on the part of the inchoate yet increasingly assertive colonial state to stamp a degree of order on its new headquarters was directed towards the elimination of the most obviously 'African' activities, so-called 'fetish practices'. Officials were particularly alarmed by the annual *Homowo* festival, referred to as 'Black Christmas' or – misleadingly – the 'Yam Custom'.[39] Following the watershed of the 1870s, *Homowo* emerged at the very centre of the debate over the control of cultural space in Accra. On the eve of the first festival season following the transfer of the colonial headquarters, Governor Freeling summed up the prevailing British view of town and country in an exchange with Alata *mantse* Kofi Oku: 'I cannot allow these indecent customs in the towns. People get drunk and riotous. Go into the country if you want them. I thought you were getting too sensible now to wish for them.'[40] Three years later in 1880 the Native Customs Regulation was applied to Accra, regulating the celebration of *Homowo* and requiring the chiefs to apply to the government for permission to proceed with the festival. A major outburst of violence during the 1884 festival led to further restrictions. Despite attempts by Gã leaders to explain that *Homowo* proceeded according to an intricate ritual calendar, the British aimed to halve the span of the festival to a mere three weeks.[41]

It must be emphasized that the reformulation of ritual space in the early colonial period was not simply contested between British officials on the one hand and the collective upholders of Gã tradition on the other. Accra's literate merchant and professional elite, many of whom were Euro-Africans and practising Christians, had long occupied a distinct niche in Gã society. Although their cultural affiliations and attitudes towards British 'protection' began to shift in response to the increasingly assertive racism of the new imperial age, many continued to be ardent proponents of a robust Victorian civilizing mission, as opposed to the activities of 'fetish priests' as any District Commissioner. The changing colonial dispensation also shaped the contours of conversion to Christianity in the wider Gã community, which was widely acknowledged on the Gold Coast as having been stubbornly resistant to evangelization. After half a century of labour with scant rewards, Accra's two principal missionary churches – the Basel Mission and the Wesleyan Methodists – began to attract growing numbers of converts in the final decades of the nineteenth century.

Yet conversion tended to be a long, negotiated process rather than an abrupt leap of faith from one clearly defined confession to another. The fact that the doctrine of eschatology presented such a fundamentally different version of the afterlife than indigenous cosmology meant that concern with issues of mortality, death and burial lay at the heart of the ongoing encounter between Christianity and Gã belief.[42] In the 1880s, we find native pastors of the Basel Mission despairing of the inability of the Osu congregation to abandon Gã funerary rites completely.[43] Widows were particularly anxious to continue to practice *ayiagu*, which marked the end of the period of mourning for a departed husband and enabled them to remarry. Without *ayiagu*, which culminated in a spiritual cleansing in the sea, women lived in fear of the jealous and vengeful spirits of their husbands. Intramural sepulture, moreover, as the British Colonial Surgeon observed in 1859, was 'not confined to the pagan past', and many members of the literate elite continued to be laid to rest beneath their grand 'storey houses' rather than in public cemeteries.[44] James Bannerman, for example, Accra's leading Euro-African merchant in the first half of the nineteenth century and one-time Lieutenant-Governor of the Gold Coast Settlements, stipulated in his will that he wished to be buried – without Gã 'custom' – beneath his residence. In a striking ceremony in 1912, 54 years after his death,

Bannerman's remains were exhumed by his descendants and solemnly reburied in the Wesleyan cemetery.[45]

Houses, Cemeteries and Mausoleums

The intervention of the colonial state into Gã ritual affairs was further demonstrated when in 1888 intramural sepulture was proscribed in Accra. Like the ongoing attempts to regulate the *Homowo* festival, the 1888 legislation must be set in the context of an emerging imperial ideology in which established concerns of law, order and control became linked to new issues of disease and medicine. In short, the emergent discipline of tropical medicine provided the expanding colonial project with a powerful claim to legitimacy, lending scientific credibility to European conceptualizations of African societies as 'morally backward'.[46] This equation is explicit in the reports of John Farrell Easmon, a Sierra Leonian physician who served as Medical Officer at Accra from 1884 to 1897 and who played a key role in the creation of the Medical and Sanitary departments in 1885 and 1888 respectively. Dr Easmon identified two main reasons why he regarded Gã mortuary practice as a major obstacle to the advance of colonial medicine in Accra. The entire absence of pathological statistics, he argued, was due to the 'disinclination ... which the natives have for anyone connected with the Government to know anything about the deaths of their relatives or friends'.[47] Post-mortems were regarded with such abhorrence that if the probability of such an examination was suspected, 'not the slightest demonstration of grief would be evinced by the relatives of the deceased until after the corpse had been ... disposed of'.[48] Noting that the 'great part played in the evolution of moral progress by the physical surroundings of a people is nowadays generally accepted', Easmon also identified intramural sepulture as contributing to the 'bad atmosphere' which reduced Accra's overcrowded quarters to a state of disease-ridden 'moral turpitude'.[49]

Indigenous funeral rites had long been regarded by both Europeans and members of the Gold Coast's Western-educated urban elite as morally and economically corrosive, the debilitating costs incurred leading to chronic indebtedness, impoverishment, pawning and slavery. As early as 1858 the British attempted to restrict the duration of funeral rites; half a century later further legislation was still being considered.[50] The so-called 'custom' remained a favourite target for the opprobrium of evangelists, Reindorf, for example, identifying it as an 'inner and dangerous foe' of the civilizing mission.[51] The application of Western medicine to these moral problems – albeit based in the 1880s on the scientifically unfounded miasmic theory of disease – was to underpin the campaign to improve the sanitation and the order of the colonial capital.

The administration of Governor William Brandford Griffith approached what was recognised as a highly sensitive issue with considerable care.[52] In April 1888 land was cleared in Christiansborg for a new municipal cemetery, one half of which was consecrated by the Anglican Bishop Ingham during a stop-over from Lagos to Sierra Leone. On 14 August Griffith convened a meeting of Gã office-holders, European and African churchmen, and leading members of Accra's merchant elite, at which he explained the putative sanitary advantages of cemeteries. John Sarbah, the unofficial African member of the Legislative Council, announced that house burial in the Fante towns to the west 'had been given up long ago, and most wisely too'.[53] The Gã chiefly hierarchy pledged – we can only guess with some reluctance – to give the measure their support. Four days later the Legislative Council made provisions for the appointment of a Registrar of Deaths, a sexton and five gravediggers, setting 1 September as the day when the ordinance would finally be applied.

The anticipated popular resistance duly materialized. On 19 September Griffith reported that despite the assurances of the Gã chiefs, house burial appeared to be continuing unabated.[54] The ritual adaptations already observed by Easmon, however, became widespread, as the bereaved strove to inter their dead without alerting the colonial authorities. Demonstrative displays of public grief – so essential in managing the smooth passage of the deceased to *gbohiiajen* – suddenly disappeared from view. The Governor responded by directing that notices should be posted around town announcing that a reward would be offered for information leading to the conviction of those contravening the ordinance. In a provocative demonstration of government resolve, six fresh graves in each of the public cemeteries were to be kept constantly open to receive the newly dead. Tensions boiled over in February 1889, following the compulsory demolition of a number of houses in the Asere *akutso* of Kinka. Led by *mantse* Akrama, the Asere people resolved to resist further incursions by the sanitary authorities, leading to a pitched battle with the colonial constabulary in which several people were wounded and thirty arrested.[55]

Official attempts to cajole the townspeople to abandon the burial of their dead beneath the floors of Accra's ancestral houses met with considerable resistance into the early twentieth century.[56] The popular response was not characterized by the overt resistance of February 1889, however, but by evasion and innovation. Crucially, the changing nature of death and burial shaped – and was shaped by – patterns of conversion to Christianity. Reflecting on the events of 1888, Reindorf reported that the horror with which the Gã viewed interment in the public cemetery was akin to that of being cast unburied into the bush.[57] The new law, he wrote, 'has ... placed our work in Christiansborg in a most hopeful position'. Fear of being caught out and consigned to the common burial ground rather than the more sanctified Basel Mission cemetery was actually encouraging the return to the fold of elderly backsliders who – when they felt death approaching – had left the church specifically to be laid to rest in their own houses. Growing numbers of Gã 'now prefer to become Christians and be buried as such, than to die as a Heathen and be thrown away – they mean by throwing away, the burial in the government Cemetery'.[58]

This abhorrence of being 'thrown away', according to Reindorf, played a large part in what he considered to be a major breakthrough for the Basel Mission in Osu, when in November 1888 he accepted a group of 16 candidates for baptism. These included some of the most respected elders in his own Asante Blohum *akutso*, including the designated successor to the office of *mankralo*, who gave up all claims to the stool. The desire to at least be buried within the confines of one's own town – if not one's house – continued to inform attitudes towards Christian conversion, catechist Isaac Odoi writing in 1897 that the fear of being interred in the Basel Mission cemetery at Osu was one of the main problems he faced in attracting adherents from the more stubbornly 'pagan' and traditionalist town of Kinka.[59]

By the mid-1890s a further innovation in mortuary practice began to emerge in response to the 1888 legislation. Rather than being buried within the town at all, some Gã leaders chose to be interred in specially constructed mausoleums on the outskirts of Accra. As was so often the case in Accra's eclectic past, the Akan kingdoms to the north provided the model for change. Unfortunately, the debates over what represented a dramatic shift in ideas about Accra's ritual topography remain outside the historical record. We can only speculate that the impossibility of concealing the death and intramural burial of leading office-holders from the British government – which by now officially confirmed the enstoolment of *mantsemei* – was an important factor. The earliest recorded mausoleum burial appears to be that of Sempe *mantse* Allotei, who died in 1895 and was interred on open ground to the immediate west of Kole lagoon.[60] The real breakthrough came in July 1902, with the death and burial of *Ga mantse* Taki Tawia. Aged 68 at his death, Taki had occupied the Gã stool for forty turbulent years. Succeeding to office at a time when the *Ga mantse* was still recognized throughout the south-eastern Gold Coast as the senior military leader and broker with the European forts, his successes on the battlefield in the 1860s–70s fuelled his reputation as a figure closely in touch with the supernatural realm.[61] Taki's funeral rites were attended by a crowd estimated to number 10,000 people, who witnessed his interment in a 'royal' mausoleum, *manprobi*, located on a rise to the north of Kole lagoon.[62] Other respected chiefs, notably Gbese *mantse* Okaija in 1910 and Osu *mankralo* Yeboa Kwamli in 1912, subsequently followed the late *Ga mantse*'s example. 'A new institution', in the words of Ako Adjei, 'developed out of the ruins of the old'.[63]

The use of mausoleums, however, remained limited to *mantsemei* and a few other high-ranking notables, the vast majority of the Gã population of Accra having to come to terms with the 1888 legislation in other ways. The gradual acquiescence to the new funerary dispensation – whether interment in church cemetery, public burial ground or mausoleum – was characterized by ongoing innovation in the mortuary rites conducted within the *adeboo shia*. By the 1930s a miniature coffin of relics (finger – and toe-nails, hair, and the sacred sponge used to wash the corpse) was ceremoniously interred beneath the floor in place of the entire body.[64] A long-established practice in the case of warriors killed on distant battlefields, this was deemed enough to ensure the return of the spirits of the deceased.[65] Yet the colonial state never exerted anything like complete control over the old *majii* of Accra. 'Even if the zealous sanitary authorities were to challenge the coffin [en route to the cemetery] and find that it duly contained the corpse', Field noted discreetly, 'it is doubtful where the remains would finally come to rest'.[66]

Gã Homowo: Cultural Politics and Political Culture

Given the highly ambiguous and hazardous supernatural environment of the *husunaa*, the interment of leading Gã office-holders in this liminal zone between town and country represented a striking innovation in mortuary practice. The furore over the burial of Osu *mankralo* Yeboa Kwamli in 1912, moreover, indicates that the social meanings of this innovation were far from uncontested. Funeral rites, as we have seen with the eighteenth-century case of Okaija, had long been an arena for political action in Accra. The adoption of Akan-style mausoleums in the 1890s, however, marks the beginning of a steadily increasing politicization of death and burial in the colonial city. Just as mortuary practice had shaped the contours of the Gã world, this politicization became intimately linked to the annual reaffirmation of that world, the *Homowo* festival.

The complex dynamics and social meanings of *Homowo* await detailed historical reconstruction elsewhere. Our main concern here is the reformulation in the first quarter of the twentieth century of those aspects of the festival concerning the ritual management of the dead. It should be noted that *Homowo* in the politically fragmented Gã townships differed from the Akan *odwira* in that it was less focused on the symbolic rejuvenation of the person of the king. Indeed, much of the ritual action turns on the reconciliation of the historic tension between the secular authority of the *mantsemei* and the sacral power of the *wulomei* in the Gã polity. As the climactic central week of the sacred season suggests, this action was also finely balanced between the domestic and the public domains.

Some three weeks after the *wulomei* of the great civic deities presided over the opening of the *Homowo* season towards the end of July, the start of public festivities was signalled by the dramatic entry into Accra of the *kosebii*.[67] Referred to as '*sobii*', 'Thursday people', because of their arrival on that day, the country dwellers poured into the capital laden with the products of their farms, drums beating and banners waving.[68] *Homowo* Friday was given over to the ritualized exchange of gifts, while houses and ancestral burial sites were decorated with the vibrant red of *tun*, camwood paste. Saturday's rites began with the solemn sprinkling of *kpekpei* ('ancestors' food': prepared from new season's corn and palm oil) on the graves and throughout the *adeboo shia*. Once the ancestors had eaten, their living descendants sat down to a feast of *kpekpei* with *tshili* (red bream), the fishing season for which was strictly limited by the ritual calender. That afternoon witnessed the first of a number of stagings of the exuberant *oshi* dance, which was characterized by scathing satire, cross-dressing and exhibitions of overt sexuality. The following morning the mood changed dramatically, the action shifting back from the public to the domestic arena. The first day of the new year, Sunday, saw the great lamentation of *no wala* (lit. 'take life'), when revered ancestors and those who had passed away in the previous year were remembered with the mournful sounds of wailing, horn calls and drumming. In an idealized 'pre-colonial' situation, a further three weeks of festival followed *Homowo* Sunday, sombre ritual continuing to alternate with riotous, carnivalesque inversion of the social and moral order.

It is clear that pre-colonial *Homowo* proceeded according to a structured ideological framework, with explosions of popular revelry subsumed into a presiding logic of reaffirmation and renewal. Yet that logic could be challenged and subverted. In other words, the 'sub-text' – to use McCaskie's formulation – could emerge momentarily to dominate the 'master text'.[69] It is equally clear, however, that the 'master text' of pre-colonial Gã *Homowo* never attained the hegemonic ambitions of Akan *odwira*. It can further be argued that *Homowo* – as a stylised expression of power in a vigorously contested political arena – represented the most potent moment to challenge the established order. At times of political tension within Accra, therefore, the festival could become an arena for political mobilization. Conflict often erupted from the interludes of anarchic inversion, when those normally excluded from power – young men, women, slaves – momentarily 'captured' the public domain. Field's description of the festival in the 1930s neatly captures something of the fine line between controlled chaos and popular protest:

> Gangs ... of ... young men parade the town stamping and chanting. The chants ... consist of all the pieces of scandal whispered in the town during the year but not hitherto spoken openly. Adultery is, of course, the favourite charge, witchcraft and poisoning comes next.... However insulting or slanderous the accusation the victim has no redress.... If he goes to the chief for sanctuary ... the chief himself is liable to have his own cupboards raided for skeletons in a manner which would be treasonable at any other time. Even the priesthood does not escape lampooning.... Usually some ... symbol of the scandalous deed is ... exhibited: if ... poisoning is the accusation a small coffin is carried.[70]

In the confines of a densely populated urban environment where honour, reputation and carefully nurtured civic virtue were all-important, such ridicule was often highly political in intent. It could also provoke a violent reaction. The best recorded example is the '*Agbuntsota*', 'the war of the smoked herring', of 1884, when the ridicule of *Ga mantse* Taki Tawia erupted into a street battle between factions from Kinka and Nleshi.[71]

These forms of popular political action were incompatible with the law and order agenda of the colonial state. Alarmed by the so-called 'pandemonium' which reigned in Accra during the *yalafemo*, 'Great Lamentation', for the late Taki Tawia in 1904, the government intensified its campaign to curtail ritual affairs in the capital. The initial target of official opprobrium was the sexually explicit *oshi* dance. After complaints of a particularly graphic *oshi* during 1904's *Homowo*, the dance was banned, the new *Ga mantse* Taki Obili (1904–18) being fined and having his permit to celebrate the remainder of the festival summarily cancelled.[72] The following year, police raided the *gbatsu* of Naa Dede Oyeadu in Asere following complaints of the continuing appropriation of the property of women who died in childbirth. The *wulomo* was imprisoned and sacred objects were confiscated, according to one observer, 'to the joy of Christians but to the Heathens' sorrow'.[73] Regulating and policing social action in the old Gã neighbour-hoods, however, remained a problem for the colonial authorities. Unlike the great Asante *odwira* festival in Kumase, which entered a period of abeyance under colonial rule following the exile of the *Asantehene*, Gã *Homowo* not only retained its ritual vigour but became the site for new forms of political mobilization.

Changes in the dramaturgy of mortuary ritual and the *Homowo* festival took place within the context of escalating political tensions in early colonial Accra. By the second and third decades of the twentieth century Gã affairs were becoming increasingly dominated by internecine stool disputes, powerful families and factions mobilizing followers in support of competing claims to chiefly office. The ritual remembrance of the dead, hitherto focused on the private domain of the *adeboo shia*, took on heightened political meaning as it was extended to the new mausoleums emerging on the outskirts of Accra. Again, the burial of Taki Tawia was the catalyst for change, the royal mausoleum at 'Manprobi' becoming the destination of an ostentatious procession each *Homowo* by the people of the *Ga mantse*'s Abola *akutso*.

By 1920 the established position of the so-called Okai Koi stool of Abola as the leading Gã political office was being openly challenged by a coalition of forces led by the Asere *akutso*. The opening of a sustained campaign against *Ga mantse* Taki Yaoboi (1919–29) by the Asere leadership can be precisely dated to *Homowo so* – '*Homowo* Thursday' – of that year. As the *sobii* were pouring into town from the villages of the Accra plains, Asere *mantse* D. P. Hammond and an entourage of elders and *wulomei* travelled north to Ayawaso hill, the site of the ancient Gã capital destroyed by the Akwamu in 1677. There the Aseres proceeded to the sacred grove of Okai Koi, where they attended to the spiritual needs of the dead king – rites hitherto performed within Accra by the *Ga mantse* – before parading back to town the following day in full state. They, and not the Abolas, their action implied, were the true heirs of Okai Koi. 'Every *Mantse* has a right to perform a new custom', the Aseres claimed in the subsequent enquiry.

> After *Mantse* Tackie Tawia's death they introduced a new custom … of going to his burial place at Mamprobi every year.… On Homowo Friday people may walk on all the roads out of Accra, but not on the Saturday and Sunday. The lorries pass now on those days, but it is not custom.[74]

As inter-quarter conflict mounted throughout the 1920s, 'custom' continued to be reshaped by political action. The annual processions to the tombs of *mantsemei* emerged as prominent fixtures of *Homowo*, becoming increasingly elaborate and defiant. Asere *mantse* D. P. Hammond died in traumatic circumstances after twenty years on the stool in 1922, and was interred in a mausoleum outside the new suburb of Kaneshi.[75] His tomb became the object of veneration for the Asere people, who marched out *en masse* each *Homowo* with military flags flying, muskets firing, and drums and iron bells beating in competition with their Abola rivals.[76] The 1924 festival coincided with the second of four attempts to destool the *Ga mantse*, *Homowo* Saturday being marred by a street battle between the Abola and Asere people. Similar confrontations erupted in subsequent years, the streets of Accra's old downtown neighbourhoods becoming virtually off-limits to protagonists from adjacent *akutsei* in the highly charged atmosphere of *Homowo*. Particularly contested was control over *Sakumotsoshishi*, the shrine of the still-powerful war god Sakumo and the site of dramatic *kple* dances in the final two weeks of the festival. Some two centuries after it had been 'captured' and relocated by Okaija in a time of comparable political conflict in the 1730s, *Sakumotsoshishi* remained a potent focal point in the ritual landscape of urban Accra.

Ritual and belief lay at the centre of the contested vision of the colonial city, shaping the contours of political action both within the Gã community and between imperial rulers and African subjects. The late nineteenth and early twentieth centuries was a time of rapid change in Accra, as the Gã formulated a range of responses to the interventions of the expanding colonial state. The dramatic changes in the cultural politics of death and burial were part of a long history of innovation in the management of the intricate relationship between the living and the dead. At the heart of that relationship stood *Homowo*, which continued to act as the great symbolic bridging of the divide between town and country and between the worlds of the living and the dead. In the political climate of 1920s Accra, however, *Homowo* was as much an arena for the strident particularism of individual town quarters as a statement of Gã cultural unity. '*Weku fe akotsa ni ame ju ohe ne, no hewo le keji ote le koni oya bo amanie*', the old women continued to whisper in the ear of the dead, but the stories of the living that the spirits carried with them to *gbohiiajen* were ones of dissonance and discord.

Notes

1 Words spoken to a departing spirit by Gã *gbonyohejuloi*, the old women who bathe the dead, as the head of the corpse is washed three times with a sacred sponge: M. J. Field, *Religion and Medicine of the Gã People* (London, 1937), p. 198.

2 See National Archives of Ghana, Accra [hereafter NAG] ADM 11/1/1139, Christiansborg [i.e. Osu] Native Affairs 1883–1912, 'The Constitution of … the Town of Christiansborg', by Yeboa Kwamli, 12 October 1910; Yeboa Kwamli to SNA, 4 October 1911; Osu *mantse* Noi Ababio to SNA, 24 July 1911, 3 November 1911 and 29 July 1912.

3 Wyatt MacGaffey, *Religion and Society in Central Africa. The BaKongo of Lower Zaire* (Chicago, 1986), p. 42; Daryll Forde (ed.), *African Worlds. Studies in the Cosmological Ideas and Social Values of African Peoples* (London, 1954).

4 See R. Huntington and P. Metcalf, *Celebrations of Death. The Anthropology of Mortuary Ritual* (Cambridge, 1979).

5 T. C. McCaskie, 'Death and the *Asantehene*: a historical meditation', *Journal of African History*, 30 (1989), pp. 417–44; Richard Rathbone, *Murder and Politics in Colonial Ghana* (New Haven and London, 1993); Kwame Arhin, 'The economic implications of transformations in Akan funeral rites', *Africa*, 64 (1994), pp. 307–21; see too the ambitious, but problematic, David William Cohen and E. S. Atieno Odhiambo, *Burying SM. The Politics of Knowledge and the Sociology of Power in Africa* (Portsmouth, NH, 1992).

6 T. C. McCaskie, *State and Society in Pre-colonial Asante* (Cambridge, 1995); Jonathon Glassman, *Feasts and Riot. Revelry, Rebellion and Popular Consciousness on the Swahili Coast, 1856–1888* (Portsmouth, NH, 1995); see too – from an anthropological perspective but with due consideration given to historical change – Michelle Gilbert, 'Aesthetic strategies: the politics of a royal ritual', *Africa*, 64 (1994), pp. 99–125, and *idem*, 'The sudden death of a millionaire: conversion and consensus in a Ghanaian kingdom', *Africa*, 58 (1988), pp. 291–313.

7 See L. F. Rømer, *Tilforladelig efterretning om Kysten Guinea* (Copenhagen, 1760), Chapter 3 trans. by Irene Odotei, 'On the Negroes' religion in general', Institute of African Studies, University of Ghana, Legon *Research Review*, New Series, 3 (1987), pp. 112–58; Field, *Religion and Medicine*; Ako Adjei, 'Mortuary usages of the Gã people of the Gold Coast', *American Anthropologist*, 45 (1943), pp. 84–98; E. T. A. Abbey, *Kedzi afo Yordan* (Accra, 1967), trans. by M. E. Kropp Dakubu, 'When the Jordan is crossed. Gã death and funeral celebrations', typescript (1971); Marion Kilson, *African Urban Kinsmen. The Gã of Central Accra* (London, 1974); Joshua A. Kudadjie, 'Aspects of religion and morality in Ghanaian traditional society with particular reference to the Ga-Adangme', in J. M.

Assimeng (ed.), *Traditional Life, Culture and Literature in Ghana* (Owerri and New York, 1976), pp. 26–53; Joyce Engmann, 'Immortality and the nature of man in Gã thought', in Kwasi Wiredu and Kwame Gyekye (eds), *Person and Community. Ghanaian Philosophical Studies*, I (Washington, 1992), pp. 153–90.

8 See Marion Kilson, 'The Gã naming rite', *Anthropos*, 63/64 (1968–9), pp. 904-20.

9 Rev. J. Zimmermann, *A Grammatical Sketch of the Akra or Gã-language* (Stuttgart, 1858), Vol. 2, pp. 97–100.

10 See John Parker, 'Gã state and society in early colonial Accra, 1860s–1920s' (PhD thesis, University of London, 1995), pp. 1–18. Suggestive material is found in files NAG ADM 11/1/1474 Fishing Industry, and ADM 11/1/832 Sempe Fetish 'Oyeni'.

11 Rev. Carl Christian Reindorf, *History of the Gold Coast and Asante* (Basel, 1895), p. 22. See also Jean Barbot, *Barbot on Guinea. The Writings of Jean Barbot on West Africa 1678–1712*, ed. by P. E. H. Hair, Adam Jones and Robin Law (London, 1992), Vol. 2, p. 579, whose account of a ceremony performed on the banks of the Klote lagoon at Osu in 1679 represents the earliest commentary on the importance of water in Gã thought and ritual.

12 Reindorf, *History*, p. 217. On warfare and the manipulation of supernatural forces, see McCaskie, *State and Society*, pp. 17 and 344–5; Parker, 'Gã state and society', pp. 70–8.

13 Zimmermann, *Grammatical Sketch*, Vol. 2, p. 159.

14 Abbey, *Kedzi afo Yordan*; Adjei, 'Mortuary usages'.

15 See Parker, 'Gã state and society', pp. 29–31 and 239–56.

16 Also known respectively as English Accra (or James Town), Dutch Accra (or, from 1868, Ussher Town) and Danish Accra (or Christiansborg).

17 NAG SCT 2/6/2 High Court Records, Accra, Judgement Book, Vol. 2, Part 1, Labadi v. Christiansborg, 1902, pp. 41–52, evidence of Carl Reindorf.

18 Barbot, *Barbot on Guinea*, 2, pp. 590–2; this is also suggested by Pieter de Marees, *Description and Historical Account of the Gold Kingdom of Guinea* (1602), ed. by Albert van Dantzig and Adam Jones (Oxford, 1987), pp. 179–83.

19 P. E. Isert, *Letters on West Africa and the Slave Trade. Paul Erdmann Isert's 'Journey to Guinea and the Caribbean Islands in Columbia' (1788)*, ed. by Selena Axelrod Winsnes (Oxford, 1992), p. 132.

20 William F. Daniell, 'On the ethnography of Akkrah and Adampé, Gold Coast, Western Africa', *Journal of the Ethnological Society*, 4 (1856), pp. 1–32, 16–17; John Duncan, *Travels in Western Africa in 1845 and 1846* (London, 1847), Vol. 1, p. 83; for the same practice by the Fante of Cape Coast, see Brodie Cruickshank, *Eighteen Years on the Gold Coast of Africa* (London, 1853), Vol. 2, pp. 213–26. The non-burial of slaves in late seventeenth-century Accra was also recorded by Barbot, *Barbot on Guinea*, p. 590.

21 Daniell, 'Ethnography of Akkrah', p. 18; see too Wesleyan Methodist Missionary Society Archive, School of Oriental and African Studies, London [hereafter WMMS] Gold Coast Correspondence [GCC], File 1845, No. 40, J. Martin to General Secretaries, British Accra, 7 July 1845.

22 See especially Field, *Religion and Medicine*, pp. 92–9.

23 Cf. McCaskie, 'Death and the Asantehene', pp. 427–8.

24 Daniell, 'Ethnography of Akkrah', p. 19.

25 For the continuation of this practice into the early colonial period, see *The African Times*, 1 August 1877 and 1 November 1877; *The Gold Coast Chronicle*, 4 November 1899.

26 Field, *Religion and Medicine*, pp. 44 and 58–9.

27 The anthropologist Margaret Field found 'the rubbish-heap at the back of a town always worth a visit', listing the various pieces of ritual apparatus 'connected with the riddance of misfortune' to be found there: *ibid.*, pp. 161–2.

28 Reindorf, *History*, pp. 18–19.

29 *Ibid.*

30 M. J. Field, 'The otutu and hionte of West Africa', *Man*, 43 (1943), pp. 36–7; *idem*, *Religion and Medicine*, p. 121.

31 For some discussion, see Parker, 'Gã state and society', pp. 29–30.

32 Reindorf, *History*, pp. 99–100; see also A. B. Quartey-Papafio, 'The native tribunals of the Akras of the Gold Coast', *Journal of the African Society*, 10 (July 1911), pp. 434–46.

33 Coffins continue to be central to innovation and contest in Gã mortuary practice today. For the post-1945 emergence of custom-made 'designer coffins', brilliantly carved and painted to represent the profession of the deceased, see Thierry Secretan, *Going into Darkness. Fantastic Coffins from Africa*

(London, 1995).

34 Isert, *Letters on West Africa*, p. 132; WMMS GCC, File 1840, No. 25, Brooking to General Secretaries, British Accra, 9 October 1840. For the debate over whether mortuary slaying in the Akan kingdoms, and in particular Asante, can best be described as 'human sacrifice' or 'jural execution', see Robin Law, 'Human sacrifice in pre-colonial West Africa', *African Affairs*, 84 (1985), pp. 53–87; Ivor Wilks, *Forests of Gold. Essays on the Akan and the Kingdom of Asante* (Athens, Ohio, 1993), Chapter 7, 'Space, time and "human sacrifice"', pp. 215–40.

35 David Kimble, *A Political History of Ghana. The Rise of Gold Coast Nationalism 1850–1928* (London, 1963), pp. 193–9.

36 Zimmermann, *Grammatical Sketch*, p. 351; Basel Mission Archive, Basel, Switzerland [hereafter BMA] D-1,13B/6A, Reindorf to Josenhans, 5 March 1862.

37 Daniell, 'Ethnography of Akkrah', p. 16; cf. Cruickshank, *Eighteen Years*, Vol. 2, pp. 225–6, who observes that mortuary slaying was no longer practised on the coast, the Fante being 'satisfied with the sacrifice of sheeps and bullocks'.

38 Field, *Religion and Medicine*, p. 205.

39 Corn, and not yam, was the main Gã staple and symbolic focus of that part of *Homowo* celebrating the new crop. Deities purchased or incorporated from the Akan, however, continued to be 'fed' yam, in contrast to the corn or millet-eating autochthonous gods.

40 NAG ADM 11/1/1770 Palaver Book 1877–87, 'Palaver held with King Solomon of Accra at Christiansborg Castle', 15 August 1877.

41 See *ibid.*, palaver, 23 August 1887; Parker, 'Gã state and society', pp. 199–208.

42 For evidence that Christian eschatology also altered established Gã concepts of the afterlife, see Field, *Religion and Medicine*, p. 202.

43 BMA D-1,31/37, Jeremias Engmann to Committee, 1 January 1880; D-1,34/62, Reindorf to Committee, 28 August 1882.

44 Public Record Office, London [hereafter PRO] CO 96/45, Bird to Lytton, No. 43, 11 July 1859, enclosed: 'Medical report for the year 1858'.

45 *The Gold Coast Nation*, 4 July 1912.

46 See Philip D. Curtin, 'Medical knowledge and urban planning in tropical Africa', *American Historical Review*, 90 (1985), pp. 594–613; David Arnold (ed.), *Imperial Medicine and Indigenous Societies* (Manchester, 1988).

47 PRO CO 96/180, Griffith to Holland, No. 111, 5 April 1887, enclosed: 'Report on the increased mortality among the Natives of Accra and Christiansborg during the Harmattan Season 1886–1887', by J. F. Easmon.

48 *Ibid.*

49 British Parliamentary Papers, 1889 LXXVI [C.5897] *Gold Coast Sanitary and Medical Reports for 1887 and 1888*, 'Sanitary Report on the Accra Station for … 1888', by J. F. Easmon.

50 PRO CO 96/43, Bird to Stanley, No. 56, 10 June 1858; NAG ADM 11/1/43 Funeral Customs [1909].

51 Reindorf, *History*, p. 341.

52 PRO CO 96/194, Griffith to Knutsford, No. 342, 19 September 1888.

53 *Ibid.*

54 *Ibid.*

55 PRO CO 96/200, Griffith to Knutsford, No. 96, 24 April 1889; CO 96/234, Griffith to Ripon, No. 171, 12 June 1893, enclosed: 'Report of the Progress of the Medical Department from 1885 to 1892', by J. F. Easmon.

56 Adjei, 'Mortuary usages', p. 92.

57 BMA D-1,48/62, Reindorf to Committee, Christiansborg, 16 January 1889.

58 *Ibid.*

59 BMA D-1,66/147, I. Odoi Phillips to Committee, 31 December 1897.

60 PRO CO 96/571, Clifford to Bonar Law, No. 688, 26 September 1916.

61 Parker, 'Gã state and society', pp. 57–112.

62 *Ibid.*, pp. 70–2.

63 Adjei, 'Mortuary usages', p. 92; see too NAG CSO 21/10/13 Homowo and other festivals in the Gã State, Adotei Twi II to DC, 30 July 1951.

64 Field, *Religion and Medicine*, p. 198.

65 See Reindorf, *History*, p. 123.

66 Field, *Religion and Medicine*, p. 199. Corpses of those who died the 'blasphemous death' in childbirth or during *Homowo* in La continued to be secretly deposited in the *ko sha*, 'accursed grove', on the outskirts of the town into the 1940s: *ibid.*, pp. 58–9; Adjei, 'Mortuary usages', p. 95.
67 Important sources include Daniell, 'Ethnography of Akkrah'; *The Western Echo*, 11 September 1886; *The Gold Coast Independent,* 17 August 1918; M. A. Barnor, *A Brief Description of Gã Homowo* (Accra, 1923); Field, *Religion and Medicine*; Charles Nii Ammah, *Ga Homowo and Other Ga-Adangme Festivals* (Accra, 1982).
68 The timing and rites of *Homowo* varied from town to town: in the 'leeward' Gã *majii* from Osu down to Tema the *kosebii* entered on a Monday and were therefore called '*jubii*'.
69 McCaskie, 'Death and the *Asantehene*'; *idem, State and Society*'.
70 Field, *Religion and Medicine*, p. 48.
71 Parker, 'Gã state and society', pp. 199–208.
72 See NAG ADM 11/1/1437, 'Suppression of objectionable customs', by S. D. Codjoe, n.d. [1938].
73 Marion Kilson (ed.), *Excerpts from the Diaries of Kwaku Niri (alias J.Q. Hammond) 1884–1918* (Accra, 1967), p. 30.
74 NAG ADM 11/1/1088, Enquiry into the Action of the Asere Mantse in going to Okai Kwei, by B. Crabbe, n.d. [September 1920], evidence of T. R. Quartey. For a description of the Asere rites at Ayawaso (or Okaikoi) – mistakenly portrayed as a timeless custom – see M. J. Field, *Social Organization of the Gã People* (London, 1940), p. 180; NAG CSO 21/10/13, 'Okaikoi Celebration', by E. C. Nunoofio, n.d. [1950].
75 On Hammond's death, widely suspected to have been caused by magical 'poisoning', see Parker, 'Gã state and society', pp. 329–30.
76 For vivid reportage, see *The Gold Coast Independent*, 30 August 1924, 29 August 1925 and 28 August 1926; also NAG ADM 11/1/923 Asere Yearly Custom.

13

'Wo pe tam won pe ba' ('You like cloth but you don't want children') Urbanization, Individualism & Gender Relations in Colonial Ghana c. 1900–39

EMMANUEL AKYEAMPONG

In 1979 and 1981, Flight Lieutenant J. J. Rawlings spearheaded the junior ranks of the army in two successful military coups in Ghana. Both occasions witnessed the destruction of major markets, sites of female accumulation, in Accra (Makola Nos 1 and 2), Sekondi, Koforidua and Kumasi. The anger of young male soldiers against women in general was astounding, and soldiers caned nude women in public.[1] The military government blamed market women for Ghana's economic difficulties. 'How and why do people believe the government propaganda,' queried a disturbed Claire Robertson?[2] The answer might be that the government's propaganda converged with the financial frustrations of ordinary men who found their manhood threatened. The violence of young male soldiers in 1979 and 1981 dramatized an important shift in gender relations: a new level of conflict between young men and young women, as distinct from the traditional struggle between young women and male elders. Equally important, the site for this new gender struggle was often urban. This chapter examines the cohesion of the forces of individualism and accumulation in gender relations in urban Ghana between c.1900 and 1939. Intra-generational, urban and gender conflict in colonial Ghana reflected the dialectical relationship between cultural definitions of success and the alienating forces of economic proletarianization.

Recent studies of gender in colonial Africa have emphasized the different gender experiences of the colonial state, capitalist production, and class formation.[3] The literature on gender in Ghana is relatively sparse compared to that of southern Africa. Recent works by Jean Allman, Penelope Roberts, Beverly Grier and Gareth Austin have examined how cash crop production and the incorporation of colonial Ghana into the global economy affected relations of production, accumulation, class formation and marriage.[4] So far, rural areas have been the main focus of gender studies in colonial Ghana. This chapter genderizes the social experience of urbanization, analyzing how motives for migration, job seeking, accumulation, avenues for socialization and support networks differed for urban men and women.

McCaskie has highlighted the importance of culture in defining the norms that underpin accumulation in twentieth-century Asante.[5] The image of the aristocratic 'big man' (Twi: *obirempon*, pl. *abirempon*) has had an enduring and alluring appeal in the history of southern Ghana.[6] The lifestyle of the *obirempon* was characterized by generosity, the use of imported drinks, rich cloths, gold ornaments, and a large number of wives, children and dependants. European commerce and education expanded the opportunities of accumulation and gave ordinary people access to 'big man' status. Young men who migrated to colonial towns from the late nineteenth century aspired to 'big man' status. They hoped to strike it rich. 'Success' incorporated an interesting blend of indigenous and Western images: money, wife (wives), generosity towards friends, social drinking, Western clothes and mannerisms. As late as the 1960s, migrant men in towns hoped to return to the rural areas with enough wealth to become elders.[7]

Women were also interested in accumulation and autonomy, but they did not aspire to a simple variation of the male definition of success. Female assertiveness and aspirations in urban Ghana have not been explored in depth. What is evident from the scattered historical evidence stretching back to the seventeenth century, is that women have always sought wealth and autonomy.[8] Historically, however, women were compelled to pursue accumulation and independence within the context of their relationships with men – including European men. In the early colonial period, political, economic and social change – stimulated by the fluidity of early colonial rule (*c.* 1874–*c.* 1930s), the dual judicial structure of colonial and customary law courts, urbanization and an expanding cash economy – provided women with the first opportunity to define their autonomy outside marriage.[9]

For some urban women, migration was an end in itself: they did not intend to return to the patriarchal villages. Urban women did not fit easily into male expectations. They hoped to acquire enough wealth in towns to become autonomous. Marriage remained attractive, but such women desired marriage on terms that were beneficial to them. Economic opportunities in the colonial market economy and the dual judicial structure of the colonial era were important for women. Individualism, accumulation and autonomy were intimately connected. As real wages declined in the face of a rising cost of living, the cultural goal of 'big man' became more elusive and tensions pervaded gender relations.

Early Migrants in Colonial Towns

Urbanization in Ghana predated colonial rule. The extension of the southern termini of the trans-Saharan trade routes from the early fifteenth century to tap the gold resources of the Akan goldfields provoked the emergence of commercial towns north of the Akan forest.[10] The European presence on the Gold Coast from the late fifteenth century, however, witnessed a progressively southward shift in economic activities.[11] Fishing villages like Cape Coast and Elmina (coastal outposts of the states of Fetu and Eguafo) expanded through coastal trade to become independent and outshone their parent states in wealth and prominence.[12] Even before colonial rule, coastal towns like Cape Coast, Elmina, Anomabu, Winneba and Accra had become active centers of Euro–African trade, and the bases of a new, educated, African elite.[13] Only four old towns registered populations of over 10,000 in the first Gold Coast census of 1891: Accra, Beyin (Axim District), Cape Coast and Elmina.[14] An important sociological feature in these old towns was the balanced gender ratios. Accra had an adult population of 6,467 men and 6,362 women, while Cape Coast had an adult population of 3,526 men and 3,603 women.[15] The contrast in social composition is striking in towns that were created by colonial economic activity.

The declaration of colonial rule in 1874 provided the confidence European capital needed to invest in mechanized mining in the interior of the Gold Coast and Asante. In 1897, the Ashanti Goldfields Corporation (AGC) was established to exploit the gold resources of Obuasi. Railway construction, begun in 1898 from the tiny Ahanta fishing village of Sekondi, linked interior mines with this natural harbour. The result was its transformation, like the Asante village of Obuasi, into a bustling cosmopolitan town. Labour shortages in Sekondi and Obuasi compelled government to encourage immigration.[16] The migrant, working-class origins of towns like Sekondi and Obuasi resulted in a predominantly male population. In the Gold Coast census of 1901, Sekondi had a male population of 3,469 and a female population of 626, a ratio of five to one.[17] As cocoa cultivation extended in rural areas, productive towns and villages began to exhibit sexually imbalanced populations. The 1911 Census Report observed that 'in the mining and agricultural districts it appears that 'the imported labourers are unaccompanied by their women'.[18] A comparison of the 1901 and 1911 figures underscores the increase in population in commercial, railway and mining towns. Sekondi's population rose from 4,095 in 1901 to 9,122 in 1911; the mining town of Tarkwa had a population of 2,426 in 1911 compared with 471 in 1901; the colonial capital of Accra registered a population of 19,582 in 1911; and the commercial city of Kumasi reflected stability with its population of 18,853 in contrast with 3,000 in 1901, when an Asante-British war dispersed its population.[19] Obuasi's population in 1911 was listed as 5,626,[20] and the AGC's employees figure of 3,850 in 1914 gives a vivid impression of the corporation's large imprint on the town's economy and society.[21] Obuasi's population was described as 'mainly a floating one' by a 1914 report.[22] By 1948, Obuasi's African population had risen to 15,724; Kumasi town had 58,626; the twin city of Sekondi-Takoradi registered a population of 43,742; and Accra contained 133,192 Africans.[23]

The unwillingness of capital to provide for the social reproduction of its labour force, and the predominantly male population in new towns like Sekondi, Tarkwa and Obuasi, provided economic opportunities for women in the overwhelmingly male colonial economy. Women came to play a crucial role as retailers of food and drink, and providers of recreation and domestic comforts, including the sale of sex.[24] In old towns like Accra and Kumasi, women again dominated the distribution network for food.[25] The 1921 census reported that the most favoured female occupations in towns were bakers, kenkey (cooked corn dough) makers and sellers, fish sellers and petty traders.[26] In these migrant, working-class communities, women provided the services that facilitated wage labour. According to elderly informants in Sekondi, 'Some of these migrants didn't even have rooms, so they spent the night with prostitutes, then went to work the next day.'[27] Jobs brought single men to towns; men attracted women to the towns.[28]

Women, Accumulation and Autonomy: Female Abirempon

The literature on the Akan and other southern peoples in the Gold Coast has neglected the ethic of accumulation among women. There were 'big women', just as there were 'big men'. Both valued the conspicuous display of wealth.

> Thus, at the beginning of the seventeenth century, a Dutchman noted that when women of high status went out [in coastal society], they leant on the shoulder of 'other women who serve them and are their slaves.' Two centuries later, another Dutchman described how, when free women danced together in a circle, the slave of one woman might run behind her waving a handkerchief and crying Mo! Mo! (a form of congratulation).[29]

And like men, 'big women' treasured gold jewellery.

If a woman wore gold ornaments, so did her 'maids'; thus one might see a wealthy woman going through the streets of Elmina followed by ten of her slave women, all finely dressed and wearing gold ornaments. A woman of high status might spend hours dressing her female slaves and arranging their hair.[30]

Significantly, several of these coastal 'big women' were of mixed race or widows of Europeans.[31] Historical evidence suggests that, at least since the seventeenth century, some women chose to strike up opportunistic relations with men, including Europeans. As early as 1702, Dutch officials on the Gold Coast expressed concern at the 'improper' accumulation of wealth by company employees in conjunction with their African mistresses.[32]

The expansion of commerce and the cash economy during the colonial period enabled women to acquire independent wealth through trade. Some were able to put up huge modern houses – the new symbol of wealth. Sekondi-Takoradi in the first four decades of the twentieth century was an active site of female accumulation. The new harbour, opened in 1928, increased the economic attractiveness of the twin city. Anita Mensah recalled the brisk trade of the 1930s and 1940s.

> Efiakuma new site (Takoradi) had been established then. The lorry that took 26 passengers, and plied the route to the harbor, could go twelve trips from 5:30 am to 8:00 am. Women sold tomatoes and traded far and near. Today, there are fewer economic opportunities in Takoradi. In those days, when you stood at Kwesi Mentsim Roundabout, all the way to the Market Circle, there was a throng of people. You could barely see ahead of you. Some women had pass books with UAC [United Africa Company], whereby they were given cloth on credit to sell. On each piece of cloth sold, they received a commission of 1s. They sold cloth and built storey building from the proceeds. They amassed property in gold trinkets.[33]

In the literature on urban women, prostitution has received much attention in the examination of women's economic options. This may be because informants reproduce old notions that tied female accumulation to sexuality for researchers. But the sale of sex has been an important resource in female accumulation in Ghanaian history.

Women constituted major pawns in the struggle over power and wealth in Anlo-Ewe society.[34] In Akan society, sexuality, procreation, female spirituality and wealth were also closely connected.[35] Among the Asante, a woman's vagina was considered her treasure chest. As an Asante *bragoro* (nubility rites) song expresses it:

> Osee yei, yee yei!
> Etwe Adwoa ei!
>
> Obi di wo, na
> wamma wo ade a
> ku no oo!
>
> Rejoice! Rejoice!
> Vagina of Adwoa (name of a girl born on a Monday)
>
> If someone 'eats' you (has intercourse with you)
> And fails to reward you,
> Slay him![36]

The instruction to 'slay him' reflects the perceived spiritual powers of women, powers encapsulated in their awesome ability to procreate.[37]

The Asante refer to sexual intercourse and genitalia through euphemisms. The vagina is alluded to as 'treasure', *tano* (fetish), or *bosom kesee* ('great god'). The male–female interdependence that had been lost in Asante with the emergence of the state[38] was resuscitated in *bragoro* songs like: *etwe yare a kote ahye akomfo* ('when the vagina is ill the penis commits suicide').[39] In Asante thought, one could argue, women were seen as spiritually superior. They were not to be trifled with. Okyeame Asonade's insights are most instructive. To sum up his statements: vagina is a god. The Asante call it *obosom* (a deity). Women can use their vagina to curse men who maltreat them. Such men soon die. A wife may wash her private parts and use the water to cook for the husband. The man will die after eating the food. On the other hand, a woman can spiritually shield her husband or lover from evil, even from the man's family if they want to harm him.[40] So when women are slighted, their curse is powerful.[41] Considering the traditional context of gender relations among the peoples of southern Ghana, it is not surprising that sexuality became a key resource in women's endeavour to acquire wealth in towns. Since power (sacred and secular) and wealth were closely connected in southern Ghana,[42] female exploitation of sexuality (their spiritual power and treasure chest) in the pursuit of wealth in towns was logical.

Urban life provided exciting opportunities for the fashioning of new social networks and the accumulation of cash. As the Melody Aces emphasized in a popular highlife song:[43] 'Money be Man.'[44] Social drinking and affairs of the heart were the spice of urban life. Two highlife songs depict the importance of these spheres: Kojo Bio's '*Ma me nsa*' (Give me drink');[45] and Kwaa Mensah's '*Me pe sika aye wo ho ade*' (I am labouring for your dowry).[46] Recreational resorts multiplied as urban life became more elaborate. The drinking bar was a central institution of urban life. The First World War, and the stationing of foreign troops in Gold Coast towns added impetus to urban social formation and the popularity of social drinking.[47] Dance bands proliferated, and dances became a key feature of nightlife.[48] In Adum in central Kumasi, the Ellis Bar, run by a Lebanese, was the centre of social drinking in the 1920s. More bars were opened in the 1930s: the Bridge Bar in Adum; and the Railway Bar opposite the station in Bompata. Collingwoode Williams opened Kumasi's first hotel in 1941, the Hotel de Kingsway.[49] In Sekondi, popular places emerged to diversify the elite bias in entertainment. From the 1910s, Sekondi's educated elite resorted to the Optimism Club for elaborate ballroom dances, Alan's for drinks, and, in the 1930s, the Metropolitan Hotel in European town for their weekend dances. The establishment of the Liberia Bar in the expanding port town of Takoradi, and the emergence of the Taboo Brass Band, gave the working class their equivalent of the Optimism Club.[50] Gradually, leisure activities moved indoors.

Towns provided women with the opportunity to make money outside the confines of kinship and marriage. Prostitution was one avenue for female accumulation that also embodied the essence of urban gender conflicts — sexuality. In Sekondi-Takoradi, prostitutes settled in the colonial period in the two suburbs of Nkontompo and Sikaduase. These names, although their exact origins are unclear, expressed popular male attitudes toward prostitutes. *Nkontompo* in Twi means 'deceit'; while *sikaduase* literally means 'under the money tree'. Women were perceived as accumulating wealth through deception. Prostitutes in Sekondi in the 1930s lived in Nkontompo, while Sikaduase became the base of Ewe and Nzima prostitutes in Takoradi, especially in the 1940s.[51] Female accumulation and autonomy ('deceit' in the eyes of men) became prominent images of prostitution in particular and gender conflict in general.

The intersection of female sexuality and accumulation in colonial towns was underscored by the names people in Sekondi-Takoradi assigned to prostitutes. An older group, mostly Krus and Ibos, were called UAC (after the United African Company), a major expatriate company. The new, younger group of prostitutes were named 'Leventis' (after the expatriate company A. G. Leventis); these companies controlled the commercial life of Sekondi-Takoradi. The 'UAC' prostitutes were led by a Cape Coast woman called Akwele and the 'Leventis' prostitutes by an Nzima, Lamle.[52] Women's assertion of the right to control their sexuality, and their acquisition of wealth through their sexuality, became key points of contention in urban gender conflict. Traditional norms in colonial southern Ghana had always subsumed female sexuality within the context of marriage. The Twi word for promiscuity, *nea edi afra* (literally 'that which is out of place') captures the conception of untamed female sexuality as an anomaly.[53] When single women in Sefwi Wiawso and Asante chose actively to pursue accumulation through trade and cocoa farming to the detriment of marriage, the traditional authorities ordered their arrest in the late 1920s and early 1930s and insisted that they marry within the shortest possible time.[54] Urban and rural men, young and old, perceived the early twentieth century as an era of gender chaos and moral crisis. More accurately and importantly, it was a period of gender negotiation as well as conflict.

Gender Conflict in Colonial Towns

Broader political, economic and social changes formed the context for gender conflict in colonial towns. Two major pieces of legislation that influenced gender conflict in the period were the abolition of slavery (in 1874 in the Colony and in 1896 in Asante) and the subsequent abolition of pawning.[55] The importance of women to production and reproduction has been demonstrated for African societies.[56] It is thus not surprising that women were valued as slaves in pre-colonial Africa. The abolition of slavery led to the feminization of pawning in colonial Asante, as women were crucial to the processes of production and reproduction.[57] The abolition of pawning coincided with the take-off phase of the cocoa industry, when labour was in great demand. Men exploited the labour of their immediate family, especially wives and children.[58] Bride price (Twi: *tiri nsa*) became artificially inflated, and male elders cashed in on the 'marriage boom' and exchanged female wards for large sums of money. *Tiri ka* ('head debt'), in which the bridegroom was asked to pay a 'debt' on behalf of his wife's family, became a common feature in marriage transactions among the Akan.[59]

Marriage and courtship became expensive. In 1929, the District Commissioner (DC) for Obuasi commented that 'It is surprising how the custom that a husband shall be called upon to pay his wife's family debts or lose his wife seems to be growing.'[60] The DC for Obuasi was later informed by a European associate from Abomposu Estates that the escalating costs of marriage transactions compelled his employees on the plantation to opt for concubinage rather than marriage.[61] In towns, where urbanization had diluted the control of kinsmen, women contracted their own marriages or concubinage, making monetary rewards or compensation a key consideration in their choice of male suitors. The economic opportunities in towns ensured that women could survive on their own without male providers. On the other hand, men received low wages in the colonial economy, and needed financial help from women as wives or lovers. In 1915, the daily wage for an unskilled labourer in the Gold Coast was 1s 3d,[62] a rate that had increased slightly to 1s 9d in 1921.[63] A stable cost of living, however, allowed incremental rises in real wages. But economic conditions for urban workers worsened sharply from 1933. The food price index rose sharply, while the real wage index plummeted.[64] In the urban context, during the period under study, it was the men who really needed the women. For men who had migrated to towns with big plans, urban life was an economic disappointment.[65] Disillusion was reflected in an intensification in gender conflict, mirrored in court cases, and a male elaboration of 'romance' or 'love'.

The establishment of a dual judicial structure in colonial Ghana proved an important resource for urban women. The ability to resort to the chief's tribunal or colonial law courts encouraged the strategic exploitation of both resources, depending on the nature of a case and which legal system was seen as being more amenable to a particular suit.[66] The coexistence of judicial systems, and the British endeavour to codify customary law, encouraged the literate court recorders of native tribunals to 'act as law "modifiers" and "amenders" of customary law'.[67] Urban women increasingly applied to the courts for redress in their conflicts with men.

The court records show that some urban women were determined not to be taken for granted by men who sought to exploit women for sex and the provision of domestic services. A revealing case was one between Korkor Afiah (plaintiff) and Adjetey Niabo (defendant) that came before the Gã Native Tribunal (Accra) on 8 December 1920. Korkor Afiah claimed '£24 being service rendered as cateress for entire year'.[68] The defendant did not show up. Korkor stated her case.

> My name is Korkor Afiah. I live at Kortey Na Accra, I am a petty trader. During the Influenza of 1918 I went from Teshie to up country, Koforidua. Defendant saw me there and asked my consent if I would marry him. I told defendant that I am indebted to somebody for £6 therefore if he could pay for me there will be no further trouble on my cause again to marry him. Defendant replied me and said is willing to pay, but at that present is nothing in his hand, therefore I must stay with him to help him and work to pay. I agreed and stayed with him. I stayed with defendant for one year and he paid the debt £6 for me. After defendant has paid the debt his sister made quarrelled [sic] with me and drove me from defendant.[69]

Apparently, the defendant made no attempt to bring Korkor back, and Korkor, feeling cheated, sued for £24, which she considered just compensation for domestic services she had rendered Adjetey for the twelve months they had lived together. The Ga paramount chief's court awarded her the £24 plus costs.

Sometimes gender conflicts resulted in violence and even death. There are cases where jealous husbands murdered their wives because the latter had withdrawn sexual services. In September 1931, Kwadwo Duodu murdered his wife in the District of Kumasi because she refused to have sex with him.[70] On 27 October 1929, Jato Basari also murdered his wife for a similar reason in the District of Kumasi.[71] These cases demonstrate the importance of sexuality as a potent weapon women could deploy against men in gender conflict. Men claimed women had become materialistic and had lost their 'values'. Kwaa Mensah's highlife song: 'Wo pe tam won pe ba' ('You like cloth but you don't want children') criticized acquisitiveness among urban women.[72] At the end of the colonial period, the Ray Ellis Sextet expressed a preference for unsophisticated rural women in their song, 'Give me the Bush Girl'.[73] Urban men accused urban women of an individualism that perverted the ideal social fusion of male and female in marriage.[74]

Colonial administrators, men of course, also commented on the apparent materialism of urban women. In Obuasi, women from the Northern Territories were selected for especial condemnation.

> These women are brought from the North by their men folk who come down looking for work in the mines or on the land. After years of comfort and good clothing, these women show a tendency to leave their husbands and marry those who can afford to give them more money. There is also the case where the woman desires to leave her husband and is not prepared to return to the North and place the matter before her own family.[75]

Several women from the Northern Territories told the DC of Obuasi that if they returned to the North, they would be detained. Both the records of colonial administrators and native authorities express concern at the easy dissolubility of marriage.[76] Women were seen as culprits who exploited the sexual imbalance in colonial towns to their material advantage. In 1943 Adisa Kotokori of Sekondi Zongo was accused of the 'the habit of befooling men', by promising marriage in return for large sums of money, then reneging on the agreement.[77]

An important male response to alleged female materialism was an elaboration of 'romantic love'. J. Benibengor Blay's novels, often based on colonial mining towns, provide good illustrations. Blay sets up two contrasting models of 'bad' and 'good' women in his *Be Content with Your Lot* (1947), and *Love in a Clinic* (1957). In the first, Blay criticizes the covetousness prevalent among town women, who were seldom content with their lot. In this novel, Amba's husband, Akwampa, is always being criticized by Amba. Amba hears that her husband might be getting a new job in one of the mining companies with a higher salary.

> I shall of course, expect him to increase his maintenance money. Four shillings a day for four in the house is a pittance which fails to meet the need. Apart from that, I shall expect him to supply me with new clothing every month. If he refuses, I shall take the cash out of the daily subsistence money.[78]

Amba's friend Aba, on the contrary, has a marriage that appears to be perfect. She is happy, and never complains about her husband. Amba eventually divorces on the basis of her conviction that she could find a more generous husband. She then entices Aba's husband to leave Aba and marry her – and thus unwittingly marries the town's worst miser, whose saintly wife had never complained.

In *Love in a Clinic* Abuo Brendadu finds 'real' love. A migrant worker in a gold-mining town, he contracts tuberculosis and is referred to the Korle Bu Teaching Hospital in Accra. In hospital with an inflamed lung, Brendadu broods over how 'Western civilisation seemed to account, more or less, for the spread of the disease. Civilisation had brought about filth and squalor in the industrial towns, which the sanitary authorities could not cope [with].'[79] He believes that social life in towns, revolving around drinking bars, has facilitated the spread of tuberculosis. But Brendadu finds romantic love with a captivating nurse, Dua-Aba, transferred to his ward at the hospital. I presume this is Benibengor Blay's version of a 'happy ending'. This is true love because the beautiful Dua-Aba accepts a sick, and presumably broke, Brendadu.

Men became more profuse in their professions of love. This was an important trend, encouraged by the need for men to woo women in a social context in which they greatly outnumbered them. The love ballads of E. K. Nyame's Band, with the enchanting voice of Kwabena Okai, depicted a new sensitivity in male emotions. A classic is '*Odo a me do wo nti*' ('It is because I love you'). My translation is 'It is because I love you / not that I am mad.// All the money I have given you / all the cloth I have given you / it is because I love you / not that I am mad.// The things that you do / it's not that I don't see / it is because I love you / not that I am mad.'[80]

In this song, men, for a change, are portrayed as loving, giving and sensitive. Women are seen as insensitive, grabbing and deceitful.

But as 'chaos' pervaded gender relations in urban and rural areas, and women experienced an unprecedented improvement in their socio-economic circumstances, traditional authorities and the colonial government galvanized their forces to terminate what they perceived as unbridled female emancipation. As economic depression and the Second World War ended, empowered native authorities firmly resurbordinated women to men, and again defined marriage as the necessary mechanism in the mediation of gender relations. Native State Councils legislated lower bride prices to make marriage affordable, passed new laws to regulate adultery and divorce, and strove to eliminate what had been a nascent female petite bourgeoisie.[81]

Conclusion

The era preceding the First World War witnessed the acceleration of urbanization and rural–urban migration. Young men migrated to the towns with the intention of circumventing elderly male control over land and women. Wage labour in the colonial economy provided a new avenue for accumulating wealth and a wife or wives, and returning home a 'big man' or a respected elder. Women also migrated to the towns, but for them migration was often an end in itself. The bonds of kinship and marriage were too confining. Women seldom planned a return to the rural areas, and concentrated instead on acquiring wealth and finding a 'suitable' husband or lover in the towns. An important resource in female accumulation was their exploitation of their sexuality. Female independence and accumulation rubbed urban men up the wrong way. Suffering from low wages and declining economic standards from the 1930s, men accused women of individualism and acquisitiveness. They preferred cloth to children, they chose concubinage over marriage. Men became antagonistic and even violent, but also responded to women's emotional needs through a new sensitivity. Some men became romantic. Female assertiveness in rural and urban areas was portrayed as a sign of moral crisis, especially by male elders. From the late 1930s, women were gradually brought under effective male control by native authorities with the support of the colonial administration.

But male perceptions that women accumulated wealth through their sexuality lingered. Independence, the emergence of the Ghanaian state as the major patron, and the solidification of class distinctions made the processes of female accumulation more complex. Female accumulation took in a class dimension. Ordinary, poor women toiled in the market places. Some white-collar single women, with inadequate salaries and exaggerated lifestyles, dated 'sugar daddies' for the money.[82] Women connected to government officials exploited their relations for financial gain. Indeed, the Acheampong government (1972–8) was dubbed *fa woto begye Golf* ('bring your backside for a Golf'), for the liberality with which government officials dispensed Volkswagen Golf cars to their mistresses. The irony is that these 'elite' women, the real accumulators in the independent era, were beyond the wrath of ordinary men. Thus, with the Rawlings coups of 1979 and 1981, soldiers and policemen vented their frustration at their lack of accumulation on the available, vulnerable market women. Urban working men, their 'big man' dreams rendered increasingly unattainable in a declining economy, expressed their solidarity with the soldiers and policemen.

Notes

1 A. Adu Boahen, *The Ghanaian Sphinx: Reflections on the Contemporary History of Ghana 1972–1987* (Accra, 1989), p. 23.

2 Claire Robertson, 'The death of Makola and other tragedies,' *Canadian Journal of African Studies*, 17, 3 (1983), p. 472. Gracia Clark, *Onions are my Husband: Survival and Accumulation by West African Market Women* (Chicago and London, 1994), Chapters 1 and 10, underscores the vulnerability of market women in Kumasi. Market women have been subjected to official scapegoating from colonial times.

3 For excellent historiographical and theoretical reviews, see Margaret Jean Hay, 'Queens, prostitutes, peasants: historical perspectives on African women, 1971–1986', *Canadian Journal of African Studies*, 22, 3 (1988), pp. 431–47; and Margot Lovett, 'Gender relations, class formation, and the colonial state in Africa', in Jane L. Parpart and Kathleen A. Staudt (eds), *Women and the State in Africa* (Boulder, 1989), pp. 23–46.

4 Jean Allman, 'Of "spinsters", "concubines" and "wicked women": reflections on gender and social change in colonial Asante', *Gender and History*, 30, 2 (1991), pp. 176–89; Penelope A. Roberts, 'The state and the regulation of marriage: Sefwi Wiawso (Ghana), 1900–1940', in Haleh Afshar (ed.), *Women, State and Ideology: Studies from Africa and Asia* (London, 1987), pp. 48–69; Beverly Grier, 'Pawns, porters, and petty traders: women in the transition to cash crop agriculture in colonial Ghana', *Signs*, 17, 2 (1992), pp. 304–28; and Gareth Austin, 'Human pawning in Asante, 1800–1950: markets and coercion, gender and cocoa', in Toyin Falola and Paul Lovejoy (eds), *Pawnship in Africa: Debt Bondage in Historical Perspective* (Boulder, 1994), pp. 119–59.

5 T. C. McCaskie, 'Accumulation, wealth and belief in Asante history: II The twentieth century', *Africa*, 56, 1 (1986), pp. 2–23.

6 See Ivor Wilks, 'Founding the political kingdom: the nature of the Akan state', in *Forests of Gold: Essays on the Akan and the Kingdom of Asante* (Athens, Ohio, 1993), Chapter 3; Ivor Wilks, 'The golden stool and the elephant tail: an essay on wealth in Asante', *Research in Economic Anthropology*, 2 (1979), pp. 1–36; T. C. McCaskie, 'Accumulation, wealth and belief in Asante history: I To the close of the nineteenth century', *Africa*, 53, 1 (1983), pp. 23–43; Kwame Arhin, 'Rank and class among the Asante and Fante in the nineteenth century', *Africa*, 53, 1 (1983), pp. 2–22; and Ray Kea, *Settlements, Trade, and Polities in the Seventeenth-Century Gold Coast* (Baltimore, 1982), pp. 85–94.

7 Margaret Peil, *The Ghanaian Factory Worker: Industrial Man in Africa* (Cambridge, 1972), pp. 181–2.

8 See, for examples, Pieter de Marees, *Description and Historical Account of the Gold Kingdom of Guinea*, trans. and ed. Albert van Dantzig and Adam Jones (Oxford, 1987), p. 64; and P. E. H. Hair, Adam Jones and Robin Law (eds), *Barbot on Guinea: The Writings of Jean Barbot on West Africa 1678–1712* (London, 1992), Vol. 2, p. 495.

9 The irony is that the colonial policy of indirect rule through chiefs, capitalist operations and missionary ideology all conspired to subordinate women. A more coherent coordination of these forces from the 1930s would eventually curtail the exhilarating socio-economic opportunities for women in the era before the Second World War. See Jean Allman, 'Rounding up spinsters: gender chaos and unmarried women in colonial Asante', *Journal of African History* 37, 2 (1996), pp. 195–214; *idem*, 'Making mothers: missionaries, medical officers and women's work in colonial Asante, 1924–1945', *History Workshop*, 38 (Autumn 1994), pp. 23–47; and Roberts, 'The state and the regulation of marriage'.

10 Ivor Wilks, 'The Mossi and Akan State 1500–1800', in J. F. A. Ajayi and Michael Crowder (eds), *History of West Africa* (London, 1976), Vol. 1, pp. 413–55; and Ivor Wilks, 'Wangara, Akan, and Portuguese in the fifteenth and sixteenth centuries', in *Forests of Gold*, pp. 1–39.

11 A. A. Boahen, 'The states and cultures of the lower Guinean coast', in B. A. Ogot (ed.), *History of Africa, Vol. V: Africa from the Sixteenth to the Eighteenth Century* (Berkeley, 1992), pp. 399–433.

12 See Albert van Dantzig, *Forts and Castles of Ghana* (Accra, 1980).

13 Margaret Priestley, *West African Trade and Coastal Society* (London, 1969); and Augustus Casely-Hayford and Richard Rathbone, 'Politics, families and freemasonry in colonial Gold Coast', in J. F. Ade Ajayi and J. D. Y. Peel (eds), *People and Empires in African History: Essays in Memory of Michael*

Crowder (London, 1992), pp. 143–60.

14 Gold Coast, *Report on the Census of the Gold Coast Colony for the Year 1891*, p. 106. National Archives of Ghana (NAG), Accra, ADM 5/2/1. The population statistics cited from census reports in this article should be seen as depicting broad patterns. As late as 1931, census officers continued to question the accuracy of population returns. See A. W. Cardinall, *The Gold Coast* (Accra, 1931), p. 123.

15 *Ibid.*, p. 134.

16 See K. B. Maison, 'The History of Sekondi' (BA thesis, University of Ghana, 1979), p. 39; Egya N. Sangmuah, 'The socio-economic impact of railways and harbour on Sekondi-Takoradi, 1895-1950' (BA Thesis, University of Ghana, 1981), pp. 5–6; and Frank Amponsah-Mensah, 'The Ashanti Goldfields Corporation in the post–colonial period: 1957–1989' (BA thesis, University of Ghana, 1989), pp. 5–7.

17 Gold Coast Colony, *Census of the Population, 1901*, p. 53. NAG (Accra), ADM 5/2/2.

18 Gold Coast Colony, *Census of the Population, 1911*, 30. NAG (Accra), ADM 5/2/3.

19 Ibid., pp. 50–1.

20 Gold Coast, *Census Report 1921 for the Gold Coast Colony, Ashanti, the Northern Territories and the Mandated Area of Togoland* (Accra, 1923), p. 115.

21 NAG, Kumasi, ROA 589. Report by Junior Sanitary Officer on Obuasi Township, 1914.

22 *Ibid.*

23 The Gold Coast, *Census of Population 1948: Report and Tables* (Accra, 1950), pp. 88, 97, 230 and 246.

24 For comparative case studies, see Kenneth Little, *Women in African Towns* (Cambridge, 1973); Luise White, *The Comforts of Home: Prostitution in Colonial Nairobi* (Chicago, 1990); Helen Bradford, '"We women will show them": beer protests in the Natal Countryside, 1929', in Jonathan Crush and Charles Ambler (eds), *Liquor and Labor in Southern Africa* (Athens, 1992), pp. 208–34; and Phyllis M. Martin, *Leisure and Society in Colonial Brazzaville* (Cambridge, 1995).

25 See Claire C. Robertson, *Sharing the Same Bowl: A Socioeconomic History of Women and Class in Accra, Ghana* (Ann Arbor, 1990); and Clark, *Onions Are My Husband*.

26 Gold Coast, *Census Report 1921*, p. 159.

27 Interview with Laurence Cudjoe, J. K. Annan, Mr. Arhu and Joseph Kofi Ackon, Sekondi, 27 May 1992.

28 *Ibid.*

29 Adam Jones, 'Female slave-owners on the Gold Coast: just a matter of money?', in Stephan Palmié (ed.), *Slave Cultures and the Cultures of Slavery* (Knoxville, 1995), p. 105.

30 *Ibid.*, p. 106.

31 *Ibid.*, p. 102.

32 West Indian Company (WIC) p. 228: Instructions Book 1661–1702. Draft circular by W. De la Palma (n.d.), in A. van Dantzig, *The Dutch and the Guinea Coast 1674–1742: A Collection of Documents from the General State Archives at the Hague* (Accra, 1978), p. 89.

33 Interview with Anita Mensah, Takoradi, 16 August 1994.

34 Sandra E. Greene, *Gender, Ethnicity, and Social Change on the Upper Slave Coast: A History of the Anlo-Ewe* (Portsmouth, NH, 1996).

35 Emmanuel Akyeampong and Pashington Obeng, 'Spirituality, gender, and power in Asante history', *International Journal of African Historical Studies*, 28, 3 (1995), pp. 481–508.

36 Peter Sarpong, *Girls' Nubility Rites in Ashanti* (Tema, 1977), pp. 24–25.

37 Akyeampong and Obeng, 'Spirituality, gender, and power', pp. 488–92.

38 *Ibid.*

39 Sarpong, *Girls' Nubility Rites*, p. 84.

40 A reference to the Asante belief that witchcraft is only effective within the matrilineage.

41 Interview with Okyeame Asonade, spokesman for Obosom Nyano, Ayigya (Kumasi), 7 June 1992.

42 McCaskie, 'Accumulation, wealth and belief', I and II; and Greene, *Gender, Ethnicity, and Social Change*.

43 Highlife music became popular in the Gold Coast from the early twentieth century, when African bands fused the lyrics of Akan songs with Western instrumentation. For detailed studies of highlife music, see John Collins, 'Ghanaian Highlife', *African Arts*, 10, 1 (1976), pp. 62–8; and *West African Pop Roots* (Philadelphia, 1992).

44 Decca, GWA 4087 (KWA 6315/160).

45 HMV, West Africa, JVA 117.

46 HMV, West Africa, JLK 1017.

47 Raymond Dumett, 'The social impact of European liquor on the Akan of Ghana (Gold Coast and Asante), 1875–1910', *Journal of Interdisciplinary History*, 5 (1974), p. 97.

48 Collins, *West African Pop Roots*, Chapters 2 and 3.

49 Interviews with A. Attakora Gyimah, Kumasi, 11 June 1992; and Osei Assibey Mensah, Kumasi, 7 June 1992.

50 Interviews with Laurence Cudjoe *et al.*, Sekondi, 27 May 1992; Anita Mensah, Takoradi, 16 August 1994.

51 *Ibid.*

52 Interview with Laurence Cudjoe *et al.*, Sekondi, 27 May 1992.

53 See J. G. Christaller, *A Dictionary of the Asante and Fante Language called Tshi* [Chwee, Twi] (Basel, 1881), p. 139.

54 Roberts, 'The state and the regulation of marriage'; and Allman, 'Rounding up spinsters'.

55 Pawns (Twi: *awowa*, pl. *nwowa*) were pledged as collateral for loans in the pre-colonial and colonial eras.

56 See Claire Robertson and Martin A. Klein (eds), *Women and Slavery in Africa* (Madison, 1983).

57 Austin, 'Human pawning in Asante'.

58 Grier, 'Pawns, porters, and petty traders'; and Christine Kali, *Cocoa and Kinship in Ghana: The Matrilineal Akan of Ghana* (London, 1983).

59 See Takyiwah Manuh, 'Changes in marriage and funeral exchanges in Asante: a case study from Kona, Afigya-Kwabre', in Jane I. Guyer (ed.), *Money Matters: Instability, Values and Social Payments in the Modern History of West African Communities* (Portsmouth, NH, 1995), pp. 188–201; Austin, 'Human pawning in Asante', p. 138; Roberts, 'The state and the regulation of marriage', p. 61; and Grier, 'Pawns, porters, and petty traders', pp. 327–8.

60 NAG, Accra, ADM 53/5/3. District Commissioner's Diary (Obuasi), entry for 5 September 1929.

61 *Ibid.*, entry for 11 September 1929.

62 NAG, Accra, ADM 5/1/23, *Annual Report for 1915*, p. 21.

63 Gold Coast, *Census Report* 1921, p. 56.

64 See Robertson, *Sharing the Same Bowl*, p. 36, Table II-I: Cost of Living Indices for Accra, 1901–78.

65 In a fleeting demonstration of elusive affluence, urban workers spent lavishly on drinks on pay day. See Cameron Duodu, *The Gab Boys* (Suffolk, 1967), p. 164.

66 See Roger Gocking, 'Competing systems of inheritance before the British courts of the Gold Coast', *International Journal of African Historical Studies*, 23, 4 (1990), pp. 601–18.

67 Roger Gocking, 'British justice and native tribunals of the southern Gold Coast Colony', *Journal of African History*, 34, 1 (1993), p. 106. See also, *idem*, 'Indirect rule in the Gold Coast: competition for office and the invention of tradition', *Canadian Journal of African Studies*, 28, 3 (1994), pp. 421–45.

68 NAG, Accra, Ga Native Tribunal Accession No. 67 (1920), Suit No. 214, Korkor Afiah vs Adjetey Niabo.

69 *Ibid.*

70 NAG, Accra, CSO 15/3/09, Rex vs Kwadwo Duodu.

71 NAG, Accra, CSO 15/3/03.

72 HMV, West Africa, JLK 1016.

73 Gramophone, JUP 126.

74 On male chauvinism in highlife songs in the post-colonial period, see Nimrod Asante-Darko and Sjaak van der Geest, 'Male chauvinism: men and women in Ghanaian highlife songs', in Christine Oppong (ed.), *Female and Male in West Africa* (London, 1983), pp. 242–55.

75 NAG, Kumasi, Item 1263, Annual Report on the Obuasi District, 1938–9.

76 See, for examples, NAG, Sekondi-Takoradi Tribunal Complaints, 45/40, No. 371.

77 NAG, Sekondi, Item No. 257, Hausa Settlement, 1927–49.

78 J. Benibengor Blay, *Be Content with your Lot* (Aboso, 1947), p. 9.

79 J. Benibengor Blay, *Love in a Clinic* (Aboso, 1957), p. 15. For a non-fictionalized account of tuberculosis in the capitalist political economy, see Randall M. Packard, *White Plague, Black Labor: Tuberculosis and the Political Economy of Health and Disease in South Africa* (Berkeley, 1989).

80 Skanophone, STK C001.

81 On developments in Sefwi Wiawso, see Roberts, 'The state and the regulation of marriage', pp. 61–7. For Asante, see J. N. Matson, *A Digest of the Minutes of the Ashanti Confederacy Council from 1935 to 1949 Inclusive and a Revised Edition of Warrington's Notes on Ashanti Custom* (Cape Coast, c. 1951), pp. 23–6; and Kwame Arhin, 'Monetization and the Asante state', in Guyer (ed.), *Money Matters*, pp. 97–110.

82 See Carmel Dinan, 'Sugar daddies and gold-diggers: the white-collar single women in Accra', in Oppong (ed.), *Female and Male in West Africa*, pp. 344–66.

PART FIVE

The Politics of Urban Order

14

Land Alienation
& the Urban Growth of Bahir Dar
1935–74

SELTENE SEYOUM

Despite the large body of literature on the history of Ethiopian urbanisation,[1] the question of land rights, land tenure and land alienation has remained a largely neglected aspect in the study of the growth and expansion of towns. This chapter examines the process of land alienation that has taken place with the expansion of one town in twentieth-century highland Ethiopia, modern Bahir Dar. The purpose is to indicate the central importance of land rights in determining the pattern of urban growth, and to demonstrate the points of conflict and ultimate incompatibilities which emerge between traditional rural ideas of landholding and modern urban notions of property in highland Ethiopia, exemplified in the struggle to maintain rights of communal access in the face of legal pressures in favour of recognizing private, individual rights of ownership in urban areas such as Bahir Dar.

Bahir Dar in the early twentieth century

Until very recently Bahir Dar was known as Bahir Dar Giyorgis, being built upon the site of a *gadam* (monastery). The foundation of the monastery has traditionally been attributed to the reign of one of the greatest of the Gondarine Kings, Iyassu I (r. 1682–1706).[2] As a monastic foundation, Bahir Dar Giyorgis gradually extended its supervision over a large portion of the farmlands of Abakabot that stretched from the southern end of the shore of Lake Tana in a south-western direction to Yibab Eyasus, bordering the Dibarnge hills to the north-west and the Qotatina hills to the south. Historically, therefore, Bahir Dar has been the religious and administrative centre of the district of Abakabot for the past three centuries, and is by no means simply a modern town. Because of this fact, before discussing the problem of land alienation in the making of the modern town of Bahir Dar, we must examine the socio-economic basis of the traditional landholding system as it functioned in Abakabot in the early part of the present century.

By the turn of the twentieth century, the area around Bahir Dar Giyorgis was characterized by the communal ownership of the land, the management of which was entrusted to the elders in society.[3] In practice, this meant that any person whose blood relationship to any landholding family could be confirmed by others, or whose maternal and/or paternal descent could be proved, was fully entitled to an equal share of land. Land was thereby heritable. For those who did own land, it was invariably the basis of what wealth they had. The communal ideals buttressing the land tenure system determined a wide set of social relationships, but not all people were landowners (*balabats*). Landowners might allocate lands for a variety of different purposes – for dwellings, gardening, farming or grazing. Land might also be rented out to tenants, some of whom were not indigenous to the area and who therefore had no kin claim to agricultural lands. Such groups often required lands for other commercial operations, most of which were conducted within the town.[4] Craftworkers, such as Muslim weavers, or tanners who prepared a variety of leather goods, or the Wayto who manufactured grindstones and reed boats (*tankwa*) for transportation and trade on the waters of Lake Tana and the Blue Nile, all worked on land they rented from local *balabats*. In return, these artisans provided economic services for the wider community. There was therefore a complex set of relationships between those who owned land and those who did not, the incomes of the local *balabats* depending in part upon the rents they accumulated from their tenants.

Along with rural production, trade brought wealth to Bahir Dar. Some *balabats* supplemented their income from agriculture and cattle breeding by short-distance trade on Lake Tana to Zage and Quorata, and by land to Adet and Faras Waga.[5] Others ran *tankwa* transportation along the exit of the Blue Nile, taking people, goods and pack animals from and to Begemidir and Gojjam.[6] Bahir Dar market was also frequented by long-distance caravan merchants who made use of the town as a crossroads of trade between south-western and northern Ethiopia until the close of the nineteenth century, and between northern and western Gojjam and northern Ethiopia from the dawn of the twentieth century. These merchants brought items such as salt bars, clothes and utensils for sale, and and bought locally produced honey, beeswax and other provisions. Even in the early years of the twentieth century, it is well remembered by local elders that Bahir Dar was a trading market and relay centre of the slave trade between *Aroge* Dangila in the west and Yifag in the north. At the Bahir Dar market the wives of many local *balabats* acted as *quina safari* (measurer), regulating the quantities of grain sold at the marketplace.[7] For this service they took a tax upon the grain sold through the market, and in turn they paid an annual market tax to the *gadam*. Less wealthy *balabats* were able to earn additional income from the *mashata* business around the marketplace, selling both *talla* (beer) and *araqe* (spirits), and providing lodgings for visiting merchants.[8] This business was chiefly run by poor female *balabats* or their tenants.

The monastery benefited from the commercial wealth of Bahir Dar through its administrative control of the town and the lands around it. The *gadam* was run by three officials: the *mamhir, liqarad* and *gabaz*.[9] The *mamhir* was the head of the *gadam* for administrative purposes, and he adjudicated all court cases (except murder cases), for which he collected fees. The *liqarad* and the *gabaz* assisted in the collection of *gibir* (tribute), paid by local *balabats* to the church, collected market fees, and heard some court cases affecting the Christian community. The main sources of church income were derived from the *balabat rist* land tilled by the *balabats*, and the *rim* land farmed by their tenants. For the lands they held the *balabats* paid a tithe (*asrat*), which went to the state, and a tax (*gibir*) which went to the church. Tenants on *rim* lands paid tax to the church (in kind or cash) only on specific items, such as wheat, dried grains and incense.

From this description it is clear that the economic prosperity of many *balabats* was based on commerce as well as production, and that many commercial activities were centred on the market in Bahir Dar. Both they and the church to whom they paid tribute saw no real distinction between urban and rural lands within the *gadam*. That was to change very dramatically in the wake of the Italian occupation of the 1930s.

Land Alienation in Bahir Dar under Italian Colonial Rule

The Italians and their army entered Bahir Dar from Gondar and Yifag in April 1936. They spent the summer in tents in open fields, and under the shade of trees in the midst of the monastery dwellings and the marketplace and town of Bahir Dar. By September, the rudiments of a colonial administration were in place, and amongst the first issues to be tackled was that of land alienation within Bahir Dar itself. The Italians had their own notion of how this administrative capital should be organized and set about redesigning the town in a very radical way. Local inhabitants were forced to abandon their dwelling places so that older buildings could be cleared for rebuilding.[10] Land was then reallocated for different purposes – administrative offices, army barracks, an airstrip and port facilities on the lake shore were all constructed, and new residential and commercial zones were marked out for development. This all required more land than had previously been occupied by the dwellings and commercial activities of the old town. To accommodate their needs, and to protect their new structures from summer floods, the Italians set about draining the swamp lands around Bahir Dar.

Communications links were also rapidly improved, giving Bahir Dar more secure connections with many of its traditional trading partners. A wooden bridge was erected that connected Begemidir and Gojjam. A new motor road was built that linked Bahir Dar with Bichana and Dajan by way of Adet and Mota. Another road connected Bahir Dar with Dabra Marqos and Dajan by way of Dangila, Injabara and Bure. Bahir Dar was also now connected with Gondar and Addis Ababa by air, and Italian motor boats plied over Lake Tana linking Bahir Dar with Zage, Quorata, Dalgi and Gorgora, replacing the traditonal *tankwa* as the means of moving goods across the lake.

The appearance of Bahir Dar was changed considerably by these developments. Spatially, the town had been reorganized dramatically without any acknowledgement of existing land use or the rights of the *balabat*s. In terms of architecture, the new modern buildings constructed by the Italians were made of stone blocks or wood, but with corrugated iron sheets used as roofing material in place of the traditional thatch. These physical changes were accompanied by the introduction of new social elements that profoundly affected the life of the town and its wider region. A large garrison of Italian troops was based at Bahir Dar and many other new residents were now brought into the town, some involved in construction and others servicing the needs of the Italian administration. These included foreigners as well as persons from other parts of Ethiopia. These newcomers transformed the commercial face of the town. For example, with the encouragement of the Italians, Arabs, Somalis and Sudanese came to open tea rooms, tailoring shops and general stores.[11] Bars opened for business to serve the many Europeans now based in the town, and these were run by the Italians themselves. The growth of the town generated employment for artisans, clerks and labourers, and these opportunities brought a wider cross-section of Ethiopian society into Bahir Dar, many of them attracted by the more liberal and cosmopolitan atmosphere of colonial urban life. Among these were larger numbers of Muslims and Wayto than had been seen in Bahir Dar before, along with significant numbers of freed slaves. With so strong a military and administrative presence in the town, women from the surrounding areas of Gojjam and Begemidir were drawn to Bahir Dar to set up bars and lodging houses, and prostitution became a highly visible element of the town's social life.

All of these changes – physical, economic and social – directly affected the manner in which the lands of the *gadam* of Bahir Dar were deployed and exploited. The pattern of landowning evident in the early twentieth century was soon submerged under a new, colonial order. To strengthen their control over the town and its environs, the Italians instituted a new urban administration, which replaced the traditional authority of church and state. The town administration, the *Residenzia*, was granted full legal rights to raise revenues through the taxation of the locality of Bahir Dar and its market. In effect, this meant that all Bahir Dar's urban *balabats* now paid tax to the Italian colonial state, and not to the church. At the same time, these *balabats* were prevented from collecting their own taxes from their urban tenants, who were now made to pay directly to the Italian administration instead. The urban area of Bahir Dar had thereby been effectively removed from the *gadam*, and the major portion of the revenues that had been derived by the *balabats* and the church through collection of *gibir*, market fees and other forms of income linked to urban lands were now denied them. Commercial income deriving from trading activities was also largely diverted to the Italians, who now dominated trade across Lake Tana. Even the meagre income earned by those *balabats* who ran the *tankwa* services across the river came to an end with the construction of the bridge. To enforce its new regulatory powers upon the population, the new urban administration set up its own police force, named the *zabtya*.[12] The wholesale alienation of urban lands in Bahir Dar was made complete by unilateral seizure and redistribution of plots within the designated urban area to new residential and commercial owners. In this process traditional rights were overlooked, and a class a private landholding urban residents was created. The divide between the urban and the rural was now very apparent, and those many *balabats* who had come to depend upon incomes deriving from their urban lands found they had lost a substantial portion of their wealth.

The draconian measures imposed by the Italian administration threw up many complications and contradictions for the people of Bahir Dar, as we will now go on to discuss, but in the circumstances of colonial conquest in the 1930s there was no process of appeal through which local landowners could seek redress. Unable to resist the impositions of the colonial power, many of the *balabats* retreated and constructed huts for themselves outside the town boundaries, beyond the big ditches dug by the Italians to drain the swamplands. Other *balabats* were undoubtedly provoked by these injustices to join those in the forests carrying forward the patriotic struggle against Fascist rule.[13]

Post-colonial Struggles for Urban Ascendancy

The complexity of the innovations made under Italian rule began to unravel soon after their defeat in north-east Africa upon the outbreak of the Second World War. Although they had only ruled Ethiopia for five years, in Bahir Dar the Italians left behind them a bitter struggle between two set of claimants for rights to urban land in the new, enlarged town – the *balabats*, who wished to re-establish their alienated rights, and the new settlers who had been given lands within Bahir Dar under colonial rule and now wished to retain those properties. With the Italian evacuation, local *balabats* were quick to seize the many municipal colonial buildings, occupying the modern houses, shops and office buildings and claiming these as their own. This added a further element to the conflict over claims to urban property that developed in Bahir Dar from the 1940s.

But, far from simply reversing the impositions of the Italian administration, after liberation the Ethiopian government took a number of steps that gradually worked to strengthen the process of urbanization in the town of Bahir Dar that had begun under the Italians. In 1941, a temporary Ethiopian administration was set up to govern the town. One year later, in 1942, a Finance Office (*gimja bet*) was established to be responsible for the collection of *asrat* and *gibir*, both of which now had to be paid in cash, and to oversee the administration of 'enemy property'. This was the first indication that Bahir Dar's *balabats* were not to be free simply to claim what they thought to be theirs. In 1943, Bahir Dar was declared a sub-district capital (*warada*), thus maintaining the administrative separation of rural and urban that colonialism had introduced, and in 1945 the town of Bahir Dar was formally raised to the status of a municipality.[14] The head of this administrative structure was the Town Chief (*shum*), who was also the chief secretary of the office of the *warada gizat*. In sum, these reforms did not restore the old order, but instead imposed an Ethiopian version of municipal government not so dissimilar in structure or function to that devised by the Italians.

These measures, however, did not proceed entirely smoothly. In parallel with the setting up of an Ethiopian municipal administration for Bahir Dar, the government reestablished the authority of the *gadam* leadership of Bahir Dar Giyorgis, entitling it to *gibir* collection over the wider region of Abakabot.[15] Like the municipal administration, this parallel administration for the wider *gadam* was based in Bahir Dar. Under these arrangements, the *balabats* paid taxes over their *rist* lands to the *gadam* in the same amounts as they had done before the Italian occupation. But the Bahir Dar Finance Office (*gimja bet*) still collected *asrat*, *qibir* and other forms of tax on urban properties. In theory, the *gibir* taxes collected in the town were supposed to be handed over to the *gadam*. The overlapping nature of these authorities left much room for confusion.

More controversially, the Finance Office of Bahir Dar also claimed *all* Italian constructed buildings as 'enemy property', making these the property of the Ethiopian government to dispose of as it wished, and denying the legitimacy of claims made by the *balabats* to the restoration of rights in those buildings or the lands upon which they were constructed. To enforce this, the Finance Office sought to impose eviction orders upon *balabats* who had seized and occupied 'enemy property'. Many *balabats* refused to comply with the eviction orders, arguing that they had unalienable rights to the lands upon which the buildings were constructed. The operations of the Finance Office were thus quickly and widely resisted within Bahir Dar as the *balabats* sought the means to assert their rights.

The position of the *balabats* did not appear strong. With the creation of the municipality of Bahir Dar, the Ethiopian government had recognized, in effect, the alienation of lands by the Italian administration in the setting up of the *Rezidenzia* of Bahir Dar.[16] Despite strong resistance from the *balabats*, the government also confirmed the new settlers' rights of landownership over their residential and commercial houses, charging them urban land taxes.[17] This confirmed that, within the municipality, the *rist* of the *balabats* and the *rim* land of the *gadam* would remain separated, but that neither would accrue benefits to the *balabats*; the former would henceforth be claimed by the municipality, and the latter would remain within the administrative sphere of the *gadam*. The *balabats* opposed all the claims of the municipality, and instead asserted their historical right to pay *asrat* directly to the state and *gibir* to the church. Both these legal obligations had been removed in the urban area of Bahir Dar, with the Finance Office taking over the principal tax-rasing powers (*asrat*) within the town. The arguments raised by the *balabats* against these arrangements were framed fundamentally by their own loss of income through the alienation of their lands. For them, the creation of the municipality under the Ethiopian government had confirmed the legality of colonial impositions. In the process, their ancestral lands had been forfeited.[18]

The resistance of the *balabats* was in large part echoed by the church authorities, whose economic position had also been undermined seriously by the creation of a municipal government. The *gadam* had a claim to *gibir* from *rist* lands, and to other types of tax upon *rim* lands, but many of these lands had now been declared urban lands under municipality control.[19] The clergy therefore joined the *balabats* in their conflict with the municipality, the *warada* administration and the new settlers in the town of Bahir Dar. In particular, church leaders demanded the right of the *gadam* to collect *gibir* and other payments from the urban land under municipality administration. They also demanded a reinstatement of their authority to collect court fees from the area within the municipality, and to take their traditional dues from the operation of the market. In an effort to placate the clerics, the municipality introduced a special annual local tax of one *birr*, payable by all urban residents, which was to be given to the church.[20] In addition to this, the right of the church to take fees for baptisms and funerals conducted within the municipality was confirmed. This hardly met the main demands of the church, whose authority within the town had been greatly reduced.

Despite widespread opposition from the *balabats* and the clergy, the process of urbanization continued in Bahir Dar during the 1950s and early 1960s. Over these years, sporadic struggles emerged as new urban development plans threatened the use or ownership of further lands within the town boundaries. At one time, around 1950, Bahir Dar was amongst the towns under consideration to be the new Ethiopian administrative capital,[21] and this generated a minor flurry in the local land market, with a flood of over-eager potential buyers and consequent vast inflation in local land values. In 1956, Bahir Dar was again raised in status, this time being made a district (*awraja*) capital, with *Shambal* Aemiro Silase Ababa appointed as governor. Aemiro embarked upon a further reorganiza-tion of the town, laying out many more streets and constructing new district administra-tive offices, including a courthouse, police station and prison. Along the new streets in the business area were a range of new shops, restaurants and hotels – the latter the first to be built in competition with the Italian-constructed Ghion Hotel. In this process of urban growth, many more plots were distributed to newcomers, further weakening the position of local *balabats* within the municipality. In response, the *balabats* mounted a strong campaign against Aemiro, demanding compensation for the lands he had allocated to these developments. Among the most prominent leaders of this resistance was Dajazmach Baqala Lamu, a *balabat* and himself a former *warada* governor at Bahir Dar. So vehement did the political contest between the two become that Aemiro eventually had Bagala banished to Addis Ababa to live there in exile.[22] Opposition to the operations of the municipal government persisted despite the attempts of Aemiro to suppress it. Bagala and others, including the influential priest *Qesa gabaz* Tibabu Hailu,[23] now focused upon the rights of the *balabats* to sell off urban lands in Bahir Dar as their own personal property.[24] This stood in contradiction to their earlier assertion that the municipal government had no right to allow urban land to be sold to outsiders, but they now sought to secure the right of sale of urban lands in order at least to gain some immediate economic advantage.

For their part, the municipal administration held to the view that only through their legal authority could any sale of urban land proceed, thereby expunging all rights that may have existed prior to the creation of the municipal authority.[25] To close down a further avenue of complaint from the *balabats* and the clergy, it was announced that compensation would not be paid against any prior existing rights, and that only those whose property was destroyed as a result of town planning developments undertaken by the municipality could be compensated. Accordingly, *balabats* were informed that they could apply to be assigned plots of urban land like any other ordinary citizen, and that plots might also be provided for their children. Recognizing that this would effectively remove their strong claim to the heritability of their lands under local customary practice, the *balabats* strongly resisted this suggestion; most saw no reason why they should pay for titles to lands they already owned.[26] Faced by opposition, the municipality tended to avoid interference in those communities where resistance was known to be strongest, to some extent slowing up the process of urbanization.

But the delicate circumstances of local politics were to be overwhelmed in the mid-1950s by the determination of the Ethiopian government to impose its economic development plans upon the wider region of Lake Tana and the Blue Nile. Having selected this region as a principal area for economic growth – and perhaps still nurturing the notion that the town might become the national capital – the government made development of Bahir Dar a priority. This policy explains the dramatic growth of the town from the mid-1950s. A master plan for the town, with projected expansion encompassing both banks of the Blue Nile, was prepared. This drew a much greater expanse of rural land into the municipality, including all the remaining land of Abakabot under Bahir Dar Giyorgis (11 *gashas*), and additionally from Gojjam the lands of Shimbit Mikael (4 *gashas*), Waramit Gabriel (6.75 *gashas*), Dishat Giyorgis (3.5 *gashas*) and Gordama Qusquam (3 *gashas*), as well as a large area from Begemidir.[27] The 28.5 *gashas* now added in the master plan from the Gojjam side alone more than doubled the urban land declared under the jurisdiction of the municipality of Bahir Dar.

As the first elements of the master plan began to be implemented, a wide range of conflicts with local landowners surfaced. The construction of new textile mills, the Polytechnic Institute and the modern hospital went ahead with little protest, as these buildings occupied land to which there were fewer and less vocal claimants. Along the peripheral areas of Bahir Dar some *balabat*s opposed the erection of the larger bridge along the Blue Nile, linking Gojjam with Begemidir, but those who owned the boats that worked the river crossing were promised employment on the bridge and the protest subsided. At Shimbit Mikael and Zanzalima, to the east of the Blue Nile, the local *balabat*s were more determined in their opposition to urban development. But here, and especially in the centre of Bahir Dar town, there was a rush to capitalize upon the economic opportunities presented by rising land values as the expansion project went ahead. A great many people, including the royal family, high government officials, leading merchants and rich traders at one end of the social spectrum, and ordinary office and factory workers at the other, rushed to gain access to as much of the best land as possible. The rush to acquire individual title to urban lands was most apparent in the centre of Bahir Dar itself, in Shimbit and in Shumabo. In this process no one any longer sought to buy land or to gain access to it through the authority of the *balabats*: All realized that legal title could only be granted through the municipal administration.

Given the serious threat these plans posed to the authority of the church, the *balabats* and *gadam* officials formed a strong alliance in opposition to the master plan, adopting a wide variety of tactics, ranging from attempts to harass and intimidate new settlers to peaceful petitions to the *awraja* administration and the municipality.[28] These actions had no apparent impact upon official thinking, but they were widespread and disruptive enough for the state to become concerned about the danger of the urban *balabats* and clerics stirring up rural discontent.[29] Whether it was the persistence of opposition, or the sheer administrative burden of imposing so large and far-reaching an urban development plan, by the early 1960s the state was ready to concede that the master plan could go no further without winning greater support from the *balabats* and the *gadam*. A survey of all the property occupied by *rist* holders within the area of greater Bahir Dar had been conducted in 1956, although many landowners were too suspicious of the government's intentions to cooperate fully with the investigation. Based upon the survey, a valuation was made of what compensation would be due for lands to be alienated in order to implement the master plan: money due to the *balabats* on the Gojjam side alone was estimated to stand at some *birr* 640,000.[30] Although this survey may indicate that consideration was being given, in principle at least, to the payment of compensation to the *balabats*, no settlement was made at this time.[31]

As the political difficulties in the town continually slowed its economic development, the government attempted to broker a solution with the church. In 1964, at the instigation of the government, the Bishop of Gojjam, *Abuna* Marqos, came to Bahir Dar to try to settle the problem of the *gadam*'s relations with the *awraja* administration and the municipality.[32] The bishop convinced the clergy of Bahir Dar Giyorgis not to oppose government plans overtly, in return for which he would negotiate for the *gadam* to be granted title to as large an area of urban land as possible within Bahir Dar. He then persuaded the *awraja* administration to implement this proposal, and the decision was speedily taken to assign plots in various commercial zones of the town to the *gadam*. The beautiful church of *Qidus* Giyorgis was soon erected on one of these plots, and at its inauguration a further political gesture was made, restoring yet more economic wealth to the *gadam*. At the request of the bishop, Emperor Haile Selassie attended the inauguration of *Qidus* Giyorgis, and as a gesture of goodwill he ordered the Bahir Dar Finance Office to pay a monthly fee of *birr* 335 to the *gadam*, ostensibly to cover the salaries of those who gave service to the new church.[33] From this point forward, relations between the municipality and the church steadily improved, with the town authorities being careful to support the church by making lump-sum donations at the large church ceremonies of Christmas and Easter.[34] Thereafter, aside from minor complaints coming through the local *atibya dagna* and *safar shum* community chiefs of the town, there was no significant church opposition to urban development in Bahir Dar.[35]

Though the support of the church had been won, the *balabats* continued to oppose the use of their *rist* lands without compensation, and in this they were sometimes still supported by individual members of the clergy. For instance, in 1964 *Qesa Gabaz* Tibabu Hailu, from Bahir Dar, and Abaja Abata from Dara (near Zanzalima) were accused of instigating the *balabats* on both sides of the Blue Nile to resist any distribution of their lands to new individuals.[36] Considering them opponents of the government development plan of the town of Bahir Dar, the *awraja* administration had the *Qesa Gabaz* and Abaja arrested and imprisoned. Both were later released, but only after they had admitted the charges against them and asked for a pardon. Their humiliation was followed by a demonstration by a large crowd of people who secretly waited in a forest along the southern suburbs of Bahir Dar and stopped the Emperor on his way to visit the Tis Esat Falls.[37] But when the Emperor learned that this was a resistance mob, organized and led by men such ás Shimalash Baqala (the son of the *dajazmach* who had been banished to Addis Ababa in 1956), determined to oppose the government's efforts to urbanize the area, he is said to have refused to listen to their petition, and the angry and frustrated crowd had to disperse.

But with the redevelopment of lands on the Gojjam side imminent by 1965, the government was keen to make a settlement with the urban landowners and arrangements were made to create a remuneration fund so that compensation could be paid to those displaced. At this juncture, divisions within the ranks of the *balabats* became apparent that were to seriously undermine their cause. The most enlightened *balabats*, led by the family of *Dajazmach* Baqala and supported by locally influential men such as *Qesa Gabaz* Tibabu Hailu and Beza Dasta, approached the Addis Ababa government claiming to represent the interests of all the Bahir Dar claimants. Tibabu Hailu and Beza Dasta were put forward as their emissaries, proposing that the monies to be allocated in compensation should be administered through an office they would oversee.[38] Other landowners, who were either not privy to this proposal or opposed it, became suspicious of the intentions of these individuals: were Baqala, Tibabu and others really acting in the best interests of all, or was this a ploy to secure the lion's share of the remuneration fund for themselves and their supporters? As factionalism reared its head, doubt was cast upon the representations made to the Addis Ababa government. As a consequence of the uncertainty, the government sent the *Qesa Gabaz* and Beza back to Bahir Dar, accompanied by a government inspector who was instructed to conduct a hearing to confirm the true position of the claimants.[39] With their arrival it was rumoured that money for compensation for *balabat rist* lands had come, and as a result a large crowd from the surrounding regions of Begemichir and Gojjam gathered in Bahir Dar to await developments. At the same time, many *balabats*, fearing that their interests might not be represented fairly in the hearing to follow, petitioned the government inspector to denounce the *Qesa Gabaz* and Beza and to state their own claims. When the court sat to hear the claims of the *balabats* of Bahir Dar, the conflicts deepened: it quickly became clear that these leading *balabats* of Bahir Dar had no idea of how the representations to Addis Ababa had come to be made. Furthermore, and far more damaging to their cause, the *Qesa Gabaz* and other applicants, such as *Liqarda* Abaja Mashasha, *Marigeta* Tamirat Jamara,[40] *Qesa Gabaz* Endalamaw Bitaw and Abarash Afawarq, denied each other's claims over the land and fell to disputing the legitimate rights of each family.[41] The *Qesa Gabaz* and the Baqala family, who had taken the lead in the campaign to secure remuneration, were deeply embarrassed by these disputes among the *rist*-holding *balabats*. The huge crowd who had gathered to participate in the hearing dispersed in disgust when it became clear that no remuneration would be given out until the conflicts could be resolved satisfactorily.

Division among the *balabats*, of course, was rooted in the ambilineal character of descent and the inevitable complexity this generated in the comprehension and adjudication of heritable rights in land. Whilst it was easy to rally people to the banner to defend the general rights of traditional landowners, the precise nature of their individual claims were a matter of detailed and protracted negotiation and less easily agreed. As soon as it was apparent that compensation would be distributed, these claims and counterclaims surfaced to swamp the previous unity of the campaign for remuneration. Seeing no easy solution, the Emperor ordered that the money assigned for compensation payments be taken out of the Finance Office coffers and placed on account in a bank, effectively freezing the remuneration fund so that no payments would be made. To ensure that the urbanization and development of the town would continue without legal hindrance, the Emperor declared all Bahir Dar to be government land.[42] In these circumstances, the government retreated to its earlier position and announced that compensation would only be given for property actually destroyed as a result of the implementation of the master plan: no remuneration would be paid in regard to the loss of use of the *rist* lands. The muncipality now brought pressure to bear on the *balabats* by formally assigning their residential and farming areas as designated for the development of administrative, commercial and recreational zones. With their lands assigned for redevelopment, and facing eviction with no compensation available, many of the *balabats* now rushed to apply for urban plots from the municipal administration, fearing that they would otherwise be denied all access to lands within Bahir Dar. Many others abandoned their shrinking *rist* lands within Bahir Dar, and went once again to settle beyond the ditches where they had lived during the five years of the Italian occupation. Ultimately, the old landowners of Bahir Dar had been forced to accept the terms of the new urban order, or to leave their traditional lands.

Conclusion

In 1967, the *balabats* of Bahir Dar made a final attempt to gain compensation from the government's remuneration fund, making a direct appeal to the Emperor during his visit to the Bazait Palace at Bahir Dar.[43] Although they were able to present a united front on this occasion, their demands were again rejected. By then, the political struggle over the growth of Bahir Dar had moved from the local to the provincial stage. The expansion of the town was now an undeniable fact, and development was moving ahead apace. A political quarrel now arose between the Gojjam and Begemidir provinces over who should control the growing town – and who should thereby gain access to its resources and wealth. The Begemidir district of Dara had been absorbed into the town with the implementation' of the master plan, and officials of Begemichir province now demanded that the administration of this part of the developing town should be restored to them.[44] This dispute was concluded in 1972, with the announcement by the central government that benefits of Bahir Dar's industrial growth would be used for the development of both provinces.

The urban development of Bahir Dar played a significant role in undermining the power of the traditional *rist*-owning *balabats*, whose lineage-based pattern of land inheritance gave way to individual, private ownership of land in the town. This process was only achieved by direct government action, first through colonial conquest, and then through the decrees of a modernizing state. The outcome was thus a triumph for new, 'modern' notions of the utilization of urban land over more traditional attitudes to land use. But, there was little local support for this transformation, and from the 1940s to the 1960s the politics of Bahir Dar's growth and development was marked by conflict and tension. The central government, working through its local agencies, the *awraja* administration and the municipality, implemented its own vision of development, but did so without respecting the rights of local landowners. The successful growth of Bahir Dar was achieved not through the support of the local *balabats*, but in spite of their opposition.

Notes

1 For the historical depth of the topic, see Jean Doresse, *Ethiopia, Ancient Cities and Temples* (London, 1969), pp. 21, 51; Sergew Hable Selassie, *Ancient and Medieval Ethiopian History to 1270* (Addis Ababa, 1972), pp. 59–60; Taddesse Tamrat, *Chruch and State in Ethiopia, 1270–1527* (Oxford, 1972), pp. 7–13; and Yuri M. Kobischanov, *Axum* (University Park and London, 1979), pp. 10–11, 184.

2 Hailemariam Fantahun (*Mamhir*), 56 years old, interviewed Bahir Dar, 28 August 1986; Endalamaw Bitaw (*Qesa Gabaz*), 67 years old, interviewed Bahir Dar, 28 August 1986; Tibabu Hailu (*Qesa Gabaz*), 71 years old, interviewed Bahir Dar, 15 June 1984; Tamir Shifaraw (*Ato*), 69 years old, interviewed Bahir Dar, 10 June 1984; and Tenaw Birasaw (*Balambaras*), 81 years old, interviewed Bahir Dar, 12 November 1984. Interviews with the older residents of Bahir Dar form the principal source for this chapter.

3 Endalamaw Bitaw, Tamir Shifaraw and Tibabu Hailu. For a general picture of landownership in central Ethiopia and the social relationships related to it, see Allan Hoben, 'The role of the ambilineal descent groups in Gojjam Amhara social organisation', (PhD dissertation, University of California at Berkeley, 1963), pp. 103–12, 140–3; *idem, Land Tenure Among the Amhara of Ethiopia: the Dynamics of Cognatic Descent* (Chicago, 1973), pp. 144–59. See also James C. McCann, *From Poverty to Famine in Northeast Ethiopia: A Rural History, 1900–1935* (Philadelphia, 1987).

4 Abarash Afawarq (*Waizaro*), 66 years old, interviewed Bahir Dar, 21 August 1986; Endalamaw Bitaw; Tibabu Hailu. Tekle-Haimanot Gebre-Selassie, 'The Wayto of Lake Tana: an ethno-history' (MA dissertation, Addis Ababa University, 1984), pp. 37–8, 40. Tekle-Haimanot particularly stresses the socio-economic roles the Wayto have been playing in the locality.

5 Abarash Afawarq; Endalamaw Bitaw; Tamir Shifaraw; and Tibabu Hailu.

6 *Ibid.* Also, Tenaw Birasaw; Gabrakidan Yigzaw (*Mamhir*) 68 years old, interviewed Bahir Dar, 31 August 1986. See Arthur J. Hayes, *The Source of the Blue Nile* (London, 1905), p. 140.

7 *Madiga* and *Quina* were units of grain measurement made of earth and grass respectively. Their equivalence to modern standardized units is not clear. Kabbada Tasama says *madiga* in Gojjam is equivalent to five *quinas* in Shawa, and Bahru Zewde states *quina* is equivalent to about five litres. For further information read Kabbada Tasama, *Ya Tarik Mastawasha* (Addis Ababa, 1962 EC), p. 293 and Bahru Zewde, 'Economic origins of the absolutist state in Ethiopia (1916– 1935)', *Proceedings of*

the Second Annual Seminar of the Department of History, Addis Ababa University, (Addis Ababa: 1984), Vol. 1, p. 18.
8 *Mashata* is an institution in which women earn their living by selling alcohol.
9 Abarash Afawarq; Endalamaw Bitaw; Hailemariam Fantahun; Tibabu Hailu; and Tamir Shifaraw.
10 Hussen Eshate (*Grazmatch*), 83 years old, interviewed Bahir Dar, 19 September 1986; Tamir Shifaraw; Tenaw Birasaw; Abrash Afawarq; Endalamaw Bitaw; and Tibabu Hailu.
11 *Ibid.*
12 Hussen Eshate; Endalamaw Bitaw; Tamir Shifaraw; and Tenaw Birasaw.
13 Abarash Afawarq; Endalamaw Bitaw; Tamir Shifaraw; Tenaw Birasaw; and Balata Kassa (*ligarad*) about 80 years old, interviewed Bahir Dar, 26 August 1986.
14 *Nagarit Gazetta*, Year 4 Proclamation No 74, Magabit 21, 1937, EC.
15 Tamir Shifaraw, who has been a financial clerk in the office of the *gimja bet* at Bahir Dar since 1941, has a good knowledge of the events.
16 Tamir Shifaraw; Tenaw Bisaraw; and Tibabu Hailu.
17 *Ibid.*; Abarash Afawarq; and Endalamaw Bitaw.
18 *Ibid.*
19 Tamir Shifaraw; and Tibabu Hailu.
20 *Ibid.*; and Tenaw Birasaw.
21 Ayalew Mangasha to Gojjam *Taqlay Gizat* office, Ginbot 27, 1945 E.C.; Seymour Harris, 'Preliminary Survey Report upon Proposed Development of the Town of Shashamana', (unpublished report, Birmingham, 1954), pp. 1–6; Mulugeta Sina Giorgis to *Balambaras* Mahatama Silase, *Ginbot* 12, 1956 EC.
22 Tamir Shifaraw; Endalamaw Bitaw; and Tibabu Hailu.
23 *Qesa Gabez* is a title given to a priest when he becomes a *gabaz* (a person in charge of the internal affairs of a church).
24 Endalamaw Bitaw; Tamir Shifaraw; and Tibabu Hailu.
25 Tamir Shifaraw; and Tibabu Hailu.
26 Tamir Shifaraw; and Gabayahu Fante (*Ato*) 69 years old, interviewed Bahir Dar, 28 August 1986.
27 A *gasha* is a unit of land measurement or an area of land equivalent to 40 hectares. For the expansion of town boundaries and its inclusion of the various areas mentioned, see '*Awraja Gizat Gimjabet Gibir* List' (manscript in the possession of Tamir Shifaraw, Bahir Dar, no date).
28 Tamir Shifaraw; and Tibabu Hailu.
29 The people of the districts of Ganj and Dara were noted for their opposition: Gabayahu Fante; and Tamir Shifaraw.
30 *Fitawrari* Habtamariam Waldakidan, 'Ya Bahir Dar Mazagaja Bet Amatawi Report 1956 EC' (typescript, in Amharic, in the possession of the author).
31 Tamir Shifaraw, Bagala Zalalaw to Molla Mashasha, *Magabit* 1954 EC; Dammalash Balay to Bahir Dar *Awraja*, *Maskaram* 2, 1955 EC.
32 Abba Marqos to Habtemariam Waldakidan No 200/56 *Yekatit* 16, 1956 EC; Habtemariam Waldakidan to *Abuna* Marqos, No 2/1077/1863/1 *Yekatit* 18, 1956 EC.
33 Tamir Shifaraw; Tibabu Hailu; and Endalamaw Bitaww.
34 *Ibid.*, Habtemariam Waldakidan to Finance Section of the Municipality of Bahir Dar No.2/4038/10 *Nehase* 24, 1957 EC.
35 *Mamhir* Hailemariam Fantahun to Bahir Dar *Awraja Gizat* office, *Hamle* 8, 1963 EC. *Atibya dagna* and *safar shum* are types of community chief.
36 Abarash Afawarq; Endalamaw Bitaw; Gabayahu Fante; Tamir Shifaraw; and Tibabu Hailu.
37. Endalamw Bitaw, Tamir Shifaraw and Tibabu Hailu.
38 *Ibid.*; Abarash Afawarq; and Gabrakidan Yigzaw.
39 Tamir Shifaraw; and Gabrakidan Yigzaw.
40 *Ligarad* and *Marigeta* are clerical titles.
41 Abarash Afawarq; Endalamaw Bitaw; and Tibabu Hailu.
42 Tamir Shifaraw; and Tibabu Hailu.
43 *Ibid.*; Endalamaw Bitaw.
44 For the reluctance of the Gondar officials to participate in the economic and administrative plans of Bahir Dar, see minutes of *Tigimt* 19, 1962 EC from the Ministry of the Interior.

15

Conservation & the Colonial Past
Urban Planning, Space & Power
in Zanzibar

WILLIAM CUNNINGHAM BISSELL

Originally shaped by colonialism, the urban order on Zanzibar was overturned by the revolution of 1964 and currently is the focus of conservation efforts under a recently adopted policy of privatization and liberalization. Urban conservation,[1] considered both as architectural practice and social programme, invokes a conundrum. On one hand it seems focused exclusively on the past, oriented toward restoring that which was; yet, on the other hand, conservation's construction of the past is located very much in the present and seizes upon history as a means of building a social future. This temporal ambiguity becomes much more pressing when the past being 'restored' is specifically colonial in nature. How is it possible to create a post-colonial future out of the colonial past?

This chapter explores the history of urban planning in Zanzibar city in order to rethink the relation between colonialism, space and power. Many recent analysts of colonial cities have devoted attention to spatial strategies and planning efforts as tools of colonial domination. Yet Zanzibar's history of urban planning confronts us with domination in another mode and a form of colonialism that can best be described as chaotic. Colonial designs on the city, rather than successfully reworking space, repeatedly failed to rationalize and order the urban milieu. As a process, however, planning served to inculcate subjects into a highly arbitrary colonial legal and bureaucratic order that, paradoxically, was all the more dominating precisely because of its irregular and capricious nature. This suggests we need to reconceptualize our understanding of both the 'failure' and 'success' of colonial urban planning, a task all the more urgent in Zanzibar, where ironically recent efforts to restore the city have involved reinstating the colonial legal context that shaped the city as a zone of inequality in the first place.

The Context of Current Conservation

On Zanzibar, the colonial regime sought to create a dual city, split between a centre (Stone Town) of imposing stone edifices occupied by the elite – mainly Arabs, Indians and Europeans – and a periphery (Ng'ambo) where poorer Africans were relegated to live in mud huts without municipal services. While this programme was contested, it had

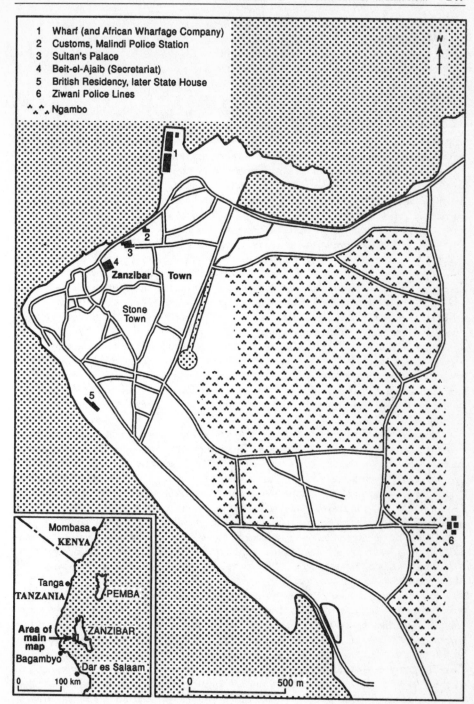

1 Wharf (and African Wharfage Company)
2 Customs, Malindi Police Station
3 Sultan's Palace
4 Beit-el-Ajaib (Secretariat)
5 British Residency, later State House
6 Ziwani Police Lines
^.^.^. Ngambo

Figure 15.1 Zanzibar Town in the late colonial period

a crucial impact on both spatial form and social relations. Given the city's centrality to the colonial project, it is no surprise that the revolution of 1964 seized upon it, seeking to overthrow the colonial order, associated as much with the pre-eminence of Arabs and Indians in the urban sphere as with European rule. Many dwellings were confiscated while others were abandoned as the elite fled abroad; the government converted these properties into multi-family dwelling units, moving poorer, rural Africans into the city centre. All land was nationalized while landmark structures (for example, the Sultan's Palace, the Beit el Ajaib) were changed into government offices or social centres. The urban revolution was capped by the progressive banning of private enterprise, as the state took over all business activity in the once booming commercial sector.

The urban achievements of the revolution were overtaken by the regime's inability to provide an economic base for its redistributive policies. By the early 1980s, *ujamaa* socialism was widely seen as a failure, blamed for chronic shortages, economic and social stagnation, and a precipitous urban decline. The historic core was in a parlous state, with most buildings showing signs of rapid decay and an average of 15 structures collapsing each year. Seeking to reverse this situation, the government has since pursued a vigorous policy of economic and political liberalization, relying on external investors and returning exiles from the Gulf States to produce a startling upsurge in tourism, development and commercial activity. Influenced by two urban master plans (1982, 1992–3) and a UN-sponsored conservation programme, much of this activity has centred on Stone Town. Over the last decade a boom in building and restoration has occurred throughout the city. As property values have soared well beyond the reach of most Zanzibaris, many have been forced to relocate outside the city. Public buildings have been privatized and converted into tourist facilities.[2] Over 30 large mansions have been converted into hotels, while wealthy exiles have bought out many poorer residents of confiscated houses and transformed them into luxury homes. This displacement of the poor has been accompanied by steep inflation, public sector decline and a rise in corruption.

Conservation efforts took off in the wake of a 1983 UN Habitat report on Stone Town that recommended an integrated programme of economic liberalization and enhanced tourism as the means of funding the rehabilitation of the city.[3] Since 1985 a newly created agency, the Stone Town Conservation and Development Authority (STCDA), has assumed overall responsibility for carrying out conservation policies, despite the fact that initially it was established by summary decree in contravention of established legislative procedure. The uncertain standing of its legal authority was complicated by bureaucratic conflict arising from overlapping spheres of jurisdiction with other institutional bodies that administer municipal affairs. As a result, considerable time and energy has been devoted since 1990 to overhauling the entire legal framework and administrative context of the city.

These efforts in bureaucratic rationalization have been doubly ironic. First, the legal reform entailed by conservation has largely involved restoration of precisely those colonial laws that shaped the city as a zone of inequality in the first place: the Towns Decree of 1929 and the Town and Country Planning Act of 1955.[4] Second, the process by which the legal framework was rewritten uncannily mirrored the very colonial planning practices that doomed earlier master plans to failure: developed by expatriate technical experts, these efforts were founded on a top-down, hierarchically controlled and state-centred strategy that emphasized formal legal instruments and planning mechanisms without due regard for the means of implementation or availability of financing. As the history of urban planning and law on Zanzibar shows, this conservation of the (legal) past is unlikely to restore the city to its 'former glory': indeed, it seems more likely that conservation instead will collapse under the weight of its unexamined contradictions.

Since the revolution a particular understanding of the colonial city on Zanzibar has become prominent in scholarly accounts.[5] This description relies upon a certain dualistic understanding of the structure (both social and spatial) of the colonial city. On one side is Stone Town, populated by the elite (Arab, Indian and European), consisting of substantial and enduring structures, the commercial and cultural centre of the islands; on the other side is Ng'ambo, the 'periphery' where predominantly Africans lived, ex-slaves and the working class, in a 'planless warren' of single-storey, non-permanent mud and wattle huts.[6] This portrait has the character of a classic stereotype: at the grossest level it carries some truth, but deeper scrutiny reveals the way in which it masks and distorts a more nuanced and complex reality. More than an apt description of the colonial city, this depiction arose historically as an expression of the ideology of the elite as to the ideal form of the city, the way things should be (but never quite were) ordered. While the colonial state sought over many years to create precisely such an orderly and rationalized urban sphere, its efforts hardly met with the kind of totalizing success implied by the portrait above. For instance, until very late in the colonial period, huts coexisted with stone dwellings in the Stone Town, despite determined efforts to clear them out; most Arabs and Indians in the town were not part of the elite, and indeed lived in conditions similar to those of their African brethren. Many of the largest structures in the Stone Town were actually *gurfas* or *chawls*, large tenement houses where poor Indians lived in very tight and ill-maintained quarters. Furthermore, stone houses existed in Ng'ambo, and in fact during the colonial period it was not easy to differentiate various housing types clearly. Colonial urban planning was a far more ambiguous and complicated phenomenon than is currently imagined.

Colonialism, Space and Power

A considerable literature on colonial urbanism has been created over the past two decades. At the most general level, interest in colonial spatiality has been provoked by the work of Henri Lefebvre on the production of space and Michel Foucault's reconceptualizations of power.[7] Many of the most recent studies broadly concern the interconnections between culture and politics, exploring how urban planning and architectural design powerfully intersected with colonial strategies of domination to create novel socio-spatial domains.[8] At its best this work seeks to place metropole and colony within a single analytic frame, taking 'as problematic the *making* of both colonizers and colonized in order to better understand the forces that, over time, have drawn them into an extraordinarily intricate web of relations'.[9] While these works have offered a wealth of empirical and historical detail on particular colonial situations, some of their theoretical assumptions have rendered the task of comprehending this 'intricate web of relations' more difficult. Garth Myers's otherwise rich analysis of town planning in Ng'ambo is a case in point.

Myers's account concerns the geography of power on the 'other side' of Zanzibar city, analyzing 'town planning and building control as instruments of state power'[10] during the colonial and post-colonial periods. In his view, urbanism in the colonial mode involves 'the manifestation of planning and building control as territorial mechanisms of the colonial state for establishing the dominance and legitimacy of empire. Planning schemes and building codes became practical, spatial tools of what Said calls the "geographical imagination" of colonialism'.[11] Myers interprets urban designs as instruments of the state's will to dominate territorially; the state here is seen as a unitary force, possessing an intentionality that is expressed in the form of its urban plans. The state's embodiment of power, however, does not mean that it 'successfully' imposed its will through urban reconstruction. Indeed, Myers critically analyzes a whole series of urban interventions in Ng'ambo as patent 'failures', but the rationale he advances to support this thesis reveals the shortcomings of his theoretical framework.

According to Myers, the intentionality of the state was bifurcated into public and private dimensions. Urban plans had the explicitly announced goal of public betterment, but failed to achieve this, overwhelmed by such practical flaws as limited finance, poor bureaucratic coordination, reliance on Eurocentric planning norms, and so forth. Yet the goal of public improvement was more crucially subverted by the private, hidden aim of urban planning – dominance – which also failed, due to the resistance of local residents in Ng'ambo, who reasserted their own local ways of building and planning (these local ways were also at least partly frustrated in their implementation due to lack of state resources and elite interference).[12]

Implicit in this account is a certain normative vision of how the state and urban planning ideally should work. That is, urban planning in the colonial mode 'failed' because it was a debased, power-ridden form of authentic city design – which, as Myers suggests, should be dialogic, consultative, working in organic concert with grassroots efforts, proceeding only on the basis of the consent of those subject to planning. Similarly, Myers views the colonial state as illegitimaté due to the fact that it was primarily concerned with domination rather than performing the 'real' function of government: the delivery of services and resources to the public. But this raises a crucial problem, namely, can government ever be viewed as a technocratic, instrumental order, somehow outside or beyond the field of power? James Ferguson underlines this point when he questions the 'neutral' status of service provision: '"Government services" are never simply "services"; instead of conceiving this phrase as a reference simply to a government whose purpose is to serve, it may be at least as appropriate to think of "services" which serve to govern.'[13]

My aim here is not to cast aspersion on Myers's attempt to articulate a more progressive basis for planning, but rather to question the way in which this effort is grounded in flawed assumptions about intentionality, state power and the colonial planning process. First, the issue of intentionality. In his analysis of the 'anti-politics machine', Ferguson has discussed cogently the implications of development interventions in rural Lesotho. In his analysis the Thaba-Tseka project of rural agricultural improvement was a 'failure' and explicitly recognized as such both within Lesotho and without by the time of its demise. Yet in what way could the scheme be described as a failure? Only in the narrow sense that, unsurprisingly, it failed to meet its stated original objectives. This gloss of failure only makes sense if one grants to intentionality a certain originary status and guiding force, as if it provides a kind of blueprint or logic leading to the eventual outcome. But the results of schemes are never guaranteed by their authors' intentions, and the structural complexities of planning apparatuses cannot be reduced merely to the determinations of specific individuals or agents. The intentions of the Thaba-Tseka planners were guided by assumptions of a developmental conceptual apparatus that was fundamentally inadequate to comprehend the realities of rural life in Lesotho. If their programme failed to deliver the promised agricultural improvement, this does not mean that the plan 'failed' to do anything: as Ferguson argues, the project had an impact with real consequences, not just those that the planners envisioned (mainly relating to the way in which rural poverty provided a point of intervention for the enlargement of state bureaucratic power in the region). Ferguson elaborates this point further:

Plans constructed within a conceptual apparatus do have effects but in the process of having these effects they generally fail to transform the world in their own image. But 'failure' here does not mean doing nothing; it means doing something else, and that something else always has its own logic. Systems of discourse and systems of thought are thus always bound up in a complex causal relationship with the stream of planned and unplanned events that constitutes the social world. The challenge is to treat these systems of thought and discourse like any other kind of structured social practice, neither dismissing them as ephemeral nor seeking in their products the master plans for those elaborate, half-invisible mechanisms of structural production and reproduction in which they are engaged as component parts.[14]

Recognizing that intentionality lacks the capacity to impose its order upon the world does not mean that we should simply dismiss it as inconsequential. This is especially true in regard to urban plans and designs, as James Holston has argued in the context of his study of modernist Brasilia: 'Architecture is itself a domain of intentions – for changing society, repatterning daily life, displaying status, regulating real estate, and so forth – which engages other intentions, all of which has consequence in the world. Intentionality constitutes a part of social action that can be neglected only at the cost of having a reductive and determinist view of historical development.'[15] Perhaps the very prominence of intention in urban planning – in the form of planning statements, manifestoes, maps, models, designs and exhibitions – has promoted the tendency to interpret it as singularly efficacious and powerful. The challenge is to put intentionality back, so to speak, in its proper place. In Holston's reading, intention and the instruments it generates for its realization constitute the 'self-understanding' of Brazilian modernist planning and must be included in any adequate analysis.[16] Taking such formulations seriously, however, does not entail remaining within the terms that they establish, seeing them as self-sufficient and determining. Intentions are always contingent and partial, engaged with other intentionalities in contradictory or complementary ways, and bound tenuously to an unruly world of social practice that often overwhelms or thwarts them.

If intentionality is only one part of the story, and its engagement with social practices in the world is neither monolithic nor predetermined, clearly it is inadequate to suggest that colonial urban planning 'failed' on Zanzibar because it was a tool of state intentionality – its will to dominate. This conceptualization problematically treats the state as a unitary object, something that possesses and wields power over the population under its control, deploying various instruments to good or ill effect, obtaining consent or provoking resistance. This simple domination and resistance model fundamentally misconstrues the nature of the state and its relation to power:

> The state is not an entity that 'has' or does not 'have' power, and state power is not a substance possessed by those individuals and groups who benefit from it. The state is neither the source of power, nor simply the projection of the power of an interested subject (ruling group, etc.). Rather than an entity 'holding' or 'exercising' power, it may be more fruitful to think of the state as instead forming a relay or point of coordination and multiplication of power relations.... The 'state' in this conception, is not the name of an actor, it is the name of a way of tying together, multiplying and coordinating power relations, a kind of knotting or congealing of power.[17]

Viewing the state as a congealed locus of power complicates our understanding of what the state actually is and how it works on the ground, challenging the tendency to objectify its authority and agency. It also throws into question any simple dualism of colonizer and colonized, controller and controlled. Thinking about relations of power rather than its 'possession' and instrumental deployment allows us to go beyond Myers's account. For if he views the colonial state as 'having' power that was used to control a subject population (however unsuccessful this effort may have been), he never analyzes the state itself as being subject to power, caught up in its complexities and contradictions. By placing colonized and colonizer (neither of which were ever internally homogeneous and consistent) within the field of power relations, I do not mean to imply that both stood in relations of equality before power – far from it. While they were differentially impacted by the process in a way that often involved radical inequality and outright violence, both were located within its field. To capture the complexity of this process, it is necessary to move beyond domination and resistance, rulers and ruled, setting a more nuanced analytic compass suggested by Holston:

> A noninternal critical analysis of this planning would have to do more than merely rescue the voices of those left out. Although this affirmation is crucial, ... a critical analysis would have to go beyond demonstrating that those marginalized have intelligent interests and important roles with respect to the social system and asking planners to respect them. Such affirmations of the nonhegemonic would not counter the planners' discourse of power. Rather, ... a counter-discourse would have to demonstrate that the delerium of power in master planning itself creates conditions over which the planners stumble and consequently conditions for its own subversion.[18]

Holston's notion of non-internal critique shifts us away from necessarily assuming that urban planning was merely an instrumental tool of the state. Colonial urban planning indeed was motivated by a whole host of intentions, including projects of social control and liberal reform. But these intentionalities were neither sufficient nor determining of social outcomes, belying the pretensions of 'master' planning. Furthermore, the state itself and the planning apparatus it spawned were never wholly unified or internally consistent. Detailed historical analysis of planning efforts reveals how conflicts over urban intervention were often motivated by struggles within the state itself, exposing crucial disjunctures and antagonisms between different levels of the bureaucracy or between local authorities and the Colonial Office. What we must attend to is the inchoate and incomplete nature of the colonial project, seeking to tease out the gaps and inconsistencies of rule. As Nicholas Dirks has pointed out, 'It is tempting but wrong to ascribe either intentionality or systematicity to a congeries of activities and a conjunction of outcomes that, though related and at times coordinated, were usually diffuse, disorganized, and even contradictory. It could be said that the power of colonialism as a system of rule was predicated at least in part on the ill-coordinated nature of power.'[19] As a process and a practice, planning itself ensnared the colonial regime within contradictions of its own creation, confronting bureaucratic power with insoluble dilemmas. Caught up within a dream of order, the rationality of colonial planning produced instead its obverse, revealing nothing so much as the disorders of rule itself, the unpredictable consequences of a certain commitment to the totalizing mastery of an entire urban milieu.

The Contradictions of Colonial Urban Planning

The most recent conservation plan is the fifth such urban programme devoted to Zanzibar since 1916, when the idea of a comprehensive town plan was first proposed by the Secretary of State for the Colonies as a cure-all for the city's ills.[20] Prior to beginning the research, I assumed each of these plans would be sharply marked by their divergent historical moments, as discontinuous and distinctive as the various regimes that sponsored them. While crucial differences existed, I was continually struck by the broad continuities that united them. The most remarkable thing that all these plans shared was the obstinate belief in the very idea of planning itself – as almost the *sine qua non* of any modern urban order. Whether under the guise of colonial, nationalist/revolutionary or free market regimes, central government and municipal officials have demonstrated repeatedly an almost unshakable faith in the ability of a comprehensive and totalizing town plan to solve all problems – despite the dismal record left behind by preceding efforts. All of the plans share other similarities, among them a lack of public sector funds and financial commitment; reliance on top-down planning; an extravagant belief in the value of technical and foreign expertise; a distrust of popular participation; a vigorous tension between developing the modern and preserving the traditional; and a deep-seated love of secrecy. These continuities raise crucial questions about the uncritical orientation of recent conservation efforts toward the colonial past. Conservationists tended to focus on what past plans did or intended to do (what was built, and when) rather than looking at *how* plans did what they did, or how they failed. This lack of a critical engagement with historical process went along with the belief that current urban problems were largely a legacy of the revolution and the twenty years of neglect that followed. This is a remarkable displacement, one which serves to cast the colonial city in an idealized light, as a well-maintained and orderly zone, the paradise lost that conservation must rehabilitate.

Two master plans were developed and approved under the colonial administration – the Lanchester plan of 1922 and the Kendall plan of 1958. The first of these, carried out by a follower of Patrick Geddes, was hailed as establishing 'town planning on scientific lines' for the first time on Zanzibar.[21] Clearly the invocation of 'scientific' here marks a key shift. Both before and after 1922, a host of urban problems consumed the attention of colonial officials, who tried to deal with these issues in a localized, *ad hoc* manner. These efforts should be seen as operations quite distinct from 'scientific' planning – indeed the former were most often subverted by the latter. In regular cycles there were predictions of imminent urban crises. A colonial official, the Medical Officer of Health or Municipal Officer, for example, would suddenly sound a warning about an urgent problem – overcrowding and congestion in the Indian 'bazaar' districts was often cited – and predict dire consequences if nothing were to be done. Site surveys, mapping and analyses would be completed, and various departments urged into action. Meetings would be convened and debates held, various measures being proposed to correct the situation. As the proposals moved through the bureaucratic process, being postponed for further consideration until complete 'data' might be available, the urgency that motivated them slowly dissipated, and eventually the entire debate would be shelved, yet another issue to be resolved by the master plan always looming just over the horizon. Piecemeal resolutions were scorned as futile – the only solution was a comprehensive planning mechanism. The master plans were seductive precisely because they promised a total solution, based on the premise that 'the *whole* area of any city including the *whole* of the outside suburban regions must be planned and controlled permanently by the civic authorities'.[22]

The totalizing nature of the plans and their pretensions to scientific mastery entailed operating on a scale that guaranteed they would never be implemented. The 1922 plan advocated 12 principal projects, at an estimated cost of £400,000. In conceptualizing the plan, no effort was made to gauge its financial feasibility. While the proposals were accepted by the Colonial Office and lauded by its Advisory and Sanitary Committee, it was left to local authorities to fund the project – and they lacked even the ability to secure a modest loan from the Colonial Development Fund to start implementing minor portions of the plan in 1931.[23] As early as 1925 officials had acknowledged there was little hope of ever funding the plan, and yet the regime continued to use it as a guide for development well into the 1930s.

254 • WILLIAM CUNNINGHAM BISSELL

The 1958 Kendall plan repeated this process. Completed after a long period of gestation (from 1935 to 1958), the Kendall plan was even more impractical and unfeasible than its predecessor – and, because of financial constraint, essentially dead on arrival. The 1958 plan initially recommended 14 projects in the first five-year segment, costing an estimated £345,000 to implement (the second, third, and fourth five-year phases required an additional £538,000). Yet within weeks of publication, government officials were expressing alarm as to the cost and demanding that the scheme be immediately revised 'to conform with a very much smaller financial outlay'.[24] The scheme was left largely intact, while the burden of paying for it was simply shifted to newly created local authorities – allowing the colonial government to claim credit for the plan while avoiding any responsibility for carrying it out. The proposals for immediate implementation were slashed to the order of £50,000 in the first five-year phase, even as colonial officials were acknowledging privately that only £15,000 might be available for actual expenditure.[25] From £883,000 to £15,000: after over twenty years of effort, the plan was stillborn, and only very minor elements of it were ever realized. The aspects of the 1958 scheme that were salvaged tended to be legal codes, costing nothing to implement (such as zoning regulations), which were later routinely ignored. Rather than constructive designs on space, the plans became exercises in ad hoc, often arbitrary prohibition, attempting to stop property owners from building as they wished.

While the plans had little effect on the ground, they spawned an entire bureaucratic and legal milieu that increasingly served as an end unto itself. The Lanchester plan gave rise to a protracted seven-year process of interdepartmental struggle that ultimately produced the Town Planning Decree of 1925 (never used) and the massive Towns Decree of 1929. And part of the reason the 1958 plan took so long to complete was the difficulty in developing the cumbersome mechanisms necessary to support an ambitious Town and Country Planning Decree, based on English precedents, and other institutional measures that led up to the various proposed schemes and the final plan. On the surface, the immense disparity between the bureaucratic resources, time and energy devoted to city planning and the meagre results that followed seem astounding. Yet on another level there is no surprise at all, for colonial plan making and inertia were not opposed activities, indeed they directly implied and depended upon each other. As the bureaucratic process became increasingly involved, a world almost unto itself, the endless making of the plan and its eventual non-implementation went hand in hand. The scale of the plans, the complexity of the planning process, and the significant time lag between conception and completion served the interests of colonial domination all too well, allowing the regime to defer and deflect social demands for improved urban conditions even while it attended to its own concerns. And indeed, if one scrutinizes the plans, one sees that the parts of them actually constructed invariably related to the colonial economy – improvement of traffic networks and transport, or the enhancement of commodity flows (port rehabilitation). At least until the revolution, pressing social needs (housing provision, in particular) were continually postponed and put off for another day.

Discipline and Power: Rethinking Colonial Regularity

The history of urban planning on Zanzibar requires us to rethink the relation between colonialism, the city and spatial control. The crucial point to be made here is that the inept, inefficient, and cumbersome nature of the colonial regime made its domination paradoxically all the more effective. To cite but one example of how the power of the colonial bureaucracy was achieved through inconsistency, the Lanchester plan of 1922 advocated clearing out a large number of huts in Ng'ambo to create a regular grid pattern of roadways (facilitating police access and surveillance) and for health reasons (the need for 'breathing spaces'). Due to lack of resources the plan was neither implemented in its totality nor even legally authorized. Quite simply the colonial regime lacked the massive resources necessary to acquire the large amounts of property on which the huts stood and pay fair compensation. Colonial officials were effectively caught in the contradiction between their desire to rework the city at will and the legal necessity of respecting the rights of property owners. Yet, despite the fact that the plan existed only on paper and had no basis in law, the Lanchester scheme directed urban policy well into the 1930s as the colonial government continued to search for the money to implement it officially. While refusing even to acknowledge the plan or disclose its contents,[26] colonial authorities regularly applied it on a case-by-case basis in an attempt to pave the way for its eventual financing and implementation. That is, as existing structures deteriorated (something that happened much more frequently in the case of huts as opposed to stone dwellings) any Zanzibari wishing to affect repairs had to apply to the Building Authority and receive written approval before proceeding. In cases where such huts stood in the way of the fictive 'Lanchester roads', permission to repair was summarily denied, despite the fact that these denials were of dubious legality – as was finally decided in the late 1930s, when the policy was finally abandoned altogether.[27] Such decisions, taken on an ad hoc basis,[28] had profoundly disruptive effects on the lives of impoverished small-holders, and served to highlight colonial law at its most capricious.

To say that colonialism was chaotic on Zanzibar is not to suggest that it was incapable of exercising domination or to dismiss the very real power it possessed; it is of central importance, however, to define precisely the nature of that domination and the mechanisms by which it was achieved. What Zanzibar reflects is the degree to which legal contradiction, bureaucratic ineptness, official obfuscation, prolonged inaction and petty adherence to formality – all reinforced by a total lack of accountability – were powerful tools of colonial power (and indeed other modalities of rule). The fact that this was 'unintentional' makes it no less powerful. If urban planning was a 'failure' in some profound sense, this very failure simultaneously served to create and perpetuate a mechanism of domination.

Over and over again, colonial officials displayed an abiding faith in the capacity of the form of the law to rework the most solid realities, the bricks and mortar of the city, and thereby to fashion new kinds of urban subjects, arranged properly in space. And yet the law was continually frustrated in its attempts to make reality conform to its own dictates. Officials made little attempt to account for the gulf between the scope of legislation and the paucity of resources available for implementation or enforcement. Consequently, in practice such decrees were applied on a case-by-case basis, the discipline envisioned in the totality degenerating into the capricious and uneven rule of the arbitrary. This very irregularity, the gaps and incoherencies that marked the unstable relation between the forms of the law and the unruly domain of social practice, was the means through which domination was achieved.

This insight would not be apparent to a conventional anthropological analysis focusing solely on jurisprudence. Here, following Joan Vincent, we can see the importance of moving beyond normative legal theory to focus critically on the 'administrative regulations, directives, guidelines, and codes of practice' and other 'state-orchestrated occasions that inculcate the very legal consciousness on which hierarchies and exclusions are based'.[29] Urban planning served as just such a state-orchestrated occasion, one that served to construct the colonized as differentially empowered right-bearing individuals, subject to the uncertain ordering of the juridical field. In the prolonged interregnum between the creation of a master plan and its final abandonment, the arbitrariness of the law was the subject of internal debate and open to external challenge. But only to the few: entrance into the legal system presupposed knowledge of English, which the Arabic- and Swahili-speaking majority did not possess. A tiny minority of wealthy and educated Zanzibaris possessed the social capital and resources to engage the system on its own terms, hiring lawyers to challenge arbitrary decision-making through the courts, waging a costly and protracted struggle. The overwhelming majority of Zanzibaris lacked the means to fight the bureaucracy at its own game; faced by an official decision to tear down their huts and relocate elsewhere, they could either comply or risk being compelled by force. Years later, when the undeclared 'law' which had destroyed their homes was abandoned as administrative policy, no restitution for those penalized was made. Unable to afford legal challenge, smallholders and the urban poor were thus particularly vulnerable to the bureaucratic fumbling and arbitrariness of colonial law.

Beyond Fixity of Form or the Letter of the Law

Just as town planning often created the very conditions of disorder it sought to resolve, so too legal measures often gave rise to contradictions and complexities that undermined them, throwing the bureaucracy into confusion and weary retrenchment. While the colonized, especially those who lacked the means to engage the bureaucracy on its own terms, were particularly subject to the capriciousness of the law, it is important to note the degree to which colonial officials got caught up in traps of their own devising, bogging down in legal conundrums that consumed them for years on end. While emphasizing the differential location of colonized and colonizer (and the internal differentiation involved with each), it is crucial to underscore that the contradictions and complexities of the law ensnared both in a manner that seems particularly emblematic of large-scale planning interventions in the modern era.

A central goal of colonial policy was to fix and rigidify the division of the city into two parts: 'Zanzibar town may be divided into two main areas within each of which living conditions conform, broadly, to two separate standards; there are the areas lying to the west of the creek in which the Arab type of stone house is in use and the area to the east of the creek, including Funguni, where native type huts are the rule'.[30] The distinction between Stone Town and Ng'ambo (often phrased in other, analogous ways – between 'town proper' and 'native location', or 'business areas' and 'residential' or 'hutting' areas), encoded a vision of a racial and class order that was a colonial fantasy, and rested on what seems at first to be an obvious and simple-minded distinction: between a stone (permanent) house and a mud hut. Colonial urban policy rested on the attempt to define these legally, clear out mixed areas of huts and stone dwellings by demolishing huts, legislate and map areas (stone town, native location) where houses and huts could legally be built, develop distinct sets of building rules, administrative apparatuses, and planning mechanisms for each area/building type, and apply different legal contexts to each (assessments on stone buildings, hut taxes then ground rent restrictions to huts). The only problem was that it did not work in quite the totalizing way that was planned. Why? Largely because the colonial regime's crisp ideological distinctions began to unravel whenever they were put into practice, and the government was continually caught up in its own policy contradictions as it tried and failed to nail down exactly in legal terms what was, and what was not, a mud hut (given the cosmopolitan nature of Zanzibar, the homologous problem of identifying who was 'Arab' and who 'native' was equally vexed). In the early days, a certain common-sense approach was sufficient, basically amounting to not much more than 'you know a native hut when you see one'. But later, as more sophisticated legal mechanisms were developed to cope with the greater complexity and scale of urban affairs, the old 'a native hut is where natives live' was increasingly subject to sterner scrutiny, though even at the height of the difficulty surrounding hut definition, it was suggested that the attempt to define these structures legally be abandoned, and that the assessors be allowed to decide on the spot on an *ad hoc* basis – 'you know one when you see one' all over again. One solution was to define huts by the building materials used in constructing them – stone versus mud. This seems simple – but Zanzibari structures really fall within a continuum drawn from a common pool of building materials, ranging from less permanent to more permanent, and rigid lines are hard to draw between them; mud huts, for example, were often built incorporating small stones in the walls, which made it difficult to arrive at a hard and fast rule as to when they ceased being huts and became stone houses. Or alternatively, a mud hut would be improved upon over time, slowly and incrementally being plastered over or solidified into a more sturdy dwelling, raising the same problem. As a colonial official protested in 1936, 'the definition of native hut in the Towns Decree is extraordinary – and it seems to me that it could be stretched to include nearly every building in Zanzibar. One cannot say that stone is not a material employed in native building. Corrugated iron is expressly included. Are all the wharf buildings native huts?'[31]

Other possible solutions to the definition problem were discussed at length. One was to define hut areas in townships and to exempt all structures in those areas from rates, making them subject to hut tax, while the rest of the town would be liable for assessment rates on the idea that these were 'stone' areas. In a good deal of the town, however, and especially in several key border neighbourhoods, things were so mixed that this solution would create patently iniquitous situations – people living in a residential 'mud hut' area would be paying the same 'hut' tax as the nearby owner of a stone building in a main commercial road who was able to rent out his place to several shops and thereby gain a considerable income.[32] The intermixed town layout defeated such rationalizations. Another response might have been to follow the Tanganyika solution where a native hut was defined, tautologically, as 'any building used ... as a dwelling ... by one family, which is owned by a native and is not occupied by a non-native'.[33] On Zanzibar, however, this would have merely transferred the problem to having to define who exactly was a 'native'. The colonial state vigorously sought at all costs to avoid this very question. After tortuous debates, colonial officials simply resorted to doing as they had always done – defining a native hut by its materials. This is not to say that the return to the status quo involved complete inertia – colonial officials insistently tinkered with the rules over the years in a futile attempt to iron out the contradictions they themselves had created. From a few sentences in its earliest version, the native hut definition grew to cover several pages by the time of the last set of colonial building rules, byzantine in its complexity, condition heaped on condition, qualified to the ultimate degree. And still the rules were challenged and undermined, much to the frustration of officials.

History in the Present

This rethinking of colonialism through a detailed analysis of the inefficiencies and irregularities of its rule becomes particularly salient in the light of current perceptions on the island of how colonialism worked on the ground. After all, conservation has adopted colonial law in the mistaken impression that it served formerly to create an orderly urban realm, laying the blame for the city's recent disrepair on the excesses of the revolution.

Curiously, the official view in this regard shares something in common with more popular perceptions. Over and over again, in discussions about the causes of contemporary problems in the city, you will hear the same refrain from Zanzibaris: 'hamna sheria hapa' – there is no law here. Or more pointedly, they state that the law only applies to the poor while the wealthy and powerful simply do as they like. In these discussions, the law (and here too there are interesting tensions between secular law and the moral code implied by Islamic shari'a) was depicted in the absolute mode, ideally capable of bestowing order, fairness and rationality – in contrast to the lawlessness and disorder of the present moment. As a surprising result, the colonial past was portrayed in an idealized and nostalgic light, a time when things worked, the law was the law, and a shilling went a long way. One building inspector, frustrated by the way in which his efforts to control building violations were routinely ignored, spoke with positive longing about the colonial building rules, saying 'in those days they really knew how to make laws'.[34] The past is deployed as a visceral critique of the present disorder and corruption, which is most often blamed on the incompetence or venality (sometimes both) of post-colonial regimes. This is a stunning displacement, one that needs to be addressed. Colonial rule on Zanzibar was anything but smooth and orderly, and there never was a time when the 'law was the law', beyond negotiation, struggle, or the politics of interpretation. Indeed, from the colonial period down to the present there is a recurrent tension between the ideology of law as unequivocal, immutable rule or standard and the much more indeterminate and flexible realm of practice – the space where deals got struck and business done. As the Medical Officer of Health complained in 1939, sounding much like a planner in the early 1990s, 'We have a town plan but no money to implement it nor legal authority to enforce it.... Business is business. I fancy Zanzibar town must be one of the few towns in the world where property owners can build where they like and defy all efforts to cause them to develop their land in an orderly way.'[35] Open city, anything goes – an apt diagnostic of the present moment.

How *should* we think about history in the present? There are three principal areas in which conservation could benefit from historical examination of colonial planning efforts. In terms of the most recent conservation plan, a historical analysis of the 1922 and 1958 plans should have raised serious questions about the capacity of 'master planning' to resolve myriad contradictions and rework an entire urban milieu. Such an analysis would have foregrounded from the outset of the planning process the issue of implementation and financing, narrowly framing proposals within the horizon of the possible. In contrast, the current master plan seems likely to follow in the footsteps of its predecessors, largely consigned to a paper existence. After two years of intensive and valuable effort, involving mapping, data collection and surveys, a master plan for the Stone Town exists which, if implemented, undoubtedly would have a beneficial impact on the physical fabric of the city. Yet external funding for the plan only covers its development; as yet no financing exists for the vastly more complicated and expensive implementation of the schemes.

More crucially, the conservation plan fails to grapple in any significant way with the question of who will actually benefit from urban restoration. The lack of funding and general weakness of the public sector on Zanzibar has meant that the current master plan – again, much like its predecessors – relies on private capital to underwrite conservation efforts. As part of a tourist promotion strategy, however, conservation coexists uneasily with the kind of rampant development that transnational capital has spurred. A central conundrum exists at the heart of conservation: many of the historic buildings scheduled for restoration are already occupied by revolutionary-era tenants who lack the resources to pay for rehabilitation. The state can either respect their rights of tenancy and allow them to remain, leaving the buildings to decay further, or choose to evict them, sell the buildings, and require the new owners to conserve these properties.[36] While acknowledging this dilemma, the conservation plan does little to address it, other than stating that the government must seek to balance social interests with conservation objectives. By not directly confronting the realities of power from the outset, the master plan operates in a political vacuum that distinctly privileges elite interests. Given the government's precarious financial position and interest in promoting tourism, the free rein given to private capital has greatly exacerbated social inequalities, favouring the wealthy at the expense of the poor, displacing long-term residents from the city centre, and reducing urban diversity. This development threatens to restore the city in terms of its physical fabric while leaving it an empty monument.

Take, for example, the UN Habitat-funded rehabilitation programme, which expended an estimated $922,372 between 1988 and May 1993.[37] This programme managed to restore a handful of sites, most of which were devoted to government use or dedicated as tourist facilities. These projects had little positive impact on the housing conditions of residents. As the draft conservation report noted in May 1993, 'over 85% of the building stock is in deteriorating or poor condition, while some 100 buildings have either partially or entirely collapsed'.[38] While these landmark restorations were being carried out, other aspects of the UN programme relating to housing fell by the wayside. One project was aimed at the 'low-income sector of the Stonetown population', designed to provide housing assistance outside the city centre. In May 1993 the internal report on the project rated the scheme's progress as 'unsatisfactory', stating that 'the expected output has dwindled off far into the future'.[39] Similarly, of a loan project intended to provide funds for housing repair the report stated that the 'production of output is nil' for this scheme, due to the fact that a suitable candidate to serve as housing consultant was never found.[40]

Nuanced analysis of earlier plans might also have promoted a greater awareness of the institutional problems engendered by colonial plan making. A good deal of time and effort has been spent under conservation in reforming the legal and bureaucratic context relating to the city. Yet here again the making of the plan has taken precedence over its implementation, and local authorities lack the institutional means and capacity to enforce the provisions laid out in the new laws. The new building regulations are fine in the ideal, but in practice there are only a handful of building inspectors to see that they are carried out. The sum of approximately $60,000 paid in 1992 to external consultants for two reports on urban strategy and legal reform might have been used instead to pay the annual salary of more than 150 additional local building inspectors, with far better results; instead of lining the pockets of external consultants, the money could have provided local jobs and institutional support.[41] Given the high rate of building, the paucity of inspectors at present means that only a portion of violations get noticed and cited, giving the law an unjust and arbitrary character that excites popular contempt for conservation efforts and defeats the purpose of reform. Despite the careful framing of the law, the practice by which it is being unevenly applied directly harkens back to colonial precedents. This attention to bureaucratic and legal issues has worked hand in hand with a top-down, state-based planning strategy on the part of conservationists. Most residents of the city remain unaware of conservation initiatives, and the master plan was developed with little popular consultation and participation. Perhaps this was the most significant way in which current planning mirrored colonial precedents – and the most disheartening, in that conservation missed a crucial opportunity to mobilize grassroots efforts, providing a context for local action and debate about the city's past and future.

Conclusion

Why, in conservation's present, is it so critically important to think about the past? Conservation, after all, will not literally restore colonialism, for it operates in utterly changed historical circumstances. There will be no simple return to the past. Yet by ignoring the past, conservation threatens to restore its forms. The replication of colonial planning practices, based on a fundamental misunderstanding of past domination and the mechanisms by which it was achieved, can only serve to repeat colonialism's worst disorders. Only by confronting directly the legacy of past planning efforts can we lay the groundwork for conservation efforts that are informed by colonial 'failures' rather than simply reproducing them in another guise.

Notes

1 Support for the research on which this paper is based was generously provided by grants from the Fulbright-IIE programme and the National Science Foundation, which I gratefully acknowledge.

'Conservation' serves as a shorthand form for a very complex conceptual and institutional apparatus. Recognizing the risk of eliding difference, I should indicate at least that the conservation process involves a range of UN agencies (UNDP, Habitat), donor groups, NGOs (Aga Khan Trust for Culture), outside architects, planners, consultants, different Zanzibari state agencies (STCDA, COLE, Municipal Council) and private developers, among others. The tensions between local, national and transnational forces in conservation are crucial, and I intend to explore them at greater length elsewhere. For present purposes, however, the structural regularities and cohesive programme expressed in the 1983 and 1993 plans justify using 'conservation' in the sense outlined above.

2 In 1984 approximately 8,000 non–Tanzanians visited the island. By 1992, a mere eight years later, over 84,000 tourists were arriving annually. This sharp increase has affected both urban and rural areas on a variety of levels profoundly.

3 Royce Lanier and D. Aidan McQuillan, *The Stone Town of Zanzibar: A Strategy for Integrated Development* (Zanzibar, 1983).

4 The 1929 Decree was described by the Attorney General at the time as a 'code of municipal law of general application for the government of towns in the protectorate' (Zanzibar National Archives [ZNA]: AB 39/182). It was a broad piece of legislation dealing with the declaration of towns, rating and taxes, building codes, and municipal provisions for street maintenance and lighting, waste disposal, water supply and public open spaces. The 1955 Act, drafted directly from English Town and Country Planning precedents, was a comprehensive decree intended to control all aspects of planning throughout the protectorate. In 1954, the colonial Housing Officer criticized the draft bill as 'so elaborate as to be in practice unworkable in this Protectorate'. In creating the act, he continued, 'are we not trying to forge a stupendous hammer in order to crack four small nuts?' (ZNA: DA 1/261). Conservation's adoption of these laws has meant taking over large sections of them wholesale, simply updating outmoded phrasing (the 'British Resident' switched to read 'the President of Zanzibar').

5 Scholarly access to Zanzibari archival and ethnographic materials was restricted in the two decades following the revolution. The few accounts written during that period relied heavily on secondary sources, and hence colonial depictions of the city took on a life of their own, being repeated in subsequent accounts until they acquired the guise of established fact.

6 Zanzibar Protectorate, *Report on the Progress of the Development Programme for the Years 1944–51* (Zanzibar, 1951), p. 30. Garth Andrew Myers has articulated the degree to which this dichotomy was constructed and reinforced through colonial planning efforts. See his 'Reconstructing Ng'ambo: town planning and development on the other side of Zanzibar' (PhD thesis, UCLA, 1993).

7 Henri Lefebvre, *The Production of Space* (Oxford, 1991 [1974]); Michel Foucault, *Discipline and Punish: The Birth of the Prison* (New York, 1979) and *Power/Knowledge* (New York, 1980).

8 See, for example, Anthony King, *Urbanism, Colonialism, and the World Economy* (London, 1990); Robert Home, *Of Planting and Planning* (London, 1997); Miriam Dossal, *Imperial Designs and Indian Realities* (Delhi, 1991); Gwendolyn Wright, *The Politics of Design in French Colonial Urbanism* (Chicago, 1991); Paul Rabinow, *French Modern* (Cambridge, MA, 1989); Thomas Metcalf, *An*

Imperial Vision (Berkeley, 1989); and Norma Evenson, *The Indian Metropolis* (New Haven, CT, 1989).

9 John L. Comaroff, 'Images of empire, contests of conscience', in John L. and Jean Comaroff, *Ethnography and the Historical Imagination* (Boulder CO, 1992), p. 183.

10 Myers, 'Reconstructing Ng'ambo', p. 3.

11 *Ibid.*, p. 176.

12 *Ibid.*, pp. 184–5.

13 James Ferguson, *The Anti-Politics Machine* (Minneapolis and Cambridge, 1994), p. 253.

14 *Ibid.*, p. 277.

15 James Holston, *The Modernist City* (Chicago, 1989), p. 11.

16 *Ibid.*, pp. 12–13.

17 Ferguson, *The Anti-Politics Machine*, pp. 272–3.

18 Holston, *The Modernist City*, pp. 8–9.

19 Nicholas B. Dirks, 'Introduction: colonialism and culture', in Dirks (ed.), *Colonialism and Culture* (Ann Arbor, 1992), p. 7.

20 ZNA: AB 39/203, quoted in R. Crofton, 'Secret memorandum on town planning', 30 August 1923.

21 ZNA AB 39/203, Resident to Secretary of State for the Colonies, 25 March 1931. Lanchester, like Geddes, was active in Indian town planning; his work in Madras and elsewhere brought him to the attention of officials in Zanzibar.

22 ZNA: AB 39/203, Crofton, 'Secret memorandum on town planning', 30 August 1923.

23 ZNA: AB 39/203, Secretary of State J. H. Thomas to Acting British Resident, Zanzibar, 26 September 1931. See also ZNA: AB 39/204 (entire).

24 ZNA: AK 19/15, Assistant Chief Secretary (Admin) to Town Planning Officer, 11 December 1958.

25 ZNA: AK 19/15, Town Planning Advisory Committee Minutes, 30 December 1958; Acting Chief Secretary to Chairman, Town Planning Advisory Committee, 21 February 1959.

26 As Myers has shown ('Reconstructing Ng'ambo', p. 195), colonial officials went to great lengths to prevent any details of Lanchester's programme from becoming public knowledge. Copies of the plan were printed in England in 1924, but were strictly controlled. As late as 1928, when Lanchester sent a few copies to Zanzibar, they were marked as strictly confidential and for official eyes only. Eventually the remaining copies in the UK were burned.

27 ZNA: AB 39/252 (entire); see also ZNA AB 39/207.

28 As the Director of Medical Services observed, 'The Lanchester roads are not marked out and it is a matter of purely arbitrary guesswork by the Building Inspector to determine where they do run', ZNA: AB 39/207, DMS to Chief Secretary, 5 September 1935.

29 Joan Vincent, 'On law and hegemonic moments: looking behind the law in early modern Uganda', in Mindie Lazarus-Black and Susan Hirsch (eds), *Contested States* (New York, 1994), p. 118.

30 ZNA: AJ 19/10, Director of Medical Services to Chief Secretary, 12 June 1935.

31 ZNA: AB 39/180, Director of Public Works to Chief Secretary, 4 January 1936.

32 ZNA: AB 39/180, W.M. to Provincial Commissioner, 21 December 1935.

33 ZNA: AB 39/180, Chief Secretary, Tanganyika to Chief Secretary, Zanzibar, 11 May 1936.

34 Masud Salum Mohamed, interview, 9/4/94. All names of informants are pseudonyms.

35 ZNA: AB 39/177, Medical Officer of Health to Chief Secretary, 13 December 1939.

36 Revolutionary tenants are frequently blamed as the source of urban decay, cast as rural Africans who didn't possess the 'cultural' resources necessary to properly inhabit 'historic' residences built by the Arab and Indian colonial elite. This scapegoating of the poor conveniently absolves the revolutionary government – who placed these tenants in overcrowded quarters and made little effort to provide for maintenance – from any responsibility for its own disinvestment in Stone Town. As a result, both the state and private interests have shown little hesitation or regret in displacing these tenants.

37 Stone Town Conservation and Development Authority: United Nations Development Project, 'Project Performance Evaluation Report', 15 May 1993.

38 ZNA: MWCELE/AKTC Planning Team, 'Zanzibar Stone Town Conservation Plan: Summary of Findings and Draft Planning Proposals', May 1993.

39 STCDA: United Nations Development Project, 'Project Performance Evaluation Report', 15 May 1993.

40 *Ibid.*

41 *Ibid.*

16

The Urbanism of District Six, Cape Town

RAFAEL MARKS & MARCO BEZZOLI

This piece has arisen out of a continuing and growing concern over the ways in which South African cities are currently developing.[1] The issue is not so much about the growth of the cities, which is continuing at an unprecedented rate, but the newly built environments in which people live. These are at best mediocre, at worst an anonymous sprawl of box houses, garages and tarmac. There has been little concern for the natural environment, the human qualities of housing, or the design of liveable and habitable urban spaces. Cape Town continues to develop along the lines set out over the past few decades. This was a combination of modernist planning principles intertwined with apartheid policy. The majority of the city's population was forced to live in a series of segregated, isolated and hostile environments, separated from each other by freeways and buffer zones. This has created a vastly inequitable and inefficient city in which the poor are marginalized from urban opportunities.

The idea of urbanism has been lost during this century. While much of Cape Town's urban development has been shaped by political expediency and the needs of capital, there was, in the past, an understanding of urban form and space, and an adherence to a certain set of principles that shaped the city and created a sense of place and community. Today this sensibility has been lost. The idea of the public realm, of people-centred places, has been subsumed to the motor car and to private consumption. The essential concepts of urban design and planning, those physical elements of the city that contribute to a humane and equitable society, no longer exist.

This chapter explores the nature of these qualities through an analysis of the urban fabric of District Six, during its time one of the most dynamic and heterogeneous urban spaces in South Africa. This analysis can help us understand how a particular built environment, for all its problems, interacts with and supports the community it houses. With this understanding, we can begin to reconstruct the South African city as a meaningful urban space, supportive of its poorer communities. The chapter also contributes to a sphere of historical discourse that has been largely neglected in the past – the spatial and physical context in which social relations take place.

The chapter does not argue for a functionalist or behaviourist approach to urban design. Good architecture will not automatically create the conditions of an enabling

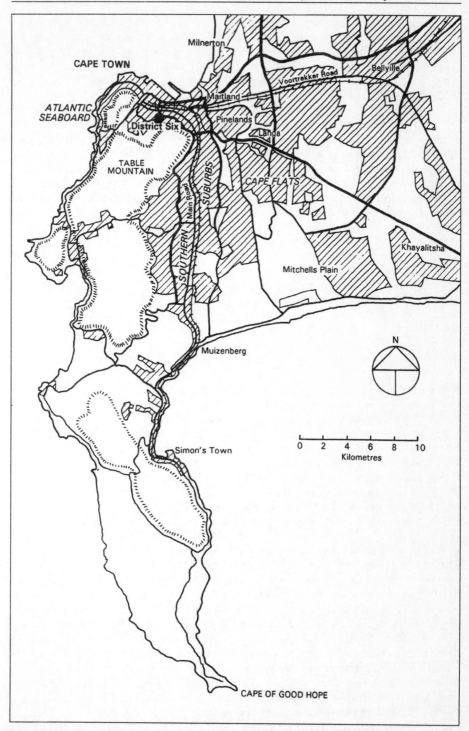

Figure 16.1 The Cape metropolitan region showing location of District Six, 1977

environment, but inappropriate planning and bad architecture will almost certainly stifle them. Furthermore, the paper does not imply that political and social considerations are unimportant, or that planning and design can somehow be divorced from the political, social and economic realms. Rather, it takes as its premise the belief that the design of urban areas have their own logic and *raison d'être* which derives from the needs and desires of the people living within them.[2]

We will begin with an exploration of the historical growth of District Six in relation to the overall development of Cape Town. Each was integral to the other, and both have been subject to many diverse forces over the centuries. Changing planning paradigms have dovetailed with the general economic and political context. At the same time, technological changes in construction techniques and transport technologies have enabled emerging ideas and visions (or nightmares) to be realized. We will then go on to analyse the physical nature of the district. That people lived in a run-down, neglected urban environment is undeniable, but these conditions were a result not so much of the urban design itself as of political and economic considerations – slum landlordism, political inaction, etc. Poverty was acute and living conditions harsh, with overcrowding, inadequate services and a dilapidated housing stock, yet various economic, social and cultural networks developed. These survival strategies, it will be argued, were facilitated and reinforced by the physical environment. In the context of economic poverty, the low-rise, high-density and multi-functional urban fabric was far more supportive of its community than the present shattered sub-urban landscapes of the Cape Flats.

The Urban Development of Cape Town and District Six

The site of Cape Town was originally used by KhoiSan pastoralists who settled in temporary structures to pasture their cattle. The first permanent settlement of Cape Town started in 1652 when the Dutch East India Company established a half-way station between Europe and the East Indies. This provided fresh meat and vegetables for the passing sailors. For the first 150 years, the town remained a small settlement structured along the lines of the Bastide plans of Northern Europe:[3] a fortified town consisting of a regular grid of streets connecting the main ordering elements of the settlement. These consisted of the Company Gardens which defined the southern edge of the settlement, the Castle and harbour which defined the northern edge of the town and linked it to the rest of the world, and two canals which channelled the 'mountain streams for potable and irrigation water.[4]

The planning of Cape Town was limited to the most important aspects of the settlement and reflected both the historical precedents of its inhabitants and its economic function – servicing the Company's needs.[5] While the generation of profit was at the heart of the developing urban centre, the settlement was structured as a conscious act of place making.[6] The principle of the plan was a regular network of streets and public squares. This set up a guiding yet flexible framework in which future private development could take place. Public buildings, particularly those serving the monopoly trading interests of the Dutch East India Company, were the major structures. They acted as 'urban pivots' around which less important buildings, such as houses, were developed.

The dominant economic activity during the eighteenth century was farming and the export of agricultural products.[7] Much of this was produced on farms in the expanding hinterland. Non-farming activities such as lodging houses, taverns, warehousing, ship repairs and small retailing outlets were concentrated mainly around the Bay. Though small, the town had a cosmopolitan population. Slaves were imported from Indonesia, India, Madagascar, Southern Africa and other parts of Africa, while settlers from all over northern Europe arrived on the shores of Table Bay. They all brought their own building and crafts traditions, adapting them to the Cape environment. Yet a fairly coherent architectural form and style developed through the specific material constraints found in the Cape – plot dimensions determined by the town plan, particularities of the site and climate, a restricted range and quality of building materials, and the dominant building and planning practices of the colonizers.[8]

The arrival of the British in 1795 saw the start of a transformation in the economy of Cape Town, accompanied by changes in social, economic, administrative and planning practices. The new colonial authorities sought to shift the export of raw products to their own developing markets, and to strengthen the town's strategic and defensive position on the Eastern sea routes.[9] The town's population began to expand, assisted by immigration schemes organized back in Britain. The growing population and economy had profound influences on the spatial growth of the city and its physical fabric. Between 1820 and 1840 alone, the quantity of shipping in the Cape ports quadrupled. An 'industrial area' began to develop adjacent to the harbour, consisting mainly of warehousing, ship chandlery, and basic packing and distribution services.

For much of the nineteenth century there was little official intervention in the form and direction of the town's development. This was despite the establishment of an elected board of commissioners in 1840 which was supposed to oversee the installation and maintenance of public infrastructure.[10] A *laissez-faire* attitude prevailed over the use and development of land and the town's growth was left primarily to market forces and private developers. As the economy expanded, particularly following the discovery of diamonds and gold in the 1860s and 1870s, pressure for land, goods and services increased dramatically. The town continued to increase in population and building density, expanding both horizontally and vertically. The profit motive became the overriding factor in land development, and those with capital became the chief architects of the rapidly expanding town. This period saw the rise of the property developer and private landlord, who took advantage of the scarcity of the newly commodified land.

The abolition of slavery in the 1830s and increasing numbers of new immigrants led to growing demands for urban housing. Lower income groups tended to settle on the edges of the town and the first expansion took place to the west on the slopes of Signal Hill where artisans built their own housing.[11] The land to the east of the town also began to be developed along Sir Lowry Road, an area that came to be known as District Six. The town rapidly spread east and south and by the end of the nineteenth century the first few kilometres out of Cape Town were characterized by high density housing inhabited predominantly by small shopkeepers, artisans and labourers.[12]

The wealthy initially remained concentrated in the centre, close to the main public amenities. With increasing congestion of the inner city, and improvements in transport and road networks later in the century, they began to move out to quieter and more spacious suburbs. New developments took place in a linear form along the main transport routes to the west, south and north-east of the town. The intensity and extent of this development was not uniform, but tended to cluster at points of higher accessibility where different transport routes interconnected. Population densities and the urban fabric supported a wide variety of activities and amenities, particularly in the centre. The natural environment still created constraints on new developments and development tended to gravitate towards places favourable to human habitation, specifically avoiding the Cape Flats. Transport technology also limited accessibility to the various parts of the city. Much of the new development occurred in an *ad hoc* fashion and as the city expanded outwards, the distinction between town, village and farmstead became increasingly blurred.

During the eighteenth and early nineteenth centuries, the area of District Six was occupied by four large farms known as Welgelegen, Hope Lodge, Bloemhof and Zonnebloem. The first formal planning of the area took place in 1812 when a new market was built adjacent to the Castle. This was planned in a similar fashion to the town centre, with a regular grid organized along the axis set up by Sir Lowry Road, the beginning of the road to the southern suburbs and the peninsula. Further development was structured by this road and Hanover Street, which became the major commercial spine through the area.

As elsewhere in the town, speculative house builders responded to the growing demand for working-class housing. Municipal records suggest that investors bought up houses and land in District Six as early as the 1840s, and by the 1850s whole streets were owned by single landlords.[13] Many of these, such as Wicht, Tennant and Stuckeris Streets, still bear the names of the original owners. Between 1842 and 1854 alone, the number of properties more than doubled, and by 1849 the population of District Six had reached 2,943.[14] Road conditions were poor and drinking water, drainage and sewerage facilities were largely absent.

Originally called District Twelve, or unofficially Kanaladorp,[15] the area was renamed District Six in 1867 when Cape Town was divided into six administrative districts. The area was defined as that 'bounded North by the Castle Moat and Canterbury Row, East by the Military Lines at the Toll Bar, South by the Devil's Peak, and West by Constitution Street.'[16] It was popular with the working class due its proximity to the new market on Sir Lowry Road, the expanding docks and the employment opportunities in the growing economy of the city centre. The natural environment was a major factor in the district's early development. The sea was a source of employment for the many fishermen who lived in the area, while Woodstock Beach and Devil's Peak were major recreation spaces for the residents. The mountain streams provided a source of water for the many washerwomen who lived in the area.[17]

The area attracted a cosmopolitan and socially mixed population, from wealthy merchants through to artisans, tradesmen, domestic servants, labourers and prostitutes. Sir Lowry Road had its share of noteworthy residents, many of whom were prominent in the colonial trade. Other residents of the street included a corn chandler, a general dealer, a butcher, two retailers, three grocers, a cattle dealer and a coach manufacturer.[18] Hanover Street was also lined with the homes and businesses of many small businessmen, such as gunsmiths, silversmiths and printers. Behind the respectable facades, however, was a grid of streets of jerry-built row housing in which the poor lived in overcrowded conditions. A correspondent of The Monthly Observer in 1861 gives a good impression of District 12 at the time:

> It is a rambling, untidy locality. The houses and streets have a newly settled appearance; and the prevailing idea suggested is that of a busy, striving, energetic population having thrown themselves upon the soil, converted into bricks all but a small portion of it, and built houses of every shape and kind on the narrow remainder. Of streets there cannot be accurately said to be any; drains there are positively none, unless it be allowable to regard the whole surface of the earth in that light ... a feeble and paralysed local government is powerless to enforce the most ordinary regulations necessary for the well-being of a rapidly growing town.[19]

Fear and concern over the worsening conditions in the working-class areas finally led to the introduction of building and planning regulations in the 1860s. This was followed, in the 1890s, by further by-laws extending public control over the broader urban environment. Yet while the municipal bodies took on the provision of urban services, little was actually done to improve the situation. The council was dominated variously by landlords or businessmen. Continual wrangling and lack of political will meant that few

Figure 16.2 The Bashew Brothers' shop in Aspeling Street, District Six, *c.* 1910

improvements took place in the poorer neighbourhoods. Landlords, who maintained power until the 1880s, were more concerned about keeping rates as low as possible. They were therefore reluctant to provide services which would have meant raising the rates. The businessmen were interested in improving services, but mainly in the areas where their businesses were located. Once they had achieved power, they consolidated their position by introducing a system of voting based on wealth.[20] By definition, this disenfranchised much of the working class.

Despite constant pressure from the residents, conditions in District Six failed to improve and it took a smallpox epidemic in 1882 to prompt the council into action. Temporary efforts were made to clean the streets, gutters and houses, but this was ineffective in an area that had few paved streets and no guttering or water supply. Sanitation was poor and many houses did not even have an outside toilet. During the 1890s, a major sewerage and drainage scheme for the city was undertaken. This eventually included District Six, but still the problems of overcrowding were not addressed. If anything they got worse – one case was reported in which over a hundred people were living in a small house with only one toilet.[21] During the plague of 1901, an inspection of Horstley Street, described by the 'special commissioner' as full of 'offensively modern' houses, found over 20 people living in a room measuring no more than 20 feet by 10 feet.[22]

The rapid growth of the city, and of poorer working-class areas in particular, led to a growing concern over worsening housing conditions. Attitudes towards the poor were shifting, although these tended to be racially based – the poor whites received sympathy and relief, while the coloureds and Africans continued to be regarded as degenerate and beyond hope of redemption.[23] The concern with the moral and physical health of the poor reflected contemporary concerns in Europe and the United States. New planning ideologies, such as the Garden City[24] and the Neighbourhood Unit[25] were imported to South Africa, where they were transformed and adapted. Ideas about zoning, separate residential areas and low density suburbs dovetailed neatly with emerging policies of racial segregation.

A plague outbreak in District Six in 1901 provided the pretext for the town's first forced removals. Over 2,000 Africans were removed to a racially segregated township on the Cape Flats – a vast, flat windswept area that until then had remained undeveloped for good reason. Hundreds of houses were knocked down by the authorities in the name of slum clearance, to be replaced a couple of years later by slightly larger row and semi-detached housing.

Increasing state intervention in urban development was characterized by the later planning of new townships. Three racially separate 'garden cities' were established on the edge of Cape Town – Maitland Garden Village for coloured municipal employees in 1919, Pinelands for whites, designed by a firm of London architects in 1922, and Langa for Africans shortly after.[26] Residential densities were low and the developments were separated from neighbouring areas by buffers of wide roads and green belts. They were located on the edge of the city and focused inwards. There were few commercial facilities and no industrial development to support the townships. They became, in effect, residential dormitories from which the coloureds and Africans would commute to the town centre to work and shop. These 'garden cities' were the precursors of future townships on the Cape Flats.

In District Six the wealthy had already begun to move out, but the area continued to be a thriving, if poor, neighbourhood. By 1912, the population of District Six was estimated to be in excess of 30,000, a quarter of the city's total population.[27] By far the majority now were working-class, drawn from all over the world. Its proximity to the city centre made it a very convenient and cheap place to live. Industries and factories, the docks, commerce

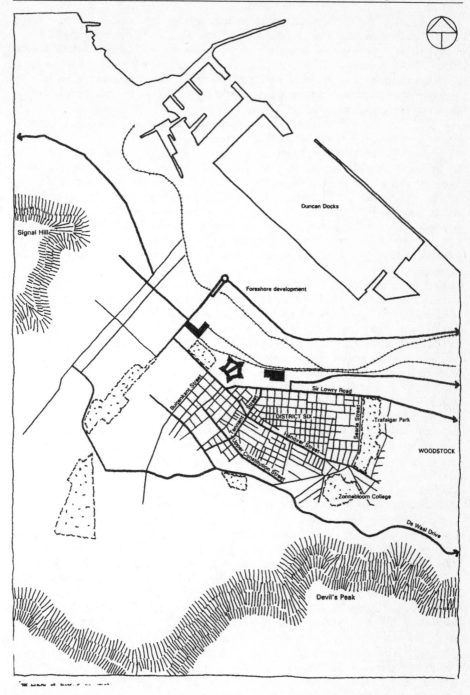

Figure 16.3 The growth of District Six, 1940

and informal sector opportunities were all within walking distance of home. Shops, schools, places of worship and community facilities were also located within the area.

Following an economic depression in the 1920s, Cape Town experienced rapid industrial development.[28] This created more job opportunities in the city, increasing the size and strength of the local working class. Increasing numbers of migrants from the poverty-stricken reserves in the Eastern Cape and immigrants from Europe swelled the city's numbers. Housing shortages reached crisis levels with two consequent results. The first was the continued deterioration and overcrowding of inner-city housing. The second was the development of large squatter settlements on the periphery of the city.

The response of the authorities in the city centre was a series of urban renewal projects, few of which came to fruition. One which did was the clearance of the infamous Well's Square in District Six – described by some as a 'hell hole of lawlessness and squalor'[29] – which was replaced with the new and modern Bloemhof flats. The space standards and health codes used in this new housing were those propagated by modern planning principles.[30] The consequence was that the new developments could not accommodate everyone who had been displaced. The 'surplus people' had to find alternative shelter, either elsewhere in the overcrowded district or in the growing squatter areas on the edge of the city.

One major development was to have a profound effect on the future of District Six and Cape Town. This was the Foreshore Scheme. First proposed in the early 1940s, it arose in response to the need to expand the port and provide deep-water harbour facilities as a result of the increased shipping traffic during the Second World War. It was an ideal opportunity for architects and engineers to put into practice the new modern ideas and technology popular at the time. The plan proposed filling in the bay and using the new land as an extension of the central business district. It also provided the opportunity to create a grand gateway to Cape Town and South Africa at a time when a large number of people were migrating to the country, the vast majority by sea. In one of the original proposals, District Six was to be effectively obliterated with a replanned street network, including a new freeway through the area.[31] Although this plan did not materialize in its original form, the freeway emerged two decades later, the forerunner of a far more devastating replanning and clearance of the area.

The Destruction of District Six

The election victory of the National Party in 1948 saw the institutionalization of apartheid and its attendant spatial planning principles of separate development. These dovetailed neatly with the popular modernist planning paradigms of zoning and separation. In the 1960s, the government embarked on a construction programme to implement the Group Areas Act. Between 1964 and 1969, 18,000 (mostly coloured) families were removed from District Six, Mowbray, Newlands, Claremont, Wynberg and other declared 'white areas', to be resettled in the newly built townships on the Cape Flats. Many Africans, deemed illegal immigrants in the city, were removed back to the 'homelands'.[32] Others found informal housing in the squatter areas on the periphery. The new townships were planned around the Neighbourhood Unit concept, separated from each other by freeways, green belts, industrial estates and railways. The use of 'scientific' standards, prefabricated, repeated elements, and traffic engineering principles contributed to the creation of the monotonous, monofunctional sterile environments that are seen today.

Three other innovations also influenced the development of the city in the next decades.[33] The first was the development of big construction companies which capitalised on the large-scale township and housing developments initiated by the state. The second was the new freeway construction technology imported from the USA. This was the era of the traffic engineer, coinciding with the term of office in the Cape Town City Council of an engineer who subscribed wholeheartedly to the new conventional wisdom. The third innovation was the shopping centre, also imported from the USA. This fitted in well with the concept of neighbourhood units and the large scale urban grid generated by the freeway. The shopping centres and freeways disrupted, and often destroyed, the existing commercial and transport networks which had developed over a long period of time and which were based on a much finer-grained, human scale of the city.

Further slum clearance proposals by the City Council in 1962 were delayed while the government decided on the racial zoning of the area. Two years later the Minister of Community Development appointed a committee to investigate the replanning of District Six, Woodstock and Salt River, all working-class, culturally mixed areas. The result of this investigation was the creation of the Committee for Rehabilitation of Depressed Areas (CORDA) to oversee the planning and redevelopment of these and six other declared areas. District Six was one of three areas given high priority. In 1965, however, the government froze all new development in the area.

The declaration of District Six as a 'white area' on 11 February 1966 was the death blow to the area and represented the culmination of a century of failed urban renewal projects and repeated attempts to segregate the city. The district's cultural and social heterogeneity, an 'alternate ... society with an identity',[34] was too great a threat to the apartheid state. This landmark declaration was unaffected by numerous protests by the community and the City Council. Landlords were barred from selling their properties to anyone other than the state, and in 1968 the first demolitions and forced removals began. During the following 20 years, over 30,000 people were removed from the district, and thousands of homes were destroyed. Protests and struggles were strong, as testified by the churches and mosques still standing today amidst the barren wasteland. Yet the opposition was unable to resist the power of the apartheid state.

Despite the vast expense of demolishing the area and government's zealous attempts to rebuild a bright white neighbourhood, the apartheid government was unable to implement future redevelopment plans. A series of at least four new masterplans for the area, symbolically renamed 'Zonnebloem' by the authorities in 1978, failed to materialize in substantial form. Lack of finance and political will, ever the problem with grand masterplans, continued to hinder the area's redevelopment. A number of small developments, such as several luxury housing complexes for whites only, an 'Asiatic Bazaar' for the removed Indian businessmen and a high-rise building for the Afrikaanse Christelike Vroue Vereniging, were completed and can be seen dotted around the area. The most significant intervention has been the substantial reconfiguration of the streets, in anticipation of future redevelopment and the construction, in the mid-1980s, of the then whites-only Cape Technikon. The latter took place amidst numerous protests from the remaining community and professional bodies, backed by the City Council. Suggestions for alternative sites were ignored by the authorities, and over 2,500 people were evicted to make space for the new development.

By 1980, conservative estimates put the cost of government expenditure on purchasing properties, demolishing buildings and administering the provision of alternative housing at R55 million. Yet by then only seven properties had been sold. At the same time, the City Council was losing R700,000 a year in unpaid rates from exempted government properties.[35] The grand visions of apartheid planning were going awry. In 1990, the UDF launched a nation-wide campaign to highlight the country's desperate housing crisis. In response to local pressure in Cape Town and threats of a mass land invasion of District

Six, a steering committee was set up to initiate and coordinate a replanning initiative for the area. This was composed of interested stakeholders in the district. The Cape Town Community Land Trust, set up in 1993 to coordinate the redevelopment of vacant land in the city, took over from the steering committee the following year. Its purpose is to consolidate state ownership land in order to facilitate a cohesive and comprehensive redevelopment. A District Six Forum has now been set up, consisting of stakeholders in the area, such as the civic associations, community and business organizations, the Cape Technikon and religious bodies. Through a slow process of consultation, the Land Trust hopes to arrive at consensus on an urban development framework for the area.

The Built Environment

The urban fabric of District Six before its destruction was characterized by a permeable grid of streets lined with predominantly terraced housing, one or two storeys high. There was little formal public open space and the streets became the major social and recreational spaces in the area. The high density of buildings encouraged a high density of population, which in turn was able to support a wide range of facilities and services. The urban fabric can be understood in terms of four aspects, all of which reinforced each other – the dominant structuring elements, the street network, density and land use. The buildings themselves and other architectural elements complemented these qualities to lend a richness and identity to the area.

Various natural and man-made elements greatly influenced the area's pattern of development, and its particular economic, social and cultural make-up. The sea and the mountain were the two dominant natural features in the area. Together they defined the northern and southern edges of the site, forming constant backdrops to the urban space of District Six. In its early days, there was a strong connection between the district and the natural environment. The proximity of the sea was particularly important since District Six was home to many fishermen, often small entrepreneurs with their own fishing boats. Woodstock Beach was a major recreational space, where the working class could escape the cramped conditions of their housing. The construction of the railway along the coast and the later infilling of the bay effectively severed this economic and recreational connection.

There was also a strong connection with the mountain, particularly during the early years of development. The slope of the land defined the pattern of the street network and the mountain created the final urban wall to the town. The mountain was always accessible by foot, just a short walk above the settlement, and the local washerwomen would use the mountain streams for washing. The later expansion of the town and construction of De Waal Drive contained further growth upwards and prevented direct pedestrian access to the mountain. The construction of pipes to channel the water also denied the washerwomen their means of livelihood; sometimes they would break open the pipes to access the water.

The western edge of District Six was defined by Buitenkant Street, the former eastern boundary of the original settlement of Cape Town. As we have seen, the proximity of the district to the city centre and the docks was one of the main reasons for its existence and popularity. People were able to walk to work, thus saving on transport costs, and the centre provided many public services that the poor could not afford individually. The eastern edge of District Six was delineated by the old French battery which later became incorporated into Trafalgar Park. This became a major recreation area, the only formal public green space in the district.

Two streets, Sir Lowry Road and Hanover Street, formed the backbone of District Six, integrating and linking it to central Cape Town and the rest of the city. Sir Lowry Road was the major road connection to the southern suburbs and beyond; Hanover Street was a more localized street – the primary public space of the district and its social and economic nerve centre. These two streets were the primary movement and commercial routes. Buses and trams ran along them, and every day they filled with people walking to work in the city centre. The dominance of these routes stimulated a higher concentration of commercial and social activities, taking advantage of the greater number of people passing by.

Behind these main roads were the quieter more residential areas with their variety of housing, interspersed with shops and community facilities. Thus, the district did not have a uniform intensity throughout. Rather, the grid and its structuring elements allowed for a variety of environmental, social and economic conditions. This contributed to the range of choice and diversity of activities, and the balance between various different needs within the city.

Although centrally located, District Six had far-reaching links with the rest of the metropolitan region. Its location on Sir Lowry Road and proximity to the railway station reinforced this connection and gave direct access to the hinterland. Likewise, the area was highly accessible from other parts of the metropolis and country. The harbour was the link to the rest of the world. It was a source of employment for many residents, and newly arrived immigrants, visitors and sailors stepping off the boats made a beeline for the cheap rooms, bars, shebeens and other illicit activities of the area.

The street grid, while not a unique quality (many parts of older Cape Town still retain their original grids), was one of the major factors contributing to the success of the urban fabric. It defined a series of square and rectangular blocks in which private, albeit speculative, development took place. These were planned at a pedestrian scale, with a high degree of permeability and accessibility through the area. It was an easily readable structure that offered a wide choice of routes and conditions through the neighbourhood. The intersections of the streets and the block corners were the junctions where several routes met. These were the sites of the ubiquitous *babie* (or neighbourhood), shops. Disturbances in the regular grid, caused by certain topographical and historical conditions, offered specific design opportunities. They were often the sites of architecturally significant buildings with special economic or social uses. Hanover Buildings, at the junction of five streets, became one of the more famous landmarks in the area.

Sir Lowry Road and Hanover Street structured the grid. Below Hanover Street, the grid followed the axis set up by Sir Lowry Road. Above Hanover Street, where the land was steeper, the axis shifted to coincide with the contour lines. The steep streets going against the contours framed views down to the sea and up to the mountain. It is interesting to note that in the district's early growth, when no definite street structure existed, new building development still took place along lines that anticipated a future grid. This set up a clear pattern for future development.

A third contributing factor to the life of the area was its high density of buildings and population. At the time of the Group Areas declaration, the overall population of the district was around 30,000.[36] The building density has been estimated at around 45 dwelling units/hectare.[37] Many of these houses were overcrowded, but the overall population density was only around 280 persons/hectare. This is similar to many European cities and much lower than many Asian cities. The large population living in the dense urban fabric provided a fertile ground for the generation of economic, social and cultural opportunities. It was able to support a diverse and complex range of activities and services that are lacking in suburban development. Located in the fine-grained grid,

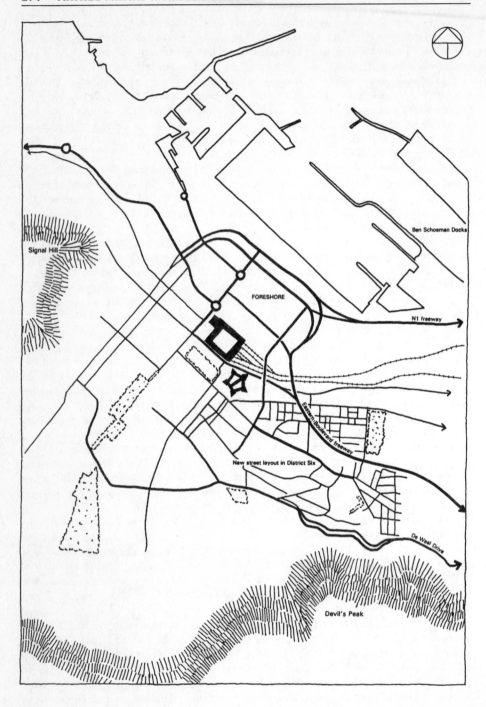

Figure 16.4 The growth of District Six, 1992

these amenities were generally situated within short distances of each other, ensuring a high degree of pedestrian accessibility and convenience. The density also contributed to the creation of a specific District Six identity, reinforced by the natural and urban boundaries of the district. At the same time, the wide diversity of cultures and religions living within the urban fabric generated a broad range of identities and allegiances, each with their territories and amenities. District Six was truly a 'many placed place'.[38]

The distribution of land uses in an area gives an indication of the range of facilities and amenities available to the local population. It also signifies the degree of equity that the urban structure affords, allowing and promoting many opportunities for economic, social and cultural interaction. A council land-use survey map of District Six in the early 1960s shows a wide diversity of services and amenities.[39] This was a function of the large number of people living in the district. A dense population in a relatively small area provided the bulk and economy necessary to support such a mix. Most facilities were within walking distance of anywhere in the vicinity, and despite the general poverty, the number of people was able to support the large number of shops and community facilities. In addition, the mix of residential and commercial functions meant that many people could both work and live in the same area, even in the same building. The enabling qualities of such an urban space is described by Bill Nasson: 'During peak work-times men would be obliged to stay on production in, for example, furniture factories, for excessively long hours. To sustain them until they returned home, a son would be sent with tea or soup in a can, and meat or cheese sandwiches. Taking food to a Searle Street factory in the 1920s would be combined with picking up cigarettes for a father's workmates: 'Always Three Castles or Commandos at that time, very strong, dark cigarettes which made them cough.'[40]

One of the features of District Six was the absence of formal 'public' open space: we have seen that Trafalgar Park was the only recreational ground in the area. Thus the streets became the major public spaces, where people socialized, children played and fought, street entertainers sought an audience, and informal vendors plied their wares – 'The street was home to absorbing sights and a vibrant communal life, it drew people like a magnet.'[41] These were the real social spaces of District Six, a reflection not only of the cramped living conditions and lack of alternative public space, but also of the cohesive and well-defined physical fabric that created these outdoor rooms.

A brief outline follows of the five main types of activity registered on the 1964 survey map.

Commercial

Sir Lowry Road and Hanover Street were the main commercial strips in the district, each functioning in a different way. The former acted as a link between the city centre and the southern suburbs and had a regional as well as local importance. This was reflected in the larger commercial spaces such as offices, banks, wholesalers and industrial units which were found along and behind the street. Hanover Street, by contrast, passed through the middle of District Six and primarily served the local population. It was inhabited mainly by smaller and medium-sized businesses, such as shops, cafés and bars. In addition, there were two cinemas, a public washhouse, and other social facilities as well as residential accommodation at the eastern end.

One of the characteristics of the area was the large number of corner shops. Again, this was a consequence of the high density of the population which could support many neighbourhood shops. These *babie* shops served many of the community's needs – groceries, housing articles, cleaning materials, wood and coal. In addition, there were butchers, bakeries, dairies, bootmakers and repairers, tobacconists, chemists and herbalists

Figure 16.5 Aerial photograph of District Six after its destruction. The remnants of the former street network can still clearly be seen, with part of the district south of the Eastern Boulevard still in existence. Kaisergracht, the Eastern Boulevard and the new road pattern can be seen slicing through the area, carving it up into amorphous tracts of land. *Source:* Cape Town City Council, 1992

scattered throughout the area. These shops sold small quantities, as cheaply and conveniently as possible.[42] Much was bought 'on tick', with the debt repaid on Friday evenings when wages were received. The next day the cycle of buying on credit resumed again until the following weekend. The corner shops also fulfilled a cultural role, centres of neighbourhood gossip and exchanges.

In addition to the formal activities, numerous informal activities took place in District Six. Many of these enterprises took place in buildings officially described as 'residential'. Self-employed businessmen and women, such as tailors, carpenters, dressmakers, shoemakers and seamstresses often worked from home.[43] Other families took in work to supplement household incomes, producing specialized items to order, such as decorated boxes, party cakes or stuffed toys. There were also numerous fruit and food vendors selling from stalls and tables on the streets. And then there were the many unofficial brothels and shebeens, sources of livelihood to many a resident.

Places of worship and schools

Historically, District Six supported a wide variety of religious groups and their places of worship. Churches, mosques and synagogues stood side by side in the area. These buildings, and their associated religious institutions, community halls and schools were often the focal point of communities, their social and cultural centres. While the synagogues disappeared long before the 1960s, many churches and all the mosques are still standing, a tribute to the resistance of the religious communities to the area's destruction.

At the time of the Group Areas declaration, District Six had 17 schools and colleges, and four community colleges. Most of these were associated with the churches, reflecting the missionary zeal with which the churches ministered to the needs of the 'deserving' poor.

Entertainment

The 'bioscopes' (cinemas) were the most popular form of entertainment right through to the 1950s, and cinema-going was both regular and habitual. Five cinemas catered for the residents of District Six. One of these, the City Cinema, was bulldozed during the construction of the Eastern Boulevard in the early 1960s. It was popular with farmers who came to the Early Morning Market. The other four cinemas were household names and still retain a strong hold in the popular consciousness of the area. These were the Avalon, the Star, the National and the British. Each had a different identity, defined by admission prices, seating quality, programme content and behaviour during the showings. Thus the Avalon was known as a 'respectable' place where 'a better class of person' went. The Star, by contrast, was patronized by the gangs who could smoke dagga in peace there. Each gangster had his own regular seat. And, as with many of the buildings in District Six, even the cinemas were used for a variety of purposes. They were also venues for talent shows, concerts and dancing.

Although there were several social and cultural centres within District Six, and plenty of entertainment on the streets, residents also sought entertainment outside the area. Attendance at the opera and classical concerts at the City Hall was widespread among both the middle class and 'respectable' working class, while cabaret at the Tivoli and 'Palm Court' bands at Delmonico's on Riebeeck Street were also popular.

Recreation

Trafalgar Park was the only recreational ground in the area, forming the eastern boundary of District Six. The swimming pool, crowded out during the summer, was built during the 1930s. Woodstock beach was another popular local recreation spot for the residents, until it was eradicated by the Foreshore development. Outings further afield were also common, affording the residents temporary escape from the cramped conditions of their housing. Afternoons spent on Adderley Street pier, tram rides to Sea Point and Camps Bay, and day trips to Muizenburg were some of the staple leisure activities.

Residential

Housing formed the dominant building block of the area. A correlation can be seen between the housing typology, date of construction and the class of tenants. The earliest houses were nearly all single-storey buildings, with a parapet roof and simple elevation to the street. The most basic houses were built directly onto the street while other houses had *stoeps* (verandahs) to mediate the transition between the public street and the private interior. The houses were contiguous, divided by 'party' walls, forming a continuous row along the street. This type of house, and its many variations, continued to be built until the beginning of this century.

Towards the end of the nineteenth century, a more elaborate housing type was built by speculative developers, reflecting contemporary colonial housing types. These were also single-storey row houses but the entrances often had covered *stoeps*, and sometimes additional front yards. Decoration was generally added by the means of cast iron columns and '*broekie* lace' metalwork on the eaves, all imported through Victorian mail order catalogues popular at the time. The construction of two-storey houses, with balconies and covered entrances, responded to the need for more housing at the end of the last century. A particular characteristic of all the row housing was the similarity in floor plans, derived from the type of working-class row housing found in Victorian Britain. While the actual width and length of the dwelling varied, the spatial layout remained fairly consistent. This comprised two main spaces – the front 'sitting room' and the back 'bedroom' – connected to each other by means of a passageway and terminating at the kitchen. This in turn gave way to a back yard which contained a separate toilet and had access to a common service lane at the rear of the property. Before water-borne sewage was introduced to the area, this service lane would have been used by night soil workers collecting sewage and rubbish.

Other types of housing were found in the area. Dense, multi-occupancy housing was found in larger two- and three-storey buildings, often with shops and other commercial activities on the ground floor. Eaton Place, with over 50 families, was one such building. There were also semi-detached and detached houses, occupied by wealthier families. These also had *stoeps* and covered verandahs, often raised above street level. Many of these houses replaced the housing demolished during the plague epidemic at the beginning of this century. There were also the Bloemhof Flats which replaced the notorious Wells Square area in the 1930s.

The Urban Elements

District Six was composed of a wide variety of building types, which together formed a coherent and integrated fabric. The buildings stood shoulder to shoulder creating an urban wall that defined the street as the public realm and mediated the transition between the street and home. Most of the buildings were relatively simple and the housing formed a low rise backdrop to larger 'landmark' buildings. These socially, culturally and eco-nomically important buildings – mosques, churches, social centres – reflected their prestige through their architecture. Minarets, spires, elaborate detailing, fancy balconies and sheer size – all signalled their presence and importance in the community. These buildings contributed to the area's identity, expressing the cultural and social dynamics of the local population. While the mosques tended to be integrated into the surrounding built fabric, the churches were detached buildings, standing apart from the surrounding structures, often creating a public space in front.

The street was the primary gathering space in District Six[44] and the interface between the street and the buildings was an important element in the making of the urban fabric. These 'transitional zones' clearly defined the private space of the house, but still allowed visual and social contact with the street. By contrast, many of today's developments turn their backs to the street, creating a hostile urban environment and eliminating any possibility of social interaction between the home and the street. Although the threshold was clearly defined, the social distinction between the public street and private home was not pronounced.[45] The high numbers of people living cheek by jowl and the shared social and economic conditions helped generate high levels of interdependence and strong community bonds. Neighbours were constantly popping over to borrow a cup of sugar, for example, and children were continually running between houses and streets.

The residential areas responded to the street in different ways. Some houses were built right up to the pavement, with little mediation between the street and home. Other houses were pulled back from the road and had well articulated transitional zones between the public street and the private house. These included elements such as *stoeps*, steps, verandahs, balconies and front yards. Although the building itself was recessed, these other elements still defined the street edge clearly and maintained visual contact between the house and street. These elements also enabled the buildings to partake in the life of the street. They provided a variety of different spaces and zones in which social and economic interactions could take place.

The houses were generally fairly uniform in height and scale, with simple, vertically proportioned openings with a variety of different decorations and finishes. The rhythm of windows, the '*broekie* lace' eaves details, elaborate gables and cornices, balconies or simply different colour paint all served to distinguish one house from the next. The house interiors were often personalized and well tended. Differences between houses may have been small, but they were important. In some cases, the only distinction between different row houses may have been in the interior furnishings; some only had mats inside, 'not a full carpet which we had'.[46]

The more important commercial streets of Hanover Street and Sir Lowry Road had a different scale, particularly at the town end. Here three-storey buildings created a greater sense of enclosure and announced their importance with their massiveness. Other architectural devices, such as the articulation of corners, the use of elaborate detailing, and particular building and paving materials, all contributed to the richness and identity of the urban environment, responding in particular ways to particular events in the urban fabric.

Many of these elements and principles were not applied as conscious acts of design. More often, they arose spontaneously out of particular opportunities that were generated by the urban environment. And although much of this environment was developed for profit, it was still built within a continuous tradition of urbanism – new and old buildings were built within existing street patterns and along common building lines. This created a cohesive and richly textured matrix, reflecting the different building traditions of the past and building up historical layers and memory within the urban fabric. This contributed to the sense of history, continuity and identity in the area.

The Way Forward

The destruction of District Six robbed Cape Town of a vibrant and vital community. It also destroyed an urban environment which expressed many of the qualities of urbanity that South Africa has lost. This chapter has attempted to explore the nature of these qualities and to understand how the built environment interacted and supported the social and cultural fabric. The physical environment cannot dictate the social and cultural relations of its inhabitants, nor indeed can it solve socio-economic problems, as the idealistic modernists proclaimed. We believe, however, that sensitive design can promote choices and opportunities for a variety of social and economic interactions, and facilitate the growth and development of a community. An urban environment which is close to economic opportunities and planned with a fine-grained street network, wide range of facilities, and high-density, low-rise, multi-functional buildings is far more supportive of poorer communities than the low-density, monofunctional sprawl that characterizes South African (sub)urbanism today.

We are not seeking a pastiche replica of a nostalgic past, rather an understanding of the urban principles which shaped the area. These can be interpreted at a detailed level in many different ways to accommodate contemporary and changing needs. These are principles which now, more than ever, need to be considered urgently. South African cities are currently developing along the lines of previous modernist and apartheid planning ideologies, in a free market environment. The cities' development lies in the hands of private housing developers. Where, in the past, private speculators built within an urban framework of human-scaled public space, today the emphasis is on individualism and the car. In contrast to the heavy-handed intervention of modernist planning, today the state, and local authorities in particular, have all but abdicated responsibility. The poor continue to be marginalized.

Stakeholders in District Six are embarking on a participatory planning process to decide the area's future. We hope this chapter contributes to the debate on its reconstruction, and that of South African cities more generally. The challenge for practitioners is to generate an urbanism that contributes to the rebuilding of communities. Until planners, developers and other professionals understand the lessons of the past, the present inequalities will continue to be perpetuated into the future. Through an analysis of historical urbanism in conjunction with an understanding of our current problems, the redevelopment of District Six can provide a critique of contemporary planning paradigms. It can serve as a model for a renewed urbanism to produce a human-scaled, efficient and equitable urban environment in which all can partake.

Notes

1 The chapter is based on an exhibition entitled 'Texture and Memory: The Urbanism of District Six', shown at the Cape Technikon, Cape Town, 30 November – 8 December, 1995, and the conference 'Africa's Urban Past', SOAS, London, 19-21 June 1996.

2 See D. Dewar and R. Uytenbogaardt, *A Manifesto for Change* (Urban Problems Research Unit, University of Cape Town, 1994). For a similar study of other areas in Cape Town, see D. Dewar and R. Uytenbogaardt, *et al.*, *Housing: A Comparative Evaluation of Urbanism in Cape Town* (Urban Problems Research Unit, University of Cape Town, 1978).

3 European Bastides were medieval fortified towns set out on a grid pattern, and generally enclosed by a defensive wall. Numerous Bastides were established in England, Wales and France during the early thirteenth century, and later in other parts of Northern Europe. Their plan formed the basis of subsequent city building in the colonies, reinforced in South America by the 'Laws of the Indies':

F. Todeschini, 'Cape Town: Physical planning traditions of a settlement in transition', *Architecture SA*, March/April 1994, pp. 31–8. See also L. Benevolo, *The History of the City* (London, 1980).

4 D. Dewar *et al.*, *The Structure and Form of Metropolitan Cape Town: Its Origins, Influences and Performance* (Working Paper No. 42, Urban Problems Research Unit/Urban Foundation (Western Cape), University of Cape Town, 1990), p. 8.

5 Dewar *et al.*, *Structure and Form*, p. 8.

6 Todeschini, 'Cape Town', p. 33.

7 Dewar *et al.*, *Structure and Form*, p. 8.

8 Todeschini, 'Cape Town', p. 34.

9 Dewar *et al.*, *Structure and Form*, p. 11.

10 *Ibid.*, p. 14.

11 For a history of the area now known as Bo Kaap, see L. and S. Townsend, *Bokaap – Faces and Facades* (Cape Town, 1977).

12 Vivian Bickford-Smith, 'The origins and early history of District Six', *The Struggle for District Six* (Cape Town, 1990), p. 37.

13 Carl Schoeman, *District Six – The Spirit of Kanala* (Cape Town, 1993).

14 *Ibid.*

15 The origins of the name Kanaladorp are unclear, but could refer either to the Malay word 'kanala', meaning 'to help one another' or 'if you please', or from the fact that the area was on the eastern side of a canal.

16 Quoted in Schoeman, *District Six*, p. 18.

17 Interview with Mr van Niekerk of Lucy Villas, 25 McGregor Street, District Six, quoted in J. Marx, 'District Six and its buildings' (photocopied report, no date: obtained from the National Monuments Council, Cape Town).

18 Bickford-Smith, 'Origins and early history', p. 36.

19 Quoted in Schoeman, *District Six*, p. 18.

20 Bickford-Smith, 'Origins and early history', p. 39.

21 *Ibid.*, p. 40.

22 E. van Heyningen, 'Cape Town and the Plague of 1901', in C. Saunders, H. Phillips and E. van Heyningen (eds), *Studies in the History of Cape Town 4* (Cape Town, 1981), p. 95.

23 Bickford-Smith, 'Origins and early history', p. 41.

24 Garden cities were the vision of Ebenezer Howard. Arising in part in reaction to the slums of Victorian cities, he saw them as vehicles for a progressive reconstruction of capitalist society into an 'infinity of cooperative commonwealths'. Through these new settlements, he sought to combine the best of both town and country. Each garden city was to have a population of 32,000 people on 1,000 acres held by a limited company owned by the residents. It was to be a largely self-contained settlement with a full range of activities, such as industrial commercial, residential, recreational and educational facilities, and surrounded by a green belt containing both farms and urban institutions. Each garden city was to offer a wide range of jobs and services, but was also connected, via a rapid transit system, to other garden cities, to form a larger unit called the Social City: P. Hall, *Cities of Tomorrow* (Oxford, 1988).

25 The concept of the Neighbourhood Unit was derived from the Garden City Movement, but adapted to an American context. Developed by Clarence Perry in the 1920s, the essence of his idea was to enhance 'the social nature and ideals of the individual'. The zoning of activities was a major element of the Neighbourhood Unit. Residential areas were to be separated from industrial and commercial activities in a system of self-contained, inward looking developments focused around community facilities. Developed at a time of great influx of immigrants and refugees into the country, the Unit was intended to socialize the newcomers into American society: Hall, *Cities of Tomorrow*, p. 128.

26 Dewar *et al.*, *Structure and Form*, p. 42.

27 Bickford-Smith, 'Origins and early history', p. 36.

28 Dewar *et al.*, *Structure and Form*, p. 45.

29 Quoted from Schoeman, *District Six*, p. 28.

30 The dominant themes in modernist planning were to do with the zoning and the separation of different functions of the city. The activities of working, living, entertainment and transport were all to take place in separately defined areas. Ideas of space and light, in contrast to the crowded and dark Victorian city, were reflected in the architecture of apartment blocks set in open green fields. Speed

of transport and connecting highways became the dominating factor in the planning of urban areas, privileging the motor car as a form of transport. Combined with the construction of functionally separate and widely spaced buildings, this new planning led to the near extinction of the street as a communal social space and made pedestrian access difficult and tiresome. The greatest protagonist of modern town planning was the architect Le Corbusier, whose writings and ideas have had a profound effect on cities all over the world. For an overview, see Hall, *Cities of Tomorrow*.

31 See N. Barnett, 'The planned destruction of District Six in 1940', in E. van Heyningen (ed.), *Studies in the History of Cape Town 6* (Cape Town, 1994); and D. Pinnock, 'Ideology and urban planning: blueprints of a garrison city', in W. James and M. Simons (eds), *Class, Caste and Colour* (New Brunswick, 1992).

32 The basis for African urbanisation and housing policies from the 1940s was the infamous Stallardist doctrine that: 'the Native should only be allowed to enter urban areas, which are essentially the white man's creation, when he is willing to enter and to minister to the needs of the white man, and should depart therefrom when he ceases so to minister': Quoted in D. Hindson, *Pass Controls and the Urban Proletariat* (Johannesburg, 1987) p. 36.

33 Dewar *et al.*, *Structure and Form*, pp. 60–3.

34 D. Pinnock, 'District Six: historical vignettes', *South African Outlook*, January 1980, pp. 9–11.

35 'Apartheid vs. People', *SA Outlook*, January 1980, pp. 3–5.

36 S. De Villiers, *A Tale of Three Cities* (Cape Town, 1985).

37 'Texture and Memory: The Urbanism of District Six', exhibition by the Urban Housing Research Unit, Cape Technikon, 30 November–8 December 1995, Cape Town.

38 Pinnock, 'District Six'.

39 'Texture and Memory' exhibition.

40 Quoted in Bill Nasson, 'Oral history and the reconstruction of District Six', in *Struggle for District Six*, p. 53. The following sections draw extensively on this chapter.

41 *Ibid.*, p. 56.

42 *Ibid.*, p. 60.

43 *Ibid.*, p. 62.

44 Soudien and Meltzer describe the street as the 'every day bioscope of people's lives': C. Soudien and L. Meltzer, 'Representation and struggle', in *District Six: Image and Representation* (catalogue from an exhibition at the South African National Gallery, 1995), p. 12.

45 *Ibid.*, p. 12.

46 Quoted in Nasson, 'Oral history', p. 52.

17

The Political Shaping of Sacred Locality in Brazzaville 1959–97

FLORENCE BERNAULT

Colonial towns have been celebrated by colonial powers as paradigms of modernity, interracial encounters, and blurring ethnicity.[1] Historians, of course, have explored the contradictions in this discourse thoroughly, and have unveiled the numerous projects and practices of racial and spatial segregation in colonial towns. But many studies have also documented how the city provided African urbanites with a space in which to approach, benefit from, and confront colonial rule while appropriating new domains of transgression and autonomy. Cities in Africa are increasingly envisioned as privileged *places de colonisation*,[2] arenas of both open and hidden games of control, appropriation and escape. This approach fits well with current trends in colonial history, especially for those who have moved from a polarized analysis of relations of power in the colony to understanding colonial relationships as the configuration of a new field of language and culture. The colonial enterprise at large is no longer exclusively described in terms of domination and resistance, of clashing spheres of political, racial and cultural mobilization, but as the emergence of a complex *lieu* of interaction where power is best described as a site, a locus delineated by the encounter itself, formulated daily through the myriads of physical, *verbal*, and political exchanges between the colonizers and the colonized. Because this historical perspective is best rendered in spatial terms, and through analyses of actual *places*, the colonial city itself emerges as a particularly appropriate field of research, and, in turn, it tends to be examined through the enhanced perspective of circulation, contact, and hybridity, rather than of opposition, segregation and polarization.

In late 1992, a violent civil war erupted in Brazzaville, the capital of the Congo. Over several months, military clashes led to the disintegration of urban space and communities, and resulted in the reconfiguration of the capital into three politico-ethnic territories controlled by rival factions. Each of these new neighbourhoods was thoroughly enclosed by barricades and checkpoints, and all experienced bloody 'ethnic cleansing' by militias eager to rid themselves of potential enemies. From 1994 to June 1997 a fragile peace prevailed and movement was restored throughout the city during daylight hours. The capital remained divided, however, and in June 1997 war broke out again, provoking the exodus of some 200,000 to 500,000 people.[3] Focusing on the power struggles among the three Congolese 'big men' (Pascal Lissouba, the current president; Denis Sassou Nguesso, the

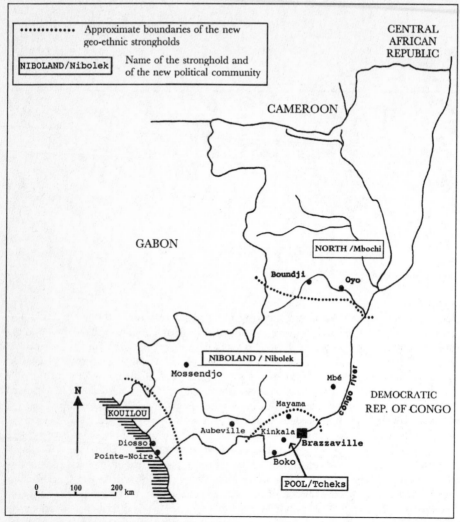

Figure 17.1 Congo's political regions, 1992–5

former president; and Bernard Kolélas, the mayor of Brazzaville), social scientists have tended to analyze the war in terms of recent personal, political, and ethnic rivalries.[4] Others have stressed the crucial role of desperate unemployed youth in the conflagrations.[5] But almost no one has linked the 1992–7 upheavals to the specific urban setting of the war – a pattern which can be traced back three decades to the deadly riots which devastated Brazzaville in February 1959. The 1959 riots place the 1992–7 conflict within a larger framework, a cycle of urban ethnic and spatial fragmentation dating back to the end of colonial rule.[6]

What is at issue in the following analysis is not simply a political narrative, nor the history of urban space, but an understanding of the connection between politics and urban territory. The real issue is to appraise the organic and ideological conjunction between a material reality and a moral unity; in other words the historical production of an urban space which has thrice polarized the capital city into fragmented, war-ridden territories emerging from the brutal fusion of urbanites, urban space and ideological representations. For the last four decades, contrary to the modern paradigm in African urban studies, the quest for central power in Congo-Brazzaville has been acted out through the building of secluded urban territories, ritualized identities, hidden and secret activities, exclusion and reclusion. As such, the Brazzaville tragedies seem to document a clash between the thin dam of modernity and the brutal flood of revived archaisms; the formation of hermetic territories led by politicians transformed into warlords, the recourse to magical practices, and the radicalization of ethnic polarization among soldiers and militants would appear to underline the dramatic resurgence of pre-colonial forms of political violence and the collapse of the modern architecture of the capital. This article will defend the opposite hypothesis. The Brazzaville wars did not result from the contradictions between an archaic political culture and a modern physical space, but from the articulation of a modern political system and an archaic space, the colonial city.

Electoral Ethnicity in the City

The crucial role of ethnicity in modern Congolese politics tends to obscure the fact that political identities in the second half of the twentieth century did not derive mechanistically from ancient communities, but emerged recently from the competition for central power in colonial and post-colonial Congo. This process took place primarily in the city, not in rural areas. Brazzaville emerged in the 1930s as the central cradle for engineering modern ethnicity. In the 1950s, heightened political rivalries led to the rigidification of urban identities – a process which soon contaminated the entire spectrum of Congolese politics.

In 1959, civil war broke at the height of a increasingly violent rivalry between the two main Congolese parties.[7] The UDDIA,[8] a party mainly implanted in the southern part of the colony and led by the flamboyant Catholic priest Fulbert Youlou, from the south of the colony, had emerged in 1955–6 as the main rival to the MSA,[9] a party based mainly in the northern part of the country, and led by Jacques Opangault, a civil servant of Mbochi origin.[10] In 1956, the French government authorized the formation of the first African cabinet. The MSA candidates won the elections with one seat, and Opangault became Prime Minister in April 1957. Over the next few months Youlou, as Secretary of Agriculture and Mayor of Brazzaville, consolidated his position. He managed to attract several MSA deputies to his camp, skilfully depriving Opangault of his political majority. On 26 August 1958 the two leaders agreed on a compromise. Youlou would replace Opangault as Prime Minister, but new elections would be organized in March 1959 to renew the National Assembly, giving the MSA an opportunity to regain its majority. On 28 November 1958, the National Assembly elected Youlou head of the government, but it refused to consider new elections.

Opangault's only hope resided in pushing for legislative elections. On 16 February 1959, at the opening of the Spring session of the National Assembly in Brazzaville, Opangault and his followers had planned to lobby for the dissolution of the Assembly and for new elections. On the same morning, 400 to 500 members of the MSA gathered in the Bar Bouya in Poto-Poto and waited to hear the outcome of the Assembly debates. In mid-afternoon, some MSA deputies arrived at Bar Bouya and announced that the UDDIA had refused to organize new elections. In response, infuriated militants organized in commandos and began to attack residents considered to be UDDIA sympathizers, and labelled as Lari (Youlou's ethnic group). In 1959 Poto-Poto was inhabited by residents of diverse origins. An expanding district in the north-eastern part of

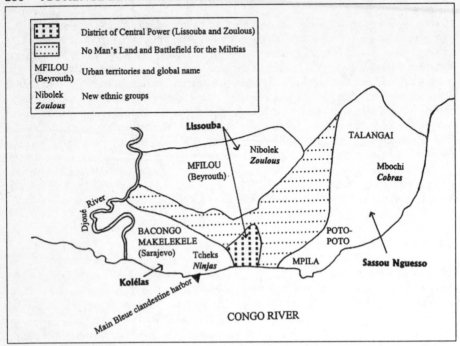

	District of Central Power (Lissouba and Zoulous)
	No Man's Land and Battlefield for the Militias
MFILOU (Beyrouth)	Urban territories and global name
Nibolek *Zoulous*	New ethnic groups

Figure 17.2 Brazzaville's territories, 1992–5

Brazzaville, it sheltered recent immigrants from all regions of the Congo.[11] Using knives, machetes and sticks, the gangs beat and stabbed to death seven people and wounded 40 more. Almost immediately, news of the slaughter spread to Bacongo, the African district in south-west Brazzaville. This neighbourhood, inhabited by stabilized urbanites from the southern part of the Congo, had proved to be Youlou's major electoral reservoir in Brazzaville since 1955. UDDIA militants began to erect barricades on Bacongo's main axes, while 'self-defence' militia organized and chased residents from the north, accused of being MSA supporters. In spite of the deployment of French troops,[12] sporadic violence broke out again in both Poto-Poto and Bacongo on 17 and 18 February. Only by the evening of 19 February did the army succeed in ending the massacres through systematic confiscation of weapons, street patrols and a military buffer zone between Bacongo and Poto-Poto.[13]

Brazzaville thus split into two new districts, each fused and separated from the other by political conflict. In the minds of the combatants, the capital's residents were segregated into new ethnic groups, modelled by the MSA/UDDIA opposition. All residents of southern origin were designated by MSA militants as 'Lari' and supporters of UDDIA, while residents of northern origin were in turn globally perceived as 'Mbochi' (Opangault's ethnic group) and supporters of the MSA. The labelling revealed a complex political innovation. It forcibly pushed every urbanite into one of the new ethnic identities, corresponding to the ethnic group of their leaders. The core Lari and Mbochi communities were far from coherent, however, nor uniformly loyal to the leaders. Each was deeply divided by tensions and conflict readily transferred into the sphere of national politics. Opangault's and Youlou's electoral reservoirs prior to 1959 had extended far across these hard-core Lari and Mbochi constituencies. Both had attracted support from different geographical areas, religious communities, generations and socio-professional categories. Finally, large numbers of the victims had remained until then indifferent to the political rivalry of Opangault and Youlou.

Indeed, the flexibility of their electoral support might explain in part the feverish actions initiated by the killers, anxious to discriminate among Brazzaville residents by 'revealing' invisible identities and ascertaining political loyalties. Linguistic culture played a major role in this reclassification. In the streets and on the barricades, militia members conducted expeditious linguistic trials. In this highly multilingual metropolis, suspects were questioned for cultural and literary knowledge (proverbs, answers to riddles, etc.) in order to ascertain their 'real' origin. Within the militias, identity anxieties also proved important; they invented new rituals to bond together, such as wearing a symbolic colour – a red headband for the MSA, a white one for the UDDIA. All voluntary and involuntary actors of the tragedy enacted or were forced to enact a new, radicalized identity, while the proclaimed incompatibility between the enlarged ethnic groups bore no meaning with reference to pre-colonial history. It had acquired meaning only in the context of the quest for state power, and of the rise of UDDIA and MSA as dominant parties in the 1940s and 1950s.[14]

The outcome of the 1959 Brazzaville riots endured as a structuring factor of Congolese politics over the next three decades. Between 1959 and 1991, political manoeuvres systematically situated themselves in the ideological opposition of a politico-regional 'north' and 'south'. Each political alliance, however it differed from this polarization in reality, could be interpreted according to it, and thus helped to preserve it.[15] Simultaneously, the physical imprint of the north–south clash vanished in Brazzaville. As soon as Youlou's government appeared to have survived the crisis successfully, refugees from each Brazzaville district began to go back to their former houses and neighbourhoods. The previously ethnically defined districts sank in people's memories and, within a few weeks, the city's violent fragmentation virtually disappeared, leaving no apparent traces on the town's human or urban structure. The conflict had transformed an open, torn urban space into an internalized master narrative of national politics. But real blood had presided over the christening of the Congo's independent state.[16]

In 1968, Congo entered a new political phase. Army officers of northern origin seized power, strengthened the single-party system and monopolized it until 1991; they reduced southerners to opposition or limited collaboration. In 1991, under mounting national and international pressure, President Denis Sassou Nguesso approved the convening of a National Conference in Brazzaville. The Conference adopted a new constitution, authorized multiple parties, and organized presidential elections. The main political parties then compromised on an outside candidate, Pascal Lissouba. Native of a marginal region (Niari in south-central Congo) which had participated in state power through opportunistic alliance or opposition, but which had always appeared peripheral to the core of the north–south canvas, Lissouba offered a possibility of political compensation for the 'south' without constituting a real threat to the northerners.[17] In August 1992 he was elected president of the Congo Republic. Less than three months later, civil war broke out again in Brazzaville.

Denis Sassou Nguesso, a Mbochi, and Bernard Kolélas, a Lari and a former political prisoner under Sassou Nguesso's regime, both claimed that Lissouba was violating the National Conference agreements and monopolizing power. In June 1993 they boycotted the second round of legislative elections, denouncing government fraud. Kolélas appealed for civil disobedience and encouraged the building of barricades in Bacongo. On 27 June he formed a dissident government in Brazzaville with Sassou Nguesso. Lissouba immediately ordered the army to dismantle the barricades in Bacongo, the rebel district. In Bacongo, young males devoted to Kolélas formed a defensive militia under the name of Ninjas. In Mpila, soldiers devoted to Sassou Nguesso adopted the name of Cobras. Young southerners from the three central regions loyal to the president (Nibolek)[18] formed their own militia, the Zoulous, and joined government troops under Lissouba's direction. On 3 November 1993 these troops attacked dissident areas. After several weeks of heavy combat, the Ninjas and Cobras succeeded in driving the government troops back. Meanwhile Mfilou, a mixed residential district, fell victim to competing Zoulous and Ninjas militias. Within a few weeks, the militias had killed 2,000 people and provoked the mass exodus of 100,000 to 200,000 residents. Suspected Nibolek supporters had to flee from Bacongo, while Lari and southern people had to leave Mfilou and the parts of the capital under Zoulou control.[19]

By the end of 1993, Brazzaville was divided into three ethnic districts controlled by armed militias. Early in 1994, peace negotiations between Lissouba, Kolélas and Sassou-Nguesso ended the slaughter but failed to erase the city's new frontiers. By mid-1995 people could again move freely in the capital, but families expelled from their homes could not return to them. Most of them had found shelter in 'their' designated district in the abandoned houses of expelled families from the other faction. Mfilou refugees occupied a temporary camp in the neutral zone of the forest reserve in downtown Brazzaville. Militias still patrolled each district, and the new urban divisions were carefully kept alive by politicians and militants. In June 1997, a few weeks before new presidential elections took place, the war started again. This time, the conflict burst out of Brazzaville and overflowed into the rest of the country. Mass migrations ensued, particularly in the south. Lari residents were chased from Nibolek regions, and many tried to seek shelter in Bacongo or in surrounding 'Lari' towns. The whole country has become split into three political strongholds, opposing the north, the 'Lari' south, and the central south (Nibolek), and subjecting all areas to ethnic purges and provincial militias patrols.

The violent formation of political space in Brazzaville and in the Congo rests upon a particular matrix of national politics, characterized by the endurance of the exclusive and rigid nature of central power, the brutality of electoral mobilizations, the fragility of political alliances and the volatility of electorates. Contrasted with the few years of electoral freedom, the harshness of the state political monopoly has represented one of the most striking continuities between the colonial and the post-colonial period. Following the colonial model, the administration of power in the Congo has worked largely on the principle of 'winner takes all'.[20] In this context, the brief periods of electoral competition (1957–9, 1990–2, 1997) combined with the widespread expectation that access to power would promptly be closed afterwards, partly explains the brutality of electoral and post-electoral mobilizations. The second crucial characteristic of the Congolese political matrix rests upon the volatility of political alliances and political identities. Colonists had thought that large and unified ethnic groups, such as the Batéké, the Kongo, the Mbochi, the Kouyou, and so on, would play a leading role in the elections. While these categories had many common cultural and historical features, on the level of modern politics they were characterized primarily by numerous divisions. Moreover, none of these large entities were demographically important enough to provide any leader with an electoral majority. As a consequence, politicians played on the diversity and omnipresence of divisions and rivalries in different segments of the population in order to amass electoral support on the national level. Fulbert Youlou, for example, typically managed in the mid-1950s to build support among the divided Lari of Brazzaville by flattering both the old religious leaders of this community, faithful to the Matsouanist movement, and the young urbanites, eager to obtain positions in the new political system opened up by the French. He used a similar strategy in the north of the colony to promote generational divisions among the Kouyou and to encourage loyalty among young voters dispossessed by elders from local positions of power in the countryside. In central Niari, he skilfully allied himself with a religious leader, Lassy Zephirin, to finance the spread of a new anti-witchcraft cult, *nzambi-bougie*, in the lands of his adversaries and to attract the votes of members of the new church.

The legislative and presidential campaign of 1991–2 revealed a comparable fragmentation of the Congolese political arena. Bernard Kolélas and his MCDDI party (Congolese Movement for Democracy and Integral Development) appeared as the major figure in the presidential and legislative election with strong support in the Pool region. But he also gained support outside the Pool by his position as a long-time opponent and political prisoner of Sassou Nguesso, thus symbolizing both the heroic southern resistance to the north, and the rebellion against state dictatorship. The former president, Sassou Nguesso, established his support in the Mbochi region, in the army, in Brazzaville, and among the members of the PCT (Congolese Labour Party), the backbone of the former regime's bureaucracy. He also managed to derive ample electoral support from diverse segments of the population through personal wealth and political connections.

While voting loyalties widely crossed over supposed ethnic sentiments, alliances among leaders also proved flexible. Sassou Nguesso supported Pascal Lissouba during the second round of the presidential elections in 1992. In November of that year, however, he switched alliance and secretly agreed with Kolélas to challenge the newly elected Lissouba government. In June 1997 the central conflict was one between Lissouba and Sassou Nguesso, while Kolélas abandoned his earlier ally and decided to join Lissouba's government.

Far from being determined by permanent rivalries of unchanged 'ethnic groups', the overall political canvas flows from the prominence of big men's rivalries and changing interests. During the peaks of competition for central power, militants and voters were offered legitimizing narratives and cynical sets of beliefs and propaganda in order to solidify, however temporarily, fluid electoral bases into ideologically rigidified communities. Closer to the present, the memory of the recent wars and the increasing brutality of polical rivalries have rigidified Congo's geo-ethnic identities. Colonial ethnic representations have triumphed. What remains to be explained is how these identities have anchored themselves into physical territories, and why Brazzaville, while no longer the sole battleground of political feuds, has endured as the central matrix in this crucial process of localization.

A Strange Modernity

In twentieth-century Congo, cities have persistently served as ideological referents for crisis, chaos, order and power. Brazzaville in particular, concentrating colonial urban planning, mass migrations and social disorder, epitomized the contradictions of colonial and post-colonial disruptions.[21] While colonial rule struggled against perceived disorder, it was sustained simultaneously by its very threat. The colonial regime used the expanding capital as a laboratory to concentrate African *sujets*, exert control over potential dissidence, engrave spatial order in the colony, and finally diffuse a specific idea of central power.

Visibility and sheer force were the two pillars of French urban doctrine in the colonial capitals, and Brazzaville was no exception. From 1910, when the city became the capital of French Equatorial Africa, the administration deployed systematic efforts to impose an architecture of domination in the city. Among the first projects was the building of an imposing administrative centre, the Plateau, intended to balance the visible impact of the

Catholic mission complex, the first nucleus of an organized European presence in Brazzaville. South of the Plateau and the Mission, in the Plaine district, a city hall, a post office and a prison completed a triangular complex of power in the colonial city.

Following independence, Brazzaville remained the prominent battleground for the symbolic display of central power in Congo. Older colonial sites have more often than not decayed, and new places of remembrance which stressed the historical rupture of 1960 have been created.[22] Successive Congolese regimes have continued to use the urban landscape for purposes of political exaltation.[23] In the 1980s and 1990s, for example, the construction of the Palace of the People (financed by China), the new sports stadium, the Avenue of the Martyrs (honouring the memory of three demonstrators killed during the 1963 revolution), and a new City Hall have reinforced the city as a showcase of legitimacy and the political fortress of Congolese governments. The socialist/military government (1968–90) made an important innovation when it used the streets of Brazzaville as a laboratory for presidential personality cults, displaying giant posters of the president, or paintings of state slogans in the streets and on public buildings. Not only did Brazzaville prove to be an enduring shelter of central power, but central power increasingly saturated strategic public urban space.

A Neo-Garrison City

The concentration of the power apparatus in Brazzaville rested on another essential foundation: the presence of the army. This apparent anachronism illuminates the endurance of the garrison city in colonial Africa, long after its disappearance in Europe.[24] Striking similarities exist between the fortress city of medieval Europe, coalescing around the castles of landlords and military chiefs, and the colonial capitals growing around the first European military outposts. Both gathered, in a hierarchical yet unstable system, burgeoning dwellings of bourgeois and peasant inhabitants around a politically and spatially autonomous centre of authority that controlled the exercise of public power through a permanent garrison, the monopoly of armed force, and the regulation of trade and rights of property. The resilience of this pattern in colonial and post-colonial Africa sheds light on military domination as a crucial and enduring source of power.

In Brazzaville, the military presence has been imposing ever since the early colonial period. As a military post it became the headquarters of FEA forces in 1908.[25] Troops were stationed in a major camp (Camp Tchad, renamed Camp de la Milice in the 1960s) facing Bacongo. After independence, the military presence spread into several other urban garrisons, and began to diffuse outside the camps. During periods of peace, military celebrations and marches (especially the colonial celebration of 14 July) and the constant presence of uniforms in the streets, have all played an important role in structuring public urban space. During periods of crisis (the 1959 riots, the 1963 revolution, the presidential coups of 1968 and 1979) soldiers and militias literally invaded the capital. Several months after the 1963 revolution, the revolutionary militias still controlled movement and traffic in Brazzaville. Loosely organized in order to hire unemployed militants attached to Marien Ngouabi's and later Sassou Nguesso's regimes via the PCT as a revolutionary tool of 'scientific socialism', they were still active in the late 1980s.

Post-colonial regimes and the popular imagination have further enhanced the physical proximity of the state and military power. The material residence of central power has gradually fused with the concentration of armed forces. During the Trois Glorieuses Revolution (1963), the crowd demonstrating in front of Youlou's palace tried to discourage trade union emissaries from entering the building and initiating negotiations with the president. Protesters believed that Youlou had set traps and mines along the path and had put electric fences around the palace to repel any outside threat.[26] In the 1980s, Sassou Nguesso entrenched himself in a new palace facing the Congo River. This large complex, surrounded by high walls, was designed to shelter a permanent army garrison and military equipment. Visitors were carefully monitored at military checkpoints equipped with barriers and light tanks. Lissouba, while not being a military man himself, has occupied the place since 1992 and preserved the garrison. The vision of workers painting afresh the huge walls of the fortified residence infuriated *Brazzavillois* in 1995, who accused the president of diverting the state budget in order to secure his protection and isolation from the capital.

For more than 60 years, state power has displayed its presence directly in the city within concentric circles of control, from the ever-present marks of soldiers and governmental posters in the streets to the protected fortresses of central power at the city's core.

Order and Chaos

Colonial rulers in Brazzaville did not content themselves with simply establishing a monumental and military presence. They also sought to imprint spatial order and legibility on the city. The capital opposed a nodal white town to two surrounding African *quartiers*. At the centre, next to the Congo River, the European quarters of La Plaine and Le Plateau ended in the north at a forest reserve that separated the white town from the new airport, Maya-Maya. Areas reserved for European residence were flanked in the east by a commercial and industrial area, Mpila, which acted as a buffer zone against the north-eastern African district of Poto-Poto and its new annexes, Moungali and Ouenzé. South-west of the white town, the second main African *quartier*, Bacongo, expanded northward and westward with new dwellings in Moukounzi-Ngouaka, Mfilou and Makélékélé. The colonial government extended its control over Brazzaville through careful racial separation between African and European districts, the systematic beautification of the white city, and the ethnic shaping of the African *quartiers* of Poto-Poto and Bacongo.[27]

The spatial domination of the white city, as well as its racial purity, came under increasing pressure after the Second World War. In 1948–54, a plan to remove 20,000 African dwellers from Bacongo to expand the growing European district towards the Congo River met with successful resistance from African *Brazzavillois*.[28] Moreover, poor whites began to leave the European district and rent houses in African neighbourhoods, a phenomenon opposed by the administration in order to preserve white prestige. Far from being stable, the colonial shaping of the city, and racial residential segregation in particular, required constant vigilance and compromises, pointing to continuous urbanite initiatives to draw the line of legal spaces and identities in the city.

The promotion of perceived ethnic homogeneity within African districts constituted the second principle of the urban colonial enterprise. The city was under domain law, and therefore the property of the state. When the colonial administration began to control the influx of immigrants to the city and to organize the location of African residence (*c.* 1912), the allocation of urban landed property was a major tool in defining urban space according to colonial representations. These representations envisioned broad ethnic regions that generated migrations to the city.[29] This system opposed the south and the north of the colony, the Pool assuming the role of a boundary. Each macro-region was defined historically in terms of ancient rivalries and divergent interests dating back to the era of the slave trade, an interpretative model which had little to do with the complex history of the area between the seventeenth and nineteenth centuries.[30]

At the turn of the twentieth century, the south was becoming more familiar to European administrators.[31] Although the administration was aware of linguistic, political and cultural distinctions in the south, the principle was to group migrants from this region in Bacongo, literally named after the 'Bakongo' people, a super-ethnic group encompassing a cultural/linguistic complex of tribes and clans loosely connected in the Pool and the southern regions.[32] Poto-Poto, on the contrary, was to shelter migrants from the northern regions or the upper Congo basin, labelled as 'people of the rivers' by the colonial administration. Early on, however, the colonial ethnic diagram began to disintegrate under the pressure of rising property values, the development of a rental market, and the rapid saturation of early tribal *quartiers*. Only Bacongo retained a strong homogeneity in 1950, with 93 per cent of residents originating from the four neighbouring southern districts of Brazzaville. Poto-Poto became a cosmopolitan neighbourhood, flooded by recent immigrants from the entire colony, and from other colonies in French Equatorial and West Africa.

In spite of the growing ethnic 'untidiness' of African neighbourhoods, language played a crucial role in differentiating the two districts and promoting a common identity within each of them. Missionaries initiated the process in Poto-Poto. In the 1910s, the first Catholic bishop of Congo, Augouard, chose to proselytize in Lingala, a language spoken by river merchants and traders in the northern part of the colony and used by missionaries in this region since the end of the nineteenth century.[33] Lingala proved quite successful as the vernacular language among different Poto-Poto residents, who used their native language at home but spoke Lingala with neighbours, friends, traders, public agents and the missionaries. In Bacongo, where the Catholic missionaries decided to use Kikongo and Kituba, two administrative languages created from simplified Kongo languages, the development of a vernacular language emerged primarily through African initiative. Lari, a derived form of Kikongo-Sundi, began to be used as a fashionable tongue in town, thanks to a simplified and more flexible syntax than rural Kikongo languages. This encouraged wit and verbal inventiveness soon became the mark of urbanity. Accent also became discriminating, rural Kikongo intonation being considered a stigma of those lacking urban sophistication. Lari thus emerged in Brazzaville both as an urban language and as a new urban class: the residents of Bacongo, fused along a double helix of Kongo integration and distancing from rural ties.[34]

Preservation of urban social stability and internal social cleansing were also important in shaping the colonial agenda.[35] The colonial project in French Equatorial Africa was constantly torn between the perception of the modern city as incongruous, on one hand, and as a necessary tool of modernization on the other.[36] Antithetical visions of order and chaos in the city derived from a deeper contradiction in the colonial project. While the city was clearly identified as a new modern phenomenon, and as such intimately related to the success and style of the colonial enterprise, the whole colonial project rested upon the preservation of racial and political boundaries between the colonizers and the colonized, hence the organization of urban spatial segregation. Political stability, the preservation of colonial rule, and the conservation of ethnic peace (ethnicity being seen primarily as a system of violent tribal rivalries), were all to be maintained through urban containment, separation and hierarchy. This ideology was in contradiction with the European experience of urban modernity, based on social and cultural circulation and mobility, and a dialectic of progress fuelled by confrontation and exchanges. It betrays the fact that colonial rule had rigidified the evolution of the city, both at the material and symbolic levels, primarily as a *champ d'action* monopolized by the state – and this despite African resistance and transgression, opposition by proletariat fringes of the white population, and the density of daily life in the capital. State control was asserted over urban space primarily by clearing the streets of unemployed young people, displaying the slogans and pictures of the ruling elite, building barricaded palaces, or preserving the city's triangular division.

The colonial manipulation of the city thus proposed a specific model of public space, a physical and ideological arena under state vigilance. Africans as constituting a legitimate civil society literally did not exist from the perspective of the colonial power structure.[37] The ruling white elite in Brazzaville used the public realm primarily as a sphere of representation and the exhibition of power, not as a field of compromise with civil society.[38] With few exceptions, colonial and post-colonial governments have successfully prevented commoners from seizing urban space as a field for public action. Under the enduring threat of militarized fortresses, African urbanites experienced the city primarily as a submissive space. Transgression and subversion could be no more than reactive in such a public sphere. Urbanites might threaten and (as in 1963) destroy central regimes, but the delimitation of a sphere where the state and the city's residents could confront and define their respective interests did not emerge in modern Brazzaville.[39] The colonial capital therefore sheltered the survival of a regressive form of power based on an archaic use of public space, marked by enclosure, containment and secrecy.

The Shaping of Sacred Localities

Such power configuration presented dramatic analogies with earlier uses of sorcery in central Africa. By sorcery I mean concealed actions manipulated by people, willingly or unwillingly in contact with the supernatural reality, in order to acquire power over other people. In the Congo, sorcery belongs to the sphere of the sacred, but differs radically from an open, public and collective religion.[40] It activates the realm of the individual, the intimate and the secret. Thus, sorcery was deployed to frame and codify political action within the archaic public sphere of the colonial/post-colonial city, where power was represented and enacted simultaneously as personalized and hidden.

New forms of sorcery emerged in the twentieth century as an innovative folklore shared by leaders and commoners, a common field of dialogue informed by complex demands and needs. Early in the century, people used sorcery and ordeals in order to solve the intense crises brought by colonization.[41] Sorcery as a political, economic, and metaphysical tool experienced in this context a profound reconfiguration. It was captured by segments of the social pyramid to take advantage of new cultural and social opportunities. Among Bakongo people, tensions between elders and the youth began to be expressed, and sometimes violently solved, through daily accusations of sorcery targeted at the 'uncles' (*les oncles*), the closest relatives in matrilineal Kongo lines of descent and therefore the most likely to be able to 'eat' the vital forces of their descent.[42]

The 1950s witnessed the development of a crucial phenomenon. African national leaders, fusing elements of pre-colonial culture with emblems of colonial authority, began to monopolize an original combination of prestige and legitimacy derived from special access to the supernatural. Carefully preserved dissimulation and secrecy served as the markers of leadership stature, explicitly bringing the illicit and the occult into the sphere of power manifestation. Sorcery has been scrutinized in diverse historical and social contexts as a social equalizer, as a vehicle for class accumulation and enhanced social stratification, and also as a vector of popular rebellion.[43] Some studies have shed light on the connection between sorcery and state power, and on the contamination of politics by sorcery idioms of kinship 'extended' to the national level.[44] Most of these approaches have associated sorcery with pre-colonial culture, and with the assumption that it belongs primarily in the village.[45] The fact that Brazzaville became, in the 1950s, a mythical territory, receptacle and source of sacred forces, helps to refine these analyses. First, the historical production of sorcery, at least in the Congolese case, should be reinserted in the realm of urbanity. Second, a crucial but seldom observed dimension of the relationships between the magical sphere and politics rests upon sorcery's capacity to provide political identities with spatial anchorage and territorial exclusiveness, thus providing modern politics with a considerable factor of cultural rigidification.

Sorcery and Leadership

In war-torn Brazzaville, militants, soldiers and members of the various Congolese factions have linked their local tragedies to the broader world. The militias proudly brandish names borrowed from TV cartoons or series (Ninjas and Cobras) or African mythical history (Zoulous). Popular wit baptized the battlefields as Place Sarajevo in Bacongo, or Beyrouth (Mfilou). These efforts at locating local stories within global history typically emerged from lower categories in the political spectrum. While the population manipulated worldly, highly publicized references, the main leaders based their power and legitimacy on quite another set of referents. They operated in the sphere of state sorcéry, dangerous and secret manipulations of powerful forces and contacts with the supernatural.

African politicians' creation of new sets of magical legitimacy was consolidated during the rise of electoral politics in the 1950s. They used a number of techniques to mobilize electoral constituencies, involving, among others, a renewed usage of local referents of power. Colonial oppression, the rise of the electoral system, and the scope of national politics have all profoundly affected the nature of these local resources. National leaders have manipulated pre-existing elements in the political tradition and transferred them to the sphere of electoral politics. Congolese leaders' fusion of emblems of prestige and authority has been accumulative and flexible, adapted to a national market of fragmented, heterogeneous, and changing electoral arenas. Fulbert Youlou, for example, sought to fuse heterogeneous symbols of public prestige from the old equatorial cultural tradition, Kongo resistance to the French conquest in the 1880s, nationalist and messianic movements of the 1930s, and recent colonial authority. In the early 1950s, he regularly visited tombs of Kongo resisters, as well as caves in the Pool where the dead visited the world of the living at night, suggesting his personal access to powerful ancestors and his own position as heir to anti-colonial figures. In 1955, choosing an emblem for his newly founded party, he pretended that a giant crocodile had appeared in the Loufoulakari River where he was praying and bathing.[46] The crocodile combined crucial elements of Kongo folklore with the electoral system. As the totemic emblem of traders, river merchants and merchants of men during the slave trade, the crocodile was believed to kill people and capture their vital force, thus providing its master with material wealth.

In twentieth-century Congo, material wealth was still perceived primarily as the successful accumulation of clients, followers and lineage members. In the 1950s, the recycled syntax of sorcery applied the pre-colonial taxonomy of big men's accumulation and competition to a leader's attraction of votes. Part of the popularity of Lissouba, Sassou Nguesso and Kolélas in the 1990s was based upon strong convictions about their magical abilities, each leader commanding in a specific magical sphere.[47] Kolélas, called *Moïse* (Moses), *Le Martyr* (the martyr) or *Le Rédempteur* (the saviour), immersed himself in Matsoua's heritage and in Lari-Kongo millenarianism, as well as in Christian tradition.

Sassou Nguesso, nicknamed *Satan* by his adversaries, was believed to use horrific magical practices, such as ingesting children's blood or emasculating opponents, in order to harness supernatural power and perpetuate his personal strength. And Lissouba's presidential victory and enduring power was routinely explained by his position as a servant of the Njobi cult, a sacred allegiance he supposedly shared with his political allies and which promoted absolute loyalty among members. All leaders enjoyed extended local referents to a wider magico-electoral sphere. The national scale of political sorcery forced them to use elements taken from Christianity or recently reshaped cults (Njobi). Sorcery has never been a fixed set of beliefs in the region, but is even less so in the 1990s, as the big men of the civil war mix their own personal cocktails of sacrality.

Invisibility, this other side of material reality,[48] plays a central role in central African culture, and might represent the most inescapable substance of the leaders' legitimacy. Continual hiding in secure redoubts is not only an obvious military strategy of powerful men in times of civil war, but political behaviour that stems from deeper cultural structures. The sorcerer also worked through dissimulation and secrecy, while in the colonial dramaturgy of power the powerful could not easily be seen. During colonial and post-colonial rule, state power could manifest itself in ritualized circumstances (public ceremonies, political campaigns, electoral shows), but otherwise it remained/remains concealed. Kolélas' former house on one of the main avenues of Bacongo, though bombed by the army in 1992 and afterwards deserted, was still in the summer of 1995 under careful scrutiny by high ranking Ninjas. One could walk by the house, but not stop and look over the fence. In order to approach the leader's general headquarters in Bacongo, one had to pass through three military barricades guarded by armed Ninjas. Extravagant stories circulated about the ubiquity of the leader and his capacity to deceive the enemy.[49] In the leaders' careful representation of power, Brazzaville's urban space was an arena within which legitimacy could be derived from the interaction of the symbolisms of material and cultural structures.

Sorcery and the New Mental Geography of Congo

In 1992, Congo split into three territorial strongholds. Each was characterized by a prominent leader who was both a national figure and a highly spiritual figure engaged in sacred activities; by a popular sense of unity and exaltation derived from the war and defined by new sub-nationalities; by the maintenance of sanctuaries where spiritual strength could flow and where the war could be memorized; and, finally, by armed militias (Zoulous, Ninjas, Cobras) in charge of ethnic and political purification.

Niboland, fiefdom of the new geo-ethnic group known as Nibolek, relied upon two main localities: Lissouba's native village north of Mossendjo and, further south, the town of Loudima where the president kept most of his troops (Zoulous) trained by Israeli officers. North of Brazzaville and the Batéké plateau, the depression of the Zaire basin belonged to Denis Sassou Nguesso. The forefront of this 'North' was the industrial and commercial neighbourhood of Mpila in Brazzaville, where Sassou transformed an army garrison into a presidential residence protected by his young militia, the Cobras. Two hundred and fifty miles north of Brazzaville, his native village, Oyo, served as the rural capital of the North. The former president liked to spend long periods of time there: he invested large amounts of money in the village, and presumably maintained large numbers of troops there. The South-Pool, led by Kolélas and land of the Tcheks,[50] was organized around three main cities: Brazzaville, Kinkala and Mayama. The pillars of the South-Pool appeared to be spiritual and to derive from sacred places rather than sheer military force. Each of the three strongholds, however, was irrigated by regional sources of sorcery and magic. Each of them, moreover, was vitally attached to one district of Brazzaville, dividing the capital into three parts. If Brazzaville lost the monopoly of political polarization, it gained a new dimension as a mythical territory, receptacle of supernatural and sacred forces whose control appeared crucial to the competing factions.

During Youlou's progression towards power, the city was transformed into a major reservoir of spiritual strength and reconfigured sacrality through three main impulses. The first was Youlou's recognition, celebration and appropriation of the Batéké's traditional hold on Brazzaville land as first occupants of the region.[51] The second impulse came from the revival of Matsouanism in the capital. Youlou regularly participated in and patronized ceremonies in the Matsouanist cemeteries in Brazzaville, especially Moukònzi-Ngouaka.[52] The third factor in the spiritualization of the capital occurred during Youlou's triumphant processions, such as that following his return from Paris on 18 March 1956. Accompanied by a cheering crowd of more than 5,000 people, Youlou slowly toured the main streets of Brazzaville in a powerful representation of his conquest of the capital. As mayor of Brazzaville, then head of the government, Youlou organized re-enactments of his conquest, notably during de Gaulle's visits in August and December 1958.[53]

Brazzaville's sacrality endured, and was considerably enhanced by the 1959 and 1992 wars. Land of battles and dead, embodiment of the state and key demographic reservoir of the Congo, the capital remains a major stake in national struggles for power. To a large extent the rural strongholds of the 1990s reproduced Brazzaville's diagram of sacrality and spatial order rather than creating an alternative one. Each fief originated its own fortress of central power, its spiritual places and its garrisons. Each derived its integrity from being connected to a part of the capital and claiming control over it. To a large extent, the Congo's split, rather than revealing the resurgence of ancient geographies, has established the contamination of the countryside by the capital's strange modernity.

Worship and Profanation in the Pool

None of the three strongholds relied more on magical and spiritual forces than the South-Pool, and none was as intimately connected to Brazzaville. The South-Pool crystallized as an entity during the battle of Bacongo in November–December 1992. As soon as Kolélas seceded from the central government, Ninjas erected barricades around the district. For several days, the army bombarded Bacongo and tried to overrun the district with troops and tanks. They were successfully resisted by the Bacongo militias, who conducted urban guerrilla warfare for weeks, killed a number of government troops, destroyed a tank and finally induced the army's retreat in December 1992. Ever since, the district has been at the core of the South-Pool identity and memory.

Traces of the war were carefully preserved in the neighbourhood until at least 1995. Refugees from Mfilou, Diata, and the central provinces proudly called themselves *rescapés*, and took advantage of this to get recognition and financial support from the MCDDI. Teenagers painted the title on their T-shirts or shorts. The militias displayed uniforms taken from dead government soldiers in the battle. In Bacongo and Makélékélé, bombed-out houses were kept as such, with burned and darkened walls, bullet holes and ruined roofs. The whole district became an ossified battlefield, where the wanderer could be told the glorious stories of the battle. One of the most famous landmarks of the war was the burned tank, trapped head first in a deep trench along the sidewalk. Kolélas's former house, next to the Marché Total, and the Main Bleue clandestine harbour (also called 'Beach Pirate') from where residents fled to Kinshasa during the war and through which

Kolélas's government organized food supply, formed two other major sites of memory.

War dances created another form of memorialization in Bacongo. In 1995, in a Bacongo bar, I witnessed a 'Danse Sarajevo' performed by a group of Ninja veterans. None wore a military uniform, but they all wore special accessories which signalled their status: bandannas, earrings, baseball caps and rasta hairstyles. The music was a regular rumba and *soukouss* played by the disc jockey.[54] The dance glorified the collective and individual action of the militias, guardians of the living memory of the Bacongo battle. The Ninjas first danced in line, under the orders of a chief. They performed elaborate movements mimicking the troops: marching, saluting, shooting, holding weapons, exercising, hiding and crawling. Then, to the sound of the chief's whistle, each dancer broke from the line in turn and performed alone for several minutes. The solo displayed the soldier's personal accomplishments during the battle. One rhythmically loaded a weapon, then imitated with his arms, shoulders and upper body the vibrations and the backward shock made by a machine gun. Another fell and crawled on the ground, expressing with his whole body his escape from the bullets and the uneasy movement on the battlefield. He then jumped to his feet, saluted, and went back to the line of dancers. The next performer stepped in, and imitated the elaborate and detailed movements necessary to take a hand grenade, prime it, launch it, and finally seek shelter from its explosion. The spiritual energy released by the dance was electrifying, and the crowd cheered and applauded continuously.

The second dance I witnessed was quite different. It occurred during a Saturday night dance party, Brazzaville's most popular entertainment.[55] The dancers were suddenly interrupted by a sequence of discs playing traditional rural Kongo music. Young people came on stage and performed rural dances for half an hour, surrounded by an approving public. This unusual intrusion would have been quite unimaginable before the war, when it would have been mocked as old-fashioned and ridiculous. The unanimous approval the dancers encountered illuminated a new spirit. It betrayed a new collective identity rooted in the rural imagination, the acceptance of links with the countryside, and the feeling that Bacongo's proud, individualized urbanites were one people with the rural south. The war generated a Kongo symbolic geography that extended far outside the capital and encompassed the old divisions between the city and the countryside, the rural and the urban.

From 1992 on, two towns, Kinkala and Mayama, served as the spiritual pillars of this new unity. North-west of Brazzaville, Mayama enshrined Matsoua's imprisonment and death (1941–2). Galvanized by the war and Kolélas's tentative attraction to Matsoua's prestige, Mayama stood as a special sanctuary, a place of spiritual resources for the South. After the war, the road from Brazzaville to Mayama was reputed to be under the close control of Kolélas's armed militias. In 1995, Mayama sheltered a crucial conciliation meeting between Kolélas and Matsouanist priests of the South-Pool. All the participants brought pieces of earth from the different parts of the region, and engaged in spiritual exercises to appease the tensions between the leaders. This episode revealed some of the internal divisions in the South-Pool, as well as how the magico-sphere represented the main field of conflict resolution.[56]

South-west of Brazzaville, Kinkala also belonged to the Matsouanist spiritual network. The native town of its leader, it sheltered a public museum and a statue of Matsoua erected on a public square. On 30 July 1995, townspeople discovered that the concrete pedestal and bronze statue had been destroyed. The next day, a man named Jacob Loutangou was arrested and presented to the public as the main suspect. Public opinion rapidly accused him of being a traitor to the south, corrupted by Lissouba's government to assault Kolélas's source of magical power:

L'acte de Jacob [Loutangou] est très monumental en face d'un monument qui porte en lui les secrets du pouvoir... Le pouvoir du Pool est un mystère incarné par deux personnalités principales devenues des légendes capables de tout et pour tout en faveur du Pool. Il s'agit de Tâ Matsoua et de Tâ Youlou. Si vous voulez prendre le pouvoir, il faut au préalable qu'ils vous l'accordent à partir de l'acceptation de vos prières à eux adressées. Tant que vous ne vous agenouillez pas devant le monument de Matsoua d'abord, et ensuite au bord de la tombe de Youlou avec des dames-jeannes de vin rouge, de vin de palme, un paquet de colas et bien d'autres objets, ne croyez pas que vous aurez le pouvoir.[57]

A few weeks before, a similar crime had been committed against Fulbert Youlou's tomb in Madibou, now a suburb of Brazzaville. People found the tomb opened and Youlou's remains visibly profaned. Youlou's tomb in Madibou represents a central anchor of spiritual inspiration and manipulation, especially since Youlou's rehabilitation by the 1990 National Conference.[58]

The profanation of Youlou's tomb was immediately interpreted as an attempt to undermine the sacred authority of Kolélas as well as the Pool's territorial integrity. Kolélas sent Ninjas militias to supervise the cemetery night and day.[59] The case reveals how corpses and bodies played an important part in the symbolic and spiritual configuration of political territories. To eliminate or weaken a rival, political leaders are thought to use mutilation. This mutilation is called *bomber* or *bombarder* (to bomb, bombard or shell), a word which can describe an actual mutilation with a grenade or a metaphorical attack on vital parts of the enemy's body (the genitals in particular) where the magic force resides. One can interpret this vocabulary as an extension of the syntax of war to personal and magical feuds between big men and enemies, but it primarily betrays the importance of the material location of political power, whether in territories or in individual bodies. Just as the districts of Brazzaville were bombed as the realms of political power, bodies and corpses could be bombed as shrines of power.[60]

A Fragile Materiality

Sorcery therefore anchors power in a fragile materiality. Power is a mystery, but it derives from physical sources of spiritual integrity in each region. Sorcery provides the new ethnic groups with a hold on the land, and the land with sacred anchors to the magical sphere. The material existence of these places, however, enables potential enemies to capture them. They are perceived as powerful channels of magical authority, but also as fortresses prone to attack by either exterior enemies or internal contenders. No territory is homogeneous, completely unified and dedicated to a single leader, identity and cause. The South for example, has suffered from dissidence emanating not only from individuals (such as the destroyer of Matsoua's statue) but also from certain geographical and territorial constituencies.[61] The North which Sassou Nguesso is supposed to control is a divided kingdom. Sassou Nguesso's most important enemy is a Kouyou military officer, Joachim Yombi-Opango, who has conducted a number of armed coups against Sassou Nguesso in the past. Nibolek, Lissouba's fief, is neither homogeneous nor safe. In the summer of 1995 several members of Lissouba's family were rumoured to have been killed in his home region, as a result of obscure internal rivalries surrounding the president.

The deployment of sorcery and territoriality in the Congo crises is not therefore synonymous with the confinement of politics into a protected, stabilized physical space. Each leader can attack the sanctuaries and vital force of his enemies. Each stronghold can to some extent be redrawn, incorporated or enlarged according to the political constraints. In the South-Pool, political tradition relies in part upon the continuity of leadership. From Youlou to Kolélas, legitimacy derives from the capacity to appear as heir to the historical figures of the South-Pool, and to attract emblems of power. In contrast, northern leaders have repeatedly seized power by annihilating or killing their predecessors. Most of their strength is associated with army power. The role of burials, shrouds, bones and earth in the power dramaturgy of the South-Pool might indicate the historical impact of permanent settlements in this region, contrasting with a more shifting land occupation in the north. In this analysis, the South-Pool might seem to be trapped in a stronger and more inescapable connection between the shaping of its political identity and its territory.[62] Yet the localization of politics, and the material connection between sorcery, collective identities and territories, participates in the increasing rigidification of power conflicts. Through this process the geopolitics of sacred localities gains every day over the earlier flexibilities of political mobilization.

Conclusion

In contemporary Congo history, Brazzaville has emerged not only as the shelter for a celebrated 'civilization of enthusiasm',[63] but also as the cradle of destructive historical dynamics. Brazzaville's urban configuration, both ideological and physical, has been based on the building of an archaic public sphere, prone to the confrontation between the state and its subjects. In the 1950s, spatial dissimulation of central power in colonial Brazzaville combined with new metaphors of power. An innovative form of sorcery emerged, intimately linked to urban space and monopolized by the powerful as a reservoir of legitimacy, prestige and domination. As a result, Brazzaville endured as the core matrix of Congolese politics. Combining colonial archaic modernity with African modern reconfigurations of ancient elements, the civil wars split the country into multiple reproductions of the capital's ideologized space, aggregating citadels of military troops, confined headquarters of central power, localized sources of sacrality, purified geo-ethnic territories and the submission of the new citizens to their leaders.

The re-evaluation of the city as a layered cradle of modernity and archaism, and its capacity to diffuse models of public life in the countryside, needs further refinement.[64] It nevertheless opens a necessary historical enquiry into Congo's submission to a new, deadly connection between materiality and ideology, and helps understand why, today, 'la mort est partout'.[65]

Notes

1 I am greatly indebted to Tom Spear and Jan Vansina for their comments on previous drafts of this article. Errors are entirely mine.
2 Achille Mbembe, *La naissance du maquis dans le Sud-Cameroun (1920–1960)* (Paris, 1996).
3 'Evaluations, September 23, 1997', by William Wallis, Reuters Limited.
4 Patrick Quantin, 'Congo: les origines politiques de la décomposition d'un processus de libéralisation (août 1992–décembre 1993)', in *L'Afrique Politique 1994. Vue sur la démocratisation à marée basse* (Paris, 1995), pp. 167–98.
5 Rémy Bazenguissa-Ganga, 'Milices politiques et bandes armées à Brazzaville. Enquête sur la violence politique et sociale des jeunes déclassés', *Les Etudes du CERI*, 13 (April 1993).
6 Material for this article was gathered during field research in Congo, July–August 1995.
7 For a detailed history of the events, see René Gauze, *The Politics of Congo-Brazzaville* (Stanford, 1973); Catherine Coquery-Vidrovitch, 'Gestion urbaine et décolonisation en Afrique noire

française: de la politique municipale à l'émeute', in Charles Robert Ageron et Marc Michel (eds), *L'Afrique noire française: l'heure des indépendances* (Paris, 1992), pp. 71–86; and Florence Bernault, *Démocraties ambigües en Afrique centrale. Congo-Brazzaville, Gabon, 1940–1965* (Paris, 1996).

8 UDDIA: *Union démocratique de défense des intérêts africains* (Democratic Union for the Defence of African Interests). This party was founded by Fulbert Youlou in 1955.

9 MSA: *Mouvement socialiste africain* (African Socialist Movement).

10 For a detailed study of the Mbochi region and peoples, see Théophile Obenga, *La Cuvette congolaise. Les hommes et les structures* (Paris, 1976).

11 On Poto-Poto's and Bacongo's ethnic composition in the 1950s, see Georges Balandier, *Sociologie des Brazzavilles noires*, (2nd edition, Paris, 1985), pp. 27–31.

12 At the initiative of Guy Georgy, the French High Commissioner of French Equatorial Africa.

13 Official accounts reported a total of 300 casualties, among which there were 100 deaths. Corpses of dozens more had probably disappeared in the river, or had been hidden from the police for fear of retaliation. Several hundred houses had been destroyed or pillaged. The army and police arrested almost 300 suspects. Youlou managed to have Opangault put in jail and moved quickly to take advantage of the crisis. He dissolved the Assembly and organized new elections in June 1959, drawing a new map of electoral districts so favourable to UDDIA that the party won 51 out of 61 seats with only 58 per cent of the votes.

14 The simple opposition between 'Mbochi' and 'Lari' made no sense in pre-colonial Congo. 'Lari' identity had appeared as a modern urban identity, while the 'Mbochi' label used in the 1950s referred primarily to the leadership role of northern regions during specific conflicts with colonial rule, and in particular to the role of Opangault and new African elite members during the Mbochi rebellion against the Catholic mission's linguistic policy in 1938. Bernault, *Démocraties ambigües*.

15 Only during rare circumstances did this polarization not work. The popular uprising of 1963 which overthrew Youlou's regime in Brazzaville crossed the lines established by the 1959 riots.

16 Tsamouna Kitongo, 'Ethnies et urbanités dans la lutte politique au Congo après 1959', *Africa* (Rome), 45 (1990), p. 667.

17 Lissouba belongs to the Nzabi, an ethnic group of south-central Congo. He began his career as a young minister in the revolutionary government in 1963, but was ousted by Massambat-Débat (1969). He spent most of the next decades in France, where he had earned a PhD in agrobiology in the 1950s. Lissouba used this image of *le professeur* to convey the image of a comforting technocrat, a skilled and honest outsider. Comic artist and opponent Ray M' depicts him as a space alien coming to earth (Congo) in a space shuttle to transform the Congo into a 'little Switzerland' (a slogan initiated by Lissouba himself during the electoral campaign). 'Les politicards', *Bande dessinée politique*, 001 (April–May 1995).

18 Nibolek: new name of Niari, Bouenza and Lekoumou administrative and electoral districts, where Lissouba's party won a majority. Lissouba, helped by Kuni and Beembe politicians, drew his main electoral support from this rich, densely populated region of south-central Congo. Since 1955 the region's political leaders have acted as opportunists in national politics, usually supporting whoever was in power while managing not to participate directly in the north–south confrontation. Kuni and Beembe leaders have joined Lissouba's new party, the UPADS (*Panafrican Union for Social Democracy*).

19 E. Dorier-Apprill, 'Jeunesse et ethnicités citadines à Brazzaville', *Politique africaine*, 64 (1996), pp. 73–88.

20 On colonial manipulation of legislative majorities by Youlou's clique, and exclusion of opposition groups from the governement, see Bernault, *Démocraties ambigües*.

21 With 80,000 inhabitants in the 1950s and over 130,000 by the 1960s (around 15 per cent of the country's total population), the capital already held the most important concentration of voters. By the 1990s Brazzaville's population numbered around 600,000 of Congo's 2.2 million people. *Annuaire statistique de l'AEF*, Vol. 1 (1950), pp. 19 and 36, and Gilles Sautter, *De l'Atlantique au fleuve Congo. Une géographie du sous peuplement* (Paris, 1966), p. 984. World Bank, 'Urban population as a percentage of total population', *World Development Report*, Washington, 1985.

22 One of the most dramatic is the statue of liberation, the 'très fâché', in the public square in front of the railway station. The statue depicts a man with raised arms, freeing himself from the chains of colonialism.

23 On the novelization of Brazzaville/Pointe-Noire rivalry and opposition, see Sony Labou Tansi, *The Seven Solitudes of Lorsa Lopez* (trans. New York, 1995).

24 Max Weber, *La Ville* (Paris, 1982), pp. 30–7. On the *incastellamento* phenomenon in medieval Italy,

see Pierre Toubert, *Les structures du Latium médiéval: le Latium méridional et la Sabine du IXe siècle à la fin du XIIe siècle* (Rome, 1973). Many historians mention that early colonial towns in Africa were mainly military garrisons, but seldom note the continuation of this dimension during later stages of colonialism. See Catherine Coquery-Vidrovitch, *Histoire des villes d'Afrique noire. Des origines à la colonisation* (Paris, 1993), p. 330.

25 Phyllis M. Martin, *Leisure and Society in Colonial Brazzaville* (Cambridge, 1995), p. 30.

26 Rémy Boutet, *Les Trois Glorieuses, ou la chute de Fulbert Youlou* (Dakar, 1990), p. 118; Balandier, *Sociologie*, p. 279.

27 Martin, *Leisure and Society*.

28 Between 1931 and 1948, the European population of Brazzaville tripled from around 1,100 to 3,300.

29 Ethnologist and historian Marcel Soret drew Congo's ethnic maps in the early 1950s. While refining some colonial representations, these maps promoted the rigidification of most colonial perceptions of ethnic boundaries and groups.

30 On colonial views of south/north rivalries, see quotations in Martin, *Leisure and Society*, p. 67. On nineteenth-century slave trade patterns and routes, see John Janzen, *Lemba, 1650–1930. A Drum of Affliction in Africa and the New World* (New York, 1982); Robert Harms, *River of Wealth, River of Sorrow. The Congo-Zaire Basin in the Era of the Slave and Ivory Trade* (New Haven, 1981); Joseph Miller, *Way of Death. Merchant Capitalism and the Angolan Slave Trade, 1730–1830* (Madison, 1988); and Jan Vansina, *The Tio Kingdom of the Middle Congo, 1880–1892* (London, 1973).

31 Especially after the building of the Matadi-Léopoldville railway in the Belgian Congo. Until then, the north had been the privileged road for European penetration, from Savorgnan de Brazza's explorations of the Ogooué River to the building of the first Catholic missions in the Boundji area.

32 While historically unified by the Kingdom of Kongo from the fifteenth to the seventeenth centuries, the Bakongo had since long shifted to a system of decentralized, autonomous settlements, and had mixed with other migrants of diverse origins.

33 Martin, *Leisure and Society*, p. 42.

34 For a brillant study of *larité* in Brazzaville, see Tsamouna Kitongo, 'Ethnies et urbanités', pp. 674–5.

35 On expulsion of unemployed youth from Brazzaville, and relocation in the countryside, see Bernault, *Démocraties ambiguës*.

36 On colonialism's ambiguous concept of modernity in Africa, see Frederic Cooper, *Decolonization and African Society. The Labor Question in French and British Africa* (Cambridge, 1996), Introduction. On colonial imaginings about Brazzaville and the cities of French Equatorial Africa, see the articles by Gilles Sautter and J. Y. Normand in Eugène Guernier (ed.), *Afrique équatoriale française* (Paris, 1950).

37 A reality embodied in the Africans' status as subjects (*sujets*) prior to 1946, then second-class citizens (*de statut personnel or coutumier*) after 1946.

38 For a classic study, see Jürgen Habermas, *The Structural Transformation of the Public Sphere. An Inquiry into a Category of Bourgeois Society* (trans. Cambridge MA, 1989).

39 Or emerged marginally and temporarily only, for example in football stadiums during matches. See Martin, *Leisure and Society*.

40 For a contrasting analysis of the constructive role of (open) Christian and Charismatic churches in Kinshasa, see René Devisch, '"Pillaging Jesus": healing churches and the villagisation of Kinshasa', *Africa*, 66, 4 (1994), pp. 555–86.

41 Karen Fields, 'Political contingencies of witchcraft in colonial Central Africa: culture and the state in Marxist theory', *Canadian Journal of African Studies*, 16, 3 (1982), pp. 567–93; Jan Vansina, *Paths in the Rainforest* (Madison, 1990); and Achille Mbembe, *La naissance*.

42 'Aînés et cadets sociaux au Congo', special issue, *Revue Rupture* (Brazzaville), 8 (May 1996).

43 Fields, 'Political contingencies'.

44 Georges Dupré, *Un ordre et sa destruction* (Paris, 1982); Michael Schatzberg, 'The cultural foundations of power and the present political transition' (paper presented at the Conference on L'Afrique dans le Monde d'Aujourd'hui, CRES, Geneva, Switzerland, 14–17 November 1994); Peter Geschiere, *The Modernity of Witchcraft. Politics and the Occult in Postcolonial Africa* (Charlottesville, 1997).

45 Michael Rowlands and Jean-Pierre Warnier, 'Sorcery, power, and the modern state in Cameroon', *Man* (NS), 23 (1988), p. 130.

46 This is also the place where a prominent Kongo resistance hero, Boueta Mbongo, was supposedly killed and his head buried, and it now marks a shrine where people still worship his memory. Boutet *Les Trois Glorieuses* (1990), p. 47.

47 Eric Gruénais, Florent Mouanda Mbambi and Jacques Tonda, 'Messies, fétiches et luttes de pouvoirs entre les "grands hommes" du Congo démocratique', *Cahiers d'études africaines*, 137, 35-1 (1995), pp. 163–93.

48 On this idea, see Mbembe, *La naissance*, p. 400.

49 The capacity to travel invisibly is one of the prominent talents of a witch (*ndoki*), or ritual specialist (*nganga*).

50 The meaning of this term is difficult to trace, but it may refer to the military 'toughness' of the southerners.

51 The Batéké spiritual capital is Mbe, 160 miles north-east of Brazzaville. On Batéké occupation of the Pool, see Martin, *Leisure and Society*, and Vansina, *Tio Kingdom*. On Youlou's strategy over the Tio Makoko, see Bernault, *Démocraties ambigües*.

52 Matsouanists extremists were active in the capital in the 1950s. They organized numerous churches in Bacongo and cults in the cemeteries where martyrs of the religion had been buried. They refused to participate in the census, pay taxes, or hold identity cards, and at national elections they voted for Matsoua ('the bones'). Among Matsoua followers, however, Youlou placed himself at the crossroads between extremists and loyalists. The latter, wary of public abstinence and eager to participate in national politics, represented the majority of the Lari-Kongo population in the city. Being a Catholic priest while going to Matsouanist ceremonies enabled Youlou to represent both African resistance to white rule and privileged access to it.

53 On the spiritual dimension of de Gaulle's image in Central Africa, see Bernault, *Democraties ambigues*, pp. 187–95.

54 Nganda 'La Pinasse', Bacongo, 24 August 1995.

55 Bar, 'Le Chaudron', Bacongo, 6 August 1995.

56 This account is based upon information gathered in 1995.

57 'Jacob Loutangou a trahi le Pool, le Poolailler et les Poossins', by Ntana-Amva, *Le Choc,* 13 (15 August 1995), p. 10 (weekly newspaper, Brazzaville). *Ta*, vocative of *Tata* (father), marks a respected person.

58 Youlou died in exile in Madrid in May 1972. His nephew organized the repatriation of the corpse, which was buried in November 1972 in Madibou, a suburb of Brazzaville. Interview, 8 August 1995. [Trans: … Jacob [Loutangou]'s act is quite monumental in the face of a monument that carries the secrets of power […] The power of the Pool is a mystery embodied by two main figures who become legends capable of anything and everything in favour of the Pool. They are Tâ Matsoua, and Tâ Youlou. If you want to seize power, Matsoua and Youlou must first grant power to you according to the acceptance of the prayers you addressed to them. As long as you do not kneel down in front of Matsoua's monument first, and then in front of Youlou's grave with demijohns of red wine and palm wine, a bag of kola nuts, and many other objects, do not think you will have power.}

59 I was denied access to the tomb by Kolélas' collaborators.

60 See the helicopter raids organized by Lissouba in September 1997 to bomb repeatedly and massively Mpila, Sassou Nguesso's refuge in Brazzaville.

61 One region is considered as a traditional traitor in the Pool: Boko. This small provincial town is led politically by Kolélas' ex-protégé, André Milongo, who has seceded from the MCDDI to organize a new party. In contrast to the Sun, emblem of the MCDDI, Milongo's party adopted an oil-lamp as its sarcastic symbol. MCDDI militants criticize Boko inhabitants as infamous and wealthy sorcerers, people who used to acquire sacred witchcraft and money through the digging up of corpses and the illegitimate use of shrouds. This belief might also refer to the participation of the region in the slave trade and the association between wealth and crime, death, or trading in people. Interviews, July 1995.

62 I owe this insight to Jan Vansina.

63 Didier Gondola, *Villes miroirs. Migrations et identités urbaines à Kinshasa et Brazzaville, 1930–1970* (Paris, 1997). On fashion movements, youth and cultural renewal in Brazzaville, see also Justin-Daniel Gandoulou, *Dandies à Bacongo. Le culte de l'élégance dans la société congolaise contemporaine* (Paris, 1989).

64 We need to know, in particular, if recent political innovations occurred in rural areas, and if they spread to the city. The role of sorcery and territories in the making of pre-colonial public cultures should help to us understand the ancient relation between the public and the private. Finally, the question remains: to what extent did people adhere to the magical dramaturgy of power? People do not passively submit to the invasion of sorcery and to big men's violence. A strong popular resentment in Bacongo accused Kolélas of being responsible for the war and for the death of thousands of people in 1995.

65 'Death is everywhere', interview with Bernard Mackiza, 1995.

Index

A. G. Leventis 226
Abaja Abata 242
Abaja Mashasha 243
Abakabot 235, 239, 241
Abarash Afawarq 243
Abdelkafi, Jellal 190
Abeche 8
Abeokuta district 8, 127-9, 134
Abidjan 8
Abola quarter (Accra) 217
Abomey 89, 93-4
Abomposu Estates 227
Abou-Tesfin, Sultan 3
Accra 5, 7-8, 10, 13, 205-18, 222-4
Accra people 163-9, 172-6, 178, 182
accumulation 1, 8, 151, 154, 156-8, 167, 170,
    175-8, 180-1, 222-7, 230-1, 236, 293-4
Acheampong government 230
Acquah, Ione 10
Ada 171
Adandozan, King 89
Adanme people 168
Adderley Street 278
Addis Ababa 5-6, 237, 243
Adet 236-7
Adjei, Ako 215
Adjovi family 88, 90, 93
administration, Accra 211, 213; Aksum 52;
    Arusha 109-10, 114-20; Bahir Dar 235,
    237-44; Belgian 77; Brazzaville 288-90,
    292; British colonial 105, 109, 114-20, 211,
    213, 228, 230, 253, 255-6; Bugandan 99;
    capitals/centres 2, 8, 40, 52, 78, 86, 99,
    109, 144, 147, 151, 237, 288; colonial 12,
    77-8, 109-10, 114-20, 149, 211, 213, 228,
    230, 237, 253, 255-6, 288, 290, 292; Daho-
    mian 86, 88, 94; District Six 265-6, 271;
    Durban 147,149; East African Community
    109; Ethiopia 238-44; European cities as
    centres of 144; French colonial 288, 290,
    292; and hierarchy 94; household 173; Ital-
    ian colonial 237-9; of labour 78; Lagos 131,
    134; languages of 292; under martial law
    131; Mbanza Kongo 78; by monastery of
    Bahir Dar Giyorgis 236, 239; Obuasi,
    Ghana 228; Pietermaritzburg 151; Por-
    tuguese 77; Pretoria 151; of races 147, 152;
    regional 110; religious 235; and trade 94; by
    walled cities 40; Zanzibar 248, 253, 255-6;
    zones 243; *see also* regulation
Adulis 52, 58, 61
Adum 226
Aemiro Silase Ababa 240
Afiah, Korkor 228
Afonso I, King 68, 70
Afonso V, King 73, 75
Africa, Atlantic coast 5; Central 3, 10, 293;
    East 1-3, 5-6, 8, 10, 39, 43, 98, 106, 109,
    110, 121; East Central 39; East coast 6, 39,
    43, 98, 206; equatorial *see* tropical; Horn 2;
    Indian Ocean coast 6; North 2, 5, 8, 36, 43,
    190; north-eastern 57; south-eastern coast
    147; southern 5-6, 10, 222; tropical 2, 8,
    36-7, 43, 48; West 1-5, 10-11, 29, 39, 43,
    45, 85, 182; West-Central 3, 67-8; West
    coast 5, 85-95, 126
African National Congress (ANC) 156
African Wharfage Company 247
Afrikaanse Christelike Vroue Vereniging 271
Afrikaner people 147, 149
Afrikaner republics 149

Afutu 165
Agadir *see* Tlemcen
Agbo, Casimir 86
Agege 129
Agege-Ota region 127
agidi 136
agriculture 4, 39-40, 45, 61, 69, 90, 92-3, 99,
    102, 109, 112, 114, 119-20, 127-8, 130,
    132, 136, 145, 153, 224, 227-8, 235-6, 243,
    250, 264
Agua Rosada e Sardonia, Prince Pedro 73
Agua Rosadas faction 71, 73-4
Agusto, L. B. 140
Ahanta 224
Ahouandjigo quarter (Ouidah) 88-9, 91
Akan people 3, 178, 207, 210-11, 214-15,
    223-4, 227; language 170
Akim *see* Akyem
Akon cult 173, 208
Akonno 167-8
Akrama 214
Akuapem people 173, 176
Akumbu 20, 27-8
Akwamu people 164-8, 173, 176, 178, 180-1,
    183, 207, 217
Akyem Abuakwa people 207
Akyem people 170, 173, 176, 178
Al-Bakri 2
Al-Yakubi 2
Alagbado 129
Alata 212
Algeria 189-90, 194
Algiers 192, 195
Aliyu Amba 5
Allada 93
Allenby, Lord 131
Allman, Jean 222
Allotei 214
Alvaro I, King 68
Alvaro XI, King 73
Alvaro XIII Ndongo, King 75-8
Alvaro XIV de Agua Rosada, King 78
Amanfro 165
Amanzimtoti 156
Ambriz 77
Ambrizette 77
Amharic language 53
Amputi Brafo 166
Amsterdam 4, 7, 155, 182
An-yang 28
Andalusian people 189
André II, King 75-6
Anecho 89
Anege 172
Aneho 171
Anglo-Boer War 149
Angola 67, 75, 78, 138
Ankober 5-6
Anlo-Ewe society 225
Anomabo 179-81, 223
Ansa Sasraku 166
anthropology 31, 49, 86
António I, King 70-1
apartheid 7, 10, 12, 147, 154-7, 262, 270-1,
    279; *see also* segregation
Arabia 52-3, 57-8, 61
Arabian Gulf 3, 6
Arabic language 189, 256
Arabs 2, 6, 43, 100, 114, 237, 246, 248-9,
    256; Arab quarter (historic Kampala) 100-2;

see also Islam
Arawan 20, 27
archaeology 1, 2, 3, 11, 12, 19-33, 40, 45,
    48; cladistics in 29; cognitive 23, 32; con-
    temporary 19; definition in 19-20; distinc-
    tiveness in 19, 21, 27-8, 31, 40; ecological
    21-3, 27-8, 31-2; functional 21-3, 25, 27-9,
    31-2; information from 45; methodology
    45; of mind 31-3; Ouidah 87; stereotypes
    19; strategies 39, 45, 48; theory testing 19
architecture 21, 23, 29, 57, 68, 71-2, 87, 113,
    195-6, 237, 246, 249, 251, 262-3, 265, 270,
    273, 278-9, 285, 289
artisans 4, 23, 28, 133, 169-71, 192, 194, 237,
    265, 277; blacksmiths 25-6, 29, 32, 171
artists 31-2
Arusha 12, 109-21
Arusha people 109-21; Arusha Chini 112;
    Arusha Juu 112-13; Arusha Maasai 112
Asä 164, 173, 177
Asante Blohum quarter (Osu) 205, 214
Asante people 5, 176, 178-9, 181, 206-7, 217,
    222, 224-7
Asere people 210, 214, 217; Asere quarter
    210, 214, 217
Ashanti Goldfields Corporation 224
Asia 9, 145, 157; South-East 21, 144
Asians 109, 111, 114
Asonade, Okyeame 226
Aspeling Street 267
assimilation 7, 13
Association of West African Merchants
    (AWAM) 135
Atbara, Battle of 43
Atkins, Keletso 150
Atlantic Ocean 12, 85, 95, 163, 208
Atlantic world 169, 171
Augouard, Bishop 292
Austin, Gareth 222
authority, in Aksum 55, 58; among the
    Akwamu 168; alternative routes to 19-33;
    of artists and specialists 31; and autonomy
    23; chiefly 118; colonial 105, 238, 293-4;
    cultural 99; and heterarchy 29, 31; intangi-
    bility of 19-22; of *Kabaka* of Buganda 98-9,
    102, 104, 106; and knowledge 31; from
    landscape 23, 28, 31-3, 68; in Mbanza
    Kongo 68, 74; of Nananom Mpow 181;
    and plurality 29; religious 99, 104, 194,
    238-42; royal 31-2, 55, 58, 74; sacred 22,
    31, 68; of shamans 32; of state 238-9, 251;
    symbolic 294-5, 298; *see also* power
Avalon Cinema (District Six) 277
Avenue of the Martyrs 290
Axim District 223
Ayawaso hill 207, 210, 217
Azawad 20, 27

Bab al-Bahr 189, 193
Bab al-Jazira 192-3
Bab al-Suwayqa 192-3
Babylon 29
Bacongo 286-8, 290-1, 294-6; battle of 296
Badagry 5
Bagala Lamu 240, 242-3
Bagamoyo 6
Bahia 89
Bahir Dar 13, 235-44
Bahir Dar Giyorgis monastery 235-7, 239,
    241-2
Bairoch, Paul 145

Bakers Ltd 152
Bakongo people 293
baldi class 190, 192, 194-5, 197, 199
Bamako 8
bananas 112, 117-18, 120
Banda 101-2
Bani River 20, 25
Bannerman, James 212-13
Bantustans 10, 156, 270
Banza 77
Bar Bouya 285
Barbary 194
Barbot, Jean 209
Bariba district 91
Baringo 6
barley 55, 58
Barroso, António 77
bars/taverns 226, 229, 237, 264, 275, 297; *see also* liquor
Barth, H. 5, 38-9
Basari, Jato 228
Basel Mission 207, 212, 214
Bashew Brothers 267
Basoko 4
Bass, E. 183
Bastian, Adolph 70, 77
Basua 166
Batéké people 288, 296
Batéké Plateau 295
Bazait Palace 243
beans 112, 137, 175
Begemichir 236-7, 241, 243-4
Begho 3
Beit el Ajaib 247-8
Belgium 77
Bembe 75
Ben Schoeman Docks 274
Benda war 178
Benin City 2, 4, 37, 39-40, 42, 45-9
Benin River 175
Benin state 3, 5, 40, 87, 89, 91, 175-7; Oba of 40
Bénin Republic 85
Bentley, W. Holman 76
Béraud, Médard 91
Berbers 2, 194
Berea 149
Berlin 114
Bey, Ahmad 191,195
Beyin 223
Beyrouth 286, 294
Beza Dasta 242-3
Bichana 237
bicycles 134-5
Bida of Wagadu 33
Biddle, Martin 39
big men 222-4, 230-1, 283, 289, 294
big women 224-5
Bigo 2, 37, 39-41, 45, 47
Bin Amir, Snay 100
Bio, Kojo 226
Biskra 2
black Atlantic 182
black market 137-8
blacksmiths 25-6, 29, 32, 171
Blay, J. Benibengor 229
Bloemhof farm 266
Bloemhof Flats 270, 278
Boahen, A. A. 178
Boardman, Sheila 55
Boers *see* Afrikaners
Boka, Mpetelo 77
Bompata 226
Bond of 1844 211
Bongo 5
Bono Mansa 3
Bonnaud family 88
Bonnaud, Pierre 88
Bonny 4
Boundu Boubou 20, 27-8
Bourgade College 195
Bowdich, T. E. 5
Boya-Cisse 89
Boyasarame quarter (Ouidah) 89-90
Boyes, John 113-14
Boyle, Acting-Governor 126
Brard, Father 105
Brasilia 251

Brazil 86-7, 89, 91, 93
Brazil quarter (Ouidah) 89-90
Brazzaville 8, 13, 283-99
bread 128, 136
bride price 227, 230
Britain 9, 39, 43, 45, 86-9, 93, 98, 100, 104-5, 109-21, 126, 129, 131, 150, 182, 190, 192, 195, 205, 211-18, 265
British Cinema (District Six) 277
British Institute in Eastern Africa 52
Bronze Age, Middle 28
bronze 57
Brown, E. J. P. 179
Brown, L. Carl 197
Buddu 105
Buganda kingdom 11-12, 98-106
building materials 130, 138, 156, 256-7, 265
building technology 45, 70-1, 103, 264-5, 270
Buitenkant Street 269, 272
Bula district 70, 72-3
Bulemezi 105
Bunyoro 100
Bura Bura Wigan *see* Nananom Mpow
Bure 237
bureaucracy 5, 31, 191, 246, 248, 250, 252-6, 259, 289
burial customs 23, 55, 57, 61
burial sites 61
Burka 112-13
Burka River 112
Burrowes, T. F. 128
Burton, Richard 40, 86, 90-2, 100
Busia, K. A. 10
Busoga 100
Buta, Alvaro 78
Bwaka Matu, Garcia 77

Cabinda 4
Cairo 102, 194
Calabar, Old 4, 5
Cameroons 128
Camps Bay 278
Cannadine, David 9
Cao people 88
Caosarame quarter (Ouidah) 88
Cape Coast 4, 8, 90, 164, 181-3, 211, 223, 226
Cape Coast Castle 180
Cape Flats 264-5, 270
Cape Lahu 181
Cape of Good Hope 3
Cape Technikon 271-2
Cape Town 6, 7, 13, 151-2, 157, 262-80
Cape Town Castle 264, 266
Cape Town Community Land Trust 272
capitalism 12, 146, 151, 153-7, 165, 170-1, 174-5, 177-9, 182-3, 222, 258-9, 262
Capitein, Jacobus Eliza Johannes 164, 182-3
Capuchin missionaries 69-70, 75
Carpenter Report 10
Carthage 2
cash cropping 128, 130, 136, 148, 222
cassava 93, 112, 127, 130, 133
Cathedrals of St Mary of Zion 52
Cato Manor 154, 157
cattle 3, 23, 25, 39-40, 111-12, 118-20, 130, 236, 264, 266
cement 134-5, 139
centralization 22-3, 31, 40, 61, 69, 74
ceramics 23, 26-7, 53, 165
Chad 8
Chaga people 109, 121
Chaille-Long 102
Chamus 112
Chang, K-C. 28
Chatsworth 154
Chavannes, Josef 77
Cheng-chou 28
Chibuene 2
Chicago 157
China 19, 28-9, 32, 53, 290
Christianity 52, 57-8, 67-8, 74, 86, 98-106, 164, 182-4, 189, 192, 195, 197-9, 208, 210-12, 214, 217, 236, 294; Anglicans 103; Baptists 76-8; in Buganda 98-106; Catholics 57, 59-60, 86-7, 98, 104-5, 197, 200, 290, 292; Jesuits 68; Lutherans 114, 164; Methodists 86, 90; Protestants 98, 104-5; Wesleyan Methodists 212-13; *see also* mis-

sionaries
Christiansborg 164-74, 183, 213-14
Church Missionary Society (CMS) 102
circulation 283, 292
cities, administrative 151; Asian 273; capital 2, 4-8, 12, 28, 67-8, 70-1, 73, 85, 88, 98-106, 149, 179, 189-90, 192, 205, 211-12, 224, 283, 290, 296, roving capital 4, 6, 61, 99; clustered 22-3, 29, 22-33; colonial 7, 9, 12, 135, 147, 191, 197, 206, 211-12, 215, 218, 246, 249, 253-4, 285, 293; commercial 224; contemporary 146; definition of 21, 144-5; European 273; garden 110, 153; garrison 290-1, 296, 299; industrial 6, 9, 146-7; Islamic 192, 195, 197; mining 6; modern 7-9, 153; monumental 2; parasitic 146; post-modern 155-8; primate 110; religious 103-6; royal 3, 28, 68, 71, 73, 85, 88, 98-106; South African 262; squatter 8; Victorian 149; walled 1-5, 12, 28, 36-50, 61, 68-9, 191, 195, 198; Western 9
citizenship 69, 153
City Cinema (District Six) 277
civil rights 150
civil society 293
Clairwood 151
Clapperton 43
Claremont 270
class 11, 23, 111, 120, 128, 146, 146, 148, 150-4, 169-71, 176, 193-6, 198-200, 222, 224, 226, 230, 238, 256, 266, 278, 290, 292
clerks 133, 237
Cleveland, William L. 199
climate 21-3, 25, 36, 127
clothing 130-1, 133-4,152, 157, 236
clustering 21-3, 26-32
coal 148
Cobras 286, 288, 294-5
Coca Cola 9
cocoa 5, 8, 128, 130, 132, 224, 227
coffee 128
coins 55, 57-8, 61, 130, 134
Colonial Development Fund 253
colonialism, administration under 149, 291-3; aggressive 43; architecture of 238-9, 265, 278, 291; authoritarian 78; British 109-21, 126-40, 205, 211-18, 228; and Buganda kingdom 98-106; bureaucracy of 246; and burial customs 211; colonial capitals 211-12, 224, 290; colonial cities 135, 147, 191, 197, 206, 211-12, 215, 218, 246, 249, 253-4, 285, 293; colonial state 206, 218, 249-53; colonial towns 109-21, 121, 145, 148-51, 223, 226-30, 237, 283; conquest 6, 98, 113, 189-90, 200, 238, 244, 294; culture of 283; domination 11, 110, 113, 116, 147-8, 246, 249-50, 254-5, 252, 260, 283, 289, 291-3; and ethnicity 289, 291-2; French 85, 95, 292, 294; functionalism of 10; garrison cities of 290; and gender 222; and hierarchy 115; and historical traditions 77; idealized 258; and immigration 291-2; imperial age of 211-13; and indigenous religion 205-6; and indirect rule 212; informal 211; Italian 237-8; judicial control 211, 223, 227-8, 246, 248; land tenure under 237-8; and language 283; liberal reform by 252; and market economy 223; and modernism 121, 299; officers of 134; and order 216, 260; and pluralism 7-8; political economy of 126, 254; post-colonial transition 288; and power 244-60, 283, 295; resistance to 250-2, 283, 293; scholarship of 190; segregation policies 7, 110, 116, 120, 283; settler 190; social control 147-8, 252, 254-6, 283; and sorcery 293-4; spatial vision of 110-12, 237, 244-60, 291-3; town planning 6-7, 9, 110, 145, 244-60, 265, 289, 291-3; values 115; and Zanzibar 246-60; *see also* Europeans
Comber, Thomas 77
commercial districts 111, 115-16, 119, 237, 243, 248-9, 257, 266, 270, 275-7, 279, 291, 295
Committee for Rehabilitation of Depressed Areas (CORDA) 271
community 174-5, 177, 262, 270, 272-3, 275, 277, 279-80, 289
Congella 149
Congo Free State 78

Congo River 291
Congo-Brazzaville 67, 283
Congress of Berlin 78
Congress of South African Trade Unions
    (COSATU) 155
Connah, Graham 39, 47
conservation 13, 246-60
Constantine, Emperor 58
Constantius 58
Constitution Street 266, 269
consumer boycott 131
consumer society 152-3, 262
control *see* regulation
Cooper, Frederick 11, 145
Copenhagen 183
Copenhagen, University of 182-3
copper 57-8
Copperbelt 10
Coquery-Vidrovitch, Catherine 145
core civilizations model 21
corn 129, 132
corporate groups 23, 26-8, 31
corruption 248, 258
corsairs 193
cosmopolitanism *see* pluralism
Cost of Living Allowance (COLA) 140
cost of living 126-40, 151, 227
Cotonou 85-6, 95
cotton 55, 57, 131
craftwork 53, 57, 100, 112, 236, 265
credit 165, 181, 209, 277
crime 11, 150, 154, 192, 196-7, 199-200
culture, Accra people 173-5; and accumula-
    tion 222; Aksumite 52-3; Akwamu 166;
    archaeological information on 48; authen-
    ticity of 200; authority of 99; bourgeois
    151; Central African 295; change and 12,
    211; city walls reflect 43; class 151; colonial
    283; 'cultural capital' 181; diversity 7, 271,
    275; and domination 110; Fante 178; Gã
    207; and gender 198; of Gold Coast mili-
    tary elites 173; heroic 178; identity 120; and
    invisibility 295; landscape aesthetic 4;
    linguistic 287, 292; *Me* and *Kpele* cults as
    cultural practices 167; Mediterranean 2;
    melting pot of 7; and migration 7; military-
    merchant 178; Muslim 2; networks 264;
    and order 177; Osu 169-71; and politics
    210, 216-17, 249, 293-9; pre-colonial 293-
    4; problematized 164; proletarian 151;
    remaking 13; royal 104; rural 2, 150; and
    site selection 3, 12, 111; slave 171; and
    sorcery 293-6; and spatial vision 4, 99, 109,
    169, 206, 211-12, 294-9; street 198, 200;
    symbolism 7, 12-13, 49, 55, 72, 74, 98,
    100-1, 103-6, 120-1, 168-9, 173, 175-6,
    179, 181, 194, 196, 211-12, 214, 218, 294-
    9; unity 218; urban 3, 9, 12, 40, 151, 154,
    207-9, 226; values 120
currency 132, 165

D'Oliveira family 89
Da Bene, Pietro Paulo 75
Da Burgio, Bernardo 75
Da Dicomano, Raimondo 74
Da Savona, Cherubino 75
Da Silva, Pedro Constantinho 72-3
Daamat 53
Dabra Behran 6
Dabra Marqos 237
Dagba family 87, 94
Dahomey 5, 85-91, 93-5, 130; *see also* Bénin,
    Republic of
Daily Service 138
Daily Times 138
Dajan 237
Dakar 5, 8
Dalgi 237
Dangbe 88
Dangila, *Aroge* 236-7
Dangme people 207
Daniell, William F. 209, 211
Danish West Indies and Guinea Company
    164-84 *passim*
Dapper, Olifert 69
Dar es Salaam 10
Dara 242, 244
Darling, Philip 39-40
Davies, Ron 148, 151

De Gaulle, General 296
De Leao, Ana Afonso 72
De Sousa, Pedro 69
De Souza family 86, 89-90, 94
De Souza, Francisco Felix 86-7, 89-90, 91-3
De Souza, Ignacio 94
De Teruel, Antonio 70
De Vide, Rafael Castello 73
De Waal Drive 269, 272, 274
Debrunner, H. W. 183
decision making 19, 21-3, 25, 28-9, 31
Delmonico's 277
Denbow, James 67
Denmark 163-84 *passim*, 209, 211
Depression, Great (1930s) 126, 129, 132, 134,
    153
'detribalization' 10, 118
Detroit 153
development 121, 241-4, 248, 250, 258
Devil's Peak 266, 269, 274
Dia 20, 22, 25, 27-8, 32
diamonds 6, 265
Diata 296
Dibange hills 235
Diogo I, King 68
Dirks, Nicholas 252
Dishat Giyorgis 241
District Six 13, 262-80
District Six Forum 272
Djenne 3
Docome quarter (Ouidah) 88
Dode Akabi 210
Domestic Area (Aksum) 55-7
domestic servants 150, 196
Dos Santos, José Francisco 87, 93
Douala 8
drought 112, 118, 127-8
Duncan Docks 269
Duncan, John 89-90, 93
Dungur 55
Dunlop 152, 154
Duodu, Kwadwo 228
Duomoro, Sodsha 171-2
Durban 6, 12, 144-58; strikes (1973) 155; sys-
    tem 153
Dutch East India Company 264
Dyos, H. J. 9-10, 13
dysfunctionality 145-6, 157

E. K. Nyame's Band 229
Easmon, John Farrell 213-14
East African Common Services Organization
    114
East African Community 109, 115
East Indies 264
Eastern Boulevard 274, 276
Eastern Cape province 270
Eaton Place 278
Ebute Metta 139
ecodynamics 22
economic growth 144-58, 241
education 8, 10, 69, 114, 152-3, 155, 182-3,
    195, 213, 223, 256, 270, 277
Edwards, Iain 147
Eguafo 223
Egya 181
Egypt 2, 102, 131
El-Ahmar 27
Elias, Michael 130
elite 2, 3, 7, 11, 21, 23, 28, 31, 55, 57, 61,
    69-71, 98, 104, 168, 173-7, 180, 191-2,
    199, 208, 212-13, 223, 226, 231, 246, 248-
    50, 256, 259, 293
Ellis Island 189, 192
Elmina 4, 164, 182, 223, 225
employment 8, 153, 155-6, 191, 194, 196,
    222, 224, 241, 270, 273
Endalamaw Bitaw 243
Endybis, King 57
Enewari 6
Engare Narok River 112
engisaka 112, 114, 117, 120
Enlightenment 182
Entebbe 101
entertainment 151, 153, 192, 197, 226, 266,
    272, 275, 277-8, 297
environment 45, 48, 111, 189, 262, 266, 273
Erh-li-t'ou 29

Eritrea 57, 61
Ethiopia 4, 5, 8, 13, 40, 52-3, 58, 61, 235-44
Ethiopian Orthodox Church 5, 52
ethnic cleansing 283, 286-8, 295, 299
ethnicity 7, 8, 22-3, 28-9, 110, 151, 194, 198-
    9, 283-4, 286-7, 289, 291-2, 295, 298
ethnography 21, 32, 49, 211 *see also* anthro-
    pology
Europe 9, 21, 68-9, 144, 146, 163, 190, 264,
    270, 290; southern 189-90, 200; western
    189, 193, 195
Europeans, and Accra elite 208; and Accra
    funerary practice 210; and archaeology 45;
    in Cape Town 6; colonial officers 109; in
    commerce 148; conception of African soci-
    eties 213; elite 293; Eurocentricity of 250;
    expatriate 190; explorers 98; factors 4; and
    Ghanaian women 223, 225; housing for
    110, 114-16, 120, 154; imported foods for
    128; inaccurate observers 87, 91; mer-
    chants 4-5, 94, 130-1, 182-4, 189, 193-4;
    as military presence 43, 163; minority 192;
    in Ouidah 85-6; poor 291; priests 182;
    racial exclusion by 196; residential areas
    110, 114-15, 120, 191-2, 291; settlers 109-
    10, 114, 118, 190, 264, 274-5; shopkeepers 116;
    spatial sense of 102, 109-10, 120-1; and
    symbolic geography 12; and technology
    200; in Tunis 189; urban forms influenced
    by 5, 7; and welfare state 153; women 200;
    working-class 152-4; in Zanzibar 246, 248-
    9; *see also* colonialism
Evangelical Moravian Brotherhood 183
Evora 68
Ewe 226
exports 5, 265; *see also* by commodities
Ezana, King 57-8, 61

factionalism 71-6, 78, 94, 98, 180, 216-17,
    242, 283, 294, 296
Falolu, *Oba* 135
family 150, 157, 174-5, 177, 180; *see also* kin-
    ship
famine 112
Fante people 90, 173, 176, 178-83, 213; Bor-
    bor 178-80; Ekumfi 178-9; language 182-3
Faras 37-40
Faras Waga 236
farina see *gari*
Fascism 238
Federation of South African Trade Unions
    (FOSATU) 155
Feise, Godfrey 192, 195, 198
Ferguson, James 250-1
Fes 2
festivals 192, 206
fetishism 179, 207, 212, 225-6
Fetu 223
Field, M. J. 165, 210-11, 215-16
firewood 129, 132
First W W 126-7,132, 190, 226, 230
fishing 22-3, 25, 27, 86, 92-3, 128, 130-3,
    136, 150-1, 175, 178, 207, 216, 223-4, 266,
    272
flax 55
Fletcher, R. 36
floodplains 21-3, 25, 28, 32, 115
Florence 196
Fon people 85, 88; language 85
fonio 28
Fonsarame quarter (Ouidah) 88
food supply 4, 12, 21, 40, 55, 93, 99, 102,
    112, 114, 126-9, 131-4, 136, 137-8, 140,
    148, 156-7, 168, 224, 227
Forbes, Frederick 86, 90, 91, 93
Ford, Henry 153
Forde, Daryll 206
Fordism, racial 151-8
Foreshore Scheme (Cape Town) 270, 278
forests 2, 7, 39-40, 43, 46, 74, 179, 207, 223,
    238, 242
Fort Jesus 43
Fort Saint Louis de Glegoy 87
Fort São João Baptista de Ajuda 87-8
Fosbrooke, Henry 119
Foucault, Michel 249
Frame Industries 152, 154
France 8, 43, 85-9, 92, 94-5, 98, 104, 144-5,
    189-91, 193-5, 197, 200, 288, 294;

French language 85
Fredensborg fort 183
Frederiksborg fort 165
Freeling, Governor 212
Freeman, T. B. 90
Freetown 5, 7, 8, 11, 90
French Equatorial Africa 289
Frimpong Manso, King 170, 174
funerary monuments 55, 61, 68, 214
Funguni 256
Fyfe, Christopher 11
Fynn, J. K. 181

Gã Native Tribunal 228
Gã people 205-18; language 164, 182-3, 206-7
Gambia 138
gambling 199
Ganda people 98-106
Ganvé quarter (Ouidah) 88-9
Gao 2, 3
Garcia II, King 69-70
Garcia IV, King 73
Garcia V, King 74-5
gari 127-9, 131-4, 136-8
Gbese people 210, 215; Gbese quarter (Accra) 210
gbohiiajen 206-7, 214, 218
Ge'ez language 58
Geddes, Patrick 253
Gedi 37, 39
Gelb, Steven 153
gender see women
General Strike, 1945 (Lagos) 140
Genoa 3, 196
geography, sacred/symbolic 23, 31-3, 68, 76, 99-101, 103, 106, 167, 206, 208-14, 295-9
Germany 70, 109-110, 113-14, 116-17, 183
Gezira 2
Gezo, King 89-90
Ghana 2, 13, 47, 206, 222-31; southern 206; see also Gold Coast
Ghion Hotel 240
Gibbon 61
Gillman, Clement 114
Gilroy, Paul 182
Glassman, Jonathon 206
Glehue 85, 88, 92; see also Ouidah
Glele, King 94
globalization 9, 146, 190, 222
Gnahoui (trader) 93
Gojjam 236-7, 243-4
Gold Coast 3, 13, 91, 130, 138, 163-84, 205-18, 223-6; see also Ghana
gold 3, 6, 57-8, 175, 177, 180-1, 223-5, 229, 265
Golden Age narrative 173-7
Gondar 4, 237
Gordama Qusquam 241
Gorgora 237
Goundam 20, 27
Gourma Rharous 27
Goux, Jean-Joseph 168
Gramsci, Antonio 163-4
grapes 55, 57
grassroots 250, 259
Great Lakes 2, 12, 99, 101, 106
Greece 2, 114, 118, 156; language 52, 58
Grier, Beverly 222
Griffith, William Brandford 213-14
groundnuts 77
Group Areas Act (South Africa) 154, 270, 273, 277
Gudit Stelae Field 55
Guinea 68; eastern 43
Gujarati people 7
Gulf States 248
Gutkind, Peter 11
Guttman, Herbert 11

Hadrami people 7
Haile Selassie, Emperor 242-3
Halq al-Wadi 189
Hambarketolo 25
Hamdallahi 37, 39-40, 42
Hammond, D. P. 217
Hanley, Sarah 200
Hanover Buildings 273
Hanover Street 266, 269, 273, 275, 279
Harar 37, 40

Harare 7
Hassi el-Abiod 20, 25
Hausa people 89
Hausaland 5, 40, 45-6
health 8, 10-11, 99, 110-11, 115, 117, 119-21, 152-3, 197, 200, 213, 253, 255, 258, 268, 270; see also sanitation
Henrique I, King 74
Henrique II, King 75-6
Herrnhut 183-4
heterarchy 23, 29, 31-2
hierarchy 22-3, 28-9, 31, 55, 58, 103, 106, 110-11, 115, 166-8, 179, 205, 208, 213, 248, 255, 290, 292
Hindson, Doug 155
Hobsbawm, Eric 9, 146
Holston, James 251-2
'homelands' (South Africa) see Bantustans
Homowo festival 208-9, 212-13, 215-18
honey 112, 236
Hope Lodge 266
Hopkins, A. G. 127
horizontal urban complex 22-33
Horse Road 208
Horstley Street 268
Hospice of St Anthony 75-6
Hotiafue 172
households 174-5, 177, 180-1
housing 68-71, 110-11, 113-16, 133, 138-40, 149-50, 153, 155-7, 195, 212-15, 225, 248-9, 254-7, 259, 262, 266, 268, 270-3, 278-9, 296
Hsing-T'ai 29
Hueda 85, 87-8, 90; see also Ouidah
Hula people 90
luluman 206
human sacrifice 210-11
hunger 131, 138
Husaynids 192
hybridity 283

Ibadan 5, 132
Iberian peninsula 3
Ibn Abi al-Dhiyaf, Ahmad 199
Ibn Battuta 2, 3
Ibo people 8, 226
Iddo 136
Ife 2, 37, 39, 43-5, 47
Ijebu district 8, 132
Ijebu-Igbo 132
Ijebu-Ode 4, 137-8
Ijebuland 136
Ikpoba River 42
imaginaries 163-84
Imoudu, Michael 140
Imperial British East Africa Company 105
imperialism 94, 211-13
imports 126-36, 149, 156
independence 120; Ghana 230; Congo-Brazzaville 290
India 21, 52, 110, 150, 264
Indian Ocean 6
Indians 144-58 passim, 246, 248-9, 253, 271
individualism 222-31, 279, 293
Indonesia 264
industrial revolution 145
industry 4, 6-7, 9, 57, 109-10, 115, 134, 140, 145-58, 229, 241, 244, 265, 270, 275, 291, 295
inflation 127, 129-32, 135-6, 140, 240, 248
informal sector 150-1, 154-7, 270
Ingham, Bishop 213
Injabara 237
Inkatha Freedom Party (IFP) 156
Inkisi Valley 76
Institute of Overseas Development (France) 87
iron smelting 23, 25-7, 29, 32, 175-6
irrigation 2
Isert, P. E. 209
Islam, in Accra 211; architecture 190; baldi notables 190, 192; in Buganda 98-106; cities 192, 195, 197; in Durban 150; in French army190; in Bahir Dar 237; and liquor 192, 196-7; Maliki 195; marriage 198; mayor in Lagos 140; in Ouidah 89; in Kampala 105; scholars 3; shari'a 258; Spanish Muslims 189; Sunni 189; trade 3, 98, 104, 211; urban space 194;

urbanization influenced by 3; walled cities/towns influenced by 2, 43; weavers 236; women under 191, 194-5, 198-200; see also Arabs
Israel 295
Istanbul 157
Italy 156, 190-2, 195-7, 235-40
Ivory Coast 181
ivory 53, 57, 61, 76-7, 147, 181
Izon (Ijo) 134

Jacobs 151
James Town fort 211
Jenne-jeno 2, 19-33, 37, 45, 47
Jesus the Saviour church 68, 72
Jews 189, 192-6
João I, King 68
João II, King 71-3
job reservation 7
Johannesburg 1, 6, 151-2
José I, King 73

Kabaka of Buganda 98-106
Kahe people 112
Kaisergracht Street 276
Kalahari 3
Kalenga 37, 43
Kampala 6, 12, 98-106
Kaneshi 217
Kaniana 25
Kano 3, 5, 37-39, 43, 46, 132
Kassala 37, 43
Kasubi 100, 103
Katamanso 207
Katonga River 41
Katsina 3, 37, 39
Katzen, May 151-2, 156
Kawumpuli 103
Kayes 67
Kazembe 6
Kendall plan (Zanzibar) 253-4
Kenya 39, 41, 43, 109, 112
Kerma 2
kerosene 131
KhoiSan 264
Kibangu 71-5
Kibuga 100-3
Kibuka 103
Kikongo language 67, 292
Kikongo-Sundi language 292
Kikuyu people 119
Kilimanjaro Union 119
Kilimanjaro, Mount 112
Kilwa 2, 3
Kimberley 6
Kimpa Vita, D. Beatriz 72-3
Kimpanzu 70-1; faction 72-4
Kimpanzu a Nkanga faction 75,78
King's African Rifles 115
Kinka 207-8, 210-11, 214, 216
Kinkala 284, 295, 297
Kinkawe quarter 205
Kinlaza 70-1; faction 72-5
Kinshasa 8, 145, 296
kinship 25, 28, 208, 226-7, 236, 294; see also family
Kisongo 112
Kisongo Maasai 112
Kitare 37, 47
Kituba language 292
Kitumba Mvemba faction 75, 78
Kitunzi 105
Kivuzi faction 75, 78
Kobadi 20, 25
Kobishchanov, Yuri 58
Kocu family 91
Kofi 169
Kofi Kuma 171-3
Kofi Oku 212
Koforidua 8, 222
Kole lagoon 208, 215
Kole, lagoon goddess 206
Kolélas, Bernard 284, 286-9, 294-9
Kongo kingdom 3, 4, 12, 67-79
Kongo people (BaKongo) 206, 288
Korle Bu Teaching Hospital 229
Kormantse 181
Kotokori, Adisa 229
Koumbi 32

Koumbi Saleh 2
Kouyou people 288, 298
Kpele cult 166-7, 174, 208, 217; *Kpele La Kpa*
　cult 166-8, 173
Kpengla, King 89, 94
Krepi 168, 181
Kru people 226
Kuba state 4
Kumasi 5, 217, 222, 224, 226, 228
Kuvo 77
Kwa Mashu 154
Kwahu 168
Kwaku 164, 169-70, 173
Kwasi 169, 171-3
Kwena people 6
Kyaddondo 105
Kyagwe people 105

La Flora, Salvatore 198
La Goulette 189
La Marsa 195
La people 165, 182, 208; region, *see* Labada
La Plaine 291
Labade 164, 166-8, 173, 184
labour, agricultural 130-2, 136; availability
　40; cheap 152, 154; colonial system 149;
　conditions at Christiansborg 171; custom-
　ary 28, 112; demand 227; division of 21;
　history 11; indentured 150; intensification
　156; migrant 7, 78, 109, 150, 156; organized
　140, 152, 155, 157; racial divisions 151-5;
　on railways 131; recruitment 114, 148;
　shortage 1, 130, 132, 224; slave 165; social
　reproduction of 224; strikes 154; struggles
　140; traditional exchange 112; urban
　growth 237; wage 10, 128, 150, 227, 230;
　on walls of Benin City 40; on walls of Bigo
　40
Lagos 1, 5, 7, 8, 12, 90, 126-40, 145, 213;
　Chamber of Commerce 134
Lagos Colony 134
Lagos Island 139
Lagos Stores Ltd 132
Lagos strike (January 1920) 131
Lagos Weekly Record 127, 130-2
Lalibala 4
Lamu 6
Lanchester plan (Zanzibar) 253-5
land 1, 70, 110-12, 116-20, 145-6, 150-1,
　156-7, 180, 196, 207, 230, 235-44, 248,
　298; alienation of 235-44; invasions 156;
　rights 235, 238; use 109-10, 112, 116-20,
　237, 240, 244, 265, 272, 275
land tenure 13, 118, 150, 235; communal
　117-18; communal vs individual 235-6,
　241-4
Lari people 285-6, 288, 294; language 292
Latakoo 6
Latin America 145
Latin language 69, 145, 182
law 67-71, 100-1, 118, 128, 131, 135, 140,
　150, 156, 175-6, 183, 193-6, 199-200, 209,
　211, 213-14, 216, 223, 227-8, 230, 236,
　240, 246, 248, 254-9, 266, 291
Le Plateau 291
Lebanese people 7, 226
Lefebvre, Henri 249
Leiden 182
Leiden, University of 182
Lelo, Pedro 75
Lemba-Bula 71
Lemon family 88
lentils 55
Leo Africanus 2-3
Leslie, J. A. K. 11
Lesotho 149, 250
Levant 194
Levine, David 11
Lézine, Alexandre 190
liberalization 246, 248
Libreville 8
Liche 6
Limpopo River 3
Lindi 6
Lingala language 292
Lipietz, Alain 152
liquor 150, 153, 192, 196-9, 226, 236-7; *see
　also* bars/taverns
Lisbon 7

Lissouba, Pascal 283, 286-9, 291, 294-5, 297-
　8
literacy 208, 212
Liverpool 157
Livorno 192
Lo-yang 29
Loango 4
local government 152, 154
London 7, 183, 192
Lopes, Duarte 69
Loudima 295
Loufoulakari R 294
Low Countries 69
Luanda 5, 78
Lugard, Frederick 40, 43, 105
Lukacs, Georg 171
Lunda state 6
Lusaka 9
luxuries 53, 70
Lygdami, Eric Olsen 165
Lykke, Hans 164-8, 173

Maasai 109, 112-14
Maasai Steppe 112
MacDonald, Kevin 27
MacDonald, Rachel 27
MacGaffey, Wyatt 206
Macina region 25
Madagascar 264
Madibou 298
Madimba 75, 77-8
Mafeking 6
Maghrib 2, 189-200
Magonga 104
Mahdi 43
Main Bleue harbour 286, 296
maize 92-3, 112, 128-9, 138, 175
Makasa, Manuel 73
Makélékélé 291, 296
Makola No. 1 222
Makola No. 2 222
Makouta 77
Makuta district 77
malaria 116, 118
Malay people 7
Maleke Aksum 55, 57, 59
Malemba 4
Mali 19, 25, 27, 39, 42-4, 47; western 43
Mali empire 32
Malindi Police Station 246
Mallaara 32
Malta 189-90, 194, 196-9
Manchester 155
Mande kingdom 20, 23, 25, 28, 31-2;
　Greater 20
Manga 72
Mani-Cabunga 68
Mankessim 179-81
Mankorongo, King 102
Manuel I, King 72
Manuel II, King 73
Manuel III Kiditu, King 78
maps 36, 46-7
Mapungubwe 3
Maputo 157, 194, 252, 262, 279
marginalization 194
Marigeta Tamirat Jamara 243
market gardens 150
market system 253, 265, 279
market women 127, 132
markets 4-5, 52, 87, 93,102-3, 109, 111, 113,
　116, 119, 127, 130, 132, 134, 136, 150,
　155, 163, 198, 222, 231, 236-8, 240, 266,
　277
Marlboro 9
Maro quarter (Ouidah) 89
Marqos, *Abuna* 242
Marrakech 2
marriage 222-3, 226-30
Marseilles 192-4, 196
Marshall, Alfred 151
Marx, Karl 168
Mashkan-Shapir 29
Massawa 58
Matara 57, 61
Matari, Marquisate of 73
Mathewson, R. D. 47
Matsouanist movement 288, 294, 296-8
Mausoleum (Aksum) 55

Mawokota 105
Maya people 144
Maya-Maya airport 291
Mayama 284, 295, 297
Maydon Wharf 151
Maylam, Paul 147, 154
Mbamba Lovata 71, 73
Mbanza a Mputo 75, 78
Mbanza Kongo 4, 12, 67-79; *see also* São
　Salvador
Mbidizi Valley 70, 72-3, 76
Mbochi 286-7, 289
Mbochi people 285, 288
Mbumba, Garcia 75, 78
Mbwila, battle of 70-1
McCarthy, Jeff 154
McCaskie, T. C. 179, 206, 216, 222
MCDDI party (Congo-Brazzaville) 289, 296
McIntosh, R. J. 47
McIntosh, S. K. 47
Me cult 165-7, 173-4, 208
Mechanics Institute (Durban) 148
Mediterranean 2, 5, 52, 61, 189-200
Melody Aces 226
Méma 20, 25, 27-8, 32
Menelik 52
Mengo 104-6
Mensah, Anita 225
Mensah, Kwaa 226, 228
merchants, in Accra 212-13; within Africa 7;
　Arab 6, 100-2, 113, 237; Asian 109, 111,
　113, 116; in Bahir Dar 241; brokers 163;
　Chaga 109, 121; Christian 193; colonial
　149; Dahomian 87; in Durban 149, 157;
　establish town quarters of Ouidah 88-9;
　European 4-5, 94, 130-1, 182-4, 189,
　193-4; Fante 178-81; French 192, 194;
　Genoese 196; Greek 111, 113; houses 5,
　135; Ijebu 137; and industrial development
　149, 157; Italian 192; in Jenne-jeno 25;
　Jewish 192; in Kampala 98, 100-1, 106;
　Lagosian 129-30; Lebanese 111; Levantine
　130; local 132, 129-30; lodgings 236; Mar-
　seilles 196; in Mbanza Kongo 76, 78; Osu
　165, 167; Muslim 5, 98, 104, 114, 211; in
　Ouidah 87-95; Pare 109, 121; quarters 7,
　111; river 292, 294; in Saqota 4; in seven-
　teenth-century African towns 4; slave
　dependants in Ouidah 91, 93; Somali 109,
　114; Swahili 109, 113-14, 121; tensions
　with Dahomian monarchy in Ouidah 94;
　in Tlemcen 3; and transnational capital 171;
　in Tunis 192; Zanzibari 106; *see also* trade
Meroe 2
Merolla, Girolamo 71
Meru people 112-13
Meru, Mount 109, 111
Mesopotamia 19, 21, 26, 29, 31
metalwork 53, 57, 112
Mexico 21
Meyer, Philip 10
Mfilou 286, 288, 291, 294, 296
migration 6-8, 10, 13, 25, 27-8, 95, 126, 150,
　156, 189-200, 211, 222-4, 229-0, 265, 270,
　273, 289, 291-2
military presence, Akwamu domination
　166-8; Arusha as German garrison town
　109-10, 113; British in Cape Town 265;
　cavalry 43; city walls 36, 40, 43; colonial
　armies 78; commercial-martial ethos 180;
　Congo-Brazzaville 283, 285-99; and cost of
　living in Lagos 138; coups 222, 231, 287;
　elites 173; European presence on Gold
　Coast 163; Fante militia units 178-9; Faras
　defences 40; firearms introduced 71; foreign
　troops in Ghana 226; fortress strategy of
　leadership 295, 298-9; French troops 43,
　190, 286; German presence in East Africa
　113-14, 120; and Gold Coast communities
　175-6; in Lagos 136; Italian presence in
　Ethiopia 237; Kampala as historic military
　centre 99, 101, 105; Mbanza Kongo 68-9,
　71, 73-4, 76; militia factions in Congo-
　Brazzaville 286-8, 294, 296-9; Ouidah as
　garrison town 86-9; prophet-led armies 72;
　role in Okaija's funeral 210; rule in Congo-
　Brazzaville 290-1; and slave trade 76; stock-
　aded villages 1, 6; and technology 43; and
　trade wars in Nigeria 40; Tunis garrison 196

millet 25, 28, 55
mining 2, 3, 6, 136, 148-9, 153, 224, 228-9
Minnesota, University of 36
minorities 8, 191-2
Mirambo 102
missionaries 69, 76-8, 86, 90, 92, 98-106, 182-3, 212-13, 290, 292
mixed-race population 2, 88-91, 150, 155, 182-4, 212, 225
Mobeni 151
modernity 10, 152, 154, 158, 182, 184, 191, 195, 211, 244, 251, 253, 262, 270, 279, 283, 285, 289-90, 292, 296
Molokweni 6
Mombasa 6, 10, 43
Monrad, H. C. 182
Monthly Observer 266
monumental architecture 2, 21, 27, 31, 53, 57, 61, 103-4, 190, 289, 291
Moody, H. L. B. 39
Moravian Brethren 183-4
Morris, Mike 155
Moshi 114, 119, 121; Old 112
Mota 237
Moukounzi-Ngouaka 291, 296
Moungali 291
Moure 181
Mourgoula 37, 43-4
Mowbray 270
Mpila 286, 288, 291, 295
Mpumalanga 156
MSA party (Congo-Brazzaville) 285-7
Mufulege River 72
Mugwanya, Stanislas 105
Muhammad 192
Muizenburg 278
Mulago 100, 102
multiculturalism *see* pluralism
Mulumbi 72
Mumford, Lewis 144-5
municipalities 150-2, 154-5, 157, 239-44, 253, 266
Munyonyo 102, 104
music 9, 168, 197, 226, 228-9, 297
Mussolini, Benito 156
Mutesa, *Kabaka* 99-104
Mwanga, *Kabaka* 99, 103-4
Mwene Vunda 74
Myers, Garth 249-50

Naa Dede Oyeadu 210, 217
Nabulagala 100-2
Nabulagala-Kasubi 102
Nai 1, 7-10, 206-7
Nakawa 102
Nakheila 37, 43
Namanga 119
Namirembe 100, 103-5
Namole 165
Nananom Mpow 179-80
Nasson, Bill 275
Natal Manufacturing Association 151
Natal province 148, 150
Natete 102, 105
National Cinema (District Six) 277
National Party (South Africa) 270
nationalism 11-12, 67, 253, 293-4
nationalization 248
nature 179, 207, 272
Naururu River 115-16
Nduruma Chini 119
Near East 21
Nende 103
Nesbitt, Frances E. 195, 198
Netherlands 4, 168, 175, 182, 210-11, 224-5
Newlands 270
Ng'ambo 246-7, 249-50, 255-6
Ngosua 112
Ngouabi, Marien 290
Nguesso, Denis Sassou 283, 286-91, 294-5, 298
Nguruman people 112
Ni Tshie 164, 173, 176-7
Niabo, Adjetey 228
Niari 287, 289
Niboland 284, 295
Nibolek 284, 286, 288, 295, 298, 300n
Niger River 2, 19-33; Middle 19-33
Nigeria 38-40, 42, 44, 46, 126-40; Eastern

Region 8; Northern Region 8, 130, 134, 136, 138; Western Region 8
Nigerian Pioneer 128, 130-1
Nile River 2, 39-40, 98; Blue 236, 241-2
Ninjas 287-8, 294-8
Nippur 29
Njobi cult 295
Nkondo, Marquisate of 70-1, 73
Nkontompo 226
Nkunga 75-6
Nleshi 207-8, 216
Noete Adowi 164, 173, 177
Noete Shai 165
Noi Ababio 205
Noki 78
nomadism 22-3, 26-7
noog 57
North America 11
Notei Doku *see* Lykke, Hans
Notei Sã *see* Asã
Notse 37, 39
Nsamnya 104
Nsongela 75
Ntusi 2
Nubia 2
Nungwa 167-8, 211
Nyanaose regime 166
Nyanawase 168
Nyeri 121
Nyonmo 170, 206
Nzima 226
Nzinga Nkuwu, King 68
Nzolo, Marquisate of 76

Obuasi 224, 227-8
occult knowledge 25, 29, 31-2
Odoi, Isaac 214
Ogba Stream 40
ogi (corn flour) 128, 136
Ogun River 127
oil refineries 152
Okai Koi 165-7
Okai, Kwabena 229
Okaija 210, 215, 218
Okaikoi 210
Okaikoi stool 217
Olasiti 112-13
Oldendorp, C. G. A. 183
Ollivier de Montaguère, Joseph 89
Ollivier, Nicolas 89
Omani people 7
Ondo Province 137
Opangault, Jacques 285-7
oral tradition 22, 25-7, 32, 39, 86-7
Oran 2
oranges 133
Oranie 2
order 9-10, 13, 110-11, 113, 116, 118, 120-1, 154, 156, 158, 166, 177, 180, 198-9, 206, 208-9, 212-13, 216, 246, 252-3, 257-8, 289, 291-3
Osu 164-73, 182-4, 205, 208-9, 211-12, 214-15
Osudoku 165
Osudoku-Shai 165
Osuko 165
Ottoman Empire 189, 192-4
Otu cult 173, 208
Ouenzé 291
Ouidah 4, 5, 12, 85-95
Our Lady of Victory church 68, 72
overcrowding 213, 253, 264, 266, 268, 270, 273
Owo 4
Oyo 4-5, 284, 295; Old 2, 37, 39, 43, 45
Ozanne, P. 39

Palace of the People 290-1
Palermo 198
Palm Court band 277
palm oil 85, 90, 92-3, 94, 129, 131, 133, 134, 137
palm wine 134
Palmerston, Lord 93
Pangani River 109
Pangani Valley 112
Pare people 109, 121
Paris 192, 199, 296
Parnell, Susan 146, 158n

participation 253, 259, 279
Pase 87, 90
pastoralism 22-3, 27, 409, 112-13, 264
Pate 37, 39, 40-1, 43
patriarchy 174, 177, 223
PCT (Congolese Labour Party) 289-90
Pedro III, King 70
Pedro IV Agua Rosada, King 72-3, 75
Pedro V, King 73, 76-8
Peel, J. D. Y. 11
pepper 127, 133, 137
Periplus of the Erythraean Sea 53, 58, 61
Phoenicians 2
Phoenix 154
Pietermaritzburg 148-51, 157
Pinetown 151
Place Sarajevo 286, 294, 297
Plaine district 290
plantains 133
pluralism 1, 7, 29, 100, 106, 152, 208, 224, 237, 256, 259, 262, 266, 271, 275
Point 149
police 11, 199, 238, 255
Polytechnic Institute (Bahir Dar) 241
Pool region 289, 291-2, 294-9
Popo, Grand 90
Popo, Little *see* Anecho
population, Abeche 8; Abidjan 8; Accra 8, 176, 223-4; agrarian 40; Aksum 2, 52; Ankober 5; Arusha 113, 115; Bamako 8; Basoko 4; Brazzaville 8, 296; Cape Coast 223; Cape Town 6, 265-6, 270; cause of urbanism 21; and civil war 71; colonial 110; Congo-Brazzaville 288; Dakar 8; and definition of cities 144; density 1, 69; District Six (Cape Town) 266, 272-3, 275; Durban 147,149-52, 156; estimating 22, 26-7; Fante 178; gender 223-4; historic Kampala 99; Indian 154; Jenne-jeno 23, 26-7; Johannesburg 6; Kampala 106; Kilwa 3; Kumasi 5, 224; Lagos 8, 126-8, 136, 138, 140; Latakoo 6; Libreville 8; Mbanza Kongo 67-9, 72, 75-6; mixed-race 150, 155, 182; mobility 70; Nairobi 8; Obuasi 224; Ouidah 86, 90-2; patterns 22; and power/status 77; reproduction of 152, 155; royal power dependent on 75-7; rural 99; and sedentarism 22; Sekondi 224; Sekondi-Takoradi 224; shifting 70; South African urban 8; specialist 22; surplus 156; Tarkwa 224; Third World cities 145; token 74; towns 20; Tunis 189, 191; Ujiji 6; urban Ethiopian 8; urban North African 8; in walled cities 36; white 148, 150, 153
Porto-Novo 85, 94-5
ports 6, 52, 101, 126-7, 130-2, 149-50, 156, 189-200, 237, 254, 264-6, 270
Portugal 3-4, 68-9, 75, 77-8, 86-9, 93, 175-6, 207
Portuguese Guinea 138
Posnansky, Merrick 40, 47
post-colonial period 9, 196, 246, 249, 258, 288, 290, 293
post-Fordism 146
Poto-Poto 285-6, 291-2
poverty 8, 11, 145, 148, 150, 192, 195, 196, 198, 213, 229, 250, 255-6, 259, 262, 264, 275, 279
power, in Aksum 52, 55; in Akwamu heartland 166; Arabian 60; in Brazzaville 290; businessmen and 268; and cities 289; colonizer/colonized 98, 244-60, 251-2, 255-6, 283, 292, 295; in Congo-Brazzaville 285; in Danish slave trade 289; despotic 28-9; elites 21; Foucault on 249; and fragile materiality 298-9; in Gã towns 208, 216; Ganda notions of 99; and gender 225-7; geography of 29-33, 249; heterarchical 29-33; inversion during carnival 216; juxtapositions 158; of *Kabaka* 103; of landlords 268; in Mbanza-Kongo 69-76; in Middle Niger 21, 28-9; military foundation of 290-1; occult 29-33; and personality cult 290, 293; ritual 110; sacred/secular 23, 25, 29-33, 226; and sexuality 225-9; and sorcery 293-9; and spatiality 29-33, 246-60; state 249-53, 287, 291; symbolic display 55, 72, 74, 290-1, 293, 299; and urban space 249-53, 259, 285; and walled cities 40; *see also* authority

press 126, 129-31
Pretoria 151
privatization 246, 248
Prochaska, David 190
professionals 31, 151, 212
profiteering 129-32, 136, 138-9
prostitution 190, 195, 197-9, 225-7, 237
Protten, Christian Jacob 164, 182-4
Ptolemy 2
public services 156, 246, 250, 264-6, 268, 272-3, 275
public space 68-9, 72, 87, 165, 262, 272-3, 275, 278-9
Pullen Scheme 136
Pullen, A. P. 138

Qasbah 191, 193, 196
Qotatina hill 235
Quaque, Philip 164, 182-4
Quarcoopome, N. O. 39
Quénum family 87, 90, 93-4
Quénum quarter (Ouidah) 90
Quénum, Azanmado 90, 94
Quénum, Kpadanou 94
Quénum, Tovalou 94
Quillie, Raymond 88
Quorata 236-7

race 7, 13, 111, 116, 120, 147, 151-5, 157, 198, 212, 252, 256, 271, 283, 291
Railway Union (Lagos) 140
railways 114, 116, 130-2, 135-6, 148-53, 155, 224, 270, 272-3; *see also* transport
rainfall 25, 28, 48, 127, 130
Rask, Johannes 164
rates 156, 257, 268, 271
Rawlings, J. J. 222, 231
Ray Ellis Sextet 228
Reconquista 189
recreation *see* entertainment
Red Sea 5, 52, 57-8, 61
regulation, of access 9, 12; administrative 255-6; Bahir Dar 240-1; Benin City 40; boundaries 154; building 115, 249-50, 254-9, 266; colonial 10, 12, 254-6; crime 197; disciplinary code at Christiansborg 171-2; District Six (Cape Town) 266; Durban 150-1; economy 134, 153; food supplies 128; Fordist 156-7; health 270; housing 270; hygiene 153; immigration 291-2; imports 156; Islamic system of 189-90; by Italian colonial regime in Bahir Dar 238; land tenure 13, 118; land use 110; liquor 197; of marginal communities 154; markets 236; by Nananom Mpow 180; by notables in Tunis 191; planning 1, 6, 11-13, 115-16, 120, 146, 151, 153-8, 240-1, 248-9, 256, 264, 266, 270, 279, 290; post-colonial town 10; pre-colonial 12; prices 128-9, 131, 134-6, 138; property rights 13, 290; of racial groups 153-4; rates 7; by religious principles 194; rent 7, 139-40; sanitation 7; spatial 21-3, 110-11, 154, 270; taxis 156; trade 290; Tunis 191, 193, 197, 199; and urban renewal 200; of women 191, 193-4, 230; of working class 153; in world centres 146; zoning 254; *see also* administration
Reindorf, C. C. 165, 207, 210-11, 213-14
religion, of Accra people 173-5; in Accra towns 169-70; in Aksum 2, 52, 57-8, 61; blacksmiths' role 25; buildings 61, 278-9; burial customs 205-18; and capital accumulation 179; centres of 2, 52, 192; and change 12, 211; churches 4; and class 200; clerics 4; Dangbe shrine (Ouidah) 88; in District Six 277; diversity of 275; Fante 179-81; Faras cathedral 40; fetishism 179, 207, 212, 225-6; foundations 4; of Gã people 205-7; Hamdallahi mosque 40; in Kumasi 5; and law 69, 236; Mbanza Kongo as holy city 67-79, 75-7; monastery of Bahir Dar Giyorgis 235-6; Osu quarter 164, 169-71; and politics 98-106, 289; and residential patterns 194; ritual 1, 3, 5, 12, 28, 32, 103, 110-11, 113, 165, 205-18, 295; royal python deity (Ouidah) 88; sacred urban sites 3, 12, 23, 25, 31, 111, 294-9, *see also* geography, symbolic; and sorcery 293-4; tax 238; and trade 98-106; and wars 98,
105; *see also* Islam, Christianity
relocation 116-20, 153-5, 190, 237, 248, 256, 259, 270-1, 283, 288, 291
Rent Assessment Board (Lagos) 139
rent 115, 126-7, 133, 138-9, 236, 292
residential patterns 110, 114-15, 120, 191-2, 194-7, 237, 243, 256, 262, 273, 278-9
revolution 248-9, 253-4, 257-8, 290
Rhodes Livingstone Institute 10
rice 25, 28, 127-9, 133-4, 137
Riebeeck Street 277
Rift Valley 112
riots 13, 192, 197, 214, 216, 284, 287
ritual topography *see* geography, sacred/symbolic; spatial symbolism
roadbuilding 119, 149, 151, 237, 255, 262, 266, 270-1; *see also* transport
Roberts, Penelope 222
Robertson, Claire 222
Robrerdo, Manuel 69
Roman Empire 2, 45, 52, 57-8, 73, 157
Rømer, L. F. 169, 173-4, 178-80
Rosada, António Agua 70
Royal African Company 178
Rubaga 6, 11, 102, 104-6
rubber 76-7
Rudé, George 11

Sahara 2, 25, 27, 32
Sahel 1, 3, 7
Saiccor 152
Said, Edward 249
Sakumo 206, 217-18
Sakumofio lagoon 207
Salisbury *see* Harare
Salt River 271
salt 86, 93, 134-6, 207, 236
Sanguwezi 112-13
sanitation 7-8, 99, 111, 117-18, 120, 196, 199-200, 213-15, 229, 253, 268; *see also* health
São Salvador 12, 67-79; *see also* Mbanza Kongo
São Tomé 78
Saqala, *Dajazmach* 242
Saqota 4
Sarajevo *see* Place Sarajevo
Sarbah, John 213
Sardinia 189, 197
savanna 4, 39, 43
Savi 85, 87-8, 90
science 213, 253, 270
Sea Point 278
Searle Street 269, 275
Second World War 8, 126, 134-40, 152, 154, 200, 230, 238, 270, 291
Sefwi Wiawso 227
segregation 7, 9, 28, 110, 111, 116, 120, 153, 154, 193, 194, 195, 200, 262, 270, 283, 283, 286, 291-3, 292; *see also* apartheid
Sekondi 222, 224, 226
Sekondi Zongo 229
Sekondi-Takoradi 10, 224-6
Sempe 214
Senegal River 27
Senegal, Middle 20
Sesse islands 103
sewage 149, 196-7, 266, 268, 278
sexual politics 189
sexuality 194, 225-30
Shagamu 137
shamanism 32
Shang period 28; Middle 32
Shanga 2
Shawan people 5-6
Sheba, Queen of 52
Shimalash Haqala 242
Shimbit Mikael 241
shopping centres 271
shops *see* trade, retail
shrines 31, 87-8, 90, 103-4, 167, 179-81, 192, 194, 208, 210, 217, 298
Shumabo 241
Sicilian quarter (Tunis) 189
Sicily 189-91, 194, 196-8
Sidi Mahrez 194
Sierra Leone 90, 213
Signal Hill 265, 274
Sikaduase 226

Silesia 183
silver 57-8
Singo 105
Sir Lowry Road 265-6, 269, 273, 275, 279
sisaman 164, 167
Sjoberg, G. 110
Skertchly, J. A. 91-2
Slave Coast 3, 85, 171, 210
slaves/slavery, abolition 5, 86, 227, 265; in Accra 208; and Akwamu domination 166; American plantations 169; in Bahir Dar 236; black Atlantic view of 182-4; burial of 209, 213; in Congo-Brazzaville 291-2; culture 171; decline of 85, 92, 94; embarkation points 85; employed in Ouidah 91; entrepots 12; Fante role 178, 180-1; freed 89, 93, 237; and German colonialism 114; in Gold Coast 163; in Golden Age narrative 177; illegal trade 93; Kwasi's fate 169; labour 165; life experiences at Christiansborg 169-73; market 198; in Mbanza Kongo 68-9, 75-6; as military guards 76; Muslim 89; Ouidah as centre of 85-6; plantations on African coast 4, 90, 93; political role of slaves 76; provisioning slave ships 93; rebellion 171-2; religious organizations and 75-6; in South Africa 264; transfigured 171; women own 224-5; women valued as 227; world view of 169-72; in Zanzibar 249
slum clearance 154
smallpox 268
smuggling 137, 190, 196, 199
Smyrna 193
social welfare 10, 153
socialism 248, 290
Society for the Propagation of the Gospel in Foreign Parts 183
Soga people 100
Sogbadji quarter (Ouidah) 88, 91
Solarin, Tai 136
Solomon 52
Somali people 109, 114, 118, 237
Sonjo 6
Soper, Robert 39
sorghum 25, 28, 112
South Africa 6-7, 8, 10, 11, 12, 144-58
South Semitic languages 53
Soweto 8
Soyo, princes of 70, 72
Spain 195
spatial politics 116-20, 246-60, 294-9
spatial symbolism 7, 12-13, 49, 55, 72, 74, 99-101, 103, 105-6, 110-11, 113, 120-1, 167, 191, 194, 206, 208, 210-12, 214, 290-9
Spear, Tom 12
specialization 21-3, 26-9, 31, 45, 68, 127, 170
Speke, J. H. 100-1
sport 151
squatters 8, 150-1, 270
St Joseph, J. K.
St Louis 4
St Mary of Rubaga Cathedral 104
St Thomas 184
Stanley, H. M. 102
Star Cinema (District Six) 277
state 146, 152, 154, 157, 178, 193, 199-200, 206, 225, 230, 236, 241, 244, 248-52, 258-9, 271-2, 287, 291, 294, 299
Staudinger, Paul 40
Stedman Jones, Gareth 11
stelae 53-5
Stone Age, Late 27-8, 32
Stone Town (Zanzibar) 246-9, 258-9
Stone Town Conservation and Development Authority(STCDA) 248
street culture 198, 200
Stuckeris Street 266
subsistence 21, 23, 28, 55, 61, 191, 200
suburbia 154
Sudan 3, 38-9, 43, 237
sugar 112, 127, 135, 148, 150
Sumeria 29
Suna, Kabaka 99-101, 103, 106
Supeet 112
surveillance 153, 199, 255
surveying 45
Sutton, John E. G. 39, 61
Svane, Frederik Pedersen 182-4
Swahili 43, 109, 114, 121, 206, 256

Swanson, Maynard 148
Switzerland 77

Table Bay 265
Taboo Brass Band 226
Tabora 101
Taki Obili 217
Taki Tawia 205, 215-17
Taki Yaoboi 217
Takoradi 226
Tana, Lake 235-6, 238, 241
Tanganyika 257; see also Tanzania
Tanganyika, Lake 6
Tantumkweri fort 181
Tanzania 43, 109; northern 12; see also Tanganyika
tapioca 128
Tarkwa 224
taverns see bars
Taveta 6
Taveta people 112
taxation 78, 114, 156, 236, 238-40, 256-7
taxis 156
Tcheks 286, 295
technology 53, 55, 98, 146, 200, 264, 270-1
teff 55
Temi floodplain 115
Tennant Street 266, 269
Teshi 164, 167-8, 173, 176, 228
Thaba-Tseka project 250
Third World 145, 147
Thompson, Hubble 114
Tibadu Hailu 240, 242-3
Tichitt 20, 25
Tigray 52-3; Tigrinya language 53
Timbuktu 3, 20, 22, 25, 27
Tis Esat Falls 242
Tivoli band 277
Tlemcen 2-3
tobacco 112
Togo 39
Togola, Téréba 27
Tomb of Gabra Masqal 55
Tomb of Kaleb 55
Tomb of the Brick Arches 53
Tongaat 156
tourism 95, 109, 114, 153, 248, 258-9
Toutswe people 3
Tové Quarter (Ouidah) 88, 87, 90
town planning 1, 6, 11-13, 115-16, 120, 146, 151, 153-8, 240-1, 248-9, 256, 264, 266, 270, 279, 290; financing 253-5, 258-9, 271
towns, capital 237, 241; clustered 22-33; colonial 6-7, 9-10, 69, 109-21, 145, 148-51, 223, 226-30, 237, 283; defined 20-1, 99; forest 7; frontier 6, 147-9; garden 114; garrison 1, 86, 109-10, 113-14; industrial 7; Kikongo definition 67; market 2, 4, 8,12; modern 235; New 155; oasis 2; pre-industrial 22; small 110; trading 4
townships 155-5
Toyota 152, 154
trade, Accra elite and European companies 173-7; accumulation through 225, 227, 236, 238; African 'firms' 4; African continental 7; agricultural produce 109; Akan region 3; Aksum 2, 52-3, 58, 61; alternative to militarism 181; and Golden Age communitarianism 174-7; Arabs 6, 100-2, 113, 237; Bahir Dar 236, 241; barriers 156; Benin City 40; brokers 166-7; Buganda 98-106; caravans 6, 112-13, 109, 236; coastal 223; colonial 78; Danish 169; and decentralization 77; Durban 147-8; Dutch East India Company 264; entrepots 29, 147-8, 163-5, 184; Euro-African 4-5, 85-6, 178-81, 223; European merchant houses 5, 135; Fante 178-81; gold 3, 181, 223; groundnuts 77; and identity 168; indigenous 101; international 58; ivory 76-7; Jenne-jeno 25; Kampala 99-103; Kilwa 3; labour requirements of 76-7; Lagos 127; local 112, 129-30; long-distance 99-101, 106; maritime 126; Mbanza Kongo 77; Middle Niger 22; monopoly 99, 264; Muslims 5, 98, 104, 114, 211; Ouidah 85-6; palm oil 85, 90, 92-4; petty 224, 228, 275, 277; and pluralism 7;

and politics 98-106; quarters in Ouidah 88-9; Red Sea 5, 52; regulation of 290; and religion 98-106; retail 3, 109-16, 127, 130-1, 133, 136, 192, 196-8, 237-8, 240, 257, 264-6, 273, 275, 277; river 292, 294; routes 4-6, 98-9, 110, 112, 223; rubber 76-7; Saqota 4; short-distance 236; and socioeconomic differentiation 208-9; Somalis 237; spatial organization altered by 103, 237; stations 169; Sudanese 237; tavern keepers 196-9; trans-Saharan 2, 3, 7, 27, 223; village staging posts 76; Zaria 40; see also merchants, slavery
tram systems 149
transhumance 22
transport 8, 130, 135, 146, 148, 149, 151, 152, 155, 156, 236, 254, 262, 264-5, 271, 278-9
see also railways, roadbuilding, tram systems
Transvaal 6
Trigger, Bruce B. 20
Tripoli 2
Trois Glorieuses Revolution 290
Tswana people 6
Tudor Davies Commission 140
Tunis 13, 189-200; French Protectorate 190-1
Tunisia 192
Tuscany 196
Twi language 226-7

UDDIA party (Congo-Brazzaville) 285-7
Uganda 39, 41, 43
ujamaa 248
Ujiji 6
Umbilo 151
Umgeni River 150
Umhlatuzana 151
Umlazi 154
Umpuka 77
umran 191
unemployment 1, 153, 155, 284, 290, 293
Unguja Ukuu 2
Unilever 152
United Africa Company 225-6
United Democratic Front (UDF) 271
United Nations Educational, Social and Cultural Organization (UNESCO) 52
United Nations Habitat 248, 259
United States of America(USA) 46, 271
Unyamwezi 102
urban renewal 270-1, 279
urbanism 262-80
Usui 102
Utengule Usafwa 6

Vallée du Serpent 32-3
van Onselen, Charles 11
Vansina, Jan 4
vegetables 127, 132-3, 136; vegetable oils 5; see also named vegetable crops
Venice 3, 5, 7, 192
Vichy government 190
Victoria, Lake 103
Vincent, Joan 255
violence 56, 174, 176-7, 197-8, 212, 216, 228, 230, 252; see also riots, wars
Volta River 168, 207
Vugha 6

wages 126, 128-9, 131, 133, 140
walled settlements 1, 2, 3, 4, 5, 6, 12, 28, 36-50, 68-9, 191, 195, 198
Wallo 4
Wamala 103
Waramit Gabriel 241
Warri Province 137
wars 88, 105, 112, 166, 175-9, 207, 224; civil 67, 70-3, 76, 283, 285, 287-8, 295, 299
water 2, 8, 113, 149, 151, 167, 199-200, 264, 266
Wayto people 236-7
Weber, Max 31-2
Webster, G. F. 116-18
Welgelegen 266
Wells Square 270, 278
Weme kingdom 90
West African Pilot 139
West Indies 172; Danish 183-4

Wetshe Odoi Kpoti 164, 173, 177, 183
wheat 55, 58
Wheeler, R. E. M. 45
White Fathers 99, 105
Whydah see Ouidah
Wicht Street 266
Willett, Frank 47
William's Fort 87
Williams, Collingwood 226
Wilson, Gordon 10
Winchester 39
Winneba 223
Witwatersrand 6, 11, 148, 152
women, absence from historical record 190; accumulation by 222-7, 230-1; artisan class 194; autonomy 223-7; and baldi 195; blamed for economic difficulties 222; and British colonial administration 228, 230; caned in public 222; and capitalism 222; and Christianity 193; and class 222, 230; and colonialism 222; contests over 198; and culture 198, 200; death in childbirth 209-10, 217; elite 231; European 200; exclusion of 193-4; in Ghana 222-31; indentured labour by 150; individualism of 228, 230; and Islam 191, 194-5, 198-200; Jewish 195; and kinship 226, 230; labour by 227; and land 112; and legal system 227-8; lower-class 196; male anger towards 222, 230-1; and market 198, 222, 231; and marriage 226-30; materialistic 228-30; in medina 191; migrant 230; population 223-4; in production 227; prostitution 190, 195, 197-9, 225-7, 237; purdah 191, 194-6, 198, 200; in 'real economy' 145; rebellious 200; and reproduction 227; and 'romantic love' 229-30; sexuality 194, 225-30; single 196; social control over 191, 200; and spatial symbolism 196; spiritually superior 226; and street life in Tunis 198; in Tunis 189-200; upper-class 195; and urban culture 154; urban services provided by 224, 227, 236-7; and urban space 111, 157, 191, 194, 196, 198-200, 211; and urbanization 13; vagina as god 226; 'wanton' 194; work 150, 157
Woodford, J. S. 194
Woodstock 269, 271; Beach 266, 272, 278
working class 3, 128, 150, 152-5, 169, 171, 194, 224, 226, 229, 249, 266, 268, 270-2, 275, 277-8
Wynberg 270

Yaba Estate 139
yams 112, 128-9, 132-3, 136-8
Yeboa Kwamli 205-6, 215
Yeha 52-3
Yemen 52
Yibab Eyasus 235
Yifag 236-7
Yombi-Opango, Joachim 298
Yoruba people 4, 8, 11, 45, 89
Yorubaland 5, 6, 40, 43, 130
Youlou, Fulbert 285-8, 291, 294, 296, 298-9
Young, Bruce 156
Yovogan of Ouidah 86-8, 94

Zage 236-7
Zaire 206
Zaire Basin 295
Zaire River 3-4, 70, 76, 78
Zambezi River 2-3
Zanzalima 241-2
Zanzibar 6, 7, 13, 98, 101-2, 106, 246-60
Zaria 37, 39-40, 46
Zaytuna mosque-university 192-3
Zbiss, Slimane Mostafa 190
Zephirin, Lassy 289
Zimbabwe 2; Great Zimbabwe 3
Zimmerman, J. 207
Zomai quarter (Ouidah) 89
Zombo 76-8
Zonnebloem 266, 271
Zoscales 58
Zoulous (Congo-Brazzaville faction) 286, 288, 294-5
Zulu people 147-8